TH
PROMISES OF GOD

A DAILY DEVOTIONAL

BY

CLARENCE E. WARNER

The Promises of God
by Clarence E. Warner

Printed in the United States of America

ISBN 1-59781-234-X

www.xulonpress.com

This book is dedicated to:

<table>
<tr><td>Clarence Leroy Warner, 1883-1953
Married 10-7-1903
Dora Bea Cox Warner, 1886-1978</td><td></td><td>Edgar Code Arnett, 1872-1956
Married 4-7-1898
Rosetta May Haworth Arnett,
1874-1956</td></tr>
<tr><td>Virgil Otis Warner, 1910-2003</td><td>Married 7-27-1930</td><td>Mabel Alice Arnett Warner,
1922-1979</td></tr>
</table>

A person could never ask for better parents and grandparents. I thank God for them and I thank them for the Christian heritage they gave me and for the thousands of prayers they said for me.

INTRODUCTION TO "THE PROMISES OF GOD"

"THROUGH THESE HE HAS GIVEN US HIS VERY GREAT AND PRECIOUS PROMISES, SO THAT THROUGH THEM YOU MAY PARTICIPATE IN THE DIVINE NATURE AND ESCAPE THE CORRUPTION IN THE WORLD CAUSED BY EVIL DESIRES." 2 Peter 1:4

God called me to write this devotional in 1998. I ordered some resource material, looked it over and then responded to my business and family obligations. In 2001 He got real serious about the call, and I started by writing two days of devotions. By then I had retired from my insurance business, so I didn't have that as a distraction. My father-in-law then died, and I had an obligation to help the family once again. In 2002, God's call to me intensified, and I started work on the project.

It soon became obvious that I was in way over my head! I talked to God on many occasions with a series of arguments. I said, "God, I don't have any courses in theology. All I know about the Bible is what I learned in my devotions, self-study, Sunday school and church services." He responded, "That is one of the reasons you should write the devotional." I said, "God, I'm a SINNER, saved by grace." He said, "Yes, you are a sinner, SAVED by grace." I said, "God, what if I leave out an important promise?" His answer was, "ALL My promises are important." I said, "God, this task is overwhelming! You can't expect me to write devotionals for the entire year! How can I do such an immense job?" God reminded me of the joke about how to eat an elephant. One bite at a time! I soon learned that it was of no benefit to argue with God. He gave me the task, He would equip me, and expected me to do it for Him. I adopted the attitude that God was to write the devotional, using me to put it in words and handle the details.

This task is truly a labor of love. My love for God has grown with each selected promise and with each daily devotional completed. I selected the above verse to start this introduction, as I feel it sets the theme of this devotional so well. God has given us many promises. I hope that your favorite ones are in the book. If they are not, please accept my apologies in advance. I have included the ones which the Holy Spirit led me to include.

In chapter 17 of the book "The God of All Comfort" Haddan Whitall Smith writes: "We say sometimes, 'If I could only find a promise to fit my case I could then be at rest.' But promises may be misunderstood or misapplied, and, at the moment when we are all leaning all our weight upon them, they may seem utterly to fail us. But the Promiser, who is behind His promises, and is infinitely more than His promises, can never fail nor change." You may not agree with the interpretation I give to a promise or feel that I have used the best illustrations. I ask you to look instead to the Promiser and to His constancy and to realize that I have written what I felt He led me to write.

In "Absolute Surrender" by Andrew Murray, he writes, "...when you get a promise from God it is worth just as much as a fulfilment. A promise brings you into direct contact with God. Only honour Him by trusting the promise and obeying Him, and if there is any preparation that you still need, God knows about it: and if there is anything that is to be opened up to you He will do it, if you count upon Him to do it. Trust the promise,...". I could not have said it better concerning the promises I have written about in this devotional!

After the report of the Israelites settling in the Promised Land, we read in Joshua 21:43-45, "So the Lord gave Israel all the land He had sworn to give their forefathers, and they took possession of it and settled there. The Lord gave them rest on every side, just as He had sworn to their forefathers. Not one of their enemies withstood them; the Lord handed all their enemies over to them. NOT ONE OF ALL THE LORD'S GOOD PROMISES TO THE HOUSE OF ISRAEL FAILED; EVERY ONE WAS FULFILLED." I believe the same is true of all the Lord's promises I have used here.

I hope these pages give you inspiration, pause for thought, peace, strength for the day and a deeper relationship with God.

I have written 373 devotions. There is one for each of the 366 days in a Leap Year and seven for non date specific holidays - Good Friday, Easter Sunday, Mother's Day, Memorial Day, Father's Day, Labor Day and Thanksgiving, these are after the December daily devotions.

I find it distracting to be reading a devotional and have the author refer to a Bible verse by Scripture reference and not have the verse in the reading. Therefore, I have tried to put each and every verse, with its Scriptural reference, in the reading in full, each time I refer to one. I know this takes space, however, I feel it makes for a smoother reading devotional.

This devotional is not, however, designed to replace your Bible study and reading. It is meant only as a devotional to uplift, give you cause to pause and think, help you think about other areas of the Bible and to give you guidance for daily living. You can claim the promises of our loving God! David tells us in Psalm 145:13, "YOUR KINGDOM IS AN EVERLASTING KINGDOM, AND YOUR DOMINION ENDURES THROUGH ALL GENERATIONS. THE LORD IS FAITHFUL TO ALL HIS PROMISES AND LOVING TOWARD ALL HE HAS MADE." When you find a promise which is especially meaningful to you in your current circumstances, memorize it and repeat it as an affirmation throughout the day, week, month or other duration of your circumstance. If you find a favorite promise which is not in this book, write your own devotional reading about it. You will find that to be a very educational and rewarding experience. Please send me a copy of any devotion you write.

May God bless you as you read this devotional like He has blessed me as I wrote it.

January 1

"For God so loved the world that He gave His one and only Son, that WHOEVER BELIEVES IN HIM SHALL NOT PERISH BUT HAVE ETERNAL LIFE." John 3:16

The most precious promise in the Bible is the most appropriate promise to begin this new year. This is the traditional time to make New Year's Resolutions. This is a perfect time to include in those New Year's Resolutions one that you will read, and meditate on, one of God's promises each day. The late Doug Hooper for years wrote a column titled "You Are What You Think." I read those columns for many years. They established the basis for my positive mental outlook with which I face life. We should read and think about God's promises each and every day. That will provide a solid foundation for our actions which will reflect a positive mental attitude toward life.

It is said if you do anything on a consistent basis for thirty days it will be a habit. Likewise, if you refrain from doing something for thirty days, you will have broken a habit. Read God's word and these daily promises for thirty days and you will have developed a good habit which will last you for a lifetime.

Some have questioned whether or not just "believing" on God's Son will guarantee eternal life. I believe that is so! Why? We read in Luke 23:39-43, " One of the criminals who hung there hurled insults at Him: 'Aren't you the Christ? Save yourself and us!' But the other criminal rebuked him, 'Don't you fear God,' he said, 'since you are under the same sentence? We are punished justly, for we are getting what our deeds deserve. But this man has done nothing wrong.' Then he said, 'Jesus, remember me when you come into your kingdom.' (This indicates belief!) Jesus answered him, 'I tell you the truth, today you will be with me in paradise.'" That is only part of the answer, however. The rest is: If you believe in Jesus with all your heart, you will do all things required by God. Also, Jesus said in John 16:8-9, "When He (God) comes, He will convict the world of guilt in regard to sin and righteousness and judgment: in regard to sin, because men do not believe in me." We read in Acts 10:43, "All the prophets testify about Him that everyone who believes in Him receives forgiveness of sins through His name."

Believe in Jesus' birth, life, death and resurrection and you will have eternal life. Just living a good life and doing the 'right' thing is not good enough. Ephesians 2:8 & 9 says: "For it is by grace you have been saved, through faith (believing) and this not from yourselves, it is the gift of God; not by works, so that no one can boast." Christian people do good works, but they do them because they are following God's will and serving others as Jesus instructed us to do.

The life Jesus would have you to lead is a joyful life. It is a satisfying life. It is a worthwhile life. It is a comforting life. It is a life of security. With a life like this you can maintain a positive mental attitude. So smile today, and every, day! Expect good things to happen — and they will! Go out and make this a great day!

Love sent my Savior to die in my stead; why should He love me so?
Meekly to Calvary's cross He was led; why should He love me so?
Why should He love me so? Why should He love me so?
Why should my Savior to Calvary go? Why should He love me so?
Robert Harkness, 1880-1961

January 2

"Come to me, all you who are weary and burdened, and I WILL GIVE YOU REST."
Matthew 11:28.

Did you stay up to watch the New Year in? Did you overdose on the football games on New Year's Day? Are you weary today and burdened with the thought of making a living for the family? Take heart! Jesus can make you feel better! He does so by relieving you of the worry and the care. He will not give you back the sleep you lost. You will have to make that up tonight or later. He will remove the negative thoughts that are so hard to carry and so heavy to lift.

Many times, our physical weariness is caused by our mental and/or spiritual state. We toss and turn at night thinking of what we have done, what we have not done, what we might have done differently or having negative, anxious thoughts. This process does two things. First, it robs you of much needed sleep. Second, it causes mental anguish which is physically draining. 1 Peter 5:7 says: "Cast all your anxiety on Him because He cares for you." What a wonderful offer! When these thoughts creep into your mind in the still of the night, whisper a prayer to God asking Him to take the anxious thoughts from your mind and give you mental, spiritual and physical rest. See how much better you will feel the next day!

Another thing that will cause you mental, spiritual and physical stress and rob you of your rest and feelings of refreshment is bitterness. Bitterness, and the accompanying resentment is often caused by our lack of forgiveness of others. Has someone wronged you? Are you bitter about it? Do you hold a grudge against that person? This is a burden you should not carry. For that bitterness you should ask God for forgiveness and ask forgiveness from the one who wronged you. How can we expect God to forgive us if we do not forgive those who wronged us? In the Lord's prayer in Matthew 6:12 we pray "Forgive us our debts, as we also have forgiven our debtors." After Jesus gave his instructions to the disciples about a brother who sins against them (Matthew 18:15-20) Matthew 18:21 & 22 tells of Peter's reaction to this, "Then Peter came to Jesus and asked, 'Lord, how many times shall I forgive my brother when he sins against me? Up to seven times?' Jesus answered, 'I tell you, not seven times, but seventy-seven times.'" In other words - forgive a person as many times as they wrong you!

Take your cares and concerns to God! Leave your burdens at the cross! God will give you rest like you have never had before! This will be true rest for your weary mind and body. (Oh yes, it might not hurt to get to bed a little bit earlier tonight also!) Because He cares for YOU!

Go out and make this a great day!

Cast your care on Jesus today; leave your worry and fear:
Burdens are lifted at Calvary - Jesus is very near.
Burdens are lifted at Calvary, Calvary;
Burdens are lifted at Calvary - Jesus is very near
John M. Moore, 1925-

January 3

"Jesus replied, 'I tell you the truth, if you have faith and do not doubt, not only can you do what was done to the fig tree, but also you can say to this mountain, 'Go, throw yourself into the sea,' and it will be done. If you believe, YOU WILL RECEIVE WHATEVER YOU ASK FOR IN PRAYER.'" Matthew 21:21 & 22

This is a great promise from Jesus' own mouth! However, many prayers are sent to God and are never answered. The hardest question to answer a young inquirer is, "Why doesn't God answer my prayer?" There are a number of things which lead to unanswered prayer. Notice the qualifier in verse 22, "IF YOU BELIEVE"! This phrase carries with it all the connotations of believe. The first thing that leads to unanswered prayer is SIN. If you have unforgiven sin, you cannot expect God to answer your prayer. One line of the Lord's Prayer says, "Forgive us our debts (sins)."

The second thing that leads to unanswered prayer is a selfish request. James 4:3 says: "When you ask, you do not receive, because you ask with wrong motives, that you may spend what you get on your pleasures." In 1 Kings 3:9 Solomon asked of God, "So give your servant a discerning heart to govern your people and to distinguish between right and wrong. For who is able to govern this great people of yours?" Do you see any evidence of Solomon asking with the wrong motives? Neither did God, for in verses 12 & 13 God told Solomon, "I will do what you have asked. I will give you a wise and discerning heart, so that there will never have been anyone like you, nor will there ever be. Moreover, I will give you what you have not asked for - both riches and honor - so that in your lifetime you will have no equal among kings."

The third thing that leads to unanswered prayer is unforgiveness. In Matthews 5:23 & 24 Jesus says: "Therefore, if you are offering your gift at the altar (PRAYER) and there remember that your brother has something against you, leave your gift there in front of the altar. First go and be reconciled to your brother; then come and offer your gift." In yesterday's reading we found that Jesus told Peter he must forgive seventy-seven times. You simply can't BELIEVE if you have not forgiven!

There are three answers to prayer from which God may choose. Yes! Wait! And I have other plans! When Jesus prayed in Gethsemane in Matthews 26:39, "My Father, if it is possible may this cup be taken from me. Yet not as I will, but as you will." God answered this prayer with "I have other plans". Abraham and Sarah had prayed for years for children and God promised a son. This is a case of the answer "wait". Abraham was 101 years old and Sarah was 91 when she bore Isaac. There are far too many cases of God's "yes" answers to prayer to ever enumerate. Many cases today where doctors are baffled by a patient's recovery are the miracle of the positive answer to prayer of the patient's family and/or friends.

Spend your time in prayer with the foregoing thoughts in mind. You will be surprised at the peace it will bring and the wonderful changes which will be wrought. Make this a great day!

Sweet hour of prayer, sweet hour of prayer, that calls me from a world of care
And bids me at my Father's throne make all my wants and wishes known!
In seasons of distress and grief my soul has often found relief,
And oft escaped the tempter's snare by thy return, sweet hour of prayer.
William B. Bradbury, 1816-1868

January 4

"I am the vine; you are the branches. If a man remains in me and I in him, HE WILL BEAR MUCH FRUIT; apart from me you can do nothing." John 15:5

Winter is the time many people prune their vines and trees. When you go out to do the pruning do you lay aside the branches you prune off so that they will bear fruit the following Summer? No, you discard them to be taken away and burned, recycled into compost or other means of final discard. Likewise, you are the branches which have no value if you are apart from God! He is the vine. You are but the branches. Apart from Him you can do nothing! Connected to God, He has promised that you WILL BEAR MUCH FRUIT!

What a wonderful promise that is. We spend so much of our time reading, studying, listening to tapes and attending meetings to increase our self-esteem, our self-confidence and our positive attitude so we can have a more productive life. Jesus says if we remain in Him we will have that productive life. This is not just something for Him to say on the given day. No, it is a promise he has made to us. Take it, claim it and live it, and you will see the changes it makes in your life and in your productivity!

In Romans 4:21 & 22 Paul writes, "Yet he (Abraham) did not waiver through unbelief regarding the promise of God, but was strengthened in his faith and gave glory to God, being fully persuaded that God had power to do what he had promised." Do you, like Abraham, have the faith and are you fully persuaded that God has the power to do what he promised? Today's promise is just one that God has made to us for every day this year. This is a good day to work on our faith and to thank God for His promises and to begin fully to claim those promises.

In Mark 9:21-24, reporting on the man who brought his son with an evil spirit to Jesus, "Jesus asked the boy's father, 'How long has he been like this?' 'From childhood,' he answered. 'It has often thrown him into fire or water to kill him, but if you can do anything, take pity on us and help us.' 'If you can?' said Jesus. 'Everything is possible for him who believes.' Immediately the boy's father exclaimed, 'I do believe; help me overcome my unbelief!'" Our prayer should be: "Oh, God, please help me today to overcome my unbelief and to claim the promises of God as my very own, for they are!" We just need the faith to hold those promises. Jesus said in Matthew 17:20, "I tell you the truth, if you have faith as small as a mustard seed, you can say to this mountain, 'Move from here to there' and it will move. Nothing will be impossible for you."

Claim God's promises for your very own today, and make this a great day!

The following is the "Theme Song" of this book:

"Standing on the promises of Christ my King,
thru eternal ages let His praises ring;
glory in the highest I will shout and sing,
standing on the promises of God."

R. Kelso Carter - 1849-1928

January 5

"'BUT I WILL RESTORE YOU TO HEALTH AND HEAL YOUR WOUNDS,' declares the Lord," Jeremiah 30:17

This is THE promise I held close when I was diagnosed with prostate cancer after my annual physical exam in 1995. I had an elevated PSA and the doctors recommended I have a needle biopsy. I was in perfect health and had no concern at all. On Friday morning, after the biopsy, the doctor called to tell me I had prostate cancer. I knew nothing about the cancer at the time. As I tell people now, 'hearing, on a Friday morning, that I had cancer just ruined my whole weekend. I did spend the weekend with my Bible looking for promises from God. This one just stuck out so plainly that I claimed it for my own. I also spent a lot of time that weekend studying about prostate cancer. When the tests were completed I chose to have surgery, followed by radiation. God's promise held true for me!

Whatever your health challenge, know that you can, and may, claim this promise as your very own. God expects you to do your part also. You need to treat your body as the Temple Of God that it is by eating right, exercising, resting and maintaining good habits (or better, getting rid of all bad habits!). Physicians have learned through many studies that a positive mental attitude and strong spirituality are strong contributors to regaining health. You should also ask for the prayers of others concerning your health. Intercessory prayers are a powerful healing device. We are told in James 5:16, "Therefore, confess your sins to each other and pray for each other that you may be healed. The prayer of a righteous man is powerful and effective."

Not everyone who prays will be healed. Why? This is one of the most difficult questions to answer. One answer is the same as why all prayers are not answered (see reading for January 3). Do you have sin in your life? Do you ask amiss (selfishly)? Do you carry unforgiveness in your heart? Clear your heart and stand fast for God and your prayers will be answered. Remember the three answers - Yes! No! And Wait! If the answer is "Yes", you are healed and returned to the condition before. If it is "Wait", you may go through a long period of time to gain the health you seek. In James 1:2 - 4 we are told, "Consider it pure joy, my brothers, whenever you face trials of many kinds, because you know that the testing of your faith develops perseverance. Perseverance must finish its work so that you may be mature and complete, not lacking anything." Maybe God feels you need perseverance and patience!

Finally, you may not be healed because it is not God's will. We cannot understand everything God does. We will only understand when we dine with God in heaven! Let us say, as Jesus said, "Nevertheless, not my will, but Thine be done."

Claim God's promise to restore your health, and make this a great day!

Open now the crystal fountain whence the healing waters flow;
Let the fiery, cloudy pillar lead me all my journey through.
Strong Deliverer, be Thou still my strength and shield;
Strong Deliverer, be Thou still my strength and shield.
William Williams - 1717-1791

January 6

> "But as for you, be strong and do not give up, FOR YOUR WORK WILL BE REWARDED." 2 Chronicles 15:7

Now that we are almost one week into the new year let me ask you a question. Are you still being true to the resolutions you made for the new year? If you are reading this today, then you have held true to at least one resolution: that you spend time each day with the word of God and reflecting on His promises. What about all those other resolutions you made? Are you about to give up on some of them? Go back and read today's promise again. It means what it says! If you are strong and do not give up, your work WILL be rewarded.

Several years ago I attended a meeting in which the "Serenity Prayer" was the topic for discussion. The leader of the group had each of us say the prayer with the first person placing the emphasis on the first word - I - and repeating the rest of the prayer. The second person then repeated the prayer, placing the emphasis on the second word - CAN. And so on throughout the entire group until the prayer had been repeated enough times to have the emphasis placed on each word. Now, take the promise for today and repeat the entire verse with the emphasis on 'BUT'.

Repeat it again with the emphasis on 'AS', and again with the emphasis on 'FOR', and so on. When you get through the 17th time of repeating the verse you will have had it memorized and will have claimed it for your own for today!

Yes, your work will be rewarded. What is the reward? In Matthew 24:21 in the Parable of the Talents Jesus says, "His master replied, 'Well done, good and faithful servant! You have been faithful with a few things; I will put you in charge of many things. Come and share your master's happiness!'" Your reward for breaking a bad habit will be a better lifestyle, better health, better physical condition, etc. Your reward for starting good habits will be a better lifestyle, better health, better physical condition, etc. Your reward for always giving your best to your work will be more productivity, more recognition, more job security, better pay, etc. But, these are earthly rewards. Great as these rewards are, important as they are, meaningful as they are, they pale to insignificance when we compare them to the rewards we will receive from our Lord Jesus Christ when we are strong and do not give up on our daily Christian life with God.

Your time today has been taken up in repeating the verse for today. So let's close today by once again committing to "be strong and not give up, for our work will be rewarded". Go out with that thought firmly in mind, and make it a great day.

> "Encamped along the hills of light, ye Christian soldiers rise,
> and press the battle ere the night shall veil the glowing skies.
> Against the foe in vales below let all our strength be hurled;
> faith is the victory, we know, that overcomes the world."
>
> John H. Yates, 1837-1900

January 7

"So do not fear, FOR I AM WITH YOU; do not be dismayed, FOR I AM YOUR GOD. I WILL STRENGTHEN YOU AND HELP YOU; I WILL UPHOLD YOU WITH MY RIGHTEOUS RIGHT HAND." Isaiah 41:10

Wow! What a promise this one is! "I AM WITH YOU!" That is straight from God, and you can take it to heart and live with it! Why, you ask, then does it feel that I am alone. Rest assured that God has not moved. Have you? God is still there to comfort, help, protect and bless you. YOU need to call on Him with your whole heart. He will hear your cries for comfort.

The times you are going through may be difficult, rough or just downright awful. These are the times you must call and depend on God's promises. The promise of today says God will be with you, and He will be with you. Avoid letting the devil obscure the presence of God. The promise of today says God will strengthen you, and He will strengthen you. Ask for His hand to be on you. This is a request for the supernatural workings of God through you. This is the promise that God makes. The promise of today says that God will Help you, and He will help you. Call on Him for that help, whether your situation involves problems in relationships, in difficult assignments at work or in the learning process and testing at school.

The most wonderful part of today's promise is His promise to uphold you with His righteous right hand. Pray for guidance as you enter into any difficult conversation, task or test. His righteous right hand WILL uphold you throughout the entire time. This is a promise from God. Tell God you need it! Claim it! Count on it! Experience it!

Now, lest you think that you have no part in this at all, lest you think you have no need to work at relationships, lest you think you have no need to study for new learning or for tests, let me disabuse you of the idea. God will be with you to strengthen and help you and to uphold you, BUT you must do your part by living a Christian life of Bible study, prayer AND applying yourself to the task at hand to place yourself in a position to claim this promise of God. Too many people sit back and do nothing, then say, "God has promised and He will take care of the situation." You can claim this promise only if you continue to place yourself where God leads you and, therefore, to be in the position for the miraculous workings of our omnipotent God.

One other thought on this matter is to take your time to speak to God in your prayer life. To shorten your prayer time to accomplish your tasks will be counterproductive. Martin Luther at one time said something like, "I have so much to get done today that if I didn't spend three hours in prayer I would never get it done." This is placed here today to emphasize to you that you must have a devotional and prayer time when you study, then make your requests known to God and then listen for His guidance. This is a habit you need to develop, if it is not established.

Pray to God, claim His presence, strength, help and upholding, and make it a great day.

I need Thee every hour, most gracious Lord.
No tender voice like Thine can peace afford.
I need Thee, O I need Thee, Every hour I need Thee!
O bless me now, my Savior - I come to Thee!

Annie S. Hawks - 1835-1918

January 8

"Give, and IT WILL BE GIVEN TO YOU. A good measure, pressed down, shaken together and running over, will be poured into your lap. For with the measure you use, it will be measured to you." Luke 6:38

There are many ways to look at the first word in the scripture above. Paul said in Romans 12:6 - 8, "We have different gifts, according to the grace given us. If a man's gift is prophesying, let him use it in proportion to his faith. If it is serving, let him serve; if it is teaching, let him teach; if it is encouraging, let him encourage; if it is contributing to the needs of others, let him give generously; if it is leadership, let him govern diligently; if it is showing mercy, let him do it cheerfully." Today, I want to look at "GIVE" as it relates to tithing!

Leviticus is known as the "rules" chapter. These are the commands the Lord gave Moses on Mount Sinai for the Israelites. In Leviticus 27:30 -33 we are told, "A tithe of everything from the land, whether grain from the soil or fruit from the trees, belongs to the Lord; it is holy to the Lord. If a man redeems any of his tithe, he must add a fifth of the value to it. The entire tithe of the herd and flock - every tenth animal that passes under the shepherd's rod - will be holy to the Lord. He must not pick out the good from the bad or make any substitution. If he does make a substitution, both the animal and its substitute become holy and cannot be redeemed." And in 2 Corinthians 9:7 we are told, "Each man should give what he has decided in his heart to give, not reluctantly or under compulsion, for God loves a cheerful giver."

We each have the obligation to support the work of God. We do this through our tithes and offerings. It is more than a suggestion. It is the law of God! This was brought home to me when I was reading the Bible through one time. As I was finishing the Old Testament I read Malachi 3:8-10, "Will a man rob God? Yet you rob me. But you ask, 'How do we rob you?' In tithes and offerings. You are under a curse - the whole nation of you - because you are robbing me. Bring the whole tithe into the storehouse, that there may be food in my house. Test me in this, says the Lord Almighty, and see if I will not throw open the floodgates of heaven and pour out so much blessing that you will not have room enough for it." I stopped short in my reading as God spoke to my heart and told me that I had not been faithful to Him with my tithes. I prayed to Him and vowed that I would never again fail to pay my tithes. Do it because you love God, not because he promises great return for you! However, His promise for today says He will give to you in return, and the reference in this paragraph says your storehouses will not be able to hold what God will pour out on you when you give to Him!

Make your commitment today to give God the tithes you owe for His work! You will go forth with a lighter heart, and you will make it a great day!

Saviour, Thy dying love Thou gavest me,
Nor should I aught withhold, Dear Lord, from Thee:
In love my soul would bow, My heart fulfill its vow,
Some offering bring Thee now, Something for Thee.

Sylvanus Dryden Phelps - 1816-1895

January 9

> "For I am the Lord, your God, who takes hold of your right hand and says to you, DO NOT FEAR; I WILL HELP YOU." Isaiah 41:13

God says, "Do not fear; I will help you." Fear is a powerful emotion. It causes adrenaline to be pumped into the blood. It puts the body on alert for "fight or flight". It causes the heart to race and makes it difficult to get our breath. It has many causes. What evokes fear in one person may not cause another to fear. Experience is the difference in the degree of fear. Training programs in the military concentrate on situations you may be facing in battle which would bring on fear. These training exercises help to reduce the fear generated when those conditions are actually met.

There are many phobias which cause fear in different people - claustrophobia, the fear of being in an enclosed or confining place; Anglophobia, the fear of England, its people or its customs, etc. You may have a phobia which is bothering you. If so, claim this promise of God! Remember where we get fear. 2 Timothy 1:7 says, "For God did not give us a spirit of timidity (fear), but a spirit of power, of love and of self discipline." His command is, "Do not fear; I will help you." How simple it is to state that promise. How difficult it is to claim that promise. You can claim it, however, because God made it and it is as solid as every other promise He made. Learn to whisper a prayer of affirmation when you are in a situation which brings on your phobia. Say, "God, in the past this situation has brought on a panic in me. I know right now that You are taking hold of my right hand. I hear You telling me 'Do not fear; I will help you.'" Repeat the prayer as you become calm and assured. God's word will never return void. Speak it!

Fear can also be caused by evil. What is the most "evil" we know? Right, the devil! When we work in an effective way for God, guess whose territory we are invading. Right, the devil's. The fear you feel when you start to testify or witness for God is thrown into you by the devil! James 4:7 says, "Submit yourselves, then, to God. Resist the devil, and he will flee from you." When you start to feel the fear, you need to submit yourselves totally, wholly and completely to God, continue your witness, resist the devil and the devil will then flee from you!

THIS IS A PROMISE!!! Claim it, practice it, use it and you will see that it works.

Are you starting a new assignment on your job or in school today? New assignments frequently bring with them fear. Will I know how to do this? What if I fail? How will I ever be able to accomplish all this in the time I have available? Whisper the above prayer and hear, in your mind, God telling you, "Do not fear; I will help you." Faith in God and in your abilities will accomplish far more than just overcoming your fear. It will accomplish the task!

Gird up your faith, try the above, and go out and make this a great day.

> Encamped along the hills of light, ye Christian soldiers rise,
> and press the battle ere the night shall veil the glowing skies.
> Against the foe in vales below let all our strength be hurled;
> faith is the victory, we know, that overcomes the world.
>
> John H. Yates - 1837-1900

January 10

"For whoever exalts himself WILL BE HUMBLED, and whoever humbles himself WILL BE EXALTED." Matthew 23:12

You are doing real well now. You have stuck to your resolution for ten days, and you are really feeling proud. Now you read this promise and think, "God will humble me for the feelings I have about my accomplishments. Wrong! Good feelings about your accomplishments are honest, sincere reactions we have as human beings. Don't confuse those feelings with the 'exalting' talked about in today's promise. Are you praising yourself for what you have done? Are you feeling the joy and pride in yourself? Are you glorifying your abilities? If so, you may have a problem.

Rather, I'll guess you are not giving the credit to yourself. I'll guess you are giving God the praise and glory and thanking Him for the joy and pride you feel. This is taught us in Psalms 86:12, "I will praise you, O Lord my God, with all my heart; I will glorify your name forever." This is an exhibition of the person who truly humbles themselves before God. When you do this, you have God's promise that you "WILL BE EXALTED." When and how might you be exalted?

That is a good question. The ultimate exalting will come about when we experience eternal life with God in Heaven. However, I feel that we should follow Paul's example given in Philippians 1:20, "I eagerly expect and hope that I will in no way be ashamed, but will have sufficient courage so that now as always Christ will be exalted in my body, whether by life or by death."

When we live in such a way that Christ is exalted in our bodies we are being truly humble. At that point, we are serving God in the highest form possible. I heard our preacher recently talk about a former member of our church, who has gone on to his reward. He said about the man, "He was a true man of God." To me, this is earthly exaltation of the highest form. To be thought of by people as a true person of God would mean that the love of God, the light of God, the teachings of God were reflected in your life. To have the love, light and teachings reflected in your life would mean that you were an humble person. Those things could not be said about you if you felt superior because you were able to accomplish a regimen of study and devotions or if you praised yourself and were prideful because you could exhibit your knowledge of the Bible. But you should rejoice in God and give praise to His name, and God will give you a good feeling you can carry with you at all times wherever you go.

Rejoice in the Lord, and go out and make this a great day.

Rejoice, ye pure in heart, Rejoice, give thanks and sing.
Your festal banner wave on high, The cross of Christ your King.
Bright youth and snow-crowned age, Strong men and maidens meek;
Raise high your free, exalting song, God's wondrous praises speak.
Edward H Plumptre

January 11

"To the man who pleases Him, GOD GIVES WISDOM, KNOWLEDGE AND HAPPINESS," Ecclesiastes 2:26

The first thing we should note about today's promise is the qualifier, "To the man who pleases Him." How do we please God? Proverbs 15:8 says, "The Lord detests the sacrifice of the wicked, but the prayer of the upright pleases Him." From this we can determine that God isn't even pleased with the most religious thing about a wicked person. We can determine that to please God we must be "upright"! Used in this context, "upright" means a person whose heart is right with God, one who has confessed their sins and God has been faithful and just and has forgiven those sins, and then the prayer from that person pleases God.

In Colossians 3:20 we read, "Children, obey your parents in everything, for this pleases the Lord." This is a direct command to all children everywhere. It does not say, "obey your parents most of the time"' It does not say, "do a pretty good job of doing what your parents tell you to do." No, it clearly says, "obey in everything." So, if you are not an adult, you should obey your parents even when you think they are not right. I am sure that God would not have you obey if the command was in direct opposition to the Lord's commands; however, this verse is set in a series of verses which also commands parents in their behavior to their children.

In 1 John 3:21 & 22 we read, "Dear friends, if our hearts do not condemn us, we have confidence before God and receive from Him anything we ask, because we obey his commands and do what pleases Him." This is telling us that if our hearts are right with God they will condemn us if we are doing something wrong. Obviously, if we are not obeying God's commands we are not being right with God and our hearts will condemn us. If we do obey the commands of God, and this is more than just the Ten Commandments, we are pleasing Him.

Looking at the promise, we see that God will then give us wisdom, knowledge and happiness. Webster's Dictionary says knowledge is a state of knowing, acquaintance with facts, all that has been perceived by the mind or the body of facts. Psalm 119:105 says, "Your word is a lamp to my feet and a light for my path." From this we see that if we please God we will continue to learn more and more about His word - the Bible. We need to read it and study it every day. This pleases God and He gives us wisdom. Wisdom is the power of judging rightly and following the soundest course of action. When we please God we are led by God in our decision making so that we make the best choices available and our lives become better. Our lives are marked by our relationship with God. Happiness, therefore, is like a well springing up within us. God's promise, therefore, is complete within us.

Study God's word, follow God's commands, and make this a great day of happiness.

A charge to keep I have - a God to glorify,
who gave His Son my soul to save and fit it for the sky.
To serve the present age, my calling to fulfill
O may it all my pow'rs engage to do my Master's will!
Charles Wesley - 1707-1788

January 12

> "Do not lie to each other, since you have taken off your old self with its practices and have put on the new self, WHICH IS BEING RENEWED IN KNOWLEDGE IN THE IMAGE OF ITS CREATOR." Colossians 3:9 & 10

There are many places in the Bible which tell us not to lie. Lying is an abomination to God. He loves the truth. Many, many verses which quote Jesus begin with the phrase, "I tell you the truth...". In John 8:31-32 we read, "To the Jews who had believed Him, Jesus said, 'If you hold to my teaching, you are really my disciples. Then you will know the truth, and the truth will set you free.'" So - to refrain from lying is of utmost importance to God and to today's promise.

I am a Rotarian. In Rotary we have the "Four Way Test", which says: "Of all the things I think and say and do, 1. Is it the truth? 2. Is it fair to all concerned? 3. Will it build good will and better friendships? 4. Will it be beneficial to all concerned? This is a good test to make in our world today. As Rotarians, we are challenged to live the "Four Way Test" every day. Jesus was way ahead of the Rotarians. He set the standard for honesty two thousand years ago.

When you accept Jesus Christ as your personal savior and become a practicing Christian you take off your old self with its practices and put on the new self. You abandon the old sinful ways. In Galatians 5:19-21, Paul says, "The acts of the sinful nature are obvious: sexual immorality, impurity and debauchery; idolatry and witchcraft; hatred, discord, jealousy, fits of rage, selfish ambition, dissensions, factions and envy; drunkenness, orgies and the like." You put on the new self, which is described in the next two verses, "But the fruit of the Spirit is love, joy, peace, patience, kindness, goodness, faithfulness, gentleness, and self-control. Against such things there is no law." Now, isn't that interesting! The acts of a Christian are not unlawful, whereas, many of the acts of the non-Christian ARE unlawful!

Now, to the promise. Your new self is being renewed in knowledge in the image of its creator. How do we obtain the knowledge to be renewed in God's image? THE BIBLE!!! Books such as this devotional can give you insights, uplift your spirit, give you pause to think, point out some things to you, but the real meat of your study must be the Bible. I discover many insights into the Bible with my daily reading of Christian books. I will mention many of them to you over the next year, but still, I spend time studying the Bible every day. That is where your new self will be renewed in knowledge because that is the inspired word of God. Anyone who does not teach the Bible and use the Bible as their ultimate source of wisdom is not following God's own commands.

So, spend time with God's own book - the Bible - and in prayer, and go out and make this a great day!

> Teach me Thy Way, O Lord, teach me Thy way!
> Thy guiding grace afford - teach me Thy way!
> Help me to walk aright, more by faith, less by sight;
> lead me with heavenly light - teach me Thy Way!
>
> Mansell Ramsey - 1849-1923

January 13

"Therefore, if anyone is in Christ, HE IS A NEW CREATION; the old has gone, the new has come!" 2 Corinthians 5:17

Following on from the devotion of yesterday, I want to talk a little more about this "NEW CREATION" which has come. When you give your life to Christ you give up the old ways. You may have been a "good person" before you gave your heart to the Lord Jesus Christ. The inward change is always a very great change. Sometimes the apparent outward change may be small, but we should never underestimate that change.

I am reminded of a meeting I attended leading up to the Reagan campaign in 1976, for which I was a Regional Coordinator. During the meeting someone gave an idea and another person mentioned that the point made was a "small thing". Ronald Reagan then said, "Never underestimate any point. Anyone who thinks small things don't matter never tried to get a night's sleep in a room with a mosquito."

The "small changes" which are outwardly apparent may be just the thing to be noticed by your Friends, Relatives, Associates or Neighbors. Those changes may be just the thing which lead to one of these "FRANs" giving their lives to God. These are the people you will influence on a regular basis. These are the very people you are most interested in winning to Christ. You will be around these people and they will see the changes in you. Christians tend to smile more, they tend to be more considerate, more thoughtful and more helpful. The grouchy, selfish, self-centered "old" has gone, the new creation has come.

Whether you are a "new creation" just recently, or if you became a "new creation" years ago, you can still become more "in Christ" each and every day. Your daily walk with God will open new vistas for you: new areas of study, new areas of ministry, new areas of worship or new areas of service to Christ. When you accept these new areas you find that some of the "old" has gone and, sure enough, "the new has come"! This does not mean you were not serving God properly before! NO! It means that your walk with God is becoming even more meaningful, more productive and more mature. Marvel in this! Savor it! Search for even more ways to become more "in Christ"! Enjoy the gladness, peace and joy that Christ brings to you.

Set yourself a goal for witnessing. List those you want to win for Christ, those you want to help have a closer walk with Christ, or those you wish to help overcome a harmful habit. Pray for them first and foremost! Ask God to present the opportunity to witness. This is a good time to pray the prayer of Jabez, 1 Chronicles 4:10, see "Prayer of Jabez" by Bruce Wilkinson, a wonderful little book! You will find that God will present the opportunity for you.

Become ever more "in Christ" and you will find that you will make this a great day!

Only God can bring us gladness, only God can give us peace;
Joys are vain that end in sadness, Joy divine shall never cease.
Mid the shade of want and sorrow undisturbed, our hearts rejoice;
Patient, wait the brighter morrow; Faithful, heed the Father's voice.

Johan O. Wallin - 1779-1839

January 14

"Come, let us bow down in worship, let us kneel before the Lord our Maker; FOR HE IS OUR GOD AND WE ARE THE PEOPLE OF HIS PASTURE, THE FLOCK UNDER HIS CARE." Psalm 95:6 & 7

I grew to young adulthood on a farm in Northern Kansas. We raised wheat, corn, oats and alfalfa and had horses, cows, hogs and chickens - a typical early mid-1900's Kansas farm. I learned the care which must be given to animals in order for them to thrive. I remember one December morning when the threat of snow was heavy on us. It was my job, as a twelve year old, to go into the pasture in the morning darkness, round up the milk cows and drive them into the barnyard. This particular morning we had a cow that was expecting a calf at any time. I had found all the other cows and got them started toward the barnyard. I found a break in the fence near where the other cows had been and there were tracks leading West. At this time it began to snow big, wet flakes, and I walked rapidly West over the fields for almost a mile. I noticed a darker spot in a protected small valley and walked toward it. Sure enough, there was the cow and her newborn calf. By this time it was snowing heavily. I picked up the calf, draped it about my neck and headed toward the home place with the cow following behind. I had to stop frequently to rest from the exertions of carrying the calf through the deepening snow. By the time I got into the barnyard I was really tired and felt like I was freezing to death. Dad had finished milking all the cows and was getting ready to come see if he could find me. He complimented me for my care of the calf and likened it to the love of God for His flock, which is us! My I was proud of myself and much less tired and cold! What a timely lesson for a young man to get!

That only shows a minuscule amount of the love and care that God shows for His flock. He is the Good Shepherd! Jesus said in John 10:11, "I am the good shepherd. The good shepherd lays down his life for the sheep." This is exactly what Jesus did! He laid down His life on the cross for us! Jesus goes on to say in verses 14-15, "I am the good shepherd; I know my sheep and my sheep know me-just as the Father knows me and I know the Father-and I lay down my life for the sheep." So let us bow down in worship, let us kneel before the Lord our Maker, for He is the good shepherd-OUR GOOD SHEPHERD-and we are under His care. This is a comforting realization for today. We ARE under God's care. He KNOWS us. He calls us by name. We belong to Him.

Today, as you go about your duties of daily living, go with the knowledge that you are a member of the flock of Jesus Christ our Lord. If you have wandered into a small valley and are feeling lost and alone, remember that God doesn't have to hunt for you. He knows exactly where you are, and He cares for you and will bring you into the fold safely.

Listen for the voice of the Good Shepherd, bow down to Him in worship, kneel before Him, and go out and make this a great day.

Saviour, like a shepherd lead us, much we need Thy tender care;
In Thy pleasant pastures feed us, for our use Thy fold prepare:
Blessed Jesus, Blessed Jesus, Thou hast bought us, Thine we are;
Blessed Jesus, Blessed Jesus, Thou hast bought us, Thine we are.
Dorothy A. Thrupp - 1779-1847

January 15

> "A new command I give you: Love one another. As I have loved you, so you must love one another. ALL MEN WILL KNOW THAT YOU ARE MY DISCIPLES IF YOU LOVE ONE ANOTHER." John 13:34 & 35

In order to know how we are to "love one another" as He has loved us, we need to know how He has loved us. Romans 5:8 tells us, "But God demonstrates His own love for us in this; While we were still sinners, Christ died for us." He further states how much He loves us in John 15:13, "Greater love has no one than this, that he lay down his life for his friends." Then in verse 14 Jesus says, "You are my friends if you do what I command." Jesus was saying that He was going to die for us because He had such great love for us.

God's command about love of Him was given in Matthew 22:36-38, "'Teacher, which is the greatest commandment in the Law?' Jesus replied: 'Love the Lord your God with all your heart and with all your soul and with all your mind. This is the first and greatest commandment.'" Jesus went on in verse 39 to say, "And the second is like it: Love your neighbor as yourself."

Now, after seeing some of what Jesus said about love, let's look at what Paul said about love in 1 Corinthians 13: "If I speak in the tongues of men and of angels, but have not love, I am only a resounding gong or a clanging cymbal. If I have the gift of prophecy and can fathom all mysteries and all knowledge, and if I have the faith that can move mountains, but have not love, I am nothing. If I give all I possess to the poor and surrender my body to the flames, but have not love, I gain nothing. Love is patient, love is kind. It does not envy, it does not boast, it is not proud. It is not rude, it is not self-seeking, it is not easily angered, it keeps no record of wrongs. Love does not delight in evil but rejoices with the truth. It always protects, always trusts, always hopes, always perseveres. Love never fails." In Matthew 5:44 Jesus tells us, "Love your enemies and pray for those who persecute you."

Are you loving as you have been commanded? How do you feel about your co-worker who drops a project on your desk at 4:45 P.M. with the comment, "I have an appointment so please take care of this."? Are you angered? Do you wait for the chance to get even by rudely doing the same thing to them at a later date? Or are you patient, kind, forgiving and keeping no record of the wrong? Your behavior with all you come in contact with will be proper if you love them as Christ has loved us. You can then be an effective disciple of Christ. Your attitude will show them what it means to be a Christian. So don't be a "nothing", a "resounding gong" or a "clanging cymbal". Let all men know that you are a disciple of Christ by your love for them.

Remember, Paul said in 1 Corinthians 13:13, "And now these three remain: faith, hope and love. But the greatest of these is love." Show that love today, and go out and make it a great day.

> Love divine, all loves excelling, joy of heav'n, to earth come down;
> fix in us Thy humble dwelling; all Thy faithful mercies crown.
> Jesus, Thou art all compassion; pure, unbounded love Thou art;
> visit us with Thy salvation; enter ev'ry trembling heart.
>
> Charles Wesley - 1707-1788

January 16

"The Lord abhors dishonest scales, BUT ACCURATE WEIGHTS ARE HIS DELIGHT."
Proverbs 11:1

In 1969, I was elected as the Oklahoma Republican State Chairman and served for three consecutive two-year terms. In 1972, Dewey F. Bartlett, who had served as Oklahoma Governor from 1967 to 1971, was elected to the U. S. Senate. Then State Senator Jim Inhofe, now a U. S. Senator, was campaigning for Bartlett and made an automobile trip throughout the state with Dewey Bartlett, Jr. Jim later told me a story Dewey, Jr., told him. When Bartlett was first elected as governor and moved the family from Tulsa into the governor's mansion, Dewey, Jr., wrote two letters to friends back in Tulsa. He did not have any stamps so he roamed through the mansion searching for some. He found a new roll in a desk in a small office in the front of the house. As he was unwrapping the roll (first class stamps were 5 cents each then) to get two stamps, Governor Bartlett came into the room. "What are you doing, son,"the Governor asked? "Oh, I just wrote a couple of letters to friends back home and needed stamps to mail them," Dewey, Jr., replied. "Son, you can't use those stamps," the Governor said. "Those stamps were purchased with tax money paid by the people of Oklahoma for use by your mother in her official correspondence as First Lady of Oklahoma. You just can't use taxpayer purchased stamps for your private correspondence." Dewey Bartlett served four years as governor and six years as a U. S. Senator before retiring to fight a losing battle with cancer. I have great respect for his memory because in all his service there was not one hint of impropriety or scandal associated with his service.

I think of the above story when I read today's promise. The Lord promises us that accurate weights (i.e. honesty in all our dealings) are His delight. Let me ask you a question. If you go into a store to make a purchase and the clerk gives you $5.00 too little in change, do you mention it to the clerk and ask for the correct change? What if the clerk gives you $5.00 too much change, do you mention it to the clerk? Let me suggest, when that happens, you give back the $5.00 with the comment, "God would not like it if I accepted more money in change than I rightly have coming, and I want to please God." That is an excellent way to witness!

Today, before I wrote this devotion, three of us went out to lunch, and the lady taking orders was in a hurry. She failed to write down the price of one of the sandwiches we ordered. When I reached the cash register to pay, I pointed that out to the lady taking the money. She looked at me and said, "Sir, I appreciate your honesty." Remember, you have to shave or put on makeup every day. If you don't like what you see in the mirror, it can make for a sad beginning. You can't be just a little dishonest. You are either honest or dishonest. Which are you?

Use accurate weights, delight the Lord, and make this a great day.

Once far from God and dead in sin, no light my heart could see;
but in God's Word the light I found. Now Christ liveth in me.
As lives the flower within the seed, as in the cone the tree;
so, praise the God of truth and grace; His Spirit dwelleth in me.
Daniel W. Whittle - 1840-1901

January 17

"A HEART AT PEACE GIVES LIFE TO THE BODY, BUT ENVY ROTS THE BONES."
Proverbs 14:30

This is a positive promise and a negative promise! The first part is very positive. A heart at peace gives life to the body. When you get fearful, angry, jealous, hateful, etc. the blood pressure increases, the heart beats faster and, in many cases, adrenaline is pumped into the blood. How can the heart be at peace in situations such as these? These are feelings given us by the devil. Is it a sin to momentarily feel the above? How momentarily do you mean? It is not a sin to be tempted. Jesus was tempted by the devil and the Bible tells us He was without sin. So, "no" it is not a sin to feel these emotions for an instant. That means we are tempted. How do you respond to the temptation. Do you harden your heart and continue the feelings or do you immediately call upon God to soften and lighten your heart?

Turn your thoughts and feelings immediately to love, joy, peace, patience, kindness, goodness, faithfulness, gentleness and self-control and your heart will become at peace, your blood pressure will be normal, your breathing will be smooth and regular and your heart will be giving life to the body. Your muscles will relax, tension will flow out of you and you will be better able to maintain total control over your body and its functions.

The second part of today's promise is a negative promise. Envy rots the bones. If you have the love of Jesus in your heart, why would you envy anyone else regardless of what they have, how much they make, how beautiful they are or how gifted they are? You have the most precious thing a person could need, want or have! And you know what? You are perfectly happy in sharing that with anyone else so there is no need for them to be envious. There is an old saying "love is not love unless it is given away". I say that especially about the love of God. It isn't really love of God unless you share it - give it away. You find it returns many fold back to you and swells the good feelings. When you have good feelings your health is better - your heart is at peace - and is giving life to your body. If you have any envious thoughts today, fall to your knees and ask God to remove them. Psalm 51:10 says, "Create in me a pure heart, O God, and renew a steadfast spirit within me." Ask God to do that for you - don't let any envy rot your bones!

Now, you might ask why have I included God's promises to the wicked (and I do have several in this book)? I have included them because they are promises of God! God will punish those who have not confessed their sins and received His forgiveness. In Romans 12:19 we read, "Do not take revenge, my friends, but leave room for God's wrath, for it is written: 'It is mine to avenge; I will repay,' says the Lord." It is our duty to tell the people of the world about His offer of salvation. It is also our duty to tell the world about His sure and fair judgement.

Let your heart be at peace, and go out and make this a great day.

Peace, perfect peace - in this dark world of sin?
The blood of Jesus whispers peace within.
Peace, perfect peace - by thronging duties pressed?
To do the will of Jesus, this is rest.

Edward H. Bickersteth - 1825-1906

January 18

"We are hard pressed on every side, BUT NOT CRUSHED; perplexed, BUT NOT IN DESPAIR; persecuted, BUT NOT ABANDONED; struck down, BUT NOT DESTROYED." 2 Corinthians 4:8 & 9

Have you ever had those times when things were coming at you so fast you could not handle them? One of those times when you think of that funny, "I take care of things as they come, if I can handle them that fast!"? Maybe it is at work where one of your co-workers left and the work poured in on you. Maybe it is at home where the washing machine broke, the toilet started running all the time, the storm door won't shut properly, the porch light bulb burned out and your child was sick on the carpet. Yes, you may be hard pressed on every side, but you ARE NOT crushed! Whisper a prayer to God for calm, efficiency in action and a settling of your circumstances. Remember, you can accomplish so much more when you are calm yourself.

So you started a new semester of classes and they are eating your lunch, your job assignment changed and you are not sure how to accomplish all you have to do, or you have a loved one ill and don't know how to treat the illness. Perplexed? Look at the promise again, God said you would not be in despair. Your prayers to God will open your eyes to how to study that class assignment, accomplish the job assignment, or treat the illness. It will also calm you and put you in position to be more efficient and effective.

All right, so you were in a hurry to get to an appointment and got a traffic ticket, the neighbor children tore up your flowers, you found out a person you thought of as a friend has been spreading gossip about you. Yes, you are persecuted - rightly or wrongly. But you are NOT abandoned! When such things happen, again, I recommend prayer. Why? IT WORKS! Ask God to help you to plan your life so you can be more efficient and leave earlier for appointments. Work with the neighbor children to get them to help you plant and tend while you talk about God's gift of growing things and thus give them an "ownership" in the flowers to help you protect them (and they may just learn more about God in the process). Ask your "friend" if you have offended them in the past which may have led to the comments they made. If so ask their forgiveness. Serve as a witness to them for Christ.

Now it has happened! That vehicle accident has you laid up for a period of time or, as in my case, the doctor calls with the diagnosis of cancer. You are "struck down!" Rest assured, you are not destroyed! Do what I did. Consider it a call from God to get your attention. The week-end following my call from the doctor resulted in more Bible study than I had done in the previous year. I was not living my life as I should at that time. God got my attention, but He did not destroy me. He put me on the path that has led to so many blessings I can't ever enumerate them.

Claim His promise, pray it as an affirmation, and go out and make this a great day.

O God, our help in ages past, our hope for years to come,
our shelter from the stormy blast, and our eternal home.
Under the shadow of Thy throne still may we dwell secure;
Sufficient is Thine arm alone, and our defense is sure.

Isaac Watts - 1674-1748

January 19

"As the Father has loved me, so have I loved you. Now remain in my love. If you obey my commands, you will remain in my love, just as I have obeyed my Father's commands and remain in His love. I HAVE TOLD YOU THIS SO THAT MY JOY MAY BE IN YOU AND THAT YOUR JOY MAY BE COMPLETE." John 15:9-11

Today's promise is beautifully stated by Pastor Phil Toole of Mountain Valley Community Church in Scottsdale, Arizona. He wrote it as: **Jesus O You**. "The '**J**' stands for Jesus," said Pastor Toole. "The '**Y**' stands for you. Do you know what the '**O**' stands for? It stands for zero. Just what it says - nothing. What I am saying here is the way to stay close to Jesus and keep joy in your heart is let nothing between Jesus and you."

In the promise, Jesus tells us how strongly He loves us and tells us to remain in His love. If we obey His commands we WILL remain in His love. When we do this, our Lord's joy WILL be in us and our joy WILL be complete. Robert J. Morgan, pastor of the Donelson Fellowship in Nashville, Tennessee, said in one of his sermons, "Happiness is an emotion, and joy is an attitude. Emotions come and go, but attitudes come and grow." When we remain in the love of Jesus and obey His commands we find our Joy comes and grows with each passing day.

Are you going through a particularly tough situation right now? Is it causing you grief instead of happiness? This is a part of life. We cope with them. We share our grief with others. We seek counseling to solve our problems. Best of all, we call upon the Lord, who hears our call for help and has promised to send the Comforter to us. Whatever your state of happiness today, you can still have the joy of Jesus in you and you find that His joy is complete!

When my wife was younger, she had a mentor named Myrtle Drake in Norman, Oklahoma. Myrtle is a lovely, sweet lady and a precious friend. Each year at Christmas she gives us another form of 'JOY' in a plaque to hang on our door, a picture for the wall, note cards to send, etc. It is always a joy to receive her gifts! It is even more a joy to receive her and her love! She exhibits the love of God in such a strong manner that it is unmistakable. When I read today's promise, I always think of Myrtle Drake and her very special way of bringing joy to each and every person she meets. Are you being that kind of person with your life? Think about it. Pray about it. It can only come when you are walking with the Lord Jesus Christ and remaining in His love.

If you are not in His love, today is the best time ever to give your heart wholly to Him and begin your daily walk in His love! If you confess your sins, He is faithful and just and WILL forgive you of your sins! That is a special promise also. Claim it and you will claim today's promise as well.

Put God's joy in your heart, and go out and make this a great day.

Joys are flowing like a river, since the comforter has come;
He abides with us forever, makes the trusting heart His home.
What a wonderful salvation where we always see His face!
What a peaceful habitation! What a quiet resting place!

Manie P. Ferguson - 19th Century

January 20

"Blessed are the meek, FOR THEY WILL INHERIT THE EARTH." Matthew 5:5

Just who are these "meek" who will be inheriting the earth? When I look in my dictionary, I find "meek" defined as: 1) patient and mild; not inclined to anger or resentment. 2) Too submissive; easily imposed on; spineless; spiritless. 3) Gentle or kind - SYN. See HUMBLE. We can rule out definition 2 as not the kind Jesus was talking about in the Sermon on the Mount when He made the above promise. So we can say the meek are those who are patient, mild, not inclined to anger or resentment, gentle, kind and humble. In 2 Chronicles 7:14 we read, "If my people, who are called by my name, will humble themselves and pray and seek my face and turn from their wicked ways, then will I hear from heaven and will forgive their sin and will heal their land." This verse applies so strongly to us today.

Psalm 37:11 says much the same as today's promise and the above verse, "But the meek will inherit the land and enjoy great peace." Now that is a double promise! Not only will we inherit the earth if we are meek, but we will also enjoy great peace! Our challenge, then, is to be meek. Think about yesterday for a moment. Were you gentle? Kind? Patient? Slow to anger or resentment? Humble? If you answered 'no' to any of these questions, where did you go wrong? What can you do to improve today?

Start with prayer. Ask God to forgive your impulsive behavior and improper actions. I do this every day as God and I are working on me to make me a better person. I like the bumper sticker which says: "Christians aren't perfect. Just forgiven!" That sure describes me. I pray that He will make me more like Him each and every day.

The second thing you can do is to place foremost in your mind that question which was very popular a few years ago: "What would Jesus do?" Or WWJD? He showed us the way by living a life of meekness. Even when He was betrayed, falsely accused, scourged, beaten, spit upon, led to Golgotha and placed on the cross to die, Jesus was meek as described above. You and I have not suffered anything like our Lord Jesus Christ suffered. We should train ourselves to be meek and to love our tormentors - to be more like Jesus!

In the book of Zephaniah, the prophet speaks to Israel about the judgment in the day of the Lord and then about the salvation in the day of the Lord. Of note to us now is the message in 3:11-12, "On that day you will not be put to shame for all the wrongs you have done to me, because I will remove from this city those who rejoice in their pride. Never again will you be haughty on my holy hill. But I will leave within you the meek and humble, who trust in the name of the Lord." This is further evidence of today's promise!

Live today, and every day, showing the traits of meekness as described above, and go out and make this a great day.

Earthly pleasures vainly call me - I would be like Jesus;
nothing worldly shall enthrall me - I would be like Jesus:
He has broken ev'ry fetter - I would be like Jesus;
that my soul may serve Him better - I would be like Jesus.

James Rowe - 1865-1933

January 21

"WHOEVER TRUSTS IN HIS RICHES WILL FALL, BUT THE RIGHTEOUS WILL THRIVE LIKE A GREEN LEAF." Proverbs 11:28

Do you long for a life of security? Are you working to build up financial security at the expense of all else? Is this the way you really think you should live? Now, don't get me wrong. I think we should work to provide for ourselves and to help those less fortunate than are we. I also think we should provide for our retirement such that we will not be a burden on our families and our government. However, I want you to reread the above promise. If you are going to trust in your riches you WILL fall! If you are righteous, you WILL thrive like a green leaf.

In "Pinstripe Parables" by David McCasland he tells a story based on Luke 12:13-21 (Parable of the rich fool) about the man who had been divorced twice because all he thought about was money. He was on a flight in first class from Chicago to London and was living a very pleasant life of ease bought with money. He made his plans to tear down some old storage buildings and build a state of the art warehouse. From this he would have sufficient money to be able to retire to the Caribbean in another year. Satisfied and happy, he finished his wine and went to sleep. When the flight attendant tried to awaken him for breakfast before landing in London she found he had died in his sleep with a brain hemorrhage.

In Mark 8:35-36 Jesus says, "For whoever wants to save his life will lose it, but whoever loses his life for me and for the gospel will save it. What good is it for a man to gain the whole world, yet forfeit his soul?" And again Jesus said in Matthew 6:19-21, "Do not store up for yourselves treasures on earth, where moth and rust destroy, and where thieves break in and steal. But store up for yourselves treasures in heaven, where moth and rust do not destroy, and where thieves do not break in and steal. For where your treasure is, there your heart will be also." and He goes on in verse 24 to say, "No one can serve two masters. Either he will hate the one and love the other, or he will be devoted to the one and despise the other. You cannot serve both God and Money."

Now are you confused? Don't be! God intends for us to be successful. God intends for us to have our needs fulfilled. God intends for us have our needs provided in our lifetimes. What God wants from us is the proper attitude toward our income, investments, retirement and success. Are those things more important to you than tithing to the church? Are those things so important that you work on Sundays instead of keeping them holy? Are those things your driving force? If so, you are in trouble! Pray for your attitude to change, for God to come into your heart and occupy first place, for God to be first in your life and for you to grow in righteousness. THEN you will thrive like a green leaf! Yes, pray the Prayer of Jabez. God wants to bless us a lot! It is His greatest desire, BUT He wants your heart in the right place first.

Gain in righteousness, thrive like a green leaf, and go out and make this a great day.

All to Jesus I surrender, all to Him I freely give;
I will ever love and trust Him, in His presence daily live.
All to Jesus I surrender, humbly at His feet I bow;
worldly pleasures all forsaken, take me, Jesus, take me now.

Judson W. Van De Venter - 1855-1939

January 22

> "Let the peace of Christ rule in your hearts, since as members of one body YOU WERE CALLED TO PEACE. And be thankful." Colossians 3:15

Peace is a wonderful condition. In our lifetimes we have seen only short periods of peace. In the 20th century there were many wars fought, including two wars involving most of the world's countries. Many wars were fought between only two countries, and many more were fought among a few nations. Is this the kind of peace Jesus was talking about? I don't think so.

In fact, in Matthew 10:34-37 Jesus said to the disciples, "Do not suppose that I have come to bring peace to the earth. I did not come to bring peace, but a sword. For I have come to turn 'a man against his father, a daughter against her mother, a daughter-in-law against her mother-in-law - a man's enemies will be the members of his own household.' Anyone who loves his father or mother more than me is not worthy of me; anyone who loves his son or daughter more than me is not worthy of me; and anyone who does not take his cross and follow me is not worthy of me." Wow! What does that mean? I believe it simply means that God expects us to put Him first in our lives. Yesterday we learned that God expects us to put Him before our financial security. Today we find that He expects us to put him before our family.

Do we neglect our family? No way! Even on the cross, we are told in John 19:26-27, "When Jesus saw His mother there, and the disciple whom He loved standing nearby, He said to His mother, 'Dear woman, here is your son,' and to the disciple, 'Here is your mother.' From that time on, this disciple took her into his home." Did Jesus abandon His mother? No! He provided for her. We have many examples of instructions for us to care for our family and our neighbors. No, what Jesus was saying to the disciples, and thus saying to us, is that we are to put Him first and foremost in our lives!

When we put Him first we come into a peace that passes all understanding. We were called to peace, as the promise says. This is in Colossians where Paul is telling the people of Colossi, and by its inclusion in the Bible, to us, about putting on the new man. So Paul says to "Let the peace of Christ rule in your hearts" since they are members of the church - the body of Christ - and, as such, they "were called to peace". Then Paul says, "And be thankful." God wants us to be at peace with all men. Are you? When you think of what you say to members of your family, friends, co-workers and neighbors, do you have a feeling of peace? Do you let the peace of Christ rule in your heart and guide what you say? It is really hard sometimes isn't it? I find it difficult and really have to work at it and ask for His forgiveness when I am not successful. Then I try harder the next time.

So let the peace of Christ rule in your heart, rule in your associations with others, rule in what you say and how you say it, and go out and make this a great day.

> Like a river glorious is God's perfect peace,
> over all victorious in its bright increase;
> perfect, yet it floweth fuller ev'ry day;
> perfect, yet it groweth deeper all the way.
>
> Frances R. Havergal - 1826-1879

January 23

"Come, follow me," Jesus said, "and I WILL MAKE YOU FISHERS OF MEN." Mark 1:17

Each of us finds Christ in our own way. Some of us, like me, are so very fortunate that we had Godly parents who taught us from our birth the love, grace and blessings of God. Others were brought by friends or relatives. Others came to God through revival meetings and church outreach programs. Still others came as a result of strangers telling them of the love and care of our Lord Jesus Christ. Think back to how you came to know Christ. If you do not have that personal relationship with God right now, this is a good time to gain it! 1 John 1:9 says, "If we confess our sins, He is faithful and just and will forgive us our sins and purify us from all unrighteousness." Confess your sins to God and you will begin a life of unbelievable joy!

Every Christian should read, memorize, and take to heart today's promise. Jesus said, "I will make you fishers of men!" What a wonderful thing to be. We can strengthen our Christian walk by ministering to others. We can, and should, do this on a daily basis by the way we live, the way we dress, the way we talk, the way we care, the way we listen and the way we emulate Jesus. People will be drawn to us as they see Jesus at work in our lives. Study the scriptures so you can respond to others when they ask about a problem they have or when they ask about the joy in your life. By doing this, you do strengthen your walk with Christ. This process is used by some addiction treatment centers. After a person reaches a certain level in their treatment program, they are asked to work with people just beginning their program. By working with the new comers, those further into the program enforce the teachings and training they have previously received in their own treatment program. Practice this in your Christian development program!

After the resurrection of Jesus Christ on His third appearance, He reinstated Peter by the following conversation recorded in John 21:15-17, "When they had finished eating, Jesus said to Simon Peter, 'Simon son of John, do you truly love me more that these?' 'Yes, Lord,' he said, 'you know that I love you.' Jesus said, 'Feed my lambs.' Again Jesus said, 'Simon son of John, do you truly love me?; He answered, 'Yes, Lord, you know that I love you.' Jesus said, 'Take care of my sheep.' The third time He said to him, 'Simon son of John, do you love me?' Peter was hurt because Jesus asked him the third time, 'Do you love me?' He said, 'Lord, you know all things; you know that I love you.' Jesus answered, 'Feed my sheep.'" This conversation is a very clear charge to us to bring Christ to the lost. We have the obligation to work as evangelists. We do so today in our homes, our work areas and in our contacts with loved ones, friends, fellow workers and strangers.

Go forth as a Christian missionary today and "Feed my sheep!" and make this a great day!

Out in the highways and byways of life many are weary and sad;
carry the sunshine where darkness is rife, making the sorrowing glad.
Tell the sweet story of Christ and His love. Tell of His pow'r to forgive,
others will trust Him if only you prove true every moment you live.
Make me a blessing, O Savior I pray, Make me a blessing to someone today.

Ira B. Wilson, 1880-1950

January 24

"A GOOD MAN OBTAINS FAVOR FROM THE LORD, BUT THE LORD CONDEMNS A CRAFTY MAN." Proverbs 12:2

First, this verse is gender neutral. It could be written: "A good person obtains favor from the Lord, but the Lord condemns a crafty person." Now, let's continue from that perspective.

What is a good person? Descriptive words comes to mind like: humble, kind, generous, patient, loving, respectful, helpful, honest, compassionate, law abiding, family oriented, protective, a sense of humor and a person of character. All those words would apply to a "good" person to one degree or another. Would such a person described be found in heaven? Of course! Would all persons described above be found in heaven? No way! What is the difference?

Goodness, itself, is not the total answer. We see in Romans 5:8, "But God demonstrates His own love for us in this: While we were still sinners, Christ died for us." Also in Romans 3:23, "For all have sinned and fall short of the glory of God." And in 1 John 1:9, "If we confess our sins, He is faithful and just and will forgive us our sins and purify us from all unrighteousness." Again in Ephesians 2:8-9, "For it is by grace you have been saved, through faith - and this not from yourselves, it is the gift of God - not by works, so that no one can boast." The difference is having Christ Jesus in your hearts!

When we read the rest of the verse, we see it does NOT say the Lord condemns a "bad" person, but "crafty". How would you describe a "crafty" person? How about: schemer, untruthful, hypocritical, gives expecting return, self-serving, looks out for number one and takes advantage of people or situations? Don't you think that pretty well describes such a person?

Let us look at a particular situation. Two people are asked to ring the bells for the Salvation Army Kettle campaign at Christmas time. The first person says, "Yes, I will be glad to do so. I know you need the money and I am not afraid to give greetings, call out to friends to come help with a few coins and look people in the eye with a smile to cause them to feel more like giving." The second says, "Yes, I will be glad to do so. Please place me at a kettle where there will be a lot of people going by who will recognize me and my profession so that while I am helping you I am also helping my business." Is there anything wrong with getting a return on your business or profession from the help you give? No! What is the difference? Motive and intent. Search your heart for the motives and intents you have for the volunteer work you do and the money you contribute. Is it done for or given expecting a return? Psalm 139:23-24 says, "Search me, O God, and know my heart; test me and know my anxious thoughts. See if there is any offensive way in me, and lead me in the way everlasting."

Know your heart and thoughts, and go out and make this a great day.

Thy works, how beauteous, how divine, that in true meekness used to shine,
That lit thy lonely pathway, trod in wondrous love, O Son of God.
O, who like thee so calm, so bright, so pure, so made to live in light?
O, who like thee did ever go so patient through a world of woe?
Arthur C. Coxe - 1818-1896

January 25

"AND WITHOUT FAITH IT IS IMPOSSIBLE TO PLEASE GOD, because anyone who comes to Him must believe that He exists and that He rewards those who earnestly seek Him." Hebrews 11:6

As love is the basis of the relationship of God to us, so faith is the basis of our relationship to God. Romans 5:8 says, "But God demonstrates His own love for us in this: While we were still sinners, Christ died for us." This is total, absolute love from God. He expects us to show Him the same kind of faith! So strongly does He expect it that He promises us that without faith it is impossible to please God!

Faith is shown in many places in the Bible. In Matthew 8 the centurion came to Jesus and asked Him to say the word and his servant would be healed. Jesus said, "I tell you the truth, I have not found anyone in Israel with such great faith." And the servant was healed. In Mark 5 the woman with the blood issue touched the hem of Jesus' cloak and when Jesus asked who touched Him and heard the story from the woman, He said, "Daughter, your faith has healed you." In 2 Corinthians 5:7 we are told, "We live by faith, not by sight." In Galatians 3:26 we read, "You are all sons of God through faith in Christ Jesus." In Ephesians 6 we read of the armor of God, and in verse 16 we are charged, "In addition to all this, take up the shield of faith, with which you can extinguish all the flaming darts of the evil one."

What is faith? Hebrews 11 tells us in great detail. Today's promise is only one verse in that chapter. The first verse says, "Now faith is being sure of what we hope for and certain of what we do not see." It is just knowing that God is there. It is trusting that peace that comes when we give our lives to Christ. It is the joy that fills our hearts and lives when we are living for Him. Is our faith ever tested? Of course it is! J. O. Fraser, a missionary to China, said, "Faith is like a muscle which grows stronger and stronger with use, rather than rubber, which weakens when it is stretched."

Suppose your earthly father had to go on an out-of-town business trip and you hated to see him leave. He knew of your sadness to see him leave so he promised to bring you a gift. You were cheered by this promise weren't you? He left for the trip and after its completion, returned home. What was the first thing you thought of when he returned? The gift! What great thing had he brought for you? You waited in anticipation. What joy you had when you crawled on his lap and he let you search his pocket to find the very special little illustrated book he had brought to you. Did you doubt he would bring something wonderful? Jesus said in Matthew 7:11, "If you, then, though you are evil, know how to give good gifts to your children, how much more will your Father in heaven give good gifts to those who ask Him!"

Have faith in God, and go out and make this a great day.

Faith of our fathers, living still in spite of dungeon, fire and sword
O how our hearts beat high with joy whene'er we hear that glorious word!
Faith of our fathers, we will love both friend and foe in all our strife;
And preach thee too, as love knows how, by kindly words and virtuous life.
Frederick W. Faber -1814-1863

January 26

"AND HOPE DOES NOT DISAPPOINT US, because God has poured out His love into our hearts by the Holy Spirit, whom He has given us." Romans 5:5

The story is told of the man who had a full service gasoline station in a town near an Army post. One day a family drove up beside the pumps and the man went out to pump the gas, clean the windows, check the oil, etc. The man from the car and his children headed for the bathrooms. The lady asked the station owner, "What kind of town is this? My husband just got transferred here and we are worried." "What kind of town did you leave?" asked the owner. "Oh," said the lady, "we were so sorry to leave. The schools were so good and the children had such good friends. We really loved our church and had so many friends. We also enjoyed all the neat places to shop." "Well," replied the owner, "I think you will find this town a lot like that one." "Wonderful!" exclaimed the lady. With that her husband and children returned, paid and drove off with smiles on their faces as they discussed what the lady had learned.

A short time later another car pulled in and a man and two children got out and headed for the bathrooms. As the owner was starting to service the car the lady asked, "What kind of town is this? My husband just got transferred her and we are worried." "What kind of town did you leave?" asked the owner. "Oh," said the lady, "we were so happy to leave. The schools were so bad and the children had no one to be friends with. We couldn't find a church we liked and the people were so unfriendly. We had to drive miles to find a decent place to shop." "Well," replied the owner, "I think you will find this town a lot like that one." "I was afraid of that!" said the lady. With that her husband and children returned, paid and drove off with frowns on their faces as they discussed what the lady had learned.

Do you feel about your town like the first lady or the second lady? What is the difference in the two of them? IT IS HOPE! Hope does not disappoint us! When you have hope in your heart you can do anything you set your mind to accomplish. We have more hope because God has poured out His love into our hearts by the Holy Spirit, who He has given us. I think the worst thing in the world would be to face the world without hope.

When I was diagnosed with prostate cancer, I turned to the Bible and to books about the disease, specifically, "Me Too-A Doctor Survives Prostate Cancer" by James E. Payne, M.D. When I read the book and studied the Bible, I then was ready to talk to my doctor again. I faced him with hope because of what I had learned. That was in mid 1995 and I am still cancer free.

Do you face a situation which requires hope? Have you lost hope for yourself? You find that hope again in the Lord Jesus Christ by asking Him to pour His love into your heart by the Holy Spirit. Ask him! Claim the promise! Then go out and make this a great day.

My hope is built on nothing less than Jesus blood and righteousness;
I dare not trust the sweetest frame, but wholly lean on Jesus' name.
When darkness seems to hide His face, I rest on His unchanging grace;
In every high and stormy gale, my anchor holds within the vale.
Edward Mote - 1797-1874

January 27

"I WILL BE A FATHER TO YOU AND YOU WILL BE MY SONS AND DAUGHTERS, SAYS THE LORD ALMIGHTY." 2 Corinthians 6:18

Those of us who have had Christian parents can appreciate this promise to the fullest. As I look back over my early life and think of the lessons taught by my earthly father and mother, I thank God for the comfort of today's promise. No matter how busy the day on our farm was scheduled to be, our family always sat down to breakfast after the morning chores were completed and started the day with dad reading a scripture and then a devotional writing accompanying the scripture. Each parent and each of the four children then said their morning prayers before we began to eat. How comforting that was to start the day in that same way every day. We felt the protection of parents who loved us dearly, and it brought to us the lesson of our Heavenly Father who loves us infinitely more and protects us throughout the day.

Regardless of the type family in which you grew to adulthood, you can claim today's promise as your very own and take great comfort in it. During your devotions period, take time to just sit or kneel and commune with your Heavenly Father. Talk to Him as though He were sitting or kneeling right beside you, because He is! It was later in life that I took the time to commune with the Lord. I love to do so in our back yard where I can see our garden and think of Jesus in the Garden of Gethsemane. What a wonderful feeling that is to sit in silence, ask a question, and get a response as plain as though another person was in the room with you and talking with an earthly voice. In the introduction to this devotional book, I told you of some of my conversations with God. They were very clear and plain conversations. I had no doubt in my mind that I had just had a talk with God.

If you didn't have the same type home to grow up in that I had, you can make your current home that way. Slow down, commune with God, ask Him what you should do and how you should schedule your mornings with your family. Take the time to be quiet and listen to the Lord. He will talk to you in a very clear manner if you will. Are your mornings too hurried with various family members going off in different directions? Then go to bed a little earlier, get up earlier, and start the day with God. He will then put His arms around you for the rest of the day, and you will really feel His presence as you go throughout your busy day. What a wonderful blessing you will be giving your children if you set the example of the importance of starting a day with your Heavenly Father and letting Him be a Father to you and you to be His sons and His daughters. You will find answers to difficult questions and situations popping into your head and, at first, you will wonder, "where did that come from?" Later, you will know for sure. It came from your Heavenly Father who has made YOU His sons and daughters.

Try it! Claim it! Talk to God quietly! Then go out and make this a great day.

I come to the garden alone, while the dew is still on the roses;
and the voice I hear, falling on my ear, the Son of God discloses.
He speaks, and the sound of His voice is so sweet the birds hush their singing;
and the melody that He gave to me within my heart is ringing.

C. Austin Miles - 1868-1945

January 28

"Your people settled in it, and from your bounty, O God, YOU PROVIDED FOR THE POOR." Psalm 68:10

When my daughter was thirteen years old I asked her to go with me a few days before Christmas. I had asked The Salvation Army Corps Commander for, and received, the name and address of a single mother and her four children who needed more at Christmas time than the traditional basket of food and a few gifts they were able to give them. We went to visit the family and then went shopping. What a wonderful time we had! We bought canned food, canned hams, a turkey, breads, fruit, staples, etc. and then we went out and bought coats and caps, other clothing, bedding, school supplies, etc. We laughed, cried, argued and bantered for the better part of the day. When we were satisfied with our purchases we drove back to the home. As we made trip after trip to carry in our purchases the eyes of the children (ages 6 to 14) got bigger and bigger, and the eyes of the mother got wetter and wetter. Today, my daughter still says that is the most memorable time she spent with me during her entire life. When my grandson was thirteen, guess how we spent a day during the holidays!

Why did I do what I just described? I felt led to do so at the time. Today's promise tells me exactly why I felt led to do so. God will provide for the poor! In that one case, at that particular time, He used me to provide much needed help for the poor. The promise says, "from your bounty, O God." Where is God's bounty? It is in the lives, possessions and assistance of His people. Are you being a part of God's bounty? In my lifetime, there have been times when I could not have afforded the help I gave at this particular time, but there has never been a time I couldn't give some help.

In Mark 12:41-44 we read, "Jesus sat down opposite the place where the offerings were put and watched the crowd putting their money into the temple treasury. Many rich people threw in large amounts. But a poor widow came and put in two very small copper coins, worth only a fraction of a penny. Calling His disciples to Him, Jesus said, 'I tell you the truth, this poor widow has put more into the treasury than all the others. They all gave out of their wealth; but she, out of her poverty, put in everything - all she had to live on.'" So whether you can give much or little, you should give to God's bounty so that God can provide for the poor through you. God asks for, and desires, our tithes (one tenth) and offerings (what He lays on our hearts to contribute) to be used in His work.

Are you doing your part in fulfilling today's promise? Remember to provide your physical help in mowing a lawn, repairing a door, painting a room, a ride to the doctor, visiting the sick, providing a job and the many other forms of assistance needed. If you are hurting and needing assistance, you can claim today's promise. Help God's bounty, and go out and make this a great day.

Be not dismayed whate'er betide, God will take care of you;
beneath His wings of love abide; God will take care of you.
All you may need He will provide; God will take care of you;
nothing you ask will be denied; God will take care of you.
Civilla D. Martin - 1869-1948

January 29

"Blessed are you when people insult you, persecute you and falsely say all kinds of evil against you because of me. Rejoice and be glad, BECAUSE GREAT IS YOUR REWARD IN HEAVEN, for in the same way they persecuted the prophets who were before you."
Matthew 5:11 & 12

Today, in the United States of America, it is hard for us to conceive of persecution of Christians. In many parts of the world, though, persecution of Christians is a regular occurrence. In many Islamic countries, there are many Christians being persecuted, even unto death. Even in America, we are insulted by people from countries of other beliefs. Our Christianity is one of the big reasons our country is a target of many. We see the torment, capture, abuse, and even murder, of some of our Christians missionaries. This promise today speaks directly to them, as well as to those of us who stay here in America and support them.

We need to pray for our missionaries. This is the greatest thing we can do for them - hold them up to God for His love, comfort and protection of them. We need to provide them with their physical needs, and the financial support necessary to build their ministries wherever they are. Additionally, we need to provide the political support available to us through our elected officials and the diplomatic channels to lessen the abuse Christian missionaries suffer. This we do by electing Godly men and women to public office and support those like minded individuals for appointment to the administrative branch of government.

We have many missionaries serving within our own country. They are in areas in which we have great poverty, crime and dangerous conditions which are a threat to safety and life. These people are insulted and persecuted in perhaps a different way than in another country with a different primary religion, however, they no less need our prayers and financial support.

All these people are very special to God! Today's promise specifically tells us that their reward will be great in heaven. I feel that the reward for those of us who earnestly support them with our prayers and personal and financial support will be likewise great in heaven. It will be because we are sharing in the insults, accusations and persecutions with our support.

Now, let's look at a different type of persecution - one right here among us. Some young Christians were the specific targets of the shooters who went on a rampage in a Colorado high school some time back. Some people are being laughed at because they don't take part in many activities considered "in" by many. These comments from our co-workers, fellow students or neighbors can be hurtful.

We can rejoice in the knowledge that God hears and sees all that happens to us and supports us. In John 16:33 Jesus said, "I have told you these things, so that in me you may have peace. In this world you will have trouble. But take heart! I have overcome the world."

Find your comfort and peace in the Lord, and go out and make this a great day.

Help us to help each other, Lord, each other's cross to bear;
Let each his friendly aid afford, and feel his brother's care.
Help us to build each other up, our little stock improve;
Increase our faith, confirm our hope, and perfect us in love.
Charles Wesley - 1707-1788

January 30

"Marriage should be honored by all, and the marriage bed kept pure, FOR GOD WILL JUDGE THE ADULTERER AND ALL THE SEXUALLY IMMORAL." Hebrews 13:4

Probably nothing that can happen to a marriage will cause as deep, devastating, lasting pain as adultery. In Matthew 19:4-6 we read Jesus' words, "'Haven't you read,' He replied, 'that at the beginning the Creator made them male and female', and said, 'For this reason a man will leave his father and mother and be united to his wife, and the two will become one flesh'? So they are no longer two, but one. Therefore what God has joined together, let man not separate.'" Jesus specifically said a husband and wife become one flesh!

In 1 Corinthians 6:13-20 we read, "'Food for the stomach and the stomach for food' - but God will destroy them both. The body is not meant for sexual immorality, but for the Lord, and the Lord for the body. By His power God raised the Lord from the dead, and He will raise us also. Do you not know that your bodies are members of Christ Himself? Shall I then take the members of Christ and unite them with a prostitute? Never! Do you not know that he who unites himself with a prostitute is one with her in body? For it is said, 'The two will become one flesh.' But he who unites himself with the Lord is one with Him in spirit. Flee from sexual immorality. All other sins a man commits are outside his body, but he who sins sexually sins against his own body. Do you not know that your body is a temple of the Holy Spirit, who is in you, whom you have received from God? You are not your own; you were bought at a price. Therefore honor God with your body."

I put the entire scripture above in today's reading because of the importance of our understanding just how significant adultery and sexual immorality are. Read the scripture again. It clearly says that ALL other sins are outside the body, but sexual immorality is a sin within the temple of God. That is the way you need to think about this sin. It is directly against the temple of God!

We also read the words of Jesus in Matthew 5:27-28, "You have heard that it was said, 'Do not commit adultery.' But I tell you that anyone who looks at a woman lustfully has already committed adultery with her in his heart." In our world today we have many advertisements, many TV shows and movies and the dress of many which causes us to be sexually aroused. What do you do? TURN AWAY! Do not partake of the looks or the sensations! Jesus goes on to say in verse 29, "If your right eye causes you to sin, gouge it out and throw it away. It is better for you to lose one part of your body than for your whole body to be thrown into hell."

If you have committed the sin of adultery and sexual immorality is there hope for you? YES! Confess your sins before God and He is faithful and just and will forgive your sins and cleanse you of ALL unrighteousness! Remain pure, and go out and make this a great day.

Jesus my Lord will love me forever, from Him no pow'r of evil can sever;
He gave His life to ransom my soul - Now I belong to Him!
Once I was lost in sin's degradation; Jesus came down to bring me salvation,
lifted me up from sorrow and shame - Now I belong to Him!
Norman J. Clayton - 1903-

January 31

"Moreover, when God gives any man wealth and possessions, and enables him to enjoy them, to accept his lot and be happy in his work - THIS IS A GIFT OF GOD." Ecclesiastes 5:19

Do you read today's promise the same way I do? I read it to say that God gives us our wealth and possessions along with our ability to enjoy them and be happy in our work. GOD gives us those things! They are a GIFT from GOD!! Should we expect them? Yes, they are a gift from our wonderful Savior. Should we pray for blessings? Yes, if you are living for the Lord you should be praying for God to bless you. In "The Prayer of Jabez" by Bruce Wilkinson are several comments supporting this very concept. I encourage you to get the book and read it over and over again. It is wonderful! In the book, Wilkinson says that "when we ask for God's blessing, we're not asking for more of what we could get for our ourselves. We're crying out for the wonderful, unlimited goodness that only God has the power to know about or give to us." and, "God's bounty is limited only by us, not by His resources, power, or willingness to give." and again later, "God favors those who ask. He holds back nothing from those who want and earnestly long for what He wants."

We were challenged in church one day to read "The Prayer of Jabez" completely through in a day and then to read it a chapter a day (there are seven chapters) for five consecutive weeks. I did that, I prayed the prayer of Jabez faithfully, I communed with God as I described in the introduction to this devotional, and I was led to write this book. I feel that the reason God gave me such a success in my business was to make it possible for me to have the resources I need to devote my time to this writing.

You have a responsibility to God also. You must give back to God. In Luke 6:38 we read, "Give and it will be given to you. A good measure, pressed down, shaken together and running over, will be poured into your lap. For with the measure you use, it will be measured to you." In other words, YOU CAN'T OUT GIVE GOD!!!!!!!! J. Oswald Sanders wrote in "A Spiritual Clinic," "The basic question is not how much of **our** money we should give to God, but how much of **God's** money we should keep for ourselves."

If you have wealth and possessions in quantity you SHOULD enjoy them. You SHOULD accept your lot and be happy in your work. You MUST, however, remember THEY ARE A GIFT OF GOD! Having wealth and possessions is, in no way, a sin. We read in 1 Timothy 6:9-10, "People who want to get rich fall into temptation and a trap and into many foolish and harmful desires that plunge men into ruin and destruction. For the love of money is a root of all kinds of evil. Some people, eager for money, have wandered from the faith and pierced themselves with many griefs." Putting the love of money first - that is the sin.

Love God above all, accept His gifts, and go out and make this a great day.

Give of your best to the Master; Give Him first place in your heart;
Give Him first place in your service, Consecrate ev'ry part.
Give, and to you shall be given; God His beloved Son gave;
Gratefully seeking to serve Him, Give Him the best that you have.

February 1

"My dear children, I write this to you so that you will not sin, but if anybody does sin, WE HAVE ONE WHO SPEAKS TO THE FATHER IN OUR DEFENSE - JESUS CHRIST, the Righteous One." 1 John 2:1

Once we have asked God for forgiveness and become a Christian we stand on 2 Corinthians 25:17, "Therefore, if anyone is in Christ, he is a new creation; the old has gone, the new has come!" What a wonderful change that is in us! We become a new creation IN Christ! We have a great change in our lives and in our hearts. Does this mean we will never sin again? Of course it doesn't. We still live in the carnal world. We are still tempted. We still fail from time to time.

Remember when the disciples came to Jesus and asked Him to teach them to pray He did so by teaching them what we now know as "The Lord's Prayer". In Matthew 6:12 we read, "Forgive us our debts (sins), as we also have forgiven our debtors (those who have sinned against, or offended, us)." Why do you suppose that Jesus taught this prayer to His disciples? He knew the carnal nature of man is to sin. He taught them the prayer to let them know that He wanted them to always ask for forgiveness. If the disciples who physically walked with Jesus needed to continually ask for forgiveness, how much more do we who walk with Him in Spirit?

Today's promise tells us that we should not sin, but if we do sin, we have Jesus Christ as our intercessor to speak to God the Father in our behalf. I recognize the carnal nature within myself. I try to be filled with the love of God at all times, however, I have to work to control my anger and feelings of disdain for those I feel are not serving us in government like they should. I tend to speak quickly and think at a later time about the love of God I should show at all times. I continually have to talk to God about that. I thank Him that Jesus Christ, who walked this earth as a man and knows the failings of all of us, speaks to God the Father in my defense. He speaks in your defense also.

Do you have an area of your life which is difficult for you to get under control? Do you have a co-worker who just "doesn't get it"? Are your parents or your children getting to you? Have you just had difficulty with a clerk in a store or a service person who came to your home? Do you have a bad habit that detracts from your Christian life? Take time in your devotions, prayer and meditation time to talk to God about it. Be still and listen for the answers. God will speak to you about it. He will help you to overcome the "sin nature" you have in yourself. It will take time. Be patient. Develop affirmations which will help you in stressful situations and then practice what you can say in various situations. Call on God, with Jesus Christ speaking in your defense, and go out and make this a great day.

More holiness give me, more striving within;
more patience in suffering, more sorrow for sin;
more faith in my Savior, more sense of His care;
more joy in His service, more purpose in prayer.

Philip P. Bliss - 1838-1876

February 2

"YOU WILL GO OUT IN JOY AND BE LED FORTH IN PEACE; THE MOUNTAINS AND HILLS WILL BURST INTO SONG BEFORE YOU, AND ALL THE TREES OF THE FIELD WILL CLAP THEIR HANDS." Isaiah 55:12

February is a month you sometimes feel you can do without. This is the month we have already enjoyed about all the snow we feel we can for the year. We have endured about all the cold we would like to have for the year. We are developing "cabin fever" and would love a walk in the park. I heard a little verse that went: "Thirty days hath September, April, June and November. All the rest have thirty-one, save February, which just seems like it has 89!" If you are feeling this way today break forth in praise of God. Follow the promise of today and go out in joy, be led forth in peace, join the mountains and hills by bursting into songs of praise and clap your hands along with the trees! The Psalmist said in 43:4-5, "Then will I go to the altar of God, to God, my joy and my delight. I will praise You with the harp, O God, my God. Why are you downcast O my soul? Why so disturbed within me? Put your hope in God, for I will yet praise Him, my Savior and my God."

Do you feel today that you are besieged on every side. Nowhere to turn without work waiting for you? Family members sick with the flu? Not feeling well yourself? Still need to send the "thanks" for those Christmas gifts and no time to do it? Well follow the Psalmist in 31:21, "Praise be to the Lord, for He showed His wonderful love to me when I was in a besieged city." Then go out in joy and be led forth in peace, burst into song and clap your hands for God loves you and cares for you! Claim His promise! Praise His holy name! Praise is comely, praise is correct and praise is due to our Lord and Savior!

When Jesus made His triumphant entry into Jerusalem His disciples were praising Him (Luke 19:38-40), "'Blessed is the king who comes in the name of the Lord! Peace in heaven and glory in the Highest!' Some of the Pharisees in the crowd said to Jesus, 'Teacher, rebuke your disciples!' 'I tell you,' He replied, 'if they keep quiet, the stones will cry out.'" We are told over and over again in Psalm to 'praise Him', 'sing praises to Him', 'sing a new song to Him', not just us, but (Psalm 69:39), "Let heaven and earth praise Him, the seas and all that move in them."

In Psalm 33:1 we read, "Sing joyfully to the Lord, you righteous, it is fitting for the upright to praise Him." This charge in His holy word is why I put a verse or two of hymns at the end of each day's promise devotion. I feel by reading the hymns you will involuntarily burst into song - in your heart, if not on your lips - and praise Him! That joy, peace, singing and clapping will pull you out of the funk and into a glorious day with the Lord Jesus Christ!

Join the world and all therein in His praise, and go out and make this a great day.

Praise Him! Praise Him! Jesus, our blessed Redeemer!
Sing, O earth, His wonderful love proclaim!
Hail Him! Hail Him! Highest archangels in glory;
strength and honor give to His holy name!
Like a shepherd Jesus will guard His children.
In His arms He carries them all day long.

Fanny J. Crosby - 1820-1915

February 3

> "He said to them, 'You are the ones who justify yourselves in the eyes of men, BUT GOD KNOWS YOUR HEARTS. WHAT IS HIGHLY VALUED AMONG MEN IS DETESTABLE IN GOD'S SIGHT." Luke 16:15

We frequently read in the papers about people who are under investigation, or have lost their jobs, because it is discovered they falsified their resumes to show college degrees which were never received. In one case I remember the person showed a degree from a college where he had only attended to audit a course. We wonder why people do such things. I think it is because they are trying to justify themselves in the eyes of men! In doing so, do you think they are bearing false witness about themselves?

From today's promise we see that God knows our hearts. What is highly valued among men is detestable in God's sight. I don't think He cares a whit whether or not we have a college degree, advanced degree, professional degree or a third grade education! I do think that He gives us the ability to think and to reason and that we owe Him and the world our best efforts to develop ourselves to make the best contribution possible. Saying that, I would also say that we should be guided by Philippians 3:7-9, "But whatever was to my profit I now consider loss for the sake of Christ. What is more, I consider everything a loss compared to the surpassing greatness of knowing Christ Jesus my Lord, for whose sake I have lost all things. I consider them rubbish, that I may gain Christ and be found in Him, not having a righteousness of my own that comes from the law, but that which is through faith in Christ - the righteousness that comes from God and is by faith."

What about your life? Are you completely honest in conversation with friends and associates? Do you stretch the truth about your exploits, capabilities or experience? We laugh when we see signs like I saw recently which read, "Welcome hunters, fishermen and other liars". While we laugh about it, we should never want that kind of reputation about ourselves. Strive today to build such a reputation that if you tell someone something, they know it to be the absolute truth. The things you do today which accrue to your profit should be done to the glory of God, otherwise you can consider them but rubbish.

Build your life today around the Lord Jesus Christ and you will find that the character you develop will justify yourselves in the eyes of men whose judgement really means something to you. Keep your heart pure today as you go about your duties, remembering that God knows your heart. When you serve the Lord Jesus Christ you have such a joy and peace that you will just radiate to those around you. You find that there is no need for exaggeration of your abilities and accomplishments to justify yourself in the eyes of men. Your life and your accomplishments will be highly valued by God!

Strive to serve God, not man, and go out and make this a great day.

> I will serve Thee because I love Thee, You have given life to me;
> I was nothing before You found me, You have given life to me.
> Heartaches, broken pieces, ruined lives are why You died on Calvary;
> Your touch was what I longed for, You have given life to me.
>
> Gloria - 1942- & William J. Gaither - 1936-

February 4

"Trust in the Lord with all your heart and lean not on your own understanding; in all your ways acknowledge Him, AND HE WILL MAKE YOUR PATHS STRAIGHT." Proverbs 3:5-6

Have you watched a mother or father play with their little child? Whether they swing them, bounce them, teach them to walk or whatever, the child has total trust in the parent. They know that their parent will keep them safe and will not hurt them. (I know that trust is broken in an abusive home and that is only one of the devastating aspects of an abusive parent!) That trust we see in a child is what God wants from us when He says, "Trust in the Lord with all your heart". I believe in this respect we should consider what Jesus said when the disciples were wondering who is the greatest in the kingdom. In Matthew 18:2-4 we read, "He called a little child and had him stand among them. And He said: 'I tell you the truth, unless you change and become like little children, you will never enter the kingdom of heaven. Therefore, whoever humbles himself like this child is the greatest in the kingdom of heaven.'" So TRUST in the Lord!

Next in the above reading, we are told, 'lean not on your own understanding'. Many things about the scriptures, prophesies, happenings on earth, etc. we don't understand intellectually. That is okay! We go by trust - FAITH - to follow the Lord. We go by things of the heart, not the mind. We are to trust the Lord with all our hearts. Are you in a mode of needing everything explained just so to you? If you can't see it, smell it, taste it, hear it or understand it with your senses are you in question about it? Don't be!

In all your ways acknowledge Him. Trust and faith come from the heart. Our understanding comes from the mind. God knew that. That is why this verse is written in the Bible. God wants you to trust in Him even when things aren't just as you think they should be. God had Samuel choose a successor to Saul, and he considered Jesse's sons, as instructed by God. As the first was before him, Samuel thought this was the one, but we read in 1 Samuel 16 6-7, "When they arrived, Samuel saw Eliab and thought, 'Surely the Lord's anointed stands here before the Lord.' But the Lord said to Samuel, 'Do not consider his appearance or his height, for I have rejected him. The Lord does not look at the things man looks at. Man looks at the outward appearance, but the Lord looks at the heart.'" God then led Samuel to select David. Samuel was initially leaning on his understanding (following his mind), but God wanted him to trust (follow his heart).

When you trust and acknowledge God, He will make your paths straight. As written in Matthew 7:14 (KJV), "Because strait is the gate, and narrow is the way, which leadeth unto life, and few there be that find it". In today's vernacular, stay on the straight and narrow! In other words, you will not be distracted by things of the world which please man, but will be focused on God and enjoy a life led by Him. He will not deliver you from problems. He will lead you through them. Do that right now, and go out and make this a great day.

Simply trusting ev'ry day, trusting thru a stormy way;
even when my faith is small, trusting Jesus - that is all.
Trusting Him while life shall last. Trusting Him 'til earth be past.
'Til I hear His final call. Trusting Jesus - that is all.

Edgar Page Stites - 1836-1921

February 5

> "The word of God is living and active. Sharper than any double-edged sword, IT PENETRATES EVEN TO DIVIDING SOUL AND SPIRIT, JOINTS AND MARROW; IT JUDGES THE THOUGHTS AND ATTITUDES OF THE HEART." Hebrews 4:12

In the introduction to this devotional I wrote, "This devotional is not, however, designed to replace your Bible study and reading." I hope that you have continued with your Bible study through this year. If you are not in the habit of daily reading and study of the Bible, then you need to start TODAY! Read today's promise again. The Bible IS the word of God. It is living and active! In his book, "Life At Eighty As I See It", Arthur Flake wrote: "When I first became a Christian, I lived in New York City, and did I feel lonely! I had to give up the crowd I was running with and form new friendships. I was advised by the man who led me to Christ to read the Bible. After business hours I would go to my room and read my Bible often for hours at a time. Though I did not understand all I read, and still do not, I did understand much that I read, and it made me feel that I was not alone but that I had a dear Friend who cared for me. Today I read the same identical verses and chapters I read then. Although I have read many of them hundreds of times, they are, I believe, sweeter today than they were then. What other book can one read with such results?" Someone else once said, "Other books were given for our information; the Bible was given for our transformation."

Today's promise tells us His word penetrates our very being, both mind and soul! When we read His word we learn things which cause us to look at our thoughts and attitudes of the heart. His word tells us many things, including how to live, love, think, give, forgive, pray, speak, praise, sing, befriend, help, and comfort.

Psalm is full of references to His word. Not only is His word sharper than a double-edged sword, but we see in Psalm 18:30, "As for God, His way is perfect, the word of the Lord is flawless. He is a shield for all who take refuge in Him." It is also a flawless shield against the arrows of the devil. We see in Psalm 56:4, "In God, whose word I praise, in God I trust (sounds like a great national motto!); I will not be afraid. What can mortal man do to me?" What can mortal man do to you when you have God's word as your shield? We read in Psalm 119:9-11, "How can a young man keep his way pure? By living according to Your word. I seek You with all my heart; do not let me stray from Your commands. I have hidden Your word in my heart that I might not sin against You." Not only read God's word, but memorize it so that you do not sin!

Psalm 119:105 says, "Your word is a lamp to my feet and a light to my path." Reading your Bible daily will give you guidance for your Christian journey. Whether you are physically in the brightest noonday or the darkest night, your thoughts and actions will be guided by God's word! We are promised in Psalm 119:89, "Your word, O Lord, is eternal; it stands firm in the heavens." Read it, memorize it, live it, and go out and make this a great day.

> Thy word is a lamp to my feet, a light to my path alway,
> to guide and to save me from sin and show me the heav'nly way.
> Forever, O Lord, is Thy word established and fixed on high;
> Thy faithfulness unto all men abideth forever nigh.
>
> Ernest O. Sellers - 1869-1952

February 6

"When you pray, go into your room, close the door and pray to your Father, who is unseen. Then your Father, who sees what is done in secret, WILL REWARD YOU."
Matthew 6:6

Public prayer has its place and I would never discourage such praying in any manner. However, we are instructed in the Bible to pray in SECRET! Do you have a regular prayer time when you can go into a room by yourself and spend time in prayer to God? If not, this is the time to start it. You don't have time for it? The truth is you don't have time not to do it. The prayer time you have with God will still your heart, take worry off your mind, relax you, prepare you for the day and allow you to be much more productive as you work. That extra productivity while you work is a part of the reward promised in today's "Promise".

Jesus taught the Disciples to pray. It was a short, simple prayer. This is what I think of the most when I think of a public prayer. Remember, Jesus spent hours and days in prayer. He encouraged time in prayer. How do we pray when we "go into our room"?

Prayer has five components. The first of these is PRAISE. The second of these is FORGIVENESS (and remember in the Lord's Prayer, Jesus taught us to say, "Forgive us our debts (sins), as we also have forgiven our debtors." Therefore, with this one honest phrase you remove the sin and you remove the failure to forgive, either of which would lead to unanswered prayer. The third component is THANKSGIVING. We are instructed in 1 Thessalonians 5:18 to "give thanks in all circumstances, for this is God's will for you in Christ Jesus." The fourth component of prayer is PETITION. With petition you unselfishly ask God for your own needs. Is it selfish to ask God for health? No! The body is the temple of God and to ask for health is to ask God for blessings on His temple. The fifth component is INTERCESSION. With intercession you are without limit in area of the earth you can impact! You carry the request to God for whomever you choose and for whatever you choose which you think is best for them. What a wonderful, fulfilling thought!

Read Paul's letters and you find many examples of intercession. He says in Colossians 1:9 "For this reason, since the day we heard about you, we have not stopped praying for you and asking God to fill you with the knowledge of His will through all spiritual wisdom and understanding." I think when I read words such as these how wonderful it must have been to have someone like Paul praying for you. Then I think of all those I know who have prayed for me, my parents, relatives and friends. I rest in the knowledge that I DO have someone like Paul praying for me! It now becomes my responsibility to pray for others, and like Paul said in

1 Thessalonians 1:2 "We always thank God for all of you, mentioning you in our prayers." Do you mention those for whom you pray by name in your prayers? Pray and make this a great day!

Prayer is the heart's sincere desire, Uttered or unexpressed;
The motion of a hidden fire that trembles in the breast.
Prayer is the simplest form of speech that infant lips can try;
And prayer's sublimest strain doth reach the Majesty on high.

John B. Dykes

February 7

"I tell you the truth, anyone who gives you a cup of water in my name because you belong to Christ WILL CERTAINLY NOT LOSE HIS REWARD." Mark 9:41

Thomas Watson said in his book, "Gleanings From Thomas Watson", "There is a blessed kind of giving, which, though it makes the purse lighter, makes the crown heavier." I think today's promise and Thomas Watson's quote say the same thing. This promise is gleaned from the report of Jesus' teaching to prepare His disciples. This is from the section teaching the attitude of servanthood. In Matthew 20:25-28 Jesus is also teaching the disciples, "Jesus called them together and said, 'You know that the rulers of the Gentiles lord it over them, and their high officials exercise authority over them. Not so with you. Instead, whoever wants to become great among you must be your servant, and whoever wants to be first must be your slave - just as the Son of Man did not come to be served, but to serve, and to give His life as a ransom for many.'"

And again in Matthew 23:11 Jesus said, "The greatest among you will be your servant." Look also at John 12:26 where Jesus says, "Whoever serves me must follow me; and where I am, my servant also will be. My Father will honor the one who serves me."

Perhaps the greatest show of servanthood came when Mary was visited by the angel to be told of the coming birth of Jesus. She responded in Luke 1:38, "'I am the Lord's servant,' Mary answered. 'May it be to me as you have said.' Then the angel left her." Now here is a virgin young lady about to be married to an upstanding man who is visited by an angel to be told she will become pregnant while a virgin and give birth to a great King. How would you respond? Would you not be a whole lot surprised, worried, scared and desperate for a way out? Look again at John 12:26 above. If you are to serve Christ you must follow Him! Now, the rest of that verse in John says, "My Father will honor the one who serves me." Mary served greatly and Mary was, and is, honored among all women who ever lived!

Do you look for the little ways to serve each and every day? Who can you serve? Start with your family! I have heard it said that marriage is a 50-50 proposition. I disagree! I think that marriage is an 80-20 proposition for each partner; that is, each partner should strive to give 80% of the serving to the marriage. The reason I don't think they should strive for 100% of the giving is because I feel each should gracefully accept the service of the other. Next look to your church to find ways to serve, then to your associates, friends, neighbors and strangers. Some of my most memorable feelings have come when I have helped a stranger, and to this day they don't know who I am, only that I mentioned "in God's name" to them.

Serve God today. Follow God today. Be with God today. Give that cup of cold water in His name. You will not lose your reward and you will find that you have made this a great day.

Since I started for the Kingdom, since my life He controls,
since I gave my heart to Jesus, the longer I serve Him, the sweeter He grows.
Every need He is supplying. Plenteous grace He bestows;
Every day my way gets brighter, the longer I serve Him, the sweeter He grows.
William J. Gaither - 1965-

February 8

"HEAL ME, O LORD, AND I WILL BE HEALED; save me and I will be saved, for you are the One I praise." Jeremiah 17:14

It is very difficult to try to explain to unbelievers why a Christian dies of an accident or an illness. They know of the promises of God just like today's promise. What do you say to these people? In his book, "Why Us?", Warren W. Wiersbe writes, "Ultimate healing and the glorification of the body are certainly among the blessings of calvary for the believing Christian. Immediate healing is not guaranteed. God can heal any disease, but He is not obligated to do so." We know that we will all die some day. God chooses that day and the method of death. We can rest on the last part of today's promise, "Save me and I will be saved!" What a wonderful thought to carry always in our minds and hearts both. What a reason to praise God!

What DOES today's promise mean? Here are some study results which have been taken from several different sources:

1. Christians, as an average, have lower blood pressure, cholesterol levels and blood pressure.
2. Of 232 elderly patients undergoing elective heart surgery those who described themselves as deeply religious were more likely to be alive six months later than the others.
3. Repetitive prayer and the rejection of negative thoughts can benefit treatment of a number of diseases.
4. Heart patients who had someone praying for them without their knowledge suffered 10% fewer complications.
5. People who attend church weekly live an average of seven years longer than people who never attend church.
6. More than half of all medical schools in the United States now offer courses or forums on spirituality and health.
7. A poll in 1997 said 63% of people want to talk to their doctors about faith, and 40% want their doctors to pray with them.
8. Those who describe themselves as devout Christians take less sick days, have fewer surgeries and live longer lives than others.

I think these findings prove today's promise. Just in the past year I have heard of several instances of doctors saying the cure had nothing to do with the practice of medicine, that it was truly a miracle. I also firmly believe that the life style of a Christian has a lot to do with the above findings. Christians have fewer destructive habits, they go to fewer places that negatively impact their health, they tend to overindulge far less, their temperament is far less likely to cause negative health effects and they tend to be less involved in destructive relationships.

Enjoy the health given by God, and go out and make this a great day.

Came the leper to Christ, saying, "Surely I know that Thou, Lord, canst make me whole!"
When his great faith was seen, Jesus said, "Yes, I will," and touched him and made him clean.
He has healed my sick soul, made me every whit whole, and He'll do the same for you;
He's the same yesterday and today and for aye, this healer of men today.

Lois Irwin - 1926-

February 9

"But I TELL YOU THAT MEN WILL HAVE TO GIVE ACCOUNT ON THE DAY OF JUDGMENT FOR EVERY CARELESS WORD THEY HAVE SPOKEN." Matthew 12:36

As I grew up, one of the little poems we learned was: Keep your words soft and tender and sweet, for you never know which ones you will have to eat! Today's promise is much more blunt and explicit. Every careless word we utter will be on our account on the day of judgement. We must remember Psalm 139:4, "Before a word is on my tongue You know it completely, O Lord." So know that your words are registered with God. I also want you to consider Proverbs 6:16-19, "There are six things the Lord hates, seven that are detestable to Him: haughty eyes, **a lying tongue**, hands that shed innocent blood, a heart that devises wicked schemes, feet that are quick to rush into evil, **a false witness who pours out lies** and **a man who stirs up dissension among brothers.**" Three of those things that are detestable to the Lord are a result of us not bridling our tongue. Are you beginning to get an idea of just how important our words are to our Lord Jesus Christ, and how strongly He wants us to control our tongue?

James tells us in 3:5-6, "Likewise the tongue is a small part of the body, but it makes great boasts. Consider what a great forest is set on fire by a small spark. The tongue also is a fire, a world of evil among the parts of the body. It corrupts the whole person, sets the whole course of his life on fire, and is itself set on fire by hell." And, again in 1:26, "If anyone considers himself religious and yet does not keep a tight rein on his tongue, he deceives himself and his religion is worthless." Wow! Our religion is worthless! Why would he say that? We read in Proverbs 12:18 just why, "Reckless words pierce like a sword, but the tongue of the wise brings healing." And in Psalm 34:12-13, "Whoever of you loves life and desires to see many good days, keep your tongue from evil and your lips from speaking lies."

Now how about the targets of careless words, how do they feel? Did you ever taste something that was so bitter that the awful taste stayed with you all day, even though you washed out your mouth and did your best to get rid of it? Listen to Job 34:3, "For the ear tests words as the tongue tastes food." When your words are careless and bitter to a person, they carry that awful taste with them for many days. That is why God wants us to control our tongue and not be guilty of 'careless words'. That is why we will have to give account on the day of judgment for EVERY careless word we have spoken. Do you need to change the way you speak? Do you need to talk to a family member, associate or friend about their words? If you do, remember to keep your words to them about their words to you like the poem I learned as a boy!

Keep your faith in God. Follow His direction. Pray for wisdom today. Remain in His tender, loving care. Then you can count on the words of Job 5:21, "You will be protected from the lash of the tongue, and need not fear when destruction comes.

Make your words today the words of life, and go out and make this a great day.

Sing them over again to me - wonderful words of life;
Let me more of their beauty see - wonderful words of life.
Words of life and beauty, teach me faith and duty;
Beautiful words, wonderful words, wonderful words of life.
Philip P. Bliss - 1838-1876

February 10

"No temptation has seized you except what is common to man. And God is faithful; HE WILL NOT LET YOU BE TEMPTED BEYOND WHAT YOU CAN BEAR. BUT WHEN YOU ARE TEMPTED, HE WILL ALSO PROVIDE A WAY OUT SO THAT YOU CAN STAND UP UNDER IT." 1 Corinthians 10:13.

Today's promise is one that I need so often. I frequently fall into the trap of letting anger and bitterness creep into my thoughts. I constantly ask for strength in that area of my life. I guess I am like a lot of other people. The magazine "Discipleship Journal" asked its readers to rank the areas of greatest spiritual challenge to them. The results came back in this order:

1. Materialism 2. Pride 3. Self-centeredness 4. Laziness
5. Anger/Bitterness 5. (Tie) Sexual lust 7. Envy 8. Gluttony 9. Lying

The respondents also noted that temptations were more potent when they had neglected their time with God (81%) and when they were physically tired (57%).

Resisting temptation was accomplished by prayer (84%), avoiding compromising situations (76%), Bible study (66%) and being accountable to someone else (52%).

Notice that prayer was mentioned as the number one way people resisted temptation. The Bible addresses this in the Lord's Prayer in Matthew 6:13, "And lead us not into temptation, but deliver us from the evil one." From this, I would say that prayer should be the number one way to resist temptation, but I would add the best prayer is pre-prayer - asking God to keep you from temptation. It is far better to **avoid** temptation than it is to **bear** temptation! Ralph Waldo Emerson once said, "Call on God, but row away from the rocks."

How do you avoid temptation? Alcoholics Anonymous teaches those who attend their meetings they can help remain sober by avoiding those they used to drink with and the places they used to drink. From this we should see that to avoid temptation, if possible, we should stay away from people and places where the greatest temptations exist for us. What about your life today? Are there places or situations where you feel great temptation to sin? Can they be avoided? If so, then avoid them. If not, then call upon God in advance. God is faithful! He will not let you be tempted beyond what you can bear! He will also provide a way out so that you can stand up under the temptation!

Read Matthew 4:1-11. When Jesus fasted for 40 days and was then tempted by the devil, He answered the challenge to turn stones to bread by saying, "Man does not live on bread alone, but on every word that comes from the mouth of God." He answered the challenge to throw himself down from the high place so the angels would catch Him by saying, "It is also written: 'Do not put the Lord your God to the test.'" And finally He just said, "Away from me, Satan!"

Avoid temptation today if possible, if not, trust in the Lord, and make this a great day.

Ere you left your room this morning, did you think to pray?
In the name of Christ, our Saviour, did you sue for loving favor as a shield today?
When you met with great temptation, did you think to pray?
By His dying love and merit did you claim the Holy Spirit as your guide and stay?
Mary A. Kidder - 1820-1905

February 11

"AND GOD IS ABLE TO MAKE ALL GRACE ABOUND TO YOU, SO THAT IN ALL THINGS AT ALL TIMES, HAVING ALL THAT YOU NEED, YOU WILL ABOUND IN EVERY GOOD WORK." 2 Corinthians 9:8

My Bible dictionary defines "grace" as follows: The theological use of this word denotes the free favor of God, bestowed upon men without any merit or claim on their part. Hence the New Testament is called the gospel of the grace of God because it reveals the plan by which this grace is bestowed consistently with the divine attributes. Those divine attributes are the atonement, mediation and intercession of the Lord Jesus Christ. It is in and through the Lord Jesus Christ alone the free, rich and eternal fullness of God's favor is dispensed.

In 1 Timothy 1:12-14, Paul says, "I thank Christ Jesus our Lord, who has given me strength, that He considered me faithful, appointing me to His service. Even though I was once a blasphemer and a persecutor and a violent man, I was shown mercy because I acted in ignorance and unbelief. The GRACE of our Lord was poured out on me abundantly, along with the faith and love that are in Christ Jesus." Paul readily recognized that he had received the favor of God and admitted that he was without merit to receive that favor.

Now, understanding what grace is, and that we receive it without any merit or claim on our part, today's promise really becomes something special! Note the conditions under which you will receive God's grace: IN ALL THINGS! AT ALL TIMES! HAVING ALL THAT YOU NEED! WOW! What a promise! You, yourself, alone, are the recipient of God's grace in such abundance.

What are you to do with all the grace from God? Just what the promise says you are to do - ABOUND IN EVERY GOOD WORK! As you go about your normal routine today look for ways you can be involved in God's good work. Does your child need training to master a new skill? Does an associate need help on a project? Is a neighbor ill and in need of a pot of soup for the family dinner tonight? Look back to February 7. Whatever you do, do in the name of Christ and you WILL receive your reward!

Do you feel that you are unworthy of God's grace? You should know that you are a one- of-a-kind person. There is no one else in the world like you. No one has your DNA. God cares, and knows, so much about you that even the hairs of your head are numbered. Regardless of the vileness of your past sin, God's grace is sufficient for you. Look at Paul before his conversion. By his own words he was a blasphemer, persecutor and violent man. He acted in ignorance because he had not received God in his heart. Jesus died for your sins just like He died for Paul's sins. You can claim the grace of God just as surely as Paul could. You will abound in every good work just as well as Paul did.

Claim God's grace right now, and go out and make this a great day.

Marvelous, infinite, matchless grace, freely bestowed on all who believe!
You that are longing to see His face, will you this moment His grace receive?
Grace, grace, God's grace, grace that will pardon and cleanse within;
Grace, grace, God's grace, grace that is greater than all our sin!
Julia H. Johnston - 1849-1919

February 12

> "To the Jews who had believed him, Jesus said, 'If you hold to my teaching, you are really my disciples. Then YOU WILL KNOW THE TRUTH, and THE TRUTH WILL SET YOU FREE." John 8:31 & 32

Do you have a harmful habit? Jesus is the key that unlocks the door to freedom from all the harmful habits we could ever have. Maybe you, or someone you know has a habit which detracts from the great life Jesus promised us. Maybe you, or they, are in denial about the habit. This is not unusual. Denial is one of the major ways most people deal with something in their lives which should not be there. Most times we don't know what to do to break the habit or even how to ask for help. If this fits you today, you are not powerless!

You can't deny it to God, however. He is omnipotent! He loved you from the first when you were conceived! He understands your weaknesses. Paul said in 2 Corinthians 12:10, "That is why, for Christ's sake, I delight in weaknesses, in insults, in hardships, in persecutions, in difficulties. For when I am weak, then I am strong." And again in Romans 8:26, "In the same way, the Spirit helps us in our weakness. We do not know what we ought to pray for, but the Spirit himself intercedes for us with groans that words cannot express."

Pray to God! God's presence within is power that gives you the freedom from negative habits. God in you is stronger than the strongest habit you may have. If you don't know how to ask God for help, just pray! 'The Spirit will intercede for you with groans that words cannot express.' The power of God overcomes any habit or inclination that detracts from your pure and productive life.

Your fight to overcome the negative habit may be a blessing to someone who is watching your life. God may use your weakness to speak to someone else. Remember, Paul said, "When I am weak, then I am strong." Your weakness may allow God to show through your life to influence a friend, a neighbor, a fellow worker, etc. "Cast all your cares on Him for He cares for you." God loves you. God wants you to live a pure, holy life. God will give you the strength to live that life if you will lean on him. By trusting in God and in God's strength in overcoming your weaknesses you can succeed, and go out and make it a great day!

> "What have I to dread, what have I to fear, Leaning on the everlasting arms;
> I have blessed peace with my Lord so near, Leaning on the everlasting arms.
> Leaning on Jesus, leaning on Jesus, Safe and secure from all alarms;
> Leaning on Jesus, Leaning on Jesus, Leaning on the everlasting arms."
>
> Rev. E. A. Hoffman

February 13

"Call to me and I WILL ANSWER YOU AND TELL YOU GREAT AND UNSEARCHABLE THINGS YOU DO NOT KNOW." Jeremiah 33:3

This promise is so precious to everyone. From the child just exploring his new world to the research scientist exploring the scientific unknown and medical researchers studying ways to treat diseases and finding cures for illnesses. The first challenge is to call on God! I firmly believe that God will help the child in his discoveries of his new surroundings if called upon. I read the story of the father who was putting in a new garbage disposal while his two year old son watched. Several attempts were unsuccessful and the father was becoming discouraged. He decided to make one more attempt and before he began said to his son, "Now you pray for me." Not knowing what to say, the son bowed his head and repeated the only prayer he was comfortable with, "Now I lay me down to sleep..." The father chuckled as he stuck his head back under the sink to make yet another attempt. To his surprise, the garbage disposal fit right into place and it was just a matter of tightening everything up and the job was completed. While the young son didn't know how to ask for what he wanted, Romans 8:26 tells us in part, "the Spirit Himself intercedes for us with groans that words cannot express." God heard the young son's prayer, and, with the intercession of Jesus, understood the request and granted it. Encourage your children to pray.

I also believe that God will answer the research scientists and medical researchers if called upon. He will tell those scientists and medical researchers great and unsearchable things they do not yet know. Thank God for Christian scientists and doctors whose work contribute so much to our world!

Whether you need God's help in cleaning your home, typing a page, taking a test or closing a sale, call on God and He will answer you! This is a what makes this promise so precious! There may be others who know what you need to know or be able to do what you need to do, but God promises to answer YOU and tell YOU great and unsearchable things YOU do not know!

This promise is a treasure to you. You have a mighty power into which to tap. You need not fear a school assignment or test, a business assignment or change of jobs nor a chore around the house. Now I am not going to tell you that God will give you the answers to a test without your having done the proper study for that test. He will, however, give you a clear mind and freedom from distractions so your mind will be free to pull the information into your conscious mind at the proper time. By being relaxed and confident at the time you have a need, you will find that you can concentrate on the task at hand and perform at a higher level than you thought.

Call on God today, He will answer you, and you can go out and make it a great day!

"Did you pray it through till the answer came?
There's a promise true for your faith to claim;
At the place of prayer Jesus waits for you,
Did you meet Him there, Did you pray it through?"

Rev. W. C. Poole - 1875-1949

February 14

"THE LORD IS CLOSE TO THE BROKENHEARTED AND SAVES THOSE WHO ARE CRUSHED IN SPIRIT." Psalm 34:18

There are many ways to become brokenhearted or crushed in spirit. From the child who drops a toy and breaks it, to the parent who loses a child in death, to a person who is wrongfully charged of some misdeed, there are many degrees of brokenheartedness. We find that the child who broke his toy soon has other distractions and goes about his way. This does not mean that the Lord does not hear his cry of despair and respond to it. No, God is interested in all the 'little' things that worry any of us. In this regard I remember the story reported in 2 Kings 6:1-7, "The company of the prophets said to Elisha, 'Look, the place where we meet with you is too small for us. Let us go to the Jordan, where each of us can get a pole; and let us build a place there for us to live.' And he said, 'Go.' Then one of them said, 'Won't you please come with your servants?' 'I will,' Elisha replied. And he went with them. They went to the Jordan and began to cut down trees. As one of them was cutting down a tree, the iron axhead fell into the water. 'Oh, my lord,' he cried out, 'it was borrowed!' The man of God asked, 'Where did it fall?' When he showed him the place, Elisha cut a stick and threw it there, and made the iron float. 'Lift it out,' he said. Then the man reached out his hand and took it." Now iron is almost eight times as dense as water, yet the axhead floated. God was interested in the 'little thing' like a lost axhead which had been borrowed and He gave Elisha the power to float it in water. Can you, therefore, doubt He is interested in all things for a child?

Regardless of how Bathsheba became David's wife, she bore him a son. This story is recorded in 2 Samuel 12. The Lord struck down the child which Bathsheba had born David, and David was brokenhearted. He fasted and spent the nights lying on the ground. On the seventh day the child died and David arose, washed, put on clean clothes and went about his business. When the servants asked him why he mourned before the death and not afterward, David's answer is recorded in verse 23, "...I will go to him, but he will not return to me." Personally, I can not imagine the grief of losing a child, however, I do know that the Lord will be close to those who do. Your little child will be with God in heaven. You, like David, will be able to go to them, but they will not return to you.

I have a dear friend who was wrongfully accused and went through a long time of anguish, self-doubt, torment, turmoil and communing with God. He told me, "I am just crushed! It just broke my heart!" What sorrow that pain caused me to observe! But, guess what! The Lord is faithful! He bound up the broken heart and he saved that one with the crushed spirit! I know He did, because I watched the episode from the beginning. Are you or do you have friends who are brokenhearted? Call on the Lord, He will be close and save those with a crushed spirit.

Now go out and make this a great day.

My friend, won't you cast your care on the Lord;
There's grace for the asking and courage to dare;
His peace like a fountain will comfort your soul,
For the Lord, He is God and He cares about you.

Vernon M. Whaley - 1949-

February 15

"Cast all your anxiety on Him because HE CARES FOR YOU." 1 Peter 5:7

After I completed college I was fortunate to receive a part time fellowship and part time teaching assistantship. I attended Oklahoma State University, where I earned a Master's degree in Chemistry. I then taught Chemistry at the college level for five years. Several of my students would be very anxious before taking tests. I would counsel them to study hard in advance, get a good night's rest before the test, relax as I handed out the tests and then do their very best with a clear mind. I would tell them the only thing they could accomplish by worrying about the test would be to lower their test scores. I'm not sure just how many followed all of my advice, but I do know that I had several very fine students who obtained good results. What I was trying to get them to do was to lay their anxiety aside. That is what God wants us to do. He wants us to lay our anxiety on Him! Why? Because He cares for us!

This is said a little differently in Psalm 37: 4-6, "Delight yourself in the Lord and He will give you the desires of your heart. Commit your way to the Lord; trust in Him and He will do this: He will make your righteousness shine like the dawn, the justice of your cause like the noonday sun." Jesus told us in Matthew 6:25-27, "Therefore I tell you, do not worry about your life, what you will eat or drink; or about your body, what you will wear. Is not life more important than food, and the body more important than clothes? Look at the birds of the air, they do not sow or reap or store away in barns, and yet your heavenly Father feeds them. Are you not much more valuable than they? Who of you by worrying can add a single hour to his life?" And, again in Psalm 55:22, "Cast your cares on the Lord and He will sustain you; He will never let the righteous fall."

These additional scriptures support today's promise! Jesus wants us to be His friends. In fact, in John 15:14-15 we read the words of Jesus, "You are my friends if you do what I command. I no longer call you servants, because a servant does not know his master's business. Instead, I have called you friends, for everything that I learned from my Father I have made known to you." Do you have close friends you turn to so you can discuss problems you have? You do if you have Jesus as your friend! Jesus is your friend if you are doing what he commands you to do. Talk over all your problems and concerns with Jesus in prayer. Take all your anxious thoughts to Him. He wants them because He cares for you! You can count on the support of Him because you have His promise.

When you have family, friends or associates who are carrying a burden of anxiety, lead them to this devotional promise. Pray with them to help them reach a place of calm peacefulness with the Lord. Is it your responsibility? YES! As Jesus told Peter - FEED MY SHEEP! You have that duty as a Christian.

Keep your friend, Jesus, ever near, and go out and make this a great day.

What a Friend we have in Jesus, all our sins and griefs to bear!
What a privilege to carry everything to God in prayer!
O what peace we often forfeit, O what needless pain we bear,
all because we do no carry everything to God in prayer.

Joseph Scriven - 1819-1886

February 16

"Yet to all who received Him, to those who believed in His name, HE GAVE THE RIGHT TO BECOME CHILDREN OF GOD." John 1:12

Jesus loves children. They are special to Him. In Matthew 18:10 Jesus said, "See that you do not look down on one of these little ones. For I tell you that their angels in heaven always see the face of my Father in heaven." Wow! Nowhere in the Bible does it say that adults have an angel who always see the face of God! I think this tells us the value God, and Jesus, places on children.

That makes today's promise very special! All of us who receive Him and believe in His name are given the right to become the children of God! I think back to my earthly father and my years growing up on our farm in Northern Kansas. I saw him on many occasions with a pencil, a sheet of paper and his checkbook before him at the dining room table as he figured how he could provide the needs of his wife and four growing children and all their demands for clothes, shoes, food (though most of it was grown right there on the farm), books and other needs. We didn't have a lot of what some people would call 'the finer things', but we had a home filled with love, adequate and warm clothing, plenty of fresh food and Christian teaching. I will always thank God for that heritage.

I think Jesus had my father in mind when he said in Matthew 7:9-11, "Which of you, if his son asks for bread, will give him a stone? Or if he asks for a fish, will give him a snake? If you, then, though your are evil (meaning born in sin), know how to give good gifts to your children, how much more will your Father in heaven give good gifts to those who ask Him!" My father knew how to give his children wonderfully good gifts and yet, God gives us so much more. How wonderful it is to be able to go to God any time, any place, for any reason to let our needs be known to Him and, like a good father, He will treat us like His own dear children, which we are.

Have you received Him as your personal Savior? Have you believed on His name? If you have, do those who are close to you share your Christian experience? Are you witnessing for Him like He has instructed us to do? If the answer to any of these questions is "NO", then you need to go to God in prayer. He is faithful and just and He will hear your prayer and He will give you the right to become His child. What a wonderful promise that is to receive and to share with those we love! You can't get there by being a "good" person. He told us in Ephesians 2:9, "Not by works, so that no one can boast." You can not "good works" your way to heaven. It is only by the confession of sins, asking forgiveness through faith and receiving salvation as the gift of God. I pray that you and your loved ones be true "Children of God" today.

Receive Him, believe on Him, become His children, and go out and make this a great day.

Children of the heavenly Father safely in His bosom gather;
Nestling bird nor star in heaven such a refuge e'er was given.
Though He giveth or He taketh, God His children ne'er forsaketh;
His the loving purpose solely to preserve them pure and holy.

Carolina Sandell Berg - 1832-1903

February 17

"Each man should give what he has decided in his heart to give, not reluctantly or under compulsion, FOR GOD LOVES A CHEERFUL GIVER." 2 Corinthians 9:7

When I was 10 years old I was playing in the yard and found a nickel. We didn't have much cash money back then. That evening I was being a smart aleck and showing everyone in the family the nickel I had found, and bragging about what I would buy with it. At my most obnoxious point I said, "Bet none of you has a nickel." At this point Dad reached into his pocket, pulled out a dime and said, "You are right. All I have is a dime." Not to be outdone I said, "Yes, but look. My coin is bigger that your coin." He replied, "You are right." I then said, "I'll trade you my big coin for your little one." He agreed, "Okay." The trade was then made. Now I really felt smart since I had fooled Dad so bad. I ran to the stairway door, opened it and started upstairs to my bedroom, closing the door behind me. Having to have the last word, I ran back down, opened the door and said, "I fooled you! Your coin was smaller, but it was worth more and now I have it. You gave me more money." Dad calmly looked at me and cheerfully said, "I knew that, but it is more blessed to give than to receive."

I thought about what Dad had said for a long time, and instinctively knew that he had just taught me a very good, strong lesson. That lesson has stayed with me for my entire life since that time and has guided many of my actions. It has set a pattern for me as I love to give gifts, give help, give advice, give time and, hopefully, give more meaning to life for those around me.

When God spoke to me about my not being faithful in my tithes I knew I had to do something to set God's money apart so I would always know it was His and not mix it up. I set up a separate account with a 10% automatic monthly transfer from my regular account. Since that money is in a separate account there is no temptation to spend it for something we might need or want. When I give my check to the church each month I do so with a very happy, cheerful feeling because, psychologically I know I am passing along God's money to Him. If you have trouble making sure you tithe each month you might like to try the same thing. My tithe account is set up with no service charge and no charge for checks.

Are we only to give 10% to God's work? Good question! I believe the 10% 'belongs' to the Lord. We can, and should, give offerings to the work of God. See in Deuteronomy 12:6 the phrase, "...your tithes and special gifts...". In 12:11 the phrase, "...your tithes and special gifts, and all the choice possessions you have vowed to the Lord...". In 2 Chronicles 31:12 it says, "... tithes and dedicated gifts...", in Nehemiah 12:44, "...firstfruits and tithes..." and in Malachi 3:8, "...tithes and offerings...". Doesn't that sound like we should do more than 10%? Whatever you decide in your heart to give, do so without reluctance or compulsion. For God loves a cheerful giver! Give as God leads you to give, and go out and make this a great day.

Give of your best to the Master, give Him first place in your heart;
Give Him first place in your service; consecrate every part.
Give, and to you shall be given. God His beloved Son gave;
Gratefully seeking to serve Him, give Him the best that you have.

Howard B. Grose - 1851-1939

February 18

> "Do not be anxious about anything, but in everything, by prayer and petition, with thanksgiving, present your requests to God. AND THE PEACE OF GOD, WHICH TRANSCENDS ALL UNDERSTANDING, WILL GUARD YOUR HEARTS AND YOUR MINDS IN CHRIST JESUS." Philippians 4:6 & 7

Today's promise sounds a lot like what we read in 1 Thessalonians 5:16-18, "Be joyful always; pray continually; give thanks in all circumstances, for this is God's will for you in Christ Jesus." These verses DO NOT say, "In some things be resigned", or "pray once in a while", or "be pretty happy most of the time". Rather, it says, "be joyful always", pray "continually" and "give thanks in ALL circumstances". Why should we do this? Because it is God's will for you in Christ Jesus! Today we are instructed to not be anxious about anything. Why? We are to take everything to God in a request in prayer and petition accompanied by our THANKS! The result? The peace of God, beyond our comprehension, will fill our hearts and minds and make us more like Christ Jesus!

Let's look at a series of happenings to see if you would be anxious, bitter and forget God:
Your siblings hate you because you are your parents' favorite.
They plot together and throw you in a well to leave you to die.
They immediately get a chance to sell you to a group of traveling foreigners.
The foreigners sell you to a high government official in another country as a slave.
You work hard for the official; he prospers and places you in total charge of his holdings.
The official's wife wants an affair with you; you refuse and she falsely accuses you.
You are thrown in prison like a common criminal.
You interpret the dreams of two servants and ask them to remember you.
They are taken out of prison, as your interpretation indicated and forget you.
Two years later the chief official has a dream and you are remembered.
You correctly interpret the dream and are made second in command of the country.
Your siblings come to you for food to feed themselves and their families during a famine.

What do you do? Read this story in Genesis 37-42 about Joseph. Because Joseph stayed close to God, prayed to God, gave thanks to God and continued to walk with God he was continually raised up and was able to provide great service to his adopted country and to his family. Without the treachery toward Joseph there may not have been any Israelites!

Do you remain joyous, prayerful and thankful in ALL circumstances? Are you having some tough time with your health, your marriage, your job, your friends, your school or any other area of your life? Go to God in prayer, with thanksgiving, and make your petition to Him. Then, the peace of God, which is beyond our ability to understand, will guard your heart and mind for Christ Jesus. Now go out and make this a great day.

> There comes to my heart one sweet strain, a glad and a joyous refrain;
> I sing it again and again - sweet peace, the gift of God's love.
> Thru Christ on the cross peace was made. My debt by His death was all paid;
> No other foundation is laid for peace, the gift of God's love.
>
> Peter P. Bilhorn - 1865-1936

February 19

"When Jesus spoke again to the people, He said, 'I AM THE LIGHT OF THE WORLD. WHOEVER FOLLOWS ME WILL NEVER WALK IN DARKNESS, BUT WILL HAVE THE LIGHT OF LIFE.'" John 8:12

I remember one night in July 1962 while I was attending Infantry Officer Basis Course at Fort Benning, GA. We were completing the study of "Evasion, Escape and Survival". It rained during the late afternoon and remained cloudy, wet and humid. We were taken to the South end of the training area in trucks and let out in small groups across a wide area with instructions to make our way through the "enemy" to the safety of "friendly" positions approximately three miles North. Since it was not quite dark, three of us made our way rapidly along a rough, brushy hillside for just under a mile. We heard voices indicating we were behind the main line, so we moved to easier ground and continued North. About the time it was very dark, we crossed the road which was the halfway point . We entered an area of thick brush and trees where it was so dark you couldn't see the man in front of you. We formed a line with the first man following a compass and the next two men holding tight to the pistol belt of the men in front of him. At one time, while I was the number two man, we were making good time when the man in front of me suddenly dropped straight down. I held on to him, the man behind me held on to me and we were able to just barely stop the drop. When we pulled the lead man back up we briefly used our flashlight and saw he had walked over a thirty foot cliff. We took a brief rest, regained our composure and continued on our way through rough terrain, creeks, brush and trees to reach our "friendly" lines and the safety which had been promised to us. That time was so dark that I hoped then, and hope now, never to be in that much darkness again.

When I read this verse, I think of that night all over again! That was what I describe as DARK! The truth is, during the time of my life when I was not following God like I knew I should, I was in a far deeper darkness. When I look back on that time now, I wonder how I was ever able to survive. I know that it was only through the love of God that He kept me from destruction. I thank Him for that.

What about your life today? Are you walking away from God by harboring some anger, resentment, lust, greed, gossip or other sin? Do you have a habit which is harmful to your body, the Temple of God? Are you walking in darkness, not knowing what will result from your next step? Look again at today's promise. Jesus is the light of the world! Jesus gave His life for your sins, not just your sins, but the sins of the entire world! Confess your sins to God! Follow Jesus and you will never walk in darkness again! You will have the light of life which is provided only through the grace of our Lord Jesus Christ! Yes, Jesus is the light. Follow Him and you will reach the safety of friendly lines which is found only in heaven.

Follow Jesus' light today, and go out and make it a great day.

Walk in the light! And thou shalt own thy darkness passed away,
because that light hath on thee shone in which is perfect day.
Walk in the light! And thine shall be a path, though thorny, bright;
For God, by grace, shall dwell in thee, and God Himself is light.

Bernard Barton - 1784-1849

February 20

> "COME NEAR TO GOD AND HE WILL COME NEAR TO YOU. Wash your hands, you sinners, and purify your hearts, you double-minded." James 4:8

In the devotion of January 27 I told you about our family devotions and prayer before breakfast each morning. This was a time of the day when we "came near to God". As I grew to young adulthood I can never remember hearing my dad use profanity. I can never remember seeing my dad be more than just momentarily angry. I can, however, remember many times as we were working in the fields when Dad would strike up a conversation with me about some story or point in the Bible. When we would go quite a distance from home to work in the field we would take our lunch and I never remember a time Dad did not say a prayer of thanks before we would eat the lunch in the field. At harvest time we would not take a noon break, but Momma would bring our meal to the field and bring a snack at 4:00 P. M. Again, Dad would say a prayer of thanks before eating. I grew up knowing that God was always near. Why was He near? Because we always came near to Him!

The story is told about the two men on a fishing trip. One was tying a lure on his line, slipped and plunged the hook into his hand. He uttered several words of profanity then stopped and said, "Sure is a good thing the preacher isn't here." What he was saying meant that he would not have used such words in front of a man of God. Yet he used those very word in front of God! How did he justify that? Perhaps he should have read the last sentence of today's promise!

What about your life? Do you have a set time of the day for your devotions and prayer time? Consistency matters! If you don't have a set time then you need to review your typical day and establish a time you can be quiet and alone so you can concentrate on your study of the Bible and can concentrate on what you say to God and listen for what He says to you. This will be the time of the day that you will be coming near to God. Do this consistently and you will find He will come near to you on a consistent basis. As you develop this relationship with God you will find it easy to do as Paul suggested. Pray continuously, i.e. always be in a state of mind to have a conversation with God just as though He were your best friend and were right there with you. You know what? He is and He is! You can count on what Jesus says in Matthew 28:20, "... And surely I am with you always, to the very end of the age."

Your nearness to God will solve so many other problems also. You will be more even-tempered, you will smile more, you will be a friendlier person, you will be more solicitous of your friends' needs (attitude of the servant!), people will be more likely to want to be with you and you will find your testimony to be so much more effective.

Claim today's promise by consistently coming near to God in the way you live and in your prayers and you will find God coming near to you. Do it, and go out and make this a great day.

> Nearer, still nearer, close to Thy heart, draw me, my Savior, so precious Thou art;
> Fold me, O fold me close to Thy breast; shelter me safe in that haven of rest.
> Nearer, still nearer, nothing I bring, naught as an offering to Jesus my King:
> Only my sinful, now contrite heart; grant me the cleansing Thy blood doth impart.
>
> Leila N. Morris - 1864-1929

February 21

"If they obey and serve Him, THEY WILL SPEND THE REST OF THEIR DAYS IN PROSPERITY AND THEIR YEARS IN CONTENTMENT." Job 36:11

Today's promise is another one with a qualifier. "If they obey and serve Him." If you meet the qualifier, then "They will spend the rest of their days in prosperity and their years in contentment." When you ask most people how many commandments there are you will get the answer, ten. My study of the Bible, however, reveal many more than that to me. This devotional book you are reading is based on the promises of God. How precious they are. How true they are. How wonderfully they bless us. They do not stand alone. They are connected to His commands. In his book, "Absolute Surrender", Andrew Murray writes, "Where do I find God's will? I find God's will in His Word. I have often heard it said that people have said, 'I believe every work within these two covers has come from God'; and I have sometimes heard it said, 'I want to believe every promise between these two covers'; but I have not often heard it said, 'I accept every commandment within these two covers.' But let us say it. If you like, write in the front page of your Bible what I once wrote in the front page of a young man's: 'Every promise of God in this book I desire to believe, every command of God in this book I desire to accept.'"

When you are living your life for Christ by obeying and serving Him you will find such a peace and joy in your heart that you know the promise of today is so true. How much you yield to Christ determines the extent of your contentment, or happiness. I am reminded of the words Abraham Lincoln is reported to have said, "I have found that a man is just about as happy (contented) as he makes up his mind to be." Bill Gothard once said, "Contentment is realizing that God has already provided everything we need for our present happiness." What about your life? Are you spending your days in prosperity and your years in contentment? Are you spending time in Bible study and prayer? Are you striving in every way to obey and serve Him?

Even if you are striving in every way to obey and serve God there will be times you get the "wants". Businesses today spend billions of dollars each year to raise our level of desire. Why do they do it? Because it works! (Have you noticed that many people who say the sex, language, alcohol and drug use and violence in movies don't influence our youths are very influenced by the advertisements?) You also find that people who spend a lot of time in malls and just "shopping" raise their "want" level. How much better that time could be spent in doing as Jesus commanded in Matthew 25:33-40 to feed the hungry, give drink to the thirsty, clothe those who need them, look after the sick and visit those in prison. I am not saying it is wrong to shop or to want nice things. We all do that. What I am saying is to be content with whatever God has given you and enjoy your prosperity. He will supply your every need.

Obey and serve Him today, and go out and make it a great day.

Who can cheer the heart like Jesus, by His presence all divine?
True and tender, pure and precious, O how blest to call Him mine!
Every need His hand supplying, every good in Him I see;
On His strength divine relying, He is all in all to me.
Thoro Harris - 1874-1955

February 22

"Blessed are those who mourn, FOR THEY WILL BE COMFORTED." Matthew 5:4

There are many reasons for different people to mourn. The most obvious reason is death. Probably the worst death is the death of one of your children. This is not, in any way, to diminish the sorrow of the loss of a parent, older relative or friend. I believe the saddest thing for me in this regard is to see, read or hear of someone who is in mourning for the death of a loved one in spiritual circumstances that they will not be rejoined in heaven. How sad! How hopeless! What strong cause to truly mourn!

Other reasons to mourn are the loss of a job, the breakup of a marriage, separation from a dear relative or friend, the loss of a valued heirloom (regardless of the financial worth of the object) or simply to mourn "what might have been" (my wife and I mourn the loss of the time we did not spend in church attendance and a close relationship with God). Any reason which brings on a state of mourning is of concern for God. Our promise today is that if you are in mourning you WILL be comforted.

From where does the comfort come? The most obvious answer is, you are comforted by God. How are you comforted? Perhaps the best way to answer this is to look at 1 Corinthians 1:3-5, "Praise be to the God and Father of our Lord Jesus Christ, the Father of compassion and the God of all comfort, who comforts us in all our troubles, so that we can comfort those in any trouble with the comfort we ourselves have received from God. For just as the sufferings of Christ flow over into our lives, so also through Christ our comfort overflows." You are comforted by God in your quiet times of prayer and meditation. You are comforted by knowing He is present with you, by you and in you at all times as you go through your period of mourning.

We are comforted by those who have gone through the same type mourning as we are experiencing as we see from above, He comforts us in our troubles, so we can comfort those in any trouble with the comfort we received from Him. In one of his sermons our pastor, Brother Joe Grizzle, told us of a couple who lost an infant shortly after birth. He said, "I had never suffered such a loss and had no idea what to say or how to comfort them with credibility, however, our Minister of Music, Mike Lewis, and his wife had also lost an infant. Mike did a wonderful job of providing comfort to the couple. He had been comforted by God for the same type mourning and could give the comfort needed.

Are you mourning? Seek God and those who have been comforted by Him similarly. Do you know those who are mourning an experience similar to one of yours? Share the comfort with them that you received from God! This is our charge and duty as servants of God.

Be comforted and give comfort, and go out and make this a great day.

Does Jesus care when my heart is pained too deeply for mirth and song:
As the burdens press, and the cares distress, and the way grows weary and long?
Does Jesus care when I've said goodbye to the dearest on earth to me,
And my sad heart aches till it nearly breaks - Is it aught to Him? Does He see?
O yes, He cares, I know He cares! His heart is touched with my grief;
When the days are weary, the long nights dreary, I know my Savior cares.
Frank E. Graeff - 1860-1919

February 23

> "What is man that You are mindful of him, the son of man that You care for him? YOU MADE HIM A LITTLE LOWER THAN THE HEAVENLY BEINGS AND CROWNED HIM WITH GLORY AND HONOR." Psalm 8:4 & 5

Genesis 1:26-27 says, "Then God said, 'Let us make man in Our image, in Our likeness, and let them rule over the fish of the sea and the birds of the air, over the livestock, over all the earth, and over all the creatures that move along the ground.' So God created man in His own image, in the image of God He created him; male and female He created them." Our promise for today tells us He made us a little lower than the heavenly beings and crowned us with glory and honor. Why? What responsibility does that give us? How should we act in our lives to justify this elevated place God has given us?

One of the ways we act is to care for those who cannot care for themselves. The care givers of the world occupy a very special place in my heart. I watched my wife give care to members of her family for fifteen years; her aunt (father's sister), and her mother and father who died over a two year period. All were Christians and very special people.

Care givers look at the present physical form and see the beloved child of God that each person is. They must do even the most menial task in helping others. This is a way that they honor God and these dear children of God. Care givers rise above the circumstances in which they work to embrace the beauty and wonder of each unique individual for whom they care because they know each is a special creation of God. There are special care givers who not only relieve the physical pain of others, they bring hope to those who have lost hope and love to all they touch and minister to. They call forth the healing and renewal of those in their care by their prayers to God for their special charges.

Parents exhibit the loving characteristics of care givers to their precious little ones God has entrusted to their care. We are all pained and grieved to hear or read of parental abuse to children. I feel that because of the special love Jesus had for children, those who are responsible for abuse to children will be dealt with very harshly when they meet their Maker. As a parent you have the obligation to take care of a child's physical needs. You have the obligation to take care of your child's mental needs and social needs. Most importantly, however, you have a strong obligation - because you were made a little lower than the heavenly beings - to take care of their spiritual needs. There are many, many places in the Bible that instruct us to teach the spiritual lessons to our children. Those who love Him and fulfill this major obligation will certainly be crowned with glory and honor!

What is man that God should be mindful of him and care for him? The special creation of His, made in His image. Live for God, love and care for others, and go out and make this a great day.

Take my life and let it be consecrated, Lord, to Thee:
Take my hands and let them move at the impulse of Thy love,
Take my love, my God, I pour at Thy feet its treasure store;
Take myself and I will be ever, only, all for Thee.

Frances R. Havergal - 1836-1918

February 24

"Therefore, my dear brothers, stand firm. Let nothing move you. Always give yourselves fully to the work of the Lord, BECAUSE YOU KNOW THAT YOUR LABOR IN THE LORD IS NOT IN VAIN." 1 Corinthians 15:58

The story is told about a missionary who had been faithful in his work for over a year and had seen only three souls saved for the Lord. He became very discouraged as the time came for him to return home on leave and meet with the mission board. During the leave he visited with his spiritual mentor about the work. The mentor determined the missionary was faithful to God, was forgiven of his sins, was steeped in the gospel, was preaching Jesus crucified, dead, buried, raised from the dead and sitting at the right hand of God; in short, was just what we want and need as a missionary. The mentor read Galatians 6:9 to the missionary, "Let us not become weary in doing good, for at the proper time we will reap a harvest if we do not give up." Somewhat heartened after this meeting and having completed his mission board meetings and rest, the missionary returned to the mission field and was surprised at his reception upon his return. Many souls were saved over the next few weeks.

From this story, it is obvious the seeds of salvation had been planted over the year of time the missionary was becoming more and more discouraged. He was "becoming weary in doing good". What about your work for the Lord? Are you becoming weary? Are your prayers going unanswered in the time you think they should be answered? Reread Galatians 6:9 above and take heart in today's promise. When you stand firm for God, let nothing move you from doing what God directs you to do, and always give yourself fully to the work the Lord tells you to do. You have God's promise - your labor in the Lord is not in vain.

Yes, we become discouraged when we pray for someone's salvation and it doesn't occur in OUR time. Remember, the world doesn't run on OUR time. It runs on GOD'S time! It is not your job to set the dates and times of obtaining results. It is your job to be faithful, stand firm, do as you are led and give of yourself fully. It is God's job to gain the results. We read Paul's comments in 1 Corinthians 3:6-9, "I planted the seed, Apollos watered it, but God made it grow. So neither he who plants nor he who waters is anything, but only God, who makes things grow. The man who plants and the man who waters have one purpose, and each will be rewarded according to his own labor. For we are God's fellow workers; you are God's field, God's building."

So continue your faithful work for the lord. Invite those friends, associates and neighbors to Sunday School and Church; pray for salvation, physical healing, safety, relationship healing, obtaining of jobs, etc.; visit the sick; give to the work of God; work with youth and all the other items of service you are called to perform. That is your job and your work will not be in vain.

Claim today's promise, and go out and make this a great day.

If I walk in the pathway of duty, if I work till the close of the day;
I shall see the great King in His beauty when I've gone the last mile of the way.
If for Christ I proclaim the glad story, if I seek for His sheep gone astray;
I am sure He will show me His glory when I've gone the last mile of the way.

Johnson Oatman, Jr. - 1856-1922

February 25

> "All the prophets testify about Him THAT EVERYONE WHO BELIEVES IN HIM RECEIVES FORGIVENESS OF SINS THROUGH HIS NAME." Acts 10:43

Today's promise is much like the most precious promise we started this devotional with on January 1, John 3:16. Part of that verse says, "...that whoever believes in Him shall not perish but have eternal life." "Believe" in this regard means "Faith". The word denotes the credit we give to the existence of God; the truth of the evidence presented in the Bible and the birth, life, death, burial, resurrection and ascension of Jesus Christ. Without belief (faith) we cannot have salvation, see Hebrews 11:6, "And without faith it is impossible to please God, because anyone who comes to Him must believe that He exists and that He rewards those who earnestly seek Him." Exercising this faith, the sinner is received and treated as if he were just and righteous; hence the process is called "justification by faith". This belief (faith) in Him includes concurrence of the will and affections in this plan of redemption, along with all its relations and bearings as they are revealed in the gospel. It also includes an actual personal trust in Christ as a Savior that leads to the renouncing of every other trust, the forsaking of sin and the cheerful and constant obedience to all His commands.

Isaiah 1:18 says, "'Come now, let us reason together,' says the Lord. 'Though your sins are like scarlet, they shall be as white as snow; though they are red as crimson, they shall be like wool.'" No matter how bad your sins, God will blot them completely. They are removed from you as described in Psalm 103:12, "As far as the East is from the West, so far has He removed our transgressions from us." No matter how bad your sins, God forgives them. Read 1 John 1:9, "If we confess our sins, He is faithful and just and will forgive us our sins and purify us from all unrighteousness." Once you have been forgiven of your sins you need never think about them again. They are gone forever!

My own sins were so bad that if I were the only person on earth, Jesus would have still gone to the cross and died for me. How precious that knowledge is to me. You can, and should, feel the same way. If you do feel that way then you BELIEVE in Him. If you believe in Him, then you receive forgiveness of sins through His name. Through your belief you will then have a personal trust in God, you will forsake all other trusts, you will forsake sin and you will cheerfully and constantly obey His commands. What a wonderful, peaceful life you will lead with God as your Savior. You can count on Him!

Your belief (faith) grows stronger each day you walk with the Lord. Someone once said, "Little faith will bring your soul to heaven, but great faith will bring heaven to your soul." So believe in Him, receive forgiveness for your sins, and go out and make it a great day.

I believe that the Christ who was slain on that cross
Has the power to change lives today;
For He changed me completely, a new life is mine,
That is why by the cross I will stay.

Gloria Gaither - 1942-
William J. Gaither - 1936-

February 26

"Discipline your son, AND HE WILL GIVE YOU PEACE; HE WILL BRING DELIGHT TO YOUR SOUL." Proverbs 29:17

Without discipline children fail to learn, fail to develop, fail to feel loved and appreciated and fail to mature. When and how to teach discipline is the question. Isaiah 28:9-10 says, "Who is it he is trying to teach? To whom is he explaining his message? To children weaned from their milk, to those just taken from the breast? For it is: Do and do, do and do, rule on rule, rule on rule; a little here a little there." When to start? As little children! How to teach it? By consistent and constant application and repetition!

My parents expected obedience from their four children. I was the youngest with my brother the eldest and my two sisters between. They tell me of a time when I was two and they were told to watch over me one afternoon. They were swinging and when it came my turn they pushed me very high. At the highest point the rope broke and I fell to the ground. They gathered around me and couldn't see me breathing. Out of stark fear they thought they had killed me and decided, amid their tears to bury me in the milk room in the barn under a loose board. They agreed on a story to tell mom that I didn't want to wait my turn and wandered off to the barn. When they told the story to mom she quickly got to the truth and rushed to the barn to get me. How relieved she was to find that I was breathing. I had been knocked out and had the breath knocked out of me so the other children could not see me breathing. Using this as a training lesson, mom taught her children that they were responsible for ALL their actions ALL the time.

My minister, Brother Joe Grizzle, preached a sermon to us on "Keys to a Structured Home". In it he said "Everything needs structure to maintain consistency" and that "Balance is always the goal". He said we need a structured spiritual life, eating habits, exercise, professional life and marriage. He further stated that children need discipline to learn to live a structured life, referring to Luke 2:27, "Moved by the Spirit, he went into the temple courts. When the parents brought in the child Jesus to do for Him WHAT THE CUSTOM of the Law required." and Luke 2:42, "When He was twelve years old, they went up to the Feast, ACCORDING TO THE CUSTOM." and Luke 4:16, "He went to Nazareth, where He had been brought up, and on the Sabbath day He went into the synagogue, AS WAS HIS CUSTOM. And He stood up to read."

These passages show the structured, disciplined life of Jesus. Brother Joe gave us three principles of discipline: Kids need consistent rules. Kids need consistent control. Kids need consistent affirmation.

Teach your children the Bible. Proverbs 1:7 says, "The fear (awe, reverence, love) of the Lord is the beginning of knowledge, but fools despise wisdom and discipline." Discipline yourself and your children and your children will give you peace and bring delight to your soul.

Claim today's promise on a consistent basis, and go out and make this a great day.

Tell me the story of Jesus, write on my heart every word:
Tell me the story most precious, sweetest that ever was heard.
Tell how the angels in chorus sang as they welcomed His birth,
Glory to God in the highest! Peace and good tidings to earth.

Fanny J. Crosby - 1820-1915

February 27

> "It is God's will that you should be sanctified: that you should avoid sexual immorality; that each of you should learn to control his own body in a way that is holy and honorable, not in passionate lust like the heathen, who do not know God; and that in this matter no one should wrong his brother or take advantage of him. THE LORD WILL PUNISH MEN FOR SUCH SINS, AS WE HAVE ALREADY TOLD YOU AND WARNED YOU. FOR GOD DID NOT CALL US TO BE IMPURE, BUT TO LIVE A HOLY LIFE." 1 Thessalonians 4:3-7

To get a review of the sin of sexual immorality, reread January 30. I want to discuss today's promise from a different angle. We are instructed by God to avoid sexual immorality, to control our own body in a way that is holy and honorable and to not wrong our brother or take advantage of him. God also says that failure to control our body is to act just like the heathen! Our failure to abide by this command brings us to today's promise, "The Lord will punish you for such sins!" Yes, this is a negative promise, however, it is of such great importance I was led to include it here.

There is an argument that, "It is my body and if what I do is with consenting adults then it is nobody else's business." This argument falls apart on several points. First, it isn't "your body", it is the Temple of God. We belong to God! God made us, He sent His Son to die for our sins and God's we are. He gave us a mind and the freedom to choose because He is never going to force us against our will, however, we WILL be judged for our actions! Second, if you are single and engage in sexual activity, it is fornication and that is a sin against the temple of God (your body). This is warned against in many places in the Bible. If you are married and engage in sexual activity, it is adultery and a sin against the temple of God (your body). This is also warned against in many places in the Bible. Third, if you engage in sexual activity with a married person you are harming that person's spouse, therefore, sinning against them. You are instructed in today's promise to not wrong your brother (or sister) or take advantage of him (or her).

Let's look a little closer at "consenting adults". Does that mean "consenting" at that very moment or does it mean "consenting" in thought, planning and actions at ALL times? When you place yourself in compromising situations, you are more likely to yield to the sin of lust than if you are always sure to keep yourself out of those situations. Do you go with, or take, a member of the opposite sex to lunch? Do you have close, private working relationships with them in a closed room? Avoid such situations! Remember the Lord's Prayer, "Lead us not into temptation." Learn to do your part to avoid temptation! There is no evil in God! God cannot tempt you with evil! Temptation with evil comes from the devil! Avoid it. Remember 1 Corinthians 10:13, "No temptation has seized you except what is common to man. And God is faithful; He will not let you be tempted beyond what you can bear. But when you are tempted, He will also provide a way out so that you can stand up under it." Claim it, and go make this a great day.

When we walk with the Lord in the light of His Word,
What a glory He sheds on our way!
While we do His good will He abides with us still,
And with all who will trust and obey.

John H. Sammis - 1846-1919

February 28

"But He gives us more grace. That is why Scripture says 'God opposes the proud but GIVES GRACE TO THE HUMBLE.'" James 4:6

Andrew Murray once wrote, "The humble man feels no jealously or envy. He can praise God when others are preferred and blessed before him. He can bear to hear others praised while he is forgotten because . . . he has received the spirit of Jesus who pleased not Himself, and who sought not His own honor." Such a man described then receives the free favor of God, bestowed upon him without any merit or claim on his part. This wonderful grace to us, when we remain humble, is only part of the promise for today. It also says, "God opposes the proud." I am reminded of the man who was discussing his spiritual state with a friend. He stated to his friend, "If I can just get over being proud and become more humble, then I will be perfect." Somehow, I think he is missing the point.

Being humble is a state of unconscious mind. We need to be emptied of "US" and filled with "GOD". We need to think of God's goodness poured out upon us, God's love extended to us, God's example set before us, and God's direction for our lives more than we think of our own business plans for success in this world. When we reach this state in our Christian lives we will see God's grace poured out on us in such ways as we never thought possible. We will find our work and testimony bringing such success for the work of God that we will be amazed. We will find, in short, that we are filled with the Holy Spirit who will work through us to accomplish great and wonderful things.

How about your life today? Are you proud of what you have accomplished? Are you working on your business plans at the expense of God's plan for your life? Do you have a "place for everything and everything in its place", including God? Is God reserved for devotional reading and prayer time and Sunday service time? Or do you constantly pray for opportunity to serve Him in special ways? I heard the testimony of a lady from our church who had returned to the church after a lengthy separation following her divorce. She was working in her office one day and had prayed for the opportunity to witness for God that day. During the day a lady from another department brought some papers in to be filed. Our church member looked at her and knew something was wrong. She asked what she could do to help. "I need to file these papers with you," the second lady replied. "No, what can I do to help you," our member responded. Soon the entire story of desertion and divorce was pouring out of the second lady. Our member offered to pray with her, took her to a vacant office and, together, they prayed to God. The second lady is now a member of our church. God gave His grace to our humble member! She was filled with "GOD"! She did His work in an unconsciously humble manner. Oh, to be like her every day of our lives! Put God first in your life today as you go about your business. Serve and honor Him, and He will bless you. Then go out and make it a great day.

Marvelous grace of our loving Lord, grace that exceeds our sin and our guilt!
Yonder on Calvary's mount outpoured - there where the blood of the Lamb was spilt
Sin and despair, like the sea waves cold, threaten the soul with infinite loss;
Grace that is greater - yes, grace untold - points to the Refuge, the mighty Cross.
Julia H. Johnston - 1849-1919

February 29

"For where you have envy and selfish ambition, THERE YOU FIND DISORDER AND EVERY EVIL PRACTICE." James 3:16

The above promise is a negative promise. As you have determined by now, I would much rather deal in positives. Let me rewrite this promise in the positive form. "For where there is the absence of envy and selfish ambition, THERE YOU FIND ORDER AND EVERY GOOD PRACTICE."

Have you ever been in a group of people who were self centered and were jockeying for position and for recognition? If you sit back in such a group, you can see the envy expressed on the faces of other members of the group when one makes a good point. You see them lean forward ready to inject their own point of view so they will gain the recognition they crave - that is, gain their selfish ambition. When you are in such a group you feel the undercurrent of disorder and you can see the back-stabbing taking place as you hear the snide remarks about the proposals one of the others has made. You have the overpowering sense that this is not a place you want to be and not a group with which you want to be associated.

During my service in the Army National Guard, I served on the staff of an officer who understood the above promise. He adopted, as his command motto, the phrase: "Isn't is amazing how much can be accomplished when no one cares who gets the credit!" Isn't that a wonderful motto? Doesn't just hearing it make you think how great it would be to work for a person like that? That is the way all the staff officers of this commander felt! As you can imagine, he had a very successful period of command, and several of his staff went on to become major unit commanders.

Why do people act in this destructive manner when cooperation is always the best? Maybe they are not at peace within themselves. If you are at peace with God, you will be at peace within yourself and will, therefore, be at peace with those around you. When you are right with God and at peace, you will reflect that peace in your voice, in your manner of speaking, in the things you say and in your interaction with others. When you feel a meeting slipping to resemble one described above you can help the situation by recognizing the real contributions made by other members. Maybe if you will adopt the motto of my former commander you will make a more harmonious workplace or meeting, and a better place to witness God's love.

There is a tendency in some people to 'go along to get along.' I'm not sure this is ever a good thing to do. There will be times you will have to speak up, disagree and stand on your principles. However, you can speak up in a loving manner. You can disagree without being disagreeable. And, you can lovingly state the position of your principles.

Give God the credit today, and go out and make it a great day.

The love of God is greater far than tongue or pen can ever tell,
It goes beyond the highest star and reaches to the lowest hell,
The guilty pair, bowed down with care, God gave His Son to win:
His erring child He reconciled and pardoned from his sin.

Frederick M. Lehman - 1868-1953

March 1

"BUT I TELL YOU THAT ANYONE WHO IS ANGRY WITH HIS BROTHER WILL BE SUBJECT TO JUDGMENT" Matthew 5:22

Someone once said that people who fly into a rage always make a bad landing. Another person pointed out that ANGER is only one letter away from DANGER! How true are these sayings. At a Men's Prayer Breakfast at our church one of our faithful attendees came with his right hand in a cast. A lot of friendly banter was passed about the hand. At prayer requests time, prior to our adjourning breakfast for prayer at the altar, he told us what happened to his hand. He had explained a matter several times to an employee who still had difficulty comprehending it. He said, "Over the past several weeks I have noticed that people were getting less able to understand and it was more maddening in almost every situation. When this employee left I was furious and just slammed a cabinet in the room. Now the Lord has given me six weeks to explain my actions which led to a broken hand. I have thought about it. When everybody else you talk to is dense, stubborn and abrasive it is time to look in a mirror at your own actions and feelings." The man went on to ask for prayer for himself to help control his anger and to be more understanding of his brothers. Many of us agreed openly or silently that we needed the same prayer.

In his lists of sins in Galatians 5:19-21, Paul lists "fits of rage" as an act of the sinful nature. I am sure he was led to list it based on the above verse which quotes Jesus in the Sermon on the Mount. Since Jesus said, in today's promise, "That anyone who is angry with his brother will be subject to judgment", don't you agree with Paul that "fits of rage" are a sin? When we have that anger we WILL be subject to judgment. So what to do about it? Just stop our angry outbursts! Now that, my friend, is easier to say than to do. We can only do it with practice and with an ever closer walk with God. The closer we walk with our Lord, the more will our personality and demeanor come to that of our Savior, Jesus Christ.

What about your life at this time? Do you have something that causes you to become angry? Is there some person or some people who "get on your nerves"? Are there situations which cause you to "lose it"? What can you do about it? You might do what I am doing. I have a situation which occurs frequently which really made me mad! I have spent time in my prayer life talking to God about it. I have explained why it makes me mad, what I have done about it and the results of that action. You know what He told me? He told me to accept the situation because nobody is perfect and it really won't matter that much later in my life, later this year or, for that matter, later this week and, therefore, to act like Jesus would and love the people involved. I wanted Him to tell me how to fix it, not how to live with it. Isn't that just like Him? To tell you something you really didn't want to hear! What does He expect us to do, just accept things? Yes, I really think He does.

Pray for forgiveness, control your anger, and go out and make this a great day.

Tempted and tried we're oft made to wonder why it should be thus all the day long
While there are others living about us, never molested though in the wrong.
Faithful 'til death said our loving Master, a few more days to labor and wait;
Toils of the road will then seem as nothing, as we sweep through the beautiful gate

W. B. Stevens - (No Date)

March 2

"FOR THIS GOD IS OUR GOD FOR EVER AND EVER; HE WILL BE OUR GUIDE EVEN TO THE END." Psalm 48:14

During my thirty years in the Army National Guard I had many occasions to move units into training areas for conduct of training exercises and operations. Prior to moving a unit, whatever its size, from the cantonment area into the field, we would conduct a reconnaissance of the route along with some guides from each subunit involved. These guides were selected based on their ability to remember terrain features, routes, points of reference, etc. After they had been over the way they would return to their units and guide them into the specific areas assigned to them. In my years of service I saw times when a guide would become confused and turn his unit in the wrong direction or at the wrong place. I also saw times when our mock "enemy" would stand in the route, dressed as one of our own people and direct the convoy to go a different route, explaining there had been a change to a "new and better" route. You can imagine the chaos which ensued in turning around an entire line of military vehicles to get back to the correct path and proceed to the place assigned to them. You might also be able to imagine the trouble the guides were in when that occurred!

Isn't that a lot like our lives? We have a Guide who will take us to the correct place. He has been over the route before. He knows all the features, routes, points of reference, turning points and, most importantly, where we need to arrive. Jesus came to earth as a man. He was born of the most humble beginnings and raised to adulthood by loving parents who made sure He had a structured life and attended the expected events throughout His years. In Hebrews 2:18 we read, "Because He Himself suffered when He was tempted, He is able to help those who are being tempted." Yes, He has been over the way before. He did not make a mistake as we see in Hebrews 4:15, "For we do not have a high priest who is unable to sympathize with our weaknesses, but we have one who has been tempted in every way, just as we are - yet was without sin." No, He will not lead us down a wrong road. He will not allow us to make a wrong turn. If we follow this Guide we will not find ourselves in a situation of chaos and confusion as we try to turn around to get back on the right path.

Will there be an "enemy" to try to tempt us to turn aside? Of course there will. Remember always James 1:13-14, "When tempted, no one should say, 'God is tempting me.' For God cannot be tempted by evil, nor does He tempt anyone; but each one is tempted when, by his own evil desire, he is dragged away and enticed." If we are tempted to turn from the path our Guide is leading us on remember it is the evil one who is doing the tempting, regardless of how he looks. This God is our God and He will be our Guide even to the end.

Are you being led astray today by one who is trying to convince you he is a part of your Guide? Find your correct path, follow the true Guide, and go out and make this a great day.

In shady, green pastures, so rich and so sweet, God leads His dear children along;
Where the water's cool flow bathes the weary one's feet, God leads His dear children along.
Tho sorrows befall us and Satan oppose, God leads His dear children along;
Thru grace we can conquer, defeat all our foes, God leads His dear children along.
George A. Young - 1903-

March 3

"THE LORD IS GOOD, A REFUGE IN TIMES OF TROUBLE. HE CARES FOR THOSE WHO TRUST IN HIM." Nahum 1:7

David said in Psalm 18:2 (also 2 Samuel 22:3), "My God is my rock, in whom I take refuge, my shield and the horn (or strength) of my salvation, my stronghold." and in Psalm 18:30 (also 2 Samuel 22:31), "As for God, His way is perfect, the word of the Lord is flawless. He is a shield for all who take refuge in Him." In the day of David, war-making equipment was quite elementary in terms of today. They had pikes, swords, bows and arrows and David's famous one, the slingshot. The best thing to protect themselves against their enemy was high ground, as a rock, and a shield. High ground has been desired by military for centuries. Let the enemy attack uphill! That is why David said in Psalm 22:5, "For in the day of trouble He will keep me in His dwelling; He will hide me in the shelter of His tabernacle and set me high upon a rock." The "rock" was the symbol for "refuge" for David.

Like David, we turn to God for our shelter and refuge in times of trouble for, we find, the Lord IS good! He does care for those who trust in Him. Today's promise in one we need to hold close to us when we are faced with the times of trouble such as sickness, loss of job, dispute with a friend, marital problems, car trouble, difficulty in mastering a school assignment, etc. In fact, He is always there for us - in good times and bad. For some reason, we just feel the need for Him more when we are troubled. We shouldn't! We should always feel our need for Him!

I am reminded here of the poem, "Footprints", in which the person looked back over his life and saw only one set of footprints in the sand during the times of trouble. When he cried to God as to why He had deserted him just when he needed Him most, He gently informed him that those were the times He was carrying his. How precious that thought. How totally like our God! He is, indeed, our refuge in times of trouble. Go to Him at any time you feel the slightest distress and He will serve as your refuge.

What a caring God He is. It is so difficult for me to fathom such a God as one who sees every Sparrow which falls to the ground and notes its passage. He is the one who has the hairs of my head numbered! (I will admit I have made it somewhat easier for Him to do the last few years.) Seriously, He does care for us in a very special way. I have written earlier in this devotional about the better health, lower blood pressure, longer life, greater wealth, etc. of Christian people. It should not be a surprise to us. We don't have to carry the load of stress. He is our refuge for it. Give it to Him, for He cares for you! We don't have to carry a burden of sin and regret. Give it to Him, for He cares for you!

Today, as you go about your life, whether the road is easy or difficult, let God be your refuge, let God carry your load, let God show you the high place for you so your enemies can not overwhelm you. Trust in Him, and go out and make this a great day.

A mighty fortress is our God, a bulwark never failing;
Our helper He amid the flood of mortal ills prevailing.
For still our ancient foe doth seek to work us woe
His craft and pow'r are great, and, armed with cruel hate, On earth is not His equal.
Martin Luther - 1483-1546

March 4

"COMMIT TO THE LORD WHATEVER YOU DO, AND YOUR PLANS WILL SUCCEED." Proverbs 16:3

In the introduction to this devotional I told you that God called me in to write this in 1998. It wasn't until 2002 that I committed to the work the Lord had called me to do and began, in earnest, the planning and working on this devotional. After that commitment things started going very well - not easy, mind you, but very well. I feel that my experience is a testimony to the above promise. My plans have succeeded! My work on this has resulted in a much closer walk with God and I have gained a deeper understanding of His word.

What are your plans that are meaningful to you? Do they involve your family goals? Business goals? Education goals? Church or community involvement goals? Financial planning goals? . God would rather not recognize any of your plans which are in opposition to His will. If your plans and goals do not conform to His plan for your life you will feel the leading of the Holy Spirit to change those plans to reflect His will. This will be done through your prayer time in His presence. Commit your plans to God in your prayers and listen for His leading.

After you have formed your plans and communed with God in prayer and received the leading of the Holy Spirit you will then be able to develop your final plans and goals. Whatever they involve, commit them to the Lord and claim today's promise. You will be pleasantly surprised about how quickly your plans will begin to unfold and the goals will begin to be realized.

We must always realize that God works in His own way and in His own time. If your plans and goals are not progressing as they should you should first make sure they are in agreement with God's will. When we are sure they are we can then trust in the Lord for His promise in His time. We should always remember the words of Winston Churchill, "Success is never final; failure is never fatal; it is the courage to continue that counts." When we keep an open, continuous communication with God we can be sure our failure is never fatal. We may need some refinement of our plans to conform to His will. Just listen to God when you pray. He will hear you and He will lead you. Knowing that, you should always have the courage to continue developing your plans and working toward your goal.

Today's promise may also open the communication to a friend, family member, associate or neighbor. Remember, a goal is not a goal if it isn't written down and told to someone. When someone discusses a goal with you it should open the lines of communication to talk about God and their relationship with Him. Use it as an opportunity to witness for Him.

Keep your communication open with God, make your plans, commit them to the Lord, know they will succeed, and you can go out and make this a great day.

O victory in Jesus, my Savior, forever!
He sought me and bought me with His redeeming blood;
He loved me ere I knew Him, and all my love is due Him -
He plunged me to victory beneath the cleansing flood.

Eugene M. Bartlett, Sr. - 1895-1941

March 5

"THOSE WHOM I LOVE I REBUKE AND DISCIPLINE. So be earnest, and repent."
Revelations 3:19

My dictionary defines "rebuke" as: 1) to blame or scold in a sharp way; reprimand. 2) to force back; check; a sharp reprimand or reproof. And it defines "discipline" as: 2) a) training that develops self-control, character, or orderliness and efficiency b) strict control to enforce obedience 5) treatment that corrects or punishes. I think of these definitions as I look back over my life and consider the times my father or my mother disciplined me. I remember spankings, scoldings and stern talks about my misbehavior. I can never remember a time, though, that I did not feel the discipline was deserved. I can think of many times discipline was deserved and was not delivered. Somehow, many of those times taught me more than the times of discipline. Through it all I never doubted the love of my parents for me or of me for my parents. Through their discipline I learned to develop self-control. I developed a strong character which has served me well throughout my life. I developed obedience which led to my being orderly and efficient in my action. Yes, I remember times when I was punished and it led to a change in behavior, or to correct actions.

Often at the time of the discipline it was hard to accept the tone and the actions. I can remember sulking about at times and being told to "Stop that sulking and put on a smile. You know you deserved what you got." It sometimes took a while to get into the correct frame of mind, but with me, and my parents, working on it I was able to do so.

If God disciplines you because of an act you committed or an attitude you show, you can count on God to give you the grace to be humble and patient. You will be made better because of receiving the discipline. Just as I never doubted the love of my parents for me or of my love for my parents you can have the same attitude toward God for His discipline. Our promise today assures us of His love by the statement, "Those whom I love I rebuke and discipline." Romans 3:23 says, "For all have sinned and fall short of the glory of God." You will, therefore, need to worry if you don't occasionally receive rebuke and discipline from the Lord. Since we are not perfect, we miss the mark from time to time. In other words - WE SIN. God will find occasion to rebuke and discipline us and lead us to do right because He loves us.

The last of today's promise says, "So be earnest, and repent." Just as I would tell my parents I was sorry for my misbehavior and would work hard to correct my actions, I need to respond to God's discipline with an apology, tell Him I am sorry, ask Him for forgiveness, and then work hard to correct my actions and develop my Christian character.

How about you? Have you been disciplined by God lately? Did you accept it with the love and repentance for which He asks? Do it now, and go out and make this a great day.

He leadeth me, O blessed thought! O words with heavenly comfort fraught!
Whate'er I do, wheree'er I be, Still 'tis God's hand that leadeth me.
Lord, I would clasp Thy hand in mine, nor ever murmur nor repine;
Content whatever lot I see, since 'tis God's hand that leadeth me.
Joseph H. Gilmore - 1824-1918

March 6

"If you remain in me and my words remain in you, ASK WHATEVER YOU WISH, AND IT WILL BE GIVEN YOU." John 15:7

Today's promise is almost too wonderful for words. The promise does not stand alone, however, as it follows the qualifier, "If you remain in me and my words remain in you,". IF ... THEN, "Ask whatever you wish, and it will be given you." This promise verse is in John's report of the conversation following the Passover Feast, which is now called "The Last Supper". After Jesus predicted that Peter would deny Him and that Judas Iscariot would betray Him the Disciples (minus Judas Iscariot) left the room with Jesus as He continued to teach them. In chapter 15 Jesus uses the grape vines to illustrate His points. Bruce Wilkinson, in his book, "Secrets of The Vine", wonderfully describes what takes place there. I recommend it to you for your reading. In today's promise, Jesus is telling the disciples (and us through them) just what is possible for them in their (and our) future. Remember, this is before God gave the Holy Spirit as the Comforter.

What does Jesus mean by "If you remain in me and my words remain in you"? Good question! What do you think it means? As I think about this statement, I think of the illustration Jesus is using. A branch of a grape vine can-not, on its own, produce grapes. That vine must be totally connected to the vine. I believe Jesus is telling us we must be totally connected to Him. We can't be totally connected to Him with church attendance on Sunday morning only. We must read and study His word on a daily basis. We must pray to Him on a continual basis, as Paul told us in 1 Thessalonians 5:17, "Pray continually." Do you also think it means that we should obey all of God's commands? I think it does as they are communicated to us by His words and it says, "and my words remain in you". This is an overwhelming challenge isn't it? This is why God gave us the Holy Spirit!

Let's think about Thomas who was so hard to convince he became known as "Doubting Thomas", and think also of Peter who, on his own, denied on three separate occasions even knowing Jesus. These men had spent most of three years with Jesus watching Him heal the sick, raise the dead, preach, teach and perform miracles. Yet they were unable to stand the test on their own. Are you able to stand the tests of today on your own? I am not! Look what happened after these two men (and the others) received the Holy Spirit. They all went out and built a church body which has changed the face of the world over the last two thousand years.

Are you sure you know all of God's commands? I don't think I do. I just follow the lead of the Holy Spirit. Sometimes when I am reading the Bible I will read a passage that jumps right out at me. THAT is the leading of the Holy Spirit. When that occurs I know that I have found a new (to me) command which I must obey from then on and I will be a little more like Jesus.

So remain in God, keep His words, and ask Him to let you go out and make this a great day.

O to be like Thee! Blessed redeemer, this is my constant longing and prayer;
Gladly I'll forfeit all of earth's treasures, Jesus, Thy perfect likeness to wear.
O to be like Thee! Lowly in spirit, holy and harmless, patient and brave;
Meekly enduring cruel reproaches, willing to suffer others to save.

Thomas O. Chisholm - 1886-1960

March 7

"BE NOT AFRAID, O WILD ANIMALS, FOR THE OPEN PASTURES ARE BECOMING GREEN. THE TREES ARE BEARING THEIR FRUIT; THE FIG TREE AND THE VINE YIELD THEIR RICHES." Joel 2:22

Happy birthday sweetheart! Because of her love for animals and my love for her, I dedicate this devotional to my precious wife, Jan.

This is a promise to our animal friends! When I read this I think of one of my favorite pictures of Jesus. He is seated on a rock with birds flying about, one sitting on His shoulder, and some on the ground with several animals - large and small. He has a beautiful smile on His face as He watches the animals. All the birds and animals have their heads turned toward Him. Oh, how precious the mutual love expressed in this picture!

Does God really love animals? Look at the evidence. When Noah was given the instruction concerning the ark he was told to take a pair of each animal species into the ark before he closed the doors. This was done to make sure of the perpetuation of the species. The Psalmist said in Psalm 84:3, "Even the sparrow has found a home, and the swallow a nest for herself, where she may have her young - a place near your altar, O Lord Almighty, my King and my God." I think he was telling us that the birds ARE close to God. They built their nests near His altar as an indication of that closeness. Matthew 10:29 records Jesus as saying, "Are not two sparrows sold for a penny? Yet not one of them will fall to the ground apart from the will of your Father." Luke 12:6 records Jesus as saying, "Are not five sparrows sold for two pennies? Yet not one of them is forgotten by God." Jesus used the lesson of the shepherd's care of his sheep over and over again to illustrate His care for us. In fact, Jesus told us, "I am the good Shepherd."

We are instructed in Proverbs 12:10, "A righteous man cares for the needs of his animal."

I think the Bible is clear in regard to the love of God for animals. I think the Bible is clear in regard to the love and care we should give to our animals. I remember, as a boy on the farm, cleaning out the pens of our sows with their pigs. They were like pets to me. I would put down fresh straw, then lie down and play with the little pigs while the sow ate. We would always water, unharness and feed our horses at noon and evening before we would take care of our own needs. I have always loved animals. In fact, my little Dachshund, Fritz, is sitting on my lap as I write this devotional right now!

Social service workers have found a high correlation between violent behavior in people and their cruelty to animals earlier in life. This tells us that we should watch young people closely as they relate to animals and urge counseling for those who mistreat them.

Remember, your pets are not in the wilds. They cannot find their own food and water with the help of God. That is your job! Feed them, water them, love them, don't leave them in cars to get overheated and, for both you and them, go out and make this a great day.

Why should I feel discouraged, why should the shadows come,
Why should my heart be lonely and long for Heav'n and home,
When Jesus is my portion: My constant Friend is He;
His eye is on the sparrow, and I know He watches me.

Civilla D. Martin - 1869-1948

March 8

"I CAN DO EVERYTHING THROUGH HIM WHO GIVES ME STRENGTH."
Philippians 4:13

When God was talking to me about writing this devotional book I had a great feeling of inadequacy. I have written many things in my life, including teacher's lesson plans, military plans, political campaign plans, fund raising letters, etc. Never, however, had I written anything scriptural. After I started writing, faltered, became discouraged and felt I should quit, I received a letter from a friend which contained a card the size of a business card. That card contained today's promise. As I sat looking at the card God whispered to me, "Believe it! You CAN do everything because I will give you strength." I don't remember what the letter said, but the card is glued to the front of the notebook I use in this effort as a constant reminder I do not have to count on my abilities. I count on God working through me! You can do the same!

Robert J. Morgan, in his book, "From This Verse", tells this story of Corrie ten Boom, author of "The Hiding Place" (a must read!). One Sunday in Copenhagen she spoke from Romans 12:1-2, urging her audience to present their bodies to Christ as living sacrifices. After the service two young nurses invited her to their apartment for lunch and to meet their parents. They lived on the tenth floor and the elevator was out. By the fifth floor, Corrie's heart was pounding, her breath coming in gulps, her legs buckling and she collapsed into a chair thinking she could go no further. She complained bitterly to the Lord, wondering if she might die en route. The Lord whispered that a special blessing awaited her so she bravely pressed on with a nurse in front and one behind. On reaching the apartment she found that neither parent was a Christian, but both were eager to hear the Gospel. Opening her Bible, Corrie carefully explained the plan of salvation. "I have traveled in more than sixty countries and have never found anyone who said they were sorry they had given their hearts to Jesus," she said. "You will not be sorry, either." That day both prayed for Christ to enter their lives. On her way down the steps, Corrie said, "Thank you, Lord, for making me walk up all these steps. And next time, Lord, help Corrie ten Boom listen to her own sermon about being willing to go anywhere you tell me to go - even up ten flights of stairs."

At her age and after all she had been through in the German concentration camp of Ravensbruck, Corrie could not make it up ten flights of stairs. God knew what need existed at the top of those stairs. He gave Corrie the strength to continue to the top so she could present the plan of salvation to those parents hungry for the work of God.

Has God called you to some task you feel unqualified to complete? Remember, God will not call you to a task He does not equip you to perform. Claim today's promise! Repeat it as an affirmation. When you feel overwhelmed call on God to deliver on His promise to you. Then you can go out and in a very special way make this a great day.

Holy Spirit, breathe on me; my stubborn will subdue.
Teach me in words of living flame what Christ would have me do.
Holy Spirit, breathe on me; fill me with power divine.
Kindle a flame of love and zeal within this heart of mine.
Edwin Hatch - 1835-1889

March 9

"If you love me, you will obey what I command. And I will ask the Father, and HE WILL GIVE YOU ANOTHER COUNSELOR TO BE WITH YOU FOREVER - THE SPIRIT OF TRUTH. THE WORLD CANNOT ACCEPT HIM, BECAUSE IT NEITHER SEES HIM NOR KNOWS HIM. BUT YOU KNOW HIM, FOR HE LIVES WITH YOU AND WILL BE IN YOU." John 14:15-17

Paul's letter to the Romans is sometimes called "The Constitution of Christianity" because Paul's writing is so complete concerning God's plan of salvation and righteousness, along with justification by faith. In Romans 7:24-25 Paul writes, "What a wretched man I am! Who will rescue me from this body of death? Thanks be to God - through Jesus Christ our Lord! So then, I myself in my mind am a slave to God's law, but in the sinful nature a slave to the law of sin." The point he is making is the sinful nature of man, or the sin of the flesh. By himself, Paul could not live a life without sin. The next four verses are in chapter 8:1-4, "Therefore, there is now no condemnation for those who are in Christ Jesus, because through Christ Jesus the law of the Spirit of life set me free from the law of sin and death. For what the law was powerless to do in that it was weakened by the sinful nature, God did by sending his own Son in the likeness of sinful man to be a sin offering. And so He condemned sin in sinful man, in order that the righteous requirements of the law might be fully met in us, who do not live according to the sinful nature but according to the Spirit."

After His resurrection Jesus appeared to the disciples, as recorded in John 20:19-23 and in verse 22 it says, "And with that He breathed on them and said, 'Receive the Holy Spirit.'" It is God's will that we receive the Holy Spirit. We are commanded, in Ephesians 5:18, "Do not get drunk on wine, which leads to debauchery. Instead, be filled with the Spirit." And in Luke 11:13 Jesus says, "If you then, though you are evil, know how to give good gifts to your children, how much more will your Father in heaven give the Holy Spirit to those who ask Him!" God in heaven loves to fill His children with His Holy Spirit. He longs to give each one of us individually, separately, the power of the Holy Spirit for our daily life.

Paul preached justification by faith. He also preached that justified man can only live by the Holy Spirit, therefore, God gives every person who is justified by faith the Holy Spirit to seal them. The beginning of the true Christian life is to receive the Holy Spirit. When do you receive the Holy Spirit? When you repent of your sins and receive Christ as your Savior you also receive the Holy Spirit. You will know the Holy Spirit because He will live with you and will be in you, as promised in today's promise. You need not depend on your "will power" to refrain from sin. Religious self-effort always ends in sinful ways. You need only follow the gentle nudging of the Holy Spirit. He will guide you every hour of every day of the year.

Constantly ask God to fill you with the Holy Spirit, and go out and make this a great day.

Holy Spirit, faithful Guide, ever near the Christian's side,
Gently lead us by the hand, pilgrims in a desert land.
Weary souls fore'er rejoice, while they hear that sweetest voice
Whispering softly, "Wanderer, come! Follow Me, I'll guide thee home."

Marcus M. Wells - 1815-1895

March 10

"DILIGENT HANDS WILL RULE, BUT LAZINESS ENDS IN SLAVE LABOR."
Proverbs 12:24

This is a good promise to follow yesterday's promise of the Holy Spirit. One of the devotionals my wife and I read on a regular basis is Unity Village's "Daily Word". One I read says, "I am honored that the very Spirit of God resides within my body, keeping me strong and full of life. With this strength of Spirit bolstering me, I easily resist cravings for unhealthy foods or other substances or habits that could be harmful to me. Then I am able to make the wisest and most healthful choices for my body. Aware of the sacred life of Spirit within me, I am inspired to treat my body with the utmost respect. My body is, after all, a temple of the Holy Spirit. I have been given the freedom to make choices regarding the care of my body temple, and with that freedom comes the responsibility to make healthful choices. With each life-affirming choice I make, my body responds with increased vitality until I positively glow with health."

When we were planning for my retirement from my insurance business, my wife and I remodeled our home to add an exercise room. We already had a good treadmill and we added a weight machine. Now we exercise three or four mornings a week. Jan walks while I do the exercises on the weight machine and then we switch places. Since we have been doing that exercise regime we both feel better, have lost weight, have raised our HDL levels and have toned our muscles. All this makes it possible for us to enjoy more and more things in life.

Years ago, during my work in politics, I called on a CEO for assistance in my organizational work. He had set the meeting at lunch time so we could have our discussion while we ate in the company cafeteria. We had not finished our discussion at the end of lunch, and I thought we would adjourn to his office to continue. Not so! We left the building and briskly walked (sort of a rapid march) around the office building for thirty minutes while we talked. He agreed to help me in my work, but that wasn't the important thing about the meeting. I realized then the truth of today's promise. He took his lunch hour by spending half the time eating and half the time walking to maintain his exercise program. His diligent hands ruled his company!

I am not saying you will be a slave without an exercise program, but I will say you will be much more successful if you take care of your temple of the Holy Spirit! There are far too many studies to quote concerning the benefits of a regular exercise program. One I just read reported a study of two groups of sedentary people of retirement age. One group remained sedentary while the other group walked twelve miles or more a week. The active group had lower blood pressure, lower heart rate, higher HDL and their LDL was found to be more "fluffy" so it was not so likely to cause them heart problems.

So do like we would say in the military, "Off your seat and on your feet, out of the shade and into the heat." Get in shape, and go out and make this a great day.

Onward, Christian soldiers marching as to war,
With the cross of Jesus going on before!
Christ, the royal Master, leads against the foe;
Forward into battle see His banner go!

Sabine Baring-Gould - 1834-1924

March 11

> "Blessed is the man who perseveres under trial, BECAUSE WHEN HE HAS STOOD THE TEST, HE WILL RECEIVE THE CROWN OF LIFE THAT GOD HAS PROMISED TO THOSE WHO LOVE HIM." James 1:12

Some time after the turn of the twentieth century a farmer was working in his barn and looked through the cracks in the boards toward his apple orchard. He noticed a young boy looking longingly at the apples hanging bright red and juicy on the branches. As he stood and watched the boy would approach the fence, look around, back off, amble down the road, turn around and amble back, look longingly at the apples again, approach the fence, look around and repeat the actions again. After some time the farmer slipped out of the barn to the fence and along the fence to the point where the young boy approached. When the boy approached again, the farmer stood up and asked, "What are you doing, young man, trying to steal some of my apples?" "No sir," replied the boy. "I'm trying not to."

That young boy was standing the test! Hard as it was to refrain from taking one of those apples, and much as he suffered for want of one of them, he had been successful. Blessed is that young boy. He will receive the crown of life that God has promised to those who love him. Today's promise is one you can claim for yourself when you persevere through temptation. We read in Romans 5:3-5, "Not only so, but we also rejoice in our sufferings, because we know that suffering produces perseverance; perseverance, character; and character, hope. And hope does not disappoint us, because God has poured out His love into our hearts by the Holy Spirit, whom He has given us." That young boy was building character which will give him hope throughout his life.

Should we be dismayed and saddened when we are tempted? James 1:2-4 says, "Consider it pure joy, my brothers, whenever you face trials of many kinds, because you know that the testing of your faith develops perseverance. Perseverance must finish its work so that you may be mature and complete, not lacking anything." And in James 1:13-15 we read, "When tempted, no one should say, 'God is tempting me.' For God cannot be tempted by evil, nor does He tempt anyone; but each one is tempted when, by his own evil desire, he is dragged away and enticed. Then after desire has conceived, it gives birth to sin; and sin, when it is full-grown, gives birth to death." You ARE NOT being tempted by God. You are being tempted by the devil. You best resist those temptations by relying on the Holy Spirit.

Are you going through temptations which are hard to resist? Is there one activity which seems to bring more temptation to you than others? Jesus was tempted just like we are, yet He was without sin. He has sent the Holy Spirit to you as you Comforter and your constant companion. James 4:7 tells us, "Submit yourselves, then, to God. Resist the devil, and he will flee from you." That is what Jesus did! Do the same, and go out and make this a great day.

> Living below in this old sinful world, hardly a comfort can afford;
> Striving alone to face temptations sore, where could I go but to the Lord?
> Life here is grand with friends I love so dear, Comfort I get from God's own word;
> Yet when I face the chilling hand of death, where could I go but to the Lord?
>
> James B. Coats - 1901-1961

March 12

"Consequently, FAITH COMES FROM HEARING THE MESSAGE, and the message is heard through the word of Christ." Romans 10:17

When I was growing up my parents always took me to church. We were members of the Friends church (Quakers) and attended Sunday morning, Sunday evening and Wednesday evening prayer service. There would always be a revival meeting which ran one or two weeks once or twice a year. One of them would be a "Camp Meeting" which would be held in a large tent we would set up in a grove of trees and fill with old pews which were stored in a barn the rest of the time. I am reminded of these services we attended when I read 1 Corinthians 14:26, "What then shall we say, brothers? When you come together, everyone has a hymn, or a word of instruction, a revelation, a tongue or an interpretation. All of these must be done for the strengthening of the church." While we didn't practice the speaking of tongues, we did the rest plus a sermon. I thank God for that heritage!

I am sad to report that I did not follow that habit all my life. I let other priorities take first place, such as work, service in the National Guard, rest, etc. I made excuses such as, "I work real hard in the community which makes up for missing church.", "God would expect me to fulfill my responsibilities to my job." All my excuses and reasons were as filthy rags! We read in Hebrews 10:25, "Let us not give up meeting together, as some are in the habit of doing, but let us encourage one another - and all the more as you see the Day approaching." I thank God again that I have again become regular in my church attendance. It is adding so much to my life.

What about your church attendance? Are you like I was for several years? Do you find excuses for occasionally skipping church? Do you skip your exercise routine? Does your heart skip its beats a few days a year? Do you skip meals? Do you skip breathing for a week or two?

(Maybe I should have left out that sentence about exercising!) Seriously, how important is church attendance to you? Does the minister or deacon have to call on you frequently about your absences? Someone once said, "The great task of the church is not only to get sinners into heaven, but to get saints out of bed." Regular church attendance adds structure and stability to your life.

Is your church a large one or a small one? It matters not, because Jesus said in Matthew 18:20, "For where two or three come together in my name, there am I with them." It doesn't matter if there are so many members that they will not miss you. God will miss you!

Another item of importance is inviting others to church. While attending a civic club meeting recently I was asked by a member of our church, "Why did it take you so long to find our church?" I replied, "In the last twenty five years no one has asked us to attend church." He immediately turned to the man next to us and invited him to church. Try it, they may come.

Become a regular at church, and go out and make this a great day.

We have come into His house and gathered in His name to worship Him.
We have come into His house and gathered in His name to worship Christ the Lord.
Let's forget about ourselves and magnify His name and worship Him.
Let's forget about ourselves and magnify His name and worship Christ the Lord.

Bruce Ballinger - 1945-

March 13

"WHOEVER ACKNOWLEDGES ME BEFORE MEN, I WILL ALSO ACKNOWLEDGE HIM BEFORE MY FATHER IN HEAVEN." Matthew 10:32

In one of his sermons our minister, Brother Joe Grizzle, told us of our need to witness, and to be willing to witness at any time. He told the story of a man who was very shy and very hesitant about witnessing for Christ. He had passed up several opportunities to share the gospel and would always feel badly about it afterwards. In responding to the call of God to witness he said, "God just give me a sign when you want me to witness. Make sure I recognize the sign and know that I am to be a witness for you." The next day the man was taking a bus downtown and was the only person on the bus at the time. The bus stopped and picked up another second man, who staggered onto the bus with tears in his eyes. "Oh, I am such a wretched man," he cried. "Oh, if there were only someone to help me and to show me how I can break out of this awful life of drunkenness. Oh, if there were only someone who could tell me how to find Christ." The first man bowed his head and whispered, "Lord, is this a sign?"

Do you feel this way about sharing the gospel of God? Do you find it hard to lead the conversation to spiritual matters? I do! I pray about it, I think about it, and I try to do what I can. I am developing the habit of responding to a "thank you" from a clerk with the phrase, "You are welcome, go with God today." Since Brother Joe is such a good minister and our church always has an altar call, I invite people to church. It is something I feel the Holy Spirit will lead me in at the time of God's choosing if I remain faithful to Him.

In emphasizing the importance of witnessing for Christ, Robert J. Morgan wrote: According to a legend, when Jesus returned to heaven following His death on the cross and resurrection from the tomb, the angels gathered in amazement. They gazed at the wounds in His hands and feet, and shuddered to recall His suffering. Finally Gabriel spoke: "Master, you suffered terribly down there. Do they know and appreciate the extent of your sacrifice?" "No," said Jesus. "Not yet. Right now only a handful of people in Palestine know." "Then what have you done to let everyone else know?" asked Gabriel. "I've asked Peter, James and John, and a few others to spread thc news. They will tell others who will tell others until the message spreads to the ends of the earth." But Gabriel, knowing the nature of human beings, askcd, "What is Plan B?" "I have no Plan B," replied Jesus. "There is no alternative strategy. I'm counting on them."

Twenty centuries later, He still has no other plan. He's counting on you and me.

We can claim today's promise by witnessing for Jesus Christ before men, acknowledging Him, explaining the plan of salvation and leading people to Christ. It is done one person at a time.

It is done in the home. It is done in the workplace. It is done on the playground. It is done in the hospitals and jails. It is done wherever you meet people and are able to lead the conversation to the story of the love of Jesus and His gift to us. Witness, and go out and make this a great day.

Jesus! The name that charms our fears, that bids our sorrows cease,
'Tis music in the sinner's ears; 'tis life and health and peace.
He breaks the pow'r of canceled sin; He sets the pris'ner free.
His blood can make the foulest clean...His blood availed for me.
Charles Wesley - 1707-1788

March 14

"ALL THIS IS FROM GOD, WHO RECONCILED US TO HIMSELF THROUGH CHRIST AND GAVE US THE MINISTRY OF RECONCILIATION." 2 Corinthians 5:18

The first words of Jesus' ministry are recorded in Matthew 4:17, "From that time on Jesus began to preach, 'Repent, for the kingdom of heaven is near.'" Just before His ascension into heaven the words of Jesus are recorded in Luke 24: 47, "And repentance and forgiveness of sins will be preached in His name to all nations, beginning at Jerusalem." From these two recordings, the first preaching and the last preaching, of Jesus Christ, we are told to be reconciled to God. We become reconciled to God through His Son, Jesus Christ! Through the teachings of Jesus, we are given the ministry of reconciliation.

Our first step in reconciliation is to admit we have sinned. We learn in Romans 3:23, "For all have sinned and fall short of the glory of God." We are also told in 1 John 1:10, "If we claim we have not sinned, we make Him out to be a liar and His word has no place in our lives." So, we are stuck! We are sinners! We must have the attitude of the tax collector recorded in Luke 18:13, "But the tax collector stood at a distance. He would not even look up to heaven, but beat his breast and said, 'God, have mercy on me, a sinner.'" We should confess our sins to God. They are not "mistakes". They are not "errors". They are not "short-comings". They are SINS! 1 John 1:9 assures us, "If we confess our sins, He is faithful and just and will forgive us our sins and purify us from all unrighteousness." We become reconciled to God when we simply cry out to God for forgiveness and help from Him. He stands ready and waiting for you to do that.

Once we are reconciled to God, then we need to be reconciled to others. We need to ask forgiveness for the wrongs we caused. Many of our sins cause pain in other people, and we can not be reconciled fully to God until we have become reconciled to others. We are instructed by Jesus in Matthew 5:23-24, "Therefore, if you are offering your gift at the altar and there remember that your brother has something against you, leave your gift there in front of the altar. First go and be reconciled to your brother; then come and offer your gift." WOW! God doesn't even want our gift if we are not reconciled to others!

Claim today's promise that He gave us the ministry of reconciliation. Become truly reconciled with God and with others and you will experience such an outpouring of blessings that you could never imagine. What about your life? Do you have unconfessed and unforgiven sin? Are you estranged from some person? Do you want true peace in your heart? Then you need to practice the "Ministry of reconciliation". A. W. Tozer wrote in "The Divine Conquest", "A thousand years of remorse over a wrong act would not please God as much as a change of conduct and a reformed life."

So please God today by claiming today's promise and practicing what Jesus taught! Gain the peace in your heart that will result, and go out and make this a great day.

You have longed for sweet peace and for faith to increase, and have earnestly, fervently prayed;
But you cannot have rest or be perfectly blest until all on the altar is laid.
Would you walk with the Lord in the light of His Word, and have peace and contentment alway?
You must do His sweet will and be free from all ill - on the altar your all you must lay.

Elisha A. Hoffman - 1839-1929

March 15

> "Therefore the Lord, the God of Israel, declares: 'I promised that your house and your father's house would minister before me forever.' But now the Lord declares: 'Far be it from me! THOSE WHO HONOR ME I WILL HONOR, BUT THOSE WHO DESPISE ME WILL BE DISDAINED.'" 1 Samuel 2:30

Today's promise was directed first at Eli when his sons took more than their share of the sacrifices and were also living sinful lives. It wouldn't be in the Bible, however, unless it was meant to be speaking directly to me and you also. This is one of those promises which is both a positive promise, "Those who honor me I will honor," and a negative promise, "But those who despise me will be disdained." How do you feel about your life at this very moment? If this were your last minute on earth, would God honor you or would He disdain you? I feel the fact you are reading this devotional answers that question!

Let's look at some of the ways we should honor God. First, we honor God by admitting our sin and asking for His forgiveness. That is first, and foremost, what He asks for, and expects, from us. That is the reason He sent His only Son to become the son of man, to live without sin and to suffer the shame and pain of the cross so that He could shed His blood as a continual sacrifice for all the sins of the world.

We honor Him when we are faithful to attend church. We honor Him with our tithes AND our offerings. We honor Him with our witnessing to others of His love and care for them. We honor Him with our praise of His Holy Name and our songs to Him. Whether we can sing well or whether we sing like I do (I have been accused of being tone deaf).

We honor Him when we thank Him for our blessings - not by saying, "Thank you for your blessings to me." No, by actually naming our blessings and thanking Him for each and every one of them. You don't write a letter after your birthday to the giver of a gift and say, "Thank you for the gift." No, you would say, "I want to thank you for the CD. I have played it several times already and it gives me great pleasure." Name your blessings to God, thank Him for each and every one of them and tell Him how they have blessed you. You praise Him when you do this.

We honor God by reading and studying His Word. We honor Him more by memorizing His Word. Psalm 119:11 says, "I have hidden your word in my heart that I might not sin against you." When we memorize verses of the Bible we honor God by both the reading AND the hiding of His Word in our hearts to direct the actions of our lives.

We honor Him especially when we pray to Him. He doesn't want just our praise, thanks, forgiveness requests, petitions and intercessions. No, He also wants us to spend quiet time with Him listening for His still soft voice on the wind to direct our lives.

How do we show we despise Him? By failing the above!

Honor God today, and go out and make this a great day.

> O Lord my God, when I in awesome wonder consider all the worlds Thy hands have made,
> I see the stars, I hear the rolling thunder, Thy pow'r throughout the universe displayed!
> And when I think that God, His Son not sparing, sent Him to die, I scarce can take it in -
> That on the cross, my burden gladly bearing, He bled and died to take away my sin!
>
> Stuart K. Hine - 1899-

March 16

"DO NOT LET YOUR HEARTS BE TROUBLED. TRUST IN GOD; TRUST ALSO IN ME. IN MY FATHER'S HOUSE ARE MANY ROOMS; IF IT WERE NOT SO, I WOULD HAVE TOLD YOU. I AM GOING THERE TO PREPARE A PLACE FOR YOU." John 14:1 & 2

In his book, "Heaven: A Place, A City, A Home", Edward M. Bounds said, "Earth is but a pilgrim's stay, a pilgrim's journey, a pilgrim's tent. Heaven is a city, permanent, God-planned,

God-built, whose foundations are as stable as God's throne." This statement of Bounds is probably made based on his reading chapter 21 of the Revelations of John in which he describes

the Holy City. If you do not recall that in some detail, I recommend you read it again. This is the

place Jesus told His disciples He was going. He has told them of His coming death and is letting them know they should not be overly sorrowful, but to trust in God and in Jesus.

Today's promise is one of the most comforting there is. We have the word of Jesus that

there IS a heaven, that God and Jesus Christ ARE there, and that He is preparing our place for us

for the time our pilgrim's journey on this earth is complete. We will then go to spend eternity in

heaven! I am reminded of the story of the teacher of a children's Sunday School class who was

teaching a lesson on heaven. The teacher asked the children, "Who wants to go to heaven?" All

the children, except for Johnny, raised their hands. Johnny just sat there staring of into space. The teacher thought perhaps Johnny hadn't heard, or hadn't understood, the question, so once again asked, "Who wants to go to heaven and live with Jesus?" Again, all the children, except for Johnny, raised their hands. Wondering whatever could be wrong with Johnny, the teacher asked, "Don't you want to go to heaven, Johnny?" "No," replied Johnny. "You mean that when you die you don't want to go to heaven and live with Jesus?" the flustered teacher asked. "Oh," answered Johnny. "You mean when I die. Of course I want to go to heaven and live with Jesus when I die. I thought you were getting up a load for today!" We can laugh at Johnny's misunderstanding, but isn't it wonderful to be able to claim today's promise?

Does it give you peace in your heart to think of spending eternity in heaven? I believe the promise of today is a direct message from Jesus to each of us to let peace and confidence fill our hearts when we think about eternity. What kind of place is Jesus preparing for you? Are you happy with the way you are serving Him? Does the way you are living your life as a Christian give you confidence in the amount of preparation Jesus has to do to get your place ready? Today is the time to begin thinking about that. He is preparing a place for ALL people who are reconciled to God. The type of place depends only upon the service you perform for Him. We can take great comfort in our knowledge that eternity will be spent with our Lord God and His Son, Jesus Christ, in heaven in the place prepared for us.

Calm your heart, claim today's promise, and go out and make this a great day.

This world is not my home, I'm just a passing through.
My treasures are laid up somewhere beyond the blue.
My Lord's expecting me; and this I surely know;
I fixed it up with God so many years ago.

Source Unknown

March 17

> "Do you not know that the wicked will not inherit the kingdom of God? Do not be deceived: Neither the sexually immoral nor idolaters nor adulterers nor male prostitutes nor homosexual offenders nor thieves nor the greedy nor drunkards nor slanderers nor swindlers will inherit the kingdom of God. And that is what some of you were. BUT YOU WERE WASHED, YOU WERE SANCTIFIED, YOU WERE JUSTIFIED IN THE NAME OF THE LORD JESUS CHRIST AND BY THE SPIRIT OF OUR GOD." 1 Corinthians 6:9-11

In this passage from his first letter to the Christians at Corinth, Paul gives a list of sins which will deny a person the right to inherit the kingdom of God. This is one of several such lists in his writings. Because of the type of city Corinth was this list was tailored to them. Paul lists these sins in more detail in the fifth chapter. If Paul were alive today and he were to write a letter to the Christians in America do you think he would alter his list very much? Paul was not surprised by the sin. He wrote in Romans 3:23, "For all have sinned and fall short of the glory of God." Have you heard people say? "Thank goodness my sins aren't very bad. I have just told little white lies. I have never swindled anyone or engaged in homosexual activity or anything like that." Suggest they read James 2:10, "For whoever keeps the whole law (royal law found in Scripture) and yet stumbles at just one point is guilty of breaking all of it." Therefore, the sentence above, "And that is what some of you were." also applies to all of us. Each of us were such bad sinners, that if we were the only sinner in the world, Jesus would have still died on the cross to save us.

When our sins are forgiven they ARE FORGIVEN. Hebrews 10:17 says, "Then He (the Lord) adds: 'Their sins and lawless acts I will remember no more.'" I like what Corrie ten Boom wrote in "Not Good if Detached", "When I bring my sins to the Lord Jesus He casts them into the depths of the sea - forgiven and forgotten. He also puts up a sign, 'No Fishing Allowed!'"

That is what today's promise is all about. When you asked forgiveness YOU WERE WASHED! Your sins were washed away by the blood of Jesus Christ! YOU WERE SANCTIFIED! Sanctification is the process by which the soul is cleansed from the pollution and delivered from the power of sin, and, at the same time, endued with those spiritual graces of knowledge, faith, love, repentance and humility. YOU WERE JUSTIFIED! Justification is the opposite of condemnation. It denotes that act of God's sovereign grace, by which He accepts and receives those who believe in Christ as just and righteous. When God has pardoned a sinner, He treats him as righteous, or as if he had never sinned - WASHED, SANCTIFIED and JUSTIFIED in the name of the Lord Jesus Christ and by the Spirit of our God!

So take comfort in today's promise. Your forgiven sins are as if they had never occurred. You have a place prepared for you by Jesus in heaven. Claim the promise for today, and go out and make this a great day.

> Have you been to Jesus for the cleansing power? Are you washed in the blood of the Lamb?
> Are you fully trusting in His grace this hour? Are you washed in the blood of the Lamb?
> Lay aside the garments that are stained with sin and be washed in the blood of the Lamb.
> There's a fountain flowing for the soul unclean; O be washed in the blood of the Lamb!
>
> Elisha A. Hoffman - 1839-1929

March 18

> "AND IF ANYONE GIVES EVEN A CUP OF COLD WATER TO ONE OF THESE LITTLE ONES BECAUSE HE IS MY DISCIPLE, I TELL YOU THE TRUTH, HE WILL CERTAINLY NOT LOSE HIS REWARD." Matthew 10:42

Today, we have no shortage of groups and organizations willing to help people in need and urgently asking for contributions from each of us. Those groups did not exist in our area of Northern Kansas where I grew to adulthood. We did, however, have neighbors. The Parable of the Good Samaritan is written in Luke 10:25-37. This is a well known story to anyone who has studied the Bible in any detail or attended church very much.

During my Junior year of high school I was selected to attend Boy's State, which was held in Wichita, Kansas. While I was there my father became seriously ill, was taken to the hospital and underwent surgery to remove a blockage between his kidney and bladder. He was in the hospital for a month, home in bed for another month and slowly regained his strength during the next three months when he again underwent surgery, this time for adhesions. My siblings were all married at the time so I returned to the responsibility of running the farm. It had been a very wet Spring so none of the Spring crops were planted. At the age of sixteen, I would arise early, do the morning chores, eat breakfast, work in the fields all day, do the evening chores, eat supper and fall into bed exhausted late at night. I loved Sundays because it was a strict rule that no work except the chores was to be done on the Lord's day. As I was preparing to go into the fields the second week home a neighbor drove into the yard and began talking to me asking me what I was planning for first one field and then another. I became more agitated by the minute as he seemed to be wasting my limited time, however, I knew my father and mother would want me to be courteous to this "time waster". After what seemed like a very long time he finally took his leave and I headed for the field. Imagine my surprise the next morning when tractors with implements began arriving in our fields to perform the work I had told the "time waster" about the previous day! By evening the entire Spring work was completed by thirty six men with their machines. The women gathered about ten that morning to fix a wonderful meal for all the workers! Rest assured, I will NEVER forget that cup of cold water given to me! I know who my neighbors were at that time. My church had never meant as much to me as it did that late Spring day.

In 1 Peter 2:12 we are told, "Live such good lives among the pagans that, though they accuse you of doing wrong, they may see your good deeds and glorify God on the day He visits us." How do you give a cup of cold water today? Do you find a way to feed the hungry, give shelter to those without it, visit those sick or in prison or encourage the defeated? Matthew 12:35 says, "The good man brings good things out of the good stored up in him, and the evil man brings evil things out of the evil stored up in him."

Be a "good man" today, and go out and make this a great day.

Blest be the tie that binds our hearts in Christian love!
The fellowship of kindred minds is like to that above.
We share our mutual woes, our mutual burdens bear;
And often for each other flows the sympathizing tear.
John Fawcett - 1740-1817

March 19

"THEREFORE CONFESS YOUR SINS TO EACH OTHER AND PRAY FOR EACH OTHER SO THAT YOU MAY BE HEALED. THE PRAYER OF A RIGHTEOUS MAN IS POWERFUL AND EFFECTIVE." James 5:16

Colin Brown, writing for "Christianity Today", said, "It is as wrong to say that the church has no part in the ministry of healing as it is to say that the only thing that prevents people from being healed is their lack of faith." In many, many places in the four gospels we are told of Jesus curing diseases, healing the sick and restoring to wholeness those who were crippled. You can read in Mark 5:24-32 the story of the woman who had a blood issue for twelve years and had spent all she had on doctors. She reasoned that if she could just touch the hem of Jesus' clothes she could be healed. She did and she was! Jesus said to her, "Daughter, your faith has healed you."

Our promise for today gives us a command, followed by the promise. We are to first confess our sins to each other. Then, second, pray for each other so that you may be healed. Then we get the promise that the prayer of a righteous man is powerful and effective! These instructions are quite clear. We should be humble in our lives and do the very best we can to follow the teachings of God and the leading of the Holy Spirit. When we sin we should confess those sins to each other. This instruction is not designed to diminish you in the eyes of your brothers in Christ, but to express humility and earnest request for prayers for strength and help to depend more and more on the Holy Spirit. By confessing our sins to each other we gain the combined prayers to make us stronger and the combined support and understanding of like- minded individuals in Christ.

This verse also carries the command to pray for each other so that you may be healed. The evidence of the effectiveness of faith and prayer in healing continues to grow. More and more doctors are losing their skepticism as they see case after case which have been thought hopeless turn to healing. Why? Prayer works! Today's promise specifically says, "The prayer of a righteous man is powerful and effective." I feel this is a way God has of pulling us together, making us more a church 'family', recognizing the importance of the role of church leaders and insuring a sharing of responsibility for each other.

If you confess your sins to each other and pray for each other you will be healed, right? What it says is, "so that you may be healed." We all know of people who have led Godly lives, become sick, been prayed over and still died. Why? I don't know. We don't know God's plans. Does God change His plans based on the prayer of righteous men? Yes! Go read Exodus again. You will see several cases where Moses' pleadings caused God to change His mind. He changes His plans some today also, but not always. We have to be willing to accept His will above our own. Claim today's promise and pray for healing, then go out and make this a great day.

Prayer is the soul's sincere desire, uttered or unexpressed,
The motion of a hidden fire that trembles in the breast.
Prayer is the burden of a sigh, the falling of a tear,
The upward glancing of an eye when none but God is near.

James Montgomery - 1771-1854

March 20

"AS FAR AS THE EAST IS FROM THE WEST, SO FAR HAS HE REMOVED OUR TRANSGRESSIONS FROM US." Psalm 103:12

This reference to distance of directions from each other we are given in today's promise is very interesting in the choice of the Psalmist. Even when this was written about three thousand years ago it was known that the directions East and West should be used in this example instead of North and South. Consider the example if North and South were used. If we started at the equator and went North we would travel just over six thousand miles and then we would be traveling South. We would travel over twelve thousand miles and we would then be going North. So to say how far North is from South would be about twelve thousand five hundred miles. Now consider how far East is from West. If we started at the equator and traveled straight East for almost twenty five thousand miles we would come to the place we started, but we would still be going East. You could continue another circuit of the Earth and still be going East. You would NEVER start going West! Therefore, the Psalmist knew the above and, hence, the reference.

Today's promise tells us that God will remove our transgressions from us as far as the East is from the West. How far? Infinity! Forever! Be assured that transgressions are sins! They are not "mistakes", "errors", "bad choices", "shortcomings" or any other politically correct name you want to give them. They are SINS! We are told in 1 John 1:9, "If we confess our sins, He is faithful and just and will forgive us our sins and purify us from all unrighteousness." So, if we confess our sins to God, He removes them from us as far as the East is from the West. He removes them from us so far that we can never get to them again, need never again think about them, need never again ask forgiveness for them, need never again feel bad about them and need never again fear their effect upon us. Now that is a promise you can live with for eternity!

Do you have concerns that you have not been able to reach God for forgiveness of your sins? In Deuteronomy 4:29 we are told, "But if from there you seek the Lord your God, you will find Him if you look for Him with all your heart and with all your soul." You can couple this promise with today's promise and have comfort in your heart and mind. Do you have a concern about forgiveness of your sins? Do you feel you must ask for forgiveness over and over again for a sin, or sins, you have committed? I heard a story of a man who could talk to God directly. He had committed a sin and asked God to forgive him for that sin. God said, "Okay, you are forgiven." The man felt particularly bad about the sin, worried about it, thought about it and cried about it. He again approached God in prayer and asked God to forgive him for that same sin. God said, "What sin?" You see, that sin had been removed as far as the East is from the West. It was even beyond the scope of God remembering it! In Hebrews 10:17 we are told about God, "Then He adds: 'Their sins and lawless acts I will remember no more.'" So be confident in your relationship to God, and go out and make this a great day.

Though your sins be as scarlet, they shall be as white as snow;
Hear the voice that entreats you, O return ye unto God!
He is of great compassion, and of wondrous love;
He'll forgive your transgressions, and remember them no more.

Fanny J. Crosby - 1820-1915

March 21

"The Lord is not slow in keeping His promise, as some understand slowness. HE IS PATIENT WITH YOU, NOT WANTING ANYONE TO PERISH, BUT EVERYONE TO COME TO REPENTANCE." 2 Peter 3:9

There is a joke about the lady who was very impatient. Her fidgeting and nervousness was a distraction to many as she went about her life. Several people had talked to her about it and asked her to calm down and be more patient. Finally she was desperate and went to the Lord in prayer. (Isn't that like a lot of us? We don't go to the Lord in prayer until we become desperate! Shouldn't we go to the Lord FIRST and we may find that we don't become desperate!) Her prayer went something like this, "Lord, I am impatient. It causes problems with my friends and family and with many clerks at stores where I shop. I know I need to develop patience, remain calm and be a steady influence to those around me. Lord, grant me patience. And, please, can you grant it to me today?" We can laugh at this joke, except it really isn't a joke to many of us. I tell people to be careful about what they ask for as it may be granted. When you pray for patience you should remember Romans 5:3 (KJV), "And not only so, but we glory in tribulations also: knowing that tribulation worketh patience." So when you pray for patience maybe you are praying for the tribulation which "worketh patience".

Our Lord is patient! Today's promise tells us we may consider Him slow, however, we should remember that God works in perfect timing. We need to accept His timing. He is patient with us. He does not want us to perish. He especially wants us to come to repentance! As Paul wrote to Titus in Chapter 3:3-7, "At one time we too were foolish, disobedient, deceived and enslaved by all kinds of passions and pleasures. We lived in malice and envy, being hated and hating one another. But when the kindness and love of God our Savior appeared, He saved us, not because of righteous things we had done, but because of His mercy. He saved us through the washing of rebirth and renewal by the Holy Spirit, whom He poured out on us generously through Jesus Christ our Savior, so that having been justified by His grace, we might become heirs having the hope of eternal life."

Have you been foolish? Have you been disobedient? Are you deceived or enslaved by any passions or pleasures? Do you live with jealousy or envy? Do you hold a grudge against a brother or a sister? Our Lord is patient with you. He wants you to accept the love of God and be saved by His mercy through the washing by the blood of Jesus Christ, thereby being justified by the Grace of God and becoming His heirs and being granted eternal life. Don't count on your good works to gain eternal life for yourself. If you do you will be told, "Depart from me, I never knew you." That great promise of John 3:16 says, "For God so loved the world that He gave His one and only Son, that whoever believes in Him shall not perish but have eternal life." There is no way except the blood of Jesus Christ! Repent today, and go out and make this a great day.

What can wash away my sin? Nothing but the blood of Jesus;
What can make me whole again? Nothing but the blood of Jesus.
For my pardon this I see - nothing but the blood of Jesus;
For my cleansing, this my plea - nothing but the blood of Jesus.
Robert Lowry - 1826-1899

March 22

> "Do not be yoked together with unbelievers. For what do righteousness and wickedness have in common? Or what fellowship can light have with darkness? What harmony is there between Christ and Belial? What does a believer have in common with an unbeliever? What agreement is there between the temple of God and idols? FOR WE ARE THE TEMPLE OF THE LIVING GOD. AS GOD HAS SAID: 'I WILL LIVE WITH THEM AND WALK AMONG THEM, AND I WILL BE THEIR GOD, AND THEY WILL BE MY PEOPLE.'" 2 Corinthians 6:14-16

Nancy, a young Christian lady, graduated from high school and left for college. There she caught the eye of Larry in one of her classes and he pursued her until she agreed to a Saturday night date. Larry was a perfect gentleman, gave Nancy great attention and was very kind throughout the dinner and a nice movie, which Nancy chose. When Larry returned Nancy to her dorm she invited him to church with her the next day. Larry promptly accepted. The following day he picked her up at the appointed time and went to church. Nancy noticed that he acted very reserved during the service. At lunch, following the service, Larry invited Nancy to a party the following Friday night. At the party there was much drinking and behavior which Nancy considered inappropriate. She asked Larry to take her home, which he did. They dated several times and Nancy felt herself falling in love and was sure Larry reciprocated the feeling. Following one of their dates Larry told Nancy he loved her and she assured him she felt the same. Larry next asked her to start saving money for marriage, and she agreed to do that. He then said, "I have a great idea. Why can't you move into my apartment with me and we can save the money you are spending on the dorm room. Nancy was flabbergasted at the suggestion, and said, "I could never live with you without being married." To which Larry replied, "What is a marriage certificate? It is just a piece of paper!" Nancy responded, "Yes, it is just a piece of paper. It is a piece of paper that represents a commitment and a legal ceremony in the sight of God and man. Do you consider a driver's license just a piece of paper? What about the title to your car or your college transcript? When you buy a home will you consider the deed to be just a piece of paper?" She then probed further into Larry's relationship with God and found that he was merely acting to get her to date him, that he had no true feelings for Christ. When Nancy got to her room she read today's promise as her evening devotions, called Larry and ended the relationship.

Are you single and looking for a mate? As your dating grows more serious do you make sure you both share the love of Christ? Do you do this early in your relationship? Do you live your life in such a way that you attract others who would naturally share your Christian beliefs? God wants you to! If you are currently married to a person who is a non-believer you should live your life as an example to your spouse that they would want to know and serve the same gentle, loving God that you have. Marriage between believers is a wonderful, blessed relationship!

Know and serve God with your spouse, and go out and make this a great day.

O give us homes built firm upon the Savior,
Where Christ is Head and Counselor and Guide;
Where every child is taught His love and favor
And gives his heart to Christ, the crucified.

Barbara B. Hart - 1956-

March 23

> "Dear friend, do not imitate what is evil but what is good. ANYONE WHO DOES WHAT IS GOOD IS FROM GOD. ANYONE WHO DOES WHAT IS EVIL HAS NOT SEEN GOD." 3 John 1:11

I have been asked by several people why I use the phrase, "make this a great day." When I was in the insurance business I had a very good friend, who was also a client, John Lloyd. John would come to the office each month to pay his insurance. He could have just mailed it, however, he made the trip an outing. He always had a smile on his face and a joke to tell me as we visited. One day as John was leaving the office I said, "John, have a great day!" John stopped, turned around, sternly looked at me and asked, "Now what am I supposed to do? Should I just go home, sit in my easy chair, lean back and say, 'Come on great day. I am ready to have you?' Now you know that in order to have a great day you have to go out and make it a great day. It is not just going to come to you. You should never say, 'have a great day', you should say, 'make this a great day.'" I took John's conversation to heart. We are responsible for the kind of day we have. Even if things aren't going well, we control how we react to them.

I think of that conversation in relation to today's promise. We are in charge of what we do, what we think and how we feel about things. We should never imitate what is evil. We should do what is good. God expects us to do good deeds. James 2:18 says, "But someone will say, 'You have faith; I have deeds.' Show me your faith without deeds, and I will show you my faith by what I do." Your good works should imitate the work which Jesus did when He walked this earth. Our positive promise today says anyone who does what is good is from God.

We also have a negative promise today. That negative promise says anyone who does what is evil has not seen God. We should avoid doing evil. We should avoid relationships with those who do evil. You are known by the company you keep. We are told in 1 Thessalonians 5:22 (KJV), "Abstain from all appearance of evil." I am sure you have read the stories of the driver of the get-away car claiming he just thought his friends were just going into the convenience store to buy something. Or the young person busted at a party where illegal drugs were being used who told their parents they didn't know "that" was going on. Those people were guilty by association. They need to change friends. In the teachings of AA they teach that you stay away from the places where you went before you were sober and that you avoid those you used to drink with. That is what it means when we are instructed to abstain from all appearance of evil.

What about your life? Are you doing good deeds for God? Are you avoiding evil and the appearance of evil? Are you providing the good influence for your family, friends, neighbors and associates or are you letting some of them influence you to occasionally do evil works?

Take heart in today's promise, and go out and make this a great day.

> Give me souls for my hire, let my life be on fire,
> Shining out to the world as a guide:
> Help me rescue some one sinking now with no hope,
> That in heaven we shall ever abide.
>
> J. R. Varner - (No date)

March 24

"A GENTLE ANSWER TURNS AWAY WRATH, BUT A HARSH WORD STIRS UP ANGER." Proverbs 15:1

In his book, "The Practice of Godliness", Jerry Bridges suggests these five strategies for obeying the biblical injunctions about gentleness:

1. Actively seek to make others feel at ease. Be sensitive to other's opinions and ideas, welcoming opinion.
2. Show respect for the personal dignity of the other person. When you need to change a wrong opinion, do so with persuasion and kindness rather than domination or intimidation.
3. Avoid blunt speech and abrupt manner. Be sensitive to how others react to your words, considering how they may feel. When it is necessary to wound, also include encouragement.
4. Don't be threatened by opposition; gently instruct, asking God to dissolve the opposition.
5. Do not belittle or degrade or gossip about a brother who has fallen - instead grieve and pray for his repentance.

I believe these are great suggestions. Perhaps I would add one more. Always keep a pleasant expression on your face and LOVE IN YOUR HEART when you are talking to someone concerning a subject which could be contentious.

From my Momma I picked up an old saying that says, "Keep your words soft and tender and sweet. You never know which ones you will have to eat." This is a great saying to keep in mind when considering today's promise. When you use harsh words to someone those very words often come back to you over and over. They come back from that person, from friends of that person and, worst of all, in your mind time after time during your quiet times. What should you do if you have used harsh words to someone? Do the same thing you do when you sin against God - ask for forgiveness!

Many times during my life I have seen tense situations diffused by gentle responses. When I was a child and I, or my siblings, would be angry about something and talk about what we "were going to tell so-and-so", my mother would use the saying, "You catch more flies with honey than you do with vinegar." This would always make us stop to think about what we were doing to the relationships involved.

During the time in my life I was not walking close with God I could sure have used Jerry Bridges point number 2. In many conflicts I tended to use domination and intimidation rather than persuasion and kindness. It led to several situations which were not resolved amicably. What about your actions? Are you gentle or do you tend to be harsh? Do you show gentleness to your family after a hard day of work and you are tired? Do you disagree with others agreeably? Think about it, and then go out and make this a great day.

Gentle Shepherd, come and lead us, for we need You to help us find our way.
Gentle Shepherd, come and feed us, for we need Your strength from day to day.
There's no other we can turn to who can help us face another day;
Gentle Shepherd, come and lead us, for we need You to help us find our way.
Gloria & William J. Gaither - 1942- & 1936-

March 25

"YOU ARE MY FRIENDS IF YOU DO WHAT I COMMAND." John 15:14

In Norman, Oklahoma I have a long time friend, Ed Copelin, who owns an office supply store and is very active in his church and community organizations. We have worked together in several organizations and on many projects. When I shared with him my call to write this devotional he shared with me the following from his life: The year his church had their long-time minister retire Ed received a call from a lady who served on their "Committee on Committees" to ask him to Chair the "Long Range Planning Committee". Ed knew that committee chair would have to meet with many, many different people to accomplish the task since there was no "CEO" present to pull together all the plans from the various boards and committees. He also knew he had many commitments in other organizations. He told the lady he would just not have time to do the job and would therefore decline to serve as requested. That night Ed had a dream that he was standing before an elevated table with a bearded man on a throne behind it looking through a book. The man turned page after page and scanned each on carefully. Finally he looked up at Ed and said, "Copelin, I don't see your name on my list". Ed awakened in a sweat. The next morning he called the lady back to ask if the position had been filled. She told him it had not. He told her he would be honored to serve in the capacity requested of him.

I can also tell you that in my work in community organizations I have called upon Ed to serve. He has always been faithful to help me out when I needed the help. What I asked of him was of absolutely no importance compared to the work of our Lord That willingness on his part is just one of the reasons I call him my friend.

Consider today's promise in regard to the above. Now think about situations in which you have been when you called upon people and they helped you. Didn't you feel more friendly toward them for their help? Today's promise is a promise from Jesus Christ. We are given many promises in the Bible. We are also given many commands. In Matthew 22:36-38 we read, "'Teacher, which is the greatest commandment in the Law?' Jesus replied: 'Love the Lord your God with all your heart and with all your soul and with all your mind. This is the first and greatest commandment.'" This is the first command which must be followed to be called a friend of God! Jesus also said in John 13:34, "A new command I give you: Love one another. As I have loved you, so you must love one another."

As you read and study the Bible make a note of both the promises of God and the commandments of God. You can claim the promises with great assurance, but you must also obey the commands! I am happy to have worked with Ed in community service to fulfill one of God's commands that we "give a cup of water in His name". I know that Ed is a friend of God and so am I. What about you? Do what God commands and you will know for sure you are His friend. Then you can go out and make this a great day.

A friend of Jesus, O what bliss that one so weak as I
Should ever have a friend like this to lead me to the sky.
A friend when other friendships cease, a friend when others fail;
A friend who gives me joy and peace, a friend who will prevail.
Joseph C. Ludgate - (no dates)

March 26

> "My son, if you accept my words and store up my commands within you, turning your ear to wisdom and applying your heart to understanding, and cry aloud for understanding, and if you look for it as for silver and search for it as for hidden treasure, THEN YOU WILL UNDERSTAND THE FEAR OF THE LORD AND FIND THE KNOWLEDGE OF GOD." Proverbs 2:1-5

As I was growing up my Momma had a large tin nearly filled with buttons. Over the years as we would wear out our clothes she would cut off the buttons and place them in the tin. She would then use the cloth for quilts, patches, cleaning rags or any other use she could think of. I can remember times when she would be sitting in her rocker by the wood stove in the Winter. She would always be reading, writing, or mending as she visited with the family. She would say, "Clarence, please bring me my button tin." Then she would look through all colors, sizes, styles and shapes of buttons until she came up with just the right one to put on a shirt, blouse or other item she was mending. She had buttons large enough to keep a coat closed during a Northern Kansas snow storm and buttons small and dainty enough for a fine blouse to wear to church.

Some people are like that. In a conversation they can choose just the right verse to illustrate a point, answer a question, address a problem or help a hurting heart. How do you suppose they are able to do that? They get that from long study of the Word of God-the Bible. They get their verses just like Momma got her buttons - one or a few at a time!

Psalm 19:7-11 says, "The law of the Lord is perfect, reviving the soul. The statutes of the Lord are trustworthy, making wise the simple. The precepts of the Lord are right, giving joy to the heart. The commands of the Lord are radiant, giving light to the eyes. The fear of the Lord is pure, enduring forever. The ordinances of the Lord are sure and altogether righteous. They are more precious than gold, than much pure gold; they are sweeter than honey, than honey from the comb. By them is your servant warned; in keeping them there is great reward." I have never heard a better description of the Bible! These verses should make you want to read the Bible!

What about your life? Do you spend time each day reading and studying the Bible? As you have gone through these devotions now for almost three months you should be able to see the many wonderful verses which speak to us at various times in our lives. How do you know what is in the Bible unless you have studied it and memorized a good share of it? Read the Bible through in a year every two or three years. There are many lists available to guide you in this endeavor. Study it as you would if you had a treasure map given to you by a person you totally trust because you are told to look for it as for silver and search for it as for hidden treasure. Pray and cry for understanding for that is what today's promise tells you to do. If you do you will be able to understand the awe, wonder and love of the Lord and find the knowledge of God!

Try it, and then go out and make this a great day.

> Holy Bible, book divine, precious treasure, thou art mine;
> Mine to tell me whence I came; mine to teach me which I am;
> Mine to comfort in distress, suffering in this wilderness;
> Mine to show, by living faith, man can triumph over death.
>
> John Burton - 1773-1822

March 27

"A man can do nothing better than to eat and drink and find satisfaction in his work. THIS TOO, I SEE, IS FROM THE HAND OF GOD, FOR WITHOUT HIM, WHO CAN EAT OR FIND ENJOYMENT?" Ecclesiastes 2:24 & 25

I have had five careers in my life (six, if you count my writing as a career). I was a farmer for the first early years of my working life. My dad let me be a partner. He let me rent a piece of land from him and I was responsible for farming it and all decisions involving it. I taught Chemistry for one semester at Sterling College in Sterling, KS and for five years at Phillips University in Enid, OK. I spent ten years in politics as a campaign manager, Oklahoma Republican State Chairman and as a political consultant. I then spent just over twenty years as a State Farm Insurance Agent. I retired from that business at the age of sixty-one to take care of family responsibilities and pursue other interests, like writing this devotional. While I was a Freshman in college I joined the Kansas National Guard and served there, the DC National Guard and the Oklahoma National Guard for the next thirty plus years. I retired at the rank of Colonel. I can say that I loved every one of the careers I have had. I was good at what I did and rose rapidly in each. I now feel that my entire life has been a training ground for writing this devotional. Truly, the satisfaction I had in my work and the success I enjoyed are from the hand of God! I did not always walk with the Lord as I should have, but thank God, I am now doing so.

I found it easy to work because of the great enjoyment I found and the success I enjoyed. Everyone is not so fortunate in that regard. If you are one of those who isn't finding satisfaction in your work maybe you should change your attitude about it. Colossians 3:23-24 says, "Whatever you do, work at it with all your heart, as working for the Lord, not for men, since you know that you will receive an inheritance from the Lord as a reward. It is the Lord Christ you are serving." Change your attitude about your job by changing your attitude about who you work for. It is the Lord Christ you work for, therefore, work at it with all your heart. You will greatly benefit with a more serene life, greater production and a happier and more joyful time while you work. This just has to be noticed by your supervisor and it will be rewarded.

Ephesians 4:1 says, "As a prisoner for the Lord, then, I urge you to live a life worthy of the calling you have received." You are called by the Lord for whatever it is you are to do with your life. If you feel His nudging of you to change your occupation you should give it the thought, consideration and prayer that it rightfully should receive. The Lord wants you to be happy, productive and successful at whatever He calls you to do. First, you need to have a forgiven heart and then a continuous, close walk with Him. Today's promise clearly says, "for without Him, who can eat or find enjoyment?"

Serve the Lord, work hard at whatever you do, find the enjoyment promised, and go out and make this a great day.

Work, for the night is coming. Work thru the morning hours;
Work while the dew is sparkling; work 'mid springing flow'rs.
Work when the day grows brighter. Work in the glowing sun;
Work for the night is coming, when man's work is done.

Annie L. Coghill - 1836-1907

March 28

"HE HAS SCATTERED ABROAD HIS GIFTS TO THE POOR, HIS RIGHTEOUSNESS ENDURES FOREVER; HIS HORN WILL BE LIFTED HIGH IN HONOR."
Psalm 112:9

At Christmas time our church gets names of needy people from several different sources, including our own church membership list. These names are given out to those who want to "adopt" a family at Christmas or are given gifts purchased by the church offering. Our church leaders ask for a special offering, a couple weeks before Christmas, equal to the largest amount you will spend on a gift for another person. This special offering is called, "A Christmas gift to Jesus." This money is used for the purchase of food items and gifts to be given to those in need. The "Thank You" letters we receive back are heartwarming and touching. Everyone involved in this effort, whether giving, buying, wrapping, boxing or delivering, have a great time while they are expressing the true meaning of Christmas. We understand the meaning of "His gifts to the poor."

What about you, have you given your gifts to God? What does He want? He wants your "belief" as He stated in John 3:16, "For God so loved the world that He gave His one and only Son, that whoever believes in Him shall not perish but have eternal life." In return for your gift to Him, He gives you a gift that is beyond value - ETERNAL LIFE - through the washing away of our sins by the blood of our Lord Jesus Christ! If you believe, His grace is sufficient for you and you will be saved and be able to be called an heir of God, even a co-heir of Jesus!

What are His gifts to the poor? That is the entire purpose of this daily devotional book! Each day contains a promise. Those promises are not only to the rich, the politically powerful or to the members of your congregation only. They are to anyone who believes and who then follows the commands of God. How does He distribute His gifts to the poor? In many ways! He does so by leading them to find a job they are capable of doing. He does so by placing it in the hearts of us to give. In many places in the Bible we are told to feed the hungry, clothe the naked, visit the sick, give a cup of water in His name, etc. When we follow the commands God gives us we are doing His will and the gifts we give are from Him. After all, how did we get the resources to be able to give as freely as we do? It is from the hand of God!

How long will God's gifts keep coming? Today's promise answers that question also - forever! God loves us so much that He provides a way for us to live by His grace. When we serve Him, as by our contributions, tithes, offerings and assistance to others, we are showing the love of God. We are told in 1 John 4:16 that, "God is love." John 15:12 quotes Jesus as saying, "My command is this: Love each other as I have loved you." If God is love, and we are to love each other as God loved us then we must honor Him by helping Him scatter his gifts abroad to the poor. Is your life right with God? Are you honoring Him each day? Lift His horn high in honor, and go out and make this a great day.

How to reach the masses, men of ev'ry birth, for an answer Jesus gave the key;
"And I, if I be lifted up from the earth, will draw all men unto me."
Lift Him up by living as a Christian ought. Let the world in you the Savior see;
Then men will gladly follow Him who once taught, "I'll draw all men unto me."
Johnson Oatman, Jr. - 1856-1922

March 29

"Keep your lives free from the love of money and be content with what you have, BECAUSE GOD HAS SAID, 'NEVER WILL I LEAVE YOU; NEVER WILL I FORSAKE YOU.'" Hebrews 13:5

I grew up on a farm, so I enjoy stories about them. There is the story told of two farmers visiting one day. One farmer had just completed a very successful year and looked very relaxed and happy, while the other one had all kinds of problems and looked very haggard. The haggard farmer asked the successful one, "How were you so successful last year?" The successful farmer replied, "I am a Christian. I count on God to tell me all things. Each day I read the Bible wherever I open it and point with my finger. Last Spring I opened the Bible and pointed to Ecclesiastes 11:6, 'Sow your seed in the morning.' You know it had been dry and the ground wasn't in the best shape for planting, but I went out the next morning and planted my crop. That very night the gentle rains came for two weeks. By the time it dried out and everyone else started planting my crop had a lot of growth and continued to be ahead of the others in maturity. Last Fall, before I thought the crop was ready I opened the Bible and pointed to Revelations 14:15, 'Take your sickle and reap, because the time to reap has come.' I went out the next morning and harvested my crop. It cost me some extra money to dry the grain, but you know what happened. An early cold front moved in with freezing rain and wind and most others lost their crops. The price of grain went up more than enough to pay for the drying I had to do. God was good to me." The haggard farmer said, "Well, I'm a Christian also. I'll try that plan." The next year the successful farmer ran into his friend and found him looking very relaxed and happy. "I see the Bible plan worked for you too," he said. The former haggard farmer laughed and said, "Yes, it really did." "Tell me about it, the successful farmer said. "Well," said the other, "I took my Bible last Spring, opened it and pointed with my finger and there was the answer, Chapter 7!"

We laugh at the joke, but today's promise is one of the hundreds of verses in the Bible dealing with money and possessions. We are commanded to keep our lives free from the love of money and be content with what we have. It doesn't command us to live in poverty and enjoy it! Money and possessions are not bad - putting them first is what is bad. We read in 1 Timothy 6:10, "For the love of money is a root of all kinds of evil. Some people, eager for money, have wandered from the faith and pierced themselves with many griefs." It is not wrong to ask God to bless you with financial success or the success of your job or business. What it wrong is when you start thinking, planning and scheming more about your financial well being than about what God has in store for you and what you do with your life. What God expects from us is to invest our resources wisely. He will bless us financially, but He expects our love, our dedication, our devotion, our work for Him, our tithes and offerings and our giving to the poor in His name. Put God first. He will never leave you or forsake you, and go out and make this a great day.

All for Jesus, all for Jesus! All my being's ransomed powers:
All my thoughts and words and doings, all my days and all my hours.
Let my hands perform His bidding, let my feet run in His ways;
Let my eyes see Jesus only, let my lips speak forth His praise.

Mary D. James - 1810-1883

March 30

> "A GOSSIP BETRAYS A CONFIDENCE, BUT A TRUSTWORTHY MAN KEEPS A SECRET." Proverbs 11:13

It is said that a secret is something that only one person knows. Any time two or more people know something you find a proportionately greater chance that it will become widely known. Have you ever told something in confidence to a friend only to have it repeated back to you from another acquaintance? Did you feel betrayed? Now, have you ever repeated something a friend told you in confidence? How do you think your friend felt when they found out about it?

Are you as trustworthy as you expect your friends to be?

Why do some people gossip? Perhaps it is because they feel insecure and want to tell someone else something that person doesn't know, and, as a result, make themselves seem more important in the eyes of the person to whom they tell the gossip. When we have given our lives to Christ we should feel confident about our future, and this should make us feel more confident in ourselves and our abilities. As we learn more about the scripture, God's love of us and His promises to us we should gain more confidence and it should build our self-worth and self-esteem. That should make us much less prone to gossip.

One reason some people gossip is because they talk too much. In World War II there was a slogan, "Loose lips sink ships." This was penned to cause people to stop to think before they said too much about what they were doing and the plans they were made aware of during the course of their work for shipping people or items. Proverbs 20:19 says it very clearly, "A gossip betrays a confidence; so avoid a man who talks too much." Does it make you feel better about yourself when others listen carefully to what you have to say and ask you questions about yourself and what you are doing? That is the way others feel when you listen to them with interest and ask questions about what they are feeling, what they are doing, where they are going, etc. There is a saying that God gave us two ears and one mouth so we should listen twice as much as we talk.

Paul, in his writings to the Corinthians in 2 Corinthians 12:20 said, "For I am afraid that when I come I may not find you as I want you to be, and you may not find me as you want me to be. I fear that there may be quarreling, jealousy, outbursts of anger, factions, slander, gossip, arrogance and disorder." Notice the list Paul writes to include gossip. Are any of them qualities you want in yourself? I greatly doubt it! They are all in opposition to the teachings of Jesus!

Today's promise clearly promises that a gossip betrays a confidence and that a trustworthy person will keep a secret. Romans 14:13 says, "May the God of hope fill you with all joy and peace as you trust in Him, so that you may overflow with hope by the power of the Holy Spirit." You will be trustworthy if you trust God, people will trust you more and you will be a better witness for Christ to bring joy and peace to your friends. Isn't that the kind of life God wants you to lead. Avoid gossip, be trustworthy, and go out and make this a great day.

I just keep trusting my Lord as I walk along.
I just keep trusting my Lord, and He gives a song;
Though the storm clouds darken the sky o'er the heavenly trail,
I just keep trusting my Lord. He will never fail!

John W. Peterson - 1921-

March 31

"So do not throw away your confidence; it will be richly rewarded. You need to persevere so that when you have done the will of God, YOU WILL RECEIVE WHAT HE HAS PROMISED." Hebrews 10:35 & 36

When I was nine years old my family was farming two farms in Northern Kansas. We lived on the one my parents owned and farmed one my grandfather owned. It was just over three miles from our home. It had been a wet, cold Fall and we didn't have the corn picked yet. One Saturday morning we were out to complete our morning chores very early, ate a quick breakfast, harnessed the team, hitched them to the corn wagon and left for the corn field. It was a bitter cold morning with a north wind whipping up the snow from the ground. We arrived at the corn field just after 8:00 A.M. and started picking corn by hand. Dad would pick two rows and I would pick the one row closest to the wagon and throw the ears into the wagon. Dad had promised me I would be picking on shares. I would get fifty percent of all I picked, or one bushel out of each six we picked together. The snow on the corn first melted on my warm mittens, then froze as the warmth left them. By mid-morning both dad and I were very cold. Dad promised we would take a long break for lunch and build a fire. The thought of that fire kept me going as I just got colder and colder. We were just short of a load at lunch time and as we pulled into the old farm yard area the sun came out. We watered the horses, unharnessed and fed them then we built a fire. It was a roaring fire and soon we were warm enough to eat. We sat around the fire for a long time talking and drying out our mittens and clothes. The wind had stopped and the sun was thawing out the ground. About 2:00 P.M. we hitched up the team and finished picking the wagon full of corn. By this time the ground was thawed so much the horses could not pull the full wagon home. We unhitched them and Dad rode one and I rode the other one home. We recovered the wagon later and sold the corn, thirty-six bushel, and Dad gave me the price he had received for six bushels. I had persevered, done Dad's will and was richly rewarded for my work, because Dad had promised me I would get my share. You can imagine what that meant to a nine year old boy!

What about you today? Are you doing your Father's will? Do you find the going tough from time to time? Are you losing your confidence? Read today's promise again. Don't throw away your confidence, it will be richly rewarded. Persevere in doing the will of God and you will receive what He has promised. What has He promised? In John 14:1-3 we read Jesus' words, "Do not let your hearts be troubled. Trust in God, trust also in me. In my Father's house are many rooms; if it were not so, I would have told you. I am going there to prepare a place for you. And if I go and prepare a place for you, I will come back and take you to be with me that you also may be where I am." Yes, Jesus promised us eternity with Him in heaven with God! Trust in God, follow the lead of the Holy Spirit, which He has given us, and go out and make this a great day.

Not a shadow can rise, not a cloud in the skies, but His smile quickly drives it away;
Not a doubt nor a fear, not a sigh nor a tear, can abide while we trust and obey.
Not a burden we bear, not a sorrow we share, but our toil He doth richly repay;
Not a grief nor a loss, not a frown nor a cross, but is blest if we trust and obey.
John H. Sammis - 1846-1919

April 1

"YOU WILL KEEP IN PERFECT PEACE HIM WHOSE MIND IS STEADFAST, BECAUSE HE TRUSTS IN YOU." Isaiah 26:3

In his book, "Changes for the Better" G. M. Alexander wrote: "In 1680, after soldiers had dragged away her husband, William, because of his outspoken preaching, Marion Veitch said: It bred some new trouble and fear to my spirit; but He was graciously pleased to set home that word 'He does all things well. Trust in the Lord and fear not what man can do'; which brought peace to me in such a measure that I was made to wonder. For all the time the officers were in the house He supported me so that I was not in the least discouraged before them. Shortly afterward news arrived that William was to be hanged. Marion rode horseback through a blinding January snowstorm to Morpeth jail and was given a few moments with her husband. Later that day, prosecutor Thomas Bell announced, "Veitch will hang tomorrow as he deserves." That evening Mr. Bell tarried at a friend's house, drinking and talking until past ten. The night was dark and cold when he left for home. He never arrived. Two days later, his body was found in the river, frozen up to his arms in a solid block of ice. William Veitch was released, and he and Marion lived to ripe old age, passing their godly heritage on to their children and grandchildren. The Lord's peace had, as usual, been followed by His providence."

This story is a great example of today's promise. The minds of both William and Marion were steadfast. God trusted in them and He brought about events which brought peace to them. This is a wonderful story with a wonderful ending. Let's look at this story, however, if it had a different ending. Suppose William had been hanged. Would that have meant that God didn't trust them, didn't think their minds were steadfast and would not keep them in peace? Certainly not! It would have changed only one example of His trust and love for them. We can not fault the will and acts of God.

Now suppose it were you and your spouse in this story (or your parents, if you are not married). Look at the current state of your relationship with God. Would he have spared you? If not, why not? Have you cleaned out all the old, unwanted baggage from your life such that you have complete JOY (zero, or nothing, between Jesus and you) in your life? Are you holding on to habits God wants you to break? Are you frequenting places where you would not want God to accompany you? Do you use words in your speech you would not use in the presence of God?

We are now one-fourth of the way through this year. This is a good time to take inventory of your life for this year. If it isn't the way you want it to be this is the time to change it. Now is the time to review your habits of daily devotions, Bible reading, church attendance and prayer time. These are habits which will help you to mature as a Christian. These are habits which help you to be steadfast and bring peace to your mind and life regardless of the conditions around you. Keep your mind steadfast, and go out and make this a great day.

Far away in the depths of my spirit tonight rolls a melody sweeter than psalm;
In celestial-like strains it unceasingly falls o'er my soul like an infinite calm.
What a treasure I have in this wonderful peace, buried deep in the heart of my soul;
So secure that no power can mine it away while the years of eternity roll.

W. D. Cornell - 19th Century

April 2

"'If you can?' said Jesus. 'EVERYTHING IS POSSIBLE FOR HIM WHO BELIEVES.'"
Mark 9:23

Today's promise comes from the story of the man who brought his son, who was possessed by a spirit that had robbed him of his speech, to Jesus' disciples for them to heal. The disciples were unable to heal the boy. When Jesus approached the place where they were, the man brought his son to Jesus and said when the spirit seized the boy it would throw him to the ground, foaming at the mouth, gnashing his teeth and becoming rigid. When the spirit saw Jesus, it immediately threw the boy into a convulsion such that he fell to the ground and rolled around, foaming at the mouth. When Jesus asked how long he had been like this the boy's father replied, "From childhood, it has often thrown him into fire or water to kill him. But if you can do anything, take pity on us and help us." The first three words of today's promise is Jesus repeating the man's words back to him. Then Jesus gives us the promise, "Everything is possible for him who believes." The boy's father immediately exclaimed, "I do believe; help me overcome my unbelief!" Jesus then rebuked the spirit and it came out of the boy, shrieking.

How like that man many of us are today. When we face problems we try to solve them ourselves. If that doesn't work, we go to someone else to try to get them solved. If that doesn't work, we finally turn to God to see if He can solve them. Does this sound like your actions? It just may be that if we take our problems to God in prayer FIRST we will be given the solution by the gentle nudging of the Holy Spirit.

When you do approach God with your problems do you approach Him in faith, or do you approach Him like that father? Do you need to pray that father's prayer? "I do believe; help me overcome my unbelief!" What that father was actually saying was, "I am trying to believe, but I am not there yet. I am working on my faith, but it is not that strong yet. I want to trust in God, but I have not developed that trust yet." Then the father reached out with the cry that sounds a lot like my cry from time to time, "Help me overcome my unbelief! Help me to have faith! Help me to trust in God!"

You would think, at my age, I would be a mature Christian. I feel a lot like that man whose grandson told him about a boy who was always doing mean things to him. "Grandpa, what should I do about it?" he asked. The man replied, "I have people like that. First you should always show him love, care and friendship. Then you should try to understand him. Then you should forgive him. Then you should pray for him." "Is that the way you do it, grandpa?" the boy asked. "Well, I'm working on it," the man replied. I am working on my Christian maturity! It has been said, "Growing older is mandatory. Maturing is optional." So join me in praying, "I believe, help me overcome my unbelief!" God will help us to mature into stronger, more trusting, more faith filled and more believing Christians. Do it, and go out and make this a great day.

Have faith in God when your pathway is lonely, He sees and knows all the way you have trod;
Never alone are the least of His children; have faith in God, have faith in God.
Have faith in God tho all else fail about you; have faith in God, He provides for His own;
He cannot fail tho all kingdoms shall perish, He rules, He reigns upon His throne.
B. B. McKinney - 1886-1952

April 3

"FOR GOD DID NOT GIVE US A SPIRIT OF TIMIDITY, BUT A SPIRIT OF POWER, OF LOVE AND OF SELF-DISCIPLINE." 2 Timothy 1:7

The King James version of the Bible uses the word "fear" instead of "timidity" in today's promise. I like that translation best for this verse. Have you ever been really afraid? I have. When I was eleven years old my elder sister had her first baby. When she and my brother-in-law left for the hospital they called us and my folks left me in the farm house alone and took my other sister with them for the birth of their first grandchild. Shortly after they left I went upstairs to my room to go to bed. It was a bright, moonlit night and I lay there looking out the window into the grove of trees we had planted as a windbreak. Suddenly I saw movement. My first thought was one of our animals had gotten out of the pasture and was wandering around. As I looked longer and more closely I realized it was a man. I was scared! I slipped down stairs and got dad's rifle I often used for hunting. I slipped back up to my room, carefully opened the window, picked out the area of movement and fired the rifle into the ground quite a way away from the movement. I then saw the individual run away from the house and heard loud crashing of limbs against them. I slept very little that night. I spent the night with a spirit of fear. I lost the trust I had in my safety, and the faith I had in the security of the house. That is what fear does to us. It destroys our trust and faith. I was up doing the morning chores when the family returned home with the news I was an uncle. I never did tell my family what a night I had. I went into the grove the next day and found footprints and a pair of pliers, obviously dropped as the individual ran away.

In Romans 13:3 we read, "For rulers hold no terror for those who do right, but for those who do wrong. Do you want to be free from fear of the one authority? Then do what is right and He will commend you." Our God has not given us a spirit of fear. He has, instead, given us the spirit of power, the spirit of love and the spirit of self-discipline. We are told in 1 John 4:18, "There is no fear in love. But perfect love drives out fear, because fear has to do with punishment. The one who fears is not made perfect in love." God gave us the spirit of love. That spirit of love should drive out our fear - our fear of failure, our fear of disappointment, our fear for our safety because our lives are always in His hands and our fear of death.

I think one of the worst things a parent can do is abuse their children. I can't even imagine the fear this creates in little ones who are abused. Thank God we have a heavenly Father who loves us and would never abuse us. In Romans 8:15 we read, "For you did not receive a spirit that makes you a slave again to fear, but you received the Spirit of sonship. And by Him we cry, 'Abba, Father.'" Are you the kind of person you want to be? Is there any spirit of fear of you in any of your family, friends, or associates? How can you live to insure that spirit of fear never develops? I think today's promise is very clear. Make sure you are living as God would have you live and you will show the spirit of love. Do it and go out and make this a great day.

Thru days of toil when heart doth fail, God will take care of you;
When dangers fierce your path assail, God will take care of you.
No matter what may be the test, God will take care of you;
Lean weary one, upon His breast; God will take care of you.

Civilla D. Martin - 1869-1948

April 4

"'Men of Galilee,' they said, 'why do you stand here looking into the sky? THIS SAME JESUS, WHO HAS BEEN TAKEN FROM YOU INTO HEAVEN, WILL COME BACK IN THE SAME WAY YOU HAVE SEEN HIM GO INTO HEAVEN.'" Acts 1:11

John and Mary had each given their hearts to God in their early years. They grew in faith, met, fell in love, went through spiritual counseling and married. They had a little boy they named David, two years later a little girl they named Julie and continued to live their lives and raise their children with God. When the little boy was eight years old he was diagnosed with a rare form of cancer. Though he battled valiantly for a year, he succumbed to the disease in the late Winter. The family was devastated, but took refuge in God and his promises. The Sunday after Easter the promise for today was the scripture for the sermon. John, Mary and little Julie were very comforted to know that their precious one had gone to be with Jesus and that they too would be joining Him in heaven. That next week-end the family went to a Spring carnival which was in town. John bought Julie a Helium filled balloon on a string. As they were walking through the carnival the string suddenly broke and the balloon, free of its mooring, lifted into the air. As the family stood watching the balloon become smaller and smaller John expressed his regrets and told Julie, "I will buy you another balloon and make sure the string is strong." "That's okay, daddy," Julie replied. "I think that must have been how Jesus went up into the sky when the disciples were standing there watching. Maybe Jesus broke the string on purpose because He wanted my balloon for David so he wouldn't feel so all alone, and for us to play with when I get there too."

Do you have the faith of Julie that you will be in heaven when you depart this life? In 2 Corinthians 4:13-14 we read, "It is written: 'I believed; therefore I have spoken.' With that same spirit of faith we also believe and therefore speak, because we know that the One who raised the Lord Jesus from the dead will also raise us with Jesus and present us with you in His presence." When you give your heart to God you can be assured that you will be with other Christian loved ones and friends when your time on earth is over. Like Julie, you will play with your parents and siblings when you are present with them in His presence.

This promise is given in a slightly different way by Jesus, in His own words, in Matthew 16:27, "For the son of Man is going to come in His Father's glory with His angels, and then He will reward each person according to what he has done." How will you be rewarded? Do you have some fear you may be rewarded like the once popular song said, "A rusty old halo, a skinny white cloud and a robe that's so wooly it scratches." Or will you be rewarded for the many cups of water you have given in the name of Christ? For the witness you gave in your work place? The training you gave your children? James 2:26 says, "As the body without the spirit is dead, so faith without deeds is dead." You will see Jesus again and you will be rewarded for your works.

Have faith, and go out and make this a great day.

My faith looks up to Thee, Thou Lamb of Calvary, Savior divine;
Now hear me when I pray, take all my sin away; O let me from this day be wholly Thine!
When ends life's transient dream, when death's cold sullen stream shall o'er me roll,
Blest Savior, then, in love, fear and distrust remove - O bear me safe above, a ransomed soul.

Ray Palmer - 1808-1887

April 5

> "Taste and see that the Lord is good; BLESSED IS THE MAN WHO TAKES REFUGE IN HIM." Psalm 34:8

I grew to adulthood on a farm in Northern Kansas. We were members of the Friends church (Quakers). Each church would hold a business meeting each month, hence they were called "Monthly Meetings." Each three months a group of churches would get together and hold services together, have a picnic dinner and then hold a common business meeting. Thus they were called a "Quarterly Meeting." Each lady would bring her best food for the dinner. The men would set up tables of planks set on saw horses out under the trees. The ladies would bring out their food and arrange it by salads, vegetables, fruit salads, meats and desserts. I can still taste some of the meatloaf, pea salad, scalloped potatoes, pies and cakes. They were really something! I also learned that if you complimented a lady in a very special way she would sometimes send the leftovers home with you. Boy, did I ever get some extra amounts of great foods! I think of those times when I read today's promise. I tasted the food. I could tell it was good.

In much the same way we can taste the Lord. We read in Job 34:3, "For the ear tests words as the tongue tastes food." Don't you just love the way some of the Bible verses sound when you read them? Don't you pick up the rhythm of the verses? Perhaps that is one of the reasons I still read the King James Version for my daily Bible reading. My ears love the way the words taste! I think that is what the Psalmist is saying today. Read the Word of God, taste his words with your ears and you will see that the Lord is good. You will be blessed when you take refuge in Him. We read in Psalm 5:11, "But let all who take refuge in you be glad; let them ever sing for joy. Spread your protection over them, that those who love your name may rejoice in you." In the writing of this daily devotion I have chosen to put a verse or two of a hymn at the end of each daily devotion. I do so because the thought for the day reminds me of a hymn and I take to heart the above admonition, "Let them ever sing for joy."

As we study the Bible and taste the Word of God we are taking spiritual nourishment. We read in 1 Pet 2:2-3, "Like newborn babies, crave pure spiritual milk, so that by it you may grow up in your salvation, now that you have tasted that the Lord is good." This is a command of God. We are to crave the spiritual milk found in His Word. We are to consume it like newborn babies. How often does a newborn baby eat? Ask a new mother. She will probably tell you they eat every hour or so. Really, they eat often because their little tummies won't hold that much and they need the nourishment for the physical growth and development of their bodies. Like them, we need the spiritual nourishment for the spiritual growth and development of our souls. Learn the promises directly from the Bible. Memorize those verses which are especially meaningful to you. That is the best way to "taste" the Word of God.

Taste the Lord, know He is good, and go out and make this a great day.

> Standing on the promises that cannot fail, when the howling storms of doubt and fear assail,
> By the living Word of God I shall prevail, standing on the promises of God.
> Standing on the promises of Christ the Lord, bound to Him eternally by love's strong cord,
> Overcoming daily with the Spirit's sword, standing on the promises of God.
>
> R. Kelso Carter - 1849-1928

April 6

"If any of you lacks wisdom, HE SHOULD ASK GOD, WHO GIVES GENEROUSLY TO ALL WITHOUT FINDING FAULT, AND IT WILL BE GIVEN TO HIM." James 1:5

The story is told of little Johnny, who was of the age to start Kindergarten. He had a younger brother and sister with whom he loved to play. As the time to start Kindergarten approached his mother talked to him about the day he would go to Kindergarten. She circled the date on the calendar and told the three children that Johnny would go to Kindergarten on that day. When the big day arrived Johnny was dressed and taken to Kindergarten. After his day there was over and he was home playing with his siblings again his mother overheard the following: Sister, "Well, did you learn anything in Kindergarten?" "Yeah," replied Johnny, "but not enough. I gotta go back again tomorrow."

We laugh at little Johnny and his misunderstanding of the nature of Kindergarten. Aren't we a lot like that, however? Don't we think we should be able to glance at the directions and know how to put the item together. We study for a few minutes for the test and wonder why we didn't make a higher grade. We sit through one sales meeting and wonder why we aren't more successful in sales. We read the Bible a few minutes a week and wonder why our spiritual life doesn't seem to satisfy us.

In some cases we confuse knowledge with wisdom. If we read the directions we gain knowledge. Using that knowledge we can develop the best course of action for putting together an item - that is wisdom. We study to gain knowledge. When we have enough knowledge we are able to use reason to determine the correct answers - that is wisdom. When we sit through enough sales meetings and meetings about our products, how they work and what problems and situations they are best used in, then we are then able to present a reasonable plan to our potential customers and show them how our products solve their problems - that is wisdom. If we study the Bible enough, talk to godly people and pray about our understanding we begin to understand more and more about God, to be more and more in awe of Him, to respect Him more and more and to love Him more and more - that is wisdom!

Look closely at today's promise. It does not promise you knowledge. It clearly says if you lack wisdom you should ask God. Wisdom is defined as the quality of being wise; power of judging rightly and following the soundest course of action, based on knowledge, experience, understanding, etc. To grow as a new Christian, you should spend time in worship services and Bible study classes, reading devotions and the Bible on your own, talking to godly people and, most importantly, in prayer. You will gain the knowledge, you will gain the experience and your relationship with God in your prayer time and study will eventually lead to wisdom. When you reach the point you know you want wisdom is the time you will ask God for it. He will give it to you. Keep praying, and go out and make this a great day.

Immortal, invisible, God only wise, in light inaccessible hid from our eyes,
Most blessed, most glorious, the Ancient of Days, Almighty, victorious-Thy great name we praise
Great Father of glory, pure Father of light, Thine angels adore Thee all veiling their sight;
All praise we would render-O help us to see 'tis only the splendor of light hideth Thee!

Walter Chalmers Smith - 1824-1908

April 7

"In your struggle against sin, you have not yet resisted to the point of shedding your blood. And you have forgotten that word of encouragement that addresses you as sons: 'My son, do not make light of the Lord's discipline, and do not lose heart when He rebukes you, BECAUSE THE LORD DISCIPLINES THOSE HE LOVES, AND HE PUNISHES EVERYONE HE ACCEPTS AS A SON.'" Hebrews 12:4-6

When I was a Senior in high school I had developed independence since I had run the farm during the Summer due to my dad's severe illness. I played six-man football and dated a young lady from a town in Nebraska, where my sister and her husband lived. They brought her down for a Friday night game and I took her back. We stopped at my sister's home for refreshments and watched TV until we all four went to sleep. My sister was the first to awaken after midnight and shook me awake. I awakened my date and quickly took her home and drove the forty miles home, arriving at about 1:30 A.M. I did have a curfew, which was midnight on Friday night. I slipped into the house, tip-toed upstairs and went to bed. Dad awakened me at the normal time of 5:30 A.M. to do the morning chores. Since it was early in the Fall we were going to cut fire-wood during the day. It was a beautiful day with the sun shining brightly. We had cut down a tree and dad and a neighbor were starting to cut the large limbs with the tractor mounted saw. I was to trim the tree and get the limbs ready for sawing. It was mid-afternoon and the combination of lack of sleep, noon meal and the sun made my eyes very heavy. I thought I could take just a few minutes of nap so I laid on the grass in the sun. The next thing I knew dad had whopped my rear end with the axe handle and said, "If you can stay out all night, you can work all day. Now get up and get to work." So much for my quiet entry the night before! I worked hard the rest of the day and kept the two of them busy sawing the limbs I prepared for them.

That was a very important time for me in learning lessons. I learned I wasn't quite as independent as I thought I was. I learned to never underestimate what my parents knew. I learned that dad cared enough about me to train me in the way I should go. I learned to do my share of the work that was to be done. I knew better than to question dad's discipline. He hadn't hurt me. He had startled me and he did it to teach me the lessons I learned. Why did he do it? Because he loved me and wanted the best for me in life and knew proper discipline was very necessary for me to have the best in life. He was leading me to be my best.

God is like that. He wants the best for us - eternal life. He wants it so bad that He sent His only Son to shed His blood on the cross that we might have eternal life. When sin comes between us and God, He disciplines us. Our struggle against sin is not to the point that we have shed our blood. Our struggle against sin IS to the point that we must confess our sins before God and He is faithful and just and will forgive us of our sins. So if you think you are getting pretty independent confess your sins to God. Then go out and make it a great day.

All the way my Savior leads me; what have I to ask beside?
Can I doubt His tender mercy, who through life has been my Guide?
Heavenly peace, divinest comfort, here by faith in Him to dwell!
For I know whate'er befall me, Jesus doeth all things well.
Fanny J. Crosby - 1820-1915

April 8

"He who walks righteously and speaks what is right, who rejects gain from extortion and keeps his hand from accepting bribes, who stops his ears against plots of murder and shuts his eyes against contemplating evil-THIS IS THE MAN WHO WILL DWELL ON THE HEIGHTS, WHOSE REFUGE WILL BE THE MOUNTAIN FORTRESS. HIS BREAD WILL BE SUPPLIED, AND WATER WILL NOT FAIL HIM." Isaiah 33:15 & 16

Two times in my political life I was offered, what I considered to be, improper considerations. The first case came as I was the Oklahoma Republican State Chairman and was approached by a close acquaintance who told me he was representing an Engineering firm in the state. He asked me to call the appropriate federal entity any time an engineering contract was up for consideration and recommend the firm he was representing. For this I was to get one percent of the gross contract as a "finder's fee". I assured this acquaintance that I would call the appropriate federal entity any time I heard there was an engineering contract up for consideration and I would tell them of his offer and my reply and ask them to remove that firm from consideration for the contract. The second case came later when I was visited by a candidate for governor. The candidate told me that if I would give my support to their campaign I would be appointed to a position in government which would have been very attractive to me. I knew it was against Oklahoma law to offer any appointment to gain support in a campaign. I assured the candidate I would not grant my support nor would I grant support in the general election should they be successful in the primary. They went on to lose convincingly!

When I read today's promise I think of those two times and feel humbled that I obeyed God's commands and acted as a Christian. It could have been tempting to think about hundreds of thousands of dollars in contracts or about the prestige of the appointment I was offered. I face God in prayers every day. I could never do that after accepting the offers made. There are many times in life when we are tempted to do wrong. It is not God who tempts us. It is the devil!

What about your life? Have you been tempted with the assurance, "It will just be between us. No one else need ever know."? God knows! It doesn't have to be a temptation which involves huge sums of money or prestige. What about the letter you mailed at the office. Did it have your stamp on it or one "borrowed" from the office? What about the mistake the clerk made when they gave you a dollar too much change? Did you point out the error? What about the juicy gossip you heard about someone? Did you pass it on to a mutual acquaintance? Do you think that might murder their reputation? What about the test you took in school when you didn't know the answer, but you were sure the person next to you did know it? Did you look at their test paper to try to get the correct answer? If you did, was that 'walking righteously?

God promises great things for your righteous behavior. One of those great things is the way we feel about ourselves and our walk with God. Now go out and make this a great day.

I would be true, for there are those who trust me; I would be pure, for there are those who care.
I would be strong, for there is much to suffer; I would be brave, for there is much to dare.
I would be friend of all - the foe, the friendless; I would be giving, and forget the gift.
I would be humble, for I know my weakness; I would look up, and laugh, and love, and lift.
Howard A. Walter - 1883-1918

April 9

"DO NOT FORGET TO ENTERTAIN STRANGERS, FOR BY SO DOING SOME PEOPLE HAVE ENTERTAINED ANGELS WITHOUT KNOWING IT." Hebrews 13:2

Robert J. Morgan, pastor of the Donelson Fellowship in Nashville, TN, tells the story of Mrs. Agnes Frazier, who was the oldest member of his church. She was a woman of deep piety and enthusiastic spirituality. At age ninety-five, her health failed, and he received a call. "Mrs. Agnes is asking for you," said her nurse. When he entered her bedroom, she was almost too weak to look up at him. Her words were indistinct at times, but it soon became clear that she had wanted to see him because she was curious about "these men." "What men?" he asked. "I keep seeing these two men," she said. "What do they look like?" he asked. "Two men, dressed in white from head to foot are standing at the foot of my bed. I don't know what to tell them. What should I say if they ask me something?" "Tell them," he said at length, "that you belong to Jesus." That seemed to satisfy her. She said, "Yes, I'll tell them I belong to Jesus." And shortly afterward, she fell asleep in Christ and those two angels, he believes, ushered her to heaven.

Have you ever been around someone who was very ill and close to death? Have they ever had similar experiences? I remember when my father-in-law was the care giver of my mother-in-law and became very ill. We put him in the hospital and someone stayed with him at all times. One evening when I was with him he kept saying, "Please, tell him to leave." I never did understand what he was meaning until I sat to write this devotional. I am now convinced he saw an angel and knew he could not leave the care of his wife of sixty-five years to anyone else, therefore, he must not go at that time. He cared for her another five years to his age ninety-five.

In many places in the Bible we find angels are the messengers of God. It was an angel who appeared to Zechariah to tell him that Elizabeth would conceive and bear a son, who was John the Baptist. It was an angel who appeared to Mary to tell her she would bear a son, who would be named Jesus. It was an angel who appeared to Joseph to tell him it was God's will he should marry Mary. An angel escorted Peter out of prison after Herod had arrested him. It was a series of angels who gave the account of Revelation to John.

So what does today's promise mean? I think God still uses angels to communicate with us. Perhaps we are not enough "in tune" with God to recognize them as such. We are too concerned that people will think us crazy if we believe in angels. How else can you explain the, uncanny protection of little children from harm? I think today's promise also tells us that we should be sociable and entertain our friends, relatives, associates and neighbors. It tells us that we should listen to their conversation because God may be using them to deliver us a message He wants us to have.

It also tells us to have faith in God. He WILL find a way to communicate His wishes to us if we keep our hearts tuned to Him. Tune in, and then go out and make this a great day.

Angels, from the realms of glory, wing your flight o'er all the earth;
Ye who sang creation's story, now proclaim Messiah's birth.
Saints before the altar bending, watching long in hope and fear,
Suddenly the Lord, descending, in His temple shall appear.
James Montgomery - 1771-1854

April 10

> "When the Son of Man comes in His glory and all the angels with Him, He will sit on His throne in heavenly glory. All the nations will be gathered before Him, and He will separate the people one from another as a shepherd separates the sheep from the goats. He will put the sheep on His right and the goats on His left. Then the King will say to those on His right, 'COME, YOU WHO ARE BLESSED BY MY FATHER; TAKE YOUR INHERITANCE, THE KINGDOM PREPARED FOR YOU SINCE THE CREATION OF THE WORLD. For I was hungry and you gave me something to eat, I was thirsty and you gave me something to drink, I was a stranger and you invited me in, I needed clothes and you clothed me, I was sick and you looked after me, I was in prison and you came to visit me.' Then the righteous will answer Him, 'Lord when did we see you hungry and feed you, or thirsty and give you something to drink? When did we see you a stranger and invite you in, or needing clothes and clothe you? When did we see you sick or in prison and go to visit you?' The King will reply, 'I tell you the truth, whatever you did for one of the least of these brothers of mine, you did for me.'" Matthew 25:31-40

This is a long reading for a promise, however, I felt it very important to get the entire story Jesus was making in this parable. He goes on to say those on the left should depart from him as they did not minister to the least of one of these. Here Jesus is calling upon us to love our neighbors as we love ourselves. Do you do this?

It is important that you do this ministering in the name of God. Simple things will happen to give you an opportunity to minister. I was filling my vehicle with gas one day. A man in an old car, which had seen far better days, pulled in across the pump. He approached me and asked, "Friend, do you have a dollar for gas?" I pulled out my billfold and gave him two dollars with the reply, "Here are two dollars. Put in your gas and go with God. His grace is sufficient." Now, that man will never know my name, as I will never know his, however, I pray that he always remembers it was a child of Christ who gave him the money for a little gas.

How do you accomplish what Jesus instructs us to do in today's promise? Ministry! We are charged by God in Ephesians 2:10, "For we are God's workmanship, created in Christ Jesus to do good works, which God prepared in advance for us to do." Give to your church's food pantry for the poor or to the Salvation Army. Donate your clothes which 'shrunk in the closet' to the church closet or to the Salvation Army. Participate in your church's visits to the sick, not just visiting the members in the hospital, but visit the other people who are in the hospital. Visit those who are shut in their homes or are in nursing homes. Visit those people in jail or prison. Your church doesn't have a program to visit hospitals? Your church doesn't have a program to visit prisons? Take the lead and help set up such a program. It is a charge of God!

Perform your missionary work today, and make it a great day.

> So Send I you to bind the bruised and broken, o'er wandering souls to weep, to wake,
> to bear the burdens of a world a-weary. So send I you to suffer for My sake.
> So send I you to loneliness and longing, with heart a-hungering for the loved and known,
> forsaking home and kindred, friend and dear one. So send I you to know my love alone.
>
> E. Margaret Clarkson, 1915 -

April 11

"Fear of man will prove to be a snare, but WHOEVER TRUSTS IN THE LORD IS KEPT SAFE. Proverbs 29:25

The destructive effect of fear and worry on our Christian faith is vividly illustrated by Daniel DeFoe's character Robinson Crusoe. Rejecting his father's pleas, Crusoe had left home in search of wealth and adventure. His life was one of recklessness and godlessness until, following a terrible storm and shipwreck, he found himself stranded on a deserted island in the Caribbean. There his soul began to respond to the Lord, and finding a Bible among the effects salvaged from the ship, he was converted and grew into a thankful, devout, hard-working Christian. His life, though missing human companionship, was peaceful and prayerful. His faith grew strong. But one day Crusoe found a footprint in the sand, and suddenly realized that he was not alone on the island. Knowing the fierce, cannibalistic practices of the native tribes, he grew into a fearful man. He looked over his shoulder with every step. He no longer slept peacefully. He altered his habits and patterns. He visualized himself being captured, boiled and devoured. "Thus my fear banished all my religious hope. All that former confidence in God, which was founded upon such wonderful experience as I had of His goodness, now vanished, as if He that had fed me by miracle hitherto could not reserve, by His power, the provision which he had made for me by His goodness," Crusoe said. That is what fear does to us - it is diametrically opposed to our faith. The fear of man, for Robinson Crusoe, had become a snare to his faith.

Today's promise reminds me of many of the conversations I have had over the years with men who have been in combat. They would readily admit to being afraid. I consider this to be constructive fear. It is a fear which pumps adrenalin to the body to prepare it for "fight or flight." It is a fear which demands the brain to recall all the training received for such a circumstances. It is a fear which calls for boldness of action, with a cautious approach. It becomes a destructive fear when it stops the thought process, when it causes them to panic and forget their training or when it will immobilize them. Then, it becomes a "fear of man which will prove to be a snare."

1 Peter 5:7 says, "Cast all your anxiety (fear) on Him because He cares for you." Trust God!

I remember the story of George Washington in "Braddock's War." He rode to and fro throughout the battlefield, giving orders, moving men, shouting encouragement. He had horses shot out from under him. A bullet go through his tunic, however, he continued to pursue the battle until he could withdraw the forces. Here was a man who trusted God, feared not and was kept safe. God kept him safe to be able to lead the fledgling nation when it was later established.

Do you have someone at work, in meetings or at home whom you fear? Worse yet, does someone at one of these places fear you? Claim today's promise as you go about your work, sit in meetings or live at home. The Lord will keep you safe. He will lead you to live so others need not fear you. Trust the Lord today, and go out and make this a great day.

'Tis so sweet to trust in Jesus, just to take Him at His word,
Just to rest upon His promise, just to know, "Thus saith the Lord."
Yes, 'tis sweet to trust in Jesus, just from sin and self to cease,
Just from Jesus simply taking life and rest and joy and peace.
Louisa M. R. Stead - 1850-1917

April 12

"Blessed are the merciful, FOR THEY WILL BE SHOWN MERCY." Matthew 5:7

The plan of salvation by Jesus Christ provides for large measures of mercy, coupled with strict demands of truth and righteousness. In Hosea 6:6 we read, "For I desire mercy, not sacrifice, and acknowledgment of God rather than burnt offerings." This Scripture was repeated by Jesus when He ate with Matthew. The Pharisees grumbled about His eating with tax collectors and 'sinners.' In Matthew 9:12-13 Jesus answers this, "On hearing this, Jesus said, 'It is not the healthy who need a doctor, but the sick. But go and learn what this means: 'I desire mercy, not sacrifice.' For I have not come to call the righteous, but sinners.'"

Mercy is a Christian grace, and no duty is more strongly urged by the Scriptures than that we show mercy towards all men, especially those who have trespassed against us. Matthew 18:21-35 tells the parable of the unmerciful servant. A king, settling accounts, called a servant who owed him millions of dollars. The servant said he didn't have the money so the king forgave him of it. The servant then went to a fellow servant who owed him a few dollars and demanded payment. When the fellow servant could not pay him the first servant had him thrown into prison. Matthew 19:32-34 tells what happened when the king heard about his servant's actions. "Then the master called the servant in. 'You wicked servant,' he said, 'I canceled all that debt of yours because you begged me to. Shouldn't you have had mercy on your fellow servant just as I had on you?' In anger his master turned him over to the jailers to be tortured, until he should pay back all he owed." Then Jesus concludes the parable with this statement in verse 35, "This is how my heavenly Father will treat each of you unless you forgive your brother from your heart."

So we come to today's promise. Jesus said this promise in the Sermon on the Mount. He was establishing a standard for the conduct of His followers. He wants each of us to be merciful to our fellow man. By showing mercy, we will be shown His mercy. Do you have someone who has somehow wronged you? How can you show them mercy? Did Jesus counsel forgiveness? Of course He did! He said to not forgive them seven times, but seventy-seven times. Does forgiving someone show mercy to them? Partly! You must also obey the command Jesus said was the second most important command; "Love one another. As I have loved you, so you must love one another." How important is love to the Christian character? Paul told us the importance in 1 Corinthians 13:13, "And now these three remain: faith, hope and love. But the greatest of these is love." Many times we are told to have faith, but, even of more importance than our faith is our love. This is stated in today's vernacular by the expression, "People don't care how much you know until they know how much you care." In other words, how much you love them!

Show your Christian character of mercy by forgiving others when they wrong you, by giving others unconditional love and by living your life in such a way that others will be able to see Christ in you. If you do you will surely be able to make this a great day.

From every stormy wind that blows, from every swelling tide of woes,
There is a calm, a sure retreat; 'tis found beneath the mercy seat.
There is a place where Jesus sheds the oil of gladness on our heads;
A place than all beside more sweet: it is the blood-bought mercy seat.

Hugh Stowell - 1799-1865

April 13

> "Anyone who claims to be in the light but hates his brother is still in the darkness. WHOEVER LOVES HIS BROTHER LIVES IN THE LIGHT, AND THERE IS NOTHING IN HIM TO MAKE HIM STUMBLE. BUT WHOEVER HATES HIS BROTHER IS IN THE DARKNESS AND WALKS AROUND IN THE DARKNESS; HE DOES NOT KNOW WHERE HE IS GOING, BECAUSE THE DARKNESS HAS BLINDED HIM."
> 1 John 2:9-11

John 1:1-5 says, "In the beginning was the Word, and the Word was with God, and the Word was God. He was with God in the beginning. Through Him all things were made; without Him nothing was made that has been made. In Him was life, and that life was the light of men. The light shines in the darkness, but the darkness has not understood it." When today's promise says, "Whoever loves his brother lives in the light," it is saying, "Whoever loves his brother lives in God." If you do not love your brother (hate your brother) you live in darkness, or in the absence of God. You are walking in darkness and do not know where you are going. You just stumble around because you are in the dark and cannot see where you are going. This is in contrast with loving your brother and KNOWING you are going to spend eternal life with God.

Jesus told us who our brother is in Mark 3:33-34, "'Who are my mother and my brothers?' He asked. Then He looked at those seated in a circle around Him and said, 'Here are my mother and my brothers! Whoever does God's will is my brother and sister and mother.'"

We should not sin against our brother. We read Jesus' words in Matthew 5:23-24, "Therefore, if you are offering your gift at the altar and there remember that your brother has something against you, (you have sinned against your brother) leave your gift there in front of the altar. First go and be reconciled to your brother; then come and offer your gift." If our brother sins against us what should we do? Jesus answered that also in Matthew 18:21-22, "Then Peter came to Jesus and asked, 'Lord, how many times shall I forgive my brother when he sins against me? Up to seven times?' Jesus answered, 'I tell you, not seven times, but seventy-seven times.'" Reread the devotion for yesterday to see how Jesus said you would be treated unless you forgive your brother from your heart.

We are also instructed by Paul to not cause our brothers distress. In Romans 14:15-18 says, "If your brother is distressed because of what you eat, you are no longer acting in love. Do not by your eating destroy your brother for whom Christ died. Do not allow what you consider good to be spoken of as evil. For the kingdom of God is not a matter of eating and drinking, but of righteousness, peace and joy in the Holy Spirit, because anyone who serves Christ in this way is pleasing to God and approved by men."

Are you loving your brothers as Jesus would have you love them, and living so they will be able to love you? Let God be with you and guide you. Walk in the light. Love and respect your brother and sister, and go out and make this a great day.

> God be with you 'til we meet again, if life's trials should confound you,
> God will put His arms around you; God be with you 'til we meet again.
> God be with you 'til we meet again, keep love's banner floating o'er you.
> Smite death's threat'ning wave before you: God be with you 'til we meet again.
> Jeremiah E. Rankin - 1828-1904

April 14

> "At one time we too were foolish, disobedient, deceived and enslaved by all kinds of passions and pleasures. We lived in malice and envy, being hated and hating one another. BUT WHEN THE KINDNESS AND LOVE OF GOD OUR SAVIOR APPEARED, HE SAVED US, NOT BECAUSE OF RIGHTEOUS THINGS WE HAD DONE, BUT BECAUSE OF HIS MERCY. HE SAVED US THROUGH THE WASHING OF REBIRTH AND RENEWAL BY THE HOLY SPIRIT, WHOM HE POURED OUT ON US GENEROUSLY THROUGH JESUS CHRIST OUR SAVIOR." Titus 3:3-6

This part of Paul's letter to Titus could probably have been written by most of us. We were foolish, disobedient, deceived and enslaved by all kinds of passions and pleasures. We thought we were happy and had a great amount of joy. We were envious and jealous of others, pushing to get ahead of them and gossiping about them. We may have even prevented the promotion of a person under us because we were afraid they would eventually receive enough notice to be promoted over us. Oh, sure, we did good works. We may have been a member of Boy Scouts or Girl Scouts, served with the United Way, helped other non-profit groups, given a few dollars to the church and occasionally attended so others in the church and community would see what a "good person" we were. Yes, we did good works! We acted like a righteous person. Isaiah wrote in 64:6, "All of us have become like one who is unclean, and all our righteous acts are like filthy rags; we all shrivel up like a leaf, and like the wind our sins sweep us away."

Paul wrote in Romans 5:8, "But God demonstrates His own love for us in this: while we were still sinners, Christ died for us." Paul must have known how we would live without Jesus, for he told us in Romans 3:22-24, "This righteousness from God comes through faith in Jesus Christ to all who believe. There is no difference, for all have sinned and fall short of the glory of God, and are justified freely by His grace through the redemption that came by Christ Jesus." We read in 1 John 1:10, "If we claim we have not sinned, we make Him out to be a liar and His word has no place in our lives." So we have sinned. What happens to us? We are told in Romans 6:23, "For the wages of sin is death, but the gift of God is eternal life in Christ Jesus our Lord."

Where do we go from here? Read 1 John 1:9, "If we confess our sins, He is faithful and just and will forgive us our sins and purify us from all unrighteousness." How do we confess our sins? Read Romans 10:9, "That if you confess with your mouth, 'Jesus is Lord,' and believe in your heart that God raised Him from the dead, you will be saved." You can't "work" your way to heaven, no matter what you do! We see in Ephesians 2:8-9, "For it is by grace you have been saved, through faith - and this not from yourselves, it is the gift of God - not by works, so that no one can boast."

Oh, how wonderful! Through the grace and mercy of God we are saved! What a special, precious promise we have today! Claim it, and go out and make this a great day.

> Some day the silver chord will break, and I no more as now shall sing;
> But O the joy when I shall wake within the palace of the King!
> And I shall see Him face to face, and tell the story - saved by grace;
> And I shall see Him face to face, and tell the story - saved by grace.
>
> Fanny J. Crosby - 1820-1915

April 15

"Here I am! I stand at the door and knock. IF ANYONE HEARS MY VOICE AND OPENS THE DOOR, I WILL COME IN AND EAT WITH HIM, AND HE WITH ME." Revelation 3:20

This promise is taken from the instructions from God to John, when He told John what to write to the seven churches. This one being to Laodicea. We read God's word in Revelation 3:14-18, "To the angel of the church in Laodicea write: These are the words of the Amen, the faithful and true witness, the ruler of God's creation. I know your deeds, that you are neither cold nor hot. I wish you were either one or the other! So, because you are lukewarm - neither hot nor cold - I am about to spit you out of my mouth. You say, 'I am rich; I have acquired wealth and do not need a thing.' But you do not realize that you are wretched, pitiful, poor, blind and naked. I counsel you to buy from me gold refined in the fire, so you can become rich; and white clothes to wear, so you can cover your shameful nakedness; and salve to put on your eyes, so you can see." Don't you know "Christians" like that? They are neither hot nor cold. They go to church on Sundays (most Sundays, anyway) and give a few dollars to support the church. They live their lives during the week as it pleases them, without trying to live to the standard set by Jesus.

Are you living your life like that? I doubt it, for if you were you would not be reading this devotional. However, if you are living even a little like this you can change it easily. God wants your total devotion. He wants to be first in your life. If you have wealth or position, you must not love it more than you love God. We are told in 1 Chronicles 29:12, "Wealth and honor come from you." Spend more time in prayer and Bible reading. He will show you the path to follow.

Do you have friends, relatives, associates or neighbors like that? Do you make an effort to witness to them? How do you witness to them? First, live your life to reflect the love of Jesus Christ. Next, invite them to your home for a meal, to visit, relax and enjoy the time - maybe play games or watch a special game or show on TV. Ask them questions about their life, their job, their interests. Become a friend to them first. Then invite them to Sunday School and church. Offer to take them and ask them to accompany you to lunch following the services. Be gently persistent with them as the Holy Spirit leads. During the entire time, even if they try to close the door, be sure to pray for them and for your witness to them. Ask God to go before you to prepare the way with them. Avoid arguing with them about religion. Avoid trying to let them know how much you know about the Bible. Show them you are a friend and they will want to be friends with you and your friends. As Jesus said in John 15:14, "You are my friend if you do what I command." Remember, God does not crowd in. He waits to be invited!

Live fully for God. Witness for God. Now go out and make this a great day.

There's a Stranger at the door, let Him in; He has been there oft before, let Him in;
Let Him in ere He is gone, let Him in, the holy One, Jesus Christ, the Father's Son.
Open now to Him your heart, let Him in; If you wait He will depart, let Him in;
Let Him in, He is your Friend, He your soul will sure defend, He will keep you to the end.
J. B. Atchinson - No date

April 16

"I WILL GIVE YOU A NEW HEART AND PUT A NEW SPIRIT IN YOU; I WILL REMOVE FROM YOU YOUR HEART OF STONE AND GIVE YOU A HEART OF FLESH." Ezekiel 36:26

I lost both of my grandfathers to heart attacks, one at age 70 and the other at age 84. I had the great privilege of knowing, and loving, both of them. When they died in the mid 1950's, there was no such thing as someone having a heart transplant. Today, many lives are saved by transplanting the heart of an accident victim into a person who has suffered severe heart damage. Medical science has also developed bypass surgery to remove blockages in the vessels around the heart and that is being replaced with the implantation of "stints" to open the vessels. What a wonderful thing it is to read about the miracles of modern medicine. We seem to get an advance reported every month or two. When someone tells you today that they have a new heart you might wonder what medical problem they might have had that led to the need for a transplant.

Today's promise concerns satisfying a need far greater than the need for a heart transplant. With a heart transplant you will gain greater physical comfort, more freedom in the activity you can perform and a longer life here on this earth. What God promises you is greater spiritual comfort, total freedom from the wages of sin, true joy in your life, peaceful feelings and thoughts in your mind, the knowledge that He has promised to care for you and eternal life! Now that is a promise worth being written up in every newspaper, magazine and periodical in the world!

Dr. Roy McDaniel, who writes a short, daily devotion which I get over the internet, wrote about this verse, "God really loves His children. He is willing to replace a hard stubborn heart with a soft teachable one. How he does this, is by our accepting His Son, Jesus Christ as our Savior and Lord. At this time He gives us the Holy Spirit to live within us. Isn't it amazing He thought of everything for us!!" The Psalmist wrote much the same thing in Psalm 51:10, "Create in me a pure heart, O God, and renew a steadfast spirit within me." We are told in Hebrews 3:12, "See to it, brothers, that none of you has a sinful, unbelieving heart that turns away from the living God." In this latter, we are being warned to ask God to remove from us our heart of stone.

When we receive forgiveness for our sins, we also receive a new Spirit, the Holy Spirit. We are told in Ephesians 6:12, "For our struggle is not against flesh and blood, but against the rulers, against the authorities, against the powers of this dark world and against the spiritual forces of evil in the heavenly realms." I learned in training schools during the thirty years I served in the Army National Guard that the best weapon to use against a weapon was a like weapon. So the best weapon to use against a tank was a tank, the best weapon against artillery was counter-battery artillery, etc. We fight against the "spiritual forces of evil," therefore, we need the Holy Spirit to fight that fight for us. Today's promise assures us of that presence.

Receive your new heart and the Holy Spirit, and go out and make this a great day.

Holy Ghost, with light divine, shine upon this heart of mine
Chase the shades of night away; turn my darkness into day.
Holy Spirit, all divine, dwell within this heart of mine;
Cast down ev'ry idol-throne; reign supreme and reign alone.
Andrew Reed - 1787-1862

April 17

"Finally, brothers, good-by. AIM FOR PERFECTION, LISTEN TO MY APPEAL, BE OF ONE MIND, LIVE IN PEACE. AND THE GOD OF LOVE AND PEACE WILL BE WITH YOU." 2 Corinthians 13:11

In the conclusion to his second letter to the Corinthians, Paul includes today's promise. Let's look at it carefully. First, there are four commands followed by today's promise. The first command is to "aim for perfection." In His admonition to us to "love your enemies", Jesus closes with the command to us in Matthew 5:48, "Be perfect, therefore, as your heavenly father is perfect." Paul also admitted in Philippians 3:12 that he was not perfect as he said, "Not that I have already obtained all this, or have already been made perfect, but I press on to take hold of that for which Christ Jesus took hold of me." When Jesus takes hold of us He does it to make us perfect. How do we get to be perfect? Again, Paul tells us in Colossians 1:28, "We proclaim Him, admonishing and teaching everyone with all wisdom, so that we may present everyone perfect in Christ." There is an old saying, "Practice makes perfect." I reject that saying! In my experience I have found that practice makes permanent. Only perfect practice makes perfect! So we gain that perfection in God's eyes by proclaiming Him, accepting Him, being admonished by Him and devoting time and attention to the study of Him.

The second command Paul gave was to listen to his appeal. That appeal was to be reconciled with other believers and to be yoked (married, partnerships, etc.) to other believers. This is such an important point. Some churches have split over arguments about the church building, the interpretation of scripture or who to hire as a minister. Make sure you agree on the fundamental teachings of the Bible, then learn to disagree in an agreeable manner. When you date and marry, form business relationships, etc. you should choose from among God's children. Relationships are difficult enough without introducing a difference in spiritual matters as well.

The third command was to be of one mind. In matters of church policy, unanimity of action is always best. If that is not possible, then consensus should be sought. This can be done if all church members will obey the fourth command of Paul and live in peace. Refrain from picking a fight or arguing. By being peaceful, kind, gentle and patient when working with others we will let them see the light of God in us and the God of love and peace will be with us.

I like how this is said in 1 John 1:5-7, "This is the message we have heard from Him and declare to you: God is light; in Him there is no darkness at all. If we claim to have fellowship with Him yet walk in the darkness, we lie and do not live by the truth. But if we walk in the light, as He is in the light, we have fellowship with one another, and the blood of Jesus His Son, purifies us from all sin." Are you walking fully in the light today? Do you have a peaceful and loving relationship with others? Do you disagree agreeably and peacefully at work, home, community and church? Live in God's light, and go out and make this a great day.

The love of God is greater far than tongue or pen can ever tell;
It goes beyond the highest star, and reaches to the lowest hell;
The guilty pair, bowed down with care, God gave His Son to win;
His erring child He reconciled, and pardoned from his sin.

Frederick M. Lehman - 1868-1953

April 18

"WICKED MEN ARE OVERTHROWN AND ARE NO MORE, BUT THE HOUSE OF THE RIGHTEOUS STANDS FIRM." Proverbs 12:7

In the 1930's three wicked men rose to power in the world. They were Adolph Hitler in Germany, Benito Mussolini in Italy and Premier Hideki Tojo in Japan. As Hitler consolidated his power and began his conquest to establish the Third Reich, he was joined by Mussolini. As the war spread over Europe Japan moved into Manchuria and China. In November the Japanese Ambassador and a Japanese diplomat representing Tojo were meeting in Washington, DC with the U.S. Department of State representatives to solve the problems created by the cessation of trade and freezing of assets by each country. At this very time Japanese carriers were bringing their warships within range of Hawaii. History bears out the wickedness of these three men. They were despicable in their treatment of civilians and military prisoners alike. Hitler's aim of establishing a super race was particularly despicable in that he caused to be killed millions of Jews, mentally ill, labor organizers, Christian leaders, Gypsies and others. The treatment of American soldiers captured on the Bataan peninsula, with the full knowledge of and approval by Tojo's government was equally as bad. What happened to these men and their delusions of grandeur? All were dead before the end of 1945 and their regimes were overthrown. What happened to the rule of the Communists started by Stalin? Crumbled and overthrown! They all are no more!

Do we still have evil in the world? Of course we do! There is still a devil and he is still working as hard as he can to destroy the goodness in the world. There will always be those who will rise for evil intent with the use of evil ways. It remains for us to be ever vigilant. Thomas Jefferson told us, "Eternal vigilance is the price of liberty (freedom)." However, true freedom comes only from God. As Paul told us in 2 Corinthians 3:17, "Now the lord is the Spirit, and where the Spirit of the Lord is, there is freedom." And again in Galatians 5:1, "It is for freedom that Christ has set us free. Stand firm, then, and do not let yourselves be burdened again by a yoke of slavery." We are also told in James 1:25, "But the man who looks intently into the perfect law that gives freedom, and continues to do this, not forgetting what he has heard, but doing it - he will be blessed in what he does."

In 2 Peter 2:9 we read, "Then the Lord knows how to rescue godly men from trials and to hold the unrighteous for the day of judgement, while continuing their punishment." The most important thing you can do is accept Christ as your Savior. The promise today is as sure as any word of God. The house of the righteous stands as firm today as at any time in history. Christians have come under persecution time and again over the years, yet the faith has endured and the belief in, and service to God is strong. Even if man should kill this mortal body the soul will stand firm with our God for all eternity. Do you worry about evil in the world? Of course! Pray about it, add to the goodness by your words and deeds, and make this a great day.

The Lord is King! Lift up, lift up your voice - sing His praise, sing His praise!
All heaven and earth before Him now rejoice - sing His praise, sing His praise!
From world to world the joy shall ring, for He alone is God and King;
From sky to sky His banners fling - sing His praise, sing His praise!
Josiah Conder - 1798-1855

April 19

"You did not choose me, but I chose you and appointed you to go and bear fruit - fruit that will last. THEN THE FATHER WILL GIVE YOU WHATEVER YOU ASK IN MY NAME." John 15:16

This verse quotes Jesus as he walked in the vineyard with His disciples after they had shared what we know today as "The Last Supper." Jesus tells the disciples that they did not choose Him, but, rather, He chose them. He chose them, taught them, loved them and appointed them to go and bear fruit for Him after His crucifixion. When Jesus chose His disciples they had a choice also. They could have chosen to continue their work as fishermen, physicians, tax collectors, etc. They did not make the choice to remain, rather, the choice to follow Jesus. Does God choose us? Yes He does. Does God not choose some? Read 2 Peter 3:9, "The Lord is not slow in keeping His promise, as some understand slowness. He is patient with you, not wanting anyone to perish, but everyone to come to repentance." That verse means exactly what it says! Jesus chooses everyone! It is your choice, then, as to whether or not you will follow Him.

Your life will be affected by your choice. In fact, your life is affected by every choice you make. When I took my grandson with me to meet a family we would help at Christmas on the year he turned fourteen, we found a family who really needed help. They had jobs, but they had made many bad choices. They had made many purchases which had left them deeply in debt. The pay from their jobs was not enough to cover the cost of rent, vehicle payments, payments for electronic equipment, food, clothing and medical care for the family. They had nothing left over for buying gifts for their two children for Christmas and for the traditional food for Thanksgiving and Christmas. After we had met with the mother and children and learned their needs it opened the opportunity for me to have a discussion with my grandson about choices. The choices they had made led them to the state of a need for help.

We each one make choices every day, some of which will affect us for the rest of our lives. We can choose to apply ourselves to our school work to gain knowledge to assist us in providing a better life for ourselves. We can choose to learn self-discipline to give us a work ethic which will hold us in good stead in our later life. We can choose to exercise and eat correctly so we treat our body like it should be treated. We can choose to develop bad habits which will detract from the great life style we could enjoy.

The most important choice we will ever make, though, is to choose to follow Jesus and accept His choosing you. Have you chosen to follow Jesus and to love Him with all your heart, with all your mind and with all your soul? No one can do that for you except you, yourself. It is a personal choice and the most important choice you will ever make. Follow Jesus' teachings, read the Word of God and He will give you whatever you ask in His name.

Accept God's choosing you, and go out and make this a great day.

Jesus calls us o'er the tumult of our life's wild, restless sea;
Day by day His sweet voice soundeth, saying, "Christian, follow Me."
In our joys and in our sorrows, days of toil and hours of ease,
Still He calls, in cares and pleasures, "Christian, love Me more that these."
Mrs. Cecil F. Alexander - 1818-1895

April 20

"The fear of the Lord is the beginning of wisdom, and knowledge of the Holy One is understanding. FOR THROUGH ME YOUR DAYS WILL BE MANY AND YEARS WILL BE ADDED TO YOUR LIFE." Proverbs 9:10 & 11

Do you want to be wise? The fear (awe, reverence and love) of the Lord is the beginning of wisdom. You must dedicate yourself to read and study the Bible. You must also seek out dedicated teachers who teach the Bible without relying on their own agendas. When you find a point that is disturbing to you or is hard to understand, you should go to God in prayer and ask for the teachings of the Holy Spirit.

When I taught Chemistry at Phillips University in Enid, OK during the mid 1960's I would tell my students to do the same thing my undergraduate professor told me to do when I came across a concept I could not understand or a problem I could not solve. He told me to read the concept or the problem very carefully just before I went to bed at night. Many time when I would do that I would awake the next morning with an understanding of the concept or the path to take to solve the problem. Psychologists tell us that our subconscious mind works on the matter while we are asleep and brings it to the conscious mind when we awaken. I think the study of the Bible or of Biblical concepts is a lot like that, except that you have the added help of the Holy Spirit working while you are asleep.

What is important for us to know about the Bible and religion? I like Paul's statement about that in his letter to the Philippians in 3:8, "What is more, I consider everything a loss compared to the surpassing greatness of knowing Christ Jesus my Lord, for whose sake I have lost all things. I consider them rubbish, that I may gain Christ." Knowing Christ Jesus as our Lord was so great that Paul considers EVERYTHING else a loss in comparison. What a great concept! Whatever Paul would, or could, learn he considered rubbish if he only gained Christ! Do you feel that way about our Lord Jesus Christ? Do you spend time daily reading His word? Do you spend time daily reading devotions? Do you spend time daily in conversation with the Lord through your prayer time? Do you study the Bible to learn the concepts, behavior, truths, commands and promises of Christianity? Do you live by those concepts? Can others see Christ in your life? You can only do that if you continue your study of His word - the Bible. As we read in Colossians 2:6-7, "So then, just as you received Christ Jesus as Lord, continue to live in Him, rooted and built up in Him, strengthened in the faith as you were taught, and overflowing with thankfulness."

Read, study, absorb, devour, honor the Bible with your time, thoughts and study and through God your days will be many and years will be added to your life. Commit to do that today, and go out and make this a great day.

How firm a foundation, ye saints of the Lord,
Is laid for your faith in His excellent Word!
What more can He say than to you He hath said
To you, who for refuge to Jesus have fled?
Rippon's Selection Of Hymns - 1781

April 21

> "To keep me from becoming conceited because of these surpassingly great revelations, there was given me a thorn in my flesh, a messenger of Satan, to torment me. Three times I pleaded with the Lord to take it away from me. But He said to me, 'MY GRACE IS SUFFICIENT FOR YOU, FOR MY POWER IS MADE PERFECT IN WEAKNESS.' Therefore I will boast all the more gladly about my weaknesses, so that Christ's power may rest on me." 2 Corinthians 12:7-9

Mary King is a very special lady. She has had severe medical problems which have resulted in the removal of most of her small intestines and colon. She rises early in the morning to go to the local hospital ER to serve as a volunteer. She carries messages to family and water to patients, gives friendship and comfort at the times of greatest stress in people's lives and still finds time to minister to the doctors and nurses working in the ER. She has won patients to Christ with her kind, loving care as a volunteer. She also organizes the weddings at our church to make them run smoothly. Mary is also a special prayer warrior. She loves our church members, keeps current on health problems and prays for each and every need brought to her attention. Following one of her surgeries, Brother Joe and several of us in the men's prayer breakfast group gathered in Mary's room to follow the instructions given in James 5:14 (see June 20) to anoint her with oil and pray over her. When I returned to her room a short time later to report on another church member in the hospital she was nauseous and uncomfortable. I ministered to her until the nausea passed. She apologized and said, "I am so weak." I assured her that she was physically weak, quoted her these verses and then told her Paul was just like she was at that time. Mary's continued faith, concern and love shown at the time of great physical distress to herself was being an inspiration to the members of the congregation. Her witness was very powerful at the very time she was physically weakest.

Do you realize that at the very time Jesus was the weakest was the strongest time of His ministry? He was weakest when He was hanged on the cross, died and was buried. It was those actions which then led to His resurrection and ascension. Paul says in 2 Corinthians 13:4, "For to be sure, He was crucified in weakness, yet He lives by God's power. Likewise, we are weak in Him, yet by God's power we will live with Him to serve you."

Are you physically weak? Do you have a limiting medical condition? Do you use that weakness as an excuse to avoid witnessing for Christ? I read recently of a Sunday School teacher who was having medical problems and felt he was not teaching properly, that maybe his lessons were not getting the preparation and presentation they should. He was considering resigning when a class member, who knew of the problem, approached him and said, "Do you realize how much better you are as a teacher during this time of your weakness?" Yes, when you are weak is when you have to lean the most on God. Lean on Him, and go out and make this a great day.

I am weak but Thou art strong; Jesus keep me from all wrong;
I'll be satisfied at long as I walk, let me walk close to Thee.
Just a closer walk with Thee, grant it, Jesus, is my plea,
Daily walking close to Thee, let it be, dear Lord, let it be.

Traditional

April 22

"Finally, be strong in the Lord and in His mighty power. Put on the full armor of God so that you can take your stand against the devil's schemes. For our struggle is not against flesh and blood, but against the rulers, against the authorities, against the powers of this dark world and against the spiritual forces of evil in the heavenly realms. THEREFORE PUT ON THE FULL ARMOR OF GOD, SO THAT WHEN THE DAY OF EVIL COMES, YOU MAY BE ABLE TO STAND YOUR GROUND, AND AFTER YOU HAVE DONE EVERYTHING, TO STAND. Stand firm then, with the belt of truth buckled around your waist, with the breastplate of righteousness in place, and with your feet fitted with the readiness that comes from the gospel of peace. In addition to all this, take up the shield of faith, with which you can extinguish all the flaming arrows of the evil one. Take the helmet of salvation and the sword of the Spirit, which is the word of God. And pray in the Spirit on all occasions with all kinds of prayers and requests. With this in mind, be alert and always keep on praying for all the saints." Ephesians 6:10-18

I could have included fewer verses in today's promise scripture, but I wanted the supporting verses which surrounded the promise. This is such an important promise for us to grasp and claim. Read it carefully. First, put on your helmet of salvation. Your breastplate must be your righteousness! Your continued righteousness protects your most vulnerable point just like a bullet-proof vest protects a police officer at their most vulnerable point. Be buckled with truth, for without truth we can do nothing. Fit your feet with readiness by attending church to hear the gospel and take up the sword of God by reading the Bible. Now take up the shield of faith and make sure you are prepared by spending time with God in prayer for yourself and others. This didn't just say to pray, it says pray in the Spirit. Why? Because we struggle not against flesh and blood, but against...the spiritual forces of evil in the heavenly realms.

Fight evil spirits with the Holy Spirit. Pray verbally for God to bind the evil spirits you face. Do you face the evil spirit of doubt? Read Matthew 16:19 where Jesus says, "I will give you the keys of the kingdom of heaven; whatever you bind on earth will be bound in heaven, and whatever you loose on earth will be loosed in heaven." So ask God to bind the spirit of doubt and to loose the spirit of confidence and knowledge. Do you face the evil spirit of sexual lust? Ask God to bind the spirit of lust and to loose the spirit of purity. Do you face the evil spirit of greed? Ask God to bind the spirit of greed and to loose the spirit of generosity.

Don't just stand out there with your breastplate of righteousness. The devil is likely to take off your head with a well placed-blow of doubt. Don't forget the sword of the Spirit, which is the word of God or the devil will have you so confused in a matter of time you won't know what to believe. Always! Always carry the shield of faith. During the darkest times, when you don't know what to say or think, you will always know your faith in God will see you through. Then stand your ground in the day of evil. Now go out and make this a great day.

And tho this world, with devils filled, should threaten to undo us,
We will not fear, for God hath willed His truth to triumph thru us.
The prince of darkness grim - we tremble not for him;
His rage we can endure; for lo his doom is sure - one little word shall fell him.

Martin Luther - 1483-1546

April 23

"AND MY GOD WILL MEET ALL MY NEEDS ACCORDING TO HIS GLORIOUS RICHES IN CHRIST JESUS." Philippians 4:19

Here is a promise you can't get your arms around! God will meet ALL my needs according to His glorious riches in Christ Jesus. His promise holds regardless of what it takes to satisfy them. That is what I meant by saying you can't get your arms around the promise! The truth is our needs diminish as we rely more and more on God and His love. But, He will supply all the things I need! Hallelujah! What a God we have! What a wonderful promise for today.

Surveys and research have found that Christians are healthier, happier, live longer, have better jobs and more money available to them than non-Christians. Where do you think this largess comes from? It comes from the promise above! Matthew 7:9-11 quotes Jesus as saying, "Which of you, if his son asks for bread, will give him a stone? Or if he asks for a fish, will give him a snake? If you, then, though you are evil, know how to give good gifts to your children, how much more will your Father in heaven give good gifts to those who ask Him!"

Luke 12:6 quotes Jesus, "Are not five sparrows sold for two pennies? Yet not one of them is forgotten by God. Indeed, the very hairs of your head are all numbered. Don't be afraid; you are worth more than many sparrows." How many hairs are on your head? Do you know? God knows! If He knows such things as the number of hairs on your head don't you think He will provide all your needs? YES! Are you to just lie around the house and wait for God to provide? NO! That is not the way God has instructed us to behave. If you can't work, though, God will provide some way for you to be provided your needs!

In "The Hiding Place" by Corrie Ten Boom she tells about she and Betsie, her sister, being moved into a Ravensbruck concentration camp. She was able to slip a Bible and a bottle of vitamins into the camp with them. Betsie was growing weaker by the day and needed the vitamins. Each morning Corrie would give Betsie a drop of vitamins on her hunk of bread. Others in the same barracks were feverish and weak, and Corrie and Betsie could not say "no" to their needs so soon there were twenty, twenty-five and more receiving daily drops of vitamins. In Corrie's concern about running out and not having any for Betsie she said, "Betsie, Maybe only a molecule or two really gets through that little pinhole and then in the air it expands!" Betsie replied, "Don't try too hard to explain it. Just accept it as a surprise from a Father who loves you." One day one of the other women in the barracks came from the hospital, where she worked and had another bottle of vitamins. Corrie decided to use all of the one she had before starting on the new bottle. Hold it upside down and shake it as she did, not one more drop came out! Now THAT is the result of a God who WILL meet ALL your needs!

Trust our loving God today, and go out and make this a great day.

Break Thou the bread of life, Dear Lord, to me,
As Thou didst break the loaves beside the sea:
Beyond the sacred page I seek Thee, Lord;
my spirit pants for Thee, O living Word.

Mary Ann Lathbury - 1841-1913

April 24

"THE ETERNAL GOD IS YOUR REFUGE, AND UNDERNEATH ARE THE EVERLASTING ARMS. HE WILL DRIVE OUT YOUR ENEMY BEFORE YOU, SAYING, 'DESTROY HIM!'" Deuteronomy 33:27

When God directed the partition of the Promised Land among the tribes He directed that six of the cities given to the Levites be cities of refuge. We read in Joshua 20:1-6, "Then the Lord said to Joshua: 'Tell the Israelites to designate the cities of refuge, as I instructed you through Moses, so that anyone who kills a person accidentally and unintentionally may flee there and find protection from the avenger of blood. When he flees to one of these cities, he is to stand in the entrance of the city gate and state his case before the elders of that city. Then they are to admit him into their city and give him a place to live with them. If the avenger of blood pursues him, they must not surrender the one accused, because he killed his neighbor unintentionally and without malice aforethought. He is to stay in that city until he has stood trial before the assembly and until the death of the high priest who is serving at that time. Then he may go back to his own home in the town from which he fled.'" Those cities would become "life savers" of those men who have unintentionally and accidentally killed another person. The blood relative of the person killed could not take a person who has sought refuge and extract their "blood revenge" on him.

I give you this brief history of "refuge" so you can better understand the significance of the thought of God as a refuge. This should make Psalm 7:1 more meaningful, "O Lord, my God, I take refuge in you, save and deliver me from all who pursue me." Also Psalm 9:9, "The Lord is a refuge for the oppressed, a stronghold in times of trouble." David's song recorded in 2 Samuel 22 starts out, "The Lord is my rock, my fortress and my deliverer; my God is my rock, in whom I take refuge, my shield and the horn of my salvation. He is my stronghold, my refuge and my savior - from violent men you save me."

Today we flee from the evil one. Where do you flee to escape the clutches of the evil one, who would take you, kill you and devour you? Today's promise gives you the answer, the Eternal God is your refuge. You are safe in His everlasting arms! He will drive out your enemy - the evil one - from before you, saying, 'Destroy him!' Where and how do you seek refuge in God? I do so by retreating to the Bible or other Christian literature. There I find security, sustenance and comfort to get me through times I come under the attack of the evil one.

We read in Psalm 46:1, "God is our refuge and strength, an ever-present help in trouble." We find that God is not only our refuge, but is the source of our strength for our day-to-day living. The third part of the Prayer of Jabez asks, "That Your hand would be with me." What we are asking for there is the total presence of the Holy Spirit in our hearts and minds to direct us. Only with His presence are we able to continue to resist the evil one. Accept the refuge provided by our Eternal God, and go out and make this a great day.

God is our refuge and defense, in trouble our unfailing aid;
Secure in His omnipotence, what foe can make our heart afraid?
Built by the word of His command, with His unclouded presence blest,
Firm as His throne the bulwarks stand; there is our home, our hope, our rest.
James Montgomery - 1771-1854

April 25

"THERE REMAINS, THEN, A SABBATH-REST FOR THE PEOPLE OF GOD; FOR ANYONE WHO ENTERS GOD'S REST ALSO RESTS FROM HIS OWN WORK, JUST AS GOD DID FROM HIS." Hebrews 4:9 & 10

Someone once said, "Our great-grandparents called it the holy Sabbath. Our grandparents called it the Lord's Day. Our parents called it Sunday. And we call it the weekend." Ah, the weekend! What a time! The U.S. News and World Report of January 21, 1985 reported, "A recent long-term study of executive heart-attack victims show that 75 percent of those who died at work died on Monday," reports the Blue Cross-Blue Shield magazine, Health Talk. Of those who died at home, 50 percent also died on Monday. A major factor in those deaths, says the magazine, what the 'Monday Blues' associated with returning to work after an exhausting weekend."

In all my years growing to adulthood on the farm my father never worked in the fields on Sunday. Even during harvest we would take the entire day off except for the milking of the cows and the feeding of the animals. During those few times we had people in to work on our farm it was understood by all that they were not to work on Sunday. None of our work horses, tractors nor other machinery was ever loaned out for use on Sundays. I remember many lazy Summer Sundays when I would have most of the afternoon to myself to play with my puppies, nap in the shade, play with my cousins and in other ways rest from the hard work on the farm during the previous week. In the Winter we would pop corn, make fudge, play games around the fire or Momma would read to us. We would still find time for naps.

Sundays also included Sunday School, morning worship and evening services as well. Because we always ate a big Sunday dinner either at home (with or without guests) or as a guest of friends or relatives, we would eat snack food, cold cereal or left-overs for the evening meal before church. This always gave Momma a break from the three-meals-a-day routine.

Today's promise is very special to us as it promises us rest from our work as we attend church (enter God's rest). There are several places in the Bible which command us to set aside the Sabbath day for rest. There are several other places which command us to attend worship on the Sabbath. Today, we combine both commands along with our promise of rest. Why is it important? Go back and read the study mentioned in the first paragraph. The rest we get on Sunday, along with the refreshment we get from hearing the Word of God, goes a long way to the relief of stress. Stress is one of the biggest killers there is.

Do you take the Sabbath for rest and for attending worship? Or do you hustle around to be sure you cram all the golf, ball games, movies and lake outings into the one day you don't have to work? Do you think you are doing God's will on Sundays? Do you honor God with the way you spend your Sunday? Rest on the Sabbath, and go out and make this a great day.

Safely through another week God has brought us on our way;
Let us now a blessing seek, waiting in His courts today;
Day of all the week the best, emblem of eternal rest;
Day of all the week the best, emblem of eternal rest.

John Newton - 1725-1807

April 26

"THE GLORY OF YOUNG MEN IS THEIR STRENGTH, GRAY HAIR THE SPLENDOR OF THE OLD." Proverbs 20:29

When I was twenty-three years old I completed Officer Candidate School in the Oklahoma National Guard and was commissioned a Second Lieutenant. I remember the long hours of training during OCS, which I thought would never end. After graduating from OCS I attended the Infantry Officer Basic Course (IOBC) at Fort Benning, GA, along with two other officers from the same company in which I was a member. While there I received instructions from our Company Commander that I was to teach forty-two hours of classes at our Annual Training (AT) at Fort Polk, LA, since I was assigned the Training Officer for the company. We graduated from IOBC on a Wednesday, arrived home on Thursday and left for AT on Friday so I had little time to prepare lesson plans for my classes. During every spare moment I had I prepared lesson plans, reconnoitered the training areas, rehearsed with my Sargent assistant or assembled material I would need for the classes. With the heavy class schedule I found I averaged only three hours of sleep each night. Ah, the glory of young men is their strength! I survived those two weeks, none the worse for wear, and went on to a very successful career in the National Guard.

This is a promise from God. During our younger years we are able to do many things, with success, that would leave us exhausted as we accumulate gray hair. However, aging isn't all that bad! The promise also says, "gray hair is the splendor of the old." What did we know about old age during our youth? Very little, in my case. When I was a young man anyone over thirty was considered old. When I reached age thirty I felt it surely must be that anyone over age sixty was ancient. Now that I am over sixty I can't imagine what I must have been thinking to have been so far off from the truth.

Each of us is growing older as each day passes. What we make of each day will go a long way toward determining what kind of person we will be when we begin sporting that gray hair. Someone once said, "The older we grow, the more we become like the place we're going." I think that is a pretty accurate statement. Where are you going as you age? Is that where you want to go? What are you doing with each day to assure you reach your ultimate goal? Regardless of where you are along the path of growing older you should be in charge of the most important factor in aging - your attitude! What is your attitude? Do you dread each passing day that takes you closer to the Big 40, 60 or 80? Why do you dread it? God is in charge of it!

You will find the proper amount of rest becomes more important, exercise is a must and a proper diet will keep you out of all kinds of problems. What I find is the importance of continued growth in my mind. I read a lot - books of all types, newspapers and periodicals. I find myself watching less TV shows and more news. I find God much more important to me and real to me.

Age with the proper attitude, and go out and make this a great day.

As I travel through this pilgrim land there is a Friend who walks with me.
Leads me safely through the sinking sand, it is the Christ of Calvary;
This would be my prayer, dear Lord, each day to help me do the best I can,
For I need Thy light to guide me day and night, blessed Jesus, hold my hand.
Albert E. Brumley - 1905-

April 27

> "Do not be afraid of what you are about to suffer. I tell you, the devil will put some of you in prison to test you, and you will suffer persecution for ten days. BE FAITHFUL, EVEN TO THE POINT OF DEATH, AND I WILL GIVE YOU THE CROWN OF LIFE."
> Revelations 2:10

Vance Havner wrote in his book, "Hearts Afire", "God is faithful, and He expects His people to be faithful. God's Word speaks of faithful servants, faithful in a few things, faithful in the least, faithful in the Lord, faithful ministers. And all points up that day when He will say, 'Well done, thou good and faithful servant.' What terrible times we have in our churches trying to keep people faithful in attendance and loyalty! How we reward and picnic and coax and tantalize church members into doing things they don't want to do but which they would do if they loved God! The only service that counts is faithful service. True faith shows up in faithfulness. Not everyone can sing or preach, but all can be faithful."

The above brings to mind a story I read about Mother Teresa. When Senator Mark Hatfield was touring her work in Calcutta, he asked, "How can you bear the load without being crushed by it?" Mother Teresa replied, "My dear Senator, I am not called to be successful, but faithful."

In worldly matters today, we tend to judge on success only. Did you get the promotion? The pay raise? Send your children to the best schools? What kind of car do you drive, and how old is it? What is the size of your home? These questions are superfluous! God wants you to be faithful. Questions more to the mark would be: Did you read the Bible and have a prayer time each day? Did you witness to your friends, relatives, associates and neighbors? Did you worship God with regular church attendance? Were you faithful in your tithes and offerings?

We are very fortunate in America to be able to worship and serve God without the fear of persecution. We might be wrongfully charged and imprisoned, but it would not directly relate to our worship. There are many places in the world where this type of worship is not available to Christians. There are places in the world where the attendance at worship service may be interrupted with violence, where missionaries are taken as hostages and/or killed, where places that Christians gather are targeted for destruction, etc. Should Christians stay away from those places? Not at all! Jesus said in Mark 16:10, "He said to them, 'Go into all the world and preach the good news to all creation.'" He did NOT say, "Go where it is proven safe to preach the good news to those who might be willing to hear."

You should be faithful as your God is faithful. Psalm 145:13 says, "The Lord is faithful to all His promises and loving toward all He has made." Paul told us in 1 Corinthians 1:9, "God, who has called you into fellowship with His Son Jesus Christ our Lord, is faithful." So be faithful to God, claim His promise of His gift of the crown of life, and go out and make this a great day.

> Great is Thy faithfulness, O God my Father! There is no shadow of turning with Thee;
> Thou changest not; Thy compassions, they fail not: As thou hast been Thou forever wilt be.
> Pardon for sin and a peace that endureth, thine own dear presence to cheer and to guide,
> Strength for today and bright hope for tomorrow - Great is Thy faithfulness, Lord, unto me.
> Thomas O. Chisholm - 1866-1960

April 28

"Now Thomas (called Didymus), one of the Twelve, was not with the disciples when Jesus came. So the other disciples told him, 'We have seen the Lord!' But he said to them, 'Unless I see the nail marks in His hands and put my finger where the nails were, and put my hand into His side, I will not believe it.' A week later His disciples were in the house again, and Thomas was with them. Though the doors were locked, Jesus came and stood among them and said, 'Peace be with you!' Then He said to Thomas, 'Put your finger here; see my hands. Reach out your hand and put it into my side. Stop doubting and believe.' Thomas said to Him, 'My Lord and my God!' Then Jesus told him, 'Because you have seen me, you have believed; BLESSED ARE THOSE WHO HAVE NOT SEEN AND YET HAVE BELIEVED.'" John 20:24-29

When I was in the Oklahoma National Guard Officer Candidate School the Tactical Officers used various methods and situations to determine our leadership potential. They would get us very tired, put us under pressure and harass us to see how we would react. One of their methods was to give us nicknames, which seemed to demean us, to see if we would react with anger, withdrawal or in some other negative manner. During mail call one evening one candidate received a package from home. The Tactical Officers nicknamed him "Momma's Boy" and had him open the package. It was a large batch of cookies which they immediately had him pass out to the entire company formation so all could share in his bounty. When all were passed out they told us to eat the cookies on their command. They saw one of the candidates was not eating because he had eaten the cookie as soon as it was given to him. They promptly nicknamed him "Hog." We later laughed at our nicknames and became good friends with our fellow officers who had been our Tactical Officers (Bull Dog, Donnie and Skeets - we nicknamed them also!).

The nickname, Doubting Thomas, will always be associated with Didymus because of the story related to today's promise. Even though he had spent three years as a disciple of Jesus, he still did not fully understand the teachings of Jesus and the foretelling of His death, burial and resurrection. Thomas did not have the benefit of the writings of Matthew, Mark, Luke and John. He did not have the wonderful explanations given by the letters of Paul. However, when he came face to face with Jesus and was shown the proof by Him, Thomas said, "My Lord and my God!"

What about you? What proof do you need to believe in the risen Savior? Have you doubted words of the Bible when it tells the story of the birth, life, teachings, death, burial, resurrection and ascension of Jesus? Jesus knew there would be those who would not believe these basic teachings of the Bible. That is the reason for the promise. Jesus told Thomas, "Because you have seen me, you have believed." Then He talked to all of us born since His death when He said, "Blessed are those who have not seen and yet have believed."

Believe the wonderful gift of Jesus, and go out and make this a great day.

Low in the grave He lay - Jesus, my Savior! Waiting the coming day - Jesus my Lord!
Death cannot keep his prey - Jesus, my Savior! He tore the bars away - Jesus, my Lord!
Up from the grave He arose, with a mighty triumph o'er His foes;
He arose a Victor from the dark domain, and He lives forever with His saints to reign.
Robert Lowry - 1826-1899

April 29

"IF THE LORD DELIGHTS IN A MAN'S WAY, HE MAKES HIS STEPS FIRM."
Psalm 37:23

Today's promise leads to great understanding. You may ask the question, "What is a man's way that will cause the Lord to delight in it?" When you look at Psalm 1:1-3 you get part of the answer, "Blessed is the man who does not walk in the counsel of the wicked or stand in the way of sinners or sit in the seat of mockers. But his delight is in the law of the Lord, and on His law he meditates day and night. He is like a tree planted by streams of water, which yields its fruit in season and whose leaf does not wither. Whatever he does prospers." Psalm 112:1 gives you more of the answer, "Praise the Lord. Blessed is the man who fears the Lord, who finds great delight in His commands."

We are told even more about a man's way which will delight the Lord when we read Psalm 119:9-16, "How can a young man keep his way pure? By living according to your word. I seek you with all my heart; do not let me stray from your commands, I have hidden your word in my heart that I might not sin against you. Praise be to you, O Lord; teach me your decrees. With my lips I recount all the laws that come from your mouth. I rejoice in following your statutes as one rejoices in great riches. I meditate on your precepts and consider your ways. I delight in your decrees; I will not neglect your word."

Now let's look at 1 John 4:8, "Whoever does not love does not know God, because God is love." And look at 1 Corinthians 13:6, "Love does not delight in evil but rejoices with the truth." Then Jesus said in John 15:10, "If you obey my commands, you will remain in my love, just as I have obeyed my Father's commands and remain in His love."

So, now we can define "a man's way" which will cause the Lord delight: Avoid wicked ways or being counted as a sinner; refrain from mocking or showing scorn to those who are doing right; study the Bible and memorize parts of it on a regular basis; hold the Lord in love, awe and reverence; study and obey the commands of the Lord; pray regularly, asking God to show you the full explanation of His word; love the Lord and love all the people He has made - even those who are hard to love and, finally, obey the gentle nudging of the Holy Spirit as being the commands of God. When we live according to these precepts He will make our steps firm. He will give us such peace of mind and heart that we will radiate our love of Him, which helps us show our love to others. By seeking His counsel in prayer and meditation our work will be more productive and whatever we do will prosper. We will walk with a sure step - He makes our steps firm!

How does your way of living measure up to the way in which the Lord will delight? Do you feel confident He delights in your way? What do you feel you need to change? Do you spend time in prayer listening to God rather than reciting a list of requests to Him? Walk in His way and He will delight in it, and you will make this a great day.

Day by day and with each passing moment, strength I find to meet my trials here;
Trusting in my Father's wise bestowment, I've no cause for worry or for fear.
He whose heart is kind beyond all measure gives unto each day what He deems best
Lovingly, its part of pain and pleasure, mingling toil with peace and rest.

Lina Sandell Berg - 1832-1903

April 30

"WHOEVER FINDS HIS LIFE WILL LOSE IT, AND WHOEVER LOSES HIS LIFE FOR MY SAKE WILL FIND IT." Matthew 10:39

When I read this verse for the first time I thought I was reading just a little bit of double talk. As I matured and studied the scripture and asked God to lead me in understanding His word I came to understand what a wonderful promise this is. I now realize when I place my trust and confidence in things of this world, thinking they make up my life, I will lose my life. When I place my trust and confidence in Him and His word I have found life to the fullest. What I have lost is the total dependence on things of earth and realize my life here is but a season in God's time. My life with God in heaven will be for all eternity. I have surrendered my will to Him.

These words of Jesus are recorded just a little differently in John 12:25, "The man who loves his life will lose it, while the man who hates his life in this world will keep it for eternal life." When Jesus talks about a man hating his life, He means that the love for God must be so great that all other loves are, by comparison, hatred. Jesus says in John 10:10, "The thief comes only to steal and kill and destroy; I have come that they may have life, and have it to the full." John 11:25-26 says, "Jesus said to her, 'I am the resurrection and the life. He who believes in me will live, even though he dies; and whoever lives and believes in me will never die. Do you believe this?'" Losing your life means surrendering all will, hope, dreams and desires to God.

Still confused? First, I love my life here on earth! I don't think that goes against what Jesus said. Why? Because, second, my love for God is so great, and getting greater with each passing day, that I look forward to being with Him throughout eternity. He has a number of jobs for me to do on this earth. In John 15:14 Jesus said, "You are my friends if you do what I command." What did Jesus command? Jesus said in Mark 16:15, "He said to them, 'Go into all the world and preach the good news to all creation.'" and in John 21:17, "Feed my sheep."

If God did not have a purpose for us, as Christians, on earth, He would take us directly to heaven as soon as we were saved by His grace. He does have a purpose for us, as we see in the preceding paragraph. We are His friends - His disciples - here on earth. We are the ones charged with carrying the good news to all creation! So be happy with your life here on earth. Spend it wisely in a proper distribution of time between work, family, worship, study, witnessing and prayer and meditation. God did not call me to the mission field. He did call me to mission work! His call to me was to support the work of those who are called by giving finances and holding them up to God in prayer. God did not call me to be a pastor. He did call me to support the work of the pastor with my attendance, finances, prayer and daily witnessing. In that, I have lost my life here on earth in totally living for Him. Obeying His charge to love my wife and family, love my neighbor and love my God is part of the way I lose my life for His sake.

So lose your life for God's sake, and you will find you have made this a great day.

My life, my love I give to Thee, Thou Lamb of God who died for me;
O may I ever faithful be, my Savior and my God!
I'll live for Him who died for me, how happy then my life shall be!
I'll live for Him who died for me, my Savior and my God!

Ralph E. Hudson - 1843-1901

May 1

"I pray also that the eyes of your heart may be enlightened in order that you may know THE HOPE TO WHICH HE HAS CALLED YOU, THE RICHES OF HIS GLORIOUS INHERITANCE IN THE SAINTS, AND HIS INCOMPARABLY GREAT POWER FOR US WHO BELIEVE. THAT POWER IS LIKE THE WORKING OF HIS MIGHTY STRENGTH." Ephesians 1:18 & 19

Don't you just love that phrase, "the eyes of your heart"? When I read that phrase I think of Psalm 121:1-2, "I lift up my eyes to the hills - where does my help come from? My help comes from the Lord, the Maker of heaven and earth." I also think of Psalm 123:1, "I lift up my eyes to you, to you whose throne is in heaven."

If the eyes of your heart are enlightened you will know today's promise. It contains three parts. First, the hope to which He has called you. Second, the riches of His glorious inheritance in the saints. And, third, His incomparably great power for us who believe. Understand, Paul is telling us that we will have the hope to which God has called us. He did not call us to fear, but to a great hope. We will also have the inherited riches from Him for our life eternal. We will also have the power like the power of His mighty strength, that power which created the heavens and the earth and all that are in, and on, the heaven and earth. What a great promise!

How do we enlighten the eyes of our heart? We read in Psalm 119:18, "Open my eyes that I may see wonderful things in your law." And in Psalm 119:37, "Turn my eyes away from worthless things; preserve my life according to your word." Paul also told us in 2 Corinthians 4:18, "So we fix our eyes not on what is seen, but on what is unseen. For what is seen is temporary, but what is unseen is eternal." From these verses we learn that we should study the word of God rather than spend our time on worthless things. That does not mean we should never spend time playing, resting, reading novels, etc. What it means is that we should set a time for our regular study of His word. We should also set a regular time to fix our eyes on things that are unseen - communication with God in prayer! When we do those things the eyes of our heart, and thus our entire heart, will be enlightened!

The eyes of the heart are the same as the eyes of your face. We are told in Luke 11:34, "Your eye is the lamp of your body. When your eyes are good, your whole body also is full of light. But when they are bad, your whole body is full of darkness." How do the eyes of your heart become bad? Sin! When you sin, the eyes of your heart are bad and your whole body is full of darkness. When you take that sin to God for forgiveness your eyes become good and your whole body is full of light! Jesus said in Mark 8:18, "Do you have eyes but fail to see, and ears but fail to hear?" Do you see what God has for you? What do the eyes of your heart see that God has prepared for you to do and to be? Are you following the pathway He has prepared for you? Claim today's great promise, and go out and make this a great day.

Lift the veil from my eyes, dear Lord, give me new eyes to see.
Souls that are lost are dying in sin, no hope, no life without Thee.
Humbly now at Thy cross I kneel, yielding myself to Thee.
Consecrate all my service, O God, that Christ may shine forth in me.
Beverly Terrell - (No Date)

May 2

"I WILL INSTRUCT YOU AND TEACH YOU IN THE WAY YOU SHOULD GO; I WILL COUNSEL YOU AND WATCH OVER YOU." Psalm 32:8

Early in the year when I was a Senior in high school our math teacher was sick for a week. Since I had an elective during the hour he taught Algebra, and study hall during the hour he taught Geometry, the Superintendent asked me to sit in those classes to keep order. The first day I was in the class the Superintendent started it off by saying I would be there to maintain order and to answer any questions they may have about the next few assignments. Slowly the students started coming to me to ask questions. When I looked up at one point I saw there were more students trying to see what I was writing than could possibly see. I had them all sit down and went to the board and started working the problems and taking questions. I really enjoyed it and decided I would give the assignments, work the problems and then teach each day he was gone. I did that in both classes for a week. The next week in study hall our English and Speech teacher came to me and told me he had heard a lot of good things about the week I had spent "teaching". He encouraged me to go to college and become a teacher. I applied to college, was accepted, won a scholarship and attended Emporia State University in Emporia, Kansas. I am sure I am like you, I had many really good teachers in elementary school, high school and college. They did a lot to direct the career path I have taken.

All the great things my teachers did pale to insignificance when compared to the teaching, counseling and watching over I received from my parents. I cannot remember a time my parents did not take me to church (except for times of illness and storms). I cannot remember a morning we did not have devotional reading and prayer before breakfast. I cannot remember a meal we ate without first saying a prayer of thanks for the food and blessings provided by the Lord. I remember many times I would be working alongside my dad when we would be doing something that reminded him of a Bible verse or a Biblical lesson, and he would relate it to me. Momma often read to us in the evenings. She would read novels like, "Little Britches" or "Little Women", and often read to us the great stories from the Bible. I think the most meaningful lessons I learned from my parents was learned by watching the example of the way they lived their lives. I thank God daily for the Godly example and teachings of my parents and grandparents.

Whether or not you had such an example during your childhood years you can, and should, pass that type of teaching on to your children and grandchildren. Are you living your life as God would want you to? Are you faithful in attending church with your family? Are you faithful in your devotions? Your prayers? Do you use daily happenings to reinforce Christian teachings to your children? Is your reading for relaxation from the type of books you would be proud to read to your children? Do you read to them regularly? Today's promise is that God will teach you, counsel you and watch over you. Ask Him, and go out and make this a great day.

Long as my life shall last, teach me Thy way!
Where'er my lot be cast, teach me Thy way!
Until the race is run, until the journey's done,
Until the crown is won, teach me Thy way!
Mansell Ramsey - 1849-1923

May 3

> "Therefore I tell you, WHATEVER YOU ASK FOR IN PRAYER, BELIEVE THAT YOU HAVE RECEIVED IT, AND IT WILL BE YOURS." Mark 11:24

One translation of Isaiah 62:6-7 says, "They must remind the Lord of His promises... They must give Him no rest until He restores Jerusalem." We should remind God of His promises and give Him no rest until He answers. That is a passage that taught John (Praying) Hyde to pray with persistence. Hyde grew up in Carthage, IL, in a minister's home. At McCormick Theological Seminary, he committed himself to overseas evangelism, and following graduation he went to India. His itinerant ministry took him from village to village, but his preaching produced few converts until he discovered the truth of Isaiah 62:6-7, and took these words literally. At the beginning of 1908, he prayed to win at least one soul to Christ every day. By December 31, he had recorded over four hundred converts. The following year, the Lord laid two souls per day on his heart, and his prayer was again answered. The next year he prayed for four souls daily with similar results. Once, stopping at a cottage for water, Praying Hyde pleaded with God for ten souls. He presented the Gospel to the family, and by the end of his visit all nine members of the family had been saved. But what of number ten? Suddenly a nephew who had been playing outside ran into the room and was promptly converted. It is obvious that Praying Hyde claimed today's promise, which is a promise made by Jesus.

In James 1:6-8 we read, "But when he asks, he must believe and not doubt, because he who doubts is like a wave of the sea, blown and tossed by the wind. That man should not think he will receive anything from the Lord; he is a double-minded man, unstable in all he does." What is your prayer life like? Do you believe that you have received it, even as you ask, or do you doubt? Have you stood on the shore during a storm, with the wind blowing hard, and watched the waves come in? You see the wind blowing the waves over on themselves and the spray is sent into the air to drift over the surface of the sea. Is this like you when you pray? Are you double-minded and unstable in your requests to God?

Your heart must be right with God before you pray. We read in Isaiah 59:1-2, "Surely the arm of the Lord is not too short to save, nor His ear too dull to hear. But your iniquities have separated you from your God; your sins have hidden His face from you, so that He will not hear." Sin is like a clog in the pipeline to God. It has to be removed so communication, requests and blessings will flow freely.

Do you thank God during your prayers for the answers He is even then delivering? Do you sometimes not know just how to phrase a request? Read Psalm 139:4, "Before a word is on my tongue you know it completely, O Lord." Also read Isaiah 65:24, "Before they call I will answer; while they are still speaking I will hear." We have a God who cares and has promised He would answer! Call on Him, and go out and make this a great day.

When pangs of death seized on my soul, unto the Lord I cried,
Till Jesus came and made me whole, I would not be denied.
Old Satan said my Lord was gone and would not hear my prayer,
But praise the Lord the work is done, and Christ the Lord is here.

Charles P. Jones - 19th Century

May 4

"When calamity comes, the wicked are brought down, BUT EVEN IN DEATH THE RIGHTEOUS HAVE A REFUGE." Proverbs 14:32

Atheists, in my opinion, must have a terrible lives. They can have success only for the period they are alive. They reject the teachings of Matthew 22:36-38, "'Teacher, which is the greatest commandment in the Law?' Jesus replied: 'Love the Lord your God with all your heart and with all your soul and with all your mind. This is the first and greatest commandment.'" Therefore, in the mind of an atheist, this life is all there is. So when death comes, their total existence is complete. Their body is placed in the grave, or burned with the ashes scattered, and that is all there is to it. Their lives have been brought down!

Christians, on the other hand, believe in the promise in John 3:16, "For God so loved the world that He gave His one and only Son, that whoever believes in Him shall not perish but have eternal life." We can ask of death as in 1 Corinthians 15:55-57, "Where, O death, is your victory? Where, O death, is your sting? The sting of death is sin, and the power of sin is the law. But thanks be to God! He gives us the victory through our Lord Jesus Christ." Even though we know we have eternal life with God, we still consider death to be a time of trouble. Many times it is accompanied with pain, trauma or surprise; and, almost always, it is accompanied with sorrow. So we hold on to Psalm 46:1-3 in times of death, like we hold on to it during any time of trouble, "God is our refuge and strength, an ever-present help in trouble. Therefore we will not fear, though the earth give way and the mountains fall into the heart of the sea, though its waters roar and foam and the mountains quake with their surging."

We are so blessed to have a refuge in death. That refuge is Jesus Christ, who was given to us as a sin offering from God. Jesus' blood took the place of the blood of the animals, which were required to be sacrificed when God gave Moses the law. In Leviticus 17:11 we are told, "For the life of a creature is in the blood, and I have given it to you to make atonement for yourselves on the altar; it is the blood that makes atonement for one's life." Jesus shed His blood to atone for the sins of each one of us. When we accept that atonement, ask forgiveness as described in Romans 10:9, "That if you confess with your mouth, 'Jesus is Lord," and believe in your heart that God raised Him from the dead, you will be saved."

We are not like the atheist. In death we have the refuge of eternal life promised us by God. During a conversation about an atheist we know my nephew, Kevin English, said, "They have a lot more faith than I do. If I am wrong I have wasted a little time here on earth even while I enjoyed it. If they are wrong they will have eternity to ponder their error."

Always realize that you are going to die. Hebrews 9:27 says, "Just as man is destined to die once, and after that to face judgment." Be confident in receipt of the eternal life promised you by your God. Now go out and make this a great day.

A thousand ages in Thy sight are like an evening gone;
Short as the watch that ends the night, before the rising sun.
O God, our help in ages past, our hope for years to come,
Be Thou our guide while life shall last, and our eternal home!

Isaac Watts - 1674-1748

May 5

"Yet, O Lord, you are our Father. We are the clay, you are the potter; WE ARE ALL THE WORK OF YOUR HAND." Isaiah 64:8

Suppose a potter took a hunk of moist clay and placed it on the potter wheel to make a pot. Much to the potter's surprise, the clay moved off the potter's wheel every time he came near to mold it. How many pots could the potter mold from the clay? None could be produced at all! In reality, the clay does stay on the wheel. The potter envisions a beautiful and functional pot. He makes each pot to be unique and each is an original work of art. Each pot will have a different shape, a different size and may be glazed and fired to have each a different color.

My brother-in-law, Lloyd C. English, retired after many years teaching art. Over the years he made many beautiful pots. We have some of his original creations in our home. I asked him if the clay ever moved off the wheel to avoid being made into the creation he wanted it to be. He laughed and said, "No, never! Why do you ask?" I told him I needed his answer for my writings. You are the clay God will use to create His beautiful, functional, unique and original creation. You must place yourself in God's hands so He can mold you and make the creation He desires of you. You must not move off the potter wheel every time God tries to mold you to His will. God will work wonders of you because God does nothing but work wonders.

Just as the potter has all rights and authority over the clay, so God has all rights and authority over you. In Romans 9:20-21 we read, "Shall what is formed say to Him who formed it, 'Why did you make me like this?' Does not the potter have the right to make out of the same lump of clay some pottery for noble purposes and some for common use?" You must trust in the wisdom and purpose of God, the potter. Just as the worth of the clay is minor in comparison with the worth of the completed pot, and its purpose is determined by the work of the potter, so our worth and purpose lies in the hands of the potter - our God!

We often find God's purpose for our lives in our form. Our form consists of our experiences, our education and training, our temperament, our physical attributes, etc. We need to seek God's purpose for us in a determined, coordinated manner through study of His word, prayer, communions with God, talking to trusted spiritual leaders and talking with our families. Just as a potter needs pliable clay to make the pot, so God needs us to be pliable to work His wonders on us. While a potter will take a piece of clay, fashion and shape the pot, apply the glaze(s) and fire the pot within a relatively short time, the shaping of us by God is a life-long process. We are like that Tee shirt message I saw once, "Be patient with me. God isn't through shaping me yet."

What about your life today? Are you pliable in God's hands? Are you willing to submit to His molding of your life as He makes of you what He wants you to be? Let God mold you to be the very unique person He wants while you go out and make this a great day.

Have Thine own way, Lord! Have Thine own way! Thou are the potter, I am the clay.
Mold me and make me after Thy will, while I am waiting, yielded and still.
Have Thine own way, Lord! Have Thine own way! Hold o'er my being absolute sway!
Fill with Thy Spirit till all shall see Christ only, always, living in me!
Adelaide A. Pollard - 1862-1934

May 6

> "All kinds of animals, birds, reptiles and creatures of the sea are being tamed and have been tamed by man, BUT NO MAN CAN TAME THE TONGUE. IT IS A RESTLESS EVIL, FULL OF DEADLY POISON. With the tongue we praise our Lord and Father, and with it we curse men, who have been made in God's likeness. Out of the same mouth come praise and cursing. My brothers, this should not be." James 3:7-10

In "Our Daily Bread", published by RBC Ministries, Joanie Yoder wrote for February 7, 2003, "A Greek philosopher asked his servant to cook the best dish possible. The servant, who was very wise, prepared a dish of tongue, saying, 'It's the best of all dishes, for it reminds us that we may use the tongue to bless and express happiness, dispel sorrow, remove despair and spread cheer.' Later the servant was asked to cook the worst dish possible. Again, he prepared a dish of tongue, saying, 'It's the worst dish, for it reminds us that we may use the tongue to curse and break hearts, destroy reputations, create strife and set families and nations at war.'"

Many verses about the tongue are in Proverbs. A few are: 11:13, "A gossip betrays a confidence, but a trustworthy man keeps a secret.";12:6, 12:14, "From the fruit of his lips a man is filled with good things as surely as the work of his hands rewards him."; 12:18, "Reckless words pierce like a sword, but the tongue of the wise brings healing."; 12:19 "Truthful lips endure forever, but a lying tongue lasts only a moment."; 12:22, "The Lord detests lying lips, but he delights in men who are truthful."; 15:2, "The tongue of the wise commends knowledge, but the mouth of the fool gushes folly." and 15:4, "The tongue that brings healing is a tree of life, but a deceitful tongue crushes the spirit."

I write these verses to give you just a taste of what the Bible says about our tongue. Today's promise is another negative promise in that it tells you something you cannot do. Just as we cannot control our nature to sin - we must depend on the Holy Spirit - so we cannot control our tongue. We must depend on the Holy Spirit.

What about your life? Do you have trouble controlling your tongue? Do you have a tendency to make boasts beyond what you have done, or are capable of doing? Do you have a problem with gossip? Do you tend to criticize people? Do you get angry and say things you wish you hadn't said? How do you work on the problem? Perhaps the first thing you should do to solve this problem is take it to God in prayer. Ask for His help in controlling your tongue. Many problems of the tongue come from the spirit of deceit, the spirit of boastfulness, the spirit of anger or the spirit of feeling superior. Matthew 16:19 says, "I will give you the keys of the kingdom of heaven; whatever you bind on earth will be bound in heaven, and whatever you loose on earth will be loosed in heaven." So speak out loud and ask God to bind those negative spirits and loose the positive spirits to help you control your tongue. So use your tongue to speak the truth, compliment others and praise God. Then go out and make this a great day.

O for a thousand tongues to sing, blessed be the name of the Lord!
The glories of my God and King, blessed be the name of the Lord!
He breaks the power of canceled sin, blessed be the name of the Lord!
His blood can make the foulest clean, blessed be the name of the Lord!
Charles Wesley - 1707-1788

May 7

"THOUGH HE STUMBLE, HE WILL NOT FALL, FOR THE LORD UPHOLDS HIM WITH HIS HAND." Psalm 37:24

Today's promise is a very comforting promise. Who among us has not stumbled in our Christian walk? Who among us could have thrown the first stone when Jesus said, "If any one of you is without sin, let him be the first to throw a stone at her."? Thank God for His promise that, though we stumble, we will not fall because He holds us up with His hand! This promise is nearly repeated in Psalm 55:22, "Cast your cares on the Lord and He will sustain you; He will never let the righteous fall."

What do we do when we stumble? We have scripture which clearly points this out also. Proverbs 24:16 says, "For though a righteous man falls seven times, he rises again, but the wicked are brought down by calamity." Job 5:19 says, "From six calamities He will rescue you; in seven no harm will befall you." Confucius (550-478 BC) wrote, "Our greatest glory is not in never falling, but in rising every time you fall." I think from our scripture and from sayings we can see we must rise whenever we fall. God's grace is still sufficient for us for each time we stumble.

Do we feel bad about our actions when we stumble? Of course we do! Psalm 38:15-18 says, "I wait for you, O Lord; you will answer, O Lord my God. For I said, 'Do not let them gloat or exalt themselves over me when my foot slips.' For I am about to fall, and my pain is ever with me. I confess my iniquity; I am troubled by my sin." The Psalmist felt very grieved about his sin. He was concerned that others would see his sin and react negatively toward God. He then confessed his sin and admitted that he is troubled by his sin. That is what we should do when we stumble (SIN). We should be convicted because of our sin. We should feel grieved that others would be negatively influenced by our sin. Most of all, we should confess our sin and be troubled by it to the extent that we learn from it and ask the Holy Spirit to keep us from more sin.

How do we avoid stumbling in the future? We are told in Psalm 119:165, "Great peace have they who love your law, and nothing can make them stumble." Bible study and prayer are two of the best ways to avoid stumbling. Paul also told us in Hebrews 10:25, "Let us not give up meeting together, as some are in the habit of doing, but let us encourage one another - and all the more as you see the Day approaching." Attendance at church and Sunday school are vital to prevent stumbling. We get so much reinforcement and encouragement from such assembling together. Make it an established habit to attend church!

When we have stumbled we should immediately admit out error and change our ways. Then be more careful in the future to not commit the same sin again. Christian Nestell Bovee, American author and editor said, "It is only an error in judgement to make a mistake, but it shows infirmity of character to adhere to it when discovered."

He holds you when you stumble, so confess your sin, and make this a great day.

The chimes of time ring out the news; another day is through.
Someone slipped and fell. Was that someone you?
You may have longed for added strength, your courage to renew.
Do not be disheartened, for I bring news to you. It is no secret what God can do.
Stuart Hamblen - 1908-

May 8

"IF WE LIVE, WE LIVE TO THE LORD; AND IF WE DIE, WE DIE TO THE LORD. SO WHETHER WE LIVE OR DIE, WE BELONG TO THE LORD." Romans 14:8

A member of our Sunday School class, Pat Lee, had cancer. It metastasized to her bones. She took radiation and chemotherapy as long as her body would tolerate it. She reached the condition that caused the doctors to decide to remove all medication except for that which controlled pain. She continued to come to Sunday School and church most every Sunday until a month before she died. Her testimony was very great to all of us in the class, in fact, to all those in the church. We could see the love of God she had. We could see the love she had for her husband, Mark, and that which he had for her. It was a joy to be around her! She truly lived to the Lord! I remember Mark telling us about the Hospice Chaplain coming to see them often. After one of his visits he commented to Mark, "I just love to come her to talk to Pat. She lifts my spirits so much and I always leave here feeling so much better." Now here was a lady, who no longer took any medication designed to improve her condition, ministering to a man whose job it was to minister to those medical science held out no more hope for.

I pray to God that I can live just a little bit like Pat lived. I pray that my life, in some way, will be a blessing to those who come in contact with me. How can I do that? I think the answer lies in a study of the life of Christ and what He thought was important. Jesus' words are reported in John 13:34-35, "A new command I give you: Love one another. As I have loved you, so you must love one another. By this all men will know that you are my disciples, if you love one another." Also read 1 Corinthians 13, the love chapter. Paul concludes with this, "And now these three remain: faith, hope and love, But the greatest of these is love." I think the answer to living a life like Pat lived is given in this paragraph! LOVE ONE ANOTHER!!

One of the things all of us will do is die. When we die what will happen to us? As Christians, we do not have to concern ourselves with this question. We KNOW what will happen to us. Today's promise tells us what will happen to us. We will die to the Lord! We belong to the Lord! Paul wrote in his letter to the Philippians 1:20-22, "I eagerly expect and hope that I will in no way be ashamed, but will have sufficient courage so that now as always Christ will be exalted in my body, whether by life or by death. For to me, to live is Christ and to die is gain. If I am to go on living in the body, this will mean fruitful labor for me. Yet what shall I choose? I do not know!" Paul is truly a man who lived in Christ. He provided for his own needs by working at his occupation as a tentmaker. He formed many churches. His writings give clear directions for us today in how to become a Christian and how to live a Christian life. Yet, Paul looked forward to the time of his death when he would be with Christ.

Is your life an example of fruitful labor for Christ? Will Christ always be exalted in your body, whether by life or by death? Love and it will be. Now go out and make this a great day.

O love that wilt not let me go,
I rest my weary soul in Thee;
I give Thee back the life I owe,
That in Thine ocean depths its flow may richer, fuller be.

George Matheson - 1842-1906

May 9

"He replied, 'IF YOU HAVE FAITH AS SMALL AS A MUSTARD SEED, YOU CAN SAY TO THIS MULBERRY TREE, 'BE UPROOTED AND PLANTED IN THE SEA,' AND IT WILL OBEY YOU.'" Luke 17:6

The story is told about a man hiking along the rim of the Grand Canyon in a remote area. He stopped to view the scenery, looked over the edge, lost his balance and fell. As he was going down the side of the high cliff he grabbed onto a tree growing out of it. He was hanging below the tree pondering his fate when he began to pray. He called, "Lord are you up there? Lord will you save me? Lord are you up there?" A voice came to him saying, "Yes, I am up here." "Is that you, Lord?" the man asked. "Yes, it is I. Do you believe I can save you?" "Yes, I believe you Lord," replied the man. "Do you really have faith I can save you?" "Yes, I really have faith you can save me Lord," the man answered. "Then let go of that tree." The man immediately shouted, "Is there anyone else up there?"

We can laugh at such a story, but how true is it of our faith? Are we like the congregation that met to pray for rain and was chastised by the minister because not one of them had brought an umbrella? Do we pray that God will provide for our financial needs then fail to pay our tithe because we are afraid we will not have enough money for food and housing? How strong IS our faith? The mustard seed is one of the smallest of all seeds. Obviously, the mustard seed does not wonder if there will be enough soil for its roots. Whether or not there will be enough rain to provide the moisture to sustain the plant. No, it just sprouts and grows. Is your faith like that?

What is faith? We read in Hebrews 11:1 & 6, "Now faith is being sure of what we hope for and certain of what we do not see." "And without faith it is impossible to please God, because anyone who comes to Him must believe that He exists and that He rewards those who earnestly seek Him."

How do we show our faith? By our works! We read in James 2:14-18 & 26 , "What good is it, my brothers, if a man claims to have faith but has no deeds? Can such faith save him? Suppose a brother or sister is without clothes and daily food. If one of you says to him, 'Go, I wish you well; keep warm and well fed,' but does nothing about his physical needs, what good is it? In the same way, faith by itself, if it is not accompanied by action, is dead. But someone will say, 'You have faith; I have deeds.' Show me your faith without deeds, and I will show you my faith by what I do. As the body without the spirit is dead, so faith without deeds is dead."

In addition to showing your faith by your works, you also show your love by your works. You can give to people without faith and without love. But you cannot have faith and love without giving! How do you express your faith and love? Do you follow the examples and teachings in the Bible? Or do you feel that you would be one to whom Jesus would say, "O you of little faith!"? Live by faith, and go out and make this a great day.

I care not today what tomorrow may bring, if shadow or sunshine or rain;
The Lord I know ruleth o'er everything, and all of my worry is vain.
I know that He safely will carry me through, no matter what evils betide;
Why should I then care though the tempest may blow, if Jesus walks close to my side.

James Wells - (No Date)

May 10

"Because He Himself suffered when He was tempted, HE IS ABLE TO HELP THOSE WHO ARE BEING TEMPTED." Hebrews 2:18

In his book, "Disciples Indeed," Oswald Chambers gives this insight regarding temptation: How are we to face the tempter? By prayer? No. With the Word of God? No. Face the tempter with Jesus Christ, and He will apply the word of God to you, and the temptation will cease. F. B. Meyer made a similar point in "The Christ Life for Your Life." Speaking of temptation in the life of a Christian, he wrote: Remember further that His purpose is to deliver from the power of sin. The guilt is gone, but the power remains, and He can only deliver from that gradually. Now, understand me - I do not believe in sanctification, I believe in the Sanctifier; I do not believe in holiness; I believe in the Holy One. Not an it, but a person, not an attribute, but Christ in my heart. Abide in Jesus. Let the Holy Ghost in you keep you abiding in Jesus, so that when Satan comes to knock at your door, Jesus will go and open it, and as soon as the devil sees the face of Christ looking through the door, he will turn tail.

We read in Matthew 4:1-11 about the temptations of Jesus after he had fasted and prayed in the desert for forty days. We know that Jesus lived a life free of sin; therefore, we know that being tempted is not a sin. The sin comes in yielding to temptation. The devil is very good at making temptation look very good. Look at the story of Adam and Eve. When Eve told the serpent they could not eat of the tree of life because they would die, the serpent told her she would not die, but know good and evil. The tree looked good so Eve ate and gave to Adam. What happened? By this exercise of free will and disobedience of God, they introduced sin into the world, and through sin, death; thus proving the truth of the word God had given them.

When we are tempted, we can consider the words of Hebrews 4:14-16, "Therefore, since we have a great high priest who has gone through the heavens, Jesus the Son of God, let us hold firmly to the faith we profess. For we do not have a high priest who is unable to sympathize with our weaknesses, but we have one who has been tempted in every way, just as we are - yet was without sin. Let us then approach the throne of grace with confidence, so that we may receive mercy and find grace to help us in our time of need." This is another way of saying the same thing as is said in today's promise - we have the help of God when we are tempted!

It is almost always easier to avoid being tempted than it is to avoid yielding to temptation. In The Lord's Prayer we say; "And lead us not into temptation, but deliver us from the evil one." In the prayer of Jabez we say; ""And that you would keep me from evil." If there are places you used to go where you are tempted, stay away from them. If there are people with whom you used to associate who led you to do things you shouldn't do, stay away from them. 2 Corinthians 5:17 says, "Therefore, if anyone is in Christ, he is a new creation; the old has gone, the new has come!"

So avoid temptation, ask God's help, and go out and make this a great day.

Yield not to temptations for yielding is sin; Each vict'ry will help you some other to win;
Fight manfully onward, dark passions subdue; Look ever to Jesus - He'll carry you through.
Ask the Savior to help you, comfort, strengthen and keep you;
He is willing to aid you - He will carry you through

Horatio R. Palmer - 1834-1907

May 11

"YOU WILL BE HIS WITNESS TO ALL MEN OF WHAT YOU HAVE SEEN AND HEARD." Acts 22:15

In 1988 Prokope, with the Good News Broadcasting Association, Inc., reported the following: "There have been several versions of this story, but according to research done by Warren Wiersbe, this is the official version: Britain's King George V was to give the opening address at a special disarmament conference, with a speech relayed by radio to the United States. As the broadcast was about to begin, a cable broke in the New York radio station, and more that a million listeners were left without sound. A junior mechanic in the station, Harold Vivien, solved the problem by picking up both ends of the cable and, by allowing 250 volts of electricity to pass through him, was the living link that allowed the king's message to get through." When you consider this story, you realize that Harold Vivien did not have to let those volts of electricity pass through him. I can imagine the pain and discomfort it must have caused him at the time. If he had not thought quickly, acted unselfishly and given himself for the voltage to pass through millions would not have heard the message of the king.

Isn't that what today's promise is all about? This promise comes from the conversation Ananias had with Paul after Paul's experience on the road to Damascus and came about just as Paul regained his sight. Paul went on to witness for God and His Son, Jesus Christ, by acting unselfishly and letting the message of God pass through him to millions of millions of people through the letters he wrote, which have become a major part of the New Testament of the Bible.

The promise is as alive and fresh to us today as it was to Paul in the first century AD. We are witnesses to all men of what we have seen and heard. Our seeing and hearing come about through our Bible study, church attendance, study groups, prayer and meditation. We can make the excuse that we experience it second-hand while Paul experienced it first-hand by talking and meeting with the people who had walked and talked with Jesus. I beg to differ with you! I experience Jesus first-hand, in the same way Paul experienced Jesus first-hand! That is the very unique thing about our God. He is not some abstract being we learn about only in some cold manner such as reading or listening to messages. No! We learn about Him first-hand by what He does in our lives on a daily, hourly or, even, minute-by-minute basis.

We are in the same position with our King as Harold Vivien was with King George V. The message of our King will not get through if it doesn't come through us! What are you doing to allow more people to hear the message from our King? Are you living your life in such a way that you are a witness for the love Jesus has for His people? Are you a living witness for the way Jesus wants His people to live? Your first concern is to be faithful to God, not the success of your witnessing. As Mother Teresa said, "I am not called to be successful, but faithful."

Make your witness a message from God, and go out and make this a great day.

I love to tell the story of unseen things above,
Of Jesus and His glory, of Jesus and His love;
I love to tell the story - because I know 'tis true,
It satisfies my longings as nothing else can do.

A Catherine Hankey - 1834-1911

May 12

"NO ONE WILL BE ABLE TO STAND UP AGAINST YOU ALL THE DAYS OF YOUR LIFE. AS I WAS WITH MOSES, SO I WILL BE WITH YOU; I WILL NEVER LEAVE YOU NOR FORSAKE YOU." Joshua 1:5

What a precious promise we have for today! We have the promise of God that He will never forsake us! Friends may come and go. We may lose touch with family. We may change jobs and lose relationships we developed there. We may graduate from school and not hear from the friends we made there. But GOD WILL NEVER LEAVE US NOR FORSAKE US! This isn't the only place in the Bible this promise is made to us. When Moses was passing leadership of the Israelites to Joshua he said in Deuteronomy 31:8, "The Lord Himself goes before you and will be with you; He will never leave you nor forsake you. Do not be afraid; do not be discouraged." We read in 1 Chronicles 28:20, "David also said to Solomon his son, 'Be strong and courageous, and do the work. Do not be afraid or discouraged, for the Lord God, my God, is with you. He will not fail you or forsake you until all the work for the service of the temple of the Lord is finished.'" When Solomon finished his prayers and blessed the people he said in 1 Kings 8:57, "May the Lord our God be with us as He was with our fathers; may He never leave us nor forsake us."

Paul said it a little differently in Romans 8:38-39, "For I am convinced that neither death nor life, neither angels nor demons, neither the present nor the future, nor any powers, neither height nor depth, nor anything else in all creation, will be able to separate us from the love of God that is in Christ Jesus our Lord." How great is God's love? Read Romans 5:8, "But God demonstrates His own love for us in this: While we were still sinners, Christ died for us." Also consider John 3:16, "For God so loved the world that He gave His one and only Son, that whoever believes in Him shall not perish but have eternal life."

Now, does all this sound like a God who would forsake us? No! We may forsake Him, But He will never forsake us! When we are going through particularly trying times of fear, discouragement, disappointment, financial setbacks, heartbreak or any other devastation we can always count on His faithfulness, love and comfort. Sometimes it is so hard to remember that! We feel like we are hanging out there just twisting in the wind all by ourselves. Why does that happen? Why should we not expect to suffer? Jesus suffered! God gave us free choice. Man disobeyed God and brought sin, and thus death (and suffering), into the world. How can we be comforted at such times? Jesus promised His disciples in John 14:16-17, "And I will ask the Father, and He will give you another Counselor to be with you forever - the Spirit of truth. The world cannot accept Him, because it neither sees Him nor knows Him. But you know Him, for He lives with you and will be in you." God gave us the Holy Spirit as a constant companion!

Trust in the ever present God, and go out and make this a great day.

I'm rejoicing night and day, as I walk the pilgrim way, For the hand of God in all my life I see,
And the reason of my bliss, yes, the secret all is this: That the Comforter abides with me.
He abides, He abides, Hallelujah, He abides with me! I'm rejoicing night and day,
As I walk the narrow way, for the comforter abides with me.

Herbert Buffman - (No Date)

May 13

"For the eyes of the Lord range throughout the earth TO STRENGTHEN THOSE WHOSE HEARTS ARE FULLY COMMITTED TO HIM." 2 Chronicles 16:9

Have you ever been a part of a "search group"? This is a group formed to search for a lost person, animal or item and covers a large area. As part of a search group you are responsible for the strip of land over which you walk. As you walk in the direction of search you must keep your eyes on the ground and keep them continually moving from side to side. You can't just let your eyes roam! They must focus intently on each item you look at to see if anything is out of place, if there are prints which should not be there, if the birds or animals are behaving different from normal or anything which indicates the presence of that which is lost. This method was used to search for debris in Texas, Louisiana and New Mexico from the explosion of the Columbia during its descent from orbit. A searcher failing to focus their eyes might lead to missing a vital piece which could help explain what went wrong and help lead to safer missions in the future.

I think about a member of a search group when I read today's promise. While I know our Lord is omnipotent, I can still see His eyes focusing on each one of us as He looks over the earth. He is searching to see if anything is out of place in our lives. He looks to see if our footprints indicate we are going in the wrong direction. He watches how we effect those with whom we come in contact. He looks for indication of the presence of the Holy Spirit. When He finds what He is looking for He strengthens those whose hearts are fully committed to Him. What a wonderful promise! There are times in everyone's life that doubts intrude, that discouragement comes and that strength seems to disappear. Those are the times when He sees the signs of a potential loss and He adds His strength to our hearts.

Have you gone through a time, or times, when you feel you just don't even have the strength to pray for strength? When life seems to have given you a double whammy when you were looking the other way? Have you been falsely accused or had malicious gossip spread around concerning you? Have you lost a loved one through death, divorce or drifting apart? You can claim today's promise that He will give you strength if your heart is fully committed to Him. When the clouds gather in our lives is the very time we feel we are deserted by God, who gives us strength. We can't understand why we have all the problems which seem to multiply as they hit us head on. In truth, these are the times He is closest to us. These are the times He only asks us to "Cast all your anxiety on Him because He cares for you." (1 Peter 5:7)

The same God whose eyes range throughout the earth seeking us in our times of hurt is the God who said in Luke 12:6-7, "Are not five sparrows sold for two pennies? Yet not one of them is forgotten by God. Indeed, the very hairs of your head are all numbered. Don't be afraid; you are worth more than many sparrows." So trust God to strengthen, and go out and make this a great day.

Jesus will walk with me when I am tempted,
Giving me strength as my need may demand;
When in affliction His presence is near me,
I am upheld by His almighty hand.

Haldor Lillenas - 1885-1959

May 14

"THE LORD WATCHES OVER ALL WHO LOVE HIM, BUT ALL THE WICKED HE WILL DESTROY." Psalm 145:20

If you observe a herd of cows you will probably find one cow who will never be satisfied with the hay she is eating. She will walk over it to get to the hay another cow is eating, butt her out of the way and begin eating that hay, only to move on to the hay of yet another cow. In the process she is tramping hay into the ground or mud, thus wasting the hay, and reducing the yield of the herd by keeping the cows in a constant state of turmoil and movement. When the acts of this one cow becomes so bad she must be culled from the herd and placed in a separate pen or taken to market. She has to be removed for the protection of the more sedate cows so they can produce up to the potential of the herd. This is a way the farmer or rancher protects his herd.

Don't you just feel God watching over us to protect those of us who love Him? Today's promise tells us He does. We can count on it! It also has a negative part to the promise in that it promises the wicked He will destroy. I am not going to speculate on what wickedness He will destroy. I know that He destroyed the cities of Sodom and Gomorrah because of their wickedness. The determination of wickedness (judgement) is reserved to God. In Matthew 7:1-2 Jesus said, "Do not judge, or you too will be judged. For in the same way you judge others, you will be judged, and with the measure you use, it will be measured to you." Jesus also told us in John 8:15-16, "You judge by human standards: I pass judgment on no one. But if I do judge, my decisions are right, because I am not alone. I stand with the Father, who sent me." From these verses we can see we have no business trying to judge others or to take vengeance on them. We are told about God in Deuteronomy 32:35, "It is mine to avenge; I will repay."

The Lord watches over those of us who love Him! Why? Because He loves us. He cherishes us. He cares about us. Jesus loved us so much that while we were still sinners He died for us! How do we show our love for Him? We should follow His commands! When asked which is the greatest commandment Jesus answered, "Love the Lord your God with all your heart and with all your soul and with all your mind. This is the first and greatest commandment. And the second is like it: Love your neighbor as yourself. All the Law and the Prophets hang on these two commandments." Do you show your love to others? You can do so by being their friend and by being a living witness for the Lord. When you win a soul for Christ you give great joy. We are told in Luke 15:7, "I tell you that in the same way there will be more rejoicing in heaven over one sinner who repents than over ninety-nine righteous persons who do not need to repent."

Since the Lord is so happy when a sinner repents just think how happy He is with us when we lead someone to accept Him! So relax, love God, be comforted that He watches over you and live your life to show your love for Him. What a wonderful Lord we have! What a comfort it is to know we will live for eternity with Him! Claim it, and go out and make this a great day.

"Let not your heart be troubled," His tender word I hear,
And resting on His goodness, I lose my doubts and fears;
Tho' by the path He leadeth but one step I may see:
His eye is on the sparrow, and I know He watches me.
Civilla D. Martin - 1869-1948

May 15

"For the grace of God that brings salvation has appeared to all men. It teaches us to say 'No' to ungodliness and worldly passions, and to live self-controlled, upright and godly lives in this present age, while we wait for the blessed hope - the glorious appearing of our great God and Savior, Jesus Christ, WHO GAVE HIMSELF FOR US TO REDEEM US FROM ALL WICKEDNESS AND TO PURIFY FOR HIMSELF A PEOPLE THAT ARE HIS VERY OWN, EAGER TO DO WHAT IS GOOD." Titus 2:11-14

In 1956, when I was in my Freshman year of college, my parents sold all their farm animals and moved to Nashville, TN in October to live with my sister. She and her husband had moved there for his work. They were having a hard time financially and my sister was about to deliver her first baby. Dad worked at what jobs he could find while momma took care of my sister and, later, my nephew. I went to Nashville by bus during Christmas break. At one of the bus depots on my way back, where I was to change buses, I had a long lay-over. Momma had packed a large lunch for me and I shared it with another college student I had met on the bus. After eating I looked around for a drinking fountain and was just about to get a drink when my new friend pulled me away and led me to another fountain. When I inquired as to why he had done so he pointed to the respective signs - "Colored" and "White". This was the first time I had ever been exposed to discrimination and separation of the races. I was shocked to see the evidence of this blight on our history.

The same type of discrimination took place during Jesus' time on earth. Read the stories of the Good Samaritan written in Luke 10:25-37, and Jesus talking with the Samaritan woman in John 4:1-26. The discrimination between Jews and Samaritans was very strong. Paul makes a very strong statement that the grace of God brings salvation to ALL men. The acceptance of that grace teaches us to forgo the discrimination described above. Grace teaches us to live upright, self-controlled, and godly lives in this present age. We cannot do so if we show discrimination! We must show the love of Jesus to ALL men. All men are our neighbors! Paul writes about "this present age" in 63 AD, but he could just as well have been writing it right now.

We must live as Jesus would have us live and we can claim today's promise. Our great God and Savior, Jesus Christ, appears to us each day that we walk with Him. He gave Himself to redeem us from all wickedness and purify us so we will be His very own. We should always be eager to do what is good - to imitate the life of Jesus! We do this by following the example He set for us when He walked this earth. Jesus brought healing where there was sickness, deliverance where there were captives, peace where there was conflict, togetherness where there was separation, love where there was animosity, understanding where there was confusion, forgiveness where there were wrongs and true peace and joy to the hearts of all mankind.

Imitate Jesus today, and go out and make this a great day.

O Jesus, Thou hast promised to all who follow Thee
That where Thou art in glory there shall Thy servant be;
And Jesus, I have promised to serve Thee to the end;
O give me grace to follow my Master and my Friend.
John E. Bode - 1816-1874

May 16

"And you, my son Solomon, acknowledge the God of your father, and serve Him with wholehearted devotion and with a willing mind, FOR THE LORD SEARCHES EVERY HEART AND UNDERSTANDS EVERY MOTIVE BEHIND THE THOUGHTS. IF YOU SEEK HIM, HE WILL BE FOUND BY YOU; BUT IF YOU FORSAKE HIM, HE WILL REJECT YOU FOREVER." 1 Chronicles 28:9

This story is attributed to the late, great basketball coach, Abe Lemmons. During one of his teams games Abe felt the calls were going against him in a big way. He yelled at the referees on many occasions to no avail. Finally he began berating one official to the point the official looked at Abe and said, "Don't say another word about it or I will give you a technical foul." Abe was quiet until the next time the referee made his way down the court. Abe asked, "Can you give a technical foul for what a coach is thinking?" "Of course not," replied the referee. "Well," said Abe. "I think you are just a horribly biased referee." Abe got the technical foul because the referee understood the motive behind his thought!

When David was giving his plans for the temple to all the officials of Israel, he made the above statement to his son, Solomon. David's instructions to Solomon were to serve God with wholehearted devotion and with a willing mind, not have the thoughts about God in his mind which Abe Lemmons had about that particular referee at that particular time. David specifically told Solomon that the Lord searches every heart and understands every motive behind the thoughts. We should keep our thoughts pure. Many times when we get angry our thoughts run wild. Just like Abe Lemmons, we think a lot of evil about the one who made us angry. In the Sermon on the Mount, Jesus told us in Matthew 5:22, "But I tell you that anyone who is angry with his brother will be subject to judgment."

We are told by Jesus in Luke 12:2, "There is nothing concealed that will not be disclosed, or hidden that will not be made known." Today's promise tells us if we seek Him, He will be found by us. We are also told in Deuteronomy 4:29, "But if from there you seek the Lord your God, you will find Him if you look for Him with all your heart and with all your soul." Isn't that a comforting thought? We know that we are never alone. We have all the wonderful promises of God to count on. We have the Holy Spirit dwelling within us. We have the love we have for, and from, our brothers and sisters in Christ to keep us warm.

Also look at today's promise to note it has a negative portion to it as well. If we forsake the Lord, He will reject us forever. That rejection does not start until our death. We can always call upon Him. We are told in Isaiah 55:9, "Seek the Lord while He may be found; call on Him while He is near." It is easier to become a Christian while we are young, however, we can become a Christian even unto our dying breath!

Keep your thoughts pure, seek the Lord, and go out and make this a great day.

No one understands like Jesus, He's a friend beyond compare;
Meet Him at the throne of mercy, He is waiting for you there.
No one understands like Jesus, when you falter on the way,
Tho you fail Him, sadly fail Him, He will pardon you today.
John W. Peterson - 1921-

May 17

> "Do not be wise in your own eyes; fear the Lord and shun evil. THIS WILL BRING HEALTH TO YOUR BODY AND NOURISHMENT TO YOUR BONES." Proverbs 3:7 & 8

I recently received a report of a teen-age lady who was diagnosed with cervical cancer. She had two doctors working on her case. One was a young, inexperienced doctor who had given his life to Christ. The other was a brilliant, older, experienced, well-trained doctor who was an atheist. The young lady was a Christian with a very active prayer group in her church. The prayer chain was alerted and soon spilled over into other churches. The prayer request was specifically for God's healing so there would never be an unusual problem associated with having a child. The day before surgery the medical team wanted one more CAT scan to more specifically locate the position and current extent of the cancer. The CAT scan came back completely negative. The young doctor, who knew of the prayers, was delighted with the news and called it a miraculous healing. The older doctor scoffed at such "nonsense" and in his own mind was convinced, after careful review of all previous tests and CAT scans, that the CAT scan had just failed to pick up the tumor and decided to go through with the surgery. The young lady agreed, though she, too, was convinced of a miraculous healing. When the surgery took place there was not a single sign of the cancer. The older, atheistic doctor finally admitted that a "miracle" was the only thing which could describe what had occurred. The older doctor was wise in his own eyes. The young lady, her young doctor and her prayer team feared the Lord and shunned evil.

Do you have a particular health need in yourself or a loved one or friend? If so, you should pray for health. God knows of your needs, even before you voice them. We read in Isaiah 6:24, "Before they call I will answer; while they are still speaking I will hear." Psalm 139:4 says, "Before a word is on my tongue you know it completely, O Lord." Do you feel that your prayers have gone unanswered? That God has not given you what you asked from Him? In James 4:2-3 we may have the answer, "You want something but don't get it. You kill and covet, but you cannot have what you want. You quarrel and fight. You do not have, because you do not ask God. When you ask, you do not receive, because you ask with wrong motives, that you may spend what you get on your pleasures." That is why the phrase, "fear the Lord and shun evil" is in today's promise. Do you see "wrong motive" in the prayer requests for healing the cancer in the young lady mentioned above? Neither did God, as He healed her! There is never "no hope". We should never give up seeking God's help through prayer for our friends and loved ones. This is not only for their physical healing, but for their spiritual healing, financial healing and relationship healing as well.

This type of concern for others and the praying for others will also bring "health to your body and nourishment to your bones." As you go through your day pray for the healing of others to help both them and you, and go out and make this a great day.

> If your body suffers pain and your health you can't regain,
> And your soul is almost sinking in despair,
> Jesus knows the pain you feel, He can save and He can heal-
> Take your burden to the Lord and leave it there.
>
> Charles A. Tindley - 1851-1933

May 18

"BUT YOU WILL RECEIVE POWER WHEN THE HOLY SPIRIT COMES ON YOU; AND YOU WILL BE MY WITNESSES IN JERUSALEM, AND IN ALL JUDEA AND SAMARIA, AND TO THE ENDS OF THE EARTH." Acts 1:8

While growing up on a farm in Northern Kansas I helped cut wood for burning in our wood-burning stove in the winter. In the winter Momma also cooked on a wood -burning stove in the kitchen. It took a lot of wood to keep our house warm. I would help dad sharpen the two-man crosscut saw and the thirty-six inch diameter saw blade we used on the tractor-mounted saw. We would go out to the tree grove and select the trees to be cut. Then, using the crosscut saw and axes, we would cut them down, trim the branches and cut the trunks and large branches into lengths we could maneuver onto the tilting framework mounted on the front of the tractor. We would then slide the log out to the proper length cut, tilt the framework to move the log into the saw which was powered by belt from the tractor flywheel. The cut pieces would drop off the framework to be loaded into the wagon, taken to the wood lot in the farmyard, split into proper size pieces and stacked for use over the winter. We would saw the smaller branches for use in the kitchen stove and as kindling. The crosscut saw was just as sharp as the large saw blade. Yet the amount of wood we could cut with the tractor-mounted saw was many time greater than the amount cut by hand. Why? The power behind the tractor-mounted saw! We worked in the power of the flesh when we used the crosscut saw. We used our own intellect, enthusiasm, energy and stamina to operate the crosscut saw. The saw blade was of the same steel, the same sharpness and used for the same purpose, yet the results were so much greater because of the power working through it.

Isn't that how we are when we try to live a Christ-centered life of our own power? We accomplish very little! When we ask for, and then allow, the Holy Spirit to work with us we accomplish so much more. It was said of people filled with the Holy Spirit that they "Spoke with boldness." In Acts 4:13 we read, "When they saw the courage of Peter and John and realized that they were unschooled, ordinary men, they were astonished and they took note that these men had been with Jesus." What did Jesus leave with these men? The answer is in John 14:26, "But the Counselor, the Holy Spirit, whom the Father will send in my name, will teach you all things and will remind you of everything I have said to you."

We ask for the Holy Spirit to work through us when we pray the Prayer of Jabez, "That Your hand would be with me." I pray that prayer daily and ask for the guidance of the Holy Spirit as I study, write and live. Jan and I were discussing a witness matter one day. She said, "I feel like I should do this." I encouraged her to do that very thing with a reminder that the urging she was feeling was coming from the Holy Spirit working in her. Ask for, and be aware of, the working of the Holy Spirit through you, and go out and make this a great day.

Holy Spirit, breathe on me, until my heart is clean.
Let sunshine fill its inmost part, with not a cloud between.
Holy Spirit, breathe on me, till I am all Thine own;
Until my will is lost in Thine, to live for Thee alone.
Edwin Hatch - 1835-1889

May 19

"SO WE SAY WITH CONFIDENCE, 'THE LORD IS MY HELPER; I WILL NOT BE AFRAID. WHAT CAN MAN DO TO ME?'" Hebrews 13:6

The question in today's promise is: "What can man do to me?" Let's look at the answers.

First, a man can cheat you. Swiss theologian, John Caspar Lavater (1741-1801), said, "He who purposely cheats his friend, would cheat his God." Also, American historian George Bancroft (1800-1891), wrote, "So grasping is dishonesty, that it is no respecter of persons; it will cheat friends as well as foes; and were it possible, would cheat even God Himself."

Second, a man can damage or destroy your good name. William Shakespeare (1564-1616) wrote, "Good name, in man or woman, is the immediate jewel of their souls. Who steals my purse steals trash; but he that filches from me my good name, robs me of that which not enriches him, and makes me poor indeed." English clergyman, James Hamilton (1814-1867), wrote, "No better heritage can a father bequeath to his children than a good name; nor is there in a family any richer heirloom than the memory of a noble ancestor."

Third, a man can physically harm you. Englishman, Thomas Fuller (1606-1661), gave us this advice, "Slight small injuries, and they will become none at all." American clergyman, Cotton Mather (1663-1728), gave this promise, "The injuries of life, if rightly improved, will be to us as the strokes of the statuary on his marble, forming us to a more beautiful shape, and making us fitter to adorn the heavenly temple." English poet, Francis Beaumont (1584-1616), wrote, "If men wound you with injuries, meet them with patience: hasty words rankle the wound, soft language dresses it, forgiveness cures it and oblivion takes away the scar."

Fourth, a man can murder you. English Puritan leader, William Goffe (1605-1679), said, "Murder is past all expiation the greatest crime, which nature doth abhor." Paul told us in Philippians 1:21, "For to me, to live is Christ and to die is gain."

So what do we do to man in return? We should follow the advice Paul gave in Romans 12:17-20, "Do not repay anyone evil for evil. Be careful to do what is right in the eyes of everybody. If it is possible, as far as it depends on you, live at peace with everyone. Do not take revenge, my friends, but leave room for God's wrath, for it is written: 'It is mine to avenge; I will repay,' says the Lord. On the contrary; 'If your enemy is hungry, feed him; if he is thirsty, give him something to drink. In doing this, you will heap burning coals on his head.'" How do we follow Paul's advice? We must claim today's promise, "So we say with confidence, the Lord is my helper; I will not be afraid."

This requires one of the hardest things for a Christian to do, forgive others. Without that forgiveness of others we cannot claim His forgiveness of ourselves. Remember, Jesus told Peter he must forgive his brother seventy-seven times! Trust the Lord as your helper in ALL situations, and go out and make this a great day.

The Lord's my shepherd, I'll not want; He makes me down to lie
In pastures green; He leadeth me the quiet waters by.
My table Thou hast furnished in presence of my foes;
My head Thou dost with oil anoint, and my cup overflows.
Psalm 23, Scottish Psalter - 1650

May 20

"NEVERTHELESS, THE RIGHTEOUS WILL HOLD TO THEIR WAYS, AND THOSE WITH CLEAN HANDS WILL GROW STRONGER." Job 17:9

The story of David and Goliath is probably one of the best known stories in the Bible among children. It catches the interest of all because of the improbability of such a thing ever happening, and it never would happen without the involvement of the hand of God. It pits the weak against the strong. It turns impending defeat into victory. It brings to the front a young man who goes on to have a tremendous impact on the world, on the children of Israel and on the birth of Christianity. David told Saul in 1 Samuel 26:23, "The Lord rewards every man for his righteousness and faithfulness." Was David always righteous and faithful to God? No he wasn't. We also well know the story of David and Bathsheba when David committed adultery and then had Bathsheba's husband assigned to the very front of the battle formation so he would be killed and David would be free to marry Bathsheba. Did David repent? Yes he did. He was punished for his wrongdoing, received God's forgiveness and received favor from God. David also said in 2 Samuel 22:21, "The Lord has dealt with me according to my righteousness; according to the cleanness of my hands He has rewarded me." David was not being self-righteous. He was recognizing that the Lord rewards those who faithfully seek to serve Him. In studying the life of David we come to the conclusion the first part of today's promise is, indeed, true. The righteous do hold to their ways.

What about your walk with God? Are you holding to His way? We read in Proverbs 4:18, "The path of the righteous is like the first gleam of dawn, shining ever brighter till the full light of day." God will light our pathway if we ask Him to and live according to His commands. Jesus said in John 8:12, "I am the light of the world. Whoever follows me will never walk in darkness, but will have the light of life." Isn't it wonderful to walk in that light? We never have to worry about finding our own way. God gave us the Holy Spirit to be with us always and He leads us with His gentle prodding as we walk life's pathways.

The second part of today's promise tells us "those with clean hands will grow stronger." We are told in many places in the Old Testament about the need for washing. So many places that the proverb was born: Cleanliness is next to Godliness. In this context, the term clean hands relates to the purity of the individual by receiving forgiveness for our sins. The only way we can have clean hands in this context is to have our sins washed away by the blood of Christ. We are told in Isaiah 1:18, "Though your sins are like scarlet, they shall be as white as snow; though they are red as crimson, they shall be like wool." Do you think Pilate's hands were clean when he washed them after deciding to turn Jesus over to be crucified? Of course not! When your hands are clean, as in this context, you will continue to grow stronger in your walk with God. What a wonderful promise this is! Claim it, and go out and make this a great day.

Are you walking daily by the Savior's side?
Are you washed in the blood of the Lamb?
Do you rest each moment in the Crucified?
Are you washed in the blood of the Lamb?
Elisha A. Hoffman - 1839-1929

May 21

"WHEN YOU LIE DOWN, YOU WILL NOT BE AFRAID; WHEN YOU LIE DOWN, YOUR SLEEP WILL BE SWEET." Proverbs 3:24

In the devotion for April 3 I told of a time I was afraid and got very little sleep for the night that I was left alone. That was a very unusual circumstance when I was growing up. We worked hard and I remember peaceful sleep, with no fear of any kind. I knew my folks were just downstairs in their bedroom and nothing would harm me. I also remember the time I was the Oklahoma Republican State Chairman, working five to seven days a week, and a member of the Oklahoma Army National Guard, meeting one or two week-ends each month. Many times I would sleep the sleep of the exhausted. Sometimes I would have only one week-end a month free and would sleep from Friday night until Sunday morning with only a short time awake to visit my family and eat. That sleep was not only sweet, but a real necessity. Very few times in my life have I had any trouble falling asleep and sleeping throughout the night. I can trace those few times to knowing I was not following God's will and knowing He was speaking to me about it. We read in Psalm 4:8, "I will lie down and sleep in peace, for You alone, O Lord, make me dwell in safety." In Isaiah 26:3 we read, "You will keep in perfect peace him whose mind is steadfast, because he trusts in you." We also read in Psalm 112:6-8, "Surely he will never be shaken; a righteous man will be remembered forever. He will have no fear of bad news; his heart is steadfast, trusting in the Lord. His heart is secure, he will have no fear; in the end he will look in triumph on his foes." Proverbs 6:20-22 says, "My son, keep your father's commands and do not forsake your mother's teaching. Bind them upon your heart forever; fasten them around your neck. When you walk, they will guide you; when you sleep, they watch over you; when you awake, they will speak to you." Do these passages tell you something about what you must do to claim today's promise? They should!

The promise for today applies to those of us who place our faith entirely on the Lord and live by His commands. When we live like God wants us to live we have a sweet peace about us that lets us lie down without fear and sleep a deep, restful sleep. Does that mean we do not occasionally awaken during the night? Of course not. Many times I will awaken during the night with thoughts of what I can write or with a verse or comment I wish to put in a lesson I am preparing. Many times I write them down so I won't forget them (sometimes I just know I will remember them, and guess what! I don't!) If I have any trouble at all in falling to sleep again I start praying and this relaxes me back into sweet sleep.

We read in 2 Timothy 1:7 (KJV), "For God hath not given us the spirit of fear; but of power, and of love, and of a sound mind." So if you have any fear at all, ask God to bind that spirit of fear and loose the spirits of trust, faith and love. He has promised to do that for us. What a wonderful God we have! Sleep in sweet peace, and go out and make this a great day.

Peace, perfect peace, with sorrows surging round?
On Jesus' bosom naught but calm is found.
Peace, perfect peace, with loved ones far away"
In Jesus' keeping we are safe, and they.

Edward H. Bickersteth - 1825-1906

May 22

"EVEN TO YOUR OLD AGE AND GRAY HAIRS I AM HE, I AM HE WHO WILL SUSTAIN YOU. I HAVE MADE YOU AND I WILL CARRY YOU; I WILL SUSTAIN YOU AND I WILL RESCUE YOU." Isaiah 46:4

When I was in high school I took a course called "Shop". It was a course designed to teach us (mostly farm boys) to work with wood. We started in an elementary fashion and worked our way to building furniture. I remember finding designs for a coffee table, end table and lamp which required only a little modification to be just the way I wanted them to be. I never did tell Momma what I was making in Shop. When I had all three pieces completed I had Dad come to school to pick me up with my furniture projects. I was a fourteen year old Freshman in high school at the time. You can imagine my pride when I took them home and gave them to Momma. I told her, "Momma, I designed them (at least I modified the designs) and I made them just for you. Those pieces were in my parents home until my dad moved in with my sister. They now reside in my daughter's home.

God designed us and God made us. Only God could have made man as man was made. Each one is a unique individual. Each one has their own DNA which is matched by no one else on earth. When God made man we are told in Genesis 1:26, "Then God said, 'Let us make man in our image, in our likeness, and let them rule over the fish of the sea and the birds of the air, over the livestock, over all the earth, and over all the creatures that move along the ground.'" Likeness and image are synonyms in the Old Testament. Since we are created in God's image we are worthy of honor and respect. Man was made on the last day of creation as God's crowning achievement. Man was made to love God and to be a friend and companion of God. Yet man was given a free will to choose for himself as to whether he would love and obey God. God didn't want to make man in a form such that he would "have" to love God. Man was created in a perfect world. There was no sin, no work, no pain, no suffering and no death. Man introduced sin, work, pain, suffering and death into the world when he chose to disobey God.

Today's promise tells us He will carry us, sustain us and rescue us. Why does He need to rescue us? We are told in Romans 3:23, "For all have sinned and fall short of the glory of God." If we think we have not sinned we need to read 1 John 1:10, "If we claim we have not sinned, we make Him out to be a liar and His word has no place in our lives." God loved man so much that He sent His only Son to die for us, that the world through Him might be saved. He has provided a way to cleanse us of our sins. He heals us during times of our pain, comforts us during times of our suffering and provides an eternal home for us when we die. What is His command to us? Read Matthew 22:37 & 39, "Jesus replied: 'Love the Lord your God with all your heart and with all your soul and with all your mind.' and 'Love your neighbor as yourself.'" So fill yourself with love for the God who made you, worship Him, and go out and make this a great day.

We praise Thee, O God, our Redeemer, creator,
In Grateful devotion our tribute we bring.
We lay it before Thee, we kneel and adore Thee,
We bless Thy holy name, glad praises we sin.
Julia Cady Cory - 1882-1963

May 23

"But we ought always to thank God for you, brothers loved by the Lord, because from the beginning GOD CHOSE YOU TO BE SAVED THROUGH THE SANCTIFYING WORK OF THE SPIRIT AND THROUGH BELIEF IN THE TRUTH." 2 Thessalonians 2:13

When I was in school we would often select two captains to choose teams to play each other in sports. The two captains would flip a coin to determine who would choose first then they would alternate choices until all were selected to a team. When each player was selected they would go to the side of the captain who chose them. When all had been selected the captains would assign each person a position where they could best use their physical gifts to help the team. Then the game would begin. This process provided a fair way to form teams to compete evenly. This system is now in disfavor because some students may always be chosen last, or nearly last. Parents and teachers are concerned about the effect on the child's self-esteem.

There is one selection where you are ALWAYS chosen first. God always chooses you first! We read in Ephesians 1:4-5, "For He chose us in Him before the creation of the world to be holy and blameless in His sight. In love He predestined us to be adopted as His sons through Jesus Christ, in accordance with His pleasure and will." Wow! God chose us even before the creation of the world to be His sons! That is the greatest choice there could ever be.

Are we worthy of God's choice of us? No! We are told in Ephesians 2:4-5, "But because of His great love for us, God, who is rich in mercy, made us alive with Christ even when we were dead in transgressions - it is by grace you have been saved." What is grace? Grace denotes the free favor of God, bestowed upon men without any merit or claim on their part. God loves us so much He does not force us to love Him. He gives us a free will to make the choices as we will. We can love Him or we can turn away from Him. Does that mean we are not loved by God if we do not love Him? No! Does it mean we were not chosen by God if we turn from Him? No! We were chosen by Him even if we do not choose Him!

How have you reacted to the fact that God chose you to be saved? Have you gone willingly to the side of God? If you have gone willingly to God's side, have you accepted the position He has assigned you to play? Jesus told us in Mark 8:34, "If anyone would come after me, he must deny himself and take up his cross and follow me." Have you taken up your cross to follow Jesus? Are you using the gifts He gave you to His advantage? We read in Romans 12:6-8, "We have different gifts, according to the grace given us. If a man's gift is prophesying, let him use it in proportion to his faith. If it is serving, let him serve; if it is teaching, let him teach; if it is encouraging, let him encourage; if it is contributing to the needs of others, let him give generously; if it is leadership, let him govern diligently; if it is showing mercy, let him do it cheerfully." Yes, God has included you as one He has chosen today.

Yield to God's choice of you, and go out and make this a great day.

I am so happy in Christ today, that I go singing along my way;
Yes, I'm so happy to know and say, "Jesus included me too."
Gladly I read, "Whosoever may come to the fountain of life today,"
But when I read it I always say, "Jesus included me too."

Johnson Oatman, Jr. - 1856-1922

May 24

"The Lord appeared to us in the past, saying: 'I HAVE LOVED YOU WITH AN EVERLASTING LOVE; I HAVE DRAWN YOU WITH LOVING-KINDNESS." Jeremiah 31:3

I recently saw an example of love which reminded me of this promise. We have dinner for families on Wednesday evenings at our church. After dinner we all separate into our various activities: choir practice, youth activities, children's activities, classes in our Christian Life University and prayer meetings. We were sitting at the table with a young couple, Rick and Melissa Clark. Their children had finished eating and were playing behind the dividers separating the eating area from children's activity area. Suddenly two adults appeared leading a crying boy, Joshua Clark, to his parents. He had been playing and running and had run into a stand, which held a speaker, causing a puncture wound on the side of his nose. The wound was bleeding and Joshua was frightened, in pain, perhaps angry the stand was where he was running, and much in need of comfort. Rick took him onto his lap while Melissa wiped away the blood and obtained a small bag of ice to put on the wound. As I watched the scene unfold I was impressed with the love and care shown to Joshua by his parents. Joshua needed to be held in the loving protection of his father's lap at that time. Rick was most happy to oblige this young son he loved so much. Rick continued to hold Joshua, hug him, love him and minister to him as the fear left and the pain subsided.

Today's promise from God is infinitely more meaningful than the wonderful love Rick showed to Joshua that evening. Without our deserving His love in any way He loves us with an everlasting love. He draws us to Him with His loving-kindness. Sometimes we don't think about His love as things are going so well for us we begin to think, "My, aren't I doing a great job with my life!" We forget James 1:17, "Every good and perfect gift is from above, coming down from the Father of the heavenly lights, who does not change like shifting shadows." We also tend to forget John 15:13, "Greater love has no one than this, that he lay down his life for his friends." That is exactly what Jesus did for us on the cross! Even before we thought about Him and His love or wanted anything to do with Him or His love, as told in Romans 5:8, "But God demonstrates His own love for us in this: While we were still sinners, Christ died for us."

Do you have fear in your life today? Are you in pain: physical, mental, financial, relational or spiritual? Are you in sorrow today? Is someone close to you suffering? Do what Joshua Clark did. Crawl into the loving protection of your Father's lap and soak up the love He has for you. He doesn't guarantee you will never have suffering. Jesus suffered, bled and died on the cross for us so why do we think we should never have any suffering? He does not promise you will never be tempted, but He has promised to always provide a way out so you can stand up under it. His love is so great we can not fathom it. We should just accept it!

Claim, and enjoy, God's everlasting love today, and go out and make this a great day.

Could we with ink the ocean fill and were the skies of parchment made,
Were ev'ry stalk on earth a quill and ev'ry man a scribe by trade
To write the love of God above would drain the ocean dry,
Nor could the scroll contain the whole tho stretched from sky to sky.

Frederick M. Lehman - 1868-1953

May 25

"He said, 'SURELY THEY ARE MY PEOPLE, SONS WHO WILL NOT BE FALSE TO ME'; AND SO HE BECAME THEIR SAVIOR." Isaiah 63:8

The Unassigned Lands in the Oklahoma Territory were surveyed and opened for settlement with a land run on April 22, 1889. Military personnel patrolled the area before the run was to begin. All people who wanted to claim land were to line up on the border of the Unassigned Lands and not cross the border until the cannon sounded at noon. These people were called the "Boomers" because they waited for the boom of the cannon. A few people slipped into the lands before the scheduled time and hid out. After the cannon boomed, starting the race for the parcels of land most desirable, those hiding out came out from those hiding places and claimed the land they wanted. Since they were in before the appointed time they were called "Sooners". People made the race on horseback, surreys, farm wagons, bicycles and on foot. They were alone or with their families. One elderly, wrinkled lady sat in a patched wagon, pulled by a donkey, smoking a corn cob pipe while she waited for the boom of the cannon. When the boom came and the race started she sat calmly smoking as the dust first was raised and then settled. When everyone was far in the distance she slapped the donkey with the reins, crossed the line, stopped the donkey, crawled out of the wagon and drove her stake to claim her quarter section of land. Not everyone got the land they wanted, or even got land as there were more people wanting land than there were parcels. There were many false claims filed, which had to be sorted out over the next weeks and months. Those whose claims were upheld could say, after making the proper improvements and living on, and working the claim for the proper time, "This is my land."

Thank God, we are told in 1 John 1:9, "If we confess our sins, He is faithful and just and will forgive us our sins and purify us from all unrighteousness." When we do that, we can claim God as our Savior and He will say, "Surely they are my people." We don't have to worry about any false claims or someone else claiming Him "Sooner" than we do. We know that because we read in 2 Peter 3:9, "The Lord is not slow in keeping His promise, as some understand slowness. He is patient with you, not wanting anyone to perish, but everyone to come to repentance."

God wants to claim you. He wants us to be His sons. He does not want us to be false to Him. He wants to be our Savior. Where do you stand with the Lord today? Have you allowed Him to file His claim on you by asking His forgiveness for your sins? Are you holding so many things so tightly you just can't seem to let go and let God work His wonders in you? He wants to claim you right now. If you let Him file that claim on you then you can live your life for Him so you can say as Paul did in 2 Timothy 4:7-8, "I have fought the good fight, I have finished the race, I have kept the faith. Now there is in store for me the crown of righteousness, which the Lord, the righteous Judge, will award to me on that day-and not only to me, but also to all who have longed for His appearing." Claim Him, and go out and make this a great day.

I hear the Savior say, "Thy strength indeed is small!
Child of weakness watch and pray, find in me thine all in all."
For nothing good have I whereby Thy grace to claim-
I'll wash my garments white in the blood of Calvary's Lamb.

Elvina M. Hall - 1820-1889

May 26

"So do not be ashamed to testify about our Lord, or ashamed of me his prisoner. But join with me in suffering for the gospel, by the power of God, WHO HAS SAVED US AND CALLED US TO A HOLY LIFE - NOT BECAUSE OF ANYTHING WE HAVE DONE BUT BECAUSE OF HIS OWN PURPOSE AND GRACE. THIS GRACE WAS GIVEN US IN CHRIST JESUS BEFORE THE BEGINNING OF TIME." 2 Timothy 1:8 & 9

In 1984 Jan and I traveled to Maui, Hawaii, on a one-week trip I had earned by meeting the sales requirements with State Farm Insurance Company. There were several other couples from our area also making the trip. One such couple was Terry and Rhonda Cavnar. Terry had been an agent for less than two years, and he and Rhonda had become very good friends of ours. One day the four of us drove to a beach reported to be a good place for snorkeling. I am not a good swimmer at all so I try to be very careful. I also have poor vision without my glasses, which I could not wear with the snorkel mask. Terry and I had slowly snorkeled our way out to a reef area some distance from the beach. We sat out there visiting about the fish and sights we had seen on our way out. Terry, a good swimmer, decided to go on out for a little way. I decided to go back to the beach. Shortly after I left the reef I moved my arm wrong, caught my mask and dislodged it. I tried to get the mask back on and succeeded in getting it full of water and gulping some down in the process. I fought it for a few more seconds and then panicked and called for help. Terry immediately tore off his mask and swam to my side. He held me out of the water so I could breathe and called for help from the beach. A strong swimmer swam out and helped me to the beach. The time Terry held me out of the water saved my life! How can I ever thank him for that? Terry gave me many years of life with his quick, unselfish actions.

Look at what Jesus did for all of us! Jesus died for us! Jesus took all our sins on Himself, who was without sin, and died on the cross that we might have eternal life, not just many years. This is the most unselfish act in the history of the universe! Our promise today tells us God saved us and called us to a holy life. He did this not because of anything we have done, but because of His own purpose and grace. In fact, He did this in spite of anything we have done! The promise also says this grace was given us in Christ Jesus before the beginning of time. Wow!

Let's look at that just a bit. We read in John 1:14, "The Word became flesh and made His dwelling among us. We have seen His glory, the glory of the One and Only, who came from the father, full of grace and truth." The Word, which dwelt among us, was Jesus Christ! We also read in John 1:1, "In the beginning was the Word, and the Word was with God, and the Word was God." Jesus Christ was with God from the very beginning. In fact, Jesus Christ was God! So, yes, this grace was given us in Christ Jesus before the beginning of time!

How comforting it is to realize God provided a way for us to be saved from death and given eternal life. Claim God's promise today, and go out and make this a great day.

Once I was straying in sin's dark valley; No hope within could I see.
They searched through Heaven and found a Savior to save a poor lost soul like me.
He left the Father, with all His riches, with calmness sweet and serene;
Came down from Heaven and gave His life-blood to make the vilest sinner clean.

Marvin P. Dalton - 1906-

May 27

"THEN HE OPENED THEIR MINDS SO THEY COULD UNDERSTAND THE SCRIPTURES." Luke 24:45

One of the things I enjoyed most during the time I taught college Chemistry was to watch students as I was explaining a complicated concept and see the change which came over their face when understanding came to their minds. Their faces would change from a scowl to a smile, their eyes would go from dim to bright, their body would change from leaning forward to sitting up straight or leaning slightly back and then they would start quickly writing notes to capture the concept in their own words and fix it firmly in their minds. This is when I was able to open their minds so they could understand the concept. It was important for me to watch for this time so I could gauge the pace of the lesson. This was a promising time for me as their professor as it showed me I was making progress and making a difference in their educational experience.

Today's promise reminds me of those times. How wonderful the promise that God opens our minds so we can understand the scriptures. Are there times when you are reading the scriptures and you pause and think, "Does this really mean that?" Or perhaps you say, "I never thought of that before!" I have also said to myself, "I never noticed that before!" In each of these cases we see an example of today's promise. He is opening our minds so we can understand the scriptures! How much more important it is to understand the scriptures, which are eternal, than it is to understand some concept of Chemistry, which is only temporary for us!

Psalm 119 is full of references to the Word. Verse 1 tells us, "Blessed are they whose ways are blameless, who walk according to the law of the Lord." Or, Blessed are they who not only understand the scriptures, but follow them. Verse 11 says, "I have hidden your word in my heart that I might not sin against you." Or, I not only understand the scriptures, but I have memorized them that I might think often of them and be able to resist sinning. Verse 16 says, "I delight in your decrees; I will not neglect your word." Or, I not only understand the scriptures, but I continue to study them to learn more. Verse 17 says, "Do good to your servant, and I will live; I will obey your word." Or, I not only understand your word, but I will obey it. Verse 89 says, "Your word, O Lord, is eternal; it stands firm in the heavens." Or, I not only understand your word, but I can count on it, and your promises, forever. Verse 105 says, "Your word is a lamp to my feet and a light for my path." Or, I not only understand your word, but I follow its teachings as I walk through life for it shines so brightly I can see the way. Verse 133 says, "Direct my footsteps according to your word; let no sin rule over me." Or, I not only understand your word, but I ask you to help me follow it so sin will not rule my life.

Finally, I urge you to pray verse 169, "May my cry come before you, O Lord; give me understanding according to your word." He promised understanding, so claim it, and go out and make this a great day.

O Word of God incarnate, O Wisdom from on high,
O Truth unchanged, unchanging, O Light of our dark sky;
We praise Thee for the radiance that from the hallowed page,
A lantern to our footsteps, shines on from age to age.

William W. How - 1823-1897

May 28

"THE LORD ALONE LED HIM; NO FOREIGN GOD WAS WITH HIM." Deuteronomy 32:12

The first thing I learned in Leadership Class was that leaders are made, they are not born. Leadership is such a prized attribute among people that most leadership classes are well attended. Often people confuse the terms manager, boss and leader. A manager and a boss are not necessarily leaders. They may direct people in their activities, but they are what we call "positional leaders". They may be in their positions because of their technical expertise. The U. S. Army changed the rank structure many years ago to recognize, and properly pay, people in positions which require technical expertise when they introduced the rank structure of "Specialist" in several pay grades. These people were not given the responsibility of leading other soldiers except in their field of expertise. While a manager or a boss will drive their people, a leader will coach their people. While a manager or a boss will say "go", a leader says, "follow me". While a manager or boss will refer to "I", a leader will refer to "us". The real definition of leadership is influence. The leader must be able to influence others to not just follow but to "want" to follow the leading provided. Some characteristics of a leader are integrity, without which a potential leader will fail, a vision for the cause, a knowledge of the cause and a genuine love and concern for people. Also, a leader must have self-discipline.

Who among us can come close to having the integrity, vision, knowledge, love and concern for people or the self-discipline of God? No one! Today's promise is that the Lord will lead us. God is with us, to lead us, not to direct us. He has the vision for the cause. He knows the way. He has been there. His love and concern for us is so great that He gave His only Son to die on the cross as atonement for all our sins. What a wonderful God He is! No foreign god could ever do such a thing for us.

Are you following the leading of God today? Do you seek His leading in all areas of your life, or do you have some areas you think He might not be interested in? He wants you to be fully committed to Him and ask for His leadership in everything you do. Are you studying the Word of God to learn more about Him and His plan for you? I find that many times God's leading comes to me while I am studying the Bible or reading devotional material. Do you take the time you should take each day to study and commune with Him?

Try diligently today to ask for His leading in every phase of your life-what should you study, what should you eat, to lead you in the meeting you will have, to lead you to witness to someone, what recreation you should have, etc. If you diligently work at it all day you will find an amazing amount of peace filling you at times you otherwise could be tense or concerned.

His most important leading of us is to give our lives to Him and for us to be willing to serve Him with our life. Follow God today, and go out and make this a great day.

"Take up thy cross and follow Me," I heard my Master say;
"I gave My life to ransom thee, surrender your all today."
Wherever He leads I'll go, wherever He leads I'll go,
I'll follow my Christ who loves me so, wherever He leads I'll go.
Baylus B. McKinney - 1886-1952

May 29

"Can a mother forget the baby at her breast and have no compassion on the child she has borne? Though she may forget, I WILL NOT FORGET YOU!" Isaiah 49:15

One of the greatest gifts of my life is that God gave me a godly mother. I cherish that gift more as each year passes. I thank God I have memory of her praying specifically for me. I remember so many times she gave me comfort, instruction, training, discipline, tenderness and love. We never had much cash money available while we lived on the farm, but we always had plenty to eat. In the Winter when I would arrive home from school there would be a big pot of hot soup waiting on the stove. I would have a big bowl of it before going out to do the evening chores. Momma would always fix three meals a day for us (except Sunday evening we got our own cold cereal and milk to eat.) She also had snacks for us in the afternoon when we were working in the fields. With all her work, she always had time to read to us in the evening, play games with us, put puzzles together with us or sit and tell us stories of past events in her life. She wasn't much for playing outside games, but I remember one Winter we had to go get a wagon load of corn we had left in a field (see March 31). It had frozen solid and snowed so Dad built a sled eight feet by ten feet out of two-by-sixes and fixed it to be pulled behind the horses. Momma fixed a lunch and the entire family took coats and quilts, piled onto the sled and headed for the field to get the wagon. As the horses trotted along my brother would jump off the sled and run along beside it and then jump back on. My two sisters and I soon started doing the same thing, laughing, calling to each other and playing tag. Momma decided that looked like fun so she stepped off the sled to join us. She didn't realize she had to "hit the ground running" so when her foot hit the ground she was pitched head over heels into the snow bank at the side of the road. When we found out she was merely stunned and not hurt badly at all we started laughing with her and making fun with her. What a life I had with my mother! I know she could never forget me.

One of the sad developments in our society today is the number of mothers who don't want their children, won't care for them properly, and, in fact, abuse them terribly. Yes, we do have mothers today who may forget their children.

Thank God for today's promise that He will never forget us. If you have, or had, a mother like mine I am sure you also thank God for her. As precious as she, or her memory, is, it pales in the light of the remembrance and love God has for us. If you did not have a mother like mine you can rest in the knowledge you can have a Heavenly Father just like mine. His promises are for you! His love is for you! His comfort is for you! His provision is for you! We are told in Psalm 27:10, "Though my father and mother forsake me, the Lord will receive me." Joshua 1:5 says, "No one will be able to stand up against you all the days of your life. As I was with Moses, so I will be with you; I will never leave you nor forsake you." Live your life for the Father who will never forget you, be secure in His love, and go out and make this a great day.

More secure is no one ever than the loved ones of the Savior,
Not yon star on high abiding, nor the bird in home-nest building.
What He takes or what He gives us shows the Father's love so precious;
We may trust His purpose wholly - "tis His children's welfare solely.
Lina Sandell Berg - 1832-1903

May 30

"Have I not commanded you? Be strong and courageous. Do not be terrified; do not be discouraged, FOR THE LORD YOUR GOD WILL BE WITH YOU WHEREVER YOU GO." Joshua 1:9

One of the most beautiful stories in the Bible to me is written in the book of Ruth. There was a famine in Judah and Naomi's husband took her and her two sons from Bethlehem to Moab to live there. The sons married Moabite women, Orpah and Ruth. When Naomi's husband and two sons died, she decided to return to Bethlehem to live with her people. Her two daughters-in-law started out with her to go to Bethlehem. Naomi suggested they stay with their own people and Orpah turned back to stay in her own country. Ruth's reply is in Ruth 1:16-17, "But Ruth replied, 'Don't urge me to leave you or to turn back from you. Where you go I will go, and where you stay I will stay. Your people will be my people and your God my God. Where you die I will die, and there I will be buried. May the Lord deal with me, be it ever so severely, if anything but death separates you and me.'" What love and faithfulness Ruth showed Naomi in that short speech! I am sure you know the story, Ruth gleaned in the fields of Boaz, he married Ruth and they had a son, Jesse, who was the father of David. Ruth is an ancestor of Jesus!

I think of this story when I read today's promise. What a wonderfully faithful God we have, who will be with us wherever we go! This promise was given to us in the conversation God had with Joshua after the death of Moses. God used the term "be strong and courageous" several times during that conversation. That is also instruction to us today as we live our lives in an uncertain world. How do we become strong? Paul tells us in Romans 1:11, "I long to see you so that I may impart to you some spiritual gift to make you strong." We have the certainty of God's presence, however, wherever we are.

Do you sometimes have fear for the future? Does it concern you that you might lose your job? Are you afraid you might not be able to pay all the bills coming due at the end of the month? Are you fearful about the outcome of events happening in the world? We need not be terrified, for God is with us. Paul told us in 1 Timothy 1:7, "For God did not give us a spirit of timidity (fear), but a spirit of power, of love and of self-discipline." Any time you may feel fear you should pray that God will bind the spirit of fear and loose the spirit of confidence (see Matthew 18:18).

God tells us to not be discouraged. We should follow Paul's advice in Ephesians 6:11, "Put on the full armor of God so that you can take your stand against the devil's schemes." And in verse 16, "In addition to all this, take up the shield of faith, with which you can extinguish all the flaming arrows of the evil one." Discouragement is one of the flaming arrows of the devil! Here, again, you should bind the spirit of discouragement and loose the spirit of faith.

Claim God's promise to always be with you, and go out and make this a great day.

When I come to the river at ending of day, when the last winds of sorrow have blown;
There'll be somebody waiting to show me the way, I won't have to cross Jordan alone.
I won't have to cross Jordan alone, Jesus died for my sins to atone;
When the darkness I see, He'll be waiting for me, I won't have to cross Jordan alone.

Thomas Ramsey - (No Date)

May 31

"HE WILL WIPE AWAY EVERY TEAR FROM THEIR EYES. THERE WILL BE NO MORE DEATH OR MOURNING OR CRYING OR PAIN, FOR THE OLD ORDER OF THINGS HAS PASSED AWAY." Revelations 21:4

This is the tenth consecutive promise of what I call my "God series". Beginning March 22 with: God made us, followed by, chose us, loves us, claims us, saves us, opens our understanding, leads us, will not forget us, will not fail us, and, now, will wipe away our tears.

Many events which occur may cause us to cry. Some people cry more easily than others, therefore, more events will cause them to cry. I happen to be one who sheds tears very easily. My Dad and Momma told me the story of the first time I ever cried for sorrow. When I was three years old Dad, who had been working as an "extra man" for Phillips Petroleum Company at their pipeline booster station at Booker, TX, while he had been farming, had bid for, and won, a job as a full time employee at the Phillips, TX, pipeline booster station. The folks told all four of their children that we were all going to move to Phillips. They say I sobbed for a long time like my heart would break. They talked to me for a long time to reassure me that all would be well, I would make friends, I would like the area. We would be able to have a cow and we would have a big garden (all things important to me at that time). They said I finally stopped crying and said, "Well, it will be okay if you will promise me we will never move again." As best I can count, I have moved twenty times in my life since that time, but they didn't evoke the same sorrow.

Today's promise from God tells us He will wipe away every tear from our eyes, whatever the cause of the tear. Then there will be no more death, pain, moving, broken relationships, lost items of real or sentimental value, etc. so there will be no more mourning or crying. Life, as we know it on this earth will have passed away. We will be entering into the eternal life God has promised us in His most precious promise of John 3:16.

John goes on to write after today's promise, "He who was seated on the throne said, 'I am making everything new!' Then He said, 'Write this down, for these words are trustworthy and true.' He said to me: 'It is done. I am the Alpha and the Omega, the Beginning and the End. To him who is thirsty I will give to drink without cost from the spring of the water of life. He who overcomes will inherit all this, and I will be his God and he will be my son. But the cowardly, the unbelieving, the vile, the murderers, the sexually immoral, those who practice magic arts, the idolaters and all liars - their place will be in the fiery lake of burning sulfur. This is the second death.'" Today's promise is so precious because of the reward promised - an eternity of living in heaven in perfect bodies with no death, mourning, crying or pain and singing the praises of God!

It is doubly precious as we know that the living of the life which gains that reward is a reward in itself. If Jesus came for you today, are you living a life to claim the promise? Follow God, and go out and make this a great day.

Jesus is coming to earth again, what if it were today?
Coming in power and love to reign, what if it were today?
Coming to claim His chosen Bride, all the redeemed and purified,
Over this whole earth scattered wide, what if it were today?
Lelia N. Morris - 1862-1929

June 1

"You are my hiding place; YOU WILL PROTECT ME FROM TROUBLE AND SURROUND ME WITH SONGS OF DELIVERANCE." Psalm 32:7

When I see this promise for today I am reminded of the story my pastor, Brother Joe Grizzle, told us during his sermon on "Changing the World, One Child at a Time". There was a husband and wife who had a little girl. They never attended church, talked about God or religion, didn't own a Bible or even thought about God in any way. One night the husband came home inebriated to find his wife and daughter in the living room. He and his wife got into a loud, raging argument about his drinking and he became very angry. He went to his room, got a gun, came back and killed his wife in front of his daughter. Upon realizing what he had done, he was filled with remorse and turned the gun on himself and pulled the trigger. The daughter was placed by the courts in a foster home of Christians. The first Sunday they took the little girl to Sunday School and the foster mother quietly explained to the teacher the little girl's background. During the class the teacher kept her eye on the little girl. At one point she held up a picture of Jesus and asked, "Can anyone tell me who this is?" The little girl surprised the teacher by holding up her hand. "Yes," said the teacher. "Who is this?" The little girl replied, "I don't know his name, but he is the one who held me in his arms the night my parents died."

I can't think of a better way to emphasize today's promise! God is our hiding place. He will protect us from trouble and surround us with songs of deliverance. The hills will ring with His joy over our deliverance because of our trust in Him. Maybe we don't have the trouble that little girl had, but whatever it is, big or small, God is standing by us just as close as a whispered prayer. So take all your troubles to Him. Take your time in prayer to spell out what is bothering you and ask Him for His guidance and for His deliverance. He is faithful!

I don't think for a minute that you will go through life without trials and troubles. In his "The Nonsuch Professor In His Meridian Splendor", William Secker wrote , "By affliction, the Lord separates the sin that He hates from the soul that He loves." What he is saying is, the first thing you should do when trials and troubles come is to make sure your heart is right with God and that there has been no sin that has crept in. If you have let sin creep in, you are spoken to in Hebrews 12:6, "Because the Lord disciplines those He loves, and He punishes everyone He accepts as a son." You are God's son if He is your hiding place!

Do you, or someone you love, have troubles? Have you explored your relationship (or their relationship) with God? Go to him in a two-way prayer to make sure all is well with your soul. Call on Him to provide you the hiding place He has promised to you. Work with your loved ones to become right with God. You, and they, will realize a peace you couldn't imagine. Put your faith in God, and then go out and make this a great day.

'Tis the grandest theme thro' the ages rung; 'tis the grandest theme for a mortal tongue;
'Tis the grandest theme, tell the world again. "Our God is able to deliver thee."
'Tis the grandest theme, let the tidings roll, to the guilty heart, to the sinful soul;
Look to God in faith, He will make thee whole, "Our God is able to deliver thee."
William A. Ogden - 1842-1897

June 2

"MAY THE GOD OF PEACE, WHO THROUGH THE BLOOD OF THE ETERNAL COVENANT BROUGHT BACK FROM THE DEAD OUR LORD JESUS, THAT GREAT SHEPHERD OF THE SHEEP, EQUIP YOU WITH EVERYTHING GOOD FOR DOING HIS WILL, AND MAY HE WORK IN US WHAT IS PLEASING TO HIM, THROUGH JESUS CHRIST, TO WHOM BE GLORY FOR EVER AND EVER. AMEN." Hebrews 13:20 & 21

When I arrived to teach Chemistry at Phillips University in Enid, OK, I was told to determine what chemicals I needed each month and they would be ordered. We had a limited, but adequate budget for our chemical needs, but very limited for equipment. About mid-year I was visiting with a chemical supply representative and discussed with him my desires for more items of equipment to enable my students to do more varied experiments. He told me that we were buying chemicals in the most expensive manner possible. He suggested we put together a list of all the chemicals we would need for the year and add a "wish list" of equipment. He offered to come back by in two weeks to help me. During the interim time I worked with the department head and compiled a list of all chemicals we would be needing the next year. When the man returned he sat down with me and looked over the list. We then discussed the equipment "wish list" we had compiled. He suggested we add to the list and made some suggestions of what we could put on it. When the total list was compiled, it totaled over twice our annual budget. We put it out for bid with some trepidation. A month later we had bids from three companies. The company represented by the man who helped us was the low bidder, and the amount of the bid was just under three fourths of our annual budget. Over the next three years, using the method we had developed, we were able to well equip the Chemistry Department to the advantage of our students and the education they received. We didn't have everything we wanted, but we did have a lot of good equipment to work with.

Paul tells us in today's promise that our God of peace will equip us with everything good for doing His will. Our God will also work in us what is pleasing to Him. We don't have to pinch and save to get the equipment we need. God will give it to us! Does that mean He will give us anything we may want? I don't think so! The promise is that He will equip us with everything good for DOING HIS WILL. Have you ever been asked to perform a task in, or for, church for which you were not sure you were qualified? This is the very time you should call on God to claim today's promise. Call on God and He will equip you to perform the task. The promise also tells us He will work in us what is pleasing to Him. The more malleable we are, the easier it is for Him to perform His work in us. We need to always keep our hearts tuned to Him and to His desires so He will be able to do that work in us, for without Him we can do nothing.

Are you open to God's will in your life? Are you keeping your heart tender and open to let Him work His way in you? Stay close to God, and go out and make this a great day.

Without Him I could do nothing. Without Him I'd surely fail;
Without Him I would be drifting like a ship without a sail.
Without Him I would be dying. Without Him I'd be enslaved;
Without Him life would be hopeless, but with Jesus, thank God, I'm saved.

Mylon R. LeFevre - 1945-

June 3

"I TELL YOU THE TRUTH, HE WHO BELIEVES HAS EVERLASTING LIFE." John 6:47

At a recent Christmas celebration at my brother-in-law's home we were discussing the reaction of an acquaintance of ours to our Christmas message which included comments about our church, spiritual life and this devotional I was writing. The acquaintance had reacted very strongly against our faith and proceeded to tell us he was an atheist and why he didn't believe in God and the Bible. My wife's nephew stated, "He has a lot more faith than I do! To take that stand is to exhibit total faith there is no God. If there is no God, then I have spent some time on this earth doing things I enjoy, which make me feel good, which make me happy and which helps others - you could call it wasted time. If there is a God, he will have eternity to realize his mistake."

Our promise today is much the same as the "most precious promise" given in John 3:16. The promise is directly from the mouth of Jesus, who emphasizes it by prefacing it with the words, "I tell you the truth." Jesus goes on to say, "He who believes has everlasting life." What a promise that is! One man, Adam, brought sin into the world, and, through sin, death. One man, Jesus, paid the total price of the penalty for sin, and, through His death on the cross and resurrection, brought eternal life to those who believe. That eternal life is a promise from Jesus on which we can count in the fullest sense and for all time!

We do not have to be like an atheist who believes we somehow came into being by chance on this earth which came into being by chance following the "Big Bang", for no particular reason and to do no particular thing of meaning. What an empty existence that would be. NO! We realize we were created by a God that loved us from the day of creation. We were put here on an earth which was created by God specifically to provide a place for us to live. It is only in the experience of worship that meaning comes to be. Only something greater than pleasure can provide meaning. Viktor Frankl, a holocaust prisoner, wrote, "There is nothing in the world, I venture to say, that would so effectively help one survive even the worst conditions as the knowledge that there is meaning in one's life." Knowing God gives meaning to life. Obeying God gives purpose to life.

Do you have the faith today that you will spend eternity with God? Our promise clearly tells us that we will spend eternity with Him if we believe. Yes, you may sin. Everyone does. But we are told in Romans 10:9-10, That if you confess with your mouth, 'Jesus is Lord,' and believe in your heart that God raised Him from the dead, you will be saved. For it is with your heart that you believe and are justified, and it is with your mouth that you confess and are saved."

If you have confessed your sins you will have eternal life. Claim it, and go out and make this a great day.

Some day life's journey will be o'er, and I shall reach that distant shore;
I'll sing while entering heaven's door, "Jesus led me all the way."
And hither to my Lord hath led, today He guides each step I tread;
And soon in heaven it will be said, "Jesus led me all the way."
John W. Peterson - 1921-

June 4

"But because of His great love for us, GOD, WHO IS RICH IN MERCY, MADE US ALIVE WITH CHRIST EVEN WHEN WE WERE DEAD IN TRANSGRESSIONS - IT IS BY GRACE YOU HAVE BEEN SAVED." Ephesians 2:4 & 5

I thank God that I grew to adulthood in a home with loving parents and siblings. It is less difficult for me to accept the love of God because I learned to accept love at an early age. There were many times I faced discipline (and many I didn't because I wasn't caught), but it was a just, fair and timely discipline meted out as chastisement in the spirit of love. The hardest whipping I received from Momma came at a time I disobeyed her command given for my safety because of her great love for me, and I knew that to be the case. Many times I did not receive the punishment I deserved because of the mercy shown by my loving parents. My parents led me to the Lord with their prayers, their examples, their teachings and their urging. I did not always follow God as I should throughout my life, but I never forgot their teachings.

Because of the choice made by Adam and Eve, we are born into this world in sin. We deserve to die for that sin. It would be a just, fair and timely discipline meted out to us. But God, who is rich in mercy, provided a way for us to escape that punishment. He sent His only Son to die in our place for our sins, and what an awful death it was on the cruel cross with a crown of thorns placed on His head. Do we deserve the death of Jesus for our sins? Not in any manner do we deserve it! That is where God's grace comes in - free favor of God, bestowed upon us without any merit or claim on our part.

What do we have to do to escape the death which is a result of our sins (transgressions)? We are told with the first words of Jesus' ministry, which are recorded are in Matthew 4:17, "From that time on Jesus began to preach, 'Repent, for the kingdom of heaven is near.'" We are also told in the last words of Jesus' before His ascension as recorded in Luke 24:47, "And repentance and forgiveness of sins will be preached in His name to all nations, beginning in Jerusalem." God wants us to join Him in heaven for our eternal life. We are told in Revelations 3:20, "Here I am! I stand at the door and knock. If anyone hears my voice and opens the door, I will come in and eat with him, and he with me."

Jesus also told us in Mark 1:15, "'The time has come,' He said. 'The kingdom of God is near. Repent and believe the good news!'" What is the good news? The greatest news ever is today's promise, "God, who is rich in mercy, made us ALIVE WITH CHRIST even when we were DEAD IN TRANSGRESSIONS." When we repent what happens? Jesus told us in Luke 15:7, "I tell you that in the same way there will be more rejoicing in heaven over one sinner who repents than over ninety-nine righteous persons who do not need to repent."

Have you accepted God's grace, repented of your sins, and have the assurance that you are saved by grace? If not, do so today, claim today's promise, and go out and make this a great day.

Amazing grace - how sweet the sound - that saved a wretch like me!
I once was lost but now am found, was blind but now I see.
When we've been there ten thousand years, bright shining as the sun,
We've no less days to sing God's praise than when we'd first begun.
John Newton - 1725-1807 & John P. Rees - 1825-1900

June 5

> Many, O Lord my God, are the wonders you have done. THE THINGS YOU PLANNED FOR US NO ONE CAN RECOUNT TO YOU; WERE I TO SPEAK AND TELL OF THEM, THEY WOULD BE TOO MANY TO DECLARE." Psalm 40:5

Recently my wife, Jan, and I took a vacation to the Northern Arizona and Southern Utah areas. We took just over two weeks and spent the entire time visiting one spectacular wonder after another. We started with the Painted Desert in the afternoon and "oohed" and "aahed" over the beautiful colors. We then traveled down the road through the Petrified Forest National Park and were stunned by the size, age and character of the 225 million year old petrified logs. At a gift shop we bought a small piece to put on a table in my office to remind us of one of God's many wonders. We then drove on West on I-40 to visit the Meteor Crater formed 50,000 years ago when a 150 foot diameter meteorite slammed into our earth at 30 to 40 thousand miles per hour, forming a crater 400 feet across and 700 feet deep in a few seconds. We then visited the awesome sight of the Grand Canyon (both South and North rims), Antelope Valley, Zion National Park, Bryce Canyon National Park, Glen Canyon Dam and Lake Powell and finally closed out our sightseeing trip with a visit to Monument Valley. I stop to reminisce about that trip when I read today's promise. We saw so many wonders in those two weeks it was almost an overload of the mind. We paused many times to ponder the great and wonderful things God had made on this earth for us to enjoy and for us to know of the power and wonder of our God.

God did not only plan the natural wonders of the earth for us. No, He planned the wonder of His Son's death on the cross, resurrection from the grave and ascension into heaven as His plan for forgiveness of our sins by His grace. This is told to us very strongly in 1 John 2:2, "He is the atoning sacrifice for our sins, and not only for ours, but also for the sins of the whole world." That is a wonder which causes the most awesomely wonderful view of the Grand Canyon to pale to insignificance in comparison.

He planned the wonder of love for us. Jesus, through His entire life exhibited love for all He met. He did not exclude anyone for any reason. We are told in Romans 2:11, "For God does not show favoritism." God showed us how to love and instructed us to love Him and to love others. We get a glimpse of God in 1 John 4:8, "Whoever does not love does not know God, because God is love." Isn't that a wonder?

Perhaps one of the greatest wonders God performs for us is the wonder of the change we see in a life when a person asks God for forgiveness, accepts His forgiveness by His grace and gives their life to Him. Paul told us in 2 Corinthians 5:17, "Therefore, if anyone is in Christ, he is a new creation; the old has gone, the new has come!"

Yes, there are many wonders from God, but the very best one is eternal life through Jesus Christ our Lord. Claim His wonder today, and go out and make this a great day.

> There's the wonder of sunset at evening, the wonder as sunrise I see;
> But the wonder of wonders that thrills my soul is the wonder that God loves me.
> There's the wonder of springtime and harvest, the sky, the stars, the sun,
> But the wonder of wonders that thrills my soul is a wonder that's only begun.
>
> George Beverly Shea - 1909-

June 6

"HUMILITY AND THE FEAR OF THE LORD BRING WEALTH AND HONOR AND LIFE." Proverbs 22:4

Two friends were talking one day about their respective churches, their pastors and the spiritual growth they had experienced. One of the men said, "I feel so good about my spiritual growth. I used to yield to temptation in so many ways. There was so much sin in my life. My walk with God has been so rewarding to me. I am not like so many people in the world today. I have just one sin in my life now. I am proud! If I could just get rid of that sin, then I really think I would be perfect." To which the friend replied, "And you exhibit such a spirit of humility!" This story is meant to warn us to guard against ever showing feelings of superiority. There is a saying, "There is so much bad in the best of us and so much good in the worst of us, it hardly behooves any of us to talk about the rest of us." James 3:2 warns us about this, "We all stumble in many ways." Paul wrote in Romans 3:10, "As it is written: There is no one righteous, not even one."

So, if we ever start to think of ourselves as being perfect, even near perfect or even pretty good, we should rethink our situation. Read what Paul wrote in Romans 3:21-24, "But now a righteousness from God, apart from law, has been made known to which the Law and the Prophets (Old Testament) testify. This righteousness from God comes through faith in Jesus Christ to all who believe. There is no difference, for all have sinned and fall short of the glory of God, and are justified freely by His grace through the redemption that came by Christ Jesus." We also should read Luke 18:9-14, "To some who were confident of their own righteousness and looked down on everybody else, Jesus told this parable: 'Two men went up to the temple to pray, one a Pharisee and the other a tax collector. The Pharisee stood up and prayed about himself: 'God, I thank you that I am not like other men-robbers, evildoers, adulterers-or even like this tax collector. I fast twice a week and give a tenth of all I get.' But the tax collector stood at a distance. He would not even look up to heaven, but beat his breast and said, 'God, have mercy on me, a sinner.' I tell you that this man, rather than the other, went home justified before God. For everyone who exalts himself will be humbled, and he who humbles himself will be exalted.'"

How do you feel about your spiritual life today? Do you feel you have arrived or do you feel you still have a way to go? Do you humbly bow before God and confess your sins and ask forgiveness for those sins or do you feel you can now leave that part out of your prayers? God wants to provide us with wealth and honor, but we must be totally submissive to Him. We must put off our proud ways and humble ourselves before Him. Does that mean that everyone who is humble will have wealth and honor on this earth? Absolutely not! We will gain eternal life, however, and there we will have wealth and honor untold.

Humble yourself before God, claim His promise, and go out and make this a great day.

Pass me not, O gentle Savior - hear my humble cry!
While on others Thou art calling, do not pass me by.
Trusting only in Thy merit, would I seek Thy face;
Heal my wounded, broken spirit, save me by Thy grace.
Fanny J, Crosby - 1820-1915

June 7

"DON'T YOU KNOW THAT YOU YOURSELVES ARE GOD'S TEMPLE AND THAT GOD'S SPIRIT LIVES IN YOU? IF ANYONE DESTROYS GOD'S TEMPLE, GOD WILL DESTROY HIM; FOR GOD'S TEMPLE IS SACRED, AND YOU ARE THAT TEMPLE." 1 Corinthians 3:16 & 17

The 21st chapter of Matthew records the triumphal entry of Jesus into Jerusalem on Palm Sunday. He entered amid a large crowd shouting, cheering and praising Him. Verses 10-13 record His first actions upon His entry, "When Jesus entered Jerusalem, the whole city was stirred and asked, 'Who is this?' The crowds answered, 'This is Jesus, the prophet from Nazareth in Galilee.' Jesus entered the temple area and drove out all who were buying and selling there. He overturned the tables of money changers and the benches of those selling doves. 'It is written,' He said to them, 'My house will be called a house of prayer, but you are making it a den of robbers.'" This story was taught to me very early in my Sunday School years. It was always great to me to see in my mind's eye Jesus overturning tables and chasing out of the temple those who were desecrating it by conducting business.

Our promise today clearly states that our body is the temple of the Holy Spirit. He lives in us from the time we first confess our sins and receive God's forgiveness for them. Suppose Jesus came into the temple of your body today. Would He find things in His temple which would displease Him? Our Christian bodies are sacred since they are God's temple! Today's promise does contain a negative promise: "If anyone destroys God's temple, God will destroy him."

There are many ways to destroy this temple of God which are obvious to us. They include such things as use of destructive drugs, drunkenness and promiscuous sex. What do you think would be God's attitude toward smoking? What would be His attitude toward over-eating to the extent of obesity? Do you think He wants us to exercise regularly? What about getting regular physical exams? I will admit that this discussion could be taken a long way. When we get past the obvious, I think the answers to the questions become a very personal consideration between you and God. How do we answer those questions of behavior? I suggest we follow the advice given in 1 Peter 2:21, "To this you were called, because Christ suffered for you, leaving you an example, that you should follow in His steps." A few years ago this verse was turned into a youth campaign termed, "What would Jesus do?"

Probably the best way we can reconcile our behavior in any one, or all, of the issues related to taking care of our bodies is to remember the last part of today's promise, "For God's temple is sacred, and you are that temple." Now, go back to the story of Jesus cleaning out the temple, and talk to God about what Jesus would clean out of your body and out of your life if He were to physically enter it today. This is a matter for you to carefully ask the leading of the Holy Spirit, and be under the Spirit's control. Do so, and go out and make this a great day.

Under the Spirit's control that the world may see Jesus in me;
Under the Spirit's control to be all He wants me to be.
Following Him all the way, victory is mine every day;
My will is fully surrendered to Him, I'm under the spirit's control!
R. Douglas Little - 1954-

June 8

"HE WILL SWALLOW UP DEATH FOREVER. THE SOVEREIGN LORD WILL WIPE AWAY THE TEARS FROM ALL FACES; HE WILL REMOVE THE DISGRACE OF HIS PEOPLE FROM ALL THE EARTH. The Lord has spoken." Isaiah 25:8

The date of September 11, 2001 will be remembered in history as the most devastating date in the life of our country. It is more devastating than December 7, 1941 because it involved peaceful civilians instead of warriors of the military as the primary victims. It also attacked the very way of life of Americans. It violated our peaceful right of travel, commerce and business. It resulted in the death of thousands of innocent people. It cost untold billions of dollars in initial cost and many times that amount in lost revenues and lifestyle changes over the following months and years. It resulted in an enormous amount of grief for those who lost loved ones that day, for those who lost a lifestyle that day, and for a nation that watched such utterly senseless waste by those who perpetrated it upon us. The actions that day were designed by the planners to stun and immobilize the American people and government. They thought their actions would cause us to fall apart and allow them greater access for further destruction of our way of life and our country. Their plans did not account for the leadership of a president who placed his faith in God. Their plans did not account for a nation that would turn strongly toward God during their time of great loss, sorrow, destruction and concern. Some of their initial plans were thwarted by a group, that included Todd Beamer who placed his faith in God. They rushed the highjackers and led to the crash of the plane instead of allowing it to crash into the intended target-either the U. S. Capitol Building or the White House. Yes, we in the United States of America have a recent example of great loss by death in our country, great sorrow leading to many tears as a result of those deaths, and the despair of knowing that a bunch of murdering thugs could cause such devastation to our property and way of life.

That great prophet, Isaiah, foretold the coming of Jesus Christ in many places in his writings and in many different ways. His prophesies were so specific and so accurate that it is virtually impossible to refute them. God gave His Son, Jesus Christ, to shed His blood on the cross to fulfill this prophesy of Isaiah which is our promise for today. By His death He took upon Himself the sins of you and me so we would have a way to claim forgiveness for our sins and have eternal life. By accepting His grace and asking Him for the forgiveness of our sins we know we will have eternal life in heaven. Thus He has swallowed up death forever for those who believe. THAT should wipe all the tears from your face!

Have you followed Romans 10:9, "That if you confess with your mouth, 'Jesus is Lord,' and believe in your heart that God raised Him from the dead, you will be saved."? If you have not done so before please do it today and claim this promise, then go out and make this a great day.

When peace, like a river, attendeth my way, when sorrows like sea billow roll
Whatever my lot, Thou hast taught me to say, It is well with my soul.
And, Lord, haste the day when my faith shall be sight, the clouds be rolled back as a scroll;
The trump shall resound and the Lord shall descend, "Even so"-it is well with my soul.
Horatio G. Spafford - 1828-1888

June 9

"THE LORD WILL MAKE YOU THE HEAD, NOT THE TAIL. If you pay attention to the commands of the Lord your God that I give you this day and carefully follow them, YOU WILL ALWAYS BE AT THE TOP, NEVER AT THE BOTTOM." Deuteronomy 28:13

In 1968 I managed a successful campaign for Congress for John N. Happy Camp in the Northwest part of Oklahoma. Happy asked me to go to Washington, DC with him as his Administrative Assistant. While I enjoyed the sights in the nation's capitol, I wanted neither to live in the area nor did I want the job as an AA. Richard Nixon had been elected president and the Oklahoma Republican State Chairman was appointed to a federal position. Since the State Chairman position was open I decided to run for it. Before I left Washington to return to Oklahoma for the race I visited the chapel in the Capitol Building to pray about the race. I felt a leading of the Lord to make the race. In April of 1969 I was elected as the head of the Oklahoma Republican State Party in, what most people considered, a major upset. At that time I was active in church and following the commands of the Lord my God. I did not consider it to be an upset as I felt His leading to run. I served in that position for six years, being re-elected twice, and enjoyed every bit of the service I gave to the job.

Today's promise has a command qualifier. If you really want to be the head, not the tail and always be at the top, never at the bottom, you must pay attention to the commands of the Lord your God and carefully follow them. You may not rise to the top of your profession or your business, but you will be serving at the very top as far as God is concerned. We must have good Christian people serving in every segment of our society. We see the problems which arise when Christian morality is not exhibited by leaders. Political careers have been destroyed for those who turned away from living moral lives.

The turning away from morality by corporate leaders during the 1990's led to the collapse of many corporations during the early 2000's and many individual charges being filed against the corporate officers. This violation of trust led to the loss of untold billions of dollars of assets by people who had trusted in the reports and statements of those same corporate officers. The result of that violation of trust, that loss of Christian morality, cost those corporate officers their position as the head of their corporations. Very rightly so! My prayers for our economy are that God will raise up Godly people, filled with Christian morality, to lead the corporations of our nation. What a difference that would make. They forgot for whom they work!

What about your behavior in your job? Do you follow Christian morality at all times? Do you make non-emergency personal phone calls on business cell phones? Not only does the business get charged for the time you use the phones, but the business loses your productivity while you are talking on the phone. Do you use business postage for personal letters? Do you give the full time of work the enthusiasm it deserves? Do it, and make this a great day.

Work, for the night is coming, under the sunset skies;
While their bright tints are glowing, work, for daylight flies.
Wok 'til the last beam fadeth, fadeth to shine no more;
Work while the night is darkening, when man's work is o'er
Anna L. Coghill - 1836-1907

June 10

"He who oppresses the poor shows contempt for their Maker, BUT WHOEVER IS KIND TO THE NEEDY HONORS GOD." Proverbs 14:31

George Sweeting, wrote "Money: Blessing or Curse?" in the April 1981 edition of Moody. In the article he wrote, "Henry Crowell, founder of the Quaker Oats Company and a significant contributor to the work of Moody Bible Institute knew how to use money wisely. As a young man, he received Christ as his Savior. When he began his business career in a little Ohio factory, he promised God that he would honor Him in his giving. God's blessing was upon him; and, as his business grew, he increased his giving. After more than forty years of giving 60 percent of his income to God, Crowell testified, 'I've never gotten ahead of God. He has always been ahead of me in giving.'" J. L. Draft, head of Kraft Cheese, who for many years gave 25 percent of his income to Christian causes said, "The only investments I ever made which have paid constantly increasing dividends is the money I have given to the Lord." Julius Segal, in his book, "Winning Life's Toughest Battles" wrote, "In stories of survivors of the Nazi death camps, an attitude of determined giving was one of the things that distinguished the survivors from those who perished. If a prisoner was on the verge of starvation, but he had a crust of bread or a scrap of a potato that he could share with his comrade in suffering, he was psychologically and spiritually capable of surviving. A survivor of Triblinka described it this way: 'In our group we shared everything, and the moment one of the group ate something without sharing it, we knew it was the beginning of the end for him.'" These three stories are examples of today's promise. They are examples of giving to honor God. The third story is an example of the Nazi actions of oppression which showed contempt for their Maker.

Paul wrote to encourage giving in 2 Corinthians 9:12-15, "This service that you perform is not only supplying the needs of God's people but is also overflowing in many expressions of thanks to God. Because of the service by which you have proved yourselves, men will praise God for the obedience that accompanies your confession of the gospel of Christ, and for your generosity in sharing with them and with everyone else. And in their prayers for you their hearts will go out to you, because of the surpassing grace God has given you. Thanks be to God for His indescribable gift!" There has always been the need for assistance for those less fortunate than you, whatever your financial status. We are instructed in many places in the Bible to give our "tithes AND offerings". We are also instructed to give to the needy. Jesus said in Matthew 25:40, "I tell you the truth, whatever you did for one of the least of these brothers of mine, you did for me." Are you faithful in giving to the needy, thereby honoring God? Do you set aside God's part of your income first? Do you give "offerings" above your tithes when special needs arise? Do you feel you are truly "honoring God" with the way you spend your income? Do you have a gentle, loving, giving heart? Honor God, and go out and make this a great day.

Give me, O Lord, a gentle, loving heart,
That I may learn to be more tender, kind,
And with Thy healing touch, each wound and smart
With Christly bands of Love and Truth to bind.

James J. Rome - (No Date)

June 11

> "That God was reconciling the world to Himself in Christ, not counting men's sins against them. AND HE HAS COMMITTED TO US THE MESSAGE OF RECONCILIATION. WE ARE THEREFORE CHRIST'S AMBASSADORS, AS THOUGH GOD WERE MAKING HIS APPEAL THROUGH US. We implore you on Christ's behalf: Be reconciled to God." 2 Corinthians 5:19 & 20

Verse 51 of the "Rubaiyat Of Omar Khayyam" reads, "The moving finger writes; and, having writ, moves on: nor all thy piety nor wit shall lure it back to cancel half a line, nor all thy tears wash out a word of it." How sad it is that deeds, once done, can never be undone. Words, once spoken, can never be unspoken. Sins, once committed, can never by uncommitted.

How wonderful it is, however, that God sent His only Son, Jesus Christ, to die on the cross so that, by His grace, we can remove the guilt of all those acts as far as the East is from the West. When we are reconciled to God by His forgiveness we become His ambassadors, as though God were making His appeal through us. We must, therefore, forgive others as directed by the Lord's Prayer to be reconciled to God. We cannot be the ambassadors of Christ if we do not forgive others. In response to the question of Peter as to how many times we should forgive others Jesus answered, "Not seven times, but seventy-seven."

Our forgiveness of others does not always mean we are reconciled to them. There are times and cases when it may be impossible to be reconciled to others who have wronged us. Such is the case of the one man against another man who had murdered the first man's daughter and was unrepentant. The first man said, "I have forgiven him for his wronging of me and my family, but I do not want to be around him nor to talk to him. I also want him to suffer the punishment for his crime." I don't feel that is a case where Jesus would demand reconciliation. God did not become reconciled with Aaron's sons, Nadab and Abihu, who offered unauthorized fire in their censers before the Lord. No, "fire came out from the presence of the Lord and consumed them, and they died before the Lord." By the grace of God, through Jesus Christ our Lord, we can be forgiven of our sins and become reconciled with God!

Have you become totally reconciled with God? Are you now an ambassador of Jesus Christ? Have you forgiven all those who have wronged you? Are you reconciled with those with whom you can become reconciled? If so, then you are living a life whereby God is able to make His appeal through you! You are able to become God's witness to the ones forgiven by you. You become God's example to those you forgive and those you become reconciled with. What a wonderful feeling that should give you! Yes, God has committed to us the message of reconciliation. We have become God's ambassadors. God depends on us to spread His message, and is making His appeal through us. Claim God's promise of reconciliation, follow our Savior, do what He wants you to do, and go out and make this a great day.

> I am resolved to go to the Saviour, leaving my sin and strife,
> He is the true one, He is the just one, He hath the words of life.
> I am resolved to follow the Saviour, faithful and true each day,
> Heed what He sayeth, do what He willeth; He is the living way.
>
> Palmer Hartsough - 1884-1932

June 12

"When you were dead in your sins and in the uncircumcision of your sinful nature, GOD MADE YOU ALIVE WITH CHRIST. HE FORGAVE US ALL OUR SINS, HAVING CANCELED THE WRITTEN CODE, WITH ITS REGULATIONS, THAT WAS AGAINST US AND THAT STOOD OPPOSED TO US; HE TOOK IT AWAY, NAILING IT TO THE CROSS." Colossians 2:13 & 14

Lee Strobel in his book, "The Case For Faith" tells the story of William Neal Moore. Billie killed a man for his money in May 1984. He was caught with the money, admitted his guilt, was sentenced to die. Early on Death Row Billie was visited by two church leaders at the behest of his mother. They told him about the mercy and hope that was available through Jesus Christ. "Nobody had ever told me that Jesus loves me and died for me," Moore explained during Strobel's visit to Georgia. "It was a love I could feel. It was a love I wanted. It was a love I *needed*." On that day, Moore said yes to Christ's free gift of forgiveness and eternal life, and he was promptly baptized in a small tub that was used by prison trusties. And he would never be the same. He counseled other death row inmates, he took correspondence courses on the Bible, he led Bible study and prayer groups, he won forgiveness from his victim's family and he brought many fellow prisoners to Christ. Billie became a man free in Jesus Christ. Billie spent sixteen years on Death Row. Just before Billie Moore was to be executed a campaign by Mother Teresa and others was successful in winning a halt to the execution, commutation to life in prison, and then the Parole and Pardon Board gave him his freedom on November 8, 1991. William Neal Moore became a preacher of a church between two housing projects in Rome, Georgia.

Billie Moore had his crime forgiven by his victim's family. He had his sentence, based on the written code, cancelled. The charges which were used against him to convict him of murder and sentence him to death were taken away and no longer held against him by the state of Georgia, which then made him a man free of prison. I cannot even imagine the feelings of Billie when he walked out of prison with his freedom. From reading his story, and the story of others, I know that however great the feeling is, it pales to insignificance at the feeling of freedom from sin when we go before God asking Him for His forgiveness and the washing away of our sins in the blood of His Son, Jesus Christ.

Yes, today's promise tells us that God made us alive with Christ! He forgave us ALL our sins. He canceled the written code, with its regulations, that was against us and stood opposed to us. He took it away and nailed it to the cross with His Son, Jesus Christ. Have you taken advantage of today's promise from God? Are you confident in the eternal life God has promised to you? By saying the prayer asking for forgiveness like Billie Moore, you can be a free man whatever your incarcerated state. Claim today's promise and become a free man with no charges against you and eternal life before you. Then go out and make this a great day.

Dying for me, dying for me, there on the cross He was dying for me;
Now in His death my redemption I see, all because Jesus was dying for me.
Coming for me, coming for me, one day to earth He is coming for me;
Then with what joy His dear face I shall see, O how I praise Him-He's coming for me!
Gladys Westcott Roberts - 1888-

June 13

> "FOR WHERE TWO OR THREE COME TOGETHER IN MY NAME, THERE AM I WITH THEM." Matthew 18:20

I was a State Farm Insurance Agent for over twenty years in Norman, OK. When I was first appointed no one was retiring so I started a "scratch" agency. It was a lot of hard work and I had an excellent staff for the entire time. I knew my clients expected to be able to reach me at all times and that the most likely times for claims were when the weather was bad. It was written in the "Personnel Policies and Procedures" manual for my office that the staff was expected to be present in the office during times of inclement weather. Several times this worked a hardship on my staff as they made their way to work in snow or on icy roads. At one time I was considering easing the policy when one of my clients stopped in after a period of icy weather and told me, "I was really worried about driving to work on the ice, but it was comforting to me to know that if something happened your office would be open to help me." That really made me feel better about my policy and to realize again the importance of service to my clients.

Now I want my church attendance to reflect the same commitment. I intend to be there when there is a church service. Our promise today assures us that when we come together in His name, He will be there with us. I don't want to miss being in the presence of God! Paul told us in Hebrews 10:25, "Let us not give up meeting together, as some are in the habit of doing." We are also told in Leviticus 26:2, "Observe my Sabbaths and have reverence for my sanctuary. I am the Lord." Our main purpose in life is to be like Jesus. We are told in Luke 4:16, "He went to Nazareth, where he had been brought up, and on the Sabbath day he went into the synagogue, AS WAS HIS CUSTOM."(emphasis added).

Today's promise does not apply only to church attendance. It applies any time any of us come together in His name. This can be in small group Bible study, prayer groups, care ministry visits, work projects for the church, etc. It can also be in your business office when you pray for His guidance as you start a meeting to solve a problem. Remember, God is interested in EVERY part of your life and wants to be a part of it so asking His guidance in solving a business problem, thereby inviting Him to your meeting, is a perfectly proper thing to do. If you and your business are committed to God, your business is conducted according to His principles and you meet in His name you can be assured He will be present based on today's promise. I particularly feel His presence when I am making calls in our care ministry service as I am making my calls in His name and I always say a prayer with and for the person I am calling on.

What about when you are alone? Always remember God's promise of the Comforter. The Holy Spirit dwells within each and every Christian. Your body is His temple! Talk to Him and commune with Him at all times.

Attend church, meet with fellow Christians, and go out and make this a great day.

> Here we come Thy name to praise; may we feel Thy presence near;
> May Thy glory meet our eyes, while we in Thy house appear;
> Here afford us, Lord, a taste of our everlasting feast;
> Here afford us, Lord, a taste of our everlasting feast.
>
> John Newton -1725-1807

June 14

"Many are asking, 'Who can show us any good?' Let the light of Your face shine upon us, O Lord. YOU HAVE FILLED MY HEART WITH GREATER JOY THAN WHEN THEIR GRAIN AND NEW WINE ABOUND." Psalm 4:6 & 7

I remember one year on the farm when it was so dry early in the growing season that the wheat was very short with small heads of grain. Our first cutting of alfalfa hay was very light. The corn was very thin with very little grain. We had to carry water to the garden to produce enough vegetables for our table and to can for use over the Winter. Just before wheat harvest the rains came and continued for over a month. Some of the grains of wheat actually sprouted in the head. When we were able to cut the wheat we only got a small amount of grain which was only good for feed for our hogs. The last cutting of hay before frost was very good and provided sufficient feed for our cows and horses for the Winter. With so little grain and no hay to sell there was not much happiness around our farm that year. This contrasts with another year when the rains came at the best times, the crops grew well, the hay was very plentiful and harvest time produced large yields which had us laughing and singing as we gathered in the bounty. There was a difference in the degree of happiness we had as a result of those two years. When I read today's promise I think back on that year when our harvest of grain abounded. We were very happy in our minds and also had great joy in our hearts for the production.

Happiness is a state of the mind as evidenced by the statement of Abraham Lincoln, "I have noticed that a man is just about as happy as he sets his mind to be." Joy, however, is a state of the heart. You can be joyful when you aren't feeling very happy and you can be happy when you do not feel joyful. I have found over my life when I don't feel very happy that if I turn my mind upon God and His Word I start finding many things about which I can be joyful. Feeling joyful, in turn, makes me feel much happier. This is my way of letting God's face shine upon me. That, as the promise says, fills my heart with greater joy than we had the year of the great production!

The absence of joy in the hearts of a great many people today lead to their searching for happiness in many ways which are detrimental to their best interest. This has led to an enormous increase in births to single teens, drug and alcohol addiction (sometimes starting at a very young age), pornography, spending beyond one's income, etc. The root cause of this behavior in many people is the lack of joy in their hearts and their desire to seek happiness wherever they think they can find it.

What about your life? Do you have the joy in your heart that comes from God shining His face on you? Are you reading the Bible as you should? Are you attending church services as you should? Are you living your life as you should? Think about how you are living your life. Live it as God wants you to and you will be joyful. Now go out and make this a great day.

I have found His grace is all complete, He supplieth ev'ry need;
While I sit and learn at Jesus' feet, I am free, yes, free indeed.
I have found the pleasure I once craved, it is joy and peace within;
What a wondrous blessing! I am saved from the awful gulf of sin.
Barney E. Warren - 1867-1951

June 15

"The Sovereign Lord is my strength; HE MAKES MY FEET LIKE THE FEET OF A DEER, HE ENABLES ME TO GO ON THE HEIGHTS." Habukkuk 3:19

We went to Crested Butte, CO each Summer for vacation for many years until the altitude started affecting both Jan and me. Several years we took members of the family with us. One of the years that we took Jan's parents, her father was 86 and mother was 81. On one of the really nice Summer days we planned a picnic at the very head of Washington Gulch (11,200 ft). Jan's mother was not feeling well so just her father and I made the trip. We drove to the top of the pass, parked the vehicle and hiked on up near the very top. We had a picnic lunch, cooler, walking sticks and a blanket. We found an ideal spot near a grove of trees where we were out of the wind. We spread the blanket, set out the picnic and sat down to enjoy the lunch and the view. There were a good many peaks above 14,000 feet we could see from our vantage point. We looked down on the town of Crested Butte and on a lake we had a hard time hiking up to just two days before. We could see many steep mountain sides and cliffs from where we sat. To hike many of the waterfalls and lakes we visited while we were there required us to be sure-footed and patient. Many times we would see deer or mountain goats which would go bounding up the side of the steep mountains when we stopped to take their pictures or just to get a better look at them. They never stumbled or fell as they fled away from us.

Today's promise tells us God makes our feet like the feet of those deer which bounded away from us up the mountain side. It also tells us He enables us to go on the heights. I am sure Habukkuk had seen deer bound up the steep mountain sides on many occasions. He had watched them as they ascended higher and higher until they could no longer be seen. He must have marveled at how strong and sure-footed they were and thought to himself how wonderful it would be to be able to run up the steep mountains and reach the top where they could see a very far distance.

In the first two chapters Habukkuk argues with God about His ways which seem unjust. He also was perplexed that wickedness, strife and oppression were rampant with God seemingly doing nothing. Our verse today comes from Habukkuk's confession of faith prayer with our promise as the last verse. The promise is proceeded by this in verses 17 & 18, "Though the fig tree does not bud and there are no grapes on the vines, though the olive crop fails and the fields produce no food, though there are no sheep in the pen and no cattle in the stalls, yet I will rejoice in the Lord, I will be joyful in God my Savior." Habukkuk viewed God's leading of him in his daily walk with God like the deer bounding up the mountain side. God showed Habukkuk how to walk with Him.

Whatever the problems of today. However dark the future looks. God will direct your walk with Him if you put your total trust in Him. Do it, and go out and make this a great day.

My sins were as scarlet 'til Jesus came; He washed them whiter than snow;
Now I find my delight in His lovely name; His joy is the strength of my soul.
Though rough be the pathway that leads me home, and heavy the load that I bear,
Whether I walk the mountain or valley low, His blessings will follow me there.

R. Douglas Little - 1954-

June 16

"KNOW THEN IN YOUR HEART THAT AS A MAN DISCIPLINES HIS SON, SO THE LORD YOUR GOD DISCIPLINES YOU." Deuteronomy 8:5

In 1977 I was assigned as commander of a new type battalion in the Oklahoma National Guard. It was a unit of TOW anti-tank missile launchers. The missiles were wire-guided and the gunner had to keep the optical sight on the target during the twelve to fifteen seconds the missile was in flight. We were given five missiles each year for a live-fire exercise (one per company). The first year we had five hits. The second year we put on a big show with the Oklahoma Lieutenant Governor, seven Generals, other dignitaries and families of the unit members present. The first two missiles were direct hits on a tank hull over a mile down range. I introduced the squad to fire the third missile of the day, gave a short membership history of the gunner and gave the signal for firing the missile. I counted down the time it should take and nothing happened. Just as I was worried, the missile struck into the ground about 200 meters behind the target. I knew at once the gunner had looked at the missile in flight instead of keeping his eye on the target. Rather than announce that fact to the crowd, which was sitting stunned, I turned to them and said, "You have just seen the flexibility of the TOW missile system. While the missile was in flight to the chosen target the gunner noticed a Command Bunker about 200 meters to the rear of the target, shifted his aiming point and blew it up." The crowd laughed and relaxed and we continued the firing process. After the firing program I gave a short lesson to explain what had happened and the importance of a gunner keeping his eye on the target. Later I had the Company Commander make sure the lesson was learned. We did not chasten the gunner as it was his first mistake. We would only chasten a gunner if the same mistake were to continue to be made.

Aren't we a lot like that gunner? Don't we know we are supposed to keep our eye on the target? Don't we miss the mark from time to time and sin? God forgives us and continues to love us in spite of our sins. However, if we continue to commit the same sin time after time we may be disciplined by God! Just as we would chasten and discipline a soldier who made the same mistake time after time, God will chasten and discipline us for continued sin or for failing to follow the leading of Him. Your children are disciplined out of your love for them and your desire that they act in their own best interest and learn what is in their best interest. God does the same thing with you.

Are you walking close enough to God to communicate with Him freely and learn what His desire for you is each day? Are you convinced of His love for you and His desire to lead you to what is the very best for you? Are you keeping your eye on the target God has set for you? You can only know that target as you walk closely with Him on a daily basis. Know in your heart that He loves you, wants what is best for you, watches over you and will correct you when needed.

Keep your eye on the target as God's eye is on you, and go out and make this a great day.

Whenever I am tempted, whenever clouds arise,
When songs give place to sighing, when hope within me dies,
I draw the closer to Him: from care He sets me free;
His eye is on the sparrow, and I know He watches me.

Civilla D. Martin - 1869-1948

June 17

"HE RESTORES MY SOUL. HE GUIDES ME IN PATHS OF RIGHTEOUSNESS FOR HIS NAME'S SAKE." Psalm 23:3

In August 2002 we attended the "Warner Reunion" in Hutchinson, KS. That reunion is held each year and we had not been able to attend for several years because of business and taking care of the needs of Jan's parents. Representatives from different branches of the family are named to a committee to plan the reunion and conduct the short business meeting after lunch on the final day. The chairman of the committee that year was Danny Warner, the son of my dad's first cousin. Danny is a quiet, shy man with a great smile and personality, and he dresses accordingly. As the time for the meeting approached I noticed that Danny was absent. When the meeting time arrived in walked "Troubles the Clown". Danny makes his living in Wichita, KS as "Troubles the Clown". Troubles is a talkative, exuberant person with a big, red nose, a checked coat and an outlandish long tie. He has baggy pants and very large shoes. Troubles treads where Danny would seem to follow! The personality of Danny Warner changed when he became "Troubles the Clown"!

Righteousness changes us. Paul told us in 2 Corinthians 5:17, "Therefore, if anyone is in Christ, he is a new creation; the old has gone, the new has come!" When we accept the grace of our Lord Jesus Christ and become a Christian, God restores our soul. He then guides us in the paths of righteousness. He leads us to a change of lifestyle. He uses His Word to guide us to fulfill His purpose in our lives. We become more and more like Jesus. We adopt the role of a servant as Jesus taught us to do. We feel and show our love for others more openly and in more ways. Yes, righteousness does change us! We do become a new creation! We constantly learn to be more Christ-like in our thoughts, words and actions. Our heart changes, our thought patterns change and our personality changes to some extent.

God guides us in paths of righteousness, and He does so for His Name's sake! We become a man or woman for God. He wants us to forsake the sinful things we did in the past. He leads us in learning more about Him and His ways through our study of the Bible, our association with other Christians, our attendance at church services and our following the leading of the Holy Spirit. We grow and mature as Christians best and most when we better learn to love like Jesus did. Paul wrote in 1 Corinthians 13:11 (this is the "love" chapter!), "When I was a child, I talked like a child, I thought like a child, I reasoned like a child. When I became a man, I put childish ways behind me." Children tend to talk, think, reason and act in a very self-centered manner. When we are living in sin we tend to do the same thing. We tend to be selfish, wanting "things" for ourselves. We seek to do things which will make us "happy" more than thinking of others. God changes that when He leads us in the paths of righteousness.

Is God leading you? Let Him, and go out and make this a great day.

I'm going to live the way He wants me to live,
I'm going to give until there's just no more to give;
I'm going to love, love 'til there's just no more love,
I could never, never out-love the Lord.
Gloria Gaither - 1942- & William J. Gaither - 1936-

June 18

> "For everything in the world - the cravings of sinful man, the lust of his eyes and the boasting of what he has and does - comes not from the Father but from the world. THE WORLD AND ITS DESIRES PASS AWAY, BUT THE MAN WHO DOES THE WILL OF GOD LIVES FOREVER." 1 John 2:16 & 17

How do you view yourself in relation to this world? Are you a citizen of this world who will some day die, or are you a citizen with eternal life in heaven who is temporarily living in this world? Do you own your home, your car, your bank account, your furniture, your business, etc, or are you the custodian of those things which truly belong to God? Your answers will tell you a lot about your priorities. We are told in Matthew 6:19-21, "Do not store up for yourselves treasures on earth, where moth and rust destroy, and where thieves break in and steal. But store up for yourselves treasures in heaven, where moth and rust do not destroy, and where thieves do not break in and steal. For where your treasure is, there your heart will be also."

Today's promise clearly tells us that the world and its desires will pass away. Thank God for the positive part of today's promise! The man who does the will of God will have eternal life with our Lord and Savior in heaven! If you consider yourself a citizen of this world you may be more prone to the temptations of the world, the cravings and lust of sinful man and the boasting of what sinful man has and does. Peter did not consider us to be citizens of this world as he wrote in 1 Peter 1:11, "Dear friends, I urge you, as aliens and strangers in the world, to abstain from sinful desires, which war against your soul." He fully recognized that everything of the world came not from God.

I just received an email titled "The Secret". A friend asked another, "How is it that you are always so happy? You have so much energy, and you never seem to get down." With a smile the friend replied, "I know The Secret!" "What secret is that?" was the second question. "I'll tell you all about it, but you have to promise to share The Secret with others. The Secret is this: I have learned there is little I can do in my life that will make me truly happy. I must depend on God to make my happy and to meet my needs. When a need arises in my life, I trust God to supply according to His riches. I have learned most of the time I don't need half of what I think I do. He has never let me down. Since I learned The Secret, I am happy." "That's too simple!" the questioner thought. But reflecting on her own life she recalled thinking a bigger house would make her happy. It didn't! She thought a better paying job would make her happy. It didn't! When was she happy? Sitting of the floor with her children, playing games, eating pizza or reading a story, a simple gift from God. Now YOU know The Secret! We can't depend on the world to make us happy. Only God in His infinite wisdom can do that. Trust Him! God, in His wisdom will take care of you! It really isn't a secret. We just have to believe it and do it...really trust God! Believe and trust Him! Lean on Him! Now go out and make this a great day.

> O how sweet to walk in this pilgrim way, leaning on the everlasting arms;
> O how bright the path grows from day to day, leaning on the everlasting arms.
> What have I to dread, what have I to fear, leaning on the everlasting arms;
> I have blessed peace with my Lord so near, leaning on the everlasting arms.
>
> Elisha A. Hoffman - 1839-1929

June 19

> The Jesus said to His disciples, 'If anyone would come after me, he must deny himself and take up his cross and follow me. FOR WHOEVER WANTS TO SAVE HIS LIFE WILL LOSE IT, BUT WHOEVER LOSES HIS LIFE FOR ME WILL FIND IT. What good will it be for a man if he gains the whole world, yet forfeits his soul? Or what can a man give in exchange for his soul?'" Matthew 16:24-26

Today's promise continues the thought of yesterday, "the world and its desires pass away, but the man who does the will of God will live forever." Do you want to save your life for yourself? Are you a citizen of the world? Is your greatest desire to accumulate "things"? Do you hold to a contemporary saying, "He who dies with the most toys wins"? What will it profit you for eternity if you gain the whole world, yet forfeit your soul? Do you think you can buy your way into heaven or work your way into the good graces of God? God clearly answered this last question by His inspired words in Ephesians 2:8-9, "For it is by grace you have been saved, through faith-and this not from yourselves, it is the gift of God-not by works, so that no one can boast." After your death what of your worldly possessions would you think you would be willing to exchange for eternal life in heaven?

Oh, the great promise, "whoever loses his life for me will find it"! What have you lost when you lose your life for God? Have you lost the stress which comes from always striving for one more deal, one more sale, harder work to obtain a better paying job, more pay to obtain more "things" or deeper debt to show the world of your success? Have you lost the yielding to lust which brings broken relationships, hurt feelings and a sense of failure? Have you lost the company of deceitful friends, dishonest associates and acquaintances who want to use you for their own gain? Have you lost the loss of health which comes with riotous living, harmful addictions and being a slave to unhealthy actions? Don't you think those are all things which you would be better off to have lost?

When you lose your life for God what do you find? You find true joy and a peace that comes over you when you have yielded everything to Him. You find a joy that is almost unspeakable in its fullest. You find quiet confidence in all that you do because you do it not for the world, but for Him who created the world, and this takes away all the stress of the demand for "things". You find true happiness and pleasure with your faithful mate that builds relationships, builds love and trust for each other and gives you a sense of peace and success. You gain true friends who will minister to your needs while expecting nothing but your love in return. You lose a life style which can destroy your health and happiness. Best of all, however, you will have gained ETERNAL LIFE! Your life doesn't end when your journey in this world is complete. You will go on to be with our Lord Jesus Christ forever!

So lose your life for God, and go out and make this a great day.

> There is joy in serving Jesus, as I journey on my way,
> Joy that fills the heart with praises, ev'ry hour and ev'ry day.
> There is joy in serving Jesus, joy amid the darkest night,
> For I've learned the wondrous secret, and I'm walking in the light.
>
> Oswald J. Smith - 1889-

June 20

> "Is any one of you in trouble? He should pray. Is anyone happy? Let him sing songs of praise. Is any one of you sick? He should call the elders of the church to pray over him and anoint him with oil in the name of the Lord. AND THE PRAYER OFFERED IN FAITH WILL MAKE THE SICK PERSON WELL; THE LORD WILL RAISE HIM UP. IF HE HAS SINNED, HE WILL BE FORGIVEN." James 5:13-15

I am amazed at people who say they believe in the Bible yet don't believe in ALL of the Bible. We are told in 2 Timothy 3:16-17, "All Scripture is God-breathed and is useful for teaching, rebuking, correcting and training in righteousness, so that the man of God may be thoroughly equipped for every good work." I firmly believe this means exactly what is says, ALL SCRIPTURE! I have talked to people who would never ask for anointing with oil when they are sick, yet today's promise clearly gives this instruction. When you are in trouble-pray! When you are happy-sing! When you are sick-call the elders of the church to pray over you and anoint you with oil in the name of the Lord! The promise is that the prayer offered in faith (as evidenced by anointing with oil) will make you well and the Lord will raise you up! Your faith (as evidenced by your asking for this to be accomplished) and your belief (as evidenced by your submission to the prayer and the anointing) will result in your sins being forgiven.

I will tell you about two different situations where I have seen it work! I have been part of a group which went to the hospital to pray for Mary King and anoint her with oil. The doctors had told her if they did the surgery she would die. We anointed her with oil and prayed for her in faith that He WOULD heal her. Not only did she survive the surgery, she went home to complete the recovery and came back to attendance at church to serve as a greeter with her precious smile, wonderful personality and obvious life for Christ. What a blessing she is to all who know her or know of her, and what an example she is for everyone to follow.

The other case involved a church member who had cancer and had developed pneumonia and was extremely sick, given very little chance of recovery. She called for the elders to pray over her and anoint her with oil, which we did as we had done for Mary. In less than two months she was in attendance at church services.

Do you have difficulty accepting some passages of Scripture? I can understand that. Some of your difficulty could be coming from misinterpreting the Scripture, reading a translation which is not totally true to the original version or lack of total faith. Sometimes we worry about how the world might look at what we do. On at least one occasion when I talked to a person about today's promise I suspect this latter to be the case. Yield totally to God. Put your full trust and faith in Him and His Word. All Scripture is God-breathed and useful...so that the man of God will be thoroughly equipped for every good work! So claim today's promise, trust the great Physician, and go out and make this a great day.

> The great Physician now is near-the sympathizing Jesus;
> He speaks the drooping heart to cheer-O hear the voice of Jesus!
> Your many sins are all forgiven-O hear the voice of Jesus;
> Go on your way in peace to heaven and wear a crown with Jesus!
>
> William Hunter - 1811-1877

June 21

"But, 'Let him who boasts boast in the Lord.' FOR IT IS NOT THE ONE WHO COMMENDS HIMSELF WHO IS APPROVED, BUT THE ONE WHOM THE LORD COMMENDS." 2 Corinthians 10:17 & 18

Today's promise was written by Paul after his Corinthian opponents, who used a professional type of oratory as their stock in trade, had made some inroads. In 2 Corinthians 10:12 Paul wrote, "We do not dare to classify or compare ourselves with some who commend themselves. When they measure themselves by themselves and compare themselves with themselves, they are not wise." In comparison to Paul, they were shallow and mediocre. These passages remind me of the saying, "Mediocrity is excellent to the mediocre!" Paul's adversaries were also described by William Secker, an English clergyman, when he wrote, "Usually the greatest boasters are the smallest workers. The deep rivers pay a larger tribute to the sea than shallow brooks, and yet empty themselves with less noise." While these people boasted of themselves and their work, Paul let his boasting be boasting of the Lord.

Have you known people like Paul's adversaries? Any time you have found a great bargain and made a smart purchase they tell you how much less they paid for a better quality product. When you tell a group about your great fishing trip they remind you that they had an even better one a short time ago. Their garage sale always resulted in more money and less left-over items than the one you just held. Doesn't it get annoying? When I observe people like this I feel a bit of pity for them as I feel they must have a lot of insecurity. This is probably the problem with Paul's adversaries. Paul was very secure in his relationship with God. He preached and wrote in a very straight forward manner which was easy to understand. Paul knew he was commended by the Lord and was sure of his eternal reward in heaven.

Do you share the internal security Paul had? Are you comfortable with your relationship with God? Do you serve God in such a manner that you are comfortable with your eternal reward for a job well done? Do you let the future commendation of God satisfy you or do you feel you must constantly remind yourself and/or others of the good things you have done and are doing? God has a purpose for your life. He has developed you with your talents and experiences for the specific work He has planned for you. I recommend you obtain a copy of Rick Warren's, "The Purpose Driven Life" and read and study it. Our entire church has recently completed the forty days of study it takes to complete the book by studying one short chapter each day. By careful study of the book and proper application of its principles, suggestions and methods to your life, you will find yourself boasting in the Lord as Paul suggested. I strongly recommend it to you.

By surrendering all to God you will find a greater joy in your life and a greater feeling of internal comfort. Then you will no longer feel the need to commend yourself as God will commend you and approve of you. Do it today, and go out and make this a great day.

All to Jesus I surrender, make me, Savior, wholly Thine.
Let me feel the Holy Spirit, truly know that Thou art mine.
All to Jesus I surrender, Lord, I give myself to Thee;
Fill me with Thy love and power, let Thy blessing fall on me.
Judson W. Van DeVenter - 1855-1939

June 22

> "But now, this is what the Lord says - He who created you, O Jacob, He who formed you, O Israel: 'FEAR NOT, FOR I HAVE REDEEMED YOU; I HAVE SUMMONED YOU BY NAME; YOU ARE MINE.'" Isaiah 43:1

Have you ever been chosen for a task and summoned to the superior's office to be given the instructions? It can be a frightening experience. When I was a Captain in the National Guard it seemed that my military career had stalled. I did my assignments to the best of my abilities, but seemed to never get the assignment which would propel me to promotion. We were to travel to Fort Carson, CO, for our Annual Training one year and I was given a minor assignment in the planning phase. I completed that and waited for the operations order to be published. Two weeks before we were to leave for AT, I was summoned to the commander's office. There I was told the person who was assigned to write the order had a personal conflict and had not been able to complete it. I was given four days to write and publish the order. I completed the task and delivered the required number of copies to the commander. I was then told to be back early the next day to brief the five sub-commanders on the order and to assume the position of assistant route commander. That period of training was so great and so much fun it still ranks just behind the three years I spent as a Battalion Commander. I was promoted to Major before the next year and was further promoted to retire a Colonel. I later found out that the commander had recognized my abilities and was just waiting for the right time and the right project to put me to work. He had chosen me and trained me with all my previous assignments.

Today's promise reminds me of Jeremiah 1:4-5a, "The word of the Lord came to me, saying, 'Before I formed you in the womb I knew you, before you were born I set you apart.'" You see, God had chosen Jeremiah in a very special way. Now in today's promise we have Isaiah telling us that God had chosen the descendants of Jacob (who God renamed Israel). They were redeemed and summoned by name. God told them, "You are mine."

In the same way, God knew you before He formed you in the womb. Before you were born He set you apart for a specific purpose (see the reading for yesterday and "The Purpose Driven Life" by Rick Warren) for which He gave you unique capabilities, experiences, talents and training. He wants you to ask to be saved by His grace so He can redeem you. He is calling you by name to complete the purpose for which He formed you. Have you given yourself to Him? Have you been redeemed by His grace? Have you answered His summons? Do you fully, completely and without reservations belong to Him? If you have, then you have no reason to fear anything in the world. 2 Timothy 1:7 says, "For God did not give us a spirit of timidity (fear), but a spirit of power, of love and of self discipline."

Let God's grace redeem you, answer His summons today and totally belong to Him. If you do you will be able to go out and make this a great day.

> Redeemed-how I love to proclaim it! Redeemed by the blood of the Lamb;
> Redeemed through His infinite mercy, His child, and forever, I am.
> I know I shall see in His beauty the King in whose law I delight;
> Who lovingly guards every footstep, and gives me a song in the night.
> Fanny J. Crosby - 1820-1915

June 23

"YOU WILL BE PROTECTED FROM THE LASH OF THE TONGUE, AND NEED NOT FEAR WHEN DESTRUCTION COMES." Job 5:21

Have you ever been falsely accused? Have people talked about you in a very negative manner and publicly criticized you wrongly? When I was consulting Republican Congressional candidates in several states I was asked by a friend in Washington, DC about the U. S. Senate race in Oklahoma. We had a good man running on the Republican ticket against a very popular Democrat who had been our Governor. The Republican had not been able to raise much money and did not have a strong organization. I felt his chances of winning were slim and none and that slim had just left town. I gave this information to my friend. He later attended a meeting of people representing several organizations interested in political races and told the group what my feelings were about the possibility of a Republican victory in Oklahoma. One of the people who attended that meeting was a friend of the Republican's campaign manager and he called to report what I had said. This campaign manager then held a meeting with several of the Republican leaders in Oklahoma and told them I had supported the Democrat in the race. This was spread to all the Republican organization and I was publicly asked to resign as Republican National Committeeman. They called an Executive Committee meeting for me to resign and refused to allow me to speak or tell them what I had actually said. The false rumors and gossiping which took place had destroyed my political career in the state of Oklahoma. Oh, how I wish I had been following the Lord then like I am now. The lash of the tongue would not have hurt so badly.

Knowing how badly I felt being the victim of a false accusation and the spreading of many falsehoods by gossip makes me much more cautious about what I say now. I try to live by Psalm 19:14, "Let the words of my mouth and the meditations of my heart be pleasing in your sight, O Lord, my rock and my redeemer." Tryon Edwards (1809-1894), American theologian and editor wrote, "To murder character is as truly a crime as to murder the body; the tongue of the slanderer is brother to the dagger of the assassin." This is why successful churches have a strong, strict policy against gossip. Gossip will split a church quicker than any other single cause. You must guard against it in every way you possible can. Remember, gossip is a sin so don't do it!

If you are the victim of the lash of the tongue you should remember today's promise. You do not answer to those of the world. You answer to God. He will protect you from the lash of the tongue. You need not fear when destruction comes to anything in this world. I thank God now that I got out of politics when I did and started my insurance business. I have had so many wonderful blessings from God since then. I don't think God was responsible for the false attacks, but I know God used them for His (and my) good! Remember, character counts! Reputation is what people think about you, Character is what you really are! Maintain the character God wants you to be and you will be safe in the arms of Jesus. Now go out and make this a great day.

Safe in the arms of Jesus, safe on His gentle breast,
There by His love o'ershaded, sweetly my soul shall rest.
Safe in the arms of Jesus, safe from corroding care,
Safe from the world's temptations, sin cannot harm me there.

Fanny J. Crosby - 1820-1915

June 24

"YOU WILL COME TO THE GRAVE IN FULL VIGOR, LIKE SHEAVES GATHERED IN SEASON." Job 5:26

In 1949 Dad planted a fifteen acre field to oats and it was the best oat crop we ever had. We had a binder which we used to bind the oats at the proper time into bundles. Bundles consist of a lot of stems of the oats tied together with twine. They are like the sheaves of the Bible except sheaves were tied together with some of the stems of oats twisted together to make a twine-like tie. The binder would catch about six bundles on the bundle carrier then we would trip the carrier lever to drop the pile of bundles in a row formed by the previous round of cutting. When the field was finished we had rows of piles of bundles. We let the oats cure and dry for a few days. On Friday night my three siblings and I asked Dad and Momma to take us to town on Saturday as a special treat. Dad said we had to "shock" the oats (gather the bundles together, set them on the stem butts with the heads of grain up and leaning to the center). After we talked about it for quite awhile Dad agreed we could go to town as soon as the oats were shocked as he thought it would take all day. We then suggested Dad and Momma do the chores and the four children would go to the field to work as soon as we got up and they agreed. We got up before 5:00 A.M. the next morning and went to the field. Dad and Momma completed the chores and were just getting ready to come to the field to get us for breakfast at 9:00 A.M. when we drove into the farm yard. How proud and tired we were to have worked so hard and so successfully! We got to go to town for almost an entire day and had a wonderful time. We had "gathered the sheaves in season"!

In today's promise Eliphaz the Temanite has told Job his troubles came because of some sin which he must confess. He told Job that he should not despise the chastening of the Almighty for his sin, but he should confess those sins and Job "would come to the grave in full vigor, like sheaves gathered in season." While Eliphaz was wrong about what had happened to Job, he was totally correct about the end of life for a child of God! Like those "sheaves" of oats we harvested at just the right time, God will gather His children to Him at just the right time.

Many times we can't understand God's timing. Many times the grief seems to overwhelm us and the only thing we can think is, "Why, God, why?" over and over again. I can't even imagine the grief of losing a child. I would never attempt to try to explain God's reasons and timing. Those are the times we just have to crawl up on our Heavenly Father's lap and let His tender love and mercies comfort and console us. He is always there! When a child or a person belonging to God dies we have today's promise that young, middle-age or old they were gathered in season. Have you faced the loss of a friend or loved one or are you facing such a loss? If so, please take comfort in today's promise. It is meant for you. Focus on God, His timing and His omnipotence rather than on the world. Then go out and make this a great day.

Just when I need Him Jesus is near, just when I falter, just when I fear;
Ready to help me, ready to cheer, just when I need Him most.
Just when I need Him Jesus is strong, bearing my burdens all the day long;
For all my sorrow giving a song, just when I need Him most.
William C. Poole - 1875-1949

June 25

"So if you faithfully obey the commands I am giving you today - to love the Lord your God and to serve Him with all your heart and with all your soul - THEN I WILL SEND RAIN ON YOUR LAND IN ITS SEASON, BOTH AUTUMN AND SPRING RAINS, SO THAT YOU MAY GATHER IN YOUR GRAIN, NEW WINE AND OIL. I WILL PROVIDE GRASS IN THE FIELDS FOR YOUR CATTLE, AND YOU WILL EAT AND BE SATISFIED." Deuteronomy 11:13-15

When I was growing up on the farm we would plant several rows of sweet corn at the edge of one of our fields. As the corn was about to reach maturity Momma would begin to call the family and neighbor ladies to get ready to can the corn. I would carry quart jars up from the cellar for Momma and my sisters to wash. The day before canning day I would carry water into the kitchen to fill our tubs so there would be plenty of water available. When "canning day" morning arrived I was excused from chores. I would take the team and a wagon to the field about 5:30 A.M. and start snapping off the corn which was just right for canning. When I had a wagon load I would head for the house, put up the team and feed them, eat a quick breakfast and start husking the corn and cutting the corn off the cob. I would put a clean four inch block in a clean tub, put the butt of the ear of corn on the block and cut the corn off the cob from top to bottom of the ear. By the time the ladies would be ready for the corn I would have a tub full ready for them. At noon we would stop to thank God for His goodness and bounty and to eat fried chicken, mashed potatoes and gravy and corn on the cob with fresh baked bread covered with butter and jam, all washed down with cold milk. Yes, we would eat and be satisfied! When my job was completed I would carry the husks and green cobs out to the hog lot for them to feed on. Then I would carry the fresh jars of canned corn down into the cellar and help load the jars for all the ladies who came for the canning. What a day that was!

Today's promise reminds me so much of that time in my life. God would send the rains, we did have our grain and garden produce, we did have grass and hay for our cattle and horses and we did eat to our satisfaction. We may have been short of ready cash, but we always had plenty of food. We always thanked God for our food and His goodness before every meal. Our meals were accompanied by much laughter, reports on the day and story telling. If one of us was cranky or wanted to pick a fight we would be told to leave the table until we could return and be nice. Our treasures were our God, our family and our way of life. Jesus told us in the Sermon on the Mount in Matthew 6:19-21, "Do not store up for yourselves treasures on earth, where moth and rust destroy, and where thieves break in and steal. But store up for yourselves treasures in heaven, where moth and rust do not destroy, and where thieves do not break in and steal. For where your treasure is, there your heart will be also."

Obey God's commands, trust in His provision, and go out and make this a great day.

I don't know about tomorrow, I just live from day to day;
I don't borrow from its sunshine, for its skies may turn to gray.
I don't worry o'er the future, for I know what Jesus said;
And today I'll walk beside Him, for he knows what is ahead.

Ira F. Stanphill - 1914-

June 26

"Do not be afraid, little flock, FOR YOUR FATHER HAS BEEN PLEASED TO GIVE YOU THE KINGDOM." Luke 12:32

Today's promise follows the parable of the rich young fool whose crops were so large he decided to tear down his barns and build bigger to hold it all. He said to himself, "You have plenty of good things laid up for many years. Take life easy; eat, drink and be merry." But God said to him, "You fool! This very night your life will be demanded from you." Jesus followed that parable by telling the disciples, "Therefore I tell you, do not worry about your life, what you will eat; or about your body, what you will wear. Life is more than food, and the body more than clothes." Jesus went on to tell them how the raven is fed, the lilies grow, the grass is clothed and how temporary those things are. He cautioned the disciples to not set their hearts on what they would eat, drink or wear because their Father knows that they need those things. He concludes in verse 31 with, "But seek His kingdom, and these things will be given to you as well." Then Jesus gave today's promise to His disciples, His little flock, "Do not be afraid, for your Father has been pleased to give you the Kingdom." He was promising them eternal life.

Do we still worry in spite of the promise of Jesus? Of course we do. In spite of our faith we still are concerned about our earthly needs. When the children need shoes it is hard to have faith without the worry. I am reminded of the joke about the pastor who was preaching a sermon using Jesus' words about worry I cited above. The pastor was telling the congregation they should not worry, they should not fret, rather, they should place their faith in Jesus. He went on to say, "Studies have shown that when you worry 98% of what you worry about does not happen." From the rear of the sanctuary came a voice saying, "Worry works, don't it!"

We get a chuckle out of jokes like this, but don't we fall into the same pattern? Do you worry that you will have month left over when the money is gone? Do you worry about your job stability? Do you worry about the safety of your children? Do you worry about your safety when storms come? Do you worry about the school test coming up? Do you worry about the medical exam you have scheduled? Why? Worry is fear! Jesus said, "Do not be afraid!" He promised you that your Father has been pleased to give you the Kingdom! All the worries I cited in this paragraph, and all those I didn't cite and you have, are temporary. They will be gone tomorrow. You have the Kingdom to look forward to for all eternity!

Turn to God in prayer at all times of worry and concern on your part. He wants you to talk to Him about your needs, about your concerns, about your thoughts and about your life. He wants to provide you with the comfort and assurances you need. Does it always work perfectly? No! We live in the world which is the devil's playground. The devil will test you and tempt you. The devil will cause bad things to happen to you. Remember today's promise, however. Your future is in the hand of God! Trust it, and go out and make this a great day.

I don't know about tomorrow, it may bring me poverty;
But the One who feeds the sparrow, is the One who stands by me.
And the path that is my portion, may be through the flame or flood;
But His presence goes before me, and I'm covered with His blood.
Ira F. Stanphill -1914-

June 27

"For God, who said, 'Let light shine out of darkness,' MADE HIS LIGHT SHINE IN OUR HEARTS TO GIVE US THE LIGHT OF THE KNOWLEDGE OF THE GLORY OF GOD IN THE FACE OF CHRIST." 2 Corinthians 4:6

Isn't it interesting that God and goodness are associated with light and the devil and evil are associated with darkness? I am sure it is because evildoers like to hide in the darkness and want their evil hidden. It is harder to hide in light. Much of the evil done is done at night. I have heard parents justify curfews with the statement, "Nothing good happens out there after 11:00 P.M." I tend to agree. A few years ago I read an article which said a high percent of the vehicles you meet after 11:00 P.M. on Friday and Saturday nights are driven by people who have been drinking. We read in John 3:19, "This is the verdict: Light has come into the world, but men loved darkness instead of light because their deeds were evil." We also read in John 8:12, "When Jesus spoke again to the people, He said, 'I am the light of the world. Whoever follows me will never walk in darkness, but will have the light of life." John clearly sets light against darkness!

In Genesis 1:3 we read, "And God said, 'Let there be light,' and there was light." Clearly, God brought light into the world, but that was physical light whereby we would be able to see physical things. God brought spiritual light into the world when He gave us Jesus to die on the cross for our sins. 1 John 1:5 says, "This is the message we have heard from Him and declare to you: God is light; in Him there is no darkness at all. If we claim to have fellowship with Him yet walk in the darkness, we lie and do not live by the truth. But if we walk in the light, as He is in the light, we have fellowship with one another, and the blood of Jesus His Son, purifies us from all sin." What a beautiful thought for today!

Today's promise reminds us that God gave us physical light then it promises us that God "made His light (Jesus) shine in our hearts to give us the light of the knowledge of the glory of God in the face of Christ." Have you noted the faces of people before and after they have accepted the gift God gave by giving His Son, Jesus Christ, to die on the cross for our sins, asked for, and received the forgiveness of their sins and accepted Jesus Christ as their personal Savior? The difference is more dramatic than any other "before" and "after" pictures you will ever see! What you see before is the darkness of the world reflected from their soul. What you see afterwards is the light of the knowledge of the glory of God in the face of Christ reflected from their soul. Whatever the physical beauty of the face is completely outshone by the beauty that is now in their soul-the beauty of God's spiritual light, Jesus Christ!

Have you accepted Jesus Christ as your personal Savior? Are you walking in the light as He is in the light? Do you enjoy the fellowship of other Christians? If so, you understand the difference between light and darkness. If not, please accept Jesus now and walk in the true light. Then you can go out and make this a great day.

Out of my bondage, sorrow and night, Jesus, I come, Jesus, I come;
Into Thy freedom, gladness and light, Jesus, I come to Thee.
Out of my sickness into thy health, out of my need and into Thy wealth,
Out of my sin and into Thyself, Jesus, I come to Thee.

William T. Sleeper - 1819-1904

June 28

"THE FRUIT OF RIGHTEOUSNESS WILL BE PEACE; THE EFFECT OF RIGHTEOUSNESS WILL BE QUIETNESS AND CONFIDENCE FOREVER." Isaiah 32:17

My Bible dictionary defines "righteousness", It is used to denote the perfect obedience to the Son of God.. We read in Genesis 15:6, "Abram (Abraham) believed the Lord, and He credited it to him as righteousness." The fruit of the righteousness we have described is "peace". My dictionary defines "peace" (used in this sense) as: an undisturbed state of mind; absence of mental conflict; serenity; and as calm; quiet; tranquil. Now we can change the first phrase of today's promise to read, "The fruit of perfect obedience to the Son of God will be an undisturbed state of mind with no mental conflict, and with a feeling of calm, quiet, tranquil serenity." Doesn't that sound like something you would love to have during these busy days with so many competing demands?

But wait, there's more! The effect of obedience to the Son of God will be quietness and confidence forever! Isaiah also told us in 30:15, "This is what the Sovereign Lord, the Holy One of Israel, says: 'In repentance and rest is your salvation (righteousness), in quietness and trust (confidence) is your strength.'" The effect of righteousness is our strength! How can we gain strength? Exercise, exercise and exercise!

Read the Bible! Psalm 119:165 says, "Great peace have they who love your law, and nothing can make them stumble." **Live a life of moderation**! Romans 14:17 says, "For the kingdom of God is not a matter of eating and drinking, but of righteousness, peace and joy in the Holy Spirit." **Respond to the chastisement of God**! Hebrews 12:11 says, "No discipline seems pleasant at the time, but painful. Later on, however, it produces a harvest of righteousness and peace for those who have been trained by it."

I worked with a godly man who would come into the room and you could just feel his strength. He was always calm and quiet. When he spoke, he spoke with humility, yet with great authority. He had a confidence about him which was contagious. We always liked to see him in charge of a project as everything seemed to go more smoothly and a lot more was accomplished. I believe that is the way God wants all of us to be. We develop that peace and quiet confidence by becoming more righteous.

Paul told us in Ephesians 6:10-12, "Finally, be strong in the Lord and in His mighty power. Put on the full armor of God so that you can take your stand against the devil's schemes. Or our struggle is not against flesh and blood, but against the rulers, against the authorities, against the powers of this dark world and against the spiritual forces of evil in the heavenly realms." He told us to put on the belt of truth, breastplate of righteousness, gospel of peace on our feet, shield of faith, helmet of salvation and sword of the Spirit-the Word of God.

Live in peace and quiet confidence, and go out and make this a great day.

There comes to my heart one sweet strain, a glad and a joyous refrain;
I sing it again and again, sweet peace, the gift of God's love.
In Jesus for peace I abide, and as I keep close to His side,
There's nothing but peace doth betide, sweet peace, the gift of God's love.
Peter P. Bilhorn - 1865-1936

June 29

"I will lie down and sleep in peace, FOR YOU ALONE, O LORD, MAKE ME DWELL IN SAFETY." Psalm 4:8

On the day a ship was about to complete its journey across the ocean it ran into a furious storm as it approached land. The ship was driven about, the sails were shredded and the masts broken. Finally the wallowing ship sank and the only survivor was a young boy who was swept by the waves onto a rock. He clung to the rock all night battered by the wind, rain and waves. The storm subsided as the morning approached and the worried harbor master put out search parties in several ships. About mid-morning the young boy was spotted and rescued. After he was dried and given food and water he was questioned about his experience. "Did you tremble while you were on the rock during the night?" someone asked him. "Yes," replied the young boy. "I trembled all night - but the rock didn't." That story reminds me of David's questions in Psalm 18:31, "For who is God besides the Lord? And who is the Rock except our God?"

Like that young boy who found safety on the rock in the ocean after the ship wreck, we find safety on our Rock, Jesus Christ! However the winds, or storms, or waves, or tumult might batter us, we can "lie down and sleep in peace, for You alone, O Lord, make me dwell in safety!" Looking back at the reading of yesterday we see that the peace of our sleep is an undisturbed state of mind, an absence of mental conflict and serenity. We have nothing to fear when we are in the sheltering arms of our Lord. We recognize that we are on a journey through this world. When our sins are forgiven by the grace of our Lord, Jesus Christ, we are assured of safety in Him. We will never die! We have our home assured in heaven for eternal life.

Jesus came to bring us that peace. The angel appeared to the shepherds to tell them the news of the birth of Jesus, and we read in Luke 2:12-14, "Suddenly a great company of the heavenly host appeared with the angel, praising God and saying, 'Glory to God in the highest, and on earth peace to men on whom His favor rests.'" In John 14:27 Jesus said, "Peace I leave with you, my peace I give you. I do not give to you as the world gives. Do not let your hearts be troubled and do not be afraid." He did not promise us a trouble-free existence! Jesus told us in John 16:33, "I have told you these things so that in me you may have peace. In the world you will have trouble. But take heart! I have overcome the world."

Is your mind filled with worries? Are you concerned about how your life is going? Are you battered by wind, rain and waves of the storms of your every day life? When you go to bed is it hard to sleep because of the anxieties of life? Read what Paul wrote in Philippians 4:6-7, "Do not be anxious about anything, but in everything, by prayer and petition, with thanksgiving, present your requests to God. And the peace of God, which transcends all understanding, will guard your hearts and your minds in Christ Jesus." Remember, only the Lord makes you dwell in safety so you can lie down in peace. Claim it, and go out and make this a great day.

There's within my heart a melody-Jesus whispers sweet and low,
"Fear not, I am with thee-peace be still," in all of life's ebb and flow.
All my life was wrecked by sin and strife. Discord filled my heart with pain;
Jesus swept across the broken strings, stirred the slumb'ring chords again.
Luther B. Bridgers - 1884-1948

June 30

"THE LORD YOUR GOD IS WITH YOU, HE IS MIGHTY TO SAVE. HE WILL TAKE GREAT DELIGHT IN YOU, HE WILL QUIET YOU WITH HIS LOVE, HE WILL REJOICE OVER YOU WITH SINGING." Zephaniah 3:17

I will never forget November 5, 1963. That is when my daughter, Catharine Lynette, was born. While most babies are too red faced and wrinkled to be pretty, she was beautiful! I was absolutely delighted with her in every way (still am!) and had such a great love for her I sang all the way home from the hospital to get some sleep in what was left of the night. I went into my class of Freshman Chemistry students the next morning and proudly told them the news and was further delighted with the spontaneous applause that burst from the students. I couldn't wait to get back to the hospital to see her again and, finally, to get to bring her home. Wow, what a joy! Even when I would walk the floor gently bouncing her in my hands to soothe her colicky stomach I would gently sing, hum or talk to her until she fell into a deep, peaceful sleep. I held her close to comfort her when her little dog got out of the house and was killed in the street. We buried her together in a very special place. I rode my bicycle forty-two miles with her, helped her set up a shelter using her bicycle and helped her learn the rules of safety and maintenance of the bicycle so she could earn her scouting badge. I attended her games, watched her perform with the flag twirlers, heard her honor speech at high school graduation and attended her college graduation. How precious she is to me, how much I love her, and how delightful I find her!

I think about my feelings toward my daughter when I read today's promise. How much He must love us! The most precious verse in the Bible, John 3:16 says, "For God so loved the world that He gave His one and only Son, that whoever believes in Him shall not perish but have eternal life." Yes, God is with you. God loves you. God gave His Son to save you as He is mighty to save. He takes great delight in you. He will give you peaceful sleep in safety when you are His. He rejoices over you with singing. Read Luke 15:10, "In the same way, I tell you, there is rejoicing in the presence of the angels of God over one sinner who repents." Just think, any time someone asks forgiveness for their sins and gives their lives to God the angels throw a party in heaven! That is how much He delights in you! As much as we love our children we don't even come close to the love that God has for us.

Do you feel unloved and alone? That is the way the world leaves us. If we live for the world we must have what one of my least favorite commercials says, "Parties that never end." If we don't have continuous activity in the world we are alone and forgotten. We don't have the comfort of a constant companion, the Holy Spirit! Friends in the world may come and go, family members die, jobs change, we move to new residences, we get new neighbors and governmental officials change. God doesn't change! We are promised in Hebrews 13:8, Jesus Christ is the same yesterday and today and forever." Accept Him, and go out and make this a great day.

Sometimes our skies are cloudy and dreary, sometimes our hearts are burdened with care;
But we may know, whate'er may befall us, Jesus is always there.
When in the midst of life with its problems, bent with our toil and burdens we bear;
Wonderful thought and deep consolation; Jesus is always there.

Bertha Mae Lillenas - (No Date)

July 1

"AN ANGRY MAN STIRS UP DISSENSION, AND A HOT-TEMPERED ONE COMMITS MANY SINS." Proverbs 29:22

Just how strongly does God feel against anger? Read Jesus' words in Matthew 5:21-22, "You have heard that it was said to the people long ago, 'Do not murder, and anyone who murders will be subject to judgment.' But I tell you that anyone who is angry with his brother will be subject to judgment." We can read the divinely inspired words of Paul in Ephesians 4:26-27, "In your anger do not sin. Do not let the sun go down while you are still angry, and do not give the devil a foothold."

Now do you understand the full nature of anger? Jesus tells us if we are angry with our brother we will be subject to judgment and then tells us through Paul that when we get angry we are giving the devil a foothold as we are much more likely to sin when we are angry. Have you listened to people who do not know God when a situation arises which makes them angry? They have a tendency to use God's name in vain or to utter filthy communication, both of which are classed as sin in the Bible. Christians have a tendency to lose control of their actions and to do or say things that hurt the ones they love (and I can look into a mirror when I type these words). Paul told us to not let the sun go down while we are still angry. In other words, "Get over it!"

What are we supposed to do about our tendency to anger? Read the words in James 1:19-20, "My dear brothers, take note of this: Everyone should be quick to listen, slow to speak and slow to become angry, for man's anger does not bring about the righteous life that God desires." These words were written by the brother of Jesus who must have spent many years with Jesus as they were growing up and working in the carpentry shop. Can't you just visualize the possible scene and hear the words in the carpentry shop as Jesus and James were working and James' struck his hand with the tool with which he was working. James probably became angry with himself, shouted at himself, threw down the tool and hopped around the shop. Jesus must have calmly said something like, "Now James, I have told you how to do that correctly. You need to be quick to listen and slow to speak out that you know the best ways. You should be slow to become angry, for man's anger does not bring about a life God desires." I like to think that something like this may have taken place and James later wrote it in his epistle.

I know that today's promise is a negative one, however, I felt it must be included to allow me to address this fault which affects so many of us, if not all of us. If you get angry, you will stir up dissension. If you are hot-tempered, you will commit many sins. It is a fault I have to work on constantly. Do you have a tendency to get angry? Do you have verbal outbursts when you get angry? Are they words you are proud to have Jesus hear? Does your anger cause you to commit the sins of hatred, discord, jealousy, fits of rage or dissension as listed in Galatians 5:20? God can set you free! God wants you to control your anger, and go out and make this a great day.

Open my eyes that I may see glimpses of truth Thou hast for me;
Place in my hands the wonderful key that shall unclasp and set me free.
Open my ears that I may hear voices of truth Thou sendest clear;
And while th wave-notes fall on my ear, everything false will disappear.
Clara H. Scott - 1841-1897

July 2

"You will again obey the Lord and follow all His commands I am giving you today. THEN THE LORD YOUR GOD WILL MAKE YOU MOST PROSPEROUS IN ALL THE WORK OF YOUR HANDS AND IN THE FRUIT OF YOUR WOMB, THE YOUNG OF YOUR LIVESTOCK AND THE CROPS OF YOUR LAND. THE LORD WILL AGAIN DELIGHT IN YOU AND MAKE YOU PROSPEROUS, JUST AS HE DELIGHTED IN YOUR FATHERS." Deuteronomy 30:8 & 9

Today's promise comes from the covenant Moses made with the Children of Israel in the land of Moab after nearly forty years of their time in the wilderness. They had seen the plagues in Egypt, the parting of the Red Sea, the water coming from a rock, the manna on the ground each week-day morning, the death of those who rebelled and wanted to take over leadership, the promise that if snake-bitten they could look up to the bronze serpent Moses provided and they would be saved, the clothes and shoes they started with never wearing out, the cloud leading by day and the pillar of fire by night and many other happenings and wonders. They had fallen out of God's grace and they had sworn allegiance. They had learned that by trusting the ten frightened scouts instead of Joshua and Caleb they were forced to remain out of the promised land until all the adults who left Egypt were dead. Now they are nearing the end of the journey. They are receiving the last speech from Moses. Moses is warning them they must follow the commands of God, which He had given Moses.

Can you imagine signers of the Declaration of Independence making a very similar speech? Most of them were Christian men, and they would have believed, and, I think, been able to say the following: "If you will obey the Lord and follow all His commands then the Lord your God will make you most prosperous in all the work of your hands and in the fruit of your womb, the young of your livestock and the crops of your land. The Lord will again delight in you and make you prosperous, just as He delighted in your founding fathers." I feel the formation of the United States of America was divinely led and the hand of God was on those men and many more who felt the same way and gave the same support.

However, we as a nation have drifted away from obeying the Lord and following all His commands. We have allowed the correct concept of refusing to allow the establishment of a State Church to evolve to the incorrect concept of denying everything Christian any place in government. We have allowed a school system which started with the Bible as the primary book from which to learn reading, to now deny God, prayer, Bible reading and anything Christian from having any place in the classroom. As a result of this we see more single mother births, more drug and alcohol addiction and a decline in morals that reach into the corporate board rooms.

As Independence Day approaches let's obey the Lord, follow God's commands, claim today's promise, and our father's faith will allow us to go out and make this a great day.

God of our fathers, whose almighty hand leads forth in beauty all the starry band;
Of shining worlds in splendor thru the skies, our grateful songs before Thy throne arise.
Thy love divine hath led us in the past, in this free land by Thee our lot is cast;
Be Thou our ruler, guardian, guide and stay, Thy word our law, Thy paths our chosen way.

Daniel C. Roberts - 1841-1907

July 3

"The thief comes only to steal and kill and destroy; I HAVE COME THAT THEY MAY HAVE LIFE, AND HAVE IT TO THE FULL." John 10:10

During the twenty plus years I was an insurance agent I had a lot of experience with thefts of all types. I am thankful I never had a theft claim which involved any injury or deaths to my clients. I did have several thefts which resulted in considerable destruction to the property which the thieves did not take. It seemed if they could not carry it off they would destroy it so the true owner could not enjoy it themselves. What a waste that was! Most of the theft claims I had were for thefts which occurred at night. These occurred when the owner was away. The house was not guarded. We are told by Jesus in Matthew 24:43, "But understand this: If the owner of the house had known at what time of night the thief was coming, he would have kept watch and would not have let his house be broken into." What prophetic words! How little the work of a thief has changed in the last two thousand years.

We really feel devastated and violated when a thief enters our house to steal and destroy. We feel we must wash everything the thief might have touched. We sleep very lightly for the next several nights. We can't understand why the police can not catch the thief (I once read statistics which said thieves commits seventeen thefts before they are caught). I encouraged my clients to browse the pawn shops for several weeks after the theft to see if they could find any of the stolen items, thus providing leads for the police. Thieves are clever enough to take the most valuable items and that makes us feel bad because we have worked hard to accumulate those things.

Jesus knew we would understand His comments about thieves and their intentions and actions. That is why He used it to introduce today's promise. We certainly get the contrast in the actions and results of a thief and the promise; "I have come that they may have life, and have it to the full." This promise verse contains the worst and the best mental images we can have. We get the worst in the image of the thief coming in to violate us and our belongings. We get the best in the image of a full, happy, productive life which is followed by His gift of eternal life with Him.

Are you living your life to the fullest today? I love the statement, "Only one life, 'twill soon be past. Only what's done for Christ will last." When measured against eternity, our life here on earth is but a short time. We need to live with the attitude that our home is in heaven with Jesus and we are just on a journey through life. When we do this we find such great peace and fulfillment that we have a happier life than we otherwise would have had. Have you emptied your heart from your desires and filled it with God and His desires. I love the anonymous poem: "Is there any life so blessed as one lived for Christ alone, when the heart from self is emptied and instead becomes His throne?"

Accept the full measure of what God has planned for you. Then you can live your life for Jesus and live it to the fullest possible. Then go out and make this a great day.

Living for Jesus a life that is true, striving to please Him in all that I do,
Yielding allegiance, glad-hearted and free - this is the pathway of blessing for me.
Living for Jesus who died in my place, bearing on Calv'ry my sin and disgrace
Such love constrains me to answer His call, follow His leading and give Him my all.
Thomas O. Chisholm - 1866-1960

July 4

"Jesus replied, 'I tell you the truth, EVERYONE WHO SINS IS A SLAVE TO SIN. Now a slave has no permanent place in the family, but a son belongs to it forever. SO IF THE SON SETS YOU FREE, YOU WILL BE FREE INDEED.'" John 8:34-36

Happy Independence Day to all citizens of the United States of America! Whether you came to this country as a man, woman or child; to escape oppression or famine; as a free person, indentured servant or slave; as a hunter, trapper, farmer, tradesman or soldier you are now free! Do we have problems in this country? Yes! Do we have crime in this country? Yes! Do we have the poor in this country? Yes! Do we have malcontents in this country? Yes! Do we have sin in our country today? Yes! BUT, we also have found more solutions than the citizens of any other country. We have the best and most fair judicial system in this country than that of any other country. We put forth more effort and more resources to fight poverty than any other country. We treat malcontents better than they would be treated in any other country. This country was founded by godly men. Our laws are based on the principles of justice we find in the Bible. Many of our settlers came to be able to worship God in the manner they felt led to worship Him. We developed a family friendly setting for Christians.

No one in this country today came into it legally as an indentured servant or a slave to another person. Do we have slaves in the country today? Yes! That is the negative part of today's promise. Everyone who sins is a slave to sin! They are slaves who have no permanent place in the family of Christ. They are not free to become the very best they can be. What a shame it is they cannot enjoy the freedom we are promised today. If you have asked for forgiveness and had your sins washed clean by the blood Jesus shed for you on the cross then the Son has set you free and you are free indeed!

We read in Galatians 4:31, "Therefore, brothers, we are not children of the slave woman, but of the free woman." No, we are of the family of God, no longer bound by the chains of sin, nor bound by our negative, destructive habits, but enjoy a freedom others can't understand. We read in Galatians 5:1, "It is for freedom that Christ has set us free. Stand firm, then, and do not let yourselves be burdened again by a yoke of slavery." We also read in 2 Corinthians 3:17, "Now the Lord is the Spirit, and where the Spirit of the Lord is, there is freedom." Do you have that freedom today as you celebrate the freedom won for us almost two hundred and fifty years ago? Many have died to maintain the freedom we have in this country, including the freedom of worship. Many also have given their lives in work so that you have the access to a church to attend, a Bible in the translation which suits you best, study books to help you learn more about the scriptures, sermons you can understand and from which you can learn and music to aid you in worship. As you celebrate freedom today, include your thanks for those people as well.

Celebrate true freedom today, and go out and make this a great day.

Once like a bird in prison I dwelt, no freedom from my sorrow I felt;
But Jesus came and listened to me and glory to God, He set me free.
Goodby to sin and things that confound, naught of the world shall turn me around.
Daily I'm working, I'm praying too, and glory to God, I'm going through.
Albert E. Brumley - 1905-

July 5

"JESUS CHRIST IS THE SAME YESTERDAY AND TODAY AND FOREVER."
Hebrews 13:8

I have lived in Norman, OK, for thirty years. In 1988-1989 I was the Chairman of the Norman Chamber of Commerce. That year we celebrated the Centennial of Norman, which was formed in the Land Run of 1889 that opened the Unassigned Lands for settlement. We emphasized the change which had occurred in Norman over the one hundred years since it was nothing but open land. Now Norman is home to the University of Oklahoma, several government facilities, several manufacturing companies, many weather research and forecast companies, hundreds of retail outlets and restaurants and over 100,000 people. Several of our friends talk about living on a farm or a dairy where there are now housing developments or shopping centers. The change in Norman is great just within the thirty years I have lived here. I cannot even imagine the difference between open country and what it is now in slightly over one hundred years. I have seen many friends come and go in Norman over the thirty years.

When I think of the change in Norman I also think of the change in my family. When I was a young boy I knew my great-grandfather Cox. I knew all four of my grandparents. All my aunts and uncles were raising their children, my cousins. Now some of my cousins are great-grandparents. Relatives have died. Relatives have married and had children. Children have gone on to college and on to fill many different occupations and professions. It is sometimes difficult to keep track of all the changes taking place. I am reminded of what James A. Michener wrote that an old Indian chief said in the book, "Centennial", "Only the rocks live forever."

Changes in your life are sources of stress. Death of a loved one, moving to a different home, changing jobs, etc., are all high stress changes which take place frequently in our lives. To combat stress we are told to keep as much stability and routine as possible in our lives. Today's promise tells us of the greatest stability we can possibly have in our lives. What a wonderful reality to cling to. "Jesus Christ is the same yesterday and today and forever!" He doesn't change His Word, the Bible. He doesn't change His commands. He doesn't change His promises. He doesn't move away and leave you. He is as close to you in New York City, London, Seoul, Brisbane, or Santiago as He is in Norman, OK. His love never fails, never diminishes, never changes or never falters. His grace is sufficient today as it was two thousand years ago. His death on the cross was for the forgiveness of your sins as it was for your parents, grandparents, great-grandparents, great-great-grandparents, etc. He provides eternal life for all who confess their sins today as He did for those who confessed their sins at the time Paul was preaching.

Have you availed yourself of the greatest stress reliever of all time? Have you become the son or daughter of the only Father who will never change? When you are a child of God you need never again worry about change. Claim it, and go out and make this a great day.

Earthly friends may prove untrue, doubts and fears assail;
One still loves and cares for you, one who will not fail.
In life's dark and bitter hour love will still prevail.
Trust His everlasting pow'r - Jesus will not fail.

Arthur A. Luther - 1891-1960

July 6

"This is love: not that we loved God, BUT THAT HE LOVED US AND SENT HIS SON AS AN ATONING SACRIFICE FOR OUR SINS." 1 John 4:10

We all know about love, don't we? We first had the love of a child for their parent. Then we progressed to love for our extended family. Who among us has not had a "crush" on a classmate or a teacher? One of the largest sections of books in many bookstores is that devoted to "Romance" novels. Then, if we are lucky, we find that special "someone" we know that God has just for us. How should we love them? Husbands are told in Ephesians 5:25, "Husbands, love your wives, just as Christ loved the church and gave Himself up for her." The love of spouse is the strongest form of human love for each other. It is not, however, the strongest human love there is. The strongest love there is, I believe, is the love we have for God.

But look at today's promise. It implies that however strong our love for God, it does not come close to His love for us. When did He first love us? We read in Ephesians 1:4-6, "For He chose us in Him before the creation of the world to be holy and blameless in His sight. In love He predestined us to be adopted as His sons through Jesus Christ, in accordance with His pleasure and will - to the praise of His glorious grace, which He has freely given us in the One He loves." How much does He love us? Look at the promise, He loved us so much He sent His Son as an atoning sacrifice for our sins! It is one thing to give your life for another, but to send your son to die for another? That is love beyond description!

What should we do about God's love for us? Read Ephesians 5:8-10, "For you were once darkness, but now you are light in the Lord. Live as children of light (for the fruit of the light consists in all goodness, righteousness and truth) and find out what pleases the Lord." When we confess our sins, ask forgiveness for our sins and confess Him with our mouth we come out of the darkness into the light in the Lord. We are now instructed to live as children of light, that is, live in all goodness, righteousness and truth. Then we are given the big instruction to "find out what pleases the Lord." Paul didn't want us to just find out what He wanted. No, we are to find out AND DO IT!

Paul told us a little more in two other places. 1 Corinthians 10:31 says, "So whether you eat or drink or whatever you do, do it all for the glory of God." And Colossians 3:23-24 says, "Whatever you do, work at it with all your heart, as working for the Lord, not for men, since you know that you will receive an inheritance from the Lord as a reward. It is the lord Christ you are serving." So whether you are waiting tables, farming, teaching, running a corporation or are the president of the United States you should do it with all your heart, as working for the Lord and you should do it all for the glory of God.

Are you living a life to justify God's love? Are you working and living for God? If you are you will receive God's inheritance as a reward. Do it, and go out and make this a great day.

O Jesus, Lord and Savior, I give myself to Thee,
For Thou in Thine atonement didst give Thyself for me.
I own no other Master - my heart shall be Thy throne:
My life I give, henceforth to live, O Christ, for Thee alone.
Thomas O. Chisholm - 1866-1960

July 7

"FOR YOU DID NOT RECEIVE A SPIRIT THAT MAKES YOU A SLAVE AGAIN TO FEAR, BUT YOU RECEIVED THE SPIRIT OF SONSHIP. AND BY HIM WE CRY, 'ABBA, FATHER.'" Romans 8:15

Through all the research done on my family tree (to the mid-1500's in one case), no one, to my knowledge, has ever found an individual who was either a slave or an indentured servant. Therefore, I cannot even begin to imagine the fear which must have been in the minds and hearts of people who were slaves. Perhaps many slave owners treated their slaves with kindness; however, an untimely death, illness or financial reverses could always result in families of slaves being torn apart and sold individually because they were not free to establish the direction of their own lives and the lives of their families. What mental turmoil it must be to not be free, but to be at the mercy of the whims or circumstances of another human being. What a blight the practice of slavery is on the human race.

Look again at the July 4 devotion. If we sin, we are a slave to sin and have no permanent place in the family, but a son belongs to the family forever. Now today's promise tells us that those of us who have received Christ as our Savior did not receive a spirit that makes us a slave to fear. No, we have no reason to fear. Our future is assured. We will spend eternity with God in heaven. If we live, we live to serve Him. If we die, we go to live with Him. So we can say what Paul said, "For me to live is Christ, but to die is gain."

I like the KJV of 2 Timothy 1:7, "For God hath not given us the spirit of fear; but of power, and of love, and of a sound mind." That power comes from the presence of the Holy Spirit within us. The love is the love of our Father. The sound mind, or self-confidence, comes from following His leading. No, we did not receive a spirit of fear, we received the spirit of sonship. We are son of God, our Father. And by Him we cry "Abba, Father." My Bible dictionary says the title, abba, was not allowed to be used by the servants or slaves of the Hebrews when they addressed the head of the family. This fact gives much force to the term in today's promise. It further says the term implies a high degree of love, confidence and submission, as well as a most endeared and intimate connection and fellowship.

Are you a slave to fear today? Is it because there is some form of sin in your life? If so, you need to confess that sin and that fear to God. He will remove the spirit of fear. He will give you a spirit of power, and love, and self-confidence. Claim John 8:36, "So if the Son sets you free, you will be free indeed." You will be free because He has promised you eternal life with Him in heaven when you accept the gift of His Son. Claim also that you have received the spirit of sonship from God by the grace of His Son, Jesus Christ, through His death on the cross for you. Then thank God you can cry, Abba, Father!

Now go out and make this a great day.

I once was an outcast stranger on earth,
A sinner by choice and an alien by birth;
But I've been adopted; my name's written down-
An heir to a mansion, a robe, and a crown.

Harriett E. Buell - 1834-1910

July 8

"EVERY GOOD AND PERFECT GIFT IS FROM ABOVE, COMING DOWN FROM THE FATHER OF THE HEAVENLY LIGHTS, WHO DOES NOT CHANGE LIKE SHIFTING SHADOWS." James 1:17

When I read today's promise, I think of the story of the grandmother who sent a sweater to her grandson for his birthday. The sweater was a size 12 neck and the grandson had a size 14 neck. The boy's mother insisted that he put the sweater on and sit down and write his grandmother a "Thank you" letter. Dutifully, the boy put on the sweater, sat down with pen and paper and wrote, "Dear Grandmother, Thank you very much for the beautiful sweater. I am wearing it as I write this letter. I would write more, but I am all choked up."

How many times have you given, or received, a gift which was not quite right? Maybe it was the wrong size, the wrong color or shade of color, the wrong shape, the wrong brand, etc. These may not be perfect gifts, but they are good gifts. In Matthew 7:9-11 we read the words of Jesus, "Which of you, if his son asks for bread, will give him a stone? Or if he asks for a fish, will give him a snake? If you, then, though you are evil, know how to give good gifts to your children, how much more will your Father in heaven give good gifts to those who ask Him!" Jesus then followed, in verse 12, with what we have come to call "The Golden Rule". "So in everything, do to others what you would have them do to you, for this sums up the Law and the Prophets." ("The Law and the Prophets" is the Old Testament!)

The best, and most perfect, gift ever from God is His Son, Jesus Christ, who He gave to live on earth and then shed His blood as atonement for our sins. That gift was given to us so that whoever believes in Him shall not die, but have eternal life! What a precious gift that was! But reread today's promise. The gift of His Son was given us by the Father of the heavenly lights. He does not change like the shifting shadows! Shadows change constantly. They get shorter as the morning progresses and longer as the afternoon progresses. They are different in July than they are in December. They look different in sunlight than they do in moonlight or in artificial light. But the Father of the heavenly lights does not change! He gave us the perfect gift of His Son, Jesus Christ, and He continues to give us good and perfect gifts today.

I had a friend, who is not a Christian, tell me he didn't think there were miracles today. I told him he was wrong. I consider the vaccination for polio to be a miracle. I consider the advancement of knowledge leading to organ transplants to be a miracle. I have heard of several cases of people known to me who have had masses disappear before surgery, and I consider those disappearances to be miracles. What is a miracle? A gift from God!

Have you accepted the good and perfect gifts which come from God? Have you given your life to God? Do you think the gift of His Son to be just too good for you? If you have accepted His gift are you telling to others about it? Do so, and go out and make this a great day.

For God so loved the world He gave His only Son to die on Calvary's tree,
From sin to set me free.
Some day He's coming back. What glory that will be!
Wonderful His love to me.

Francis Townsend - 1906-

July 9

"TRUTHFUL LIPS ENDURE FOREVER, BUT A LYING TONGUE LASTS ONLY A MOMENT." Proverbs 12:19

Do you tell great big, nasty, far-reaching lies? What about mean-spirited, degrading lies? What about how big the fish you caught was? Or maybe how good an athlete you were in your playing days? I remember a visit I had to my sister and her husband, with whom I had played on the high school football team. We were talking about the games we had played and the particular plays we had made. He looked at me during a pause in the conversation and said, "Clarence, did you ever notice how much better we played now than then?" Many of us would never tell the big lies or cheat on the big matters, however, I don't see anything in today's promise which puts a limit on the size or importance of the lies. Make sure your words will stand the light of His Spirit.

If we tell the truth will we live forever? Of course not! What does it mean then that truthful lips endure forever? Honesty, and the reputation for honesty, will far outlive the person and will provide an example for generations to come. How many have read of the Abraham Lincoln's love for books in his younger years? He once said, "The things I want to know are in books; my best friend is the man who'll git me a book I ain't read." His family lived in a one room cabin and one day rain soaked Weems' "Life of Washington" that Josiah Crawford had loaned him. Abe did not lie. He confessed he had been careless with the book, and picked corn for three days to pay for it, leaving not an ear on a corn-stalk in the field. His honesty is legendary to the point he is affectionately known as "Honest" Abe.

I remember visiting a friend one day while he was reminiscing about a long dead acquaintance. He summed up his feeling about the man with the statement, "He was an honest man." One day during a National Guard Training Session we were talking about an officer who had already replied. One of the officers in the group said, "What I remember about him is if he said something you could count on it." I think these three men are examples of the truth of the first part of today's promise.

When I was young we had a friend who could really say things so you could just see them. He was talking about a local man with a reputation for dishonesty. He said, "Well if he said it was raining I wouldn't believe it unless I saw the dogs running for the porch." Of another man with a similar reputation he said, "I think he would lie for a nickel if he could get a dime for the truth." . In the corporate world today we see the results of lying on corporate financial statements. We see corporations going into bankruptcy, executives fired and charged with criminal activity, share prices plummeting resulting in great losses to retirement accounts and entire segments of industry getting bad reputations which will hurt honest efforts for years to come. Do you enjoy being around people with a lying tongue? Do you count on what they say? Make sure you don't have lying lips, but be honest, trust Jesus in all things, and go out and make this a great day.

Brightly doth His Spirit shine into this poor heart of mine;
While He leads I need not fall, trusting Jesus - that is all.
Singing if my way is clear, praying if the path be drear;
If in danger, for Him call, trusting Jesus - that is all.
Edgar Page Stites -1836-1921

July 10

"All this I have spoken while still with you. BUT THE COUNSELOR, THE HOLY SPIRIT, WHOM THE FATHER WILL SEND IN MY NAME, WILL TEACH YOU ALL THINGS AND WILL REMIND YOU OF EVERYTHING I HAVE SAID TO YOU." John 14:25 & 26

When I am reading the Gospels I often wonder what it would have been like to have lived at that time, to have known Jesus, to have walked with Him and to have heard Him speak. When I start to reminisce about such things His Spirit moves within me to remind me I don't have to have lived then. My own feelings are then lifted based on today's promise. We not only have the words of Jesus which are recorded in the Gospels, but we have the Counselor, the Holy Spirit, whom God the Father sent in the name of Jesus, to teach us all things and remind us of everything Jesus said. John quoted Jesus again in 16:12-15, "I have much more to say to you, more than you can now bear. But when He, the Spirit of Truth, comes, He will guide you into all truth. He will not speak on His own; He will speak only what He hears, and He will tell you what is yet to come. He will bring glory to me by taking from what is mine and making it known to you. All that belongs to the Father is mine. That is why I said the Spirit will take from what is mine and make it known to you."

If we did not have the Bible and our Christian heritage and Jesus were to come to the earth today would we listen to Him? Would we respect, believe and practice the things He taught us? Or would we be like the Pharisees and think that because He was a carpenter's son and uneducated and we knew and followed the laws we were right and He was wrong? Thank God we do have the Bible with the Gospels based on His words and we have two millenniums of Christian study and heritage. But that is not all we have. No, we also have the Counselor, the Holy Spirit! Paul told us in Ephesians 2:18, "For through Him (Jesus) we both have access to the Father by one Spirit." Paul also told us in 1 Corinthians 3:16; "Don't you know that you yourselves are God's temple and that God's Spirit lives in you?"

Like Abraham, Moses and many other Old Testament patriarchs we can talk directly to God the Father through the Holy Spirit He sent in the name of Jesus Christ. We hear God through the gentle nudging of the Holy Spirit. In the Introduction to this book I told you of my conversations with God. Those conversations were very real to me though there were no verbal words spoken.

John 4:24 says, "God is spirit, and His worshipers must worship in spirit and in truth." We read in Ephesians 6:18, "And pray in the Spirit on all occasions with all kinds of prayers and requests." Galatians 5:22-23 tells us the results, "But the fruit of the Spirit is love, joy, peace, patience, kindness, goodness, faithfulness, gentleness and self-control. Against such things there is no law." Claim the promise of the Holy Spirit, and go out and make this a great day.

He is with me ev'rywhere, and He knows my ev'ry care, I'm as happy as a bird and just as free;
For the Spirit has control, Jesus satisfies my soul, since the Comforter abides with me.
He abides, He abides, Hallelujah, He abides with me!
I'm rejoicing night and day, as I walk the narrow way, for the Comforter abides with me.

Herbert Buffman - (No Date)

July 11

"SURELY GOD IS MY SALVATION; I WILL TRUST AND NOT BE AFRAID. THE LORD, THE LORD, IS MY STRENGTH AND MY SONG; HE HAS BECOME MY SALVATION." Isaiah 12:2

I am not what anyone would call a great singer. In fact I would not be called a good singer. If I follow the promise of yesterday to be totally honest I would have to tell you that I am a very bad singer. As a result I would seldom sing during church service. At the start of our Rotary Club meetings we have prayer, salute the flag and then sing a song. One day I was at the table with the Salvation Army Commander and when the song was announced I commented, "John, even the Lord doesn't consider my singing to be a joyful noise." When the song was over John said, "I heard on American Family Radio just a few days ago a story about a similar comment to yours. He said when you sing you, and others may think it sounds like this: There followed the sound of numerous rusty car doors all being opened at the same time. He continued by saying, but when you sing here is what it sounds like to God: There followed George Beverly Shea singing "How Great Thou Art." Now during church service I will either sing as best I can or just stand there and let the music wash over me in worship of God. My singing might still be described more by Psalm 47:1, "Clap your hands, all you nations; shout to God with cries of joy."

T. C. Horton has written a book, "The Wonderful Names of Our Wonderful Lord." This is a book which contains 365 names for the Trinity taken from the Bible. Number 63 is from today's promise and he writes, "My Strength and my Song! We know Jehovah is our "strength" but do we make Him also our "song"? As we make Him so and sing of Him, we lose our fear. We are able to "trust and not be afraid," only as we sing of Him. Our Redeemer is our strength. Make Him your SONG today." When we sing to God we do so in worship, praise and joy.

We read in Psalm 92:4, "For you make me glad by your deeds, O Lord; I sing for joy at the works of your hands." In Psalm 98:8-9 we read, "Let the rivers clap their hands, let the mountains sing together for joy; let them sing before the Lord, for He comes to judge the earth." The Psalmist says even the rivers and mountains clap and sing to God! What a wonderful God we serve! In our church we clap a lot for joy at the songs we sing, and some follow Psalm 63:4, "I will praise you as long as I live, and in your name I will lift up my hands." Some worship Him in a more sedate way during the songs. I once heard a man say, "I had such joy in my heart during that song I found it difficult to keep my hands at my sides." Well maybe he shouldn't have.

The Lord is our strength, our song and our salvation. We should trust Him completely and not be afraid. His promises are true. His mercy is great. Whatever He gives us to do we find His yoke is easy and His burden is light because of the joy we experience when we give ourselves totally to Him. Have you done that yet? Are you struggling with fear? Have you availed yourself of His promise of eternal life? Trust God, don't be afraid, and go out and make this a great day.

Thou art giving and forgiving, ever blessing, ever blest;
Well-spring of the joy of living, ocean-depth of happy rest!
Thou the Father, Christ our Brother - all who live in love are Thine:
Teach us how to love each other; lift us to the joy divine."

Henry van Dyke - 1852-1933

July 12

> "Or suppose a woman has ten silver coins and loses one. Does she not light a lamp, sweep the house and search carefully until she finds it? And when she finds it, she calls her friends and neighbors together and says, 'Rejoice with me; I have found my lost coin.' I TELL YOU, THERE IS REJOICING IN THE PRESENCE OF THE ANGELS OF GOD OVER ONE SINNER WHO REPENTS." Luke 15:8-10

Have you ever lost money you really needed? I remember a time just after we started our insurance agency and money was really scarce for us. We had met my wife's parents in Lawton, OK, for lunch one day after we had not seen them for several weeks. They had gone to Lawton for a doctor appointment and knew how busy we were so thought that would be convenient to meet about half way between our homes. Just before they drove off after lunch Jan's father gave her an envelope. We went to our car, I opened her door, she got in and immediately opened the envelope. She withdrew two twenty dollar bills and showed me the gift. Just then the strong Oklahoma wind pulled one twenty out of her hand and sent it sailing across the street. We searched the area for over an hour and never found the money. We had several places we could sure have used it. Today's promise reading does not tell us for what purpose the woman needed the money (perhaps it was to buy a plot of land or some goats to provide food), but from the context I would assume it was for something very important to her. She lit the lamp to provide more light and to catch the gleam of the silver coin. She got her broom and swept under each piece of furniture to see if it had rolled there. She got down on hands and knees to look in each corner and then went through each pocket of her clothes. Finally she finds the coin that is so important to her and she carries it as she runs into the street to call to her neighbors, "Rejoice with me; I have found my lost coin." I am sure the neighbors did come into the street and shout and sing with her because they knew how important it was to her. There was a great spontaneous celebration on her street with friends shouting and hugging her and congratulating her.

The lost coin in this parable by Jesus is the symbol of a person lost without the forgiveness which is freely given by the grace of God through the death of Jesus on the cross. No look at how Jesus completes the parable, "I tell you there is rejoicing in the presence of the angels of God over one sinner who repents." Wow, a party in heaven when one sinner repents! What does that tell us about the mission of each and every Christian on earth? Read Proverbs 11:30, "The fruit of the righteous is a tree of life, and he who wins souls is wise." Where are we to do this? Read the words of Jesus recorded by Luke in Acts 1:8, "But you will receive power when the Holy Spirit comes on you; and you will be my witnesses in Jerusalem (*your local community*), and in all Judea (*your state*), and Samaria (*neighboring states*), and to the ends of the earth (*everywhere else in the world*)."

Work to win souls for God, and go out and make this a great day.

> Seeking the lost, and pointing to Jesus souls that are weak and hearts that are sore;
> Leading them forth in ways of salvation. Showing the path to life evermore.
> Thus I would go on missions of mercy, following Christ from day unto day.
> Cheering the faint and raising the fallen, pointing the lost to Jesus, the way.
>
> William A. Ogden - 1841-1897

July 13

> "Day after day every priest stands and performs his religious duties; again and again he offers the same sacrifices, which can never take away sins. But when This Priest had offered for all time one sacrifice for sins, He sat down at the right hand of God. Since that time He waits for His enemies to be made His footstool, BECAUSE BY ONE SACRIFICE HE HAS MADE PERFECT FOREVER THOSE WHO ARE BEING MADE HOLY." Hebrews 10:11-14

After I was commissioned as a 2LT I was given about every job a young officer is usually expected to do. In March our unit went to the rifle range and I was assigned as range officer. Saturday morning was chilly and misty as we arrived at the range very early, set up the targets, gave the orientation and safety lecture, made sure we had experienced coaches and started firing the first order. As I stood on the range tower giving the necessary orders for a smooth operation of the firing I grew colder, wetter and more miserable. It didn't improve much as we completed the first order and started the second order. Near the end of the second order I saw a military staff car drive into the parking area and four officers got out and approached the firing line. I had a non-commissioned officer assistant who greeted them and gave a report on our progress. When the order was completed I climbed down from the range tower and approached the group. I immediately saw the leader of the group was a Chaplain. I saluted and greeted each in the party. I asked the Chaplain what I could do for him and he said, "I would like to conduct church services." I replied, "Chaplain, today is Saturday." "LT Warner," he responded, "in the Army, any day the Chaplain shows up is Sunday." Some of my men had built a pile of brush and logs to warm us at noon so we lit the fire, gathered all the men around the crackling flames and the Chaplain gave a message. I don't remember what he said, but I sure remember the rest of the day was a lot more warm and cheery because of the wonderful words of encouragement he brought. That wonderful Chaplain was going about his duties day after day bringing the Word of God to the soldiers in his organization. He sacrificed himself to do the duty to which God had called him.

While that Chaplain could show the way to salvation, he could not, on his own, take away our sins. There was a High Priest, however, who could, and did. That High Priest is Jesus Christ who offered for all time one sacrifice for sins - His death on the cross - that we might be forgiven. After His resurrection and ascension He sits at the right hand of God. While that Chaplain could show us the way, Jesus WAS the way as stated in John 14:6, "Jesus answered, 'I am the way and the truth and the life. No one comes to the Father except through me.'" In the Sermon on the Mount, Jesus was telling His listeners to love their enemies. He closed that portion in Matthew 5:48, "Be perfect, therefore, as your heavenly Father is perfect." How can we be perfect in God's eyes? By accepting the grace and forgiveness of His sacrifice, "because by one sacrifice He has made perfect forever those who are being made holy."

Accept Jesus' sacrifice, and go out and make this a great day.

> And when before the throne I stand in Him complete,
> "Jesus died my soul to save," my lips shall still repeat.
> Jesus paid it all, all to Him I owe;
> Sin had left a crimson stain - He washed it white as snow.
>
> Elvina M. Hall - 1820-1889

July 14

"Do you not know? Have you not heard? THE LORD IS THE EVERLASTING GOD, THE CREATOR OF THE ENDS OF THE EARTH. HE WILL NOT GROW TIRED OR WEARY, AND HIS UNDERSTANDING NO ONE CAN FATHOM." Isaiah 40:28

In 1956 I graduated from high school and had a job on a custom combining crew which started near Vernon, TX, cutting wheat in one of the smaller fields (1,500 acres) on the Waggoner Estate. When we left there we went to McPherson, KS and started cutting on a very hot June day in a forty acre field which was one-half mile North and South and one-eighth mile East and West. It had been windy all that year and dust had blown into the heads of wheat. The wind was from the South and all the dust and chaff was blown right over me as I cut toward the North. It seemed like I would never finish that field. The farmer was most anxious to get it cut as it was giving a very good yield. After cutting all day and into the night we finished the field. The farmer's wife had fixed a large evening meal for my boss and me, but I said I could not come into the house because I was so dirty and tired. The farmer had me take off my clothes and shake them out. He poured water over me as I bathed. Then I put on my clothes and went to the table to eat. By that time I was so tired and weary I could barely hold my fork and scarcely tasted my food. They tried to make conversation, but I had a hard time understanding them and the best I could do was to mumble. When I got into bed I felt like I had cut all the wheat on earth.

I am sure you have been very tired and weary at some point in your life. It seems that those who do not know the Lord are carrying such a load of guilt and pain that they become tired and weary just going about their normal days. Jesus recognized what a burden sin is to us when He said in Matthew 11:28-30, "Come to me, all you who are weary and burdened, and I will give you rest. Take my yoke upon you and learn from me, for I am gentle and humble in heart, and you will find rest for your soul. For my yoke is easy and my burden is light." Did you not know this? Had you not heard it? He is the everlasting God. He created the earth and the universe. He does not grow tired and weary. He understands us in a manner which no one can fathom. That is today's promise. What a God! What a Savior! How wonderful it is to know that, however tired and weary we might be, we can call on Him in prayer and He will hear us forever.

Listen to what David said in Psalm 62:1 & 5, "My soul finds rest in God alone; my salvation comes from Him." "Find rest, O my soul, in God alone; my hope comes from Him." Are you sick in your soul today? Are you weary of the life you are leading? Don't you know? Follow David's example and let your soul find rest in God because all your hope will come from Him. You can also take hope in what God said to Joshua in Joshua 1:5, "No one will be able to stand up against you all the days of your life. As I was with Moses, so I will be with you; I will never leave you nor forsake you." Claim that promise as being made to you, because it was, and then go out and make this a great day.

Precious Lord, take my hand, lead me on, help me stand;
I am tired, I am weak, I am worn;
Thru the storm, thru the night, lead me on to the light,
Take my hand, precious Lord, lead me home.

Thomas A. Dorsey - 1899-1993

July 15

"FOR THE LORD LOVES THE JUST AND WILL NOT FORSAKE HIS FAITHFUL ONES. THEY WILL BE PROTECTED FOREVER, BUT THE OFFSPRING OF THE WICKED WILL BE CUT OFF." Psalm 37:28

I recently heard a report of a case which started several years ago in the Houston, TX, area. The report started with a 911 call from a boy telling the operator his parents were angry and he was afraid they would beat him. He put the receiver down without disconnecting the call and you could hear the shouts of the parents, the sound of the blows striking and the screams of the young boy. By the time the policemen could get to the residence the operator had counted over sixty-five blows heard. The policemen found four other children living in filth and squalor showing signs of abuse and neglect. The parents were sentenced to several years in prison and the five children were put in different foster homes. The report continued that the mother had been released from prison, appealed to a judge in Houston and been awarded custody of all the children. From what I learned through that report it seems to me that judge was not just in his decision and was not faithful to his charge and his oath. He did not provide the protection to the helpless children. In this case it appears the wicked should have been cut off from their offspring.

What a wonderful contrast David gives us in today's promise. Our Lord is a righteous Judge and He loves the just. He will not forsake those of us who are faithful to Him. We will be protected forever. We don't have to worry about someone getting out of prison and coming back to put us in bondage and start the abuse and neglect again. God has promised us that, though we are born in sin, when we confess our sins to Him, He will forgive us our sins and we will be cut off from the wicked. In Him, we have eternal life.

Are you feeling abused and neglected by the world? Do you grow weary and faint chasing after that elusive "something" which will give you peace? Look at yesterday's reading. Don't you know? Haven't you heard? It is your total surrender of your life to God which will give you peace of mind and heart. You were made to love and worship God. You were designed to have fellowship with other believers and help them when they need your help. When you do come to Christ it is your duty to bring others to Him. I recommend you read "The Purpose Driven Life" by Rick Warren. That book is one of the very best I have read to help you in your search. I not only encourage you to read it, but to absorb it and put its principles into practice. It will help you to find the purpose for which our just Lord has placed you here. When you are faithful to Him, you will find that He will not forsake you. You will be granted eternal life by Him.

You will no longer worry about your future. You will not be described by Nazi death camp survivor, Viktor E. Frankl, when he wrote, "The prisoner who had lost faith in the future-his future-was doomed." You will be described by Jesus' words in John 10:10, "I have come that they may have life, and have it to the full." Now go out and make this a great day.

My soul, in sad exile, was out on life's sea. So burdened with sin and distressed,
'Til I heard a sweet voice saying, "Make me your choice," and I entered the haven of rest.
I yielded myself to His tender embrace, and, faith taking hold of the Word.
My fetters fell off, and I anchored my soul, the haven of rest is my Lord.

Henry L. Gilmour - 1826-1920

July 16

> "Let us hold unswervingly to the hope we profess, FOR HE WHO PROMISED IS FAITHFUL." Hebrews 10:23

We hear the word "faithful" a lot today. We are told that an item is a "faithful copy" when it is a true likeness of the original. "They are sure faithful in attendance", means you can count on them being there. If you say "she is a faithful student" you mean she studies hard, learns well, pays attention in class, responds with the correct answer to the teacher's questions and produces a quality piece of work in response to each assignment. A "faithful husband" is loyal to his wife, provides for his wife and family and is at her side when his wife needs him.

Think about "He who promised." Paul was talking about Jesus. He is a true copy of God the Father. You can always count on Him being there. He pays close attention to us, knows all about us, listens to our prayers and intercedes for us with God the Father, always provides us with the correct answers to our questions with the leading of the Holy Spirit and produces a wonderful purpose-driven life leading to eternal life for those who follow Him. He is loyal to us in every way, provides all our needs and is always by our side when we need Him. HE IS FAITHFUL!

In Lamentations 3:22-23 Jeremiah wrote, "Because of the Lord's great love we are not consumed, for His compassions never fail. They are new every morning; great is Your faithfulness." Jeremiah would agree that like those faithful in attendance, God is always there with His great love and compassion. He gives us a new day every morning. He forgives us of our sins of the previous day and provides us strength for the day. Paul said in 1 Timothy 1:12, "I thank Christ Jesus our Lord, who has given me strength, that He considered me faithful, appointing me to His service." Paul held unswervingly to the hope he professed and always found Jesus to be faithful and considered Paul to be faithful. Paul would have agreed with David in Psalm 18:25, "To the faithful you show yourself faithful, to the blameless you show yourself blameless."

We read in Psalm 146:5-6, "Blessed is he whose help is the God of Jacob, whose hope is in the Lord his God, the Maker of heaven and earth, the sea, and everything in them - the Lord, who remains faithful forever." The Psalmist was blessing those who held unswervingly to the hope they professed and assured them their Lord was faithful. David was very specific in Psalm 25:10 when he wrote, "All the ways of the Lord are loving and faithful for those who keep the demands of His covenant."

How has your week been going? Are you finding the Lord faithful? Are you holding unswervingly to the hope you profess? Are you taking time to read and study His Word? Do you remain faithful in your prayer, meditation and quiet time? Are you really listening for the Lord's guidance?

Claim today's promise of His faithfulness, and go out and make this a great day.

> Great is Thy faithfulness, O God my Father! There is no shadow of turning with Thee;
> Thou changest not; Thy compassions, they fail not: as thou hast been Thou forever wilt be.
> Great is Thy faithfulness! Great is Thy faithfulness! Morning by morning new mercies I see;
> All I have needed Thy hand hath provided - great is Thy faithfulness, Lord, unto me.
>
> Thomas O. Chisholm - 1866-1960

July 17

"So do not worry, saying, 'What shall we eat?' Or 'What shall we drink?' or 'What shall we wear?' For the pagans run after all these things, and YOUR HEAVENLY FATHER KNOWS THAT YOU NEED THEM." Matthew 6:31 & 32

I will quickly admit that I have never had to worry about what I would eat as I grew up on a farm and we always had a sufficient quantity of good food. Only once did I have to worry about what to drink as I forgot to take a bottle of water to the field on a hot afternoon when I was working about one and one-half miles from the house. Boy, did I ever get thirsty before I finished that field in late afternoon! Momma always seemed to be able to buy, find, make or mend clothes for me. In fact, when I was growing up a frequent problem was too much to eat. I remember one time a neighbor who was starting to age and had reduced his farm size asked Dad to cut his wheat. We had finished cutting our own and the other jobs we had arranged for and still had some time we could cut. It took two people to run our machine as it was a tractor-pulled machine and one person had to ride on the combine to raise and lower the platform. We drove into our neighbor's field early in the morning as it was a dry day and we could start cutting. The wheat was good and the field was the size to take just over a day cutting. We worked all morning and then went into the house for dinner (as we called our noon meal). The neighbor's wife had prepared food for harvest crews before, but they were large crews. She had fried chicken, ham, roast beef, six different vegetables, salads, breads and relish. When I would clean my plate she would urge more food on me. I thought I would burst! Then she brought out strawberry shortcake with ice cream! When we got back to the field Dad was laughing at me as I hurt to move. We started work and worked steadily until 3:30 P.M. when I was just starting to feel a little bit better. We stopped to unload the combine tank and she was there with sandwiches and lemonade for a "snack". As I was eating my first sandwich Dad took pity on me and told her we would just wrap the others up to eat as we worked so we could get back to cutting. I have never been that full of food again in my entire life.

No, I find it hard to relate to those who grew up with the worry of what to eat, drink or wear. What I do understand is the commands of Jesus to feed the hungry, give water to the thirsty and clothe the naked. That is my responsibility as a child of God! I do that to the limit of my resources on a continuous basis. Isn't that one of the ways our Heavenly Father provides the needs of His children?

God knows we need food, water and clothing and He has promised to provide them. Jesus follows today's promise with this: "But seek first His kingdom and His righteousness, and all these things will be given to you as well." This is not an idle promise as is witnessed to by many people I have known over the years. Do you worry first about the needs of this world or do you first seek Him? Center yourself in God's will, and then go out and make this a great day.

Seek ye first the kingdom of God and His righteousness,
And all these things shall be added unto you. Allelu, alleluia.
Man shall not live by bread alone, but by every word
That proceeds from the mouth of God. Allelu, alleluia.

Karen Lafferty - 1948-

July 18

"Blessed are the pure in heart, FOR THEY WILL SEE GOD." Matthew 5:8

In our world today purity is given high priority. Many years ago Ivory came out with a bath soap that was advertised, "99.9% Pure!". We like to drink pure water. We look for electronic equipment which will give us pure sound. We want a pure picture on our television set. I remember one young man coming into my office to insure his new car and he told me, "I really love that car. It is pure power." How do we make things pure? We cleanse them. We extract impurities by dissolving them in water and washing them away. We may use a solvent other than water to wash impurities out of a substance. We cleanse sound or a TV picture by use of a filter to take out the unwanted background noise or images.

So how do we cleanse a heart to make it pure? It must be washed in the blood of Jesus Christ! Paul tells us in Hebrews 9:22, "In fact, the law requires that nearly everything be cleansed with blood, and without the shedding of blood there is no forgiveness." The law from the time of Moses required that every sacred object be purified with sacrificial blood taken from an animal without blemish. 1 Peter 1:18-19 says, "For you know that it was not with perishable things such as silver or gold that you were redeemed from the empty way of life handed down to you from your forefathers, but with the precious blood of Christ, a lamb without blemish or defect." Since Jesus was without sin He was perfect in every way and was correctly described by Peter as being a "lamb without blemish or defect." We then read in 1 John 1:7, "But if we walk in the light, as He is in the light, we have fellowship with one another, and the blood of Jesus, His Son, purifies us from all sin." Therefore, the blood of Jesus, a lamb without blemish or defect, purifies our heart from all sin.

Proverbs 4:23 says, "Above all else, guard your heart, for it is the wellspring of life." In Biblical language the heart is the center of the human spirit. It is the center of one's being, even including the mind. From your heart springs your will, emotions, thought, motivations, courage and action. If we store up good things in our hearts, our words and actions will be good. Psalm 119:11 says, "I have hidden your word in my heart; that I might not sin against you." Jesus said in Mark 7:20-23, "What comes out of a man is what makes him 'unclean.' For from within, out of men's hearts, come evil thoughts, sexual immorality, theft, murder, adultery, greed, malice, deceit, lewdness envy, slander, arrogance and folly. All these evils come from inside and make a man 'unclean.'" These are the very things we need the blood of Jesus to cleanse from our hearts to make our hearts pure.

How about your heart today? Can you claim today's promise? Have you had the impurities mentioned above cleansed from your heart by the blood of the "lamb without blemish or defect?" Are you certain that you will see God? If your heart is pure you WILL see God!

Purify your heart, claim today's promise, and go out and make this a great day.

Nothing can for sin atone - nothing but the blood of Jesus;
Naught of good that I have done - nothing but the blood of Jesus.
Oh! Precious is the flow that makes me white as snow;
No other fount I know, nothing but the blood of Jesus.

Robert Lowry - 1826-1899

July 19

"AND I WILL PUT MY SPIRIT IN YOU AND MOVE YOU TO FOLLOW MY DECREES AND BE CAREFUL TO KEEP MY LAWS." Ezekiel 36:27

Have you ever worked with a person who had such a personality and aura of leadership about them that just made you want to do exactly what they said in the precise way they had explained to do it? I did. In 1976 when Ronald Reagan ran for the Republican nomination for president I worked for him. I had been the Oklahoma Republican State Chairman from 1969 to 1975 and had met Ronald Reagan when he came into Oklahoma City for a state-wide fund raising dinner in February 1974. I started working for him after I left the office of state chairman. He was such a powerful personality that it just made you want to do everything the campaign leadership asked of you and to do it in just the way they asked for it to be done. I was a Regional Coordinator for the Reagan campaign and was responsible for the campaign in Texas, Oklahoma, Colorado, South Dakota and North Dakota. When we won all one hundred delegates in the Texas Primary election and then took all thirty-six delegates in the Oklahoma Republican convention the following week-end the spirit of the campaign really changed. The campaign was energized in a very special way. Many young people had come into Texas to work in the campaign and the spirit was running very high. Those same young workers left Texas to spread to other parts of the country to campaign in the same effective way we had campaigned in Texas, and it made the nomination race so close it was not really decided until the vote was taken on the floor of the convention in Kansas City in August 1976.

Ezekiel 36:26 says, "I will give you a new heart and put a new spirit in you; I will remove from you your heart of stone and give you a heart of flesh." Our promise yesterday was that those who are pure in heart would see God. Today's promise tells us that when we become Christians and our hearts are washed pure by the blood of Jesus Christ we receive the Holy Spirit in our hearts. His Holy Spirit moves us to follow His decrees and makes us careful to keep all His laws. As much as I admired and respected Ronald Reagan and wanted to work for him in the most effective manner possible, it is as nothing in comparison to the way I feel about Jesus Christ!

I feel like David wrote in Psalm 40:8, "I desire to do your will, O my God; your law is within my heart." How do we know the decrees and laws of God? We must study and memorize the Bible each and every day of our lives. That is the only way we can say like David, "your law is within my heart." You ask, "Do we need to read, study and memorize every day?" I ask you in return, "Do you eat food every day?" Now read what Moses wrote in Deuteronomy 8:3, "He humbled you, causing you to hunger and then feeding you with manna, which neither you nor your fathers had known, to teach you that man does not live on bread alone but on every word that comes from the mouth of the Lord." Yes, accept the Spirit God gives, study His Word, follow His decrees and laws, and go out and make this a great day.

Breathe on me, breath of God; fill me with life anew,
That I may love what Thou dost love and do what Thou wouldst do.
Breathe on me, breath of God, until my heart is pure,
Until with Thee I will one will - to do and to endure.

Edwin Hatch - 1835-1889

July 20

"I WILL LEAD THE BLIND BY WAYS THEY HAVE NOT KNOWN, ALONG UNFAMILIAR PATHS I WILL GUIDE THEM; I WILL TURN THE DARKNESS INTO LIGHT BEFORE THEM AND MAKE THE ROUGH PLACES SMOOTH. THESE ARE THE THINGS I WILL DO; I WILL NOT FORSAKE THEM." Isaiah 42:16

Have you ever watched a blind person walking with a guide dog or with a white cane. When they are in unfamiliar territory they tend to walk much more carefully than when they are walking along paths they have trod before. In Washington, DC, one time I watched a blind person walking with a guide dog through a construction area when they were building the subway system. There were large steel plates put down to walk over. These made the walkway uneven like a rough path. Of course it was during the light of day, but to the person who is blind it is always in the darkness. As I watched to make sure the blind person got through safely I noticed that he was listening closely to the sounds around him, and his hands were resting lightly on the dog's harness so he could feel the change in height that would signal to step up onto a steel plate. I was amazed that he could maneuver the area so well. I thought at the time, "I'm sure glad I am not blind and have to learn to get around as that person is doing so well.

At the time, however, I was blind. I was not following God in the manner in which He wanted me to follow Him. I was stumbling around in the darkness over unfamiliar paths that were plenty rough in places. It was pretty scary at times for me then. Thank God, He did not give up on me! He did lead me by ways I had not known. He still leads me along unfamiliar paths. I have no fear of those paths now because I know who holds my hand. He led me out of the darkness into the light of His perfect love. Those pathways I trod which were plenty rough, He has turned into smooth pathways.

How about you today? Are you blind? Are you stumbling along unfamiliar paths with no one to guide you? Does it seem the way is rough and it is so dark you can't see the way? Maybe you have let sin into your heart. Maybe you are concentrating too hard on making money instead of serving Him. Maybe you have been hurt by someone and have not forgiven them. If so, you need to follow the advice of John in 1 John 1:7, "But if we walk in the light, as He is in the light, we have fellowship with one another, and the blood of Jesus His Son, purifies us from all sin." John further says in 1 John 2:9-11, "Anyone who claims to be in the light but hates his brother is still in the darkness. Whoever loves his brother lives in the light, and there is nothing in him to make him stumble. But whoever hates his brother is in the darkness and walks around in the darkness; he does not know where he is going, because the darkness has blinded him." Don't be blinded by lust, greed, envy, jealousy, unforgiveness or hate.

Claim today's promise as yours. These are the things He will do for you. He will not forsake you. Take Him at His word, and go out and make this a great day.

Trying to walk in the steps of the Savior, trying to follow our Savior and King;
Shaping our lives by His blessed example, happy, how happy, the songs that we bring.
How beautiful to walk in the steps of the Savior, stepping in the light;
How beautiful to walk in the steps of the Savior, led in paths of light.
Eliza E. Hewitt - 1851-1920

July 21

"FOR I WILL FORGIVE THEIR WICKEDNESS AND WILL REMEMBER THEIR SINS NO MORE." Hebrews 8:12

When I was a youngster growing up at home I was fortunate to have two caring, loving and strict parents. I do remember a few spankings and I do remember what some of them were for. I loved to sit with my cousins during church service. Sometimes we would not be paying attention to the sermon and begin to get a little loud. All it took to get my attention was for Momma to snap her fingers. I KNEW it was her and I would immediately become quiet, turn red in the face start paying attention to the preacher. One time as an adult I was visiting with Momma about one of the times I had misbehaved and received a spanking for it. I remember relating the story to Momma just as if it had occurred the day before. When I finished I asked, "Do you remember that time, Momma?" "No," she responded. "I don't remember it at all." You see, that had created such an impression on me that I remembered it into adulthood, but to Momma it was just a time when correction was needed and given, punishment was meted out, forgiveness was granted and it was all forgotten.

Aren't you glad we have a God like that? He may chastize us and convict us of our sins, but when we ask forgiveness He not only forgives us, forgets it. The time for us to carry a load of guilt about our sins is before they are forgiven. Today's promise is that God will not only grant us forgiveness, but will remember our sins no more! If we sit with Him later in life and tell Him about some sin we committed and then asked, and received His forgiveness for, He will honestly tell us He does not remember the time. Like Momma, He corrects, chastises, forgives and forgets. We have no need to carry a load of guilt about sins which have been forgiven. God has removed them as far as the East is from the West.

To yourself, you may have been the worst sinner possible, but when you receive the forgiveness of God and your heart is made pure by being washed with the blood of Jesus Christ, you will be as perfect and pure as anyone else. A sinner is a sinner to God. While we were still sinners Jesus died on the cross for us. We know from His Word that no one comes to the Father except through Jesus Christ and His blood. We do not have a God like a politician I knew who said, "Forgive and remember!" No! God forgives and forgets!

Did you do some things before you came to God through Jesus Christ of which you are ashamed? Many, or most, of us did. Are you carrying a load of guilt because of the things you did? If you are then please read today's promise again. God clearly says He will forgive AND "will remember your sins no more!" Now that is a promise to give you a peaceful night's sleep!

Do you have family or friends who seem to be carrying a load of guilt after accepting Jesus? Point out today's promise to them. Help them to understand that our loving Father has forgotten their sins. Claim it, teach it, and go out and make this a great day.

What a wonderful change in my life has been wrought, since Jesus came into my heart!
I have light in my soul for which long I have sought, since Jesus came into my heart!
I'm possessed of a hope that is steadfast and sure, since Jesus came into my heart!
And no dark clouds of doubt now my pathway obscure, since Jesus came into my heart!
Rufus H. McDaniel - 1850-1940

July 22

"THE SALVATION OF THE RIGHTEOUS COMES FROM THE LORD; HE IS THEIR STRONGHOLD IN TIME OF TROUBLE." Psalm 37:39

I have a friend who is an officer in a corporation. He once told me he thought there were three reasons to have an attorney. First, to keep you out of trouble by helping you to always know the parameters of correct actions within the law. Second, to tell you how to do the things you wanted to do so that you were functioning entirely within the law. Third, to help get you out of trouble when you didn't follow their advice given in the first and second situations. It is sad to me to realize that too many officers in corporate America today are apparently not asking, or even caring, what the law is, and it seems the only reason they want an attorney is to plead their case to reduce, or eliminate, any penalty they get for not following the law.

Jesus said in John 14:6, "I am the way and the truth and the life. No one comes to the Father except through me." Paul wrote in Hebrews 7:25, "Therefore He is able to save completely those who come to God through Him because He always lives to intercede for them." We can, therefore, say that our salvation comes from God through Jesus Christ. Our promise today is that our salvation comes from God, who is also our stronghold in time of trouble.

We read in Hebrews 4:16, "Let us then approach the throne of grace with confidence, so that we may receive mercy and find grace to help us in our time of need." I feel that last part could read, "and find our stronghold in time of trouble." Why can we be so confident that we will receive mercy and help? Because we have attorneys helping us plead our case with God! Who are these attorneys? Read Romans 8:26-27 and 34, "In the same ways, the Spirit helps us in our weakness. We do not know what we ought to pray for, but the Spirit Himself intercedes for us with groans that words cannot express. And He who searches our hearts knows the mind of the Spirit, because the Spirit intercedes for the saints in accordance with God's will. Who is He that condemns? Christ Jesus, who died - more than that, who was raised to life - is at the right hand of God and is also interceding for us." So you see, we have a team of attorneys representing our case when we make our pleas to God. We have the very best attorneys - two-thirds of the Trinity speaking to the other third of the Trinity.

Even when we don't know what we should ask for, the Spirit knows because the Spirit lives within us and knows our hearts and our minds. That is why God knows what we are going to say even before the word is on our tongues. The Spirit will intercede for us with groans that words cannot express, in other words when we don't even know what we want and need.

Do you have concerns today about your salvation? Are you having trouble today in a relationship, in school, at work or in your relationship with God? Your salvation comes from God and He is your stronghold in trouble. Approach Him with confidence and with your attorney team and you will get your help. You can then go out and make this a great day.

Have you a heart that's weary, tending a load of care?
Are you a soul that's seeking rest from the burden you bear?
Who knows your disappointments? Who knows each time you cry?
Who understands your heartaches? Who dries the tears from your eyes?
William F. Lakey - (No Date)

July 23

"Do not let your heart envy sinners, but always be zealous for the fear of the Lord. THERE IS SURELY A FUTURE HOPE FOR YOU, AND YOUR HOPE WILL NOT BE CUT OFF." Proverbs 23:17 & 18

Today's promise first contains two charges. Our first charge in the promise is to not let our heart envy sinners. In other words, don't lust after the things of the world. Turn your eyes upon Jesus and the things of earth will grow strangely dim in the light of His glory and grace! The second charge is to always be zealous for the fear (awe, respect and reverence) of the Lord. We meet this charge by righteousness in our Lord Jesus Christ. When we satisfy those two charges there is surely a future hope for us, AND our hope will not be cut off.

The very best definition of HOPE that I can come up with is: Have Only Prayerful Expectations! Today's promise is evidence of the accuracy of that definition. Many books have been written about the change in the physical condition of prisoners when they reach a point that they have lost hope. It is said that you can tell by the look in their eyes the very day they lose hope. What is the loss of hope but the loss of faith? That is the reason for the two charges in our promise. If we place our trust in the things of the world we are more likely to lose faith, become discouraged, lose hope and give up.

It is when our faith is in the Lord and His promises, including the promise of eternal life, that we retain our faith, remain encouraged, remain hopeful and keep going. It is that we know we are citizens of heaven and, as the song says, this world is not my home, I'm just traveling through. When we are zealous for the Lord we also maintain a "servant's attitude" which helps us to maintain our hope. It is because we are concentrating on others and their needs. As a result our needs and problems tend to shrink because of our lack of attention to them.

Our hope will not be cut off either! This promise is stated more emphatically and in more detail in 1 Peter 13-5, "Praise be to the God and Father of our Lord Jesus Christ! In His great mercy He has given us new birth into a living hope through the resurrection of Jesus Christ from the dead, and into an inheritance that can never perish, spoil or fade-kept in heaven for you, who through faith are shielded by God's power until the coming of the salvation that is ready to be revealed in the last time." Yes, our future hope is the inheritance of eternal life!

Do you sometimes feel like you have lost hope? Do you feel that you have stumbled and do not deserve to be counted as one who is always zealous for the fear of the Lord? You can, and should, retain your hope. Read Proverbs 24:16, "For though a righteous man falls seven time, he rises again." We are not perfect. Paul realized this when he wrote Philippians 3:12, "Not that I have already obtained all this, or have already been made perfect, but I press on to take hold of that for which Christ Jesus took hold of me." So maintain hope, press on, and go out and make this a great day.

My hope is built on nothing less than Jesus' blood and righteousness;
I dare not trust the sweetest frame, but wholly lean on Jesus' name.
His oath, His covenant, His blood, support me in the whelming flood;
When all around my soul gives way, He then is all my hope and stay.
Edward Mote - 1797-1874

July 24

"I WILL NOT LEAVE YOU AS ORPHANS; I WILL COME TO YOU." John 14:18

Dr. Kristina Orth-Gomer and Professor Jeffrey Johnson, in Sweden, conducted a study reported in the April 1987 "Reader's Digest". They found lonely people seem more likely to die of heart disease than do the socially active. The study allowed for medical and life-style risk factors or age, smoking, physical inactivity and signs of heart disease. It found the subjects with few social contacts had a 40% greater risk of dying from cardiovascular disease than the rest did. "Loneliness," said "Newsweek" magazine in reporting a similar study, "can speed your demise no matter how conscientiously you care for your body." One study of elderly heart-attack patients found that those with two or more close associates enjoyed twice the one-year survival rate of those who were completely alone. "We go through life surrounded by protective convoys of others," says Robert Kahn, a University of Michigan psychologist who has studied the health effects of companionship. "People who manage to maintain a network of social support do best." I have never been lonely in my life other than the few, short times I have been away from home. I have always been surrounded by loving family and found it easy to make good friends. It is difficult for me to imagine the life of an orphan. I have a wonderful, dear friend, Harry Hicks, whose mother died when he was six years old. His father was not occupationally or financially prepared to provide for the seven children. His two elder siblings were too old for the orphanage, his youngest brother was adopted by an aunt and Harry, his brother just younger than he and his two sisters just older than he, were placed in the Orphans' Home, sponsored, funded and operated under the direction of the Methodist Church Organization of Oklahoma. He lived there until he graduated from high school in 1937. He wrote a book, "Mommie, What's An Orphan?", which contains many short stories of events which took place in the Orphans' Home. In the book he reports the end of the first day: "My brother and I huddled in our bed and cried ourselves to sleep." He also reported other poignant examples of loneliness among the children. To be an orphan without loving family and friends would have to be the loneliest feeling there could be. We are told in James 1:27, "Religion that God our Father accepts as pure and faultless is this: to look after orphans and widows in their distress and to keep oneself from being polluted by the world." Thank God for the Methodist Church and their Orphans' Home for Harry!

Today's promise by Jesus tells us that He will not leave us as orphans. He will not leave us alone. It is contained in the section in which He promises the Holy Spirit as a Comforter. Jesus also adds the line, "I will come to you." This is a promise of His second coming. In Matthew 28:20 Jesus also said, "And surely I am with you always, to the very end of the age." As Christians we are always home because we are the sons of God. We count on His presence and the Word of God, the Bible, to keep us company and provide us with comfort.

Claim His promise of inclusion in His family, and go out and make this a great day.

Happy the home when God is there and love fills everyone,
When with united work and prayer the Master's will is done.
Lord, let us in our homes agree this blessed peace to gain;
Unite our hearts in love to Thee, and love to all will reign.

Henry Ware, Jr. - 1794-1843

July 25

"REMAIN IN ME, AND I WILL REMAIN IN YOU. No branch can bear fruit by itself; it must remain in the vine. Neither can you bear fruit unless you remain in me." John 15:4

Today's promise comes from Jesus after the Last Supper. Judas Iscariot has left and Jesus is walking through a vineyard with the other disciples. Jesus is using the example of the grape vines to illustrate His points concerning their relationship with Him after His ascension, which they did not yet comprehend. This subject is covered in a thorough, complete, understandable manner by Bruce Wilkinson in, "Secrets of The Vine." If you have not read that book I highly recommend it to you. Having grown up on the farm I can relate to this example of Jesus. Though we did not grow grapes, we grew so many other variety of fruits, vegetables and grains the example of Jesus is understandable to me. Can you just imagine a person cutting off a branch of a grape vine and leaving it in place on the arbor and expecting to go out at harvest time to pick large bunches of ripe, juicy grapes? If the branch is not connected to the vine, from where will it draw its life-giving nourishment? Only when the vine is connected to the vine can it receive the needed moisture and food brought up from the roots to produce those grapes we love to eat. The disciples had lived around grape vineyards all their lives so they could understand the example Jesus was using.

The promise is that if we remain in Jesus, He will remain in us. In order to remain in Jesus, we have to BE in Jesus. We are in Jesus when we confess our sins, ask for His forgiveness and commit our lives to Him, thus fulfilling the first commandment that we love the Lord our God with all our heart, mind, soul and strength. How do we remain in Jesus? As we read further in the chapter in verse 8 we see Jesus said, "This is to my Father's glory, that you bear much fruit, showing yourselves to be my disciples." So one requirement to remain in Jesus is to be His disciple. In John 13:34-35 we read, "A new command I give you: Love one another. As I have loved you, so you must love one another. By this all men will know that you are my disciples, if you love one another." Love one another! How simple and, yet, how difficult. To love like Jesus we have to pattern our lives after the life of Jesus, who loved children, sinners and all others. He ministered to any who came to Him. He instructed us to feed the hungry, clothe the naked, visit the sick and those in prison and give water to the thirsty because, by that, we are doing it to Him.

In verse 15 Jesus says, "I no longer call you servants, because a servant does not know his master's business. Instead, I have called you friends, for everything that I learned from my father I have made known to you." Therefore, I consider it important that we learn what Jesus taught to remain in Him. Where do we learn that? From the Bible and prayer primarily, but also from church attendance, fellowship with fellow Christians and reading devotionals and bible study books. Remember, Jesus chose you. Remain in Him, and go out and make this a great day.

More about Jesus would I know, more of His grace to others show,
More of His saving fullness see, more of His love who died for me.
More about Jesus let me learn, more of His holy will discern;
Spirit of God my teacher be, showing the things of Christ to me.

Eliza E. Hewitt - 1851-1920

July 26

"NOW ABOUT BROTHERLY LOVE WE DO NOT NEED TO WRITE TO YOU, FOR YOU YOURSELVES HAVE BEEN TAUGHT BY GOD TO LOVE EACH OTHER."
1 Thessalonians 4:9

Sometimes in the Winter, when it was really cold, I would try to take some shortcuts in doing my chores. Invariably Dad would catch me and say, "Now Clarence, do I have to tell you again how to do that right." No, I didn't want him to tell me again how to do it right. I just wanted to get into the house where it was warm. What I was really doing was just looking out for myself instead of taking care of the animals like they needed and deserved. Perhaps some of the people of Thessalonica were doing the same thing. They were more concerned about taking care of themselves and their own needs than they were about fellow Christians. The word Paul used which has been translated to "brotherly love" is the word which applied to the love children of the same father had for one another. It's use in the New Testament always meant the love among fellow believers in Christ.

Today it is not uncommon for siblings to greet each other with a kiss. In New Testament days it was a common greeting to greet others with a kiss. Paul wrote in three places to, "greet each other with a Holy kiss." Peter wrote it once. Today I feel we should greet other Christians with Christian love. It should be a clean, pure expression of "brotherly love" as used by Paul. I feel such a love for my fellow Christians in our church I greet them with a hug as an expression of joy I experience by seeing them and being in their presence.

Paul clearly tells the Thessalonians, like my Dad clearly told me, that he did not have to write to them about brotherly love. He gave them the promise for today, "for you yourselves have been taught by God to love each other." Yes, we have been taught by God to love each other. Jesus was quoted by John in John 15:17, "This is my command: Love each other." John 13:35 quotes Jesus, "By this all men will know that you are my disciples, if you love one another." There was no wishy-washy, half-way statement from Jesus. He did not say, "Try to get along with one another." NO! He clearly said, "Love each other."

What about your feelings toward some other Christians? Do you have a personality conflict with them and just feel you cannot love them as commanded? Have you gone to them to talk about it? You should! Jesus said in Matthew 18:15, "If your brother sins against you, go and show him his fault, just between the two of you. If he listens to you, you have won your brother over." Again, very clear instructions from Jesus in handling your relationship with a fellow Christian. He didn't say, "Complain about it to anyone who will listen." He didn't say, "Tell the preacher and let him settle it." No! He said to go to your brother! Show love and respect!

Follow the commands of Jesus, be a disciple of Jesus, love one another, therefore, showing your love for Jesus. Now go out and make this a great day.

I will be my brother's keeper, ever watching through the night
For a fellow traveler searching for the way of God's true light;
Of a single lonely brother may I always be aware
Offering love without restriction, fellowship with tender care.

R. Douglas Little - 1954-

July 27

"THOSE WHO BELONG TO CHRIST JESUS HAVE CRUCIFIED THE SINFUL NATURE WITH ITS PASSIONS AND DESIRES." Galatians 5:24

I was raised in the Friends Church (Quakers) so my religion experiences were dictated by their beliefs. Their view on baptism is derived from the words of John the Baptist recorded in John 3:11, "I baptize you with water for repentance. But after me will come one who is more powerful than I, whose sandals I am not fit to carry. He will baptize you with the Holy Spirit and with fire." I was 63 years old when I was baptized with water. Jan and I joined CrossPointe Church of Norman, OK at that time. Since I had not been baptized I asked Brother Joe Grizzle to please baptize me. I think of that experience when I read today's promise. The symbolism of baptism is very meaningful. We are crucified with Christ, dead to sinful nature, buried together and rise to a new life. Baptism will never get a person into heaven by itself. We first must belong to Christ Jesus! Those who belong to Christ Jesus have crucified the sinful nature with its passions and desires. We then are worthy to be baptized.

In the first chapter of Romans Paul writes about the guilt of the Gentiles and goes on to say, "Therefore God gave them over in the sinful desires of their hearts to sexual impurity for the degrading of their bodies with one another. They exchanged the truth of God for a lie, and worshiped and served created things rather than the Creator-who is forever praised. Amen. Because of this, God gave them over to shameful lusts. Even their women exchanged natural relations for unnatural ones. In the same way the men also abandoned natural relations with women and were inflamed with lust for one another. Men committed indecent acts with other men, and received in themselves the due penalty for their perversion. Furthermore, since they did not think it worthwhile to retain the knowledge of God, He gave them over to a depraved mind, to do what ought not to be done. They have become filled with every kind of wickedness, evil greed and depravity. They are full of envy, murder, strife, deceit and malice. They are gossips, slanderers, God-haters, insolent, arrogant and boastful; they invent ways of doing evil; they disobey their parents; they are senseless, faithless, heartless, ruthless. Although they know God's righteous decree that those who do such things deserve death, they not only continue to do these very things but also approve of those who practice them." Was Paul writing about the Gentiles or was he writing about many in our world today? It seems Paul is suggesting sexual impurity as the sin which is committed early in the moral decline of a person. He also lists it first in Colossians 3:5, "Put to death, therefore, whatever belongs to your earthly nature: sexual immorality, impurity, lust, evil desires and greed, which is idolatry."

Our promise today clearly states that if we belong to Christ Jesus we have crucified the sinful nature of such passions and desires. Your body is a temple of the Holy Spirit, who is in you. Crucify (control) passions and desires, and go out and make this a great day.

Down at the cross where my Savior died, down where for cleansing from sin I cried.
There to my heart was the blood applied: Glory to His name.
I am so wondrously saved from sin, Jesus so sweetly abides within;
There at the cross where He took me in; Glory to His name.
Elisha A Hoffman - 1839-1929

July 28

"WHOEVER LOVES MONEY NEVER HAS MONEY ENOUGH; WHOEVER LOVES WEALTH IS NEVER SATISFIED WITH HIS INCOME. This too is meaningless." Ecclesiastes 5:10

I once was led to try an experiment which made such an impression on me I have never forgotten it. I was eleven years old and had found a penny near the school grounds. When I got home I showed it to Dad as we started toward the barn to do the evening chores. "That is quite a find," Dad said. "Hold it by the edges between your index finger and your thumb. Now hold it at arms length in the direction of the barn." I did as he instructed. "Now close one eye and look with your eye like you were looking at the horizon. What do you see?" Dad asked. I began to describe the barn, the cows, the horses, the water tank, the corner of the garden and the field of corn I could see beyond the barn. Before I had completed the description Dad interrupted with, "Now hold the penny one inch from your eye and look toward the sun." I did as he instructed. "Now what do you see?" asked Dad. "I see only the penny," I replied. "You see son," Dad said. "When that penny is held properly you can still see all the things that are important to you. When you hold it too close it can even blot out the sun. A sun that is so big and so bright it can light the entire world. That is why the Bible says, 'The love of money is the root of all evil.' When you love money you hold it too close and it blots out what is really important in life."

Today's promise assures if you place your love in money, and the things it will buy, you will never have enough. If the salary of your job is the most important part of the job, you will never be satisfied with the amount of income you make. It has been said that money will buy...a bed but not sleep; books but not brains; food but not appetite; finery but not beauty; a house but not a home; medicine but not health; luxuries but not culture; amusements but not happiness; a crucifix but not a Savior; religion but not salvation; a good life but not eternal life; and a passport to everywhere but heaven. Your life will be empty if your god is the money!

Is all this to say that money is bad? Absolutely not! Read the reference Dad quoted. It is 1 Timothy 6:9-10, "People who want to get rich fall into temptation and a trap and into many foolish and harmful desires that plunge men into ruin and destruction. For the love of money is a root of all kinds of evil. Some people, eager for money, have wandered from the faith and pierced themselves with many griefs." In our world of commerce money is a very important commodity. We need it to feed, clothe, house, educate and continually provide for our families. It is bad only when it becomes a love of money for money's sake, when we want to get rich, when we wander from the faith to obtain more and more of it. Avoid falling into the trap of today's promise! It is God who gives the abundance. Thank God for His bounty given freely to you when you obtain money. Avoid being a slave to money or making it your idol. Present your tithes and offerings to God as thanks to Him. Then go out and make this a great day.

Joy floods my soul, for Jesus has saved me, freed me from sin that long has enslaved me;
His precious blood He gave to redeem - Now I belong to Him!
Now I belong to Jesus, Jesus belongs to me;
Not for the years of time alone, but for eternity.

Norman J. Clayton - 1903-

July 29

"I TELL YOU THE TRUTH, IF ANYONE SAYS TO THIS MOUNTAIN, 'GO THROW YOURSELF INTO THE SEA,' AND DOES NOT DOUBT IN HIS HEART BUT BELIEVES THAT WHAT HE SAYS WILL HAPPEN, IT WILL BE DONE FOR HIM." Mark 11:23

When I was growing up the Bible was read to us every day. We prayed at mealtime and bedtime. We attended the church twice on Sunday and on Wednesday evening, and special evangelistic meetings and camp meetings, for which we helped set up the tent and move in the pews. I gave my heart to God at an early age and attended church camps. When I graduated and went to college and joined the National Guard I met an entirely different type person than I knew while I was growing up. I studied Botany, in which our professor introduced me to the subject of evolution and pointed out the obvious evolution which gave us the different breeds of dogs, cats, etc. I studied geology and was taught the age of some of the rocks and realized they were far older than I had learned from the Bible that the earth was. I began to have serious doubts about the truths of the Bible. Now, of course, I realize the different breeds of dogs, cats, cows, etc. are caused by micro-evolution-the evolving within a species. There is not one shred of evidence in fossils to support macro-evolution-evolving from one species to another. I also realize Genesis was written by Moses, who was born in approximately 1800 BC, and he did not even know the earth was round. He had never traveled out of the Mediterranean area and had no history books. All his knowledge of the history came from oral history and the inspiration of God (and I am not discounting that!). Based on the youngest age of Neanderthal Man's bones, I believe their race was destroyed by the flood of Noah's time, and that was approximately ten thousand years ago.

As Christians, we have to explain many things and we must be able to do it credibly. We lose credibility when we state the age of the earth, according to the Bible, to be between five and six thousand years. That prevents our being able to explain the age of the remains in the petrified forest, the age of the Grand Canyon or that a meteor hit Arizona about 50,000 years ago. There are two changes Moses could have made which would make the Bible conform to scientific evidence. First, God created the earth in "periods of time" instead of "days", and second, instead of saying "When Seth had lived 105 years, he became the father of Enosh." he could have written, "When Seth had lived 105 years, he became the father of the line to which Enosh was born." This same change would apply to the line from Enosh to Noah. These two changes would give us the conformity of Bible and science. God did create the world and all therein!

We must do all we can to remove doubts from our believers. Doubt questions the divinity of God! It cannot stand. If we teach properly we can help to reduce doubt and allow full acceptance of today's promise. Have faith in God, remove doubt from your heart and believe. God will make it happen. Now go out and make this a great day.

When faith turns to doubt and hope to despair,
When joy fades to sadness and love turns to fear,
There's rest for God's child, each burden He'll bear,
For the Lord, He is God and He cares about you.
Vernon M. Whaley - 1949-

July 30

"AND WE KNOW THAT IN ALL THINGS GOD WORKS FOR THE GOOD OF THOSE WHO LOVE HIM, WHO HAVE BEEN CALLED ACCORDING TO HIS PURPOSE." Romans 8:28

In 1995 I was very busy in the first half of the year. This is the time I usually scheduled my annual physical exam. I decided that everything had been going so well in the past that I would just not have an exam. In mid-April my doctor's office called to tell me I had not yet scheduled the exam and gave me a date for it. Oh well, I thought. Why not? So I went in at the appointed time (having gone in the week earlier for them to draw blood for the lab work). After giving me the exam and asking me if I had any medical problems my doctor went over the results of the lab work on the blood. He said everything was within normal range except for my PSA report. It rated 4.3 with 0 to 4 being within the normal range. He referred me to the Urologist who examined me and did a needle biopsy. The result of the needle biopsy showed Prostate cancer. That really set me back on my heels! My wife, Jan, and I chose to have the surgery. The Pathologist's report following the surgery showed the cancer had reached the wall of the Prostate gland so the hospital tumor committee recommended I take radiation, which I did.

Do I think God caused that cancer? Absolutely not! It was a bad thing that happened to me. However, from that experience I turned back to the God of my youth, later found a wonderful church to attend and have never been happier in my life. It was after that time that God called me to write this devotional. Would He have called me before? No, because my heart wasn't right with Him and I would not have heard, nor received, His call. I have told our pastor, Brother Joe Grizzle, that the most meaningful thing I have ever done is to write these devotionals. Even if no one ever reads them I have learned so much from the writing that I will never be the same again. This brings me to today's promise. We should always be aware and always remember that in ALL things God works for the good of those who love Him, who have been called according to His purpose. Did I love Him? Yes, but not like I should have, nor was I following Him like I should have. From the bad for me came good for me and I firmly believe I am called for His purpose of writing these devotions at this time in my life.

Have you recently gone through a bad experience of grief, loss of employment, broken relationship, health problems, legal problems, addictions or any other bad that happened to you? Do you love Him? Even if you have not been serving Him as you should, even if you have sin in your life, even if you would not hear Him if He called, do you love Him? Are you doing what He wants you to do with your life? Do you feel there is a call that God has for you that you have not answered? Always, always remember that God does not cause the bad things in your life. He WILL step in to make something good come from whatever happens to you. Whatever happens to you, God will make it good if you love Him. Remember, and go out and make this a great day.

A pilgrim was I and a wandr'ring, in the cold night of sin I did roam,
When Jesus, the kind Shepherd found me, and now I am on my way home.
He restoreth my soul when I'm weary; He giveth me strength day by day.
He leads me beside the still waters; He guards me each step of the way.
John W. Peterson - 1921- ; & Alfred B. Smith - 1916

July 31

"BLESSED IS THE MAN WHOM GOD CORRECTS; so do not despise the discipline of the Almighty." Job 5:17

When I was an insurance agent I had a lot of really fine clients. Sometimes an incident would occur which impressed me so much I never forgot it. One of my clients was a couple who had a seven year old son and a ten year old daughter. One day the father brought the daughter into my office. I could tell by her expression that she would rather have been almost anywhere than where she was. He gently told her, "Now tell Clarence what happened." With tears about ready to spill she told me that she got mad at her brother and threw a rock at him. It missed him and went sailing through the window of a neighbor. Her daddy had told her that she would have to pay for the window or report it to the insurance company. Under their home-owner policy there is a coverage called, "Damage to property of others." I explained that coverage to her and that there was no deductible on it as it is considered a liability coverage like if you are the driver responsible for an accident which damages another person's vehicle or other property. She was greatly relieved and they left the office promising to bring me the bill for repairs. I recorded the claim and waited for the bill. The next day they brought me a bill for just over $17.00. I was amazed until the father explained. Since the daughter didn't have to pay for the window he had taken her back to the neighbor's house, measured the window, drove to the glass company and obtained a window pane and putty. They then went back and he supervised her removing the shards of glass, cleaning the frame, placing the pane in the frame and putting on the putty. He was obviously proud of her attitude, willingness and efforts in the repair. I was even more impressed with the father and his method of discipline. I paid the bill and they left happy.

What a wonderful example that is of today's promise! That young girl was really blessed to have a father like that. He corrected her with love and firmness in a manner which she did not despise and she learned a lot from it. (So did I!) We read in Jeremiah 30:11, "'I am with you and will save you,' declares the Lord. 'Though I completely destroy all the nations among which I scatter you, I will not completely destroy you. I will discipline you but only with justice; I will not let you go entirely unpunished.'" We should realize that, even more so than that father, God will discipline us only with justice. And, like that father, He will not let us go entirely unpunished. Like that daughter, we should be accepting and not despise the discipline of the Almighty. We can take comfort in Proverbs 3:11-12, "My son, do not despise the Lord's discipline and do not resent His rebuke, because the Lord disciplines those He loves, as a father the son he delights in." (It could read, "...the daughter he delights in.")

Have you been corrected by God lately? In your quiet times of communing with Him, has He pointed out errors or misdeeds you have committed? Accept His correction. He is expressing His love for you. Love Him, don't despise Him. Now go out and make this a great day.

Sweet is the tender love Jesus hath shown,
Sweeter far than nay love that mortals have known;
Kind to the erring one, faithful is He;
He the great example is, and pattern for me.

William A. Ogden - 1841-1897

August 1

"But the Lord is faithful, and HE WILL STRENGTHEN AND PROTECT YOU FROM THE EVIL ONE." 2 Thessalonians 3:3

Strengthen and protect! What powerful, meaningful words. How much we use them today and wonder if our nation really has the strength to protect us. I remember a story I heard in 1975 when I was attending the Army Command and General Staff College at Ft. Leavenworth, KS. We were getting a briefing from the Air Force liaison officer and he told about an incident a few years earlier when those manning the DEW (Distant Early Warning) line in Alaska issued an alert of incoming Intercontinental Ballistic Missiles. The warning was taken seriously and aircraft were launched, only to be called back when those on the DEW line determined they were getting a bounce back off their radar from the moon, which was just rising over the horizon. In 2002 we were on vacation eating breakfast at the Airport Café in Sedona, AZ when we met a couple from just West of Sedona. We were the only two couples in the room at the time their meal was served and we asked to be included when they bowed their heads for prayer. We found out he was a retired Air Force officer. Further questions revealed he had been in Alaska on the DEW line. I told him the story we had been told. He replied, "I can't believe you heard that story and relayed it to me just now. I was the officer on the line who gave the alert and finally figured out what it was!" Yes, our country went to a lot of effort, time and expense to provide protection from the possible surprise attack by a foreign power (later described by President Reagan as the "Evil Empire"). The personnel manning the DEW line were faithful to their mission; however, there could be no promise of protection because they never knew the full extent of the threat.

Today's promise is entirely different from the situation of our government trying to be strong enough to protect us. Our God IS strong enough! He is faithful! He will strengthen and protect us from the evil one. Furthermore, we read in 1 Corinthians 10:13, "No temptation has seized you except what is common to man. And God is faithful: He will not let you be tempted beyond what you can bear. But when you are tempted, He will also provide a way out so that you can stand up under it." Our God understands our temptations. We read in Hebrews 2:18, "Because He Himself suffered when He was tempted, He is able to help those who are being tempted." Again in Hebrews 4:15 we read, "For we do not have a high priest who is unable to sympathize with our weaknesses, but we have one who has been tempted in every way, just as we are-yet was without sin."

It is easier to avoid temptation than it is to withstand it. Follow the example Jesus gave us in teaching the disciples to pray when He told them in Matthew 6:13 to say, "And lead us not into temptation, but deliver us from the evil one." Do you have certain sins that tempt you more than others? Avoid them! Resist the devil and he will flee from you! Turn your eyes upon Jesus. He is faithful! He will strengthen and protect you! Now go out and make this a great day.

Thru death into life everlasting He passed, and we follow Him there;
Over us sin no more hath dominion-for more than conq'rors we are!
Turn your eyes upon Jesus; look full in His wonderful face,
And the things of earth will grow strangely dim in the light of His glory and grace.
Helen H. Lemmel - 1864-1961

August 2

"AND IN HIM YOU TOO ARE BEING BUILT TOGETHER TO BECOME A DWELLING IN WHICH GOD LIVES BY HIS SPIRIT." Ephesians 2:22

During my first two years at Emporia State University I worked at Swint's Bus Stop Café which was in the block just South of the campus. In my Sophomore year I also worked part time for the Chemistry department grading papers. It was during that second year that I had a regular café customer who was a homebuilder. He was getting ready to start a house for a Professor of Biology and asked me to work part time for him. I added that as a third part time job. As the house progressed he found he could not devote the required time to his bookkeeping so he asked me to do that work for him. I worked for him until he completed that house and moved on to other jobs. That work allowed me to have a very close look at what it took to build a dwelling. I worked on that job through pouring the foundation, framing, roofing, bricking, interior work and landscaping. I was amazed at that time of how much detail work went into the inside. This detail included the cabinets, wiring, wall covering, wood trim, painting and staining, light fixtures, tile work and laying of carpets. It had to be carefully scheduled to make sure each job built upon the completion of the one just completed.

We are told by Paul in 1 Corinthians 6:19-20, "Do you not know that your body is a temple of the Holy Spirit, who is in you, whom you have received from God? You are not your own; you were bought at a price. Therefore honor God with your body." Today's promise is that we are being built together in God to become a dwelling in which God lives by His Spirit, the Holy Spirit! The first step to building that dwelling for His Spirit is to lay the foundation-we must believe in Him. We believe with our hearts and confess with our mouths and ask His forgiveness and it will be granted. The second step is the framing: Our worship of Him which should be our entire lives. Colossians 3:23 says, "Whatever you do, work at it with all your heart, as working for the Lord, not for men." When we do that we are building the framework of His temple by worshiping Him. The third step is the exterior work-roofing and bricking: Our fellowship with other believers which puts God's glow on us as we associate with fellow believers in prayer, study, fun and food. The fourth step is the interior work: Our discipleship through becoming more like Jesus every day. We accomplish this with our Bible study and meditation, prayer and communion with God and our devotional reading and reading of Christian books. The fifth, and final, step is the landscaping work: Our ministry and evangelism. We need to minister to other Christians through our service to them. We should develop the attitude of "servanthood" as Jesus showed. We need to evangelize the world by answering the charge of Jesus to feed the hungry, give water to the thirsty, clothe the naked, shelter the homeless and visit the sick and those in prison and by telling the news of God's gift to the world through His Son, Jesus Christ.

Are you a dwelling for God's Spirit? Become one, and go out and make this a great day.

Holy Ghost, with light divine, shine upon this heart of mine;
Chase the shades of night away, turn my darkness into day.
Holy Spirit, all divine, dwell within this heart of mine;
Cast down every idol-throne, reign supreme and reign alone.
Andrew Reed - 1787-1862

August 3

"Again, I tell you THAT IF TWO OF YOU ON EARTH AGREE ABOUT ANYTHING YOU ASK FOR, IT WILL BE DONE FOR YOU BY MY FATHER IN HEAVEN." Matthew 18:19

Writing "Hardly a Coincidence" in Changed Lives: USA Testimonies, Jim L. Stegall told: While in Vietnam at age 19 he had buddies cut down around him and his terror increased. He turned twenty, then twenty-one and felt he could not go on. On February 26, 1968, his heart told him he would die before dusk. His base came under attack and Jim heard a rocket coming toward him. He knew he had three seconds to live. However, a friend shoved him into a grease pit and the rocket fuse malfunctioned. For five hours he knelt in that pit. Finally taking his New Testament from his pocket he began to read Matthew. When he read Matthew 18:19-20, he knew things would be all right. Years after he returned home he visited his wife's grandmother, Mrs. Harris, and she told him of a night she had awakened in terror, sensing that Jim was in trouble. She began praying for Jim and reading her Bible all night. Just before dawn she read Matthew 18:19-20. She immediately called her Sunday school teacher, who came to her house where together they claimed the Lord's promise as they prayed for Jim until reassured by God's peace. After telling Jim the story, she opened her Bible to show him where she had marked the passage. In the margin were the words: "Jim, February 26, 1968"!

When you pray, do you remind God of His promises? Do you verbally claim His promises to you? You should! When you are praying with someone it is important to get their agreement concerning the subject of your prayer. You should then remind God of His promise to us. Is it because God has forgotten His promise? Certainly not! It is to assure God that you know His promise, you claim His promise and you have faith that He will fulfill His promise. You cannot know His promises unless you study His Word and memorize portions of it. The study and memorization of His Word should be a regular part of each day of your life.

When I find a promise during my Bible reading, I find it helpful to me to say a prayer right then for a particular situation to which that promise applies. It is often just a short, intense prayer, but it is one which claims His promise. You see, what we are doing when we pray is recognizing that God is the one in charge. He wants all things to work for good to those who love Him, and are called for His purpose. Our prayers to Him may put us in a position to carry out His will, cause Him to move others to do His will, or cause Him to act by divine providence to carry out His will. This latter is what He did to save the life of Jim Stegall on February 26, 1968. Mrs. Harris and her Sunday school teacher agreed that Jim's life should be saved, they claimed the promise in His Word, they prayed together asking God to save Jim's life, and it was done by God, as Jesus had promised when He caused the rocket fuse to malfunction. You can cause positive changes by claiming God's promises in prayer. Do it, and go out and make this a great day.

There's a wideness in God's mercy like the wideness of the sea;
There's a kindness in His justice which is more than liberty.
If our love were but more simple we should take Him at His word,
And our lives would be all sunshine in the sweetness of our Lord.

Frederick W. Faber - 1814-1863

August 4

> "THE SOUL WHO SINS IS THE ONE WHO WILL DIE. THE SON WILL NOT SHARE THE GUILT OF THE FATHER, NOR WILL THE FATHER SHARE THE GUILT OF THE SON. THE RIGHTEOUSNESS OF THE RIGHTEOUS MAN WILL BE CREDITED TO HIM, AND THE WICKEDNESS OF THE WICKED WILL BE CHARGED AGAINST HIM." Ezekiel 18:20

When I was in grade school I attended a one-room country school which offered grades one through eight in the same room. One teacher taught all the students who attended the school. The older students would help the younger students with their work from time to time to allow the teacher to spend more time on a particular project. We had to learn to concentrate on our own assignments while other students were reading or discussing their work with the teacher. We loved recess as it gave us time to get out of the stuffy schoolhouse to run and play and work off part of the excess energy which built up in us as we had to be so still inside the school. One day one of the boys brought a large pine cone to school. He had found it while on vacation the previous Summer. It was open with very stiff, sharp points along its entire length. He thought it would be fun to place it on the teacher's chair to see what would happen. What happened was she sat down on it without ever seeing it. She did get up much faster than she sat down. She asked the guilty student to identify himself (now why did she think it was a boy?). No one spoke up, however, all the students knew who did it. When no one confessed she decided to make us stay in from afternoon recess (the very time we most wanted to go out) until someone confessed, someone told who did it or for two weeks. We stayed in for two weeks as no one told. To be punished for something you did not do is really hard to take!

Today's promise assures us we will not have to take the punishment for someone else's sins. We are assured the soul who sins is the one who will die. You will not share the guilt for the sins of your parents, siblings, friends or anyone else. They will not share the guilt for your sins either. The next line is very important: "The righteousness of the righteous man will be credited to him, and the wickedness of the wicked will be charged against him." We read in Deuteronomy 24:16, "Fathers shall not be put to death for their children, nor children put to death for their fathers; each is to die for his own sin." While you will not share in the guilt of the sins of others, neither will you share in the righteousness of others.

Have you read in the Bible about the "grandchildren" of God? You haven't? Of course not! There is no mention of them. We read in Galatians 4:4-5, "But when the time had fully come, God sent His Son, born of a woman, born under law, to redeem those under law, that we might receive the full rights of sons." It does us no good to be the children of godly parents if we do not also become God's son and heir. We cannot be a grandchild of God! Are you a son and heir of God? Be assured, and go out and make this a great day.

Blessed assurance, Jesus is mine!
O what a foretaste of glory divine!
Heir of salvation, purchase of God,
Born of His spirit, washed in His blood.
Fanny J. Crosby - 1820-1915

August 5

> "He said to them, 'Go into all the world and preach the good news to all creation. WHOEVER BELIEVES AND IS BAPTIZED WILL BE SAVED, BUT WHOEVER DOES NOT BELIEVE WILL BE CONDEMNED.'" Mark 16:15 & 16

Do you take the charge given you in Acts 1:8 seriously? "But you will receive power when the Holy Spirit comes on you; and you will be my witnesses in Jerusalem, and in all Judea and Samaria, and to the ends of the earth." This charge is another way of saying what the "command" portion of today's promise says. How do you respond to these commands of Jesus? I take them very seriously! No, God did not call me to go into the mission field. He did call me to support the work of our missionaries. Where are we to support them? Today's promise tells us "into all the world". Acts 1:8 tells us, Jerusalem-local area, Judea-in our country, Samaria-those different from us, and the ends of the earth-everyone else. I support our missionaries there in two ways. First, I support them with my regular and fervent prayers as specific as I can get based on the information I get from all the sources I have-journals, emails, visitors, etc. Second I support them with part of my tithes, but mostly with offerings. In the local area I support my church evangelism mission as well as the Campus Crusade for Christ representative to the University of Oklahoma. In our country I support a specific missionary to another state as well as general missions through our church. To those different from me I support missions directed to specific ethnic groups. To the rest of the world I support our Free Will Baptist missionary work in general and short term (up to two years) mission groups which go out from our church. This keeps me faithful to the charge of Jesus Christ our Lord.

When we are faithful to the charge we know that God will provide the results. We may not personally see the results in our lifetime, but we will definitely see them in heaven. For our promise for today is for everyone, whoever believes and is baptized will be saved, but whoever does not believe will be condemned. I know one of the first questions you might ask is, "Do you have to be baptized to be saved?" I do not believe you do because first, it is a "work"and second, I point to the thief on the cross next to Jesus who, when he asked Jesus to remember him, received the promise of Jesus in Luke 23:43, "I tell you the truth, today you will be with me in paradise." Then why are we baptized? It is part of our charge to confess the Lord Jesus Christ and we do this by the outward sign of baptism.

Your second question might be, "Is all we have do just believe?" I answered this question in detail in the January 1 devotion. Read Genesis 15:6, "Abram believed the Lord, and He credited it to him as righteousness." Also, when the earthquake set Paul and Silas free in prison and the jailer asked what he must do to be saved they told him in Acts 16:31, "Believe in the Lord Jesus, and you will be saved-you and your household." Yes, BELIEVE!

So support missions, believe in the Lord, and go out and make this a great day.

> O for a thousand tongues to sing my great Redeemer's praise,
> The glories of my God and King, the triumphs of His grace.
> My gracious Master and my God, assist me to proclaim,
> To spread thru all the earth abroad the honors of Thy name.
>
> Charles Wesley - 1707-1788

August 6

"YET I AM ALWAYS WITH YOU; YOU HOLD ME BY MY RIGHT HAND. YOU GUIDE ME WITH YOUR COUNSEL, AND AFTERWARD YOU WILL TAKE ME INTO GLORY. Whom have I in heaven but you? And earth has nothing I desire besides you." Psalm 73:23-25

Some of our favorite memories are usually associated with our children. I remember when my daughter, Katy, was a Brownie and earning all the badges she could. She asked me to help her earn the bicycle badge. We got out the booklet which told of the requirements, the most difficult of which was a twenty mile bicycle tour. We planned a tour that would take us through two towns and total forty-five miles. We would stop in the park of one of the towns for a lunch she would pack for us. There we would complete the requirements of maintenance checks and building a shelter with a bicycle and a tarp. We got up one morning, checked our bicycles over, secured the safety flags, packed water and our lunch and left on the tour about 8:00 A.M. At first, she rode ahead, but she was constantly turning around to see if I was still with her, so we changed with me leading. We stopped several times to rest and drink water. We arrived at the park before noon, completed her requirements, ate lunch, rested in the shade, refilled our water bottles and started the last of the trip. At about thirty miles I thought she would have to give up the rest of the trip and call her mother to pick us up as we had completed the requirements. She would say, "Daddy, if you will just stay right beside me I think I can go one more mile." We would go the mile and she would say, "Daddy, if you will stop with me to rest I think I can go some more." Five miles from home we stopped in the shade, drank water and rested a few minutes. A sudden shower poured rain for about two minutes. Katy said, "That rain really refreshed me. I think I can make it home." We left and didn't stop again until we were in our driveway. She earned her badge and we stored up memories which we will never lose.

Today's promise reminds me of that time. Katy wanted to be with me and have me hold her hand. She responded to my counsel, wanted my approval, worked harder as I encouraged her and just beamed as I congratulated her at the end of the ride. The Psalmist says he is always with God; God holds him by his right hand. God guides him with His counsel, and, best of all, will take him into the glory of God. What a wonderful promise to claim today!

Do you sometimes feel so all alone you just don't know what to do? Do you feel you need to be led by your right hand or you will be forever lost? You have this promise that is available to you. Just close your eyes for a few seconds and ask God to be right there with you. Feel His hand taking you by your right hand. He will provide you with comfort and peace. He will lead you in His direction. He will guide you with His counsel. Best of all, He will take you home into His glory!

Claim today's promise, and go out and make this a great day.

When my way grown drear, precious Lord, linger near;
When my life is almost gone,
Hear my cry, hear my call, hold my hand lest I fall;
Take my hand, precious Lord, lead me home.
Thomas A Dorsey - 1899-1993

August 7

> "Who is a God like you, who pardons sin and forgives the transgression of the remnant of His inheritance? YOU DO NOT STAY ANGRY FOREVER BUT DELIGHT TO SHOW MERCY." Micah 7:18

"Show No Mercy" is a popular T-shirt message now. I have seen it used in conjunction with sports teams. The implication seems to be that the person wearing the shirt with that slogan wants their team to continue to score in order to defeat the opponent by as many points as possible. I have watched games which were played that way. They always seem boring to the one who is not closely involved with the team. When I see a game played that way I wonder how much better it would be to use the substitute players more so they might gain experience playing in a real game situation. At times I have watched such a game and heard the broadcaster say, "We can expect no mercy from "A" today because they are still mad about losing that close game to "B" last year." Sure enough, A continued to score as many points as possible against B, verifying what the broadcaster said, they were still mad about last year.

We do not have a God like that! Who is a God like ours? Who is a God who pardons sin and forgives our transgressions? Our God does not stay angry forever, but He delights in showing mercy! We have a loving God! Does He get angry? Yes! What makes Him angry? Sin! When Adam sinned, God introduced the penalty of sin, which is death. Does He stay angry? No! He continues to take delight in showing mercy. How does He show His mercy? He sent His only Son to die on the cross for our sins. The death of Jesus on that cross proved God's mercy to us in that Jesus' death was in total payment for the penalty for our sin. Read Romans 6:23, "For the wages of sin is death, but the gift of God is eternal life in Christ Jesus our Lord." We have to accept God's gift to us, but when we do we will live for eternity with Him.

Our God is not an angry God who pours hurt after hurt upon us. His love for us is too great for that to ever occur. Sometimes in our lives it seems that just as things start to go well for us and we start being effective for Him we run into a series of "bad luck" and nothing goes right. We get hit from the left, then the right and from the left again. Is God angry at us? I doubt it. Remember, we live in the world where sin abounds; where the devil walks about like a roaring lion seeking whom he may devour. If we are being effective in our Christian witnessing we are a very big target for Satan. Satan will strike us at our most vulnerable point. If we tend to be pessimistic he will cause us to doubt. If we like the good things of life he will urge us into greed. He will strike us where he can hurt us the quickest and the most. Call upon God and He will hear. He promised us that what we bound on earth would be bound in heaven and what we loosed on earth would be loosed in heaven, so ask Him to bind Satan's darts of doubt, greed, or whatever is striking your vulnerability. God WILL delight in showing you mercy!

Accept His mercy, show Him your love of Him and go out and make this a great day.

> There is a scene where spirits blend, where friend holds fellowship with friend;
> Though sundered far, by faith they meet around one common mercy seat.
> Ah! there on eagle wings we soar, and sin and sense molest no more:
> And heaven comes down our souls to greet, while glory crowns the mercy seat.
>
> Hugh Stowell - 1799-1865

August 8

"FOR IT IS BY GRACE YOU HAVE BEEN SAVED, THROUGH FAITH - AND THIS NOT FROM YOURSELVES, IT IS THE GIFT OF GOD - NOT BY WORKS, SO THAT NO ONE CAN BOAST." Ephesians 2:8 & 9

John Bisango wrote in "The Power of Positive Praying" that he was reading a book one day when his daughter, Melodye Jan, age five, came to him. She asked if he would please build her a doll house. John promptly nodded and promised to build her one, then went back to reading his book. After awhile he glanced out the study window and saw her arms filled with dishes, toys, and dolls, making trip after trip until she had a great pile of playthings in the yard. He asked his wife what Melodye Jan was doing. "Oh, you promised to build her a doll house, and she believes you. She's just getting ready for it." "You would have thought I'd been hit by an atom bomb," John later said. "I threw aside that book, raced to the lumber yard for supplies, and quickly built that little girl a doll house. Now why did I respond? Because I wanted to? No. Because she deserved it? No. Her daddy had given his word, and she believed it and acted upon it. When I saw her faith, nothing could keep me from carrying out my word."

John told us the promise of God in 1 John 1:9, "If we confess our sins, He is faithful and just and will forgive us our sins and purify us from all unrighteousness." Couple this with the most precious promise in the Bible, John 3:16, "For God so loved the world that He gave His one and only son, that whoever believes in Him shall not perish but have eternal life." Do you have the faith of Melodye Jan? Have you taken today's promise given by God through Paul to be an absolute certainty? Just like that doll house was a gift from her father, so salvation for us is a gift from our heavenly Father. Just like her father was faithful to his word and completed the doll house he promised, so our heavenly Father is faithful to His word in Jeremiah 31:34, "For I will forgive their wickedness and will remember their sins no more."

Since salvation is a gift you just have to accept it. You don't have to do any work for it or in payment of it. You just have to accept it. If salvation were something for which you had to work, it would cause all sorts of problems with the sin of pride. Can't you just imagine someone saying, "I'm closer to God than you because I gave more to the church." "I traced the steps of Jesus up Calvary hill." "I have great salvation because of all my visits to those in hospitals and prisons." If those righteous acts are what we are counting on to get us into heaven we will hear the words of Isaiah 64:6, "...all our righteous acts are like filthy rags; ..."

Are you filling your home in heaven with rich rewards for your use throughout eternity? Are you transferring your earthly possessions into heavenly rewards? While works will not gain us salvation, confession with faith will. We must always remember James 2:17, "In the same way, faith by itself, if it is not accompanied by action, is dead." God will reward us for our faithful actions toward others. Accept grace through faith, and go out and make this a great day.

Many times I'm tried and tested as I travel day by day,
Oft I meet with pain and sorrow, and there's trouble in the way;
But I have the sweet assurance that my soul the Lord will lead,
And in Him there is strength for every need. O His grace is sufficient for me.
Mosie Lister - 1921-

August 9

"Dear friends, now we are children of God, and what we will be has not yet been made known. But we know that when He appears, WE SHALL BE LIKE HIM, FOR WE SHALL SEE HIM AS HE IS. EVERYONE WHO HAS THIS HOPE IN HIM PURIFIES HIMSELF, JUST AS HE IS PURE." 1 John 3:2 & 3

I saw a picture one time of a farmer standing beside his field of wheat. He was wearing overalls, with his hands in his rear pockets, palms toward the body, and with just a slight slouch toward the right. I could not see his face, but he must have been looking with concern at what he hoped would be a good crop. Just to the farmer's left stood a little boy, obviously the man's son. The little boy hardly came to the man's waist. He was dressed in the same type overalls, hands in his rear pockets, palms toward the body, and with just a slight slouch toward the right. I am sure he had the same expression of concern on his face as he, in his own way, pondered the wheat crop. What a precious sight! That little boy saw in his father everything he wanted to be.

Are you a child of God? When Jesus appears again will you be like Him? If you are a child of God you will be like Him. If you have this hope in you, you will purify yourself, just as Jesus is pure. Just like that little boy wanted to be just like his father, you should want to be just like your Father in heaven. What a wonderful promise that we who are children of God will be like Jesus when He reappears. We shall be like Him and see Him as He is!

To be His children we need to come to Him in total repentance of our sins. We need to confess them to Him, and, in sorrow, repent and sin no more. We don't need to do any "works" to be granted salvation. We don't need to bring anything to God as a sacrifice. We are told in Psalm 51:17, "The sacrifices of God are a broken spirit; a broken and contrite heart, O God, you will not despise." Just bring your honest repentance and your promise of a change of conduct so that you live a reformed life. This is told to us in Ephesians 4:22-24, "You were taught, with regard to your former way of life, to put off your old self, which is being corrupted by its deceitful desires; to be made new in the attitude of your minds; and to put on the new self, created to be like God in true righteousness and holiness."

Just as that little boy did everything in his power-from dress to stance to expression-to be like his father as he saw him, we need to see Jesus as He is and do everything in our power to be just like Him. That little boy did not know everything there was to know about his father. He just knew he loved him and wanted to be like him. Likewise, we don't know everything about our Father. We have faith and hope and love for our Lord. We are told in 1 Corinthians 13:12-13, "Now we see but a poor reflection as in a mirror; then we shall see face to face. Now I know in part; then I shall know fully, even as I am fully known. And now these three remain: faith, hope and love. But the greatest of these is love." So take Jesus as your own, strive to be like Him, and go out and make this a great day.

I'd rather have Jesus than silver or gold; I'd rather be His than have riches untold;
I'd rather have Jesus than houses or land; I'd rather be led by His nail-pierced hand:
Than to be the king of a vast domain or be held in sin's dread sway!
I'd rather have Jesus than anything this world affords today.

Mrs. Rhea F. Miller - 1894-1966

August 10

"HIS MERCY EXTENDS TO THOSE WHO FEAR HIM, FROM GENERATION TO GENERATION." Luke 1:50

Are you interested in genealogy? Many people spend some time in their lives searching the records to determine their family lines. I have been interested in a passing way. I have traced most of my family genealogy back five generations to be able to fill in the family tree section of our family Bible. The family of my maternal grandmother has been traced back using the Monthly Meeting minutes of the Quaker church to one of the original Quakers, John Scarborough. This represents thirteen generations prior to my generation and traces that family line back to the earliest days of the Quaker church.. The genealogy line of both my father and mother were Quakers as far back as I have records. They are people who loved the Lord. It is a legacy I am very fortunate to have. There have been many Quaker preachers in my family. I have previously told you of the strong Christian witness I experienced in our home as I was growing up. That is something I will cherish and thank God for throughout my entire life.

Today's promise, written by Luke, was stated similarly by David in Psalm 103:17-18, "But from everlasting to everlasting the Lord's love is with those who fear Him, and His righteousness with their children's children-with those who keep His covenant and remember to obey His precepts." In both this scripture and today's promise "fear" means awe, reverence, respect and worship of God and a desire to do His will. Notice the qualifier in the Psalm passage, "those who keep His covenant and remember to obey His precepts." In the August 4 devotion, I told you God does not have any grandchildren. Each generation is charged by God to pass the training in His covenant and His precepts on to the next generation. With that command from God comes a promise as we see in Proverbs 22:6, "Train a child in the way he should go, and when he is old he will not turn from it." God is faithful and He will be merciful to those who fear Him.

As a child did you have the spiritual training in your home which brought you to Christ? Did your parents train you in Bible reading, devotions, prayer and church attendance? If they did, you are truly blessed. If they didn't, you need to start the process with your children and grandchildren. It is both a charge and a trust from God. You must be devoted to God and to carrying out His commands regarding your life and your responsibilities to the next generation. You must train them, and claim God's promise that they will not turn from your training. Follow Ephesians 6:4, "Bring them up in the training and instruction of the Lord."

You must train your children more than to just be a "good" person. Read Jesus' words in John 3:3, "In reply Jesus declared, 'I tell you the truth, no one can see the kingdom of God unless he is born again.'" A person who is merely "good" will hear the words of Jesus recorded in Matthew 7:23 (KJV), "And then will I profess unto them, I never knew you; depart from me, ye that work iniquity." Pass on the fear of God, and go out and make this a great day.

This child we dedicate to Thee, O God of grace and purity!
In Thy great love its life prolong, shield it, we pray, from sin and wrong.
O may Thy Spirit gently draw its willing soul to keep Thy law;
May virtue, piety, and truth dawn even with its dawning youth.
Samuel Gilman - 1791-1858

August 11

"WHOEVER BELIEVES IN HIM IS NOT CONDEMNED, BUT WHOEVER DOES NOT BELIEVE STANDS CONDEMNED ALREADY BECAUSE HE HAS NOT BELIEVED IN THE NAME OF GOD'S ONE AND ONLY SON." John 3:18

Lee Strobel, in "The Case For Faith" wrote of his interview with William Neal Moore. He killed a man for his money in May 1984, was caught with the money, admitted his guilt, was sentenced to die and then gave his life to God. Following his conversion, Billy Moore counseled other death row inmates, took correspondence courses on the bible, led Bible study and prayer groups, won forgiveness from his victim's family and brought many fellow prisoners to Christ. As the time neared for his death sentence to be carried out there was a groundswell of support for him. As he was counting down the hours to his scheduled execution his death sentence was stayed. He later won commutation of his sentence, and then was freed on November 11, 1991. He then became a preacher of a church between two housing projects. During the interview Lee Strobel asked him what had changed Billy Moore. "It was the prison rehabilitation system that did it, right?" Lee asked. Moore laughed, "No, it wasn't that." "Then it was a self-help program or having a positive mental attitude." "No, not that, either." "Prozac? Transcendental Meditation? Psychological counseling?" "Come on, Lee," Moore said. "You know it wasn't any of those." "Then what was responsible for the transformation of Billy Moore?" "Plain and simple, it was Jesus Christ," Billy declared adamantly. "He changed me in ways I could never have changed on my own. He gave me a reason to live. He helped me do the right thing. He gave me a heart for others. He saved my soul."

That is the power of faith to change a human life. Paul wrote in 2 Corinthians 5:17, "Therefore, if anyone is in Christ, he is a new creation; the old has gone, the new has come!" Billy Moore, the Christian, is not the same as Billy Moore the killer. God had intervened with His forgiveness, with His mercy, with His power, with the abiding presence of His Spirit. That same kind of transforming grace is available to everyone who acts on the ample evidence for Jesus Christ by making the decision to turn away from their sin and embrace Him as their forgiver and leader! What a change in a life!

Billy Moore was condemned by man's justice system. Worse still, Billy Moore was condemned by God because he had not believed in the name of God's One and Only Son. The very instant Billy Moore confessed his sins and asked for forgiveness for those sins he was no longer condemned by God. Each one of us stands as condemned by God as was Billy Moore until we, likewise, confess our sins and ask forgiveness for those sins. We may not have committed murder and robbery, but any and all sins are grievous in the sight of God and must be forgiven.

Are you condemned by God today? There is no need for you to be condemned. Just take Him at His promises, follow Billy Moore's example, and go out and make this a great day.

Jesus, the very thought of Thee with sweetness fills my breast;
But sweeter far Thy face to see and in Thy presence rest.
O hope of ev'ry contrite heart, O joy of all the meek,
To those who fall how kind Thou art! How good to those who seek!

Attributed to Bernard of Clairvaux - 1091-1153;
Translated by Edward Caswall - 1814-1876

August 12

"Since the children have flesh and blood, He too shared in their humanity so that by His death He might destroy him who holds the power of death - that is, the devil - AND FREE THOSE WHO ALL THEIR LIVES WERE HELD IN SLAVERY BY THEIR FEAR OF DEATH." Hebrews 2:14 & 15

In the Spring of 2003 our pastor, Brother Joe Grizzle, preached a series of sermons on the subject of Heaven. As we discussed the series upon its completion, my wife, Jan, confessed to me she had always been fearful of death until she heard the sermons. We are flesh and blood, so our bodies will die at some time. That is the wonderfulness of today's promise. Jesus came to earth as a human being. He lived as a human; and felt pain, hunger, thirst, sadness, happiness, heat and cold as a human; and He died as a human. By His death He destroyed him who holds the power of death - the devil! By His death He freed those who all their lives were held in slavery by their fear of death! By the shedding of His blood, He provided the way that all of us might never die, but have eternal life. Yes, this body will die and return to dust, but our spirit will go to Jesus Christ and see God and, at the second coming of Jesus we will be given a new body to live in the new heaven and the new earth throughout eternity. As Jan said, "How wonderful it is to be free of the fear of death."

Look at some of the New Testament verses relating to the death of the body. First, we read about Jesus in John 19:30, "When He had received the drink, Jesus said, 'It is finished.' With that, He bowed His head and gave up His spirit." Second, we read about the stoning of Stephen in Acts 7:60, "Then he fell on his knees and cried out, 'Lord, do not hold this sin against them.' When he had said this, he fell asleep." Third, we read about Paul in 2 Timothy 4:6, "For I am already being poured out like a drink offering, and the time has come for my departure." Fourth, we read about Peter in 2 Peter 1:13-14, "I think it is right to refresh your memory as long as I live in the tent of this body, because I know that I will soon put it aside."

Jesus "gave up His spirit", Stephen "fell asleep", Paul "departed", and Peter "put aside his tent". Do you notice that none of them "died"? Why? Because Jesus conquered death! Praise God! We are no longer held as slaves to our fear of death. Why? Because Jesus died for us so that we will never die!

Are you a slave to the fear of death today? You need not be! You can have peace if you take your burden of sins to the cross of Jesus Christ. Just confess your sins to Him, ask for His forgiveness of those sins, and accept His promise of an eternal life free from the slavery to your fear of death. You don't have to do anything else to receive that promise of freedom. It is a gift from God. Read James 1:16-17, "Don't be deceived, my dear brothers. Every good and perfect gift is from above, coming down from the Father of the heavenly lights, who does not change like shifting shadows." Accept His gift, and go out and make this a great day.

On the resurrection morning when all the dead in Christ shall rise,
Sown in weakness, raised in power, ready to live in paradise,
Free from every imperfection, youthful and happy I shall be,
Glorified with him forever, death will be lost in victory.

Luther G. Presley - (No Date)

August 13

"FOR THE LORD YOUR GOD IS THE ONE WHO GOES WITH YOU TO FIGHT FOR YOU AGAINST YOUR ENEMIES TO GIVE YOU VICTORY." Deuteronomy 20:4

Today's promise was made to the children of Israel before they were to cross the Jordan river and fight for the land God had promised to them. Deuteronomy 20:1 says, "When you go to war against your enemies and see horses and chariots and an army greater than yours, do not be afraid of them, because the Lord your God, who brought you up out of Egypt, will be with you." We need to remember the Israelites had been slaves in Egypt for several hundred years. They did not have trained soldiers with them. They did not have the chariots and the better weapons of the time. They had no trained military leaders. Put yourself in their position. They are to go against walled cities defended by men who had been trained in tactics they intended to use in defense. Not only that, but they would be going against men who were defending their own homes. Don't you think you would have been very apprehensive? That is why the promise of God was so important to them. God's providing for the Jordan river to stop so they could all walk across on dry land was the first sign of His presence. Next came the most unusual battle for the walled city of Jericho. I am sure each of these incidents increased the number of people who really believed the promise.

The promise God gave to the children of Israel through Moses is just as good to us today. I might ask you the rhetorical questions, "What God do you serve? Do you serve the God who won the battle of Jericho, or the One who promised Mary she would, as a virgin, have a male child, or the One who fed the multitude with five fish and some loaves of bread? Or do you serve the God who heals our sick today, or the One who provides for your necessities today, or the One who heals relationships right now, or the One who whispers directions for your actions?" The obvious answer to those questions is, "They are one and the same!"

Yes! The same God who helped the children of Israel win against their enemies will help us today to win against our greatest enemy. Satan! Ephesians 6:12 tells us, "For our struggle is not against flesh and blood, but against the rulers, against the authorities, against the powers of this dark world and against the spiritual forces of evil in the heavenly realms." How do we fight them? Read Jesus' words in Matthew 18:18, "I tell you the truth, whatever you bind on earth will be bound in heaven, and whatever you loose on earth will be loosed in heaven." The more effective we become in our work for God, the harder Satan will fight by sending his spirits against us. We must command those spirits to be bound by so stating in our prayers, and they WILL be bound! We must command the spirits of God-truth, love, confidence, hope, faith, etc.-will be loosed, and they WILL be loosed.

Yes, the Lord your God is the One who goes with you to fight for you against your enemies to give you victory. Claim it today, and go out and make this a great day.

I heard an old, old story, how a Savior came from glory,
How He gave His life on Calvary to save a wretch like me;
I heard about His groaning, of His precious blood's atoning,
Then I repented of my sins and won the victory.

Eugene M. Bartlett, Sr. -1895-1941

August 14

"THE HOUSE OF THE RIGHTEOUS CONTAINS GREAT TREASURE, BUT THE INCOME OF THE WICKED BRINGS THEM TROUBLE." Proverbs 15:6

I read a story once about a young mother who, while her husband was at work, took her four children on a picnic at the edge of the woods beside a beautiful meadow, which had a stream running through it. After they had completed the meal she had prepared they all ran to the stream for a drink. The getting of a drink turned into play with running, splashing and squeals of delight. As the children continued to play the mother went back to the picnic area, sat on the blanket she had taken and watched those she loved so much. After a period of time the children stopped their play and congregated with their mother on the blanket for her to read a Bible story. After the story she told the children, "Do you know the most beautiful and valuable thing I have is in this meadow today?" "What is it?" they all chorused together. "See if you can go find it," prompted the mother. At this, they all ran about looking. One brought a beautiful butterfly. "Is this it?" she asked. "No," replied the mother. "Keep looking." Another brought a special rock with the same question and received the same answer. One got a pointed stick to dig in the ground for buried treasure, to no avail. One brought a bright feather a bird had lost. Finally the mother confessed that the most beautiful and valuable thing she had were her four children.

That young mother was training her children the way she should. She was telling them about God, she was providing them with food and exercise, and she was building in them a feeling of self-worth and self-esteem. Today's promise would have been well understood by that mother. Can't you just hear the squeals of delight as the father returns from work each day? As he comes through the door he grabs the first one and swings them up to his shoulders as the others grab him around the legs. They all bow their heads to thank God for His blessings and the meal He has provided before they eat. Listen, with your eyes closed to the stories which go around the table during the meal, and the laughter which swells spontaneously. I can see the mother and father beside their bed at night praying for those four dear children they had just tucked into their own beds.

She, and her husband, would serve God first, each other second and their family next. Whatever their income level might be, they have great treasure in their house. I read four questions with their answers in Daily Word one time. See if you agree with the answers!

What is the first human institution God created? Marriage
What is the most influential institution in the world today? The home
What is the most valuable institution in the world today? The home
What institution should be given the greatest attention and energy? The home

Make your home a home of righteousness and you will have great treasure. Your income will not bring you trouble. Now go out and make this a great day.

Good Shepherd, take this little child into your loving hands;
And in the days that lie ahead protect this little lamb.
Good Shepherd, we commit ourselves in everything we do
To be your family here on earth and love this child for you.

Claire Cloninger - 1942-

August 15

"The wicked borrow and do not repay, but the righteous give generously; THOSE THE LORD BLESSES WILL INHERIT THE LAND, BUT THOSE HE CURSES WILL BE CUT OFF." Psalm 37:21 & 22

Leslie B. Flynn told the story of a sailor who was shipwrecked and washed ashore on a South Sea island. The natives dashed to the shore, pulled him from the surf, hoisted him to their shoulders and carried him to their town. They placed him on a rude throne and proclaimed him king of their country. He learned that, according to custom, a king ruled for one year. The idea appealed to the sailor until he began to wonder what had befallen previous kings. His inquiries brought the information that when a king's reign ended, he was banished alone to a lonely, barren island where he starved. Since he had the power of kingship for a year he began issuing orders. He had one group built a large boat. He then had farmers and builders sent to the island. The farmers tilled a portion of the island and planted crops. The builders built a nice homestead. At the end of the year the sailor/king's reign was finished, and he was exiled to the island. It was not a lonely, barren island, but was, instead, a paradise of plenty. We marvel at the wisdom of that shipwrecked sailor! Isn't that what we are about in this life? That sailor quickly discovered the throne of the natives was not a permanent home for him. He was just there for a short time. He made the correct preparations for the time he would leave his life on the throne of the natives.

As the old hymn said, "This world is not my home. I'm just traveling through." We need to be like that sailor and lay up provisions for ourselves in our permanent home. Today's promise tells us the righteous give generously; those the Lord blesses will inherit the land. The Lord will bless those who give generously. Look at Jesus' words in Luke 6:38, "Give, and it will be given to you. A good measure, pressed down, shaken together and running over, will be poured into your lap. For with the measure you use, it will be measured to you." Like that sailor, our reward is not always in this life. When we give our tithes and offerings to the Lord we are building our reward for when our journey on earth is complete.

This promise also has a negative part, "The wicked borrow and do not repay...but those He curses will be cut off." This can be interpreted to mean the wicked borrow from the tithes they should be paying to the work of the Lord. These are the ones who will be cursed by the Lord and cut off. I get this interpretation from reading Malachi 3:8-9, "Will a man rob God? Yet you rob me. But you ask, 'How do we rob you?' In tithes and offerings. You are under a curse-the whole nation of you-because you are robbing me."

Are you borrowing from God? Do you take God's tithe from your pay first? The Bible is very clear that we are to tithe a tenth of all our income. In many places where tithe is mentioned it is coupled with "and special gifts" and "and offerings". God didn't put a limit of a tenth on what you can give. Give generously, earn your inheritance, and go out and make this a great day.

Give of your best to the Master, naught else is worthy His love;
He gave Himself for your ransom, gave up His glory above;
Laid down His life without murmur, you from sin's ruin to save;
Give Him your heart's adoration, give Him the best that you have.

Howard B. Grose - 1851-1939

August 16

> "KNOW THEREFORE THAT THE LORD YOUR GOD IS GOD; HE IS THE FAITHFUL GOD, KEEPING HIS COVENANT OF LOVE TO A THOUSAND GENERATIONS OF THOSE WHO LOVE HIM AND KEEP HIS COMMANDS." Deuteronomy 7:9

I love to read stories of a home which has remained in a family for many generations or of a farm which has been passed down from father to son for several generations. In my family, a generation is about twenty-five years. If one of my ancestors had started farming in Massachusetts in 1621 and had passed the farm down through the generations to me, it would only be fifteen generations. I have not read of a piece of property staying in a family in the United States for that length of time. Yet, today's promise tells us that God "is a faithful God, keeping His covenant of love to a thousand generations of those who love Him and keep His commands." That would be twenty-five thousand years! Since this writing, by Moses, was done in approximately 1400 BC I would presume Moses was talking about most of those generations being in the future, which would take to the middle of the twenty-fourth millennium. Whatever the time period involved, we have a God who will keep His covenant for a long time.

With whom will our faithful God keep His covenant of love? To those who love Him and keep His commands! Those who are faithful to God! Does that mean God does not love those who fail to love Him and keep His commands? Absolutely not! Read Romans 5:8, "But God demonstrates His own love for us in this: While we were still sinners, Christ died for us." I believe it means those who are faithful to God in loving Him and keeping His commands are assured of His love for eternity. Those who do not love Him and do not keep His commands will see the time arrive when they are cut off from His presence for eternity.

Is it easy to continually love Him and keep His commands? No, it isn't. Many things we do not understand in this world. We can't always tell if they are the chastisement of God or if they are perpetrated upon us by the devil to cause us to fall (remember the story of Job!). During the times things are going poorly with us we find it hard to keep our focus on the goodness of God. We have the tendency to ask, "Why, God, why?" We have the tendency to blame Him for our pain when we don't understand it. Those are the very times we must curl up in our Father's lap and ask Him to let His presence be felt by us.

Recently, there were many things which seemed to crush in around me. Situations I had prayed for seemed to be getting worse. I had a lot of activity with very little to show for it. As I was preparing for bed one night it all seemed to come down upon me and I felt very depressed. I prayed that He would take me in His arms and gently rock me, love me and comfort me all night long. I haven't slept that well in years! I awakened rested, positive and joyous. I recommend you try that prayer also. He IS a faithful God! Now go out and make this a great day.

> Summer and Winter, and Spring-time and harvest, sun moon, and stars in their courses above,
> Join with all nature in manifold witness to Thy great faithfulness, mercy, and love.
> Great is Thy faithfulness, great is Thy faithfulness, morning by morning new mercies I see;
> All I have needed Thy hand hath provided - Great is Thy faithfulness, Lord, unto me!
>
> Thomas O. Chisholm - 1866-1960

August 17

"And when you stand praying, if you hold anything against anyone, forgive him, SO YOUR FATHER IN HEAVEN MAY FORGIVE YOU YOUR SINS." Mark 11:25

Corrie ten Boom and her sister, Betsie, and her father were taken from their home in Holland by the Nazi's because they helped hide the Jews during World War II. Her father died soon after being taken and she and Betsie were transferred to the concentration camp of Ravensbruck, where Betsie died. After Corrie was released she opened a convalescent home in a donated mansion in Bloemendaal. The home was run by donations so Corrie spoke all over Europe. Following a meeting in Munich she was approached by a former S.S. guard, who had stood, ogled and sneered at the shower room door in the processing center at Ravensbruck. He did not recognize Corrie, but she recognized him. "How grateful I am for your message, Fraulein," he said. "To think that He has washed my sins away!" He thrust out his hand to shake Corrie's. All the angry, vengeful thoughts boiled up in Corrie. She struggled to raise her hand, but could not. She prayed a silent prayer, "Jesus, I cannot forgive him. Give me Your forgiveness. As she took his hand the most incredible thing happened. From her shoulder along her arm and through her hand a current seemed to pass from her to him, while into her heart sprang a love for that man, who had been so despicable to Corrie and the other women in the camp. This story is reported by her in her book, "The Hiding Place." She concluded this story by saying, "And so I discovered that it is not on our forgiveness any more than on our goodness that the world's healing hinges, but on His. When He tells us to love our enemies, He gives, along with the command, the love itself."

Have you had an experience as bad as Corrie ten Boom? If not, then why do you think it is so difficult to forgive those who have wronged you in some manner? If you have any bitterness in your heart toward anyone you can love them and forgive them. Do as Corrie did, call upon God to give you the forgiveness. Remember what Corrie learned - When He tells you to love your enemies, He will give, along with the command, the love itself. Just let go and let God!

When you carry an unforgiving spirit against anyone, you are letting that person control your life and your relationship with God. You don't necessarily need to become reconciled with that person, but you MUST forgive them! We are instructed in Ephesians 4:32, "Be kind and compassionate to one another, forgiving each other, just as in Christ God forgave you." What is the greatest reason for forgiving those who have hurt, or wronged, us? We are told the answer in today's promise: "So your Father in heaven may forgive you your sins." In addition, forgiveness is essential to please God, experience good health and find happiness. Forgiveness is a choice and you must forgive, even if the offender does not ask. As you forgive others, also forgive yourself. Once you forgive others and yourself, you will receive God's forgiveness. Then you should not carry the burden of guilt any longer. Forgive, be forgiven, and go out and make this a great day.

God forgave my sin in Jesus' name, I've been born again in Jesus' name;
And in Jesus' name I come to you to share His love as He told me to;
He said, "Freely, freely you have received-Freely, freely give;
Go in My name and because you believe, others will know that I live.
Carol Owens - 1931-

August 18

"THE WORDS OF A GOSSIP ARE LIKE CHOICE MORSELS; THEY GO DOWN TO A MAN'S INMOST PARTS." Proverbs 18:8 and Proverbs 26:22 (Both are identical!)

Do you engage in gossip? You do if you even listen to it just as much as if you spread it through your own words. Today's promise is a simile. It compares the words of a gossip to very tasty food, which, when eaten, sets well on the stomach (a man's inmost parts). Like tasty food, those words are easily digested and become a part of us. We carry them around with us wherever we go since they have become a part of us. Also, like tasty food, the words of a gossip whets our appetites for even more. Gossiping becomes a habit as strong as an addiction. Like other addictive behavior, it is best treated by never partaking in the first place.

The choicest morsels of gossip tends to be those which speak to the behavior, or misbehavior, of an individual, those which affect the reputation. William Shakespeare spoke to this when he wrote, "The purest treasure mortal times afford is spotless reputation; that away, men are but gilded loam or painted clay." A few years later, Lord Francis Jeffrey, Scottish jurist, critic and editor, wrote, "Good will, like a good name (reputation), is got by many actions, and lost by one." Yes, the careless words of a gossip can easily steal the good reputation of an individual. Again quoting Shakespeare, "Good name, in man or woman, is the immediate jewel of their souls. Who steals my purse steals trash; but he that filches from me my good name, robs me of that which not enriches him, and makes me poor indeed."

What should we do about gossip? First we should stop the person who starts to tell us about "Joe". Next, we should suggest that we go to "Joe" and repeat it in his presence so any inaccurate information can be immediately corrected. Even if the facts are accurate, that still doesn't give us the right to repeat them. Heed the words in James 1:26, "If anyone considers himself religious and yet does not keep a tight rein on his tongue, he deceives himself and his religion is worthless." Ask God to search our hearts and remove any tendency to gossip.

The old children's ditty said, "Sticks and stones may break my bones, but words will never hurt me." How wrong that ditty is! Gossip about a person will cause a hurt which will be carried for many years, maybe even a lifetime. Gossip about a person will hurt as badly as hateful and negative words said to a person. What do we do if we are the target of gossip? First, we should live our lives such that gossip will not be true. Next, I would suggest we discover the source, go to that person to correct the facts and assure that person of your forgiveness. We cannot always find the source or correct the facts. In that case we need to remember the words of Thomas Paine, "Reputation is what men and women think of us; character is what God and angels know of us." There is a poem written by an anonymous source: A careless word may kindle strife; A cruel word may wreck a life; A timely word may lessen strife; A loving word may heal and bless.

So watch your words, speak with tender love, and go out and make this a great day.

Search me, O God, and know my heart today;
Try me, O Savior, know my thoughts, I pray.
See if there be some wicked way in me;
Cleanse me from every sin, and set me free.

J. Edwin Orr - 1912-

August 19

"I HAVE TOLD YOU THESE THINGS, SO THAT IN ME YOU MAY HAVE PEACE. IN THIS WORLD YOU WILL HAVE TROUBLE. BUT TAKE HEART! I HAVE OVERCOME THE WORLD." John 16:33

I have a regular work-out program which includes about thirty minutes of stretching and work on the weight machine and thirty minutes of brisk walking on the treadmill. The strain of my work on the weight machine has built and toned my muscles by making them work. Likewise, the strain of my brisk walk on the treadmill exercises and builds my heart and lungs. It makes them stronger, more resilient and able to provide my normal body needs more easily. When we miss several work-outs and then return to the routine I find the exercising leaves the muscles sore because they have not been used to the work. I also find I can't walk as briskly as before because I become short of breath. The lay-off has weakened my heart, lungs and body. When I have had a vigorous work-out I find that I am hungry and need nourishment. A good lunch really sets well.

Our Christian experience is a lot like that. If our faith doesn't get stretched and have to work, it weakens to the point it is difficult for it to carry us through the bad times. Our promise for today is three-fold. First, we are promised that we will have peace. That peace is found in Jesus, as we see in Colossians 1:19-20, "For God was pleased to have all His fullness dwell in Him, and through Him to reconcile to Himself all things, whether things on earth or things in heaven, by making peace through His blood, shed on the cross." Second, we are promised we will have trouble. That trouble is the adversity we will face which strengthens our faith. If you think being a Christian means God will deliver you from all adversity you need to think again. God didn't promise to deliver us FROM adversity, but to deliver us IN adversity. The third promise is special because He tells us to take heart for He has overcome the world. Whatever trouble and adversity we may face, we know that it has been faced and overcome before, we can and will overcome it if we shelter ourselves in Jesus.

When we face the troubles which have been promised we gain the strength to deal with them. We are not given the strength needed for the troubles of tomorrow, only the strength needed for the troubles we face right now. The truth is, the three promises are one. We will face trouble which we cannot, on our own overcome, but we should take heart because Jesus has overcome the world. In Him we have peace because He faces that trouble with us, gives us the strength to overcome with His help. We should never think we will overcome alone. That is exactly what the devil wants us to think. The devil shudders when we begin to pray for help.

Let's follow the invitation given in Isaiah 27:5, "Or else let them come to me for refuge; let them make peace with me, yes, let them make peace with me." Yes, let's realize that in Jesus we have peace. Do you have that peace today? Do you call on Him at the first sign of trouble? Let Him fight for you and with you, and then go out and make this a great day.

The Lord's our Rock, in Him we hide-a shelter in the time of storm,
Secure whatever ill betide-a shelter in the time of storm.
The raging storms may round us beat-a shelter in the time of storm;
We'll never leave our safe retreat-a shelter in the time of storm.

Vernon J. Charlesworth - 1838-?

August 20

"THE ONE WHO SOWS TO PLEASE HIS SINFUL NATURE, FROM THAT NATURE WILL REAP DESTRUCTION; THE ONE WHO SOWS TO PLEASE THE SPIRIT, FROM THE SPIRIT WILL REAP ETERNAL LIFE." Galatians 6:8

The story is told about the time of a severe drought. The farmers had sowed their wheat only to watch it come up sparingly and wither and die from lack of moisture in the heat. It had reached the point the farmers just stopped sowing wheat because of the scarcity and expense of the seed wheat. The Agriculture Department became concerned about the future food supply if there continued to be no wheat sowed. They developed a plan to pay the farmers just to sow the wheat. One farmer went to the field with his tractor and wheat drill and worked all day. He went to the Agriculture Department representative and collected his money for sowing wheat. After the drought had continued for some time and there was no wheat in his field he got permission to drill the field and receive pay again. This he did. Just after he had drilled the field the second time the rains came. Imagine the surprise of the Agriculture Department representative when nothing came up in the field. Investigation of the field and questioning of the farmer brought an admission that the farmer had merely pulled the drill around the field with no wheat in the drill. He did not want to waste good wheat seed by putting it in the dry ground. That farmer had cheated the Agriculture Department and paid the price since he was tried and convicted of fraud.

The verse which proceeds today's promise in Galatians 6:7 says, "Do not be deceived: God cannot be mocked. A man reaps what he sows." The farmer sowed nothing and could reap nothing so he suffered the penalty. If that farmer had filled his drill with weed seed he would only have reaped weeds. (It was my experience you did not have to sow weeds. They always came up on their own!) What are you sowing at this time in your life? Do you watch wholesome movies and TV shows, or do you watch shows with violence, sex and bad language? Do you expect to reap a gentle spirit from watching violence? A man reaps what he sows! Do you expect to reap a pure life from watching sex filled shows? A man reaps what he sows! Do you expect to reap a habit of speaking with soft, clean, kind words from watching shows filled with bad language? A man reaps what he sows!

Read the parable of the sower in Mark 4:1-20. Jesus was explaining what happened when we spread the Word of God. Some of the Word is heard by those too busy with other things and Satan immediately takes it away. Others hear the Word, receive it and rejoice, only to fail to develop the habits of Christians and so the Word will wither and die. Others hear it, receive it and begin their walk, but worries, bad habits and evil desires choke it out so it will wither and die. There are those who hear it, receive it and rejoice. They develop good habits of worship, study, prayer and fellowship and grow in the love of the Lord. These latter make it all worthwhile!

Sow generously of the Spirit, reap a great harvest, and go out and make this a great day.

Sowing in the morning, sowing seeds of kindness,
Sowing in the noon-tide and the dewy eve.
Waiting for the harvest and the time of reaping,
We shall come rejoicing, bringing in the sheaves.
Knowles Shaw - (No Date)

August 21

"But as for you, continue in what you have learned and have become convinced of, because you know those from whom you learned it, and how from infancy you have known the holy Scriptures, WHICH ARE ABLE TO MAKE YOU WISE FOR SALVATION THROUGH FAITH IN CHRIST JESUS." 2 Timothy 3:14 & 15

As I was growing up I found that Dad was very mechanical minded. It seemed he could fix about anything. He also had a knack for knowing what would most likely break on a piece of equipment. Dad would go to farm sales, arriving before the sale began to look into all the boxes and buckets of odds and ends. Many times he would find items he knew he would be needing in the future. A lot of these containers could be purchased for a dollar or less. He would bring them home and put them in a small shed we used for such storage. There would come a day when he would say, "Clarence, there is a half-inch bolt about two inches long in either the second or third box from the door in the storage shed." I would dutifully go looking for it as I knew it had to be there. Sure enough, there would be just the bolt he needed to repair the equipment. Sometimes I couldn't find what he thought he had. He would stop what he was doing and come look with me. He never failed to find the item I couldn't find. It seemed he had just the right bolt, clamp or item he needed to repair the equipment. He knew what it was and where it was.

Don't you know people like that with Scriptures. They seem to have learned the Scriptures so well they know just what verse is needed for the situation. These people are usually mature Christians. They start out like we read in 1 Peter 2:2-3, "Like newborn babies, crave pure spiritual milk, so that by it you may grow up in your salvation, now that you have tasted that the Lord is good." It is like Paul said in 1 Corinthians 3:2, "I gave you milk, not solid food, for you were not yet ready for it. Indeed, you are still not ready." They become ready, however, by the continual reading and study of the Word of God.

Jesus told us how important it is to read the Bible, meditate, pray and attend church services to hear the Word preached. In Matthew 4:4 we read, "Jesus answered, 'It is written: Man does not live on bread alone, but on every word that comes from the mouth of God.'" The study of the Word should be a pleasure for us. We cannot leave it to be done just "sometime" during the day! We must have a specific time set aside to spend in Bible reading, meditation and prayer. Otherwise, the cares and busyness of everyday life will crowd in upon us. The devil will whisper to us how many things we have to do, and will suggest, "It won't hurt to miss just this one time." The more we study and mature as a Christian, the more we will feel as the Psalmist in Psalm 119:103, "How sweet are your words to my taste, sweeter that honey to my mouth!"

Yes, His Word will make you wise for salvation through faith in Christ Jesus just as the promise for today has stated. If you keep reading, studying, memorizing and meditating you will find it so. Claim it, and go out and make this a great day.

Thou art the bread of life, O Lord, to me;
Thy holy Word the truth that saveth me;
Give me to eat and live with Thee above;
Teach me to love Thy truth, for Thou art love.

Alexander Groves - 1842-1909

August 22

"THE LORD IS A REFUGE FOR THE OPPRESSED, A STRONGHOLD IN TIMES OF TROUBLE." Psalm 9:9

On the farm where I grew to adulthood we had a cellar. It served two purposes. The first purpose was as a storage place for all the jars of fruit, vegetables, jams, jellies and butters Momma prepared each Summer to feed us through the next year. The second purpose was used only a few times. It was as a shelter from tornadoes. I do remember one late Spring day which had been very hot for so early in the year. We had worked in the fields all day and quit to do our evening chores just as a dark cloud was forming on the horizon. We did the milking and I fed all of our hogs as Dad was separating the cream from the milk. I came in to get the milk for the calves and hogs just as the wind hit. Dad told Momma to watch the storm and he took the milk for the hogs and I took the milk for the calves. Dad came by for me as the wind was getting very strong. We stacked all the buckets together and Dad carried them and held onto my hand. By the time we reached the house we were forced to lean far into the wind to keep from being blown over. Momma and my sisters were already in the cellar. Dad sent me down, put away the buckets and came to stand at the door of the cellar, watching the storm. As it hit full fury he came down the steps and secured the door. We stayed in the cellar safe and dry as the storm passed. The only damage done was a few shingles and loose boards blown off, dirt blown into the house and the wagon was blown up against a building. That cellar was our refuge; our stronghold during the time of the terrible storm. We were really glad to have it.

Many times during our lives we will face the onslaught of a storm of trouble. Like we had on the farm, we have a refuge. We have a stronghold in those times of trouble. That refuge and stronghold is our Lord Jesus Christ! Today's promise assures us He is just that and just the time we need Him, He's always there. Do you qualify to use the Lord as a refuge and stronghold? David asked two questions and answered them in Psalm 15, "Lord, who may dwell in your sanctuary? Who may live on your holy hill? He whose walk is blameless and who does what is righteous, who speaks the truth from his heart and has no slander on his tongue, who does his neighbor no wrong and casts no slur on his fellow man, who despises a vile man but honors those who fear the Lord, who keeps his oath even when it hurts, who lends his money without usury and does not accept a bribe against the innocent. He who does these things will never be shaken."

David went on to say in Psalm 16:1, "Keep me safe, O God, for in you I take refuge."

If you will believe in Jesus Christ, ask Him to forgive you of your sins, and accept His forgiveness then you can say as David did in Psalm 18:2, "The Lord is my rock, my fortress and my deliverer; my God is my rock, in whom I take refuge. He is my shield and the horn of my salvation, my stronghold." You will be able to withstand whatever the devil may throw your way.

Accept Him and you will be safe! Now go out and make this a great day.

I serve a risen Savior, He's in the world today;
I know that He is living, whatever men may say;
I see His hand of mercy, I hear His voice of cheer,
And just the time I need Him He's always near.

Alfred H. Ackley - 1887-1960

August 23

"Do not have two differing weights in your bag - one heavy, one light. Do not have two differing measures in your house - one large, one small. You must have accurate and honest weights and measures, SO THAT YOU MAY LIVE LONG IN THE LAND THE LORD YOUR GOD IS GIVING YOU. FOR THE LORD YOUR GOD DETESTS ANYONE WHO DOES THESE THINGS, ANYONE WHO DEALS DISHONESTLY." Deuteronomy 25:13-16

I went to undergraduate college at Emporia State University in Emporia, KS in the late 1950's. Many of the students came from Kansas farms and small towns just like I did. Many of us had to work to pay our way through college. My Sophomore year I met a young lady who had transferred from another college. She had found a job close to the café where I worked. She told me one time of the reason for transfer. In the previous town she had a job as a checker in a grocery store. One day the owner of the store told her he wasn't satisfied with her work. When she asked him why he told her he expected his help to "earn their pay through 'mistakes' they made at the check stand causing the items to be charged a higher price than that listed." She told him she could not do that at all. She felt it was her job to ring up the correct amount for each item of purchase, and to do so in such a pleasant and professional manner that the customers would develop the habit of returning. In that way she would be earning her pay.

The last sentence of today's promise seems to be addressed specifically to that store owner. He didn't use different weights and measures, but he did ask his employees to deliberately charge an inflated price for the items he had for purchase in his store. He was, in effect, asking his employees to lie. He should have read Proverbs 12:22, "The Lord detests lying lips, but He delights in men who are truthful."

There are many opportunities in life to be dishonest or to take advantage of another person. We build our reputation based upon how we react to those situations. It isn't always the store owners who have the opportunity to cheat. If you are an employee, do you take advantage of your employer? Do you use sick leave in the manner for which it was planned, or do you use it as "personal leave time"? Do you use company postage to mail personal letters? Do you use the office supplies for personal uses? Do you spend work time playing games on the computer? Do you frequently arrive late or leave early? These are all examples addressed by today's promise. The third sentence could have been written: "You must be accurate and honest with the time and property of your customers and employers, so that you may live long in the land the Lord your God is giving you."

The best things in life can't be held in your hand. No matter how wonderful is the item obtained in a dishonest manner, we can never be happy and content with it if we are to live a decent, moral life. Proverbs 21:6 says, "A fortune made by a lying tongue is a fleeting vapor and a deadly snare." Be honest, claim today's promise, and go out and make this a great day.

There are things as we travel this earth's shifting sands
That transcend all the reason of man'
But the things that matter the most in this world,
They can never be held in our hand.

Dale Oldham - (No Date)

August 24

"We love, BECAUSE HE FIRST LOVED US." 1 John 4:19

I remember when I was about nine years old we went to Gate, OK to visit my maternal grandparents. Once as my siblings and I were sitting in the house my grandfather suddenly asked, "Have I ever showed you a picture of my first wife?" Talk about shocked! We didn't know grandpa had been married before. "Why, no," we stammered. He got up, went into the bedroom and brought back a picture of a young couple in wedding clothes. We dutifully oohed and aahed at the picture and my sisters commented on how pretty she was. "What was her name, grandpa?" I asked. With a gleam in his eye, grandpa replied, "Why, her name was Rosetta." Suddenly it dawned on us. Grandpa's first wife was his only wife, our grandma! We all had a good laugh over the joke he had played on us. Over fifty years later, after the death of both of them and my mother, my sisters were going through an old trunk which had been stored in Dad's basement. They found a packet of yellowed letters. When they began reading the letters they discovered they were the ones written between our grandparents in the late 1890's when they were courting in the Washington, KS, area. Grandma was teaching in Cuba, KS, about twenty-two miles West of Washington. I typed those letters so my siblings and cousins would have copies. It was really wonderful to see the undercurrents of love and concern for each other which ran through the letters. It was a love which continued to blossom until death took each of them within a few months fifty-eight years later.

We hear so much today about "love". Much of what we hear concerns a glorified romantic love which has been cheapened by movies, TV and novelists. Little of it has to do with real love or with lasting romantic love. Today's promise is so great because John, the disciple of love, tells us we know how to love because Jesus loved us first. The greatest promise in the world (see January 1) is also about love, also written by John in John 3:16, "For God so loved the world that He gave His one and only Son, that whoever believes in Him shall not perish but have eternal life." Another tremendous promise concerning God's love is Romans 5:8, "But God demonstrates His own love for us in this: While we were still sinners, Christ died for us." We read in 1 John 3:16-18, "This is how we know what love is: Jesus Christ laid down His life for us. And we ought to lay down our lives for our brothers. If anyone has material possessions and sees his brother in need but has no pity on him, how can the love of God be in him? Dear children, let us not love with words or tongue but with actions and in truth."

How should we love in response to God's love of us? We should give generously to feed the hungry, clothe and house those who need it, provide drinking water where it is not available and visit those who are sick or in prison. We should minister to fellow Christians as a servant ministers to their employer. We should pray intercessory prayers for those with spiritual, health, relationship or other needs. Love, as God loves, and go out and make this a great day.

Alas! And did my Savior bleed? And did my Sov'reign die?
Would He devote that sacred head for such a worm as I?
But drops of grief can ne'er repay the debt of love I owe;
Here, Lord, I give myself away; 'Tis all that I can do.
Isaac Watts - 1674-1748

August 25

"Children, obey your parents in everything, FOR THIS PLEASES THE LORD." Colossians 3:20

When I was four years old my brother, then ten, planned an overnight camping trip with two friends. I decided I wanted to go with them. They didn't want me to go (surprise!) so I asked Momma if I could please go with them. Her answer was a very short, "No." I really wanted to go so I waited until I knew they were to leave and followed from a distance until we were quite a way from home. Then I caught up to them and walked with them. They kept telling me at every step I should go back home as I would be in big trouble if I didn't. I ignored them as I thought they just didn't want me to be a part of their trip (which, of course, they didn't). When we were about a mile away from home we heard Momma calling my name. We all stopped until we could see her running toward us. I knew instantly that I was in BIG trouble so I started running back to her. I am sure I gave her some story about wanting to walk "just part way" with my brother and his friends, but that story didn't even buy me some time. She had broken off a tamarack switch as she had run past the tree and she switched me good. As she switched me she kept telling me she had said "NO", that is exactly what she meant and she expected me to obey her. That was the hardest switching I ever received in my life. As we were walking back home I tried again to explain my way out of trouble, but she just switched me again for lying. I learned a lot about obeying my parents that day. I don't think I ever again blatantly disobeyed them.

We read in Exodus 20:12, "Honor your father and your mother, so that you may live long in the land the Lord your God is giving you." We are, likewise, told in Ephesians 6:1-3, "Children, obey your parents in the Lord, for this is right. Honor your father and mother-which is the first commandment with a promise-that it may go well with you and that you may enjoy long life on the earth." This latter verse combines "obey" with "honor" in the instruction. I believe this is clear intent on the part of God to further instruct us to obey! Today's promise tells us that if we obey our parents "in everything" the Lord will be pleased. As Christians, our main desire is to please our Lord so it is imperative that we obey and honor our parents.

Now I am sure there is some age at which we are no longer expected to obey our parents. At this writing I am in my 60's and my father is still alive. I still feel very strongly that I must do something when Dad "suggests" I should do it. I feel when I carry out his wishes I am still "honoring" him. He is living with my sister and I check on him regularly to make sure he has what he needs, and I travel to see him at frequent intervals. In the same way we also need to honor our heavenly Father, as that pleases Him. We read in Ephesians 1:4-5, "For He chose us in Him before the creation of the world to be holy and blameless in His sight. In love He predestined us to be adopted as His sons through Jesus Christ, in accordance with His pleasure and will." Obey, honor and trust both your fathers, and go out and make this a great day.

But we never can prove the delights of His love until all on the altar we lay;
For the favor He shows, and the joy He bestows, are for them who will trust and obey.
Then in fellowship sweet we will sit at His feet, or we'll walk by His side in the way;
What He says we will do, where He sends we will go. Never fear, only trust and obey.
James H. Sammis - 1846-1919

August 26

"BUT GODLINESS WITH CONTENTMENT IS GREAT GAIN." 1 Timothy 6:6

My Bible dictionary defines "godliness" as: Piety, resulting from the knowledge and love of God, and leading to the cheerful and constant obedience of His commands. We read in 2 Peter 3:10-13, "But the day of the lord will come like a thief. The heavens will disappear with a roar; the elements will be destroyed by fire, and the earth and everything in it will be laid bare. Since everything will be destroyed in this way, what kind of people ought you to be? You ought to live holy and godly lives, as you look forward to the day of God and speed its coming. That day will bring about the destruction of the heavens by fire, and the elements will melt in the heat. But in keeping with His promise we are looking forward to a new heaven and a new earth, the home of righteousness." Yes, you ought to live holy and godly lives as that is godliness! You should also be content with fulfilling the purpose for which God has called you. In this way you are showing godliness with contentment. Today's promise states that combination will be great gain for you.

Where will you see the great gain? You will see that great gain when you receive eternal life. You will see that great gain when the current heaven and earth are destroyed and God keeps His promise to bring forward a new heaven and a new earth, the home of righteousness. What a place that new heaven will be! Read about John's vision in Revelations 22:1-6, "Then the angel showed me the river of the water of life, as clear as crystal, flowing from the throne of God and of the Lamb down the middle of the great street of the city. On each side of the river stood the tree of life, bearing twelve crops of fruit, yielding its fruit every month. And the leaves of the tree are for the healing of the nations. No longer will there be any curse. The throne of God and of the Lamb will be in the city, and His servants will serve Him. They will see His face, and His name will be on their foreheads. There will be no more night. They will not need the light of a lamp or the light of the sun, for the Lord God will give them light. And they will reign for ever and ever. The angel said to me, 'These words are trustworthy and true. The Lord, the God of the spirits of the prophets, sent His angel to show His servants the things that must soon take place.'" Just how great will heaven be? It is such a great place that gold, the symbol of wealth, power, value, beauty and permanence, will be so common-place and of such ordinary value that it will be used to pave the streets. God will wipe away every tear from our eyes. There will be no more death or mourning or crying or pain. We will be living with God as His people, and He will be our God.

Are you exhibiting godliness with contentment today? Do you have the knowledge and love of God in your heart. Does that knowledge lead to the cheerful and constant obedience of His commands? Are you content fulfilling the purpose for which God has called you? Or are you holding back a part of your life which you have not yet dedicated wholly to God? Accept God's love for you and the gift of His Son, who died for your sins. It's free! It's wonderful! It leads to great gain! Accept it, and go out and make this a great day.

O bear my longing heart to Him, who bled and died for me;
Whose blood now cleanses from all sin, and gives me victory.
O come, angel band, come and around me stand;
O bear me away on your snowy wings to my immortal home.

Jefferson Hascall - (19th Century)

August 27

"DO NOT BE AFRAID; YOU WILL NOT SUFFER SHAME. DO NOT FEAR DISGRACE; YOU WILL NOT BE HUMILIATED. You will forget the shame of your youth and remember no more the reproach of your widowhood." Isaiah 54:4

Have you ever done something for which you feel shame and disgrace, and it left you feeling humiliated? I have. I am sure most of us have done things in our past which we wish we could go back and change. You can't! Most of the things we have done in our past are things which affected very few people and are soon forgotten by those others who were aware. I can't even begin to imagine the shame and disgrace caused by those corporate officers who looted their corporations for their own gains and left stockholders and employees with the loss of their lifetime savings. Some appeared to have been defiant, but they were humiliated in the eyes of most in the country. They were certainly humiliated in the eyes of their stockholders and employees! Those corporate officers actions proved the truth of two scriptures; 1 Timothy 6:10, "For the love of money is a root of all kinds of evil. Some people, eager for money, have wandered from the faith and pierced themselves with many griefs.", and Ecclesiastes 5:10, "Whoever loves money never has money enough; whoever loves wealth is never satisfied with his income." It was so sad to watch those people try to defend their actions with all sorts of nonsensical excuses.

In today's promise Isaiah is prophesying concerning the returning remnant of the Children of Israel from Babylon. This promise is contained in the chapter following his Messianic prophesies; therefore, it should be taken as being directed at all Christians. If we live our lives in accordance with the commands and lessons in the Bible, we need never be afraid. We will not suffer shame. We need not fear disgrace. We will not be humiliated. What will humiliate us to cause us shame and disgrace? Read Galatians 5:19-21, "The acts of the sinful nature are obvious: sexual immorality, impurity and debauchery; idolatry and witchcraft; hatred, discord, jealousy, fits of rage, selfish ambition, dissensions, factions and envy; drunkenness, orgies, and the like. I warn you, as I did before, that those who live like this will not inherit the kingdom of God." How should we act? Read Galatians 5:22-26, "But the fruit of the Spirit is love, joy, peace, patience, kindness, goodness, faithfulness, gentleness and self-control. <u>Against such things there is no law</u>. Those who belong to Christ Jesus have crucified the sinful nature with its passions and desires. Since we live by the Spirit, let us keep in step with the Spirit. Let us not become conceited, provoking and envying each other." (Emphasis added.)

God wants us to live by the fruit of the Spirit, as He had Paul tell us there was no law against those fruits. By this He meant neither Scriptural and governmental law. He also wants us to avoid all acts of the sinful nature. When we study His commands we see this very clearly. He wants you to resolve today to live your life for Him by the fruit of the Spirit. He promises you will not suffer shame or humiliation. Accept Him, and go out and make this a great day.

Joys are flowing like a river since the Comforter has come;
He abides with us forever, makes the trusting heart His home.
Bringing life and health and gladness all around, this heav'nly Guest
Banished unbelief and sadness, changed our weariness to rest.

Manie P. Ferguson - (19th Century)

August 28

"Do not judge, or you too will be judged. FOR IN THE SAME WAY YOU JUDGE OTHERS, YOU WILL BE JUDGED, AND WITH THE MEASURE YOU USE, IT WILL BE MEASURED TO YOU." Matthew 7:1 & 2

Several years ago there was a joke making the rounds about a man who was caught with his hand in the till (he was embezzling!). He was charged, and the judge set a trial date. The man hired an attorney who was noted for his ability to woo a jury. The attorney made an impassioned plea during the summation telling about the man's low salary, illness of his wife and other reasons for the need for money. The jury returned a "guilty" verdict and the judge sentenced the man to five years in prison. When the sentence was announced the man turned to his attorney and said, "I thought you would get me a lot better deal than five years in prison." The attorney replied, "I think five years in prison for what you did is justice." In a loud voice the man said, "I didn't want justice. I wanted mercy!" Do you feel that way about the judgment you will face. We read in Hebrews 9:27, "Just as man is destined to die once, and after that to face judgment." We know for sure that we WILL face judgment! This is promised to us in 2 Corinthians 5:10, "For we must all appear before the judgment seat of Christ, that each one may receive what is due him for the things done while in the body, whether good or bad." We must prepare to meet our God.

When you stand before God, what kind of judge do you want deciding your case? J. I. Packer, in his book "Knowing God" wrote, "Why do men fight shy of the thought of God as a Judge? Why do they feel the thought to be unworthy of Him? The truth is that part of God's moral perfection is His perfection in judgment. Would a God who did not care about the difference between right and wrong be a good and admirable Being? Would a God who put no distinction between the beasts of history, the Hitlers and Stalins (if we dare use names), and His own saints, be morally praiseworthy and perfect? Moral indifference would be an imperfection of God, not a perfection. But not to judge the world would be to show moral indifference. The final proof that God is a perfect moral being, not indifferent to questions of right and wrong, is the fact that He has committed Himself to judge the world." You will stand before God to be judged!

Today's promise by Jesus came from His sermon on the mount. Not only is He reminding us we will be judged, but He is letting us know that He will do the judging-not us! We are told in Deuteronomy 32:35, "It is mine to avenge; I will repay." We are not to do the judging of our brothers and sisters as that is reserved to God. Jesus went on after today's promise to tell us not to look at the speck in our brother's eye when we cannot see the plank in our own. Do you have a tendency to judge others? Several times in the past few years I have been asked what I think of the actions of certain people. My standard reply is, "I would not feel right to act in that way; however, I don't know enough about their motives to judge them for those actions. I will leave the judging to God." Leave the judging to Him, and go out and make this a great day.

Careless soul, why will you linger, wandering from the fold of God?
Hear you not the invitation? O prepare to meet thy God.
If you spurn the invitation 'til the Spirit shall depart,
Then you'll see your sad condition, unprepared to meet thy God.
J. H. Stanley - (No Date)

August 29

"Not everyone who says to me, 'Lord, Lord,' will enter the kingdom of Heaven, BUT ONLY HE WHO DOES THE WILL OF MY FATHER WHO IS IN HEAVEN." Matthew 7:21

When I was in graduate school working on a Master's Degree in Chemistry I had a neighbor who loved to visit. He would come knocking on my door and visit for a long time. I knew when he came in I would not get my studying done for the next day's classes. One day I had a particularly difficult study assignment and heard him knocking on the door. I didn't answer the door and he soon called out to me, "Clarence, Clarence, let me in. I have something to tell you." I continued to ignore him and he went away after awhile. I felt so guilty about it I found it difficult to concentrate on my studies. Finally I stopped studying, went over to his house, knocked on the door and apologized to him for not answering his knock and call. I explained to him that I had a very difficult assignment to study and, when he came over, I always spent too much time talking to get the study completed. He accepted my apology and we agreed on a time which would be convenient to visit. When my neighbor knocked on the door and I did not let him in I soon relented and went to him to work out an accommodation. I went to him because I felt guilty that I had not been more careful to explain my time limitations to him and to set the ground rules for his times of visiting.

There is a set of ground rules for getting into heaven. They are carefully explained in the Bible. If you read it carefully, follow the directions and live by the instructions (commands) listed therein, you will get a positive answer when you knock on the door of heaven and call out, "Lord, Lord." Can you imagine what it would be like to just live a "good" life, die, knock on the door of heaven calling out, "Lord, Lord" and be told, "Depart from me. I never knew you."? "Good" people will not get into heaven! Can you imagine what it would be like to just be a great contributor to worthy causes, die, knock on the door of heaven calling out, "Lord, Lord" and be told, "Depart from me. I never knew you."? People who give great sums of money will not get into heaven! Can you imagine what it would be like to just do great works of caring ministry to the sick and needy, die, knock on the door of heaven calling out, "Lord, Lord" and be told, "Depart from me. I never knew you."?

Then how DO we get into heaven? Read Romans 10:9, "That if you confess with your mouth, 'Jesus is Lord,' and believe in your heart that God raised Him from the dead, you will be saved." Also read 1 John 1:9, "If we confess our sins, He is faithful and just and will forgive us our sins and purify us from all unrighteousness." Once we have accepted, by faith, the gift of the grace of God and had our sins washed away by the blood of His Son, Jesus Christ, we will then want to do the will of God and be given entrance into heaven. Is being "good", giving money and doing good works important? Of course, but NOT by themselves, they are a part of the WILL of the Father! So do the will of the Father, and go out and make this a great day.

O the blessed contemplation, when with trouble here I sigh;
I've a home beyond the river, that I'll enter by and by.
O how sweet 'twill be to meet them-all the ransomed host above;
Sweeter still to see the Savior, praise Him for redeeming love.
John W. Peterson - 1921-

August 30

"WE KNOW ALSO THAT THE SON OF GOD HAS COME AND HAS GIVEN US UNDERSTANDING, SO THAT WE MAY KNOW HIM WHO IS TRUE. AND WE ARE IN HIM WHO IS TRUE - EVEN IN HIS SON JESUS CHRIST. HE IS THE TRUE GOD AND ETERNAL LIFE." 1 John 5:20

It is easier to understand and have faith in someone if you have known them, talked to them, worked with them, lived with them, eaten with them, taken walks with them and visited friends with them. Consider how you might get to know honey bees. You could stand in front of the hive and talk to them for hours, and they would never know you, trust you or have faith in you. But, if you could make yourself into a bee, live in the hive, collect nectar with them, visit the queen bee with them, eat with them, and buzz with them; then you may gain their confidence. They would know you and you would know them. In the same way, to know God as He really is, we must know His Incarnation-Jesus Christ. In that same way we hypothetically made ourselves to be a honey bee, He actually made Himself into a man in the form of Jesus. Jesus lived with us, talked with us, ate with us, worked with us, took walks with us and visited friends with us. He suffered temptations, pain, sorrow and death just like we have and will.

You say, "Yes, but that was 2000 years ago!" Not so! I talked to Him today. He lives within my heart right now. He works with me every day. We eat our meals with Him. He visits friends with me. I walk with Him each day. To me, Jesus Christ is not doctrines, interpretations, theories, speculations, themes, information or imaginings. Jesus Christ is the impact of light upon darkness. Jesus Christ is the lesson of love to all men. Jesus Christ is the teaching of our need to forgive. Jesus Christ is the example of living for all men for all time. I thank God that He never lost interest in me. He brought me out of the miry clay and set my feet on the rock to stay. He brought me back to the faith I had as a young man, and I promise God I will faithfully follow Him and do His will, as I understand it and am led by the Holy Spirit, to the best of my ability.

What about your life today? Do you know the Son of God has come? Has He given you understanding, so that you know Him who is true? Are you in Him who is true-even in His Son, Jesus Christ? Are you in God and know that God is in you; that He is the true God and has granted you eternal life? Do you walk and talk with God on a regular basis? That is what Christianity is all about! God instructed Moses to make of a curtain in the temple to separate the Holy Place from the Most Holy Place, which contained the ark of the Testimony. Only the high priests were allowed in the Most Holy Place to talk to God. The instant Jesus died on the cross the curtain in the temple was torn in two from top to bottom. Why? Through the death of Jesus Christ we were given direct access to God, to forgive us our sins, to listen to our woes and offer us comfort, and to allow us to unburden our hearts to Him about the trials and difficulties of our lives. Know Jesus Christ, have Him in you, gain eternal life, and make this a great day.

I need Jesus: my need I now confess, no friend like Him in times of deep distress;
I need Jesus; the need I gladly own, though some may bear their load alone, yet I need Jesus.
I need Jesus: I need Him to the end, no one like Him-He is the sinners' friend.
I need Jesus; no other friend will do, so constant, kind, so strong and true-yes, I need Jesus.
George O. Webster - 1866-1942

August 31

"Let us not become weary in doing good, FOR AT THE PROPER TIME WE WILL REAP A HARVEST IF WE DO NOT GIVE UP." Galatians 6:9

Each Summer, as I was growing up on the farm, we would find the sunflowers growing up in our crops. When the work schedule allowed, Dad would help me sharpen a "corn knife", a machete-like tool with a four inch wooden handle and an eighteen inch blade, three inches wide, sharpened on one side. We would head for the crop fields and spend several days walking the rows of crops cutting sunflowers and other bothersome weeds. It was hard, hot work! Our arms would get so tired we could barely lift the knife for another stroke against another sunflower. When it seemed I would surely drop, we would stop for a water break in the shade of the truck and rest and visit for awhile. When the crops were cleared of the sunflowers they seemed to just jump in growth as they were no longer in the shade of those tall sunflowers which sapped the water out of the ground and away from the crops. You always wanted to cut the sunflowers well before the crops began to form the grain. Otherwise, the sunflowers would reduce the yield of grain. Oh, how weary we became cutting those sunflowers, but we always felt so good when the work was finished and we could see a clean field of crops! At the time of harvest we would have a better crop of grain, and it would be easier to harvest without the sunflowers.

To get the full impact of today's promise we need to read the two verses which precede this one, "Do not be deceived: God cannot be mocked. A man reaps what he sows. The one who sows to please his sinful nature, from that nature will reap destruction; the one who sows to please the Spirit, from the spirit will reap eternal life." While we did not "sow" the seeds of those sunflowers, nature did. We could have been too tired to have cut them out of the crops and just left them to grow (please our sinful nature). Had we done so, we would have reaped a smaller crop of grain (destruction). Instead, we did not become weary of cutting them out, and at the proper time we reaped a better harvest.

The verse following today's promise is also very important in understanding what God wants of us as believers. "Therefore, as we have opportunity, let us do good to all people, especially to those who belong to the family of believers." How do we do good? Read Matthew 25:31-40 (see April 10). You give food to the hungry, water to the thirsty, shelter to the homeless, clothes to those who need them, and visit the sick and those in prison. When William Booth formed the Salvation Army in 1865 in the East end of London, he did so because he said you could not expect someone to listen to the message of salvation when they were cold, hungry or without shelter. Do you think that has changed in the intervening time? Of course not! When Jesus sent out the seventy-two he said in Luke 10:2, "The harvest is plentiful, but the workers are few. Ask the Lord of the harvest, therefore, to send out workers into His harvest field." Are you a worker in His harvest field today? Be one, and go out and make this a great day.

I want to be a worker for the Lord, I want to love and trust His holy word,
I want to sing and pray, be busy every day, in the vineyard of the Lord.
I want to be a worker every day, I want to lead the erring in the way
That leads to heaven above, where all is peace and love, in the vineyard of the Lord.

I. Baltzell - (19th Century)

September 1

"Train a child in the way he should go, AND WHEN HE IS OLD HE WILL NOT TURN FROM IT." Proverbs 22:6

One time a husband and wife decided to grow a garden. They prepared the beds and decided where they wanted to grow potatoes, tomatoes, beans, carrots, squash, etc. They went to town to buy the seed and discovered the cheapest seed they could buy was a bag of thistle bird feed seed, so they bought a large quantity of it. Taking it home, they decided it really didn't matter what seed they planted, for they knew they wanted to raise potatoes in the potato patch, tomatoes in the tomato patch, beans in the bean patch and so forth. They carefully planted their seed and kept the garden watered and weed free. To their delight, they harvested large amounts of potatoes, tomatoes, beans, carrots, squash, etc. RIGHT? Preposterous and nonsense! They only harvested THISTLES!

Isn't that what a lot of husbands and wives are doing now? Aren't they planting thistle seeds in their children when they want them to produce tomatoes? What are you planting in your children or grandchildren? If you are a young person, what is being planted in you?

Do we really think we can plant immorality by watching it on TV and in the movie theater and expect to produce morality in ourselves and in our children? Can we really plant dishonesty by "fudging" on our income tax and expect to produce honesty in ourselves and in our children? Is it true that we can plant the seeds of character in our children by spending "quality time"with them at a picnic or a fishing trip on Sunday, rather than taking them to the house of God? David Roper, writing in the "Daily Bread" of October 13, 2002 said, "As parents, the question we should ask ourselves is not 'How can we produce a godly or successful child?' but rather, 'How can we be more godly parents?' The first question has to do with the end result over which we have no control; the second has to do with a process over which we do have control. Our prayer should be: 'Lord, make us the kind of parents You want us to be.'" What a great piece of advice this is for us in considering today's promise.

The next question in considering today's promise, then, is: How do we train a child in the way he should go? The answer is: Live your life according to the scriptures, and follow the gentle nudges of the Holy Spirit as you rear you children. Part of the responsibility rests on the shoulders of the children. The Psalmist said in Psalm 119:9-11, "How can a young man keep his way pure? By living according to your word. I seek you with all my heart; do not let me stray from your commands. I have hidden your word in my heart that I might not sin against you." You should do all you can to encourage the memorization of the scripture through example, contests, church attendance, family worship and any other forms you can think of. If you want potatoes, tomatoes, beans carrots, squash, etc. you must plant them. Don't plant thistles!

Follow God's lead in training your children, and go out and make this a great day.

God His own doth tend and nourish, in His holy courts they flourish;
From all evil things He spares them, in His mighty arms He bears them.
Neither life nor death shall ever from the Lord His children sever;
Unto them His grace He showeth, and their sorrows all He knoweth.
Carolina Sandell Berg - 1832-1903

September 2

"When the perishable has been clothed with the imperishable, and the mortal with immortality, then the saying that is written will come true: 'Death has been swallowed up in victory.' 'Where, O death, is your victory? Where, O death, is your sting?' The sting of death is sin, and the power of sin is the law. But thanks be to God! HE GIVES US THE VICTORY THROUGH OUR LORD JESUS CHRIST." 1 Corinthians 15:54-57

When I was five years old, Dad worked for Phillips Petroleum Company as an engineer at their pump station on the pipeline passing through Phillips, Texas. We lived in one of the five houses on the station property. Behind the houses, there was a big garden that stretched the full width of the five houses. The garden was lower than the back yards, so there was a retaining wall made from rocks just stacked together without the use of mortar. This wall made an excellent place for rattlesnakes to live and there were a lot of them there. Each family would kill several every year. That summer, when I was five, was a particularly prolific year for the "rattlers", and one day, we heard a shout from a neighbor who had been hoeing his vegetable patch. We gathered to see what the commotion was about and found that he had discovered a six-foot long diamondback rattle-snake in his garden. As we watched, he moved it around with his hoe. The rattler would strike the hoe handle again and again, occasionally getting its fangs caught in the handle. The neighbor would shake it loose and continue to show us how the snake would coil before it struck. It was a very good lesson for all of us who were not totally familiar with its habits. I will never forget the lessons our neighbor taught us and his warnings about being careful around the snakes. Can't you just imagine the sting of those fangs if they were to strike a part of your body? Reverend William Secker, a seventeenth-century British minister, once said, "Who would fear the hissing serpent, if he knew it had no sting?"

When God created us, He gave us a free will to choose. If we choose to live a life apart from God, we find that death will have a sting far worse than that diamondback could ever have delivered. If we choose to accept the gift of salvation provided through the death of His Son, Jesus Christ, we find that death will be swallowed up in victory. That victory is eternal life with our Lord. Where before we were perishable, we have been clothed with the imperishability of righteousness. Where before we were mortal, we have been granted immortality through Jesus Christ our Lord and Savior. That is what Paul meant when he wrote, "Death has been swallowed up in victory. Where, O death is your victory? Where, O death, is your sting?"

The sting of the diamondback is the plunge of its fangs into your flesh, which could result in death to the person who is struck. The sting of death is sin and eternal separation from God. The real sting is that at death, we will never again have the opportunity to accept God's gift! But, thanks be to God! By accepting His gift, He has given us the victory through our Lord Jesus Christ. Accept Him today, and go out and make this a great day.

Where will you spend eternity? This question comes to you and me!
Tell me, what shall your answer be? Where will you spend eternity?
Repent, believe, this very hour, trust in the Savior's grace and power,
Then will your joyous answer be, saved thro' a long eternity!
Elisha A. Hoffman - 1839-1929

September 3

"AND IF I GO AND PREPARE A PLACE FOR YOU, I WILL COME BACK AND TAKE YOU TO BE WITH ME THAT YOU ALSO MAY BE WHERE I AM." John 14:3

I grew up in the Friends (Quaker) church. Each individual Friends church is called a "Monthly Meeting" because they hold a business meeting each month to record births, deaths and marriages and to discuss the business of the church. Through the minutes of those monthly meetings, one branch of my family has been traced back to London, with the birth of Isaac Scarborough in 1560. In the 1680's, there was increasing persecution of the Quakers in London, so John Scarborough brought his fourteen-year old son, also John Scarborough, to America, where he bought about 500 acres of land from William Penn. I like to picture in my mind the parting with his wife, Sarah Ashley Scarborough. There must have been many tears with Sarah saying over and over, "John, please promise you will come back for me." John answered her, "My Sarah, I am going over to prepare a farm and home for you. I will come back to get you and take you with me so we can always be together." John the father and John the son did come over, got the land, clear a good-sized field, plant their crop, build a cabin and establish a home. John, the elder, then left his sixteen-year old son, John, to take care of their new home and returned to London to get Sarah. By that time, the persecution had diminished, and Sarah refused to journey to the new home. John and Sarah stayed in London and notified their son, John, that the new land in America now belonged to him. John later married Mary Pierson and had a daughter, Sarah Scarborough, who later married George Haworth. Six generations later, my maternal grandmother was born as Rosetta May Haworth.

As much as Sarah Ashley Scarborough hated to see her husband, John, leave for America it must pale in comparison to how the disciples felt about Jesus leaving them. Jesus was preparing the disciples for His death, and then He made them a very special promise, today's promise. Jesus knew He was finishing His purpose on earth. He had come to fulfill the law and the prophesies and to make the new blood covenant. By accepting the gift of God's Son, who shed His blood to atone for our sins, we are assured that He has prepared a place for us. He will come back and take us to be with Him, that where He is (heaven), we may also be.

The angel of death, who was the tenth plague against the Egyptians, passed over the homes of the children of Israel, who had put the blood of a perfect lamb on their doorway, top and sides. In the same way, by accepting the gift of our sins being washed away by the blood shed by the Perfect Lamb of God (blood from His head and hands, symbolically-top and sides), death will pass over us, and we are promised eternal life with our Lord. Then there will be no pain or death, no sorrow or parting, just eternal worship and joy in the presence of our Lord and Savior. Have you accepted that gift today? Is there a place being prepared for you in heaven?

Make sure He will come back for you, and then go out and make this a great day.

I'm satisfied with just a cottage below, a little silver and a little gold;
But in that city where the ransomed will shine, I want a gold one that's silver lined.
Don't think me poor or deserted or lonely, I'm not discouraged, I'm heaven bound;
I'm just a pilgrim in search of a city, I want a mansion, a harp and a crown.

Ira F. Stamphill - 1914-

September 4

"And of this gospel I was appointed a herald and an apostle and a teacher. That is why I am suffering as I am. Yet I am not ashamed, because I know whom I have believed, AND AM CONVINCED THAT HE IS ABLE TO GUARD WHAT I HAVE ENTRUSTED TO HIM FOR THAT DAY." 2 Timothy 1:11 & 12

Have you had a tough life? Saul was a very favored person. He was born as a citizen of the leading county in the world and studied under the leading religious scholar of the day. He also learned a trade, which was to provide for his needs during his life. He rose in his religion to become very respected and helpful to one of the leading sects in enforcing discipline to their beliefs. As he was traveling in connection with this enforcement work, he was struck down and blinded by a brilliant light. He heard the voice of God saying, "Saul, Saul, why do you persecute me?" Look at his response, "Who are you, Lord?" He knew who it was! He was asking for verification. From this experience, Saul became Paul, and Paul became one of the greatest Christian leaders and writers of all time. He made four missionary trips, establishing numerous churches, raising funds, preaching the gospel, bearing imprisonment, living through being ship wrecked and stranded for three months, speaking up for his work and churches and writing numerous letters, which became one quarter of the New Testament. For his work for God, Paul was imprisoned several times and his life ended with him being beheaded outside of Rome. I ask again, have you had a tough life?

When Saul came into the presence of God, he was totally convinced of the truth of Christianity and the veracity of the life of Jesus. He completely accepted Jesus Christ and was led to those who would teach him all that was known about Christianity. Paul was as surely led by the Holy Spirit as has anybody in the world ever been led. He realized the cost of service to Jesus Christ, since he had been one of the main persecutors of the early Christians. He accepted this and was able to say, "Of this gospel I was appointed a herald and an apostle and a teacher. That is why I am suffering as I am." Did that make him feel sorry for himself? NO! He went on to say, "Yet I am not ashamed, because I know whom I have believed, and am convinced that He is able to guard what I have entrusted to Him for that day." What had Paul entrusted to God? His life! "But," you say. "He was beheaded!" Of course he was, but he had earlier said, "For me to live is Christ, but to die is gain." He knew that to live would mean more heralding of the gospel, more preaching and teaching of the love of Christ. He also knew that to die, gave him eternal life.

Are things going tough for you right now? Then cast all your cares upon Him, for He cares for you. Know, as Paul did, in whom you have believed. Be convinced that He IS able to guard what you have entrusted to Him. Entrust your life, and all you have, to Him. He WILL guard it, and He WILL grant you eternal life.

Claim it, and go out and make this a great day.

I know not why God's wondrous grace to me He hath made known,
Nor why, unworthy, Christ in love redeemed me for His own.
But I know whom I have believed, and am persuaded that He is able
To keep that which I've committed unto Him against that day.

Daniel W. Whittle - 1840-1901

September 5

> "Therefore go and make disciples of all nations, baptizing them in the name of the Father and of the son and of the Holy Spirit, and teaching them to obey everything I have commanded you. AND SURELY I AM WITH YOU ALWAYS; TO THE VERY END OF THE AGE." Matthew 28:19 & 20

There is a joke told of young man who decided to use the Bible to find out what God wanted him to do with his life. He stood at the table with an unopened Bible on it, closed his eyes, reached down, opened the Bible and placed his finger on a verse. He then read the verse, Luke 10:2, "He told them, 'The harvest is plentiful, but the workers are few. Ask the Lord of the harvest, therefore, to send out workers into his harvest field." From this, the young man was sure he was called into the mission field. He went to training and found it very difficult and hard to concentrate. He finally finished the training and was assigned to a foreign station. He worked there for several miserable years and returned home for a year of sabbatical leave. During that year, he stayed several months with a friend on his farm. He found the work so fulfilling and satisfying he left mission work, bought a farm and became a farmer. He said he had discovered the Lord was telling him to be a farmer, not a missionary, with the call to the harvest field. We can laugh at such a joke, but we must be sure of God's call. It won't come to us by such a random approach as that young man used. It should be done by prayer, meditation and a total yielding of our lives to Him. I was not called to be a missionary. I have felt more and more the call to support missionaries with my prayers and with financial gifts. It is very fascinating to meet those who have been called to the mission fields. They are very special people and deserve our support. Since the cost of training, equipping and sending missionaries to foreign fields is so high, there has been a move in the last several years to send people on trial missions early in their potential careers to make sure they are both called and suited for mission work.

Our promise today was a call from Jesus to his followers to become missionaries. He sent them into every nation to spread the gospel of Jesus Christ. His assurance to them was, "And surely I am with you always; to the very end of the age." Almost every one of the disciples of Jesus died a martyr's death, but every one of them knew that He was with them to the end, and they willingly gave their lives to spread His teachings. The persecution of the early Christians is one of the factors which caused Christianity to spread so far and fast.

What is your calling from God in relation to missions? Are you called to go to a foreign field? If you are, you will never have joy until you are there. Are you called to local mission work? If you are, you will never have joy until you are involved therein. Are you called to support the work with your prayers and contributions? If you are, you will never have joy until you commit yourself to such work. Like the missionaries in the field, God will be with you always, even to the end of the age. Answer His call, and go out and make this a great day.

> It may not be on the mountain's height or over the stormy sea,
> It may not be at the battlefront my Lord will have need of me;
> But if by a still, small voice He calls to paths I do not know,
> I'll answer, dear Lord, with my hand in Thine, I'll go where You want me to go.
>
> Mary Brown - (19th Century)

September 6

"I write to you, dear children, BECAUSE YOUR SINS HAVE BEEN FORGIVEN ON ACCOUNT OF HIS NAME." 1 John 2:12

In "Decision Magazine", December 1996, Mark Strand tells of an experience that occurred following his first year of college. His dad and mom had left for vacation, and Mark wrecked their pickup truck, crumpling the passenger door. Returning home, he parked the truck. When his dad returned home and saw the damage, Mark acted surprised and denied any knowledge of the accident. Mr. Strand then asked the hired man about it, and to Mark's delight, the man admitted he was responsible. He had heard a loud noise while passing the truck with the wings of the cultivator up, and now he assumed he had caused the damage. The weeks that followed were torturous as Mark struggled with his guilty conscience. He repeatedly considered telling the truth, but was afraid. Finally on day he impulsively blurted out, "Dad, there's something I need to tell you." "Yes?" "You know that pickup door? I was the one who did it." His dad look at him. Mark looked back at him. For the first time in weeks he was able to look his dad in the eyes as the topic was broached. To Mark's utter disbelief, his dad calmly replied, "I know." Silent seconds later his dad said, "Let's go eat." He put his arm around Mark's shoulder, and they walked to the house, not saying another word about it. Not then, not ever.

Do you think your sins are hidden from our omnipotent and omnipresent God? He knows! That is why He sent His Son into the world to be born, live, die, rise from the dead and ascend into heaven. His Son's blood was shed for our sins-your's, mine and the sins of each person in the world. What does God want? Read 1 John 3:23, "And this is His command: to believe in the name of His Son, Jesus Christ, and to love one another as He commanded us." John tells us in today's promise that our sins have been forgiven on account of His name. Mark's life was miserable when he withheld the truth about the accident from his dad. When Mark confessed his error to his dad, he found out his dad already knew; but by that confession, Mark received the forgiveness from his dad, and their relationship was healed. God knows about our sins, and He wants us to believe in His Son as the way of salvation. He wants us to ask for His forgiveness of our sins.

When we ask for His forgiveness, we receive His forgiveness, and the relationship between God and us is healed. John, who understood God's love so well, was writing to us as children of God. How are we children of God? Because our sins have been forgiven on account of the name of Jesus Christ, who shed His life-blood as atonement for our sins. Like the thief on the cross, we don't have to do any works for that salvation. It is a gift from God! Jesus will come again as a bridegroom coming to his bride, the body of believers, called the church. When He comes, will you be ready to receive your gift of eternal life? You will be if you have received forgiveness for your sins. Make sure you are ready, and go out and make this a great day.

When the Bridegroom cometh, will your robes be white,
Are you washed in the blood of the lamb?
Will your souls be ready for the mansions bright
And be washed in the blood of the Lamb?

Elisha A. Hoffman - 1839-1929

September 7

"'FOR I KNOW THE PLANS I HAVE FOR YOU,' DECLARES THE LORD, 'PLANS TO PROSPER YOU AND NOT TO HARM YOU, PLANS TO GIVE YOU HOPE AND A FUTURE.'" Jeremiah 29:11

During the years I had my insurance agency, I was involved in economic development in Norman, Oklahoma. I served on the Board of Directors of the Norman Chamber of Commerce, including a term as president. During those years, I saw several businesses get their start. One of the things I found, almost without fail, was those businesses which had a well thought out and complete business plan were those most likely to succeed. Those which tried to get their start without such a plan almost invariably failed. I learned several cliches during that time which were proved true. One was: Plan your work, and then work your plan. Another was: Those who fail to plan are those who are planning to fail. Still another was: If your plan is not written, it isn't.

Today's promise is especially meaningful to me because of my background in economic development. What a wonderful thought it is to me that God has plans for me! They are plans with which I will succeed, as He promises me they are plans to prosper me and not to harm me. They are plans to give me hope and a future. His plan is written down for me also! Where do I find His plan for me? The same place you will find His plan for you: The Bible!

God calls us to Him as we read in Isaiah 49:1, "Listen to me, you islands; hear this, you distant nations: Before I was born the Lord called me; from my birth He has made mention of my name." God said in Jeremiah 1:5, "Before I formed you in the womb I knew you, before you were born I set you apart." How wonderful it is to know that before we were born, the Lord called us and has made mention of our names since the day we were born; that before we were conceived in our mother's womb, God knew us and set us apart!

So what is His plan for us? Jesus said in John 3:7, "You must be born again." When we are born of the flesh, we will surely die, everyone of us, but when we are born of the Spirit, we will have eternal life. Being born again is the first part of God's plan for us. Jesus told us in John 13:34, "A new command I give you: Love one another. As I have loved you, so you must love one another." John also told us in 1 John 4:7-8, "Dear friends, let us love one another, for love comes from God. Everyone who loves has been born of God and knows God... because God is love." Loving one another is the second part of God's plan for us. Read also 1 John 5:3-4, "This is love for God: to obey His commands. And His commands are not burdensome, for everyone born of God overcomes the world. This is the victory that has overcome the world, even our faith." Obeying His commands is the third part of God's plan for us.

So if we love God and are born again, love one another and obey God's commands we will be following His plans for us to prosper and give us hope for the future. That is a plan that is designed for success! Work His plan, and go out and make this a great day.

His power can make you what you ought to be;
His blood can cleanse your heart and make you free;
His love can fill your soul, and you will see
'Twas best for Him to have His way with thee.
Cyrus S. Nusbaum -1861-1937

September 8

"I waited patiently for the Lord; HE TURNED TO ME AND HEARD MY CRY. HE LIFTED ME OUT OF THE SLIMY PIT, OUT OF THE MUD AND MIRE; HE SET MY FEET ON A ROCK AND GAVE ME A FIRM PLACE TO STAND." Psalm 40:1 & 2

In Northern Kansas, where I grew up, there was a lot of clay on the hillsides. When it rained, the clay would stick to your shoes as you walked across the fields. As more and more clay would stick to the shoes, the weight would become greater and greater. The weight of that clay was such a burden it made it very difficult and tiring to walk. If the clay didn't drop off on its own, which it usually didn't, you would have to shake your foot to get it off, or get a stick and scrape it off. Even if it was considerably farther to walk, it was better to go into the pasture to walk on the grass, and get out of the clay, mud and mire.

That must have been the image in David's mind as he wrote these verses. His burdens were so great they weighted him down, and his life became very difficult and tiring. He waited patiently for the Lord to turn to him and hear his cry. God took those burdens away, just like crawling over the pasture fence, wiping the clay and mud off your shoes and walking on the grass. David's image given us is of God lifting him out of the slimy pit of mud and mire, and setting his feet on a rock. David then had a firm place to stand. He wasn't burdened by the sins and evil of the world which clung to him like the mud clung to my feet when walking across the wet fields.

What about your life today? Are you burdened with sins and cares of the world? Do you feel like you are in a slimy pit, covered with mud and mire, struggling to climb out? Are those sins and cares so heavy they are difficult to carry and make you so tired you feel you will never find rest? God will hear your cry. He will take away your burden of sins and cares of the world. He will give you a new life and a new hope. He will lift you out of the slimy pit, out of the mud and mire; He will set your feet on a rock and give you a firm place to stand. Yes, you can stand on this promises of God! This promise is about salvation! Are you carrying a burden of sin, like the mud and mire of the slimy pit about which David is speaking? Ask Him to remove the burden of sins and cares of the world from you. His promise is for YOU! He has promised to hear you knock on the door and He will open it. So knock and the door to eternal life will be opened to you.

You can also count on Jesus' promise in Matthew 11:28, "Come to me, all you who are weary and burdened, and I will give you rest." Are you weary from carrying the load of sin all by yourself? You don't have to do that! Jesus Christ our Lord will take away that load and give you a new life. He told us in John 14:6, "I am the way and the truth and the life." He will grant you a new life! Paul told us this in 2 Corinthians 5:17, "Therefore, if anyone is in Christ, he is a new creation; the old has gone, the new has come!" Yes, that old burden of sins and cares will go. A new life of joy, peace and rest will come! Claim His promise, and go out and make it a great day.

In loving kindness Jesus came my soul in mercy to reclaim,
And from the depths of sin and shame through grace He lifted me.
From sinking sand He lifted me, with tender hand He lifted me;
From shades of night to plains of light, O praise His name, He lifted me!
Charles H. Gabriel - 1856-1932

September 9

"In this you greatly rejoice, though now for a little while you may have had to suffer grief in all kinds of trials. THESE HAVE COME SO THAT YOUR FAITH - of greater worth than gold, which perishes even though refined by fire - MAY BE PROVED GENUINE AND MAY RESULT IN PRAISE, GLORY AND HONOR WHEN JESUS CHRIST IS REVEALED." 1 Peter 1:6 & 7

My brother-in-law, Lloyd C. English, is an artist. He taught art at the grade school, high school and college level. He also produced many pieces of art work—paintings, pottery and other fine arts. He worked with many mediums, including water color, oils, clay, silver and gold. One day we were visiting, and he told me about a seminar he attended. The artist conducting the seminar was working with gold. He was heating the gold to make it just right for the use he was going to make of it. One of the other seminar attendees asked, "Sir, how do you know when the gold has been heated to just the right point?" The artist replied, "You know it is just right when you can see yourself reflected just perfectly in the gold."

Our promise for today tells us that for a little while we may have to suffer grief in all kinds of trials. We sometimes call that "being tried by fire." There is an expression going around which says, "The hardest steel comes through the hottest fire!" Looking at how the artist knows just when he has heated the gold to just the right point, we get our answer of just how God knows when we have suffered just the right amount of grief and trials. It is when He can see himself reflected perfectly in our lives!

If we keep our faith, and if that faith is proved genuine, it will result in praise, glory and honor when the face of Jesus Christ is reflected by our lives. Have you gone through the fires of the suffering of grief in all kinds of trials? Do you wonder just why God lets so much happen to you? Do you feel you have been deserted by God because of all you are going through? Have you kept the faith? Is your faith in God genuine? If it is, it will result in praise, glory and honor because others will see Jesus Christ reflected in your life. Literally, Jesus Christ is in us. Jesus told us in John 14:19-20, "Before long, the world will not see me anymore, but you will see me. Because I live, you also will live. On that day you will realize that I am in my Father, and you are in me, and I am in you."

Is Jesus Christ in you today? If He is, you will live for eternity, just as He lives for eternity. Yes, you will suffer grief in all kinds of trials. You live in the world and will suffer the temptations of Satan. Read 1 Corinthians 10:13, "No temptation has seized you except what is common to man. And God is faithful; He will not let you be tempted beyond what you can bear. But when you are tempted, He will also provide a way out so that you can stand up under it." Jesus told us in John 16:33, "In this world you will have trouble. But take heart! I have overcome the world." Put your faith in Jesus Christ, and go out and make this a great day.

My faith has found a resting place, not in device nor creed;
I trust the ever living One, His wounds for me shall plead.
Enough for me that Jesus saves, this ends my fear and doubt;
A sinful soul I come to Him, He will not cast me out.
Lidie H. Edmunds - (19th Century)

September 10

"One man gives freely, yet gains even more; another withholds unduly, but comes to poverty. A GENEROUS MAN WILL PROSPER; HE WHO REFRESHES OTHERS WILL HIMSELF BE REFRESHED." Proverbs 11:24 & 25

Growing up on the farm, I remember when we would butcher a fat steer in the fall of the year, we would take several packages of meat, including steak, roasts and hamburger, to the pastor of our Friends church. When we would butcher the hogs, we would take him some pork loins, side meat and sausage. In the spring and summer, when we had chickens of frying size, we would take him dressed chickens on a regular basis. We would also include his wife in the group who came to can the corn each summer. We were cash poor, but we sure did eat good, and we shared what we did have for the work of the Lord. I never remember a time we did not have plenty to eat! What did we give? I think that is answered by David's prayer of thanks for gifts for building the temple. 1 Chronicles 29:10-14, "David praised the Lord in the presence of the whole assembly, saying, 'Praise be to you, O Lord, God of our father Israel, from everlasting to everlasting. Yours, O Lord, is the greatness and the power and the glory and the majesty and the splendor, for everything in heaven and earth is yours. Yours, O Lord, is the kingdom; you are exalted as head over all. Wealth and honor come from you; you are the ruler of all things. In your hands are strength and power to exalt and give strength to all. Now, our God, we give you thanks, and praise your glorious name. But who am I, and who are my people, that we should be able to give as generously as this? Everything comes from you, and we have given you only what comes from your hand.'" Truly, everything we have and gave came from the hand of God!

Today's promise compares two men: One gives freely while the other withholds. I like the saying, "You can give without loving, but you can't love without giving." Free giving is an expression of love which the Lord will reward. Free giving is the kind advocated in James 3:11-13, "Can both fresh water and salt water flow from the same spring? My brothers, can a fig tree bear olives, or a grapevine bear figs? Neither can a salt spring produce fresh water. Who is wise and understanding among you? Let him show it by his good life, by deeds done in the humility that comes from wisdom."

Giving is not limited to money. We give by our ministry to fellow Christians and our outreach to non-believers. This was the charge of Jesus, that we feed the hungry, give water to the thirsty, clothe those who need them, provide shelter to the homeless, and visit the sick and those in prison. Read Ephesians 2:10, "For we are God's workmanship, created in Christ Jesus to do good works, which God prepared in advance for us to do." This clearly says that GOD PREPARED IN ADVANCE THE GOOD WORKS FOR US TO DO!!!!!!! We are failing God if we do not do those works, large or small, He has prepared in advance for us to do.

Claim today's promise, and go out and make this a great day.

In the harvest field now ripened, there's a work for all to do;
Hark, the voice of God is calling, to the harvest calling you.
Little is much when God is in it, labor not for wealth or fame;
There's a crown and you can win it, if you go in Jesus' name.

Kittie Louise Suffield - 1884-1972

September 11

"HE FULFILLS THE DESIRES OF THOSE WHO FEAR HIM; HE HEARS THEIR CRY AND SAVES THEM." Psalm 145:19

When my daughter, Katy, was a baby, she had a lot of trouble with colic. Of course, the main outbreaks happened at night. I was teaching chemistry at Phillips University in Enid, OK at the time. I would be sound asleep and would hear her cry. I would get up, go to her crib, lift her out and place the heel of one hand on her chest, with her head on my fingers. My other hand would hold her little bottom. I would walk around our apartment gently bouncing her up and down. She would soon be feeling better and would drift off to sleep. If I were to lay her down too soon, her pains would come back and she would be crying again before I could get to sleep. Some nights, I would walk with her and gently bounce her for two or three hours at a time. Her crying would just break my heart, and I couldn't let her just lie there hurting and crying. Don't you think that is a lot how God responds to us? As much as I love Katy, it is not even close to how much God loves us. Yes, He fulfills the desires of those who love, respect and worship Him. He hears our cry, our faintest cry, and saves us.

After Elijah had slaughtered the prophets of Baal in the Kishon Valley, he had to flee to Beersheba from the wrath of Queen Jezebel. He fell asleep under a broom tree there. Twice an angel awakened him to eat and drink from provisions which had appeared. Strengthened, he traveled forty days and nights to Mt. Horeb and spent a night in a cave. We read in 1 Kings 19:11-13, "The Lord said, 'Go out and stand on the mountain in the presence of the Lord, for the Lord is about to pass by.' Then a great and powerful wind tore the mountains apart and shattered the rocks before the Lord, but the Lord was not in the wind. After the wind there was an earthquake, but the Lord was not in the earthquake. After the earthquake came a fire, but the Lord was not in the fire. And after the fire came a gentle whisper. When Elijah heard it, he pulled his cloak over his face and went out and stood at the mouth of the cave." If God expects us to hear Him in just a gentle whisper, don't you think He will hear our faintest cry?

If you are hurting today, give your cry to God. He will hear your cry and save you. It is His greatest wish to fulfill the desires of you when you truly love, respect and worship Him. It matters not whether your cry is brought on by your own, or a loved one's, physical pain, grief, loneliness, despair, relational suffering, physical need or spiritual need, God will hear your cry. You should not expect God to answer your cry in just the way you think He should. He will answer you in the way He knows He should. We should always yield to the omniscience of God.

Jesus did this the night before He was crucified when He prayed in Gethsemane. Three times He asked His Father to take the cup from Him, but closed the prayer with, "Yet not as I will, but as you will."

Pray your cry to God. He will hear and save you. Now go out and make this a great day.

We are Thine, do Thou befriend us, be the Guardian of our way;
Keep Thy flock; from sin defend us; seek us when we go astray.
Blessed Jesus, blessed Jesus, hear, O hear us when we pray;
Blessed Jesus, blessed Jesus, hear, O hear us when we pray.

Dorothy A. Thrupp - 1779-1847

September 12

"BUT WHOEVER LIVES BY THE TRUTH COMES INTO THE LIGHT, SO THAT IT MAY BE SEEN PLAINLY THAT WHAT HE HAS DONE HAS BEEN DONE THROUGH GOD." John 3:21

There is a story of a train wreck which was caused when one train had trouble and was stopped on the track on a very dark night. Another train, going the same direction, hit the first train in the rear. A lawsuit resulted and the signalman from the first train was called to testify. The plaintiff attorney asked the signalman if he was working on the stalled train. "Yes," was the reply. Did he take his lantern and walk back along the tracks? "Yes." Did he see the train approaching? "Yes." Did he wave the lantern? "Yes, I waved it frantically until the second train was well past me." The same set of questions was asked of the signalman in slightly different ways a number of times. Finally the signalman was allowed to step down from the witness box. As he took his seat in the court room next to the president of the railroad, the president leaned over to him and told him he had done a great job as a witness without getting flustered or changing his story. "I just told the truth," the signalman replied. "But, boy, I was afraid he would ask if the lantern was lit!" Well, maybe he told the truth, but he didn't tell the whole truth.

We can laugh at that story, but is that true of your life? Is your light not lit? In John 8:12 we read, "When Jesus spoke again to the people, He said, 'I am the light of the world. Whoever follows me will never walk in darkness, but will have the light of life.'" Read also John 12:44-46, "Then Jesus cried out, 'When a man believes in me, he does not believe in me only, but in the one who sent me. When he looks at me, he sees the one who sent me. I have come into the world as a light, so that no one who believes in me should stay in darkness.'" When we read these two passages we clearly see that the "light" in today's promise is found in Jesus Christ. Whatever we do in that light has been done through God. The only way you can have light in your life is to believe in God's Son, Jesus Christ.

Now read Jesus' words in Matthew 5:14-16, "You are the light of the world. A city on a hill cannot be hidden. Neither do people light a lamp and put it under a bowl. Instead they put it on its stand, and it gives light to everyone in the house. In the same way, let your light shine before men, that they may see your good deeds and praise your Father in heaven." When He gave the Sermon on the Mount, Jesus knew He would be crucified, die, be buried, rise from the grave and ascend into heaven. He would be no longer physically in the world. The only way His light could be in the world would be if we have Jesus Christ in us and become His light to the darkness of the world. Are you reflecting the light of Jesus Christ with your life? As a witness, are you letting the light of Jesus Christ shine forth from you to save those who are speeding toward a wreck of their life through their lifestyles?

Let your light shine before men, and go out and make this a great day.

Let me live, blessed Lord, in the light of Thy word,
Let my life be a light on a hill;
Leading souls now astray to the straight and narrow way,
Help me do some good deed while I live.

J. R. Varner - (No Date)

September 13

"SO THEN, EACH OF US WILL GIVE AN ACCOUNT OF HIMSELF TO GOD."
Romans 14:12

Have you ever been called to account for something: money, time, work, etc.? When I was in graduate school working on an MS in chemistry, I attended Officer Candidate School in the Oklahoma Army National Guard. I was in an infantry company and was assigned as the Training Officer. The unit had gone through a long stretch of ineffective leadership and had failed its last Annual General Inspection. I was instructed to bring all publications and records up to date and develop a training program in accordance with U. S. Army and Oklahoma National Guard instructions and standards. In addition to attending monthly week-end training at OCS, I also spent many weekends at the armory working long hours to accomplish the task. This meant I spent many late nights studying for my classes in graduate school. As time for the next AGI approached, I was called into the company commander's office to account for my preparedness. I accounted for all I had accomplished and then recited a list of those tasks which still remained to be completed. He said, "Warner, why haven't you completed this assignment?" I was sleep deprived, pressured and frustrated and replied, "Sir, do you realize how much effort I have expended on this assignment?" He replied, "I don't care about effort. I want results!" My tasks were completed on time!

I thank God that He has a different measuring stick than that company commander. As Mother Teresa responded when asked how she could bear her load without being crushed by it, "I am not called to be successful, but faithful." Yes, God has called each of us to be faithful to Him and His work. Jesus is quoted in Acts 1:8, "But you will receive power when the Holy Spirit comes on you; and you will be my witnesses in Jerusalem, and in all Judea and Samaria, and to the ends of the earth." Paul instructed us in Romans 12:10-13, "Be devoted to one another in brotherly love. Honor one another above yourselves. Never be lacking in zeal, but keep your spiritual fervor, serving the Lord. Be joyful in hope, patient in affliction, faithful in prayer. Share with God's people who are in need. Practice hospitality."

Today's promise tells us each of us will give an account of himself to God. If you question that, read the parable of the talents in Matthew 25:14-30 again. Jesus clearly spells out that an accounting will be required of us. The accounting will be based on the instructions given us in the Word of God-the Bible. That is why it is so necessary for us to read, study and meditate on His Word on a daily basis. We WILL be held accountable!

Are you being faithful to the purpose to which God has called you? Are you faithful in your answer to Jesus' instructions concerning evangelism? Are you living your life based on the instructions Paul gave us? Are you faithful to the leading of the Holy Spirit in your life?

Prepare for your accounting before God, and go out and make this a great day.

When Jesus comes to reward His servant, whether it be noon or night,
Faithful to Him will He find us watching, with our lamps all trimmed and bright?
Blessed are those whom the Lord finds watching, in His glory they shall share;
If He shall come at the dawn or midnight, will He find us watching there?
Fanny J. Crosby - 1820-1915

September 14

"He redeemed us in order that the blessing given to Abraham might come to the Gentiles through Christ Jesus, SO THAT BY FAITH WE MIGHT RECEIVE THE PROMISE OF THE SPIRIT." Galatians 3:14

Several years before we met, my wife lived with her late husband in Wichita, KS. He had been an All American basketball player at the University of Oklahoma and was playing for the Vickers professional team in Wichita. She was being visited by her friend, Myrtle Drake, the wife of the OU basketball coach. She was going to take Myrtle to Norman, OK, watch a basketball game, spend the night and drive back to Wichita. They left Wichita, stopped at the turnpike toll gate to get a ticket, and then drove on, talking all the time. After an hour of talking and driving they saw a sign which read, "Topeka, xx miles". They had taken the wrong entrance onto the turnpike and had driven toward the North instead of the South. They turned around, drove toward Norman and arrived during the second half of the game. Like a person boarding the wrong train is said to be "on the wrong track," Jan and Myrtle got on the "wrong track" in their drive to reach Norman, OK.

What about the direction of your life? Are you on the "wrong track" or the "right track?" When Abraham was discouraged because he had no children, he told God, "the one who will inherit my estate is Eliezer of Damascus." Genesis 15:4 reads, "Then the word of the Lord came to him: 'This man will not be your heir, but a son coming from your own body will be your heir.'" Verse 6 reads, "Abram believed the Lord, and He credited it to him as righteousness." Jesus told us in John 3:16, "For God so loved the world that He gave His one and only Son, that whoever believes in Him shall not perish but have eternal life." Ephesians 2:8 reads, "For it is by grace you have been saved, through faith-and this not from yourselves, it is the gift of God..." Now look at Romans 5:17, "For if, by the trespass of the one man, death reigned through that one man, how much more will those who receive God's abundant provision of grace and of the gift of righteousness reign in life through the one man, Jesus Christ." The gift from God was His Son to die on the cross for the atonement of our sins. We receive that gift by believing, and it is credited to us as righteousness! Then you are started on the right track!

Now Jan and Myrtle started on the right track, but they took the wrong fork in the road and then ended up on the wrong track. As Christians, we might do the same thing. How do we keep from doing that? Just as by faith we are saved, so it is by faith we receive the promise of the Holy Spirit. He it is who keeps us on the right track if we will ask for His presence and help. We read in the prayer of Jabez in 1 Chronicles 4:10 that Jabez asked , "That Your hand would be with me." By this request, he was asking for the presence and leading of the Holy Spirit. Have you prayed to God that His hand would be with you through the presence of the Holy Spirit? Do it today. He will keep you on the right track. Now go out and make this a great day.

Spirit of God, descend upon my heart; wean it from earth, through all its pulses move;
Stoop to my weakness, mighty as Thou art, and make me love Thee as I ought to love.
Teach me to feel that thou art always nigh; teach me the struggles of the soul to bear,
To check the rising doubt, the rebel sigh; teach me the patience of unanswered prayer.
George Croly - 1780-1860

September 15

"Humble yourselves, therefore, under God's mighty hand, THAT HE MAY LIFT YOU UP IN DUE TIME." 1 Peter 5:6

The word "humble" is described as: having or showing a consciousness of one's defects or shortcomings; not proud; not self-assertive; modest. Today we find many courses which teach "self-assertiveness" and self-pride and self-worth. Society tends to give a lesser value to a quiet, unassuming person. People in the military are taught to have pride in their unit-a lot of esprit de corp. Several years ago when the University of Oklahoma won two consecutive national championships in football, there were bumper stickers on vehicles all over Norman stating "Its hard to be humble when you are a SOONER!" Many of the very wealthy, very talented, very powerful people in the world are also very arrogant, proud, self-assertive and immodest. Don't you suppose it would be very difficult to be humble if you were one of the wealthiest people on earth? Wouldn't it be hard not to be proud if you owned vast estates? How would you refrain from self-assertiveness if you were one of the most powerful people on earth? Could you be modest if you were one of the most talented people alive in a given endeavor?

Yet my Bible dictionary defines "humility" as the opposite of pride and one of the cardinal graces of the renewed heart. It consists in a man's not thinking of himself more highly than he ought to think; and humility is urged with great force upon all who profess to be Christ's disciples (as in today's promise). In this, as in all other respects, our divine Savior's life furnishes us with a perfect example, and the sacred Scriptures abound with promises of grace and favor to the humble and threatens sorrow and punishment to the proud. Isn't it easy to be modest when you are serving food to fellow believers or in a soup kitchen? Don't you feel pretty meek when you consider the omnipotence, omniscience and omnipresence of God? Aren't your own defects and shortcomings magnified when you consider the perfection of the life of Jesus Christ, the majesty and glory of God, and the continual presence in yourself of the Holy Spirit?

Today's promise tells us if we humble ourselves and worship God in His total majesty and power, He will lift us up at the appropriate time. We should not be proud in our wealth. What is it but gold, silver, pearls, opals, sapphires, etc? Those items are paving and building material in heaven! What if we do own vast estates? He owns the cattle on a thousand hills, and the earth and the fullness thereof belong to Him! So what if you have great power here on earth. Read Mark 12:24, "Jesus replied, 'Are you not in error because you do not know the Scriptures or the power of God?'" What is the effect of great talent to perform some endeavor on earth? We are promised in Philippians 4:13, "I can do everything through Him who gives me strength."

Instead of being self-assertive, humble yourself under God's mighty hand. Follow the example of Jesus in humility and servanthood. Let Him mold you and make you what He wants you to be. Then go out and make this a great day.

Disrobed of all His heavenly dress, the Savior came to earth;
Clothed in a veil of mortal flesh, and bowed His head in death.
The solemn scene about to close, to make the whole complete,
He meekly from communion rose and washed His servants' feet.
Zion's Hymns - 1854

September 16

"YOU WILL BE BLESSED IN THE CITY AND BLESSED IN THE COUNTRY."
Deuteronomy 28:3

I grew up in the country, on a farm, in rural north central Kansas. My parents moved us to that area when I was eight years old. I learned to milk cows, tend the garden, care for all of our animals, drive horses, work in the field and all the other work necessary to work a farm. My parents were very strict about each of their children getting their work done in a timely manner. We worked hard, and we really enjoyed the play time we had. We were taught to read the Bible, have devotions time, pray on a regular basis and attend church regularly. Dinner after church on Sunday was always a special treat with relatives or friends from the church at our house, or us at their house. We would eat a large meal and then have play time until time for chores before going to evening church services. I learned to fulfill my responsibilities on the farm and to work hard. I attended a one-room schoolhouse comprised of all eight grades, all taught by one teacher. Because it was a rural area where all the children had to help on the family farms, our school year was only eight months long. This got us out of school in time to help with the spring tilling and planting. In spite of a shortened school year and the one room schoolhouse (or because of it!), I got a very good education. My early spiritual training, the love of my family, learning to work hard and my education were all a real blessing during the time I grew up in the country.

After graduating from high school, I attended undergraduate college, then graduate college, taught chemistry at the college level, worked in politics for ten years and then was an insurance agent for over twenty years. During all this time, I lived in cities of various sizes. I was not always faithful to the Lord during those years, but that all changed after my prostate cancer surgery and radiation treatment in 1995. It was during that time that I turned back to God as I knew Him during my early years. The abilities God gave me, the directions He led me and the situations He put me in over the years provided me with the resources I need to do what He has called me to do during my retired years. I find the blessings of God increase from one day to the next at this time of my life. I am truly blessed in the city.

The promise for today has been very clearly kept in my life! God is so good to me. I hope He is as good to you today as He has been to me. As I look back over my life, I can clearly see that the best parts of my life have been those where I walked closely with Him. As I look at the really tough times during my life, I see they were the times I was farthest from Him. Was He chastening me at those times? Perhaps! Was He always leading me to this time of serving Him? Most definitely!

Are you walking closely with the Lord at this very time? Do you feel close to Him? Are you serving Him where He wants you? Is He blessing you for your faithfulness to Him? Walk closely with Him and expect showers of blessing. Now go out and make this a great day.

There shall be showers of blessing; this is the promise of love;
There shall be seasons refreshing, sent from the Savior above.
There shall be showers of blessing; send them upon us, O Lord;
Grant to us now a refreshing, come, and now honor Thy Word.
Daniel W. Whittle - 1840-1901

September 17

"My son, pay attention to what I say; listen closely to my words. Do not let them out of your sight, keep them within your heart; FOR THEY ARE LIFE TO THOSE WHO FIND THEM AND HEALTH TO A MAN'S WHOLE BODY." Proverbs 4:20-22

Geoffrey T. Bull, in his book, "When Iron Gates Yield," wrote the biography of Geoffrey Bull, a British missionary to Tibet. He was captured and imprisoned by Chinese Communists. His captors took his possessions from him, threw him in a series of prisons, robbed him of his Bible, and made him suffer terribly at their hands for three years. In addition to extreme temperatures and miserable physical conditions, bodily abuse and near starvation, Bull was subjected to such mental and psychological torture that he feared he would go insane. How did he keep his mind at peace? He had no Bible now, but he had studied the Bible all his life. So he began to systematically go over the Scriptures in his mind. He started at Genesis and recalled each incident and story as best he could, first concentrating on the content and then musing on certain points, seeking light in prayer. He continued through the Old Testament, reconstructing the books and chapters as best he could, then into the New Testament, Matthew to Revelation. Then he started over again. He later wrote, "The strength received through this meditation was, I believe, a vital factor in bringing me through, kept by the faith to the very end."

Today's promise is perfectly illustrated by this story! Geoffrey Bull would never have been able to perform these mental exercises and meditation had he not read and studied the Bible a great amount prior to that time. He would not have been able to recall and reconstruct the Word had he not committed much of it to memory. Did Geoffrey Bull need the Word of God from the Bible at the time he was reading and memorizing it? Of course he did! Study of the Word of God is ALWAYS uplifting, spiritually fulfilling, joyous and refreshing. But how much more did he need it when he did not have access to the printed Word, and his very life was in grave danger!

What about you today? Are you reading, studying and memorizing the Word of God on a regular basis? We live our lives in the world, which is Satan's domain. How can we live the life God wants us to live? The Psalmist told us to study, learn, memorize, recite, love, obey and meditate on the Word of God in 119:9-17, "How can a young man keep his way pure? By living according to your Word. I seek you with all my heart; do not let me stray from your commands. I have hidden your word in my heart that I might not sin against you. Praise be to you, O Lord; teach me your decrees. With my lips I recount all the laws that come from your mouth. I rejoice in following your statutes as one rejoices in great riches. I meditate on your precepts and consider your ways. I delight in your decrees; I will not neglect your Word. Do good to your servant, and I will live; I will obey your Word."

Spend significant time each day with the Bible, and go out and make this a great day.

Christ, the Blessed One, gives to all wonderful words of life;
Sinner, list to the loving call, wonderful words of life.
Sweetly echo the gospel call, wonderful words of life;
Offer pardon and peace to all, wonderful words of life.

Philip P. Bliss - 1838-1876

September 18

"ALL YOUR SONS WILL BE TAUGHT BY THE LORD, AND GREAT WILL BE YOUR CHILDREN'S PEACE." Isaiah 54:13

American clergyman, A. T. Pierson, once said, "The peace of God is that eternal calm which lies far too deep in the praying, trusting soul to be reached by any external disturbances." I believe this is one of the best illustrations I have seen of today's promise! When we are all taught by the Lord, we will have great peace of God, for us and for our children. You see, it is the parents who set the tone for the temperament and mental state of the family. When the parents are at peace with God, when they know they can depend upon Him in any situation, when they reflect this in the way they receive news and express views, then they are teaching their children the way of the Lord.

Do we serve a God of peace? Most assuredly! Read Leviticus 26. When God was giving Moses instructions and promises, He told Moses to not make idols, but to observe the Sabbath, revere the sanctuary, follow His decrees, and obey His commands; then He would send rain, crops and fruit. Then in verse 6, "I will grant peace in the land, and you will lie down and no one will make you afraid." God wants us to love and worship Him. In return, He grants us peace. God sent His Son in peace. Jesus was prophesied in peace in Isaiah 9:6, "For unto us a child is born, to us a son is given, and the government will be on his shoulders. And he will be called Wonderful Counselor, Mighty God, Everlasting Father, Prince of Peace." He was also prophesied in peace in Zechariah 9:10, "I will take away the chariots from Ephraim and the war horses from Jerusalem, and the battle bow will be broken. He will proclaim peace to the nations." He was proclaimed to the shepherds in peace when the angels said in Luke 2:14, "Glory to God in the highest, and on earth peace to men on whom His favor rests." After the Last Supper, Jesus prepared the disciples for His departure by saying in John 14:27, "Peace I leave with you; my peace I give you." Finally Jesus gave the disciples the Holy Spirit in peace in John 20:21-22, "Again Jesus said, 'Peace be with you! As the Father has sent me, I am sending you.' And with that He breathed on them and said, 'Receive the Holy Spirit.'" Our God is a God of peace!

Was Jesus totally about peace? Read Jesus' words in Matthew 10:34, "Do not suppose that I have come to bring peace to the earth. I did not come to bring peace, but a sword." Yes, He came to bring peace between God and the believer, and peace among men. Yet He inevitably brought conflict between good and evil, between light and darkness, between right and wrong, and between the children of Christ and those of the devil. That conflict produces our peace!

Paul started many of his letters as in Galatians 1:3, "Grace and peace to you from God our Father and the Lord Jesus Christ..." He ended several of them as in 2 Corinthians 13:11, "Finally, brothers, good-by. Aim for perfection, listen to my appeal, be of one mind, live in peace. And the God of love and peace will be with you." Be at peace, and go out and make this a great day.

Through Christ on the cross peace was made, my debt by His death was all paid.
No other foundation is laid for peace, the gift of God's love.
When Jesus as Lord I had crowned, my heart with this peace did abound;
In Him the rich blessing I found, sweet peace, the gift of God's love.
Peter P. Bilhorn - 1865-1936

September 19

"FOR THE WAGES OF SIN IS DEATH, BUT THE GIFT OF GOD IS ETERNAL LIFE IN CHRIST JESUS OUR LORD." Romans 6:23

Do you remember your first significant job? I do! I had worked for others a day or two from time to time while I was growing up on the farm. Mostly, I worked for the family as a part of my responsibility as a member of that family. During my senior year of high school I was accepted as a student at Emporia State University and was granted a $600 scholarship. I knew I would need more money to be able to attend college so I applied for, and was hired for, a job with a local custom combine crew. We left the day after I graduated and began cutting wheat in late May near Vernon, TX. I stayed with the crew until we had finished the wheat cutting in Kenmare, ND. My parents picked me up there to take me home, to pack, and to go on to college. Just before we left for home, my boss took me into his trailer, where he kept all his paper work, and paid me $900 in wages and the $500 bonus he had promised if I stayed with him all summer. I know I earned those wages! I had really worked hard that summer and had cut a lot of acres of wheat, as well as servicing and repairing the combine. The wages I earned that summer, along with a job I obtained in Emporia, allowed me to attend my freshman year in college.

Throughout my life, I have worked hard at every job to insure I would earn my wages. I am sure you are the same way. You give an honest day's work for each day's pay you receive. As Christians, we should work hard, because Paul tells us in Colossians 3:23-24, "Whatever you do, work at it with all your heart, as working for the Lord, not for men, since you know that you will receive an inheritance from the Lord as a reward. It is the Lord Christ you are serving."

Paul tells us Romans 3:23, "...for all have sinned and fall short of the glory of God..." Then, later in Romans, he tells us that the wages of those sins is death. We have all earned the wages we are to receive for the sins we have committed—death. There is no question that we have sinned. Sin, and with it-death, entered the world through Adam and we are all born into the world; thus, we are born into sin and earn the wages of that sin—death. Then Paul gives us today's promise that the gift of God is eternal life in Christ Jesus our Lord. How can he be so certain about that gift and what that gift is? Because of the words of Jesus as reported in John 3:16, "For God so loved the world that He gave His one and only Son, that whoever believes in Him shall not perish but have eternal life." Jesus is sometimes called "the second Adam," in that death entered the world through Adam, and death was ended through Jesus for those who believe.

Even if you feel unappreciated by your boss today, know that you are not working for him, you are working for the Lord. Therefore, you know that you will receive your inheritance from the Lord, and that inheritance is eternal life. The monetary wages you receive are only to take care of your needs during this life. The real reward you receive will be eternal life. Heaven is your home. You are just passing through here. Claim it, and go out and make this a great day.

I won't have long to stay; my work is nearly done.
I'm happy now to say my race is almost run.
So long my eyes have set on heaven's open door,
And I can't feel at home in this world any more.

Source Unknown

September 20

"He is the image of the invisible God, the firstborn over all creation. FOR BY HIM ALL THINGS WERE CREATED: THINGS IN HEAVEN AND ON EARTH, VISIBLE AND INVISIBLE, WHETHER THRONES OR POWERS OR RULERS OR AUTHORITIES; ALL THINGS WERE CREATED BY HIM AND FOR HIM." Colossians 1:15 & 16

My Bible dictionary states: To create is to cause anything to exist that never existed in any form or manner before. It is to make, without materials to make of. In chemistry, I learned the scientific principle: Matter is neither created nor destroyed in any chemical reaction. It merely changes form. We talk about "creating jobs" when a new industry is formed, and there are a lot of new jobs. We also talk about an artist "creating" a painting, a sculpture or other art work. These uses of "create" are proper according to the definitions we use today; however, there are no current examples of anyone creating any physical object from nothing. This very concept is what today's promise is all about.

The Trinity has existed forever. We read in Psalm 90:2, "Before the mountains were born or you brought forth the earth and the world, from everlasting to everlasting you are God." We read in John 1:1-2 & 14, "In the beginning was the Word, and the Word was with God, and the Word was God. He was with God in the beginning. The Word became flesh and made His dwelling among us. We have seen His glory, the glory of the One and Only, who came from the Father, full of grace and truth." We also read in Genesis 1:2, "Now the earth was formless and empty, darkness was over the surface of the deep, and the Spirit of God was hovering over the water." God's Word and God's Spirit are parallel, yet distinct, figures. Read Psalm 33:6, "By the Word of the Lord were the heavens made, their starry host by the breath of His mouth" (Spirit).

We can take great comfort in today's promise. The promise is multifaceted. By Him ALL things were created! Things in heaven (sun, moon, other planets, stars, meteors, asteroids, etc.) and on earth (soil, rocks, metals, liquids, plants, animals, birds, human beings, etc.). Things visible (solids, liquids and gas) (above the surface of the earth) and invisible (below the surface of the earth) (all forms of energy-light, heat, electrical, etc.). He also created thrones, powers, rulers and authorities! That one is really hard to comprehend. We wonder why He creates, or allows the creation of certain leaders of the past. We just have to trust Him on that one as His ways are not possible for us to comprehend. The promise then closes again with the comforting statement, "All things were created by Him and for Him."

Yes, God has created all things, and we can take great comfort in that promise. We can take great comfort because we have another promise in Romans 8:28, "And we know that in all things God works for the good of those who love Him, who have been called according to His purpose." So, if something seems out of whack in your world today, take comfort. God created your world and He is in control! Now go out and make this a great day.

All creatures of our God and King, lift up your voice and with us sing.
Thou burning sun with golden beam, thou silver moon with softer gleam.
Let all things their Creator bless, and worship Him in humbleness.
Praise, praise the Father, praise the Son, and praise the Spirit, Three in One!

St. Francis of Assisi - 1182-1226

September 21

"HE IS BEFORE ALL THINGS, AND IN HIM ALL THINGS HOLD TOGETHER."
Colossians 1:17

A very good friend of mine, Ed Copelin, owns an office supply store (see March 25). The symbol of his business is a paper clip. He has the drawing on his store, his business cards and all of his advertising. I asked him why he used a paper clip. His reply was that it was a symbol of the needs he supplied his customers. He further said, "It is clear, simple and functional like I would like my business to be." Ed has a very good business, but I think it has much more to do with him, his caring, friendly personality and his business ability than it does with any symbol he might use for his business. His business preceded the discount office supply businesses. He is the glue which holds his employees and product line together. He is like that paper clip symbol.

When I read today's promise, I think of Ed and his paper clip symbol. Jesus Christ was before all things. John wrote in John 1:1-2, "In the beginning was the Word, and the Word was with God, and the Word was God. He was with God in the beginning." He went on in verse 14 to say, "The Word became flesh and made His dwelling among us." In today's promise Paul reminds us that Jesus existed before all things. Paul further states that in Jesus Christ all things hold together. When you get right down to it, the purpose of Jesus Christ coming to earth to live as a man, like that paper clip, is clear, simple and functional.

Jesus said in John 10:10, "The thief comes only to steal and kill and destroy; I have come that they may have life, and have it to the full." Jesus also said in John 10:28, "I give them eternal life, and they shall never perish; no one can snatch them out of my hand." There is the story— clear, simple and functional! Jesus came to give us life to the fullest and to give us eternal life beyond this world. The way to obtain that eternal life is also clear, simple and functional. Read Romans 10:9, "That if you confess with your mouth, 'Jesus is Lord,' and believe in your heart that God raised Him from the dead, you will be saved."

Your life as a Christian is clear, simple and functional. Just follow the words of Jesus in Matthew 22:17-40, "...Love the Lord your God with all your heart and with all your soul and with all your mind. This is the first and greatest commandment. And the second is like it: Love your neighbor as yourself. All the Law and the Prophets hang on these two commandments." Would you take the Lord's name in vain if you loved Him completely? Would you steal from your neighbors if you loved them? Would you lie about them? Would you have an affair with their spouse? 1 John 4:16 says, "...God is love." It is clear: we are to love. It is simple: we are to love. It is functional: we are to love, for if we love completely we have such a wonderful life.

Now about that paper clip. Wear one on your clothing today in a prominent place. When someone asks you about it, tell them about today's promise and bear witness.

Now go out and make this a great day.

Jesus is all the world to me, I want no better friend;
I trust Him now, I'll trust Him when life's fleeting days shall end.
Beautiful life with such a Friend; beautiful life that has no end;
Eternal life, eternal joy, He's my Friend.

Will L. Thompson - 1847-1909

September 22

"AND HE IS THE HEAD OF THE BODY, THE CHURCH; HE IS THE BEGINNING AND THE FIRSTBORN FROM AMONG THE DEAD, SO THAT IN EVERYTHING HE MIGHT HAVE THE SUPREMACY." Colossians 1:18

Have you been the "head" of something? Almost all adults have been. They may have been head of as small a unit as a family (small in size, definitely not small in importance) to the head of an organization on a national or international level. I heard a joke once about a man who said he was definitely the head of his household. He made all the important decisions such as: what should the president have as a foreign policy, whether or not to support a given tax bill, and how best to settle the middle east problems. His wife made the unimportant decisions such as: where they lived, what kind of car they drove, where they went to dinner, and what would be their annual budget. We laugh at such jokes and realize they are all in fun, but being the head of any entity is a very important position. There are many decisions to be made. The entity must put forth a united front, be consistent and responsible in behavior, take consistent positions on issues, be fair and honest to all involved, have consistent and unwavering membership requirements, establish conduct requirements for members and state long-term goals and a plan to reach them.

In today's promise, Paul tells us that Jesus is the head of the body, the church. Paul also tells us that Jesus is the beginning of the church. He is the firstborn among the dead, meaning He is the first to rise from the dead to eternal life. He is the head, the beginning and the firstborn so that He might have supremacy in everything! Doesn't it give you a great feeling to know that the only perfect man who ever lived is the head of the body of Christians? Who else has established such perfect and clear long-term goals for our lives—eternal life in a perfect place? Who else could be so clear, fair and unwavering in membership requirements for the body of Christians? No one else could be as fair and honest to everyone! No one else could be so consistent throughout the ages! We have been given the Bible to teach us the proper behavior so we can put forth a united front. Praise God for the perfect plan He developed when He gave His only Son to die for our sins! Praise God for the willingness of Jesus Christ to obey His Father, even unto death!

What are Jesus' long term goals? We read in 2 Peter 3:9, "The Lord is not slow in keeping His promise, as some understand slowness. He is patient with you, not wanting anyone to perish, but every one to come to repentance." He wants EVERYONE to have eternal life! How do we reach that goal? Read 1 John 1:9, "If we confess our sins, He is faithful and just and will forgive us our sins and purify us from all unrighteousness." What conduct does He expect? We are told in Galatians 5:22-23, "But the fruit of the Spirit is love, joy, peace, patience, kindness, goodness, faithfulness, gentleness and self-control. Against such things there is no law." So follow Jesus. He is the perfect head! Now go out and make this a great day.

That in all things He might have preeminence, preeminence, preeminence;
That in all things He might have preeminence, Jesus Christ our Lord.
And He is the Head of the body, the church: Who is the Beginning, Beginning;
And He is the Head of the body, the church, the Firstborn from the dead.

Arranged by W. Blaine Hughes - 1946-

September 23

"Who is he that condemns? CHRIST JESUS WHO DIED - MORE THAN THAT, WHO WAS RAISED TO LIFE - IS AT THE RIGHT HAND OF GOD AND IS ALSO INTERCEDING FOR US." Romans 8:34

I read in the newspaper about a person whose illegal actions cost the state about $400,000 in money which was diverted into the pockets of himself and others, who were equally unscrupulous. At the conclusion of their trial, the judge condemned them and sentenced them to five years probation, fifty hours of community service and a $1,000 fine. In another paper, I read about a man who was out of work and needed money to pay the rent and buy food and clothing for his family. He robbed a local business, was tried, convicted and sentenced to five years in prison. I confess, I don't understand the seeming disparity in the sentencing of these two people.

Who among us would condemn Jesus? Paul tells us in today's promise that He died, was raised to life, sits at the right hand of God and is interceding for us. That sounds to me like four pretty good reasons that none of us should condemn Him! Jesus told us in Luke 6:37, "Do not judge, and you will not be judged. Do not condemn, and you will not be condemned. Forgive, and you will be forgiven." Jesus also tells us in John 3:17, "For God did not send His Son into the world to condemn the world, but to save the world through Him." Jesus does not condemn us, therefore, we should not condemn Him, or anything about Him. Does this mean we will not be judged, and if found guilty, condemned? Not at all. It means that Jesus does not condemn us. He gave His life for us that we might escape the condemnation after judgment and have eternal life. We read in Hebrews 9:27-28, "Just as man is destined to die once, and after that to face judgment, so Christ was sacrificed once to take away the sins of many people; and He will appear a second time, not to bear sin, but to bring salvation to those who are waiting for Him."

Because Jesus died, rose from the dead, sits at the right hand of God and is interceding for us, we have the promise of eternal life. Read the words of Jesus on this matter in John 12:47-50, "As for the person who hears my words but does not keep them, I do not judge him. For I did not come to judge the world, but to save it. There is a judge for the one who rejects me and does not accept my words; that very word which I spoke will condemn him at the last day. For I did not speak of my own accord, but the Father who sent me commanded me what to say and how to say it. I know that His command leads to eternal life. So whatever I say is just what the Father has told me to say." When we stand before God to be judged and our sins are pointed out to us, we will have Jesus Christ to intercede for us. He will stand with us before God and tell God that those sins have been washed away in His blood. He will say, "I paid the total price for those sins." Pay heed to the words of Jesus in John 14:6, "I am the way and the truth and the life. No one comes to the Father except through me."

Accept the gift of Jesus Christ, and go out and make this a great day.

One day when heaven was filled with His praises, one day when sin was as black as could be,
Jesus came forth to be born of a virgin, dwelt among men-my example is He!
One day the grave could conceal Him no longer, one day the stone rolled away from the door;
Then He arose, over death He had conquered,, now is ascended, my Lord evermore!

J. Wilbur Chapman - 1859-1918

September 24

> "Dear children, let us not love with words or tongue but with actions and in truth. This then is how we know that we belong to the truth, and how we set our hearts at rest in His presence whenever our hearts condemn us. FOR GOD IS GREATER THAN OUR HEARTS, AND HE KNOWS EVERYTHING." 1 John 3:18-20

When we give our hearts to God by accepting the gift of the death of His Son, Jesus Christ, on the cross for us, believing in the gift, asking forgiveness for our sins, and confessing the Lord Jesus Christ with our mouths, we not only lose all the guilt for our sins, but we get the gift of the presence of the Holy Spirit living in our hearts. Today's promise tells us that God is greater than our hearts, and He knows everything. God even knows our unspoken thoughts through communication with the Holy Spirit. We serve an omniscient, omnipresent and omnipotent God! He is, without any doubt, all knowing, ever present and all powerful God!

In the writing leading up to today's promise, John warns us against loving only with words or tongue. If we truly follow God's two commands, given by Jesus Christ, that we are to love God with all our heart, mind, soul and strength, and that we are to love our neighbors as ourselves, then we must be loving with actions and in truth. John then tells us that loving in that way is how we know that we belong to the truth. When we love with actions and in truth, our hearts are at rest in the presence of God. When we pray at those times, it is just like we are talking to an old and dear friend, because that is exactly what it is.

If we do love with words or tongue, and do not love with actions and in truth, our hearts are not at rest in His presence, rather, they condemn us. It is at those times we say, "I have a guilty conscience." My Bible dictionary says the conscience "is that within us which judges the moral character of our actions, and approves or censures, condemns or justifies us accordingly. This universal tribunal is established in the breast of every man. It may be weakened, perverted, stupefied, defiled, and hardened, in various ways; and its decisions are more or less clear, just, and imperative, according to the degree of improvement in the understanding and heart, and especially according to the degree in which its purity and sensitiveness have been preserved and cultivated." God made man to be a moral being. Each person is born with an innate urge and desire to do good. Man is also born into the world, which is the devil's domain. Therefore, we are sinners by reason of the actions of Adam. It is conscience which makes us want to do right.

The communication between the Holy Spirit, Jesus, and God is total and instantaneous. The urging of the Holy Spirit is a direct message from our omniscient God. Philippians 4:13 says, "I can do everything through Him who gives me strength." How is that possible? Because of the promise of God through John in 1 John 4:4, "You, dear children, are from God and have overcome them, because the one who is in you is greater than the one who is in the world." Love with actions and in truth, be at peace with God, and go out and make this a great day.

> Sometimes when misgivings darken the day, and faith's light I cannot see;
> I ask my dear Lord to brighten the way, He whispers sweet peace to me.
> I could not go on without Him I know, the world would o'erwhelm my soul;
> For I could not see the right way to go, when temptations o'er me roll.
>
> Will M. Ramsey - (No Date)

September 25

"Therefore, prepare your minds for action; be self-controlled; SET YOUR HOPE FULLY ON THE GRACE TO BE GIVEN YOU WHEN JESUS CHRIST IS REVEALED."
1 Peter 1:13

Before you are involved in any action—military, sport, business call, speech, etc., you must prepare your minds for that action. You must be able to exercise self-control. When I had to be prepared for action in teaching Chemistry in college, running a training exercise in the National Guard, making a speech in politics or making a business call when I was an insurance agent, I prepared my mind for action and gained self-control by closing my eyes and assuming the position of a soaring eagle. I would rise above everyone and everything and look down on myself in the position ready for action. I would watch the action from beginning to end, seeking the best course of action, anticipating problems, looking for the right words to use, making sure I was using all the knowledge and training I had received which applied to the particular action. When I had my mind prepared for the action, I would have obtained self-control and self-confidence in my performance of that action. I then set my hope on the thoroughness of my training, preparation and capabilities and faced the action.

Today's promise from Peter is a call to action issued to the early-day Christians. It is an exhortation to prepare themselves for the action of serving God. Our promise is that the grace of God will be given us when we have accepted Jesus Christ. We will then receive complete deliverance from sins and have total blessedness.

How do we, as Christians, prepare our minds for action? I think we should do just like I did in all the areas in which I have worked in my life. We should study to learn all we can. We should ponder (meditate) about different aspects of our study. We should attend classes to learn all we can from other's experiences. We should talk to experts in the area and get their advice. We should think about different situations in which we might find ourselves and consider what we would do, say, propose or how we would handle it. We do that, as Christians, by studying the Bible and meditating on His Word, attending Sunday school classes and other classes, praying to God to get His leading and asking for the continual leading of the Holy Spirit, and thinking about people we know and love and how we could and should witness to them.

Have you prepared your mind for action for God? Have you set your hope fully on the grace to be given you when you accept Jesus Christ? Are you ready to go into action for God? What is your action to be? Is it to live your life as a witness to your family? Is it to work at your job as if you are working for the Lord? It is to witness to a friend or co-worker? Whatever the action might be, you can be fully ready by following the preparation guidelines listed here. When your hope is based on the grace of God and you have prepared your mind for action, you will be successful in whatever action God calls you to.

Now go out and make this a great day.

'Twas grace that taught my heart to fear, and grace my fears relieved;
How precious did that grace appear the hour I first believed!
Through many dangers, toils, and snares, I have already come;
'Tis grace hath brought me safe thus far, and grace will lead me home.
John Newton - 1725-1807

September 26

"Whoever has my commands and obeys them, he is the one who loves me. HE WHO LOVES ME WILL BE LOVED BY MY FATHER, AND I TOO WILL LOVE HIM AND SHOW MYSELF TO HIM." John 14:21

Many promises are accompanied by a command. This one is accompanied by a general command to obey the commands God has given us. If we do so, God says this is evidence of our love for Him and then we get to the precious promise of today. We will be loved by God the Father and God the Son! Everyone needs love! We need love as a baby in the cradle, and we need love as we pass from this world - cradle to grave love - that is what we need. Do we have to obey His commands to be loved by Him? No! He loves us in spite of ourselves. Romans 5:8 tells us, "But God demonstrates His own love for us in this: While we were still sinners, Christ died for us." What is different about today's promise? The last phrase - "and show myself to him (us)."

Jesus loves us unconditionally! He reveals Himself to us when we obey His commands and when we love Him. How does He do that? Like He did with Elijah - in a gentle whisper. The showing of the Lord to us comes to us when we are in communion with Him. We need to be still and wait on the Lord. He is not in a hurry with us. He wants us to abide in Him by our regular, quiet communing with Him. When the Lord shows Himself to you, you will not doubt it. It will leave such an impression that you will want it as a regular occurrence. He wants it as a regular occurrence also! His love for us is so great. His love is not a sentimental love nor a love of mere acceptance. No, His love is a sacrificial love. He gave His all for us when He died on the cross.

As a mother loves her little child, so God loves us. The little child can't verbally communicate yet, however, any mother will tell you of the various ways their child communicates with us. Maybe that is one of the things Jesus meant when He said in Matthew 18:3-4, "And He said: 'I tell you the truth, unless you change and become like little children, you will never enter the kingdom of heaven. Therefore, whoever humbles himself like this child is the greatest in the kingdom of heaven.'" God wants us to communicate in more ways than just verbally. God also wants us to trust Him and His love like little children trust their mothers to provide for their needs.

How about you today? Do you obey God's commands and love Him? Do you communicate with God in all ways and trust Him for His bountiful goodness? Do you let the cares and woes of the world take away from your time in quiet, private prayer and communion with God? Do you ever let yourself just feel like a child again and tell the Lord over and over that you Love Him? If not, why not?

Love God, obey His commands, and go out and make this a great day.

Jesus loves me! this I know, for the Bible tells me so.
Little ones to Him belong; they are weak, but He is strong.
Jesus loves me! He who died heaven's gate to open wide;
He will wash away my sin, let His little child come in.

Anna B. Warner - 1820-1915

September 27

> "The acts of the sinful nature are obvious: sexual immorality, impurity and debauchery; idolatry and witchcraft; hatred, discord, jealousy, fits of rage, selfish ambition, dissensions, factions and envy; drunkenness, orgies, and the like. I WARN YOU, AS I DID BEFORE, THAT THOSE WHO LIVE LIKE THIS WILL NOT INHERIT THE KINGDOM OF GOD." Galatians 5:19-21

I read an illustration once which suggested you take a beautiful, nice, straight, clean, sanded board and drive a nail into the middle of it. When you have done that, carefully pull the nail out. Do you now have the board exactly like it was before? No! You have a beautiful, nice, straight, clean, sanded board with a nail hole, a scar, right in the center of it!

Today's promise is a negative promise. You WILL NOT inherit the kingdom of God if you live your life performing acts of the sinful nature! See also Romans 13:13, "Let us behave decently, as in the daytime, not in orgies and drunkenness, not in sexual immorality and debauchery, not in dissension and jealousy." 1 Corinthians 6:9-10 says, "Do you not know that the wicked will not inherit the kingdom of God? Do not be deceived: Neither the sexually immoral nor idolaters nor adulterers nor male prostitutes nor homosexual offenders nor thieves nor the greedy nor drunkards nor slanderers nor swindlers will inherit the kingdom of God." Colossians 3:5 & 8 reads, "Put to death, therefore, whatever belongs to your earthly nature: sexual immorality, impurity, lust, evil desires and greed, which is idolatry. But now you must rid yourselves of all such things as these: anger, rage, malice, slander, and filthy language from your lips." These are all lists of sins given us by Paul.

How should we live? Look at Galatians 5:22-25, "But the fruit of the Spirit is love, joy, peace, patience, kindness, goodness, faithfulness, gentleness and self-control. Against such things there is no law. Those who belong to Christ Jesus have crucified the sinful nature with its passions and desires. Since we live by the Spirit, let us keep in step with the Spirit." Paul says in Romans 13:14, "Rather, clothe yourselves with the Lord Jesus Christ, and do not think about how to gratify the desires of the sinful nature." 1 Corinthians 6:11 says, "And that is what some of you were. But you were washed, you were sanctified, you were justified in the name of the Lord Jesus Christ and by the Spirit of our God." Paul tells us in Colossians 3:9-10, "Do not lie to each other, since you have taken off your old self with its practices and have put on the new self, which is being renewed in knowledge in the image of its Creator."

If it is your choice to live a life of sin, it will cause scars, visible or invisible, on you in the same way that nail caused such a scar on the beautiful wood. You can gain the promise of eternal life through Jesus Christ our Lord. Your sins WILL be forgiven. You WILL inherit the Kingdom of God. He will remove those sins, but you will carry the scars of your sins.

Wash your sins in the blood of Jesus Christ, and go out and make this a great day.

> What can wash away my sin? Nothing but the blood of Jesus;
> What can make me whole again? Nothing but the blood of Jesus.
> This is all my hope and peace-nothing but the blood of Jesus;
> This is all my righteousness-nothing but the blood of Jesus.
>
> Robert Lowry - 1826-1899

September 28

"Have nothing to do with a false charge and do not put an innocent or honest person to death, FOR I WILL NOT ACQUIT THE GUILTY." Exodus 23:7

I recently read in the newspaper about a person who worked in a police department crime laboratory who worked closely with the detectives and the district attorney to convict several people charged with crimes. The testimony given by this person was very convincing and authoritative. The detectives loved to have this person working the lab on their cases. When this person was put on the witness stand and gave such definite statements, it was easy for the jury to see the facts, as presented, and bring back a verdict of "guilty". It all fell apart when a person who had served seventeen years for rape was able to get the evidence examined by a independent laboratory. The independent laboratory found there was no match between the evidence at the crime scene and the person serving in prison. The case was reopened and the innocent man was set free. This led to investigation of all the cases which were examined by that one laboratory worker, who later gave testimony. It was charged that the person would ask what the detectives and the district attorney wanted to prove and prepare the evidence to show those "facts". The charge was made that the crime laboratory worker gave false evidence in many cases which led to false convictions and caused innocent and honest people to be imprisoned.

I thought back to those newspaper stories when I read today's promise. This is another negative promise. If we are guilty of false charges, and if we do something which leads to harm of an innocent or honest person, God will NOT acquit us of our guilt. In 1 Kings 21 there is the story of Ahab's attempt to buy the vineyard owned by Naboth. Naboth refused to sell it to King Ahab. When Ahab's wife, Jezebel, heard of the refusal of Naboth to sell the vineyard she told the elders and nobles, "Proclaim a day of fasting and seat Naboth in a prominent place among the people. But seat two scoundrels opposite him and have them testify that he has cursed both God and the king. Then take him out and stone him to death." When the elders and nobles had carried out her instructions, she told Ahab to take possession of the vineyard. Elijah delivered the Lord's message to Ahab, "Have you not murdered a man and seized his property? In the place where dogs licked up Naboth's blood, dogs will lick up your blood—yes, yours!" This story states very explicitly how God views false charges which lead to death of an innocent person.

How should we act? Read Psalm 19:14, "May the words of my mouth and the meditation of my heart be pleasing in your sight, O Lord, my Rock and my Redeemer." Also read Ephesians 4:29, "Do not let any unwholesome talk come out of your mouths, but only what is helpful for building others up according to their needs, that it may benefit those who listen." "But," you say, "I don't give false testimony leading to someone's death!" Have you killed someone's reputation by passing on scurrilous gossip? This, also, destroys a person as surely as death.

So say what Jesus would have you say. Now go out and make this a great day.

Perhaps today there are loving words which Jesus would have me speak,
There may be now, in the paths of sin, some wanderer whom I should seek;
O Savior, if Thou wilt be my Guide, Tho dark and rugged the way,
My voice shall echo the message sweet, I'll say what You want me to say.

Charles E. Prior - 1856-1927

September 29

"In this same way, husbands ought to love their wives as their own bodies. HE WHO LOVES HIS WIFE LOVES HIMSELF." Ephesians 5:28

Jan and I were married on December 14, 1975. We have been through two of my careers and into retirement. We do have a great life together. We decided early in our marriage to have at least one date each week. We reserve that night for each other to just go to a restaurant, have a quiet dinner and talk about the week or our plans, hopes and dreams. We laugh, tease each other (always in a loving gentle manner), discuss vacation plans, hold hands across the table and relish the time together. Over the years we have been married we have had many friends talk to us about our "weekly date". I love to give Jan cards. On Valentine's day, her birthday and our anniversary, I always get several cards to place around the house. Each year, I always find one new place to hide a card or one new way to give it to her. While we have always been very close and loving, we have become even closer since we have been walking closely with our Lord. I cannot love Jan completely unless I am walking with God as He directs me to walk. If I had a hole in my heart where God is supposed to be, my relationship with Jan wouldn't be complete.

Our promise today clearly states we are to love our wives as our own bodies. Do you feed your own body when you are hungry? So take care of the physical needs of your wife! Do you take the proper remedy when you are not feeling well? So provide for your wife's health! Do you enjoy it when your wife pampers and pets on you? So pamper and pet her! Do you get the right exercise to gain or maintain your strength and cardiovascular fitness? So make sure your wife has the opportunity for the same! Do you have a fulfilling job or profession? So don't begrudge the same for your wife! Do you study the Bible, read devotions and pray daily? So include your wife in those activities to insure her spiritual growth! If you love your wife, you will show those around you that you love and respect yourself.

We read in Proverbs 3:3-4, "Let love and faithfulness never leave you; bind them around your neck, write them on the tablet of your heart. Then you will win favor and a good name in the sight of God and man." Today's promise was preceded by a command in Ephesians 5:25-27, "Husbands, love your wives, just as Christ loved the church and gave Himself for her to make her holy, cleansing her by the washing with water through the word, and to present her to Himself as a radiant church, without stain or wrinkle or any other blemish, but holy and blameless." These two passages tells each of us very clearly how we are to act toward our wife. Ephesians 5:22-23 says, "Wives, submit to your husbands as to the Lord. For the husband is the head of the wife as Christ is the head of the church, His body, of which He is the Savior." This causes some concern among women today, perhaps because husbands are not loving wives as instructed by God. Our love and concern for our wives should be as complete and absorbing to us as God's love is for us.

Love your wife in a special way today, and you will go out and make this a great day.

There is beauty all around when there's love at home;
There is joy in every sound when there's love at home.
Peace and plenty here abide, smiling sweet on every side.
Time doth softly, sweetly glide when there's love at home.

John H. McNaughton - 1829-1891

September 30

"THEN YOU WILL CALL UPON ME AND COME AND PRAY TO ME, AND I WILL LISTEN TO YOU. YOU WILL SEEK ME AND FIND ME WHEN YOU SEEK ME WITH ALL YOUR HEART." Jeremiah 29:12 & 13

For three years, Fannie Wallace, pastor of Praise Assembly Full Gospel Ministry of Del City, OK, had been praying that God would provide a way she could start a school that would not only teach academics, but also help strengthen students' Christian faith. She had called upon God in prayer. She had sought an answer from Him with all her heart. She had studied other ways to start the school, but to no avail. Then, in the summer of 2002, God brought her into contact with another minister who owned a building which had been used as a nursing home. Without even realizing her longtime vision for a school run by the church, he gifted the property to her church. A week after the property was gifted to the church, one of the members told Pastor Wallace about a school equipment auction in Arcadia, OK. When church leaders showed up and explained their needs the person in charge of the auction donated hundreds of desks, computers, tables and other items to the church. Later, Tinker Air Force Base (located just outside of Del City in Midwest City) also donated twenty computers to the school. "Everything came at once," Pastor Wallace said. "Seven days after He gave us the building, He furnished it. God says He will open up the windows of heaven and pour you out a blessing. He said He will make provision." Members of the congregation, big and small, worked with mops, brooms and cleaning supplies to convert the nursing home into an academy. The school, Harbor Christian Academy, opened September 3, 2002 with 34 students in grades preschool through sixth.

Today's promise is as good for Pastor Fannie Wallace in the twenty-first century A.D. as it was when He gave it to Jeremiah in the seventh century B.C. Pastor Fannie Wallace didn't just mention to God in her prayers one night that she would like to start a Christian school. The Holy Spirit had put that desire in her heart. She verbalized it fervently, frequently and persistently to God in her prayers to Him. Today's promise is the basis of Jesus' parable of the persistent widow in Luke 18:2-8a. Jesus used that parable to urge us to call upon God fervently and persistent.

Do you have a goal which rests in your heart? Are you praying for its accomplishment? Are you consistent in your prayers? Remember, Pastor Fannie Wallace prayed for three years for the school, and when God granted her request, He granted the building and the contents within a week of time. Do you not know how to pray to ask for your heart's desire? We are assured in Isaiah 65:24, "Before they call I will answer; while they are still speaking I will hear." Do you feel too weak to explain to God just what your heart desires? You are assured of help in Romans 8:26, "In the same way, the Spirit helps us in our weakness. We do not know what we ought to pray for, but the Spirit Himself intercedes for us with groans that words cannot express."

Ask God fervently, frequently and persistently, and go out and make this a great day.

I must tell Jesus all of my trials, I cannot bear these burdens alone;
In my distress He kindly will help me, He always loves and cares for His own.
I must tell Jesus all of my troubles, He is a kind, compassionate friend;
If I but ask Him, He will deliver, make of my troubles quickly an end.

Elisha A. Hoffman - 1839-1929

October 1

"THE LORD IS NEAR TO ALL WHO CALL ON HIM, TO ALL WHO CALL ON HIM IN TRUTH." Psalm 145:18

I grew up on a farm many years before cell phones were even thought about. In fact, I grew up before there were heated and air conditioned cabs on the tractors! Many times there would be a need to communicate with one of us working in a distant field. We developed a system of communication using what we had, our straw hats. If it was time for the person working in the field to come into the farm yard, the person in the farm yard would get to a position to be seen and wave his hat. When the person in the field saw him, he would wave his hat in return, complete the circuit of the field, unhitch from the implement and come into the farm yard. We had different waves for the need for fuel, water, etc. The problem with needing something in the field and trying to communicate with someone in the house was that they never saw your signal. Running out of fuel in the field or having other types of trouble usually meant a long walk into the farm yard to get the help needed. People just weren't there looking at you when you needed them!

Isn't it wonderful we have today's promise! We don't have to wonder if God will be there looking at us when we need Him. He is always there for us. He will hear our loudest cry and He will respond to our softest whisper. The Lord is always near to those who call on Him! Does He always answer us? No! Sometimes the connection is broken. You know what breaks the connection? Sin! God will always hear our cry for forgiveness, but He doesn't hear our request for blessings when sin stands between us and Him. That is the qualifier on today's promise. The Lord is near to all who call on Him, to all who call on Him IN TRUTH. When Jesus was teaching His disciples to pray He included the admonition to always make sure there is no unforgiven sin between yourself and God (in Matthew 6:12) when He included this phrase: "Forgive us our debts, (sins) as we also have forgiven our debtors." (Those who have sinned against us or wronged us in any way.)

We read in Hosea 6:3, "Let us acknowledge the Lord; let us press on to acknowledge Him. As surely as the sun rises, He will appear; He will come to us like the winter rains, like the spring rains that water the earth." Hosea knew if we lived in harmony with the will of God, and acknowledged Him we would be in communication with Him. Do you ever get up in the morning and wonder if the sun will come up? Of course you don't! (Unless you live close to the north or south pole!) Hosea is reminding us we should have the same faith in our communication with God as we have in the sunrise. God wants communication with those who love Him. He wants to answer us, show us things and give us our true heart's desire. Jeremiah said "This is what the Lord says," in 33:3, "Call to me and I will answer you and tell you great and unsearchable things you do not know." So always call on God in truth, and go out and make this a great day.

Whisper a prayer in the morning, whisper a prayer at noon,
Whisper a prayer in the evening, to keep your heart in tune.
God answers prayer in the morning, God answers prayer at noon,
God answers prayer in the evening, to keep your heart in tune.
Source Unknown

October 2

> "As Jesus and His disciples were on their way, He came to a village where a woman named Martha opened her home to Him. She had a sister called Mary, who sat at the Lord's feet listening to what He said. But Martha was distracted by all the preparations that had to be made. She came to Him and asked, 'Lord, don't you care that my sister has left me to do the work by myself? Tell her to help me!' 'Martha, Martha,' the Lord answered, 'you are worried and upset about many things, BUT ONLY ONE THING IS NEEDED. MARY HAS CHOSEN WHAT IS BETTER, AND IT WILL NOT BE TAKEN AWAY FROM HER.'" Luke 10 38-42

School came easy for me in my early years and I found it very difficult to keep focused on my work unless it was just the work I wanted to do. I attended one-room schools for the first eight grades. Most years we had students in each of the eight grades in the same room with one teacher. We were given a "Report Card" each month showing our grades in each subject, our attendance record and a comment from the teacher. There was also a place for a parent to make a comment and sign his name. I loved to read (still do) and would much rather spend my time doing that. I would get distracted from my other, more tedious work, by my desire to read. I would also hurry through my assignments in other classes so I could spend my time reading. In the fourth grade I had a teacher, Miss Donna Blew, who once wrote the comment, "Clarence is a little careless in his writing for spelling and arithmetic. He can try a little harder." Dad signed the card with this comment, "Make him do it over until he does it right. He gets careless around home too." Again, my hurrying up everything so I could get to my reading!

Don't you think that is a little what Martha was going through? Her greatest desire was to make everything just right for the meal. She could see so many things which needed to be done to make the meal for Jesus a really special occasion. She became irritated with Mary for just sitting at the feet of Jesus, listening to what He said. Finally in her frustration to make everything just right she blurted out to Jesus (who, in her mind, was guilty of distracting Mary from productive meal preparation), "Lord, don't you care that my sister has left me to do the work by myself? Tell her to help me!" Jesus' reply was, "Martha, Martha, you are worried and upset about many things." Then He gives us today's promise, "But only one thing is needed. Mary has chosen what is better, and it will not be taken away from her."

Do you get distracted by all the preparation for church service, and become so worried and upset about many things that you feel need to be done that you fail to pay attention to Jesus? Are you so concerned with the preparation that you forget to sit and worship with music, prayer, scripture, fellowship, tithing and hearing the Word of God. Are you concerned about the length of the service because of your desire to get to a restaurant or home to a ball game?

Maybe we should remember that only one thing is needed! Maybe we should choose that which cannot be taken from us. Choose Jesus, and go out and make this a great day.

> Joyful, joyful, we adore Thee, God of glory, Lord of love;
> Hearts unfold like flowers before Thee, opening to the sun above.
> Melt the clouds of sin and sadness, drive the dark of doubt away;
> Giver of immortal gladness, fill us with the light of day.
>
> Henry Van Dyke - 1852-1933

October 3

"From the fruit of his lips a man is filled with good things AS SURELY AS THE WORK OF HIS HANDS REWARDS HIM." Proverbs 12:14

In our Sunday School class there is a man, Troy Shinn, who can do wonders with wood. Give him a set of plans, or tell him clearly what you want built, and he will build it with fine details. Troy makes his living by the work of his hands. He built an entertainment center for us which will be in our house for the rest of our lives. The very best things about Troy are his love for the Lord and his love for his wife, Alice. Troy is a Deacon in our church and is very knowledgeable about the Bible. His prayers are such that you know you are hearing a man talk directly to God. Yes, the work of his hands truly rewards Troy. Even more, the fruit of his lips, through his prayers, fills him with the things that are true, valuable, long-lasting and bring joy.

What about your life today? Do you have an occupation of working with your hands? Do you work with your hands, not as if working for yourself or your boss, but as if working for God? If you don't have such an occupation, do you have a hobby which requires you to work with your hands? Does the work of your hands reward you? When I am tending my roses or weeding my flower beds, I must concentrate on what I am doing but it doesn't take the full attention of my mind and I am able to commune with God during those times.

What about the fruit of your lips? Do you go to God in prayer on a regular basis? Do you ask for the things you need? Do you pray like Jabez did, that God would bless you? We read in James 1:17, "Every good and perfect gift is from above, coming down from the Father of the heavenly lights, who does not change like shifting shadow." Jesus told us in the sermon on the mount in Matthew 7:7-8, "Ask and it will be given to you; seek and you will find; knock and the door will be opened to you. For everyone who asks receives; he who seeks finds; and to him who knocks, the door will be opened." He told us again in Matthew 21:22, "If you believe, you will receive whatever you ask for in prayer."

Does this mean we can ask just anything from God and He will give it to us? Does it mean He will satisfy any appetite we have if we just ask Him? The answer to these questions is in three scriptures. First, 1 John 5:14-15, "This is the confidence we have in approaching God: that if we ask anything according to His will, He hears us. And if we know that He hears us-whatever we ask-we know that we have what we asked of Him." The first key is "according to His will." Second, 1 John 3:21-22, "Dear friends, if our hearts do not condemn us, we have confidence before God and receive from Him anything we ask, because we obey His commands and do what pleases Him." The second key is "obey His commands and do what pleases Him." Third, James 4:3, "When you ask, you do not receive, because you ask with wrong motives, that you may spend what you get on your pleasures." The third key is "you ask with wrong motives." So ask according to these scriptures, be filled with good things, and go out and make this a great day.

We gather together to ask the Lord's blessing
He chastens and hastens His will to make known;
The wicked oppressing now cease from distressing:
Sing praises to His name-He forgets not His own.

Netherland's Folk Hymn

October 4

> "Therefore Jesus said, again, 'I tell you the truth. I am the gate for the sheep. All who ever came before me were thieves and robbers, but the sheep did not listen to them. I AM THE GATE; WHOEVER ENTERS THROUGH ME WILL BE SAVED.'" John 10:7-9

This begins a nine part series between us and God. The parts are: God makes us free, guides us always, works within us, can save us, gives us rest, will never leave nor forsake us, is our strength, carries our works to completion and will judge us.

I grew up in a gated community. We had a gate to the yard, a gate to the garden, a gate to the corral, a gate to the pasture, a gate to the hog pen and a gate to many of our fields. When I read today's promise with Jesus saying He is the gate, I fully understand it. I opened enough gates during my younger years to know full well the significance of entering at the proper place. Our cows all knew exactly where to enter and exit the pasture. After we finished milking and left the barn we would find them waiting at the gate for us to come open it so they could enter the pasture for the day. When I read Jesus' words, "I am the gate for the sheep", I can just see them standing around waiting to enter. Those sheep wouldn't leave the gate for a thief or a robber because they would be at a place where they had cut the fence. The sheep could not be coaxed to that place, because they knew they entered through the gate, just as out cows knew also.

The cows, just like the sheep, knew when they left the corral in the morning they were going to the pasture where they would find plenty to eat. At evening they knew when they entered the corral they would have their water and feed, they would be milked, and they would be safe for the night. Isn't that the very image Jesus was trying to get us to see when he said these words? We know He is the true Savior. We should not listen to any temptation to believe otherwise. Jesus is the gate. He is the gate to the food, water, safety and comfort of life. Just as He told the Samaritan woman at Jacob's well in John 4:10 & 13-14, "If you knew the gift of God and who it is that asks you for a drink, you would have asked Him and He would have given you living water. Everyone who drinks this water will be thirsty again, but whoever drinks the water I give him will never thirst. Indeed the water I give him will become in him a spring of water welling up to eternal life."

Jesus is the gate. We know we will not live our lives hungering and craving for something to fill our souls. We are promised by Jesus in John 6:35, "I am the bread of life. He who comes to me will never go hungry, and he who believes in me will never be thirsty." Jesus is the gate. We know that we are safe when we enter through Him. As David wrote in Psalm 4:8, "I will lie down and sleep in peace, for you alone, O Lord, make me dwell in safety." Jesus is the gate. He will provide comfort to the weary as He promised in Matthew 11:28, "Come to me, all you who are weary and burdened, and I will give you rest." Yes, Jesus is the gate. When we enter through Him we have eternal life. Cherish that thought, and go out and make this a great day.

> Jesus! What a friend for sinners! Jesus! Lover of my soul!
> Friends may fail me, foes assail me, He, my Savior, makes me whole.
> Jesus! I do now receive Him, more than all in Him I find;
> He hath granted my forgiveness, I am His, and He is mine.
>
> J. Wilbur Chapman - 1859-1918

October 5

"THE LORD WILL GUIDE YOU ALWAYS; He will satisfy your needs in a sun-scorched land and will strengthen your frame. You will be like a well-watered garden, like a spring whose waters never fail." Isaiah 58:11

When I was ten years old my parents and I went to the home of an older couple in our church for Sunday dinner. My brother and sisters went with their friends so I was the only child present for the dinner. After dinner the man took Dad and me around the farm yard to show us what he had done to fix it up after he had purchased it and moved on it. As we entered the area where he raised his hogs he took us into the hog barn to show us a new litter of pigs. One of his sows had given birth to thirteen pigs just two days before. One of the pigs, a female, was much smaller than the others; we called those "runts". He was sure the runt would die if left to fend for itself with its litter mates. He asked me if I would like to take the pig home to try to raise it by hand. I quickly agreed! When I got it home I made a small pen for it in our mud room, placed papers on the floor and added plenty of straw for warm nesting. Momma helped me by finding an old toy baby bottle which had come with a doll one of my sisters had received. We would fill it with warm milk and feed the little pig. I spent many hours with that little pig feeding, petting, playing and caring for it. She did survive to move into the hog pen. She would run to the fence when she saw me or heard me for she knew I would satisfy her needs for food, water and attention. She grew to full size and had several litters of pigs for me to sell. Until the day she died she would always follow me wherever I wanted to guide her. She had total trust in me.

Do you feel like you need a guide? Are you living in a sun-scorched land? Do you often feel too weak to face life alone? How wonderful it is we have our God to guide us. Today's promise assures us He WILL guide us. He WILL satisfy our needs. When the earth is sun-scorched and dry during a drought, it finds refreshing relief from a good rain. When our souls are sun-scorched and dry when we are away from God, He sends His word and His Spirit to provide us with refreshing relief. Just as the earth becomes a well-watered garden following the refreshing rains, so our souls become like that well-watered garden, like a spring whose waters never fail.

The little red runt pig developed a faith in me for her food, water and attention. Similarly we should develop a faith in God for His living water, promised to us by Jesus Christ, which will never cease. It will lead us to eternal life through Jesus Christ, our Lord. Do you have the faith of that little red runt pig? Or do you doubt that the Lord will guide you and provide for you? Isaiah warned the people in 7:9, "If you do not stand firm in your faith, you will not stand at all." The same can be said to us today. Either we will stand firm in our faith that the Lord will guide us or we will become like a barren and sun-scorched land, without strength in our frame.

Accept God's guiding gift to you this very day. Your soul will become like a well-watered garden with a spring whose waters never fail. Now go out and make this a great day.

Guide me, O Thou great Jehovah, pilgrim through this barren land;
I am weak, but Thou art mighty, hold me with Thy powerful hand:
Bread of heaven, feed me till I want no more;
Bread of heaven, feed me till I want no more.

William Williams - 1717-1791

October 6

> "Therefore, my dear friends, as you have always obeyed - not only in my presence, but now much more in my absence - continue to work out your salvation with fear and trembling, FOR IT IS GOD WHO WORKS IN YOU TO WILL AND TO ACT ACCORDING TO HIS GOOD PURPOSE." Philippians 2:12 & 13

Did you always, or have you always, obeyed your parents? I must confess that I, and my siblings, did not do so. I remember one time when I was five years old Dad and Momma went to the neighbors home for a visit after dinner. Momma told my sisters, age seven and nine, to have the dishes done when they got back home. My sisters loved to play with their dolls, and they went into their bedroom to play after our parents left. I was afraid they would get in trouble so I reminded them three times they should get the dishes done. They just continued playing. I got so concerned about the trouble they would have and their punishment that I pulled a stool up to the sink and washed the dishes. I was just finished drying the dishes when we heard our parents at the door. The girls dashed madly into the kitchen to start the dishes and were so surprised to find them done they just stood there as Dad and Momma came in. Momma was so glad to see the dishes done she praised the girls for doing what she had told them to do. They never told her who did the dishes. In fact, she complemented them so much they soon began to believe they had actually been the ones to accomplish the task. I never told Momma that I was the one who washed the dishes because I didn't want my sisters punished for failure to obey.

Paul first expresses his joy that the people of Philippians had accepted Jesus Christ as their Savior, and had obeyed the Word he had taught them. They had obeyed both when he was there on two of his missionary journeys and during the time he had been absent to other places. Since they had obeyed God's Word, as taught to them, Paul told them to continue to work out their salvation with fear and trembling. Now, I don't think for a minute Paul meant by this that they were to perform works so they would gain salvation! Rather, I think Paul meant they were to continue to study, pray and support each other with awe, reverence and love at being in the presence of God in their worship.

In today's promise Paul assures the Philippians (and all who have read his words) that in their zeal for salvation it is God who works in them (and us) to will and to act according to His good purpose. God has given us the Holy Spirit to communicate with us constantly urging us and guiding our thoughts. We may call this our "conscience", but it is the presence of the Holy Spirit given to us by God. If we tune ourselves to receive His urges and guidance we find that we both will and act according to God's plan for us. We tune ourselves to the Holy Spirit by obeying God's Word, by prayer and meditation and by constantly showing our love to God and to our fellow man. Let there be nothing between you and God like sin or disobedience.

Live so God can work in you, and go out and make this a great day.

> Nothing between by soul and the Savior, naught of this world's delusive dream;
> I have renounced all sinful pleasure-Jesus is mine! There's nothing between.
> Nothing between my soul and the Savior, so that His blessed face may be seen;
> Nothing preventing the least of His favor: Keep the way clear! Let nothing between.
>
> Charles A. Tindley - 1851-1933

October 7

"Because Jesus lives forever, He has a permanent priesthood. THEREFORE HE IS ABLE TO SAVE COMPLETELY THOSE WHO COME TO GOD THROUGH HIM, BECAUSE HE ALWAYS LIVES TO INTERCEDE FOR THEM." Hebrews 7:24 & 25

When my daughter, Katy, was in Junior High school she had to take a physical education course. She had a lot of health problems that year and missed several days as she was sick, and also had to miss several days for appointments with the doctor. When she got her grade for the physical education class she called me in tears. She had received a D in the course. I asked her what the school policy was regarding absences and was told the teacher was not to lower a grade for excused absences, which included illness and doctor appointments. I asked her if she had talked to her teacher, and, through her sobs, she told me she had and the teacher told her the grade would stand. She asked me if I would help her. Of course I would! I called the school to verify the excused absence policy and was told it was as Katy had described it to me. I then called the teacher and set up an appointment for Katy and me to meet with her. I arrived in plenty of time on the day of the appointment and Katy and I went into the teacher's room at the appointed time. Katy never said a word. I asked the teacher to tell me when Katy had been absent, which she did. I then compared the dates given me with the dates Katy had supplied of her illnesses and doctor appointments. They all checked out. Katy had not been absent one time that wasn't excused. I asked the teacher if she was aware of the school policy regarding excused absences and grades. She said she was. I asked her if Katy participated in a satisfactory manner when she was present, and was assured she did. I then asked her if the grade she had given Katy was fair. After a long silence, the teacher looked at Katy, then at me, and said, "It isn't fair. I gave her that grade because I thought she should have been here. I was wrong. I will give her the grade she should have gotten." That grade was an A.

Now, a father will not live forever, but he will sure be a father forever. I was able to intercede for Katy to correct a wrong that had been done to her. Jesus lives forever! He has a permanent priesthood! God gave Him to die on the cross as atonement for our sins. God promised us that if we believed in Him we would have eternal life. Jesus is able to save us completely when we come to God through Him. We need never fear when we consider Hebrews 9:27, "Just as man is destined to die once, and after that to face judgment," because we have today's promise as the one in verse 28, "so Christ was sacrificed once to take away the sins of many people; and He will appear a second time, not to bear sin, but to bring salvation to those who are waiting for Him."

When we face the judgment, Jesus will be there to intercede for those of us who believe in Him, and have come to God through Him. Jesus paid the price for our sins by His death on the cross, so it is fair that we have eternal life. Believe it! Now go out and make this a great day.

Saved by the blood of the Crucified One! Now ransomed from sin and a new work begun,
Sing praise to the Father and praise to the Son, saved by the blood of the Crucified one!
Saved! Saved! My sins are all pardoned, my guilt is all gone!
Saved! Saved! I am saved by the blood of the Crucified One!

S. J. Henderson - (Nineteenth Century)

October 8

"THEREFORE, SINCE THE PROMISE OF ENTERING HIS REST STILL STANDS, LET US BE CAREFUL THAT NONE OF YOU BE FOUND TO HAVE FALLEN SHORT OF IT." Hebrews 4:1

In my Senior year in high school I participated in track. My special event was the mile run. I won several of the earlier track meets and was working hard to improve my times. To train for the race I would start the afternoon training session by running around a course which measured 4.8 miles. The coach would time me on that run and then have me run a series of sprints of one-eighth mile each. I would then be allowed to walk and rest until near the end of the training session. He would then have me run a mile, which he would time. If I beat the slowest time I had run in a previous meet that year, I could consider the session finished and go to the showers. If I failed to beat that time, I had to run another series of sprints. You can be sure I ran that timed mile very hard to avoid additional sprints, earn the privilege of going to the showers, and then rest until time to catch the bus. If I fell short of the required time, I didn't get the promised rest. This training paid off as I earned a spot at the state track meet and finished in my best time ever.

Today's promise of rest far exceeds that promised by my coach! Paul is pointing out that salvation in available. We have God's promise that if we believe in Jesus Christ we can rest in His word and be assured of eternal life. Why did God give His Son, Jesus Christ to die on the cross for our sins? Because He loved us so much, even when we were sinners! Two days ago our promise included Paul cautioning the Philippians to work out their salvation with fear and trembling. Now Paul cautions us to be careful that we do not fall short of salvation. Does that cause you to be fearful? Are you concerned you may not measure up? Do you wonder if your salvation is sufficient to gain the promise of entering His rest? Do you fear that you will be found to have fallen short? Claim 1 John 4:18, "There is no fear in love. But perfect love drives out fear, because fear has to do with punishment. The one who fears is not made perfect in love."

Your fears are quelled as you study God's Word. We read in 1 John 4:14-15, "And we have seen and testify that the Father has sent His Son to be the Savior of the world. If anyone acknowledges that Jesus is the Son of God, God lives in him and he in God." Have you acknowledged that Jesus is the Son of God? Have you followed the instructions of Paul in Romans 10:9, "That if you confess with your mouth, 'Jesus is Lord,' and believe in your heart that God raised Him from the dead, you will be saved."? If you have, then cast aside your anxiety. You will have eternal life! Claim Philippians 4:6-7, "Do not be anxious about anything, but in everything, by prayer and petition, with thanksgiving, present your requests to God. And the peace of God, which transcends all understanding, will guard your hearts and your minds in Christ Jesus." Rest in this promise! Live it! Now go out and make this a great day.

Standing on the promises I now can see perfect, present cleansing in the blood for me;
Standing in the liberty where Christ makes free, standing on the promises of God.
Standing on the promises I cannot fall, list'ning ev'ry moment to the Spirit's call,
Resting in my Savior as my all in all, standing on the promises of God.

R. Kelso Carter - 1849-1928

October 9

"THE LORD HIMSELF GOES BEFORE YOU AND WILL BE WITH YOU; HE WILL NEVER LEAVE YOU NOR FORSAKE YOU. DO NOT BE AFRAID; DO NOT BE DISCOURAGED." Deuteronomy 31:8

Someone wrote a poem entitled, "Footprints". In it the author tells of a man having a dream and looking back over his life as being a walk along a beach. He saw two sets of footprints all along the way-one for him and one for the Lord. When he looked closer he saw only one set of footprints in many places. Upon studying those times he discovered the one set appeared only at those times of his life which were the hardest, saddest and most lonely times. This bothered him so he cried out, "Lord, you said that once I decided to follow you, you would walk with me all the way. However, during the most difficult times of my life there is only one set of footprints. Why did you leave me and forsake me?" The Lord replied, "My son, I love you and would never leave you alone. It was during those most difficult times of your life that I was carrying you!"

That is a perfect example for today's promise. This is a precious, precious promise for us to cling to at all time, but especially when we are feeling low, sad, lonely, hurt, disappointed, grieved or fearful. It is a promise that our God will go before us to prepare the way, that He will be with us as we walk life's pathway, that He will NEVER leave us nor forsake us, and that He asks us not to be afraid nor discouraged. In fact, Paul tells us in 2 Timothy 1:7, "For God did not give us a spirit of timidity (fear), but a spirit of power, of love and of self-discipline." Jesus told the eleven disciples, shortly before His ascension, in Matthew 28:20, "And surely I am with you always, to the very end of the age."

If you need New Testament proof that the Lord goes before us, you should read the words of Jesus recorded in John 14:1-3, "Do not let your hearts be troubled. Trust in God; trust also in me. In my Father's house are many rooms; if it were not so, I would have told you. I am going there to prepare a place for you. And if I go and prepare a place for you, I will come back and take you to be with me that you also may be where I am." Not only does He go before us, He is preparing a place for us in His Father's house, He is coming back for us, and He wants us with Him. Do you wonder if He is with you during temptations? Does He understand what you are going through? Read Paul's words in Hebrews 2:18, "Because He Himself suffered when He was tempted, He is able to help those who are being tempted." Will it be enough help? Again read Paul's words in 1 Corinthians 10:13, "No temptation has seized you except what is common to man. And God is faithful; He will not let you be tempted beyond what you can bear. But when you are tempted, He will also provide a way out so that you can stand up under it."

When you are grieved, sad, lonely or hurt is the very time you should claim this promise. Ask God to hold you in His arms on His lap, just like a child would ask their earthly father. Curl up in His arms and bask in His comfort. Now go out and make this a great day.

Sweetly, Lord, have we heard Thee calling, "Come, follow Me!"
And we see where Thy footprints falling lead us to Thee.
Then at last, when on high He sees us, our journey done,
We will rest where the steps of Jesus end at His throne.

Mary B. C. Slade - 1826-1882

October 10

> "Nehemiah said, 'Go and enjoy choice food and sweet drinks, and send some to those who have nothing prepared. This day is sacred to our Lord. DO NOT GRIEVE, FOR THE JOY OF THE LORD IS YOUR STRENGTH.'" Nehemiah 8:10

Today's promise is recorded by Nehemiah following a long period of devastation and rebuilding by the Israelites. In 722 the Northern kingdom of Israel fell to the Assyrians because of the wickedness of the people in Israel. In 586 the Southern kingdom of Judah fell to the Babylonians because of the wickedness in Jerusalem and the kingdom of Judah. God allowed the punishment of the people of Israel and Judah because of their wickedness. We write and study much about the love, kindness, goodness, peace, hope, joy, etc. of God and very little about the wrath of God. We read in Romans 1:18-19, "The wrath of God is being revealed from heaven against all the godlessness and wickedness of men who suppress the truth by their wickedness, since what may be known about God is plain to them, because God has made it plain to them." God had made His law plain to the Israelites and they chose to disobey that law. He destroyed their country and caused them to be exiled. After seventy years in captivity the Israelites who were true to God were allowed to return to Jerusalem. In 445 the wall around Jerusalem was complete. Ezra, the priest read the law to the assembled people. When the reading of the law was completed, Nehemiah, the governor, made the statement, which is today's promise, to the Israelites. It may seem to you that God was very stern with the wickedness of the Israelites. He was, and we are told by Paul of His sternness in Romans 1:22, "Consider therefore the kindness and sternness of God: sternness to those who fell, but kindness to you, provided that you continue in His kindness. Otherwise, you also will be cut off."

The people were so grateful for a restored Jerusalem they were weeping as the law was being read. The promise God caused Nehemiah to give us expresses the real love, kindness, goodness, peace, hope and joy of God. God truly wants us to enjoy our food and beverages. He also wants us to provide for those in need. He does not want us to be in sorrow. He wants us to be nourished and strong, for His joy is in our strength.

His joy in our strength is not just our physical strength. It is also in our spiritual strength. Note the people had just heard the reading of His law, and hearing it had caused them great emotion. They fully realized what God expected from them. It is the same way when we read and study the Word of God. We should take the lessons deep within ourselves and fully digest them to make us spiritually strong, just as we take our food and beverage into our very being to digest it to make us physically strong. We should also give of our provisions to those in need to make us strong in the ministry of Christ.

Have you been through a time of low spirit like the Israelites during their exile? Renew your spiritual, physical and ministerial strength, and go out and make this a great day.

> O Master, let me walk with Thee in lowly paths of service free;
> Tell me Thy secret-help me bear the strain of toil, the fret of care.
> Teach me Thy patience: still with Thee In closer, dearer company,
> In work that keeps faith sweet and strong, in trust that triumphs over wrong.
> Washington Gladden - 1836-1918

October 11

"Being confident of this, THAT HE WHO BEGAN A GOOD WORK IN YOU WILL CARRY IT ON TO COMPLETION UNTIL THE DAY OF CHRIST JESUS." Philippians 1:6

Several years ago we had to make several trips from Oklahoma to Nebraska. As we were making the first trip we entered a construction zone north of Salina, Kansas. The state of Kansas was building highway 81 as a four lane, divided highway. As we drove on the two-lane part, I thought to myself, "My, that will sure be nice to drive on when it is finished." Each subsequent trip, about ten weeks apart, showed the work being carried on toward completion. We continued those trips for almost two years. By that time the highway was completed and was wonderful to drive over. All those times we drove through the construction zones I thought about the message I had seen on the shirts worn by some young people, "Be patient with me. I am God's work in progress." We had to be patient with the construction workers and the slow speed zones in the area of construction. That highway was a work in progress. Now, the few times I travel that way, I am thankful for the work that was done on that highway and the results of it.

That is what Paul is telling the Philippian people in this passage. He told them he thanked God for them every time he remembered them because of their partnership with God. He was confident that the partnership with God would carry His good work in them on to completion until the day they were taken home to be with Him for eternity. What a wonderful, powerful, comforting promise this is for today!

Are there people you have known in the past you feel this way about? Those who worked on a project with you, attended a class or seminar with you, or those who worshiped with you may have a special place in your heart. Have you told them so? Why don't you call or write them today to tell them how much they meant, and still mean, to you? They may be struggling with a need in their heart that your contact might meet. Your contact may provide the source of strength which can get them through a really tough time. I think that is one of the reasons Paul included this promise in his letter. He really understood how to continue to mentor and support fellow Christians, even in his absence.

Do your feel discouraged about your walk with Christ at this time? Do you feel you should be much farther along in your maturity as a Christian? Are you having trouble breaking a bad habit? Is there a particular temptation you are having trouble avoiding? Read today's promise again. God has begun a good work in you and He WILL carry it on to completion until the day you meet Christ Jesus face to face. Just remember that tee shirt message and be patient; you are God's work in progress. That highway didn't get completed for our second trip, nor our third, nor our sixth, but it DID get completed. We just had to be patient until it was completed. Remember, we will be a work in progress until God calls us home. Be patient, trust God, follow Him and learn to wait for His guidance. Now go out and make this a great day.

They that wait upon the Lord shall renew their strength;
They shall mount up with wings like eagles;
They shall run, and not be weary; they shall walk, and not faint.
Teach me, Lord, teach me, Lord, to wait.

Stuart Hamblen - 1908-

October 12

"JUST AS MAN IS DESTINED TO DIE ONCE, AND AFTER THAT TO FACE JUDGMENT, SO CHRIST WAS SACRIFICED ONCE TO TAKE AWAY THE SINS OF MANY PEOPLE; AND HE WILL APPEAR A SECOND TIME, NOT TO BEAR SIN, BUT TO BRING SALVATION TO THOSE WHO ARE WAITING FOR HIM." Hebrews 9:27 & 28

In the United States of America we have a double jeopardy law. This means that a man can only be tried once for any crime for which he may have been tried (assuming a verdict was reached). There are cases where a man has not even been tried once because of a lack of solid evidence. Several years ago (before the use of DNA evidence) I read about a detective who had been assigned a very difficult case many years before. He had worked on it very hard for two years. He had found enough evidence to convince himself who had committed the crime, but the evidence was weak. It involved a weak motive, weak circumstantial evidence and a weak alibi for the suspect. Nothing the detective could find was of such strength that it could convince a jury of the guilt of the suspect. In an interview about the case the detective said, "I am sure, in my mind, who committed the crime, but I would never be able to convince a jury so I could get a conviction." If the detective was correct in his analysis, the guilty person never faced judgment.

This is not the case with us facing the consequences of our sins! We will die, and then we will face the judgment of God, who is a just and fair God, and He will give us the sentence we deserve. We are told in Jeremiah 17:10, "I the Lord search the heart and examine the mind, to reward a man according to his conduct, according to what his deeds deserve." This is the first part of today's promise. We can be assured that we WILL face judgment! Like the United States of America judicial system, God has provided that we will not face double jeopardy. How did He do that? That is the second part of today's promise. He sent His Son, Jesus Christ, to shed His blood to atone for the sins of the world. All we have to do is to believe on Him. As Paul said in Romans 10:9, "That if you confess with your mouth, 'Jesus is Lord,' and believe in your heart that God raised Him from the dead, you will be saved."

Yes, Christ WAS sacrificed once to take away the sins of many people, and that includes us. What does He do with our sins? We are told in Psalm 103:12, "As far as the east is from the west, so far has He removed our transgressions from us." He will appear a second time, not because He has to atone for our sins again, but to bring salvation to all those who are waiting for Him. Bring salvation? Yes, the consummation of our belief in Him. The glorious fulfillment of our life for Him. This was the promise of God in John 3:16 when it says, "that whoever believes in Him shall not perish but have eternal life."

Do you believe in Jesus Christ? Have you confessed Him with your mouth? Have you asked God to forgive your sins? Are you ready for the judgment which will come after your earthly death? If you have you will have eternal life. Now go out and make this a great day.

Would you be free from your burden of sin? There's pow'r in the blood, pow'r in the blood;
Would you o'er evil a victory win? There's wonderful pow'r in the blood.
Would you be whiter, much whiter than snow? There's pow'r in the blood, pow'r in the blood;
Sin-stains are lost in its life-giving flow. There's wonderful pow'r in the blood.

Lewis E. Jones - 1865-1936

October 13

> "I am the bread of life. Your forefathers ate the manna in the desert, yet they died. But here is the bread that comes down from heaven, which a man may eat and not die. I AM THE LIVING BREAD THAT CAME DOWN FROM HEAVEN. IF ANYONE EATS OF THIS BREAD, HE WILL LIVE FOREVER. This bread is my flesh, which I will give for the life of the world." John 6:48-51

When I was growing up on the farm, Momma occasionally purchased "store bought" bread. Most of the time she baked it. We had a large kitchen, and we would congregate there when we came home from school. My favorite time after school was when it was very cold and I would arrive home (I only walked one and one-eighth mile, and it wasn't uphill both ways!) to the smell of fresh baked bread and a large kettle of vegetable beef soup on the stove. We would take off our coats and galoshes, fill a bowl with soup, get a glass of milk, butter a thick slice of bread, put some jam on it and have an afternoon snack fit for a king. This time together gave us the opportunity to share what happened at school, what happened on the farm while we were gone, catch up on news from the community Momma heard during the day, and relax before doing the evening chores. It was really nice to change into our "work clothes", bundle up against the cold and go about our evening chores with our stomachs full of warm food. It seems like I can just close my eyes, think real hard and smell that fresh baked, home made bread. It was really satisfying to the taste!

When Jesus walked the earth everyone baked their own bread. They ate a lot of it as they didn't have cereals and other foods to eat and got their grains from the bread. I am sure everyone instantly thought of the smell, taste and filling quality of fresh baked bread when Jesus made the promise we have for today. They knew the importance of bread to their physical bodies. The people Jesus was talking to knew the stories of the exodus during which their ancestors survived on the manna which came down from heaven fresh each day except Sunday. They must have been able to understand the example Jesus used when He said, "I am the living bread that came down from heaven." Jesus was telling them of the importance of believing on Him, accepting Him and His Word and taking Him into their hearts as food for their spiritual bodies. With this promise and His statement, "This bread is my flesh, which I will give for the life of the world." Jesus was starting the teaching to prepare them for His death on the cross for the sins of the people of the world.

Jesus is still the bread of life. We still have to believe on Him, accept Him, study His Word, and take Him into our hearts to be partakers of Him and have eternal life. We symbolize this partaking of the bread of life when we have communion. We must be sure our hearts are right with God before we take communion as we are literally partaking spiritually of the body and blood of Jesus Christ. Partake of the bread of life, and go out and make this a great day.

> Break Thou the bread of life, dear Lord, to me,
> As Thou didst break the loaves beside the sea;
> Beyond the sacred page I seek Thee, Lord;
> My spirit pants for Thee, O living Word.
>
> Mary A. Lathbury - 1841-1913

October 14

"WITHOUT WOOD A FIRE GOES OUT; WITHOUT GOSSIP A QUARREL DIES DOWN. AS CHARCOAL TO EMBERS AND AS WOOD TO FIRE, SO IS A QUARRELSOME MAN FOR KINDLING STRIFE." Proverbs 26:20 & 21

We burned wood in a heating stove in our living room during the years I was growing up. In the Winter Momma also burned wood in a wood-burning cook stove in the kitchen to keep that end of the house warm. We did have a stove which burned butane which we used in the Summer. During the real cold weather, Dad would "bank" the stove at night. He would let the fire burn down to glowing coals, shut off the air vents to the firebox, turn the damper in the smokestack to a position of nearly closed, add a few good size pieces of wood and close the firebox door. The next morning Dad would find a bed of glowing embers mixed with the ashes which were formed over night. He would add several small sticks and dry wood as kindling, and would place the larger pieces of wood on top of this. He would shake out the ashes and take them out to dump in a small pit we had dug. If Dad didn't add enough wood to properly bank the fire, or if he had not shut down the flow of air through the firebox, the fire would go out over night. Dad would then have to start the fire with papers and kindling in the cold room the next morning. Whether the fire was properly banked or not, as Dad got a small fire going in the morning, he would add several pieces of wood, open the air vents and the damper, and the fire would become a warmth-giving, roaring fire.

In the days of Solomon everyone burned wood to keep warm. They understood this proverb very well. Our promise today is a double promise. Just as the fire would go out when there was no more wood, we are promised that a quarrel dies down without gossip. Likewise, just as our fire would become a warmth-giving, roaring flame when the wood was added, so a quarrelsome man will cause a strife to become a roaring inferno of bickering.

Speaking of people who had become wicked, Paul told us in Romans 1:29-31, "They have become filled with every kind of wickedness, evil, greed and depravity. They are full of envy, murder, strife, deceit and malice. They are gossips, slanderers, God-haters, insolent, arrogant and boastful; they invent ways of doing evil; they disobey their parents; they are senseless, faithless, heartless, ruthless." Notice the list of other sins included with gossiping. God does not take it lightly! Gossiping is a sin! It divides people, causes others to take sides, builds up strife and anger, and can lead to hate. John particularly warned against gossip in the church as being divisive and destructive. We must be careful of what we say and how we say it about others. We must never be guilty of passing on falsehoods we have heard about others. We should not even pass on information which may be true if it would hurt another person and is not helpful to healing and growth in the church. Don't kindle a quarrel with gossip! Let the fire die out!

Let Jesus take your sin of gossiping away. Now go out and make this a great day.

I came to Jesus, weary, worn, and sad, He took my sins away, He took my sins away;
And now His love has made my heart so glad, He took my sins away.
If you will come to Jesus Christ today, He'll take your sins away, He'll take your sins away;
And keep you happy in His love each day, He'll take your sins away.

Margaret J. Harris - 1903-

October 15

> "Even though I walk through the valley of the shadow of death, I will fear no evil, FOR YOU ARE WITH ME; YOUR ROD AND YOUR STAFF, THEY COMFORT ME."
> Psalm 23:4

When you were a child, did you ever have occasion to walk in a strange, wild place, like the woods, when it was very dark? On the farm I had many such occasions to be out on very dark nights both in areas which were familiar and some which were unfamiliar. In such situations it is easy to let your imagination run away with you such that you "see" all sorts of scary things. It was many years later in military training that I learned the secret of seeing better at night. (You don't look directly at what you want to see, rather you look at a very slight, five degree, angle from the point you want to see so your "night vision" part of your eye will be better focused on the point.) Back then I had spent enough time outside to know what animals were present, but they would still give me a big fright when I would get close and one would suddenly run away. The shapes of the trees took on all sorts of sinister beings in my mind, and as I walked by they seemed to move because my motion was ascribed to them in my mind. I am sure David was thinking about just such times when he wrote this verse. He had spent a lot of time out at night shepherding the sheep when he was young. As a young adult, he spent a lot of time in the wilderness evading Saul, who wrongly thought David meant him harm. David probably moved at night and hid out during the day.

Just as David says in today's promise, we have no cause to fear evil for God is with us. I think David also meant us to understand that when we are walking through the darkest times of our lives we still have no reason to fear evil, because those are the very times God is closest with us. David knew well the use of the rod for counting, guiding, rescuing and protecting sheep. He knew well the use of the staff to assist himself walking in rough places. The staff also made a very good weapon for close fighting, and I am sure David was highly skilled in its use. We don't use the term "rod" very much now, but it literally means a shoot or branch of a tree. David knew that meaning very well as it is applied scripturally, and was, therefore, very comforted knowing he was a shoot or branch of God, who was with him during those dark times.

Are you walking through a very dark time in your life right now? Does your faith seem to be much too small? Do you sense evil all about you? Does God seem too far away from you? Take heart, child of God! You do not need to fear evil. God is with you! As a child of God you are a branch of Jesus Christ's family. The rod of God will comfort you (Luke 12:7 says, "Indeed, the very hairs of your head are all numbered."), guide you (Isaiah 58:11 says, "The Lord will guide you always."), rescue you (2 Peter 3:9 says, "He is patient with you, not wanting anyone to perish, but everyone to come to repentance.") and protect you (Isaiah 40:11 says, "He tends His flock like a shepherd: He gathers the lambs in His arms and carries them close to His heart.")

Accept and expect the comfort of God, and go out and make this a great day.

> Savior, like a Shepherd lead us, much we need Thy tender care;
> In Thy pleasant pastures feed us; for our use Thy folds prepare.
> Blessed Jesus, blessed Jesus, Thou hast bought us Thine we are;
> Blessed Jesus, blessed Jesus, Thou hast bought us, Thine we are.
> Dorothy A. Thrupp - 1779-1847

October 16

"THOUGH YOU HAVE NOT SEEN HIM, YOU LOVE HIM; AND EVEN THOUGH YOU DO NOT SEE HIM NOW, YOU BELIEVE IN HIM AND ARE FILLED WITH AN INEXPRESSIBLE AND GLORIOUS JOY." 1 Peter 1:8

I read a story years ago about a young lady (I will call her Mary) in her late teens who wanted to do something to help the morale of the troops so she wrote a letter and sent it to Europe. Somehow the letter reached a young soldier not yet twenty (I will call him John). John read the chatty letter and was greatly encouraged that someone would appreciate what he was doing so much they would send such a letter. He answered it, and, to his surprise, received a return response. From this developed a correspondence which lasted until the war was over. As letter followed letter the two writers discovered many common interests, including their love for God. Though they had never seen each other, they fell in love. Though Mary had not seen John, she believed he would make a great husband. After the end of the war, John returned home, visited his family, and announced to them (after the inevitable question as to what he was going to do now) that he was going to go meet his future wife, marry and bring her home. That is exactly what he did, and they had a wonderful life full of love, happiness, service to the Lord and many children and grand-children.

I think of that story when I read today's promise. Mary fell in love with John by reading the words he wrote, the thoughts he expressed and the indication of the feelings which were growing in him. Likewise, John fell in love with Mary in the same way. First, because he knew of her love for her country and the men who were fighting to support and defend her country. Second, his love for her grew as he learned more about her through her words, and continued to make her more and more a part of him. Isn't that a lot like we are with God? He loves the world and all of us in it. He had given us His Word to read and study on a regular basis. He wants us to know more and more about Him. He wants us to make Him more and more a part of us. We have not seen Him, but we love Him. We have not seen Him, but we believe in Him. This fills us with an inexpressible and glorious joy which is far greater than that of John for Mary.

Thomas was not with the other disciples when Jesus first appeared to them. When they told Thomas they had seen Jesus he refused to believe. Later Jesus appeared to all and showed Thomas His hands and side. Thomas said, "My Lord and my God!" Jesus answered in John 20:29, "Because you have seen me, you have believed; blessed are those who have not seen and yet have believed." Isn't it wonderful that Jesus would understand our hesitancy to believe in Him when we can't see Him and gave us this precious story? Have you found it hard to believe in Him? Read His Word, invite Him into your home and heart, live with Him, and express the words of today's promise. You will be filled with inexpressible and glorious joy!

Now go out and make this a great day.

My Jesus, I love Thee, I know Thou art mine; For Thee all the follies of sin I resign;
My Gracious Redeemer, my Savior art Thou; if ever I loved Thee, my Jesus 'tis now.
I love Thee because Thou hast first loved me, and purchased my pardon on Calvary's tree;
I love Thee for wearing the thorns on Thy brow; if ever I loved Thee, my Jesus, 'tis now.
William R. Featherstone 1846-1873

October 17

"A FALSE WITNESS WILL NOT GO UNPUNISHED, AND HE WHO POURS OUT LIES WILL PERISH." Proverbs 19:9

When I was in grade school I attended a one-room school with one teacher for all the grades 1-8. Sometimes there were not students in all grades, and there might be two, three or four in some grades. The teacher had her hands full to prepare assignments, listen to recitations, grade homework, prepare and give tests and handle discipline. One day there was an altercation between two students, and both combatants ended up bloody and dirty. The teacher put one of the eighth grade girls in charge of the rest of us in the classroom and took the students, one at a time, into the hallway to get their story of what started the fight. It turned out that all the stories were the same except for that of the best friend of the boy who started the fight. His story was just the opposite of that of all the rest of us. This was in the days when paddling was common and the teacher paddled the boy who started the fight. She then paddled the boy who did not tell the truth, and she made him stay in the classroom at both the morning and afternoon recess for an entire week. He wasn't involved in the fight, but he had not told the truth. She justified the punishment by telling us it was very important to always tell the truth and used this verse to back up her position. This made a very great impression on all the rest of us relating to the importance of honesty.

Have you ever been in a position to bear the brunt of punishment because of a false witness? It makes you feel pretty bad doesn't it? It especially makes you feel bad when the one who makes the false statements escapes punishment. Did you want to seek revenge against that person? We should always remember Romans 12:19, "Do not take revenge, my friends, but leave room for God's wrath, for it is written: 'It is mine to avenge; I will repay,' says the Lord." Today's promise clearly states that a false witness WILL NOT go unpunished. We may not be satisfied to see someone who lied about us walking around without suffering any consequences, but we must remember that God's timing is perfect. The person who lies about you, or testifies falsely about you in court, WILL be punished in God's own time. I am totally convinced that God meant it when He gave Moses the commandment listed in Exodus 20:16, "You shall not give false testimony against your neighbor."

What should you do when someone testifies falsely about you or spreads lies about you? This is clearly a sin against you. That question was answered in Matthew 18:21-22, "Then Peter came to Jesus and asked, 'Lord, how many times shall I forgive my brother when he sins against me? Up to seven times?' Jesus answered, 'I tell you, not seven times, but seventy-seven times.'" The King James Version says, "seventy times seven." I don't think it makes any difference. Can you imagine someone who truly forgives keeping a record of check marks for that many times? Be honest, let God be your strength to keep you honest. Now go out and make this a great day.

Jesus! What a strength in weakness! Let me hide myself in Him;
Tempted, tried, and sometimes failing, He, my strength, my victory wins.
Jesus! What a guide and keeper! While the tempest still is high;
Storms about me, night o'ertakes me, He, my pilot, hears my cry.

J. Wilbur Chapman - 1859-1918

October 18

"The woman said, 'I know that Messiah (called Christ) is coming. When He comes, He will explain everything to us.' Then Jesus declared, 'I WHO SPEAK TO YOU AM HE.'"
John 4:25 & 26

When I was in undergraduate school I majored in Chemistry and took a course titled, "Chemical Calculations". We used a book titled "Industrial Chemical Calculations", which was filled with problems taken from real life situations. Many of the problems would take several pages of calculations each to solve. Those of us taking the class would often get together to work on the problems, and it wasn't unusual for us to find several things we didn't understand. I remember frequently saying, or hearing said, "We will ask Dr. Ericson when he gets to class. He will explain it to us." Sure enough, when we got to class with him, he would not condemn us for our inability. Instead, he would guide us through the very difficult parts of the problems so we could work through to the answer.

When I read today's promise I think back on that time and can relate to the Samaritan woman, who came to draw water from the well while Jesus was resting there, awaiting the return of His disciples from buying food. When Jesus asked her to give Him a drink, she was amazed that a Jew would even speak to a Samaritan woman, and said, "How can you ask me for a drink?" When Jesus offered her living water, she was confused, because He had nothing with which to draw water. Jesus then said in John 4:13, "Everyone who drinks this water will be thirsty again, but whoever drinks the water I give him will never thirst. Indeed, the water I give him will become in him a spring of water welling up to eternal life." The conversation with Jesus left her very confused, perhaps a bit frightened, and, definitely, wanting what Jesus could give her. She knew the Scripture well enough to know a Messiah had been promised, who would explain all things to all people, so she told Jesus, "I know that Messiah (called Christ) is coming. When He comes, He will explain everything to us."

Are you confused about parts of your Bible study? Are you questioning some of the things which are happening in your life today? The Messiah (called Christ) has come! You can take all your questions to Him and He will give you the answers. Remember today's promise when you have your quiet time and commune with the Lord, "I who speak to you am He!" We don't have to be confused, because the Bible explains things to us pretty clearly. What we don't understand, we can ask Him in our quiet time and prayer. Jesus came that we might have eternal life, so we need not have any fear with Him. We read in 1 John 4:16, "God is love." Again, we read in 1 John 4:18, "There is no fear in love. But perfect love drives out fear, because fear has to do with punishment." Like the Samaritan woman, we should definitely want what Jesus can give us! John 3:17 tells us, "For God did not send His Son into the world to condemn the world, but to save the world through Him." Claim it! Now go out and make this a great day.

Fear not, little flock, from the cross to the throne, from death into life He went for His own;
All power in earth, all power above, is given to Him for the flock of His love.
Fear not, little flock, whatever your lot; He enters all rooms, "the doors being shut."
He never forsakes, He never is gone-so count on His presence in darkness and dawn.
Paul Rader - 1879-1938

October 19

"Then He adds: 'THEIR SINS AND LAWLESS ACTS I WILL REMEMBER NO MORE.' AND WHERE THESE HAVE BEEN FORGIVEN, THERE IS NO LONGER ANY SACRIFICE FOR SIN." Hebrews 10:17 & 18

One of the subjects I loved, and was good at, in the military, was map reading. I think it has to do with my method of solving problems, making plans and organizing events. I close my eyes and project myself, in thought, above the activity and watch it develop in my mind to completion. When I am working with maps, I am actually doing, for real, what I do in my mind in solving other problems. I am looking down on the problem from above and can see how it develops to the end. I found, in map reading, that an error of one degree on the compass made no difference, of any effect, on a short distance. However, if the distance was measured in miles or kilometers, it made a vast difference. I also learned you had to walk in a straight line to get to the proper place. You could wander off the straight course only if you had established a point on your course, in the distance, which was a recognizable feature, and always aimed for that point when you had to bypass an obstacle. When you reach that feature you need to "shoot another azimuth" and establish another recognizable feature in the distance. In this manner, you are always walking a straight course, regardless of how much your path wanders to avoid obstacles. When you arrive at the final objective of your course, you don't necessarily remember the mud and the muck, the brush and thorns, or the gullies and steep places you had to avoid on the way. You just know that you have arrived at your goal.

I think that is a lot like our walk with Christ. He assures us, in today's promise, that He will not remember our sins and lawless acts. These have been forgiven, and we no longer have to make any sacrifice for our sin. Jesus made that sacrifice for us when He died on the cross. We are told in Hebrews 3:12, "See to it, brothers, that none of you has a sinful, unbelieving heart that turns away from the living God." Jesus said in Mark 7:21-23, "For from within, out of men's hearts, come evil thoughts, sexual immorality, theft, murder, adultery, greed, malice, deceit, lewdness, envy, slander, arrogance and folly. All these evils come from inside and make a man 'unclean'." We don't have to worry about getting on the wrong course when we have confessed our sins. We are told in 1 John 1:9, "If we confess our sins, He is faithful and just and will forgive us our sins and purify us from all unrighteousness." A life like Jesus lived is our goal! If we keep our eye on that goal, we will reach our objective!

Does that mean we will never be tempted to take a wrong turn? No! But we are told in 1 Cor 10:13, "No temptation has seized you except what is common to man. And God is faithful; He will not let you be tempted beyond what you can bear. But when you are tempted, He will also provide a way out so that you can stand up under it." So, always keep your eye on the goal of eternal life with Jesus Christ our Lord. Now go out and make this a great day.

Though the way seems straight and narrow, all I claimed was swept away;
My ambitions, plans and wishes at my feet in ashes lay.
Blessed be the name of Jesus! I'm so glad he took me in;
He's forgiven my transgressions, He has cleansed my heart from sin.
Margaret J. Harris - 1903-

October 20

"All Scripture is God-breathed and is useful for teaching, rebuking, correcting and training in righteousness, SO THAT THE MAN OF GOD MAY BE THOROUGHLY EQUIPPED FOR EVERY GOOD WORK." 2 Timothy 3:16 & 17

When I graduated from high school in a Senior class of eighteen, I went to college to study science and become a high school teacher. I changed my major, while in college, to Chemistry, but I still took all the preparatory courses for high school teaching. I felt I must have a thorough knowledge of my subject field to properly teach. While I learned a lot about how to teach from the education courses I took, I felt I learned far more from watching teachers who were really good at their profession. I also learned a lot from the way my parents taught me in our home. I felt I was well prepared to teach Chemistry, both from subject knowledge and teaching methods. I used many of the techniques I had learned when I taught college Chemistry.

Our promise today assures us we will be thoroughly equipped for every good work IF we use the Scriptures for teaching, rebuking, correcting and training in righteousness. Solomon told us in Proverbs 2:1-10, "My son, if you accept my words and store up my commands within you, turning your ear to wisdom and applying your heart to understanding, and if you call out for insight and cry aloud for understanding, and if you look for it as for silver and search for it as for hidden treasure, then you will understand the fear of the Lord and find the knowledge of God. For the Lord gives wisdom, and from His mouth come knowledge and understanding. He holds victory in store for the upright, He is a shield to those whose walk is blameless, for He guards the course of the just and protects the way of His faithful ones. Then you will understand what is right and just and fair - every good path. For wisdom will enter your heart, and knowledge will be pleasant to your soul." We learn directly from God when we read the Scriptures, as we are told in 2 Peter 1:20-21, "Above all, you must understand that no prophecy of Scripture came about by the prophet's own interpretation. For prophecy never had its origin in the will of man, but men spoke from God as they were carried along by the Holy Spirit."

To be thoroughly equipped, we must study the Bible. How do we do it? Set aside a specific time so it becomes a habit. Ask God for understanding. Read and meditate on the Word. Write it down to remember it. Memorize verses. Avoid becoming discouraged. You can read various explanations of the Bible, but remember, the Bible is the only word of God. Avoid other books which claim to be God's word. We are told in Revelation 22:18-19, "I warn everyone who hears the words of the prophecy of this book: If anyone adds anything to them, God will add to him the plagues described in this book. And if anyone takes words away from this book of prophecy, God will take away from him his share in the tree of life and in the holy city, which are described in this book." So study the Bible to prepare yourself for every good work.

Now go out and make this a great day.

Thy Word have I hid in my heart,
That I might not sin against Thee;
That I might not sin, that I might not sin,
Thy Word have I hid in my heart.
Ernest O. Sellers - 1869-1952

October 21

> "FOR HE HAS NOT DESPISED OR DISDAINED THE SUFFERING OF THE AFFLICTED ONE; HE HAS NOT HIDDEN HIS FACE FROM HIM BUT HAS LISTENED TO HIS CRY FOR HELP." Psalm 22:24

Have you ever watched a mother playing peek-a-boo with her child? The mother will cover her face with her hands or a handkerchief and pretend she is gone. The child will reach up to remove the cover from their mother's face, and laugh when they see the face they love so much! This game can go on for a long time, but the child becomes agitated if they cannot remove the covering from the face they love to see. If they cannot get the face covering removed they start to whine and cry. They get even more frustrated and agitated the longer it is they cannot see their mother's face.

Today's promise reminds me of the times I have seen that game played. God has promised He will not play games with us. He will not hide His face from us. He will listen to our cry for help. He does not despise or disdain us when we are suffering or afflicted. Yes, our promise is that He has not hidden His face from us, but has listened to our cry for help. Are there times events have occurred in such rapid profusion and with such negative results that it appears your cry for help goes unanswered? Do you ask and seem to receive no answer? Do you seek and not seem to find? Do you knock and it seems the door doesn't open? I believe all of us go through such times as those at some point in our lives. This does not mean God does not hear, or that He is hiding His face from us.

When we have suffering in our lives we should remember that Jesus also had suffering in His life. We should be open to the compassion and comfort of God. Paul told us in 2 Corinthians 1:3-5, "Praise be to the God and Father of our Lord Jesus Christ, the Father of compassion and the God of all comfort, who comforts us in all our troubles, so that we can comfort those in any trouble with the comfort we ourselves have received from God. For just as the sufferings of Christ flow over into our lives, so also through Christ our comfort overflows." The sufferings of Christ does flow over into our lives. Let us have faith in God and accept His comfort.

If God seems far away we should claim Deuteronomy 4:29, "But if from there you seek the Lord your God, you will find Him if you look for Him with all your heart and with all your soul." God does not want us to seek Him in a half-hearted manner. He wants our full devotion, our full attention, and our full commitment. The very times you are feeling the most suffering and affliction is the time you should seek Him with the greatest intensity. Perhaps you are in too big a hurry. David told us in Psalm 27:14, "Wait for the Lord; be strong and take heart and wait for the Lord." God works on His timetable, not on ours, and His timing is perfect. David told us further in Psalm 38:15, "I wait for you, O Lord; you will answer, O Lord my God." As God always answered David, He will answer you! Now go out and make this a great day.

> O soul, are you weary and troubled? No light in the darkness you see?
> There's light for a look at the Savior, and life more abundant and free!
> Turn your eyes upon Jesus, look full in His wonderful face,
> And the things of earth will grow strangely dim in the light of His glory and grace.
>
> Helen H. Lemmel - 1864-1961

October 22

"Our fathers disciplined us for a little while as they thought best; BUT GOD DISCIPLINES US FOR OUR GOOD, THAT WE MAY SHARE IN HIS HOLINESS." Hebrews 12:10

In "The Adventures of Tom Sawyer" by Mark Twain, Tom is always getting his fingers rapped when he tries to steal sugar from the bowl. When his aunt Polly steps into the kitchen, Tom's half-brother, Sid, reached for the sugar bowl, his fingers slipped and the bowl dropped and broke. When aunt Polly came back into the room she began to spank Tom, and he yelled, "Hold on, now, what'er you belting me for? Sid broke it!" Aunt Polly paused and said, "Umf! Well, you didn't get a lick amiss, I reckon. You been into some other audacious mischief when I wasn't around, like enough." Later, in the book, Becky sees Alfred Temple pour ink on Tom's spelling book, but doesn't tell Tom about it. Tom then catches Becky looking at the anatomy book of the school master, Mr. Dobbins, and she quickly closes it, tearing one of the pages. Later in the day, when Mr. Dobbins discovered the ink on Tom's book, he whipped Tom. The class settled into their work and Mr. Dobbins took out his anatomy book to study. He soon discovered the torn page. As he started asking the students, one-by-one, if they had torn his book they all denied it until he got to Becky. Just as Becky was about to be found out, Tom jumped to his feet and shouted, "I done it!" Tom took the whipping for Becky. You see, we try our best to discipline our young people, but we are imperfect and do an imperfect job of it. Tom took severe discipline three times when it wasn't deserved, so it could not have been for the good.

Our promise today assures us that God disciplines us for our good. It then goes on to promise that we will then share in His holiness. Aunt Polly was correct, Tom did many things he should have been punished for, but was not caught and punished. He didn't get the punishment he deserved. Like Tom, we will not get the punishment we deserve for our sins either. Becky didn't get a whipping for tearing the book because Tom stepped up and took the punishment for her. We will not suffer the punishment we deserve for our sins-death-because Jesus Christ paid the price by taking the punishment of death on the cross so we can have eternal life.

In Psalm 119:67 we read, "Before I was afflicted I went astray, but now I obey your word." Again in Psalm 119:75 we read, "I know, O Lord, that your laws are righteous, and in faithfulness you have afflicted me." A plea to God came in Jeremiah 10:23-25, "I know, O Lord, that a man's life is not his own; it is not for man to direct his steps. Correct me, Lord, but only with justice-not in your anger, lest you reduce me to nothing." That is just what God does to us. He corrects us with justice! So take the discipline of God in just the way He gives it. Learn from it, correct your ways, and obey His word. He disciplines you for your own good so you can share in His holiness throughout eternity!

Now go out and make this a great day.

I praise Thee, Lord, for cleansing me from sin;
Fulfill Thy Word and make me pure within.
Fill me with fire, where once I burned with shame;
Grant my desire to magnify Thy name.

J. Edwin Orr - 1912-

October 23

"And this is the testimony: GOD HAS GIVEN US ETERNAL LIFE, AND THIS LIFE IS IN HIS SON. HE WHO HAS THE SON HAS LIFE; HE WHO DOES NOT HAVE THE SON OF GOD DOES NOT HAVE LIFE." 1 John 5:11 & 12

I went to grade school in a one-room school house. When I finished the third grade we moved from Southern Kansas to a farm in Northern Kansas. I went to the fourth grade in a new school and we learned a new way to play "Tag". When you were touching wood, you were safe from the person who was "it". You could only stay at one object, tree, building, fence post, etc. of wood for ten seconds, then you had to run to a different object. The person who was "it" could not get closer than two steps from you when you were "safe", that is, touching wood. This gave the younger children a head start to move to the next "safe" place. This game was a lot of fun, and a great way to work off excess energy which built up while sitting in the classroom working on our lessons. One time I was caught in the open by one of the older boys and ran as hard as I could toward the post at the corner of the school yard. The fence ran from the East to the West side of the school yard and then went North along the pasture. There was no fence along the West side of the yard. I knew I could grab the post to stop me, so I stuck out my left hand to catch the post. I caught a barb on the fence just at my wrist and cut my hand to the base of the thumb. We just put some iodine on it, bandaged it and let it go. I still carry the scar from that cut. You see, the "safe" place was not so safe for me at that time.

There is a situation where we are always safe! That is when we have believed in the Son of God, and asked for the forgiveness of our sins. When we have the Son, we have life. Those who do not have the Son, do not have life. It is through the Son that God has given us eternal life. We read the words of Jesus in John 12:25, "The man who loves his life will lose it, while the man who hates his life in this world will keep it for eternal life." I believe what Jesus meant here is the person who loves the things of earth more than the things of God is not one who believes in Jesus Christ. In comparison to our love of God and our devotion to Him, we should love this life so little that it would appear to be hate. I don't think that Jesus meant that we should absolutely hate everything about our life here on earth. We should always be ready to lay down our life for Christ. Paul told us in Philippians 1:21, "For to me, to live is Christ and to die is gain." He knew he was safe in that he had the Son, and when he died the physical death here on earth he would gain life eternal with Jesus Christ his Lord. Are you safe with Jesus Christ today?

We have a precious assurance in today's promise. God has given us eternal life through His Son, Jesus Christ. If we have the Son, we are "safe", and the powers of Satan can not capture us. John told us earlier in this letter, in 1 John 4:4, "You, dear children, are from God and have overcome them, because the One who is in you is greater than the one who is in the world." So accept the Son of God and have eternal life. Now go out and make this a great day.

O Lord my God! When I in awesome wonder consider all the worlds Thy hands have made,
I see the stars, I hear the rolling thunder, Thy power throughout the universe displayed.
And when I think that God, His Son not sparing, sent Him to die, I scarce can take it in;
That on the cross, my burden gladly bearing, He bled and died to take away my sin.
Carl Boberg - 1859-1940

October 24

"IF ANYONE DOES NOT PROVIDE FOR HIS RELATIVES, AND ESPECIALLY FOR HIS IMMEDIATE FAMILY, HE HAS DENIED THE FAITH AND IS WORSE THAN AN UNBELIEVER." 1 Timothy 5:8

My wife, Jan, is the eldest child of two and I am the youngest of four. Jan had a paternal aunt who never married. Mildred worked for many years until several years after her father died. She then moved home to care for her mother until she died. We loved Aunt Mildred and took care of her business and arrangements for medical needs for over fifteen years. We took her on vacations and out for meals many times. Late in her life we moved her into a nursing home and insured her proper care until her death. We also checked into the needs of Jan's parents the last twelve years they were alive and made frequent trips to visit them so we could insure their proper care. We also took them on five vacations and had a wonderful, fun time. Just before my mother moved into a nursing home we visited her and Dad. One morning Momma said, "I would give anything for a good bath and to have my hair washed. This led to one of the most memorable times for me with Momma, as Jan and I got her into the shower, on a chair, and Jan gave her a real good bath and washed her hair. We got her dressed in clean clothes and Jan set her hair. Later Momma would just sigh and say, "That felt soooo good!" That made me feel good too! We have also provided for our children and grandchildren for things they couldn't do for themselves. We have helped our siblings and other relatives from time to time. God has been good to us to provide for our needs in such a manner as to allow us to do those things.

I think of those wonderful times as I read today's promise. Isn't that what is meant in Exodus 20:12, "Honor your father and your mother, so that you may live long in the land the Lord your God is giving you."? That is not what is meant when, after Cain had killed his brother Abel, he responded to God's inquiry as to where Abel was by answering, "I don't know, am I my brother's keeper?" Yes, we are our brother's keeper! To our earthly family, our Christian family and to those to whom we should witness! That is exactly what is meant in today's promise when it says if we do not provide for our relatives, and especially our immediate family (our Christian brothers and sisters) we have denied the faith and are worse than an unbeliever!

We need to care for our immediate earthly family to obey God's commands. We must also care for our Christian family to obey God's commands. How do we do that? First, we must be prayerful for our brothers and sisters in Christ. Second, we must make sure they have food, clothing and shelter. If that takes our resources beyond our tithe, then so be it! Many places in the Bible talks about tithes and special gifts, tithes and dedicated gifts, firstfruits and tithes, etc. I believe God expects us to share our worldly goods. Not only does our sharing help others, but it lays up treasures for ourselves in heaven and sure makes us feel better about ourselves here on earth! Take care of your relatives! Now go out and make this a great day.

Out in the highways and byways of life, many are weary and sad;
Carry the sunshine where darkness is rife, making the sorrowing glad.
Give as 'twas given to you in your need, love as the Master loved you;
Be to the helpless a helper indeed, unto your mission be true.
Ira B. Wilson - 1881-1950

October 25

"But in your hearts set apart Christ as Lord. Always be prepared to give an answer to everyone who asks you to give the reason for the hope that you have. But do this with gentleness and respect, keeping a clear conscience, SO THAT THOSE WHO SPEAK MALICIOUSLY AGAINST YOUR GOOD BEHAVIOR IN CHRIST MAY BE ASHAMED OF THEIR SLANDER." 1 Peter 3:15 & 16

Today's promise contains instructions which we must follow to claim the promise. First, we must set apart Christ as Lord in our hearts. Second, we must always be prepared to give an answer to everyone who asks us to give the reason for the hope that we have, AND we must do this with gentleness and respect, keeping a clear conscience. If we do these things in the Christian manner prescribed, THEN those who speak maliciously against our good behavior in Christ may be ashamed of their slander. When we have set apart Christ as Lord in our hearts, our hope is for eternal life, as promised in many places in the Bible. It is that hope to which we cling. It is that hope which gives us our joy, peace, contentment and enthusiasm for Jesus Christ our Lord. It is that hope which makes our lives meaningful and worth living.

In his book, "Man's Search for Meaning", Viktor Frankl tells of his years spent in the indescribable horrors of Auschwitz and Dachau. His parents, brother and wife died in the camps. His existence was full of cold, fear, starvation, pain, lice and vermin, dehumanization, exhaustion and terror. He was able to survive because he never lost the quality of hope. Those prisoners who lost faith in the future were doomed. When a prisoner lost hope, Frankl said, he let himself decline, becoming subject to mental and physical decay. He would die from the inside out. It would usually happen suddenly. One morning a prisoner would just refuse to get up. He wouldn't get dressed or wash or go outside to the parade grounds. No amount of pleading by his fellow prisoners would help. No threatening by the captors would have any effect. Losing all hope, he had simply given up. He would lay there in his own excrement until he died. American soldiers later told Frankl that this behavior pattern existed also among prisoners of war, and was called "give-up-itis." "When a prisoner lost hope, he lost his spiritual hold," said Frankl.

Like those prisoners, when we lose our hope in eternal life with Jesus Christ, we become a prisoner to sin. Our spiritual lives decline, and we are subject to spiritual decay. We are told in Isaiah 40:30, "Those who hope in the Lord will renew their strength. They will soar on wings like eagles; they will run and not grow weary, they will walk and not faint." When we have that hope we should share it with Christian love. We must be gentle and respectful in our witnessing. When we testify in this manner, we need never fear what others may say about us.

Do you have hope in the Lord Jesus Christ? Then gently and respectfully witness about that hope to others, and those who speak against you will be ashamed of their slander.

Now go out and make this a great day.

Hope, as an anchor so steadfast, rends the dark veil for the soul.
Whither the Master has entered, robbing the grave of its goal;
Come then, O come, glad fruition, come to my sad, weary heart;
Come, O Thou blest hope of glory, never, o never depart.

Alice Hawthorne - No Date

October 26

"Command those who are rich in this present world not to be arrogant nor to put their hope in wealth, which is so uncertain, but to put their hope in God, who richly provides us with everything for our enjoyment. Command them to do good, to be rich in good deeds, and to be generous and willing to share. IN THIS WAY THEY WILL LAY UP TREASURE FOR THEMSELVES AS A FIRM FOUNDATION FOR THE COMING AGE, SO THAT THEY MAY TAKE HOLD OF THE LIFE THAT IS TRULY LIFE." 1 Timothy 6:17-19

One of the driving forces behind people in American economy is to save and invest and to qualify for a pension. We seem to want to make sure we have more and more to provide for our needs during our senior years. This is a good thing to do! We do not want to be a burden on our children or our fellow citizens. This is a bad thing to do if we become obsessed with more and more financial security to the exclusion of tithing and making gifts to charities and to people in need. In Luke 12, Jesus tells the parable of the rich man whose grounds produced a good crop. He decided to tear down his barns and build bigger ones to store his wealth. Then he said to himself, "You have plenty of good things laid up for many years. Take life easy; eat, drink and be merry." Verses 20-21 say, "But God said to him, 'You fool! This very night your life will be demanded from you. Then who will get what you have prepared for yourself?' This is how it will be with anyone who stores up things for himself but is not rich toward God."

We read in Matthew 6:19-21, "Don't store up treasures here on earth, where they can be eaten by moths and get rusty, and where thieves break in and steal. Store your treasures in heaven, where they will never become moth-eaten and where they will be safe from thieves. Wherever you treasure is, there your heart and thoughts will also be." Much the same thing is said in Luke 12:33-34, "Sell what you have and give to those in need. This will store up treasure for you in heaven! And the purses of heaven have no holes in them. Your treasure will be safe-no thief can steal it and no moth can destroy it. Wherever your treasure is, there your heart and thoughts will also be." In truth, real greatness in God's kingdom is earned by service and sacrifice here on earth!

In today's promise, Paul instructs Timothy (and us as well) how we should view our wealth. It is fine to have financial security. We must not be arrogant about it nor put our hope in that financial security, because it is so uncertain. Our hope must be in God. He is the One who provides us with everything for our enjoyment. We must do good things for others. We must be rich in good deeds. We must be generous and willing to share. When we live like that, we are laying up treasures for ourselves as a firm foundation for life eternal. That life eternal is truly life!

Have you given your wealth over to God's control? Are you willing to follow His lead in your financial matters? God doesn't necessarily want all your wealth. He does want you willing to give it to Him if He asks for it. Give God control, and go out and make this a great day.

I will be a gentle helper, seeking out the weary one,
Lifting up the soul downtrodden, giving strength to journey on.
As the Spirit daily leads me, Heavenly Father let me be
Sharing freely of the bounty grace has showered down on me.
R. Douglas Little - 1954-

October 27

"YOU WILL BE BLESSED WHEN YOU COME IN AND BLESSED WHEN YOU GO OUT." Deuteronomy 28:6

This promise is part of the blessings for obedience, which is followed by the curses for disobedience given to the Israelites by Moses shortly before his death. Deuteronomy 28:1-5 says, "If you fully obey the Lord your God and carefully follow all His commands I give you today, the Lord your God will set you high above all the nations on earth. All these blessings will come upon you and accompany you if you obey the Lord your God: You will be blessed in the city and blessed in the country. The fruit of your womb will be blessed, and the crops of your land and the young of your livestock-the calves of your herds and the lambs of your flocks. Your basket and your kneading trough will be blessed." Then follows today's promise.

One year when I was still in grade school Dad had planned for over a year to have a large number of sows and gilts (female hogs which had not yet farrowed a litter of pigs) to farrow early in the Winter so the pigs would be ready for sale in early Spring. We prayed that God would bless this effort on our parts so we would have the funds which were so desperately needed. We had kept a large part of our corn crop for feed for our hogs. When farrowing time approached we had thirty-seven ready to farrow. We set up pens in the hog shed, a large part of the barn and two small sheds on the farm. What a time we had when the births began! Dad would sometimes get up two or three times a night to check all the pens. We had to spend many hours making sure everything went well with the farrowing. Some had too many pigs to properly care for, and we took them into the mud room in the house, where we prepared a pen, laid several layers of paper on the floor, covered it with straw, and placed the "extra" pigs in the makeshift pen. We would feed them out of baby bottles we had to buy. For many mornings we would go out to find another fine litter of pigs. We would work very hard to keep their pens clean, their water fresh and proper food supplied. We would come back in to find the little "extras" gaining strength and size. That turned out to be a really good year for the sale of young pigs. Dad took a load to the sale barn and received a good price. While there he was approached by a man who wanted to buy all the rest of our pigs. I remember the day that man came with two trucks to haul away another two hundred pigs. My, how thankful we were in our prayers to God for His blessings to us. I feel like Moses was talking to us at that time when I see this blessing.

Do you commit your plans to the Lord before you start an undertaking? Do you fully obey the Lord and carefully follow all His commands? Proverbs 16:3 says, "Commit to the Lord whatever you do, and your plans will succeed." Jeremiah 29:11 says "'For I know the plans I have for you,' declares the Lord, 'plans to prosper you and not to harm you, plans to give your hope and a future.'" You CAN claim these promises of God. Then you can claim the promise to be blessed when you come in and go out. Now go out and make this a great day.

Perfect submission, perfect delight, visions of rapture now burst on my sight;
Angels descending bring from above echoes of mercy, whispers of love.
Perfect submission, all is at rest, I in my Savior am happy and blest;
Watching and waiting, looking above, filled with His goodness, lost in His love.
Fanny J. Crosby - 1820-1915

October 28

"If your enemy is hungry, give him food to eat; if he is thirsty, give him water to drink. IN DOING THIS, YOU WILL HEAP BURNING COALS ON HIS HEAD, AND THE LORD WILL REWARD YOU." Proverbs 25:21 & 22

During World War II, many German prisoners were brought to the United States for the duration of the war. They were, undoubtedly, the enemy of all Americans. Many of the prisoners were allowed to live with, and work for, Americans. This reduced the amount of food which the U.S. government needed to provide to the prisoners. The story is told about one such prisoner who was assigned to live with a farm couple who had a son fighting in the war in Germany. They were Christians, and took today's promise to heart. The prisoner assigned to them was not a Christian. Day after day the couple started their day with the reading of devotions, and they always included the prisoner during this time. They thanked God for their food before beginning each meal. They had quiet time and prayer before going to bed each night. Always in their prayers they asked God to keep their son safe. They also thanked God for the prisoner, asked God to bless him, and to keep his family safe in Germany. After several weeks of this behavior the prisoner asked how he, too, could gain the peace, contentment, assurance and faith of the farm couple. At that time they led him to Christ. After the war, the German prisoner went back to Germany, found his family, won them to Christ, and helped rebuild his country while serving as a witness to others of the love and forgiveness of Christ.

Now, that couple could have worked that prisoner as hard as they could as revenge for what his countrymen were doing to American soldiers like their son. They didn't do that. Instead, they gave him food, water and shelter. They treated him with love and kindness. In doing this, they led him to Christ, thereby, laying up for themselves treasures in heaven. They lived by Romans 12:19, "Do not take revenge, my friends, but leave room for God's wrath, for it is written: 'It is mine to avenge; I will repay,' says the Lord." The evil, which was the Nazi rule in Germany was overcome by the might of the U.S. and our allies. That farm couple did their part of overcoming evil by their treatment of the prisoner assigned to them. They lived by Romans 12:21, "Do not be overcome by evil, but overcome evil with good." Isn't that what God wants us to do to those who oppose us now?

Has someone done a wrong against you? Have you cut them off entirely? Do you shun them so you won't have to talk to them? Do you tell others about what the person has done to you? Do your actions meet the test of today's qualifier and promise? Jesus told us we must forgive such people. I don't think they have to become your best buddies, but you must treat them with love and respect. You also must not gossip about how they wronged you. Like that farm couple, forgive them and love them. Let your life tell the story of Jesus Christ.

Now go out and make this a great day.

I love to tell the story-'tis pleasant to repeat
What seems, each time I tell it, more wonderfully sweet;
I love to tell the story-for some have never heard
The message of salvation from God's own holy Word.

A Catherine Hankey - 1834-1911

October 29

"But if we walk in the light, as He is in the light, WE HAVE FELLOWSHIP WITH ONE ANOTHER, AND THE BLOOD OF JESUS HIS SON, PURIFIES US FROM ALL SIN."
1 John 1:7

When I was growing up we always looked forward to Sunday. Our entire family enjoyed church, we did no work except the morning and evening chores, and two or three Sundays a month we would get together with others than our immediate family. Once or twice a month we would have Sunday dinner at the home of another church member, or have them over to our home to eat. Once a month we would gather at the home of a sibling of Dad or Momma with all the rest of the family. What fun we would have with more food than we could all eat (preceded with a prayer of thanksgiving), happy conversation among youth and elders alike, board games in the winter, and outdoor games in good weather. Many times our parents would join us in a game of baseball, touch football or "run sheep, run". As I look back on those times I can see many lessons of sportsmanship being taught to us by our parents. We were taught, and expected, to win without boasting and lose without complaint (however, friendly banter was acceptable and encouraged). The times together were sprinkled with Christian teaching, as the situation presented itself. We would take that teaching to heart, whether it came from our parent, an uncle or aunt, or from one of our cousins.

Those times seem like only yesterday when I read today's promise. The qualifier of today's promise is very clear, "But if we walk in the light, as He is in the light,". Speaking of Jesus, John wrote in John 1:4, "In Him was life, and that life was the light of men." John again wrote in John 3:19-21, "This is the verdict: Light has come into the world, but men loved darkness instead of light because their deeds were evil. Everyone who does evil hates the light, and will not come into the light for fear that his deeds will be exposed. But whoever lives by the truth comes into the light, so that it may be seen plainly that what he has done has been done through God." Therefore, what the qualifier says is, if we walk with Jesus just as Jesus walked with His Father, then we can claim today's promise.

In Jesus Christ we have fellowship together, which is pleasing in the sight of God. How does the blood of Jesus, God's Son, purify us from all sin? We are told that in John 3:16, "For God so loved the world that He gave His one and only Son, that whoever believes in Him shall not perish but have eternal life." We read in John 12:44-46, "Then Jesus cried out, 'When a man believes in me, he does not believe in me only, but in the One who sent me. When he looks at me, he sees the One who sent me. I have come into the world as a light, so that no one who believes in me should stay in darkness.'" Are you walking in the light today? Has the blood of Jesus Christ purified you from all sin? Believe in Jesus, your sins will be forgiven and you will have eternal life. Now go out and make this a great day.

The whole world was lost in the darkness of sin-the Light of the world is Jesus;
Like sunshine at noonday His glory shone in-the Light of that world is Jesus.
No darkness have we who in Jesus abide-the Light of the world is Jesus;
We walk in the Light when we follow our Guide-the Light of that world is Jesus.
Philip P. Bliss - 1838-1876

October 30

"FOR THE LORD HIMSELF WILL COME DOWN FROM HEAVEN, WITH A LOUD COMMAND, WITH THE VOICE OF THE ARCHANGEL AND WITH THE TRUMPET CALL OF GOD, AND THE DEAD IN CHRIST WILL RISE FIRST." 1 Thessalonians 4:16

You have received an invitation to a wedding. You read the announcement in the paper. The day has arrived and you are seated in the church. When you hear the "Wedding March" you know the bride is coming to meet her groom. Are you surprised? It is May. You have received an invitation to the graduation ceremony for a family member. You read about the graduation in the paper. The day has arrived and you are seated in the auditorium. When you hear "Pomp and Circumstances" you know the graduates are coming to participate in the graduation ceremonies. Are you surprised? You hear there is to be a special dedication ceremony in your community, and the President of the United States will be coming to make a dedication speech. A local group has sent you an invitation to come to the event. You have read about the ceremony in the paper. The day approaches and your excitement builds. The day arrives and you are seated as one of hundreds in the audience. When you hear "Ruffles and Flourishes" you know the President of the United States is approaching the stage. You are ready to hear what he has to say. You really want to hear what he has to say. Are you surprised he is there?

We read the words of Jesus in John 14:1-4, "Do not let your hearts be troubled. Trust in God; trust also in me. In my Father's house are many rooms; if it were not so, I would have told you. I am going there to prepare a place for you. And if I go and prepare a place for you, I will come back and take you to be with me that you also may be where I am. You know the way to the place where I am going." Who but Thomas, the careful disciple, sometimes called "the doubter", asked in verse 5, "Lord, we don't know where you are going, so how can we know the way?" Then follows Jesus' answer in verse 6, "Jesus answered, 'I am the way and the truth and the life. No one comes to the Father except through me. If you really knew me, you would know my Father as well. From now on, you do know Him and have seen Him.'" Titus 2:11-14 says, "For the grace of God that brings salvation has appeared to all men. It teaches us to say 'No' to ungodliness and worldly passions, and to live self-controlled, upright and godly lives in this present age, while we wait for the blessed hope - the glorious appearing of our great God and Savior, Jesus Christ, who gave Himself for us to redeem us from all wickedness and to purify for Himself a people that are His very own, eager to do what is good." So, we have read about the coming again of Jesus. We have received an invitation from Jesus Christ, Himself in Revelation 3:20, "Here I am! I stand at the door and knock. If anyone hears my voice and opens the door, I will come in and eat with him, and he with me." Now when we hear a loud command, with the voice of the archangel and with the trumpet call of God, we know Jesus is returning. Are you surprised? Are you ready? Make sure you are, and then go out and make this a great day.

There's a great day coming, a great day coming, there's a great day coming by and by;
When the saints and the sinners shall be parted right and left, are you ready for that day to come?
There's a bright day coming, a bright day coming, there's a bright day coming by and by;
But its brightness shall only come to them that love the Lord, are you ready for that day to come?
Will L. Thompson - 1847-1909

October 31

"Now I commit you to God and to the word of His grace, WHICH CAN BUILD YOU UP AND GIVE YOU AN INHERITANCE AMONG ALL THOSE WHO ARE SANCTIFIED. I have not coveted anyone's silver or gold or clothing. You yourselves know that these hands of mine have supplied my own needs and the needs of my companions. In everything I did, I showed you that by this kind of hard work we must help the weak, remembering the words the Lord Jesus himself said: 'It is more blessed to give than to receive.'" Acts 20:32-35

Today's passage comes from Paul's farewell to the Ephesian Elders. Paul was a skilled tent-maker. In most of his missionary travels he supported himself, and others traveling with him, by making tents. Most of these tents he sold to the Roman military. It was hard work to make the tents to the specifications required, however, Paul did this work so he would not be a burden to those to whom he was bringing the Good News.

Paul's hard and effective work reminds me of a story I heard about a salesman who was traveling from town to town, and decided to take the back roads one day. He passed several farms with dilapidated out-buildings, poorly patched fences, houses which needed paint, broken down machinery parked around, small stacks of hay just piled around and crops which looked like it would be unprofitable to even harvest. Suddenly he came to a farm which had nice out-buildings, strong fences built in straight lines, fresh painted house, good machinery parked in a perfect line, plenty of hay neatly stacked near the corral and crops which looked to be ready to produce an abundance. The salesman stopped when he saw the farmer walking toward the barn. "You have a very nice farm here," the salesman said. "Why, thank you," replied the farmer. "I have passed several marginal farms before I got to yours," said the salesman. "How do you explain that you have such a nice farm in the midst of so many marginal farms?" The farmer looked at the salesman a moment, then replied, "Mister, I think there are a great many more marginal farmers than there are marginal farms."

Aren't a lot of churches described by that story? It seems we have more marginal Christians than marginal churches. How about you and your church today? Are you, and other members of your church, committed to God and to the word of His grace? Do you spend your time working to help the weak? Would you rather receive than give? Do you spend more time worrying about your investment account, the clothing you wear and the car you drive than you do about making sure your life is centered in God's will? Would your actions be judged by God to make you a "marginal" Christian?

Remember, Jesus instructed us to "store up for ourselves treasures in heaven" by our gifts to the poor, our visits to those sick or in prison, and our work to further His church. By this we are built up and gain ourselves an inheritance among all those who are sanctified. That is the great promise for today! Make sure you are an active, effective Christian blessing others so you can gain that promise. Now go out and make this a great day.

Tell the sweet story of Christ and His love, tell of His power to forgive;
Others will trust Him if only you prove true, every moment you live.
Make me a blessing, O Savior, I pray,
Make me a blessing to someone today.

Ira B. Wilson - 1880-1950

November 1

"ASK AND IT WILL BE GIVEN TO YOU; SEEK AND YOU WILL FIND; KNOCK AND THE DOOR WILL BE OPENED TO YOU." Matthew 7:7

A long time ago some elders had been meeting with the pastor and finally determined their meeting place was too small. "Look," one of them said. "This place is too small for us. Let's go to the river, cut down some trees, and build a place there for us to live." The pastor said, "Go." The elders went out to collect their tools for the work. One of them did not have an axe so he borrowed one from a friend. When they gathered together, with their tools, they asked the pastor, "Won't you please come with us?" "I will," replied the pastor. So off they all went. When they arrived at the river they began to cut down trees. The one with the borrowed axe was cutting down a tree right at the river's bank. As he made a mighty swing with the axe, the head came off and fell into the river. "Oh, pastor," he cried out, "it was borrowed!" The pastor asked, "Where did it fall?" The elder showed him the place, the pastor said a quick prayer, cut a stick and threw it there, and made the iron float. "Lift it out," the pastor said. The elder then reached out his hand and lifted out the axe head, and the elders continued their work. This is a great story to illustrate today's promise. The beautiful truth is the story is true! I wrote it a little different from the way it is written in 2 Kings 6:1-7. It is the story of one of the miracles of Elisha.

Today's promise comes to us from Jesus during His sermon on the mount. Jesus was emphasizing prayer. Not just prayer, but persistent prayer. Jesus gives the illustration that a human father would not give his son a stone if he asked for bread, nor would he give a snake if asked for a fish. If we as humans know how to give good gifts to our children, how much more will our Father in heaven give good gifts to those who ask Him! James 1:17 says, "Every good and perfect gift is from above, coming down from the Father of heavenly lights, who does not change like shifting shadows." Whatever we honestly, and unselfishly, want is far short of what God truly wants to give to us. He knows far better than we, what we truly need.

Jesus wants us to persistently ask for gifts from above, but He also wants us to have the correct attitudes in our requests. We are told in James 4:3, "When you ask, you do not receive, because you ask with wrong motives, that you may spend what you get on your pleasures." God also wants us to ask with an attitude of thanks. Philippians 4:6-7 says, "Do not be anxious about anything, but in everything, by prayer and petition, with thanksgiving, present your requests to God. And the peace of God, which transcends all understanding, will guard your hearts and your minds in Christ Jesus."

Are your prayer requests to God persistent? Are your prayer requests for the good and perfect gifts from God? Are your prayer requests for unselfish gifts? Are your prayer requests sent to God with thanksgiving? God wants what is best for you and for your life. Claim today's promise, and go out and make this a great day.

What a friend we have in Jesus, all our sins and griefs to bear!
What a privilege to carry everything to God in prayer!
O what peace we often forfeit, O what needless pain we bear,
All because we do not carry everything to God in prayer.
Joseph M. Scriven - 1820-1886

November 2

"I delight greatly in the Lord; My soul rejoices in my God. FOR HE HAS CLOTHED ME WITH GARMENTS OF SALVATION AND ARRAYED ME IN A ROBE OF RIGHT-EOUSNESS, as a bridegroom adorns his head like a priest, and as a bride adorns herself with her jewels." Isaiah 61:10

I was the youngest child in our family. My brother was almost seven years older than I, so I never wore clothes passed down from him. My two sisters were between us in age. My eldest sister would often pass her dresses on to my younger sister. Momma made many of their clothes, and taught them how to make their own when they were still quite young. I remember one time we bought flour in sacks of printed material. Momma searched through the sacks until she found enough of the same pattern so my sisters could make dresses alike. My, they were proud to wear those dresses! I think back to how pretty they were, and how they wore them to church and school until they became faded and worn. Then they wore them for working around the house.

How much more beautiful are the garments of salvation in which God clothes us! How much more precious is the robe of righteousness He places on us! Today, we should all delight greatly in the Lord! Our soul should rejoice in God! What a wonderful truth it is that His grace has provided for our salvation! Our belief in Jesus Christ has caused Him to place on us a robe of righteousness. Like a bridegroom and bride, we have donned our finest attire of white when we believe in our hearts that Jesus is the Son of God, and confess our sins to Him. We become a new person, with the new garments of today's promise.

Paul tells us how we have changed in Ephesians 4:22-24, "You were taught, with regard to your former way of life, to put off your old self, which is being corrupted by its deceitful desires; to be made new in the attitude of your minds; and to put on the new self, created to be like God in true righteousness and holiness." Paul went on to explain what it means to "put off your old self" in Ephesians 4:25-32, "Therefore each of you must put off falsehood and speak truthfully to his neighbor, for we are all members of one body. In your anger do not sin. Do not let the sun go down while you are still angry, and do not give the devil a foothold. He who has been stealing must steal no longer, but must work, doing something useful with his own hands, that he may have something to share with those in need. Do not let any unwholesome talk come out of your mouths, but only what is helpful for building others up according to their needs, that it may benefit those who listen. And do not grieve the Holy Spirit of God, with whom you were sealed for the day of redemption. Get rid of all bitterness, rage and anger, brawling and slander, along with every form of malice. Be kind and compassionate to one another, forgiving each other, just as in Christ God forgave you." Have you put off the old man, and put on the new? Do you wear God's garments of salvation and robe of righteousness? It will change your life!

Now go out and make this a great day.

O now I see the crimson wave, the fountain deep and wide;
Jesus, my Lord, mighty to save, points to His wounded side.
I rise to walk in heaven's own light, above the world and sin;
With hearts made pure and garments white, and Christ enthroned within.

Phoebe P. Knapp - 1839-1908

November 3

"BY WISDOM A HOUSE IS BUILT, AND THROUGH UNDERSTANDING IT IS ESTABLISHED; THROUGH KNOWLEDGE ITS ROOMS ARE FILLED WITH RARE AND BEAUTIFUL TREASURES." Proverbs 24:3 & 4

During the time I have been writing this book of devotions, Jan and I have built a new home to move into after thirty years in the same house. We bought a lot in a new development on which to build our retirement home. Before anything was done toward starting to build, we invited our pastor, Brother Joe Grizzle, members of our Sunday school class and others from the church to come to the lot and have Brother Joe bless the lot. He asked for God's direction for all those involved in the building process. I based my request to him on Psalm 127:1, "Unless the Lord builds the house, its builders labor in vain. Unless the Lord watches over the city, the watchmen stand guard in vain." When the building of the house was completed and it was ready for us to move into, we again had the same group out to bless the house as our new home. We spent considerable time during the design phase to insure we planned each room to the maximum advantage. Since it is smaller than our former house, we had to choose, with care, those items we wanted in the new home. We chose those which carried the best memories, as those were what we considered our most beautiful treasures. Since the home is the place of unforgettable life-influencing memories, we made sure we made room for those items which carried those memories.

Is your home a center of affection and stability, rather than a center of abuse or neglect? Is your home a place where daddy keeps his promises? Is it a place with a mother's touch? Is it a place where you want to be? When you leave your home, will it be a place you will want to visit often? These are the questions each member of the family should consider. If each member of the family will obey the greatest commandments which Jesus gave in Mark 12:29-31, (to love God and to love others), the answer to each of those questions will be a "yes."

Today's promise refers to a house, but it really means our lives. Like building a house, we must use wisdom to build our lives. We must have a thorough understanding to establish our lives. As we gain knowledge, our lives are filled with rare and beautiful treasures. How do we do that? Psalm 111:10 tells us, "The fear (awe, reverence, respect) of the Lord is the beginning of wisdom; all who follow His precepts have good understanding. To Him belongs eternal praise." The more we study the Bible and meditate on His Word, the more we pray and have quiet time with God, the more we live our lives as Jesus lived His, the more wisdom and understanding we will have. Then our lives WILL be filled with rare and beautiful treasures. Then you will have given your lives to God. Then your homes will reflect your life because both your life and your home will have been built by the Lord. Others will see the rare and beautiful treasures each contain. Make God first in your life, study His Word, and go out and make this a great day.

Take my silver and my gold, not a mite would I withhold;
Take my moments and my days, let them flow in ceaseless praise.
Take my will and make it Thine, it shall be no longer mine;
Take my heart, it is Thine own, it shall be Thy royal throne.

Frances R. Havergal - 1836-1918

November 4

"HE PUT A NEW SONG IN MY MOUTH, A HYMN OF PRAISE TO OUR GOD. MANY WILL SEE AND FEAR AND PUT THEIR TRUST IN THE LORD." Psalm 40:3

When I was out working in the field, whether it was plowing, discing, planting, cultivating or harvesting, the time would go slowly and the work would become monotonous. I would often break up the monotony by singing. Whether it be the current songs of the times or hymns, I would sing to pass the time. I have never been accused of being a good singer! One day, as I was plowing under the hot July sun, my brother, Leslie, came out to the field with a sandwich and a cold drink of tea. As I was enjoying my afternoon lunch, I noticed Leslie looking all around the tractor as if searching for something. "What are you looking for, Leslie?", I asked. With a big grin he replied, "I was looking for that sick calf I heard bawling out here on the tractor." We both had a good laugh at his joke, but it didn't stop me from continuing to sing as I worked.

In the early days of the Quaker church, there was no singing during the meetings. Thank goodness, that changed long before I was born. I love to worship in song. Some of the time I join in the singing to the best of my ability, and some of the time I just let the words and music wash over me. I love the new songs which have been written in the last few years. I think many of them are examples of today's promise, spoken by David. They do cause people to see the wonders of God, to worship with awe, reverence and respect, and to put their trust in the Lord. Our services should be a time to show our love for God. They should be a time to express our wonderful joy which comes from serving Him. They should be a time to fully show our devotion to Him.

We are told in Psalm 47:1, "Clap your hands, all you nations; shout to God with cries of joy." The wonderful, joyous image in Psalm 98:9 just sends a thrill through me, "Shout for joy to the Lord, all the earth, burst into jubilant song with music; make music to the Lord with the harp, with the harp and the sound of singing, with trumpets and the blast of the ram's horn-shout for joy before the lord, the King. Let the sea resound, and everything in it, the world, and all who live in it. Let the rivers clap their hands, let the mountains sing together for joy; let them sing before the Lord, for He comes to judge the earth. He will judge the world in righteousness and the peoples with equity." Who among us cannot be stirred by the words in Isaiah 55:12, "You will go out in joy and be led forth in peace; the mountains and hills will burst into song before you, and all the trees of the field will clap their hands."

It is wonderful to serve a Lord who wants us to be joyful! Sometimes you just must hear the mountains and hills bursting into song and feel the wonder of the trees clapping their hands! Do you truly serve God with your songs, regardless of how well you sing? He really wants you to do so. Support your music ministry to help others put their trust in God.

Now go out in song and make this a great day.

Sing the wondrous love of Jesus, sing His mercy and His grace;
In the mansions bright and blessed He'll prepare for us a place.
When we all get to heaven, what a day of rejoicing that will be!
When we all see Jesus, we'll sing and shout the victory!

Eliza E. Hewitt - 1851-1920

November 5

"Praise be to the God and Father of our Lord Jesus Christ! IN HIS GREAT MERCY HE HAS GIVEN US NEW BIRTH INTO A LIVING HOPE THROUGH THE RESURRECTION OF JESUS CHRIST FROM THE DEAD." 1 Peter 1:3

Growing up on the farm I saw a lot of births; calves, pigs, colts, puppies and cats. I also saw many chickens emerge from the shells. I have never been present for the birth of a child. My daughter, Katy, was born before it was considered acceptable for the father to be present in the birthing room. To watch a living creature enter the world is a remarkable event. It becomes even more remarkable as you watch that creature grow to maturity. As time passes, it becomes harder and harder to remember the tiny, wiggling baby as it entered the world and you helped to clean and dry it. It is fun to watch the newborn creature instinctively make its way to begin nursing its mother. There is an expectation that the food will be present and that life and growth will result. I can remember much rejoicing in thanks to God, during our before breakfast devotion time, offered by Dad for the successful birth of baby animals on our farm.

As amazing as physical birth is, it is far less so than the spiritual birth of an individual. Praise be to the God and Father of our Lord Jesus Christ! He has provided, in His great mercy, a way for us to receive the gift of new birth into a living hope. How did He do this? Through the death on the cross by our Lord Jesus Christ, followed by His resurrection from the grave! Have you experienced the new birth into a living hope through the resurrection of Jesus Christ from the dead? If so, you know how remarkable such an event is. As a maturing Christian, I delight to witness the new birth into a living hope of an individual. It is truly a remarkable event! Just like following a physical birth, it becomes even more remarkable as you watch a person grow in Spiritual maturity. Just as Dad rejoiced over the birth of our farm animals, there is rejoicing in heaven over the new birth into a living hope of one person on earth. We read in Luke 15:10, "In the same way, I tell you, there is rejoicing in the presence of the angels of God over one sinner who repents." If you have experienced the new birth into a living hope, you set off a party of singing and rejoicing in heaven!

What does it cost a new born creature to be born? Nothing! While it may cost the mother in terms of pain, and the parents in terms of doctors and hospital, it costs the child nothing. What does it cost for the new birth into a living hope through the resurrection of Jesus Christ from the dead? Nothing! It did cost Jesus Christ in that He became a man, lived as a man (a perfect life), became sin for us, and died on the cross. Our Spiritual birth is free! Ephesians 2:8-9 says, "For it is by grace you have been saved, through faith-and this not from yourselves, it is the gift of God-not by works, so that no one can boast." Have faith in God. Accept that grace. Believe on Jesus Christ, and you will experience that new birth into a living hope! What a joy that will be!

Now go out and make this a great day.

Life is offered unto you. Hallelujah! Eternal life your soul shall have.
If you'll only look to Him. Hallelujah! Look to Jesus, who alone can save.
I will tell you how I came, Hallelujah! To Jesus when He made me whole:
'Twas believing on His name, Hallelujah! I trusted and He saved my soul.
William A. Ogden - 1841-1897

November 6

"I tell you the truth, IF ANYONE KEEPS MY WORD, HE WILL NEVER SEE DEATH." John 8:51

Many years ago a friend of mine was battling pancreatic cancer. One of our mutual friends stopped by his home to visit with him. Later our friend reported to me part of their conversation which went something like this: "Hey! It is good to see you. What are you doing just lying there?" asked our mutual friend. Our friend with cancer looked him in the eye and replied, "Just lying here fighting to save my life." We all tend to fight against death as we near the end of our life. I once read a report concerning medical insurance that said a large portion of the total payout on medical insurance occurs in the last two years of a person's life. We tend to go to medical extremes to prolong our lives when faced with death. The truth is that everyone now alive will face a physical death at some point. Some years ago a joke made the rounds which said: "Don't take life too seriously. You'll never get out of it alive anyway." That is correct. We will never get out of this physical life alive!

There is another death that is far more awful than our physical death. That is the second death which occurs for those who die without claiming today's promise. Jesus tells us the truth in today's promise, "if anyone keeps my word, he will never see death." This is promised in John 3:16, "For God so loved the world that He gave His one and only Son, that whoever believes in Him shall not perish but have eternal life." We also read in John 14:6, "Jesus answered, 'I am the way and the truth and the life. No one comes to the Father except through me." If we "believe" in Jesus Christ (see January 1) we are assured that the physical death is the only kind of death we will ever face. We are assured that we will have eternal life through Jesus Christ our Lord!

When we know in our hearts that we will have eternal life with Jesus Christ our Lord, then we will no longer fear the physical death. You see, you are not really citizens of the world, who will someday go on to heaven. No! You are citizens of heaven, who are aliens and strangers in this world. We read this in 1 Peter 2:11, "Dear friends, I urge you, as aliens and strangers in the world, to abstain from sinful desires, which war against your soul." You see, Peter knew we were citizens of heaven once we believed in Jesus Christ with our whole hearts.

Are you, a family member, or someone close to you facing health issues which are likely to end in physical death? Has the ill person given their heart to God? Do they face death with dread in their hearts? They need not have dread in their hearts. They will soon be with our Lord Jesus Christ to live eternally. Of course, it is natural to dread leaving the ones we love behind here on earth. It is also natural to dread losing a loved one to the physical death. We know, however, if our hearts are right with God, we will again see our loved ones in heaven. We can claim today's promise and know we will never see the spiritual death which everyone should avoid.

Claim the promise of eternal life, and go out and make this a great day.

Beyond the sunset, O blissful morning, when with our Savior heaven is begun;
Earth's toiling ended, O glorious dawning, beyond the sunset, when day is done.
Beyond the sunset, O glad reunion, with our dear loved ones who've gone before;
In that fair homeland we'll know no parting, beyond the sunset, forevermore!
Virgil P. Brock - 1887-1978

November 7

> "So when you give to the needy, do not announce it with trumpets, as the hypocrites do in the synagogues and on the streets, to be honored by men. I tell you the truth, they have received their reward in full. But when you give to the needy, do not let your left hand know what your right hand is doing, so that your giving may be in secret. THEN YOUR FATHER, WHO SEES WHAT IS DONE IN SECRET, WILL REWARD YOU." Matthew 6:2-4

In today's world it is hard to follow the command of not letting your left hand know what your right hand is doing when you give to the poor through the many charitable organizations which provide for the poor. When we give our contributions to The Salvation Army, Red Cross, church pantry project, etc. we should get a receipt for tax purposes. Therefore, our gift is known by others. There are many times we give gifts to help others in such a manner that they do not go through a charitable organization. This is when we slip some money to a friend who is out of work, pay the way to camp for a young person who can not afford to go, or other such instances. I have some people through which I give to help others in an anonymous manner. In fact, I prefer not to know the specific people helped in many cases so I won't feel protective or ever, God forbid, feel like I deserve some thanks from them. To some I give to directly, and I am as gracious as possible in accepting their thanks. I do not give any of my tithe to non-religious organizations. There are some organizations, to which I give, that honor the givers with plaques, pins or other means of recognition. When I give to those organizations I consider their recognition as my reward in full.

Regardless of how you give, it should be done discreetly and with no fan-fare. You are not to give in order to be honored among others. You are not to give in such a manner as to embarrass those to whom you are giving. Always be sure to give with the correct attitude in your giving: Give with LOVE! I firmly believe the saying: You can give without loving, but you cannot love without giving! When you give in this manner, you can claim today's promise. When you give discretely, with love, God will see your actions and will reward you.

The question then might arise: What is the reward? The Bible speaks to that in at least two ways. First, we read in Luke 6:38, "Give, and it will be given to you. A good measure, pressed down, shaken together and running over, will be poured into your lap. For with the measure you use, it will be measured to you." Notice, the first word is 'give', which means your action must come first. Then you may receive your reward with added blessings here on earth. Second, we read in Luke 12:33, "Sell your possessions and give to the poor. Provide purses for yourselves that will not wear out, a treasure in heaven that will not be exhausted, where no thief comes near and no moth destroys." From this we see our reward may be in heaven. This is great for us as verse 34 says, "For where you treasure is, there your heart will be also." So give your offerings to the needy. You will be rewarded. Now go out and make this a great day.

All power is given in Jesus' name, in earth and heaven in Jesus' name;
And in Jesus' name I come to you to share His power as He told me to:
He said, "Freely, freely you have received-freely, freely give;
Go in My name and because you believe, others will know that I live."
Carol Owens - 1931-

November 8

> "I WILL RANSOM THEM FROM THE POWER OF THE GRAVE; I WILL REDEEM THEM FROM DEATH. Where, O death, are your plagues? Where, O grave, is your destruction?" Hosea 13:14

Have you ever dug a grave? When I was fifteen years old, my brother and sister-in-law lost their second little boy just hours after he was born. He was born, and he died on December 3, 1953. It was very cold, and the ground was frozen as my brother and I went to the cemetery to dig his grave. I still have the pick axe I used to break through the frozen ground. I still remember the pain and sorrow we shared as we worked together. We talked a lot about the "what ifs" of that little boy. We were both Christians, and we knew he was with God, but we still had the pain of the loss. I still walk the few steps to visit his grave when I am in the cemetery. As Christians, we know that only our earthly bodies occupy that grave. Our souls are with God, and we shall have new bodies after Jesus returns and we are with Him in the new heaven and the new earth.

For that reason, we know the truth of today's promise! God sent His Son, Jesus Christ, to ransom us from the power of the grave. Jesus redeemed us from death to eternal life! We can say with total confidence, "Where, O death, are your plagues? Where, O grave, is your destruction?" Yes, our earthly bodies will return to dust, but we won't need them. We will have our new, perfect, bodies when we are in eternity with God, Jesus, and the Holy Spirit.

We are told in 1 John 2:15-17, "Do not love the world or anything in the world. If anyone loves the world, the love of the Father is not in him. For everything in the world-the cravings of sinful man, the lust of his eyes and the boasting of what he has and does-comes not from the Father but from the world. The world and its desires pass away, but the man who does the will of God lives forever." How can this be? Because we have been ransomed and redeemed by the death of Jesus Christ on the cross. Jesus told us in John 11:25-26, "Jesus said to her, 'I am the resurrection and the life. He who believes in me will live, even though he dies; and whoever lives and believes in me will never die. Do you believe this?'" Paul told us in Colossians 3:3-4, "For you died, and your life is now hidden with Christ in God. When Christ, who is your life, appears, then you also will appear with Him in glory." What a wonderful event to look forward to!

What about you today? Have you accepted the free gift of salvation? Do you know, for certain, that you have been ransomed and redeemed by Jesus Christ? If you have, then you know that you will never taste death. When your time on earth is over, you will pass from this life on earth to life everlasting with our Father in heaven. You need have no fear of death or the grave. You need not be concerned about the destruction of this earthly body. If you have not been ransomed and redeemed read 2 Peter 3:9, "The Lord is not slow in keeping His promise, as some understand slowness. He is patient with you, not wanting anyone to perish, but everyone to come to repentance." So be sure of your salvation, and go out and make this a great day.

> From the depth of sin and sadness to the heights of joy and gladness
> Jesus lifted me, in mercy full and free;
> With His precious blood He bought me, when I knew Him not, He sought me,
> And in love divine He ransomed me.
>
> Julia H. Johnston - 1849-1919

November 9

"WORSHIP THE LORD YOUR GOD, AND HIS BLESSING WILL BE ON YOUR FOOD AND WATER. I WILL TAKE AWAY SICKNESS FROM AMONG YOU."
Exodus 23:25

I thank God regularly that I grew up in a Christian home. I never remember a meal in our home that Dad did not thank God for our food and ask His blessing on it. Even when we were working in the field and Momma would bring an afternoon snack out for us to eat, Dad would thank God and ask His blessing on it. While cash money was scarce around our family, we never lacked for food. I honestly believe that was because my parents worshiped the Lord! I believe God gave Momma the wisdom to plan for the family's food needs, plan for the garden, and plan for canning the food at garden harvest time. I also believe God gave Dad the wisdom to plan for the family's food needs in the calves and hogs he selected to fatten to provide meat for the family. Additionally, I remember very few times of illness in our family. Sure, we had the normal colds, childhood diseases and accidents, but while their children were growing up, my parents had very few "sick days." Momma died at age sixty-nine in 1979, and many times I still miss her. Dad died at age ninety-three in 2003, while I was writing this devotional. I really miss the good times we had and the lessons he taught me.

Today's promise was given to Moses by God after He had given Moses the Ten Commandments. It came as God was giving Moses the laws in support of the commandments while Moses was on mount Sinai. Even though this promise was made to the children of Israel nearly fifteen hundred years ago, it is as applicable today as it was then. We read in Hebrews 10:35-36, "So do not throw away your confidence; it will be richly rewarded. You need to persevere so that when you have done the will of God, you will receive what He has promised." Paul showed his belief of this promise in Philippians 4:19, "And my God will meet all my needs according to His glorious riches in Christ Jesus."

This promise does not mean we will never suffer from illness. It does not mean we will not have physical problems. Paul reported in 2 Corinthians 12:7, "To keep me from becoming conceited because of these surpassingly great revelations, there was given me a thorn in my flesh, a messenger of Satan, to torment me." We do not know what that "thorn in the flesh" was, but we do know that God would not remove it and told Paul, "My grace is sufficient for you, for my power is made perfect in weakness." We also know that studies show Christians have better health in general than non-Christians, so there is scientific evidence of the fulfillment of today's promise. I also know that if you are a member of a church such as mine, you will have help in providing for your food needs during your times of adversity. You will also have the prayers of many brothers and sisters when you are going through times of illness. So worship God. He will bless your food and water and help in times of sickness. Now go out and make this a great day.

Thou flowing water, pure and clear, make music for thy Lord to hear,
Alleluia! Alleluia!
Thou fire so masterful and bright, that givest man both warmth and light,
O praise Him, O praise Him! Alleluia! Alleluia! Alleluia!
Francis of Assisi - 1182-1226

November 10

"FOR IF YOU FORGIVE MEN WHEN THEY SIN AGAINST YOU, YOUR HEAVENLY FATHER WILL ALSO FORGIVE YOU." Matthew 6:14

In his book, "What's So Amazing About Grace?", Philip Yancey writes: "Walter Wink tells of two peacemakers who visited a group of Polish Christians ten years after the end of World War II. 'Would you be willing to meet with other Christians from West Germany?' the peacemakers asked. 'They want to ask forgiveness for what Germany did to Poland during the war and to begin to build a new relationship.' At first there was silence. Then one Pole spoke up, 'What you are asking is impossible. Each stone of Warsaw is soaked in Polish blood! We cannot forgive!' Before the group parted, however, they said the Lord's Prayer together. When they reached the words 'forgive us our sins as we forgive...' everyone stopped praying. Tension swelled in the room. The Pole who had spoken so vehemently said, 'I must say yes to you. I could no more pray the Our Father, I could no longer call myself a Christian, if I refuse to forgive. Humanly speaking, I cannot do it, but God will give us His strength!' Eighteen months later the Polish and West German Christians met together in Vienna, establishing friendships that continue to this day." In another part of the book Yancey writes: "One day I discovered this admonition from the apostle Paul tucked in among many other admonitions in Romans 12. Hate evil, Be joyful, Live in harmony, Do not be conceited-the list goes on and on. Then appears this verse, 'Do not take revenge, my friends, but leave room for God's wrath, for it is written: 'It is mine to avenge; I will repay,' says the Lord.' At last I understood: in the final analysis, forgiveness is an act of faith. By forgiving another, I am trusting that God is a better justice-maker than I am. By forgiving, I release my own right to get even and leave all issues of fairness for god to work out. I leave in God's hands the scales that must balance justice and mercy."

Read today's promise again. It says, "For if you forgive men..." This promise is Jesus' explanation of the Lord's prayer in Matthew 6:12, "Forgive us our debts, as we also have forgiven our debtors." Can there be any question? God forgives us AS we forgive others. It DOES NOT say, "Forgive us our debts, and we might forgive others." No! The message is clear, God will forgive us as we forgive those who have wronged (sinned against) us! Look at the word we are using-forgive. It contains "give." That means it is a one way action. You are "giving" without condition. This may seem unfair, but, in the same way, isn't it unfair for God to extend forgiveness to us for our sins, without our suffering any punishment for them? The most common New Testament Greek word for forgiveness means, to release, to free yourself! Jesus instructed us to forgive so we would release the pain and free ourselves from the festering sore of an unforgiving attitude.

Are you holding something done to you with an unforgiving attitude? Is that choking your relationship with God? Forgive! Free yourself! Now go out and make this a great day.

I then shall live as one who's been forgiven; I'll walk with joy to know my debts are paid.
I know my name is clear before my Father; I am His child, and I am not afraid.
So greatly pardoned, I'll forgive my brother;
The law of love I gladly will obey.

Gloria Gaither - 1942-

November 11

"PEACE I LEAVE WITH YOU; MY PEACE I GIVE YOU. I DO NOT GIVE TO YOU AS THE WORLD GIVES. DO NOT LET YOUR HEARTS BE TROUBLED AND DO NOT BE AFRAID." John 14:27

In his book, "The Good War: An Oral History of World War II", author/historian Studs Terkel related the experience of David Milton who was an eighteen-year old merchant seaman aboard ship in 1942. His ship was transporting Sherman tanks across the Atlantic ocean to Europe one time and Milton related the adventure: "In the middle of the Atlantic, these tanks broke loose in a big storm. They were Sherman tanks, twenty or thirty tons. As the ship would roll, these tanks would just slide through the hole and bang up against the bulkhead. Then they would roll the other way, just shaking the ship apart. So we pulled out of the convoy. We headed into the sea, while the deck seaman went down below to secure those tanks. They were riding them like cowboys, trying to hook cables through. Finally, they got the tanks lashed down..." The great danger to Milton's ship came, not from the storm on the outside, but by the disturbance on the inside. His ship could handle the stress of the storm on the outside only when they were battened down within.

Do you sometimes feel like you have a storm raging inside yourself? Does your heart feel twisted inside you and raging like a storm tossed sea? Are you fearful of what might happen, what you might do, or what others might think, or say, about you? Claim today's promise! However troubled or fearful you may be, Jesus promised a peace that is real and present. In the 1960's one of the favorite greetings between people was "peace!" That greeting merely expressed a longing or a wish. Jesus promised His peace is given to you. He didn't give to you as the world gives, but He gives a deep, satisfying, comfortable peace. Most of the letters in the New Testament start by the author invoking God's peace on his readers. 2 Peter 1:2 is such an example, "Grace and peace be yours in abundance through the knowledge of God and of Jesus our Lord." The author invokes peace, but it is God who gives peace through Jesus Christ.

Paul told us in Philippians 4:6-7, "Do not be anxious about anything, but in everything, by prayer and petition, with thanksgiving, present your requests to God. And the peace of God, which transcends all understanding, will guard your hearts and your minds in Christ Jesus." What should you do if you are fearful and anxious? You should go to God in prayer, with thanksgiving, and make your request to Him. Like today's promise, Paul promises us the peace of God. It isn't an ordinary peace. No! It is a peace of God which transcends all understanding you may have. It is a peace which will guard your heart and mind through Christ Jesus.

Do you have that type of peace today? You can, and you should, by giving your hearts and lives to Jesus Christ. Go to God in prayer with Jesus as your intercess, and you will have a peace that passes all understanding. Now go out and make this a great day.

I trust Him through faith, by faith hold His hand, and sometimes my faith is weak;
And then when I ask Him to take command, it seems that I hear Him speak.
He whispers sweet peace to me, He whispers sweet peace to me,
When I am cast down in spirit and soul, He whispers sweet peace to me.
Will M. Ramsey - (No Date)

November 12

"However, as it is written: 'NO EYE HAS SEEN, NO EAR HAS HEARD, NO MIND HAS CONCEIVED WHAT GOD HAS PREPARED FOR THOSE WHO LOVE HIM." 1 Corinthians 2:9

Do you have children or grandchildren? Did you dream of what they might become, what they would do with their lives, and what their field of study might be? When they were born did you make plans for them? Were they plans for a good education, a good upbringing, and a good life? Of course they were! But we are merely human. There are ever changing conditions and events which will effect the outcome of plans we might make for our children and grandchildren. If we, as mere human beings, know how to prepare plans for our children, how much more does our omnipotent God know how to make plans for us! We read in Jeremiah 29:11, "'For I know the plans I have for you,' declares the Lord, 'plans to prosper you and not to harm you, plans to give you hope and a future.'" How good are our plans? We read in Proverbs 16:9, "Many are the plans in a man's heart, but it is the Lord's purpose that prevails." We really need to make sure our plans are made after we talk to God and ask Him for His guidance.

That brings us to today's promise. Paul told us in our promise if we love God then, "no eye has seen, no ear has heard, no mind has conceived what God has prepared for those who love Him." God has prepared plans for us which includes what no eye has currently seen. They include what no ear has heard. Those plans include what no mind has yet conceived. They are plans which will prosper us and not harm us. They are plans designed to give us hope and to give us a future. What better future could we ever conceive asking for than to have eternal life in heaven with God? We know, from reading Revelations, a little bit about what heaven will be like. We know God's glory will illuminate heaven, for we read in Revelations 21:11, "It was filled with the glory of God and sparkled like a precious gem, crystal clear like jasper." We know it will be huge. We know it will be filled with riches beyond imagination in this world. Best of all, we know from Revelations 21:22 that God will be there! That verse reads, "No temple could be seen in the city, for the Lord God Almighty and the Lamb are its temple."

Thank God, His plans included atonement for our sins, in that Christ died to pay the price for our sins. God loved us so much that He gave His Son to die for us. All He asks of us is that we believe in His Son to have eternal life in heaven. How great is that love? We read in 1 John 4:9-10, "This is how God showed His love among us: He sent His one and only Son into the world that we might live through Him. This is love: not that we loved God, but that He loved us and sent His Son as an atoning sacrifice for our sins." So go ahead and talk to God about the plans for yourself and your children. Make those plans with His guidance, but always keep yourself open to changes which God will bring your way. They will amaze you! He will always lead you to follow the plans He has prepared for you. Now, go out and make this a great day.

All the way my Savior leads me-O the fullness of His love!
Perfect rest to me is promised in my Father's house above.
When my spirit, clothed immortal, wings its flight to realms of day,
This my song through endless ages: Jesus led me all the way.
Fanny J. Crosby - 1820-1915

November 13

> "Even youths grow tired and weary, and young men stumble and fall; BUT THOSE WHO HOPE IN THE LORD WILL RENEW THEIR STRENGTH. THEY WILL SOAR ON WINGS LIKE EAGLES; THEY WILL RUN AND NOT GROW WEARY, THEY WILL WALK AND NOT BE FAINT." Isaiah 40:30 & 31

Have you ever been tired? What we called on the farm "bone tired?" I am sure that you, like me, have been so on several occasions. I remember one such time in 1976 for me. I had been assigned by the Reagan campaign team to go into Iowa to see if we could win more delegates for Reagan during the district and state conventions. I arrived there on Monday afternoon, twelve days before the conventions. Because Ronald Reagan had won several of the states preceding the Iowa conventions, money was not the problem for me it had been in earlier states. I brought in volunteers to work with us, put in phone lines, chartered planes to take us to key towns in Iowa, and worked from very early to very late. The district conventions were held on Friday evening, with the state convention on the next day. The last district convention was over and I was back in my hotel room just before 5:00 A.M. I left a 6:00 A.M. wake-up call and started a very busy day at that time. Because we had worked so hard, we had considerable success and were able to help the convention run very smoothly. The state convention was over in the early afternoon. The members from the national Reagan staff who were there wanted to take me to dinner that evening. How could I refuse them? My wife, Jan, and I went with them, visited through the appetizer and the main course. As I was completing my dinner I felt Jan shake me. I had fallen asleep! We quickly excused ourselves, with apologies, and left for the hotel where I slept until Sunday afternoon. Yes, I was tired and weary!

Physical exhaustion is something from which you can recover with the proper rest. I think Isaiah is talking about a different weariness, fainting and stumbling here than the physical nature I wrote about above. Are you weary and faint from the burden of sin you are carrying? Do you have some sin of greed, envy, anger, gossip, etc. in your heart for which you have not asked God's forgiveness? Isaiah tells us, in today's promise, how to rid ourselves of such a load: Place our hope in the Lord! Call on Him for forgiveness! Ask Him to take your burden from you! Jesus told us in Matthew 11:28, "Come to me, all you who are weary and burdened, and I will give you rest." Without that burden of sin, grief, misery and anxiety; your heart will feel so light you will feel like you can soar on the wings like eagles, run and not grow weary, and walk and not faint. We read in 1 Peter 5:7, "Cast all your anxiety on Him because He cares for you."

Paul had a physical weakness and three times asked God to remove it. God refused and gave His answer in 2 Corinthians 12:9, "My grace is sufficient for you, for my power is made perfect in weakness." Yes, we are strongest when we depend on God!

Place your hope in the Lord, and go out and make this a great day.

Did we in our own strength confide, our striving would be losing.
Were not the right man on our side, the man of God's own choosing.
Dost ask who that may be? Christ Jesus, it is He-Lord Sabaoth His name.
From age to age the same, and He must win the battle.

Martin Luther 1483-1546

November 14

"WHOEVER GIVES HEED TO INSTRUCTION PROSPERS, AND BLESSED IS HE WHO TRUSTS IN THE LORD." Proverbs 16:20

Have you ever purchased something which carried the notice "some assembly required"? How many times have your started taking pieces out of the package and putting them together without reading the instructions? I have on several occasions. Isn't it maddening to reach the end of the assembly process and find some pieces which should have been assembled into the object during the early part of the process? Have you found that you used the side pieces for the top and made the object all out of kelter (kelter is farm talk for just being WRONG!)? I have done it wrong so many times that now I carefully smooth out the instructions (that is what is written on that paper you threw away with the packaging!), read them, identify the separate pieces, and THEN begin the assembly process. I have found that following instructions make the process of assembly go much more smoothly.

Today's promise clearly tells us we will prosper if we give heed to instructions. Now I don't think Solomon was thinking about our need to follow instructions for assembling an object when he wrote this proverb. No, I think he was referring to the instructions we find in God's holy Word, the Bible. Today's promise goes on to assure us we will be blessed if we trust in the Lord. There are many instructions given in the Bible. I encourage you to read it, and to memorize large portions of it. The Psalmist tells us in Psalm 119:11, "I have hidden your word in my heart that I might not sin against you." Also in verse 14, "I rejoice in following your statutes as one rejoices in great riches." Yes, the Bible has many instructions for all areas of our lives.

What is the most important instruction, or commandment? Jesus was asked that very question, and He gave His answer in Matthew 22:37-40, "...'Love the Lord your God with all your heart and with all your soul and with all you mind.' This is the first and greatest commandment. And the second is like it: 'Love your neighbor as yourself.' All the Law and the Prophets hang on these two commandments." If you love God with all your heart, mind and soul, you will want to read, study and obey His instructions-the Bible. If you love your neighbor as much as you love yourself, you will find it much easier to follow the instructions given us, and you will be blessed by the Lord. If, on the other hand, you choose to ignore His instructions, you will not be blessed by the Lord. You will have your burdens to carry. You will not have a safe haven into which you can retreat when the storms of life roar about you. You will have struggles which you alone must face. You will have burdens which you alone must carry. You will have no safe haven during the stormy parts of your life. Paul told us in Galatians 6:7, "Do not be deceived: God cannot be mocked. A man reaps what he sows." If you fail to follow the instructions of God, you will reap the consequences.

Heed God's instructions, be blessed by the Lord, and go out and make this a great day.

It floateth like a banner before God's host unfurled;
It shineth like a beacon above the darkling world.
It is the chart and compass that o'er life's surging sea,
'Mid mists and rocks and quicksands, still guides O Christ, to Thee.
William W. How - 1823-1897

November 15

"Yet he (Abraham) did not waver through unbelief regarding the promise of God, but WAS STRENGTHENED IN HIS FAITH AND GAVE GLORY TO GOD, BEING FULLY PERSUADED THAT GOD HAD POWER TO DO WHAT HE HAD PROMISED." Romans 4:20 & 21

Have you ever had someone promise you something and then not deliver on that promise? How did it make you feel? Did that person have it within their power to deliver on the promise? If so, that makes you feel even worse toward that individual, doesn't it? I am sure we have all had promises made to us that have been broken. Sometimes, we might have made promises ourselves which we did not fulfill. Knowing how badly we feel when a promise is not fulfilled should make us all the more careful about the promises we make and the performance we show on those promises.

In today's promise, Paul is referring to the story in Genesis 17:16-22, which describes the promise of God to Abraham that, at the age of one hundred, he would have a son with Sarah, at her age of ninety. Abraham at first laughed at God's promise, as did Sarah, but the promise of God was fulfilled. As Abraham came to realize the truth of God's promise, he was strengthened in his faith and gave the glory to God. He did this because he was fully persuaded that God had the power to do what he had promised. It was God's promise which caused Abraham's faith to grow, and caused him to give glory to God. Abraham was absolutely convinced that God did, in fact, have the power to deliver on any promise He made.

What about your life? Is your faith in God growing? Are you giving glory to God? Are you fully persuaded that God has the power to do what He has promised? This devotional book is full of promises of God, and it does not contain all of the promises. Are you fully persuaded that you can count on each and every one of these promises? When you first believe in Jesus Christ and become a child of God, your faith is weak. Like a newborn baby, which must exercise his muscles to gain strength, you must exercise your faith for it to grow stronger. Your faith grows as you mature spiritually. We are told in 1 Peter 2:1-3, "Therefore, rid yourselves of all malice and all deceit, hypocrisy, envy, and slander of every kind. Like newborn babies, crave pure spiritual milk, so that by it you may grow up in your salvation, now that you have tasted that the Lord is good." As you mature you should grow in faith and likeness of Christ. Paul told us in Hebrews 5:12-14, "In fact, though by this time you ought to be teachers, you need someone to teach you the elementary truths of God's word all over again. You need milk, not solid food! Anyone who lives on milk, being still an infant, is not acquainted with the teaching about righteousness. But solid food is for the mature, who by constant use have trained themselves to distinguish good from evil." Is your faith still in the "milk" stage? Are you fully persuaded God has the power to deliver on His promises? Have faith, and go out and make this a great day.

Living by faith, in Jesus above.
Trusting, confiding in His great love;
From all harm safe in His sheltering arm,
I'm living by faith and feel no alarm.

James Wells - (No Date)

November 16

"Fear the Lord, you His saints, FOR THOSE WHO FEAR HIM LACK NOTHING."
Psalm 34:9

Have you ever been in a position that you lacked nothing? During my early years I used to dream of having enough money that I would never lack anything. The more I thought about it, the more I realized that if I had that amount of money, I would then have so many physical things that I would lack proper security to protect those things. I also realized I would always be suspicious about the type of friends that amount of money would attract. I would then lack true friends. The more I pursued that line of thinking, the more I realized that there was no such thing as financial security. I then pursued the line of reasoning that if I had political power I would lack nothing. The more I considered politics, the more I realized there would never be political security. I also read the words of the English clergyman, Caleb C. Colton, "Power will intoxicate the best hearts, as wine the strongest heads. No man is wise enough, nor good enough, to be trusted with unlimited power." I realized that the attainment of great political power would cost me my integrity.

I have come to fully realize the truth of today's promise. It is only through the fear (awe, reverence, respect and worship) of the Lord that we come to the point that we lack nothing. What a wonderful feeling it is to know that we have a God who can, and does, provide us with all our needs. Look at the words of Jesus in Luke 12:22-24, "Then Jesus said to His disciples: 'Therefore I tell you, do not worry about your life, what you will eat; or about your body, what you will wear. Life is more than food, and the body more than clothes. Consider the ravens; They do not sow or reap, they have no storeroom or barn; yet God feeds them. And how much more valuable you are than birds!'" If we have the promise of eternal life, what on earth is of such great importance that we should consider that we have a lack?

How about your life? Have you given your heart to God? Have you believed on the Lord Jesus Christ? Do you live your life to worship Him, grow to be more like Him, fellowship with His disciples, serve His people, and tell others the Good News about Him? This is the purpose of your life, you know! Read Rick Warren's, "The Purpose Driven Life' and you will come to fully appreciate the truth of today's promise. Where does Rick Warren get these purposes for your life? From the words of Jesus when He gave us the Great Commandment in Matthew 22:37-40, "Love the Lord your God with all your heart and with all your soul and with all your mind...Love your neighbor as yourself." Also from Jesus' words when He gave us the Great Commission in Matthew 28-19-20, "Go and make disciples of all nations, baptizing them in the name of the Father and of the Son and of the Holy Spirit, and teaching them to obey everything I have commanded you." Are you living deeper for Jesus? Are you fulfilling your purpose here on earth? If you are, you will lack nothing! Now go out and make this a great day.

Deeper, deeper in the love of Jesus daily let me go;
Higher, higher in the school of wisdom, more of grace to know.
Deeper, higher, ev'ry day in Jesus, till all conflict past,
Finds me conqu'ror, and in His own image perfected at last.

Charles P. Jones - (19th Century)

November 17

> "So then, no more boasting about men! All things are yours, whether Paul or Apollos or Cephas or the world or life or death or the present or the future - ALL ARE YOURS, AND YOU ARE OF CHRIST, AND CHRIST IS OF GOD." 1 Corinthians 3:21-23

Do you like your current preacher? Did you like the previous preacher more than this one? Do you discuss the qualities of each one within your family or among friends? Do you argue about which one was better, about which one was closer to Christ, or about which one had the best command of the Scriptures? This was what was going on in the church in Corinth when Paul wrote this letter. The divisions within the church had become so pronounced that word had reached Paul in Ephesus. Some members stated they were following Paul. Others said they were following Apollos (who was the current preacher in Corinth). Paul chastised the members of the church in Corinth in this chapter of his letter. What he said to them in this chapter, preceding today's promise, is as true today as it was in 55 A.D. Paul said in 1 Corinthians 3:5-9, "What, after all, is Apollos? And what is Paul? Only servants, through whom you came to believe-as the Lord has assigned to each his task. I planted the seed, Apollos watered it, but God made it grow. So neither he who plants nor he who waters is anything, but only God, who makes things grow. The man who plants and the man who waters have one purpose, and each will be rewarded according to his own labor. For we are God's fellow workers; you are God's field, God's building."

This lays the groundwork for today's promise. Paul told the people of Corinth that all things are theirs (meaning all things of God). He repeated it, "all are yours, and you are of Christ, and Christ is of God." What a wonderful promise! Paul stipulated that all things of God are ours, regardless of who our preacher is! Some may have a greater command of the Scriptures. Some may have better presentations in the pulpit. Some may be better in small groups. Some may have a more commanding appearance. But, all are of God. It is God who builds the church through Jesus Christ our Lord!

Regardless of the qualities of your current preacher, you can make him a better preacher by praying for him. Too often members of the congregation have "roast preacher" for Sunday dinner. I am sure such behavior hurts God! I am also sure that such behavior hurts your ability to receive the "all things" promised in today's promise! Always remember, you don't go to church to pay homage to the preacher. You go to church to immerse yourself in the worship of God! Entering such worship with a prayerful attitude will make you more receptive to the music, the message and the entire worship experience. Your prayerful attitude will also help make the message from the preacher a better message.

Remember, all things are yours. You are of Christ. Christ is of God. It is God we worship. The preacher is there to help in that worship. Now go out and make this a great day.

O worship the King all glorious above,
And gratefully sing His power and His love;
Our Shield and Defender, the Ancient of days,
Pavilioned in splendor and girded with praise.
William Kethe - (16th Century)

November 18

"HE WILL NOT LET YOUR FOOT SLIP - HE WHO WATCHES OVER YOU WILL NOT SLUMBER." Psalm 121:3

Have you ever stood guard duty? It has to be the loneliest duty in the world. There you are, all by yourself, with all sorts of imaginings running through your mind. You are sleepy and bored, yet you still have to remain alert at all times. In the military it is a serious offense to go to sleep on guard duty. There are several stories of disastrous defeats suffered by military units because the guard was asleep and did not give the proper warning. What a wonderful feeling to know that God will never sleep as He watches over us! He is in constant communication with the Holy Spirit, who lives within us, as promised in 1 Corinthians 3:16, "Don't you know that you yourselves are God's temple and that God's Spirit lives in you?" So, Christians have a constant, personal guard living within themselves at all times!

Is your Christian life always an easy one? Do you find your walk with God many times leads you into situations where it would be easy for you to slip in your Christian walk? Look at today's promise again. He will not let your foot slip! There is corroborating proof in Scripture, for we read in 1 Corinthians 10:13, "No temptation has seized you except what is common to man. And God is faithful; He will not let you be tempted beyond what you can bear. But when you are tempted, He will also provide a way out so that you can stand up under it."

Of course, your Christian life is not always an easy one! You should, however, realize that any temptation you have is common to man-it is not unique to yourself. You should also realize that God is faithful. He will not let your foot slip. He will not let you be tempted beyond what you can bear. He who watches over you will not slumber. God doesn't do the tempting. We read in James 1:13-15, "When tempted, no one should say, 'God is tempting me.' For God cannot be tempted by evil, nor does He tempt anyone; but each one is tempted when, by his own evil desire, he is dragged away and enticed. Then after desire has conceived, it gives birth to sin; and sin, when it is full-grown, gives birth to death." No, God is not tempting you. Rather, He will not let you be tempted beyond what you can bear. But when you are tempted, He will also provide a way out so that you can stand up under it.

We read in James 4:7-8a, "Submit yourselves, then, to God. Resist the devil, and he will flee from you. Come near to God and He will come near to you." This is the very best way God provides for you to resist temptation. Submit yourself to God with a humble heart. Come near to God in thoughts and prayer, and He will come near to you. In this manner you are able to resist the devil, and the devil will then flee from you. God will always provide an escape from temptation if you keep your eyes on Him and your heart the temple of the Holy Spirit.

Trust today's promise of God! Always know that He is watchful and ready to help you in any way. Now go out and make this a great day.

His word shall not fail you-He promised; Believe Him, and all will be well:
Then go to a world that is dying, His perfect salvation to tell!
Turn your eyes upon Jesus, Look full in His wonderful face,
And the things of earth will grow strangely dim in the light of His glory and grace.
Helen H. Lemmel - 1864-1961

November 19

"But the man who looks intently into the perfect law that gives freedom, and continues to do this, not forgetting what he has heard, but doing it - HE WILL BE BLESSED IN WHAT HE DOES." James 1:25

Many people who came to this continent in the seventeenth and eighteenth centuries were coming for freedom-freedom of religion, freedom from oppression, freedom from unjust laws, etc. They were looking to start a new life in a new world where they would not always be concerned that they might be falsely arrested and thrown into prison by unscrupulous landlords, or other persons of power. They were also escaping lands where they were unjustly persecuted with no hope of protection by the authorities. Many were escaping a system which allowed them to be thrown into debtor prison for the inability to pay some small amount owed. They were looking for a place with better laws which would guarantee them freedom. They were the foundation of a nation which prizes freedom and independence above personal safety. They were the foundation of a nation which developed the greatest constitution in the history of the world. They were the foundation of a nation which formed a government based on the Christian principles found in the Bible. They were a people who refused to accept the constitution without the first ten amendments, which are correctly called the "Bill of Rights." They were a people who struggled against odds which would overwhelm most others to win their freedom from oppressive taxes and regulations. They were blessed because they laid the foundation of the greatest country the world has ever seen. They were able to do this because they kept their trust in the Lord. The laws they formed were not perfect laws, however. The struggle continues to this day to strengthen, amplify, improve and correct the laws of the land.

Do you look to the laws of this great land to give you freedom? As a Christian, you need only to look to the only perfect law-the law of God, as found in the Bible. If we believe in Jesus Christ and receive Him, and look intently into that perfect law, we will find a freedom which our country's forefathers could only dream about. We must continue to look intently into that perfect law, not forgetting what we have heard, but doing it. Then we claim today's promise that we will be blessed in what we do! God is faithful! David said in Psalm 18:22-24, "All His laws are before me; I have not turned away from His decrees. I have been blameless before Him and have kept myself from sin. The Lord has rewarded me according to my righteousness, according to the cleanness of my hands in His sight." Psalm 119:7 says, "I will praise you with an upright heart as I learn your righteous laws."

Do you, like David, keep all His laws before you? Have you not turned away from His decrees? Are you blameless before Him and have you kept yourself from sin? Have you studied and learned His righteous laws? Are you doing your best for God? If so, you will be rewarded, as David was, and God will bless you in what you do. Now go out and make this a great day.

If at the dawn of the early morning, He shall call us one by one,
When to the Lord we restore our talents, will He answer thee-well done?
Have we been true to the trust He left us? Do we seek to do our best?
If in our hearts there is naught condemns us, we shall have a glorious rest.
Fanny J. Crosby - 1820-1915

November 20

"He upholds the cause of the oppressed and gives food to the hungry. THE LORD SETS PRISONERS FREE." Psalm 146:7

Have you ever been a prisoner? Most of us would answer that question with a resounding "no." We think of "prisoner" as being someone behind bars in a jail or prison, or as being behind concertina wire as someone in a military prison camp or a concentration camp. Donald D. Dienst said in "A Sort of Villanelle," "Not all prisons have walls and bars." Whether your prison is of walls and bars or whether it is of habits and addictions, it is still a prison. Paul said in Romans 7:22-23, "For in my inner being I delight in God's law; but I see another law at work in the members of my body, waging war against the law of my mind and making me a prisoner of the law of sin at work within my members." He also said in Galatians 3:22, "But the Scripture declares that the whole world is a prisoner of sin, so that what was promised, being given through faith in Jesus Christ, might be given to those who believe." You don't have to be addicted to alcohol or cocaine to be a prisoner to sin. Are you a prisoner to the sin of greed by wanting more and more things, a bigger paycheck, a better car, or a bigger home? Are you a prisoner to the sin of lust based on your sexual desires or activity? Are you a prisoner to the sin of pride just thinking about how "good" a person you are?

We know that all of us have sinned, and are, therefore, prisoners of sin, because we are told in Romans 3:23, "For all have sinned and fall short of the glory of God." We can't gain freedom from our prison of sin by our will power or our own strength. We don't have to pay a fine, do community work, or hope the charges are dropped against us. We just cannot do it on our own, we must have help from God! Isaiah told us in 64:5-6, "You come to the help of those who gladly do right, who remember your ways. But when we continued to sin against them, you were angry. How then can we be saved? All of us have become like one who is unclean, and all our righteous acts are like filthy rags; we all shrivel up like a leaf, and like the wind our sins sweep us away." No, the answer for our release from the prison of sin is found in Ephesians 2:8-9 and 1 John 1:9, "For it is by grace you have been saved, through faith-and this not from yourselves, it is the gift of God-not by works, so that no one can boast." And, "If we confess our sins, He is faithful and just and will forgive us our sins and purify us from all unrighteousness."

Yes, it is the Lord who sets prisoners free! Read John 8:32-32 & 36, "To the Jews who had believed Him, Jesus said, 'If you hold to my teaching, you are really my disciples. Then you will know the truth, and the truth will set you free. So if the Son sets you free, you will be free indeed." Isn't it wonderful to just cast all our cares on Jesus, and know that He does, indeed, care for us? Isn't it wonderful to know, that as a child of God, we are assured of eternal life in heaven? Know that Jesus will lift you out of your prison, set your feet on higher ground and take the darkness away. Trust God, and go out and make this a great day.

Now I am climbing higher each day, darkness of night has drifted away;
My feet are planted on higher ground and glory to God, I'm homeward bound.
He set me free, He set me free, He broke the bonds of prison for me;
I'm glory bound my Jesus to see, for glory to God, He set me free.
Albert E. Brumley - 1905-

November 21

"God made Him who had no sin to be sin for us, SO THAT IN HIM WE MIGHT BECOME THE RIGHTEOUSNESS OF GOD." 2 Corinthians 5:21

Paul wrote in Romans 5:12,15 & 18-19, "Therefore, just as sin entered the world through one man, and death through sin, and in this way death came to all men, because all sinned-... But the gift is not like the trespass. For if the many died by the trespass of the one man, how much more did God's grace and the gift that came by the grace of the one man, Jesus Christ, overflow to the many! Consequently, just as the result of one trespass was condemnation for all men, so also the result of one act of righteousness was justification that brings life for all men. For just as through the disobedience of the one man the many were made sinners, so also through the obedience of the one man the many will be made righteous." You see, only a perfect lamb was sufficient for the sacrifice for the sins of each, and every, person in the history of the world. That unblemished lamb was Jesus Christ, who lived as a man, just like you and me, yet without sin. Why did Jesus cry "My God, my God, why have you forsaken me?" on the cross? It was because God had forsaken Jesus to actually BE the sins of all of us, and to die for those sins.

Thank God for the plan which included the resurrection of Jesus Christ to sit at the right hand of God and intercede for us. If we believe in Him, confess our sins, and ask forgiveness for those sins, Jesus will intercede for us. When we are judged by God, Jesus will say, "My Father, they are innocent, because I paid the price for them. In Me they have become the righteousness of God!" We have no righteousness of our own. When we are told in Ephesians 6:13-15, "Therefore put on the full armor of God, so that when the day of evil comes, you may be able to stand your ground, and after you have done everything, to stand. Stand firm then, with the belt of truth buckled around your waist, with the *breastplate of righteousness* (emphasis added) in place, and with your feet fitted with the readiness that comes from the gospel of peace." we are putting on the righteousness we inherited from Jesus Christ. We have no righteousness on our own. We are told in Isaiah 64:6a, "All Of us have become like one who is unclean, and all our righteous acts are like filthy rags;" Any righteousness we pretend, apart from that received from Jesus Christ, is just that-a total act of pretending!

The promise today is very precious to us. It allows us to stand before God on that day of judgment, which has been promised to us, and declare our righteousness with full confidence. We do this because God's plan was for Jesus, the Lamb unblemished by sin, to be sin for us. By allowing Jesus Christ to pay that price, we gained the righteousness of God. Are you confident of your righteousness today? If you were to die today, would you be fearful about standing before God's judgment? Claim today's promise! Cast fear from your mind! Gain the confidence which Jesus wanted you to have. He did not give us a spirit of fear, but a spirit of power, of love and of self discipline. Have a peaceful mind, and go out and make this a great day.

He left His Father's throne above, so free, so infinite His grace!
Emptied Himself of all but love, and bled for Adam's helpless race!
'Tis mercy all, immense and free, for, O my God, it found out me.
Amazing love! How can it be that Thou, my god shouldst die for me!
Charles Wesley - 1707-1788

November 22

"From one man He made every nation of men, that they should inhabit the whole earth; and He determined the times set for them and the exact places where they should live. God did this so that men would seek Him and perhaps reach out for Him and find Him, THOUGH HE IS NOT FAR FROM EACH ONE OF US." Acts 17:26 & 27

When I learned to ride a bike, I was afraid that I would fall. I asked Dad to hold the bike and help me. He said, "Don't be afraid. I will always be close to you to catch you if you start to fall." That promise gave me the courage to get on the bike and begin to peddle like I had seen my siblings do. Dad would run along beside me. Several times I would start to fall to the left, or to the right. Each time, Dad would catch me and raise me back to the balanced position. Before long, I was riding along on my own. I took a few spills, but Dad was always quick to run over, help me up and make sure I had not hurt myself seriously. How proud I was when I could ride down to the end of the street and back without any mishap. One day, some time later, my sister told me that Dad had stood just around the corner of the house to watch several trips I made before he was satisfied I could handle the bike on my own.

I think of that experience when I read today's promise. It is God's plan that our nation was formed when it was, how it was and as it was. It is God's plan that we are living here and now in this country. It is God's plan that we seek Him and reach out for Him and find Him. Just like Dad was never far from me while I was learning to ride my bike. Now, the truth is, Dad could not be right beside me at all times. Try as he might, he could not protect me and keep me from any harm. God, on the other hand, can, and is, right beside us every second of the day. We read in Psalm 91:9-10, "If you make the Most High your dwelling-even the Lord, who is my refuge-then no harm will befall you, no disaster will come near your tent." We are promised in Deuteronomy 31:8, "The Lord Himself goes before you and will be with you; He will never leave you nor forsake you. Do not be afraid; do not be discouraged." Not only is He not far from each one of us, He will NEVER leave us nor forsake us! What a God!

With God near us always, and the Holy Spirit in us, we can always count on Galatians 5:22-23, "But the fruit of the Spirit is love, joy, peace, patience, kindness, goodness, faithfulness, gentleness and self-control. Against such things there is no law." When we seek Him, reach out to Him, and find Him, we find out what real love is. We experience true joy, just knowing that He is our Father and heaven is our eternal home. We have peace in our souls, and develop patience. We show kindness to others. There is a goodness about us which others see and appreciate. We are faithful, gentle and show self-control. By exhibiting these fruits of the Spirit, we are a living, breathing sermon every day of our lives. People notice that difference, and comment on it. That gives us an opportunity to share the Good News so they can know God.

See God, reach out to Him and find Him, and you will go out and make this a great day.

Nearer, my God, to Thee, nearer to Thee! E'en though it be a cross that raiseth me;
Still all my song shall be, nearer, my God, to Thee, nearer, my God, to Thee!
There let the way appear, steps unto heav'n; all that Thou sendest me, in mercy giv'n-
Angels to beckon me nearer, my God, to Thee, nearer, my God, to Thee!

Sarah F. Adams - 1805-1848

November 23

"THE LORD WILL GRANT THAT THE ENEMIES WHO RISE UP AGAINST YOU WILL BE DEFEATED BEFORE YOU. THEY WILL COME AT YOU FROM ONE DIRECTION BUT FLEE FROM YOU IN SEVEN." Deuteronomy 28:7

This promise comes to us from the blessing Moses gave to the Israelites shortly before his death. What a wonderful promise it is, too! There are two situations I can imagine when this promise is carried out. The first would be when you are in an airplane. The enemy would be against flesh and blood in other aircraft. The enemy could come at you from one direction and flee to the north, south, east, west, straight up, straight down and spherical when obliterated. If I were a fighter pilot, this would be my claimed promise with each mission assignment.

The second situation I can imagine would pertain to everyone of us. In this situation, the promise would be carried out when we are tempted by evil spirits. We read in Ephesians 6:12, "For our struggle is not against flesh and blood, but against the rulers, against the authorities, against the powers of this dark world and against the spiritual forces of evil in the heavenly realms." This situation occurs every time we are tempted. We should always be aware, and confident, that being tempted is NOT a sin. Jesus Christ, Himself was tempted, as we learn in Hebrews 4:15, "For we do not have a high priest who is unable to sympathize with our weaknesses, but we have one who has been tempted in every way, just as we are-yet without sin."

We stand on 1 Corinthians 4:10, "No temptation has seized you except what is common to man. And God is faithful; He will not let you be tempted beyond what you can bear. But when you are tempted, He will also provide a way out so that you can stand up under it." This verse tells us three truths. First, our temptation is not a unique disgusting thing that only we face. It is a temptation which is common to others! Second, it is not something that will overwhelm us, with no way of escape. No, God WILL NOT let us be tempted beyond what we can bear! Third, when we are tempted, God WILL also provide a way out so that we can stand up under it! We should always understand our enemy. Our tempters are the rulers, the authorities, the powers of this dark world and the spiritual forces of evil in heavenly realms. We take comfort in James 1:13-14, "When tempted, no one should say, 'God is tempting me.' For God cannot be tempted by evil, nor does He tempt anyone; but each one is tempted when, by his own evil desire, he is dragged away and enticed." Our temptation starts with our own thoughts and desires.

So, how do we get our enemy to flee in seven directions? First, since temptation begins in our thoughts and desires, we should turn our mind on other thoughts. Second, we should confide in a godly friend who will understand and support and strengthen us. Third, we should call upon God. The Psalmist said in Psalm 50:15, "...call upon me in the day of trouble; I will deliver you, and you will honor me." God stands ready to help 24/7! Call on Him, and watch your enemy flee in seven directions! Now go out and make this a great day.

Once from my poor sin-sick soul Christ did ev'ry burden roll, now I walk redeemed and whole.
In my night of dark despair, Jesus heard and answered prayer, now I'm walking free as air.
From the straight and narrow way, praise the Lord, I cannot stray, for I'm walking ev'ry day.
When the stars are backward rolled, and His home I shall behold, I will walk those streets of gold.

H. D. Huffstutler - (No Date)

November 24

> "FOR THE LORD GOD IS A SUN AND SHIELD; THE LORD BESTOWS FAVOR AND HONOR; NO GOOD THING DOES HE WITHHOLD FROM THOSE WHOSE WALK IS BLAMELESS." Psalm 84:11

What a wonderful promise we have for today! Our God is a sun and shield. He bestows favor and honor. He withholds no good thing from those whose walk is blameless. Just how do we qualify as having a walk that is blameless? That is a question which is answered in 1 John. Look at 1 John 1:5-9, "This is the message we have heard from Him and declare to you: God is light; in Him there is no darkness at all. If we claim to have fellowship with Him yet walk in darkness we lie and do not live by the truth. But if we walk in the light, as He is in the light, we have fellowship with one another, and the blood of Jesus His Son, purifies us from all sin. If we claim to be without sin, we deceive ourselves and the truth is not in us. If we confess our sins, He is faithful and just and will forgive us our sins and purify us from all unrighteousness." Yes, God is light! God is a sun!

Jesus said in John 12:32, "But I, when I am lifted up from the earth, will draw all men to myself." Jesus also said in John 14:6, "I am the way and the truth and the life. No one comes to the Father except through me." We have to come to God for Him to bestow favor and honor upon us. We come to God through His Son, Jesus Christ, who was lifted up on the cross so His blood could be shed as a sacrifice for our sins, not just our sins, but the sins of the world. We also read in John 3:16, "For God so loved the world that He gave his one and only Son, that whoever believes in Him shall not perish but have eternal life." Now THAT is what I call God bestowing favor and honor!

If our walk is blameless, then God will not withhold any good things from us. We are blameless if we have confessed our sins, because He is faithful and just! He will then forgive us our sins and purify us from all unrighteousness. We have no righteousness of our own. It is a gift of God, and we are to put it on. We are told in Ephesians 6:14b, where we are told to put on the armor of God, "...,with the breastplate of righteousness in place," that we are to have "righteousness" as a part of that armor. We get that gift of righteousness by belief. We read in Genesis 15:6, Abram (Abraham) believed the Lord, and He credited it to him as righteousness." So then, if we are righteous, we are blameless, and God will withhold no good thing from us.

Does that mean we will have all the "good things" of this world? Of course not! If we are righteous and blameless before God, earth is only a temporary residence. The Bible uses the terms alien, pilgrim, foreigner, stranger, visitor and traveler to describe our brief stay on earth. What we own on this earth, we have it in trust from God. Jesus told us in Matthew 19:21, "If you want to be perfect, go, sell your possessions and give to the poor, and you will have treasure in heaven." Then we will be home with all good things. Trust God, and go make this a great day.

> My heav'nly home is bright and fair, I feel like traveling on.
> Nor pain, nor death can enter there, I feel like traveling on.
> The Lord has been so good to me, I feel like traveling on.
> Until that blessed home I see, I feel like traveling on.
>
> William Hunter - 1811-1873

November 25

> "Just as Moses lifted up the snake in the desert, so the Son of Man must be lifted up, THAT EVERYONE WHO BELIEVES IN HIM MAY HAVE ETERNAL LIFE." John 3:14 & 15

Have you ever been bitten by a poisonous snake, or was present when someone else was? It is not a pleasant experience! I haven't been bitten, but I have seen quick reaction of medical personnel to counteract the venom before it could cause death. You could just see the fear on the face of the person bitten. They were sure they would die. I can only imagine the panic if there were no medical help available. Numbers chapter 21 reports that as Moses led the Israelites from Mount Hor they complained and spoke against God and against Moses. The Lord sent venomous snakes among them and they bit, and killed, many of the people. The people then repented to Moses and asked him to call on God to save them. Moses prayed to God and we are told in verses 8-9, "The Lord said to Moses, 'Make a snake and put it up on a pole; anyone who is bitten can look at it and live.' So Moses made a bronze snake and put it up on a pole. Then when anyone was bitten by a snake and looked at the bronze snake, he lived."

In today's promise, Jesus reminds us of that time of venomous snakes, and the way God saved His people. They had to look at the bronze snake, which Moses had lifted up on a pole. When they looked at the snake, they were saved. Now, I just have to think that they would not have looked at the snake unless they believed it would save them. In the same way, Jesus tells us that the Son of Man (Jesus) must be lifted up (crucified), and that everyone who believes in Him may have eternal life. (This promise is repeated in verse 16!) We later read in John 8:28, "So Jesus said, 'When you have lifted up the Son of Man, then you will know that I am the one I claim to be, and that I do nothing on my own but speak just what the Father has taught me.'" What happened when Jesus was crucified? There was blackness during the day, and, at the moment of His death, there was an earthquake, and the curtain which screened off the holy of holies room was split from top to bottom. This signified that we now have direct access to God!

What else happened when Jesus was lifted up on the cross? We read that Jesus said in John 12:31-32, "Now is the time for judgment on this world; now the prince of this world will be driven out. But I, when I am lifted up from the earth, will draw all men to myself." Jesus died for me and you! His suffering and death paid the price required to cleanse us from our sins! Jesus' death on the cross gained for us the victory over Satan, the prince of this world! Yes, the judgment on this world is that ALL who believe in Jesus Christ receive forgiveness of sins and eternal life. Those who do not believe will suffer eternal separation from God in Hell. Our promise is listed again in 1 John 5:11-12, "And this is the testimony: God has given us eternal life, and this life is in His Son. He who has the Son has life; he who does not have the Son of God does not have life." Believe in Jesus, and go out and make this a great day.

Love divine, so great and wondrous, deep and mighty, pure, sublime,
Coming from the heart of Jesus, just the same through tests of time!
Love divine, so great and wondrous! All my sins He then forgave.
I will sing His praise forever, for His blood, His power to save.
Frederick A. Blom - 1867-1927

November 26

"HE WILL COVER YOU WITH HIS FEATHERS, AND UNDER HIS WINGS YOU WILL FIND REFUGE; HIS FAITHFULNESS WILL BE YOUR SHIELD AND RAMPART." Psalm 91:4

Immediately following a forest fire, a Forest Ranger was walking through the area blackened by the fire, looking for "hot spots," which would need to be covered by soil to keep the fire from flaring up again. At the base of a blackened tree he found a mound of ashes in the shape of a bird. When he moved it with his shovel it crumbled, and from under it came four baby birds, whose lives had been saved by the mother bird. She instinctively knew her babies could not escape the fire, as they could not yet fly. She, therefore, gathered them together, covered them all with her body, wings and feathers. There, the baby birds found refuge from the fire. Their mother was their shield.

The Psalmist spent a lot of time out of doors and must have seen something like this, or seen a time when the mother bird protected her babies from a storm. He knew that God would provide just this type protection for us. This protection came to everyone, for all time, when God's own Son died on the cross so His death would pay the price for our sins. We are like those baby birds. Jesus spread His arms, covered us with His blood, and, by His faithfulness unto death, provided our shield and rampart against death. Oh sure, we will suffer physical death, but we will never suffer the death of the soul. We will immediately rise to run free with God and Jesus Christ, our Lord and Savior, for all eternity!

Jesus is also our refuge from the cares of our daily life. We can go to Him in prayer at any, and all, times of the day and night. He will hear our cry and promises to answer us. He will take us in His arms to comfort us when we are sick of mind, body or soul. His faithfulness Is our shield and rampart. He takes on His shoulders the cares and concerns of this world. He gives us a feeling of safety, peace and joy which is indescribable to those who do not know Him. It is our responsibility to continue to turn to Him for refuge. We must live our lives totally in His presence. This life style, and our verbal witnessing to others is the best way to testify to others about God. Jesus said in John 6:44, "No one can come to me unless the Father who sent me draws him, and I will raise him up at the last day." Your life, love and testimony is the best way for the Father to draw others to Jesus! Are you living your life in such a way that God can use your life to draw others to Jesus? When you are facing a firestorm of activity in this world do you find refuge in the arms of Jesus? When you face the raging fires of broken relationships, death in the family, or financial crisis, do you find the faithfulness of Jesus to be your shield and rampart? Your answer will be "yes," if you have followed the instructions and promise in 1 John 1:9, "If we confess our sins, He is faithful and just and will forgive us our sins and purify us from all unrighteousness." Then you can make this a great day.

Safe in the arms of Jesus, safe from corroding care,
Safe from the world's temptations, sin cannot harm me there.
Free from the blight of sorrow, free from my doubts and fears;
Only a few more trials, only a few more tears!

Fanny J. Crosby - 1820-1915

November 27

"Don't grumble against each other, brothers, OR YOU WILL BE JUDGED. THE JUDGE IS STANDING AT THE DOOR!" James 5:9

Have you ever been around children (or adults) who just continually grumble? It can sure get on your nerves in a hurry! Recently, a friend of mine, Alice Shinn (Mrs. Troy-see October 3), told me that when she was a young girl she had a friend whose mother had a good remedy for the children's grumbles. When they started whining, complaining and grumbling, she would round up all the kids and give them a dose of castor oil. She would tell them, "With the way you are grumbling, I just know there is something wrong with you so I will just give you this dose and see if that fixes the problem. I am sure that dose of castor oil would only have to be given a few times to really reduce the grumbling.

When we grumble against each other and have conflict with them, we are letting all the negative thoughts about people come to the front of our mind. Those negative thoughts, left to run free, will completely cover up all the reasons we have to love others. This is in direct opposition to the greatest commandment Jesus gave us when asked, as we are told in Matthew 22:36-39, "'Teacher, which is the greatest commandment in the Law?' Jesus replied: 'Love the Lord your God with all your heart and with all your soul and with all your mind. This is the first and greatest commandment. And the second is like it: Love your neighbor as yourself.'" If we love others as ourselves, how can we grumble against them? According to today's promise, we can't, or we will be judged. We are reminded the judge is standing at the door. This means that at any time we may have to stand before God and answer for the life we lived and how we treated others. We never know when that may be, as Jesus told us in Matthew 24:36, "No one knows about that day or hour, not even the angels in heaven, nor the Son, but only the Father." Not even Jesus knows! Only God knows when we will stand before the judgement seat.

Instead of grumbling to, or about, each other, we should show the love God intends for us to show. We are commanded to do so, and Jesus told us in John 15:14, "You are my friends if you do what I command." Therefore we should love our friends and relatives and we will be okay. Right? Not necessarily! Jesus told us in Matthew 5:43-48, "You have heard that it was said, 'Love your neighbor and hate your enemy.' But I tell you: Love your enemies and pray for those who persecute you, that you may be sons of your Father in heaven. He causes His sun to rise on the evil and the good, and sends rain on the righteous and the unrighteous. If you love those who love you, what reward will you get? Are not even the tax collectors doing that? And if you greet only your brothers, what are you doing more that others? Do not even pagans do that? Be perfect, therefore, as your heavenly Father is perfect." How can we be perfect? We can't be perfect, only forgiven. We must believe in Jesus Christ, the only way to God the Father, and He will make us perfect by giving us His righteousness. Now go make this a great day.

Deeper, deeper in the love of Jesus daily let me go;
Higher, higher in the school of wisdom, more of grace to know.
Deeper, higher, ev'ry day in Jesus, till all conflict past,
Finds me conqu'ror, and in His own image perfected at last.

Charles P. Jones - (19th Century)

November 28

"Therefore, as God's chosen people, holy and dearly loved, clothe yourselves with compassion, kindness, humility, gentleness and patience. Bear with each other and forgive whatever grievances you may have against one another. Forgive as the Lord forgave you. And over all these virtues put on love, WHICH BINDS THEM ALL TOGETHER IN PERFECT UNITY." Colossians 3:12-14

When I was in grade school, we would often form teams to play games. The teacher would choose two captains, they would draw straws to see who chose first, and then they would alternate choices until all children were selected. Oh, how great it was to have your best friend chosen as captain, because you knew you would be the first one chosen. You were the chosen one! You would just strut over to stand by them as all the other choices were made. You didn't have to have any particular skills for the game if your best friend was the captain. They would choose you! What were your requirements? Being a best friend! In this manner, nearly everyone would be chosen first at some time every few days.

In today's promise, Paul tells the people in the church in Colosse that they are God's chosen people. What did they do to deserve that distinction? They did the same thing we have to do to become one of God's chosen people. They had to believe in God's only Son, Jesus Christ, and give their hearts and lives to Him. When we believe in Jesus Christ, and come to God through Him, we become one of God's chosen people. Through the righteousness of Jesus, which He bestows upon us, we become holy and dearly loved. We then need to strive to become like Jesus, clothing ourselves with compassion, kindness, humility, gentleness and patience. We must bear with each other and forgive whatever grievances we may have against one another. Yes, we must forgive as the Lord forgave us. Remember, Jesus taught us to pray with the Lord's Prayer, which clearly states in Matthew 6:12, "Forgive us our debts, ***AS*** we also have forgiven our debtors." (Emphasis added.) When Paul had given all these requirements, he then went on to instruct and promise, "And over all these virtues put on love, which binds them all together in perfect unity."

We saw yesterday the importance of love to Jesus, to our friends and to our foes, to those who treat us nice, and to those who persecute us. Now we see that Paul stresses we should have the virtues of compassion, kindness, humility, gentleness, patience and forgiveness, and we should cover them all with love. Because, he says, it is love which binds all virtues together in perfect unity! If all God's chosen act as instructed in today's promise, we can occasionally make the error of impatience, or lack of compassion, or an unkind remark, and we will still have unity. How? Because our Christian friend will forgive us as we forgive them. Their love for us will be so strong that it isn't damaged by our occasional sin against them. Paul assures us that love binds all our Christian characteristics in perfect unity. Believe it, and go out and make this a great day.

Love divine, all loves excelling, joy of heaven to earth come down,
Fix in us Thy humble dwelling, all Thy faithful mercies crown.
Jesus, Thou art all compassion, pure, unbounded love Thou art;
Visis us with Thy salvation, enter every trembling heart.
Charles Wesley - 1707-1788

November 29

"And so we know and rely on the love God has for us. God is love. WHOEVER LIVES IN LOVE LIVES IN GOD, AND GOD IN HIM. IN THIS WAY, LOVE IS MADE COMPLETE AMONG US SO THAT WE WILL HAVE CONFIDENCE ON THE DAY OF JUDGMENT, BECAUSE IN THIS WORLD WE ARE LIKE HIM." 1 John 4:16 & 17

This is the third consecutive day we are seeing the importance of love. We saw that Jesus said the greatest commandment was to love God, and the second was to love our neighbor. We saw that love binds all our Christian traits in perfect unity. Now today we have the promise that if we live in love, we live in God, and God lives in us. By this, love is made complete among all of us who love God. This gives us total confidence for that time we will stand before God on the day of judgment. Why? Because if we live in love, thus living in God, we are like Him in this world.

Does that mean we are perfect? Yes! Because we are forgiven. Does that mean we are never tempted or never sin? No! But in our love of Him, and our love of others, we can count on His constant forgiveness through His grace. How much does God love us? We see that in two places which say almost the same thing. The first is John 3:16, "For God so loved the world that He gave His one and only Son, that whoever believes in Him shall not perish but have eternal life." The second is 1 John 4:10, "This is love: not that we loved God, but that He loved us and sent His Son as an atoning sacrifice for our sins." This second tells us that God sent His Son to die for the sins of everyone. What is the difference between the first and the second? The first promises eternal life to those who BELIEVE! Jesus died for the sins of everyone, but to take advantage of that atoning, we have to believe in Jesus. When we believe, we will ask for forgiveness of our sins. We are told that when we ask for forgiveness we will receive that forgiveness of sins in 1 John 1:9, "If we confess our sins, He is faithful and just and will forgive us our sins and purify us from all unrighteousness."

The love of God is great, and all He asks of us is to believe and love. Paul told us in Philippians 2:8-9, "What is more, I consider everything a loss compared to the surpassing greatness of knowing Christ Jesus my Lord, for whose sake I have lost all things. I consider them rubbish, that I may gain Christ and be found in Him, not having a righteousness of my own that comes from the law, but that which is through faith in Christ-the righteousness that comes from God and is by faith." When God forgives us our sins and purifies us from all unrighteousness, He give us His righteousness because of our faith. If you BELIEVE in Jesus Christ and confess your sins, you will receive the righteousness because of your faith just as Abraham did as reported in Genesis 15:6, "Abram believed the Lord, and He credited it to him as righteousness.

So live in love, thus living in God, and have confidence on that day of judgment, because in this world you are like Him. Now go out and make this a great day.

There is welcome for the sinner and more graces for the good;
There is mercy with the Savior; there is healing in His blood.
For the love of God is broader than the measure of man's mind;
And the heart of the Eternal is most wonderfully kind.

Frederick W. Faber - 1814-1863

November 30

"The Jesus declared, 'I AM THE BREAD OF LIFE. HE WHO COMES TO ME WILL NEVER GO HUNGRY, AND HE WHO BELIEVES IN ME WILL NEVER BE THIRSTY.'" John 6:35

I can never remember a time during my childhood years that I was hungry. Oh, sure, I can remember times when I said to Momma, "May I get something to eat? I am starving to death!" I really wasn't starving, however. In fact, I never knew real hunger. This kind of hunger of those who haven't eaten a decent meal for days, weeks or months. There is a difference in the type hunger I had as a growing boy, who was used to having three meals, plus snacks, every day, and the type hunger of the person who has eaten only scraps and bits for a long time-the type hunger which must have been a continual feeling of the German concentration camps during World War II. They were actually "starving to death." Their hunger is a need of food for survival. My hunger was a need to satisfy a craving for food to help me grow.

Today's promise of Jesus is so precious because He states that He is the bread of life. If we come to Him, we will never go hungry-we will never die, but have eternal life. Without Jesus, we have a constant hunger. We are always looking for something to satisfy that hunger. We each look to something-work, money, success, power, sex, alcohol, drugs, parties, etc.-to fill the void that hunger leaves in our lives. We will never fill that void until we come to Jesus Christ, believe in Him, ask for, and receive, forgiveness of sin, and we will then find we are never hungry again. We are no longer "starving to death." We have found the bread which fills that hunger void inside of us. We will still work and make a good income, but it will be done while fulfilling our purpose of life in Jesus Christ our Lord. It will not be the incessant, compulsive effort we were making before just to try to fill the void in our lives.

Now, with Jesus Christ as the center of my life, I find that many times I feel the way I did when I would come into the house and tell Momma, "I am starving to death." That comes from the hunger I have to learn to worship Him better, to be in fellowship with other Christians, to study to become more like Jesus each day, to serve Him better by helping fellow Christians, and to be a better witness to those who have not given their hearts to God. Those five things I find which satisfies my hunger are the five purposes God has for our lives as discussed in detail in the book, "The Purpose Driven Life" by Rick Warren. If you haven't read it, it is a MUST READ! Rick Warren didn't just pull those five purposes out of his hat. He got them from the Bible-the Great Commandment (Mark 12-28b-32) and the Great Commission (Matthew 28:18-20).

Have you come to Jesus? Do you really believe in Him? Is your Christian life the most important thing in the world to you? If it is, you know that hunger and thirst is gone. If it isn't, why don't you fully come to Jesus today, believe in Him, ask forgiveness of sins, and take on His righteousness? You will find true peace in Him. Now go out and make this a great day.

Bless Thou the truth, dear Lord, to me, to me,
As Thou didst bless the bread by Galilee;
Then shall all bondage cease, all fetters fall;
And I shall find my peace, my all in all.
Mary A. Lathbury - 1841-1913

December 1

"'Bring the whole tithe into the storehouse, that there may be food in my house. Test me in this,' says the Lord Almighty, 'AND SEE IF I WILL NOT THROW OPEN THE FLOODGATES OF HEAVEN AND POUR OUT SO MUCH BLESSING THAT YOU WILL NOT HAVE ROOM ENOUGH FOR IT.'" Malachi 3:10

As I was growing up on the farm I knew this verse very well, as well as the meaning of the verse. We raised most of our food in the garden, field, pasture, or pens for hogs or chickens. It was nearly a constant effort to gather food at the proper time, process it, and store it. When Momma canned the vegetables we grew, it would be a community event. Ladies would come from around the area to help clean the jars and the vegetables and then can the vegetables in the clean jars. Momma always invited the wife of the pastor of our church. Providing her with the vegetables for her family was always considered a part of our tithe. We did the same thing when we butchered hogs or cattle. We would invite the pastor to come help, and then provide him with a generous portion of every cut to pay for his work and pay our tithe. I can remember many times Momma would call the pastor's wife on Saturday and tell her we would be bringing chickens in for their Sunday dinner. When the pullets would mature to the point of laying eggs, we would take some of them for the pastor to keep in his chicken yard to provide eggs for the family. We would also take them milk, cream and butter. We didn't have very much cash money, but such as we had we shared as a tithe.

In today's promise Malachi very clearly tells us that God tells us to test Him regarding our faithfulness to tithe. The promise for our faithfulness is that God will throw open the floodgates of heaven and pour out so much blessing on us for tithing that we will not have room enough for it! Do you believe it? This is a matter of faith. Look at Luke 6:38, "Give, and it will be given to you. A good measure, pressed down, shaken together and running over, will be poured into your lap. For with the measure you use, it will be measured to you." Notice the first word, "give." The verse DOES NOT say, "It will be given to you so you can give." The first act must be yours! You must show the faith in God, and you must show it with the proper attitude. Look at 2 Corinthians 9:7, "Each man should give what he has decided in his heart to give, not reluctantly or under compulsion, for God loves a cheerful giver."

Can we count on today's promise? I know that we always had plenty to eat at home. We always had clothes to wear, a warm home to live in, general good health, and friends and family who loved us. All four of my parents children grew up to be respected, contributing members of the church and the world. We know Jesus as our personal savior, are active in our churches, have good homes, and have lived past retirement age. Most of all, we have retained the Christian habits taught to us by our parents. I challenge you to claim today's promise and see if you aren't likewise showered with blessings. Do it, and go out and make this a great day.

There shall be showers of blessing-precious reviving again;
Over the hills and the valleys, sound of abundance of rain.
There shall be showers of blessing: O, that today they might fall,
Now as to God we're confessing, now, as on Jesus we call!
Daniel W. Whittle - 1840-1901

December 2

"I, EVEN I, AM HE WHO BLOTS OUT YOUR TRANSGRESSIONS, FOR MY OWN SAKE, AND REMEMBERS YOUR SINS NO MORE." Isaiah 43:25

In the United States of America, when someone commits a felony they lose certain rights, among which are the right to vote and hold public office. Many people in the United States do not vote, but it is because they choose not to do so. It is a different matter entirely when they are not allowed to vote. It must be very disheartening to know that you are not allowed to vote, regardless of how intensely you feel about a matter. In some cases, those convicted of a felony hire an attorney to represent them in application to a governor or the president in an effort to obtain a pardon. A pardon is defined in Webster's Dictionary as: **1.** to release (a person) from further punishment for a crime **2.** to cancel or not exact penalty for (an offense); forgive. Not every person who applies for a pardon will be granted one. However, when a person is granted a pardon, for the rest of their lives they no longer suffer the penalty for the crime. They have been forgiven. They can then register to vote and cast their votes in any elections. Except for the memory of themselves and others, they start to live as if they had never committed the crime. From the standpoint of the government, the crime is remembered no more.

In today's promise, Isaiah tells us of our God who blots out our transgressions. Why does Isaiah tell us He does this? It is for God's sake! How can that be? It is because God made us, God loves us, and God wants to have a relationship with us. All He requires is our request for a pardon. We are told in 1 John 1:9, "If we confess our sins, He is faithful and just and will forgive us our sins and purify us from all unrighteousness." Unlike asking for a pardon from a governor or a president (in which case you may, or may not, be granted one), when you ask for forgiveness from God for your sins, He **will** forgive you of your sins and purify you from all unrighteousness. What a wonderful promise this is! Not only does He forgive you of your sins in this life, but He assures us we will have eternal life with Him in heaven!

The promise also includes the fact that He will no longer remember our sins. The story is told about the man who had been a sinner for many years and had done a great many very bad deeds. When he heard the Good News and confessed his sins with his mouth and believed with his heart that Jesus is Lord, he received forgiveness for his sins. He had such joy in his heart and worked very hard to live his life for God. When he would pray, he would remember his past sins and feel so bad about them that he would ask God again to forgive him for those sins. One night as he was praying he said, "Oh God, please forgive me for those awful sins I committed in my younger years." God answered, "What sins?" Yes, He is faithful to remember them no more! We are told in Psalm 103:12, "As far as the east is from the west, so far has He removed our transgressions from us." What a God! Ask Him to blot out your transgressions, and go out and make this a great day.

You ask why I am happy so I'll just tell you why, because my sins are gone;
And when I meet the scoffers who ask me where they are, I say, my sins are gone.
They're underneath the blood, on the cross of Calvary, as far removed as darkness is from dawn;
In the sea of God's forgetfulness, that's good enough for me. Praise God, my sins are gone.

N. B. Vandall - (No Date)

December 3

"Those who know your name will trust in you, FOR YOU, LORD, HAVE NEVER FORSAKEN THOSE WHO SEEK YOU." Psalm 9:10

When I was working in politics, I would always advise my client candidates to make every effort to meet as many voters as they possibly could. We found that people who personally met the candidate were more likely to vote for them. We also found something interesting about the thought process of people. After a candidate would go into a small town and shake hands with everyone he could find there, we would find, by survey a week later, that nearly everyone in the area of the town would say they personally met, and shook hands with, the candidate. After a person personally met the candidate, the level of trust in the candidate would increase a large amount. When others in the area would hear their friends and neighbors talking about meeting the candidate, shaking hands with him, and what was said between themselves and the candidate, it seemed those people who didn't meet the candidate would have their level of trust increase to the point they began to actually think they had met him. Once a person indicated support, I would have my candidates keep them on the "yes" mailing list up to the time of asking them to get out to vote on election day.

Today's promise has nothing to do with politics, nor with the wishy-washy attitudes of so many involved in it. However, consider the two truths: 1. Those in politics are faithful to the voters who have indicated support of them, and 2. Voters tend to trust the politicians they personally meet. So, how much infinitely greater is the trust of those who come to know the Lord Jesus Christ as their personal Savior, and how much infinitely greater does our Lord Jesus Christ keep our names on His book of life, and promises never to forsake us? We can trust our God David is talking about in today's promise. We are told in James 1:17, "Every good and perfect gift is from above, coming down from the Father of the heavenly lights, ***who does not change like shifting shadows***." (Emphasis added). God doesn't change! He remains the same forever, as we read in Psalm 100:5, "For the Lord is good and His love endures forever; His faithfulness continues through all generations." There has been no change in the love of God from the day of the Psalmist to today! We also have the assurance of His faithfulness from Paul in Hebrews 13:8, "Jesus Christ is the same yesterday and today and forever."

Do you know the name of our Lord Jesus Christ? Have you personally met Him? Have you put your trust in Him? Have you sought Him? Do you know He will never forsake you? If you did not answer "yes" to all these questions, you should pray to Him right now to remove all doubts and become His personal friend. Now go tell others about your meeting, your friendship and your trust in God. Their trust might increase such that they want to meet Him also! That is really God's plan, that we should be a witness for Him and win others to Him.

Claim today's precious promise, and go out and make this a great day.

O how sweet to trust in Jesus, just to trust His cleansing blood,
Just in simple faith to plunge me 'neath the healing, cleansing flood!
I'm so glad I learned to trust Thee, precious Jesus, Savior, Friend;
And I know that Thou art with me, wilt be with me to the end.

Louisa M. R. Stead - 1850-1917

December 4

"YOU KNOW THE WAY TO THE PLACE WHERE I AM GOING." John 14:4

When you want to go somewhere, how do you know how to get there? It's easy if you have been there before. If you are going somewhere new, you will need help in knowing how to get there. You will need a map! During my thirty years in the National Guard, my favorite subject of study was "Map Reading." I found the study to be interesting, challenging, fun and stimulating. When I was in the field and needed to find my location on a map, I would carefully study the area around me, close my eyes, and picture it as a map. Then I would look at the map to see the area of the map which looked like the map formed when I closed my eyes. When I looked at a map to see an area I was directed to visit, I would carefully study the map features, close my eyes and picture the way the area would look, and found that I would almost always recognize it when I saw it from any angle. When I am planning a trip, I take out the maps and plan the route desired, along with the points of interest I desire to see along the way. When I read a story about an area, I get a map, or world atlas, to see where it is. I find that I can find almost any place in the world with a map.

In today's promise, Jesus promises us we know the way to the place where He is going. How can we know any such thing? We study His map! What is His map? The Bible!! When Jesus gave today's promise, as recorded in John 14:5, Thomas said to Him, "Lord, we don't know where you are going, so how can we know the way?" The answer came in verse 6, "Jesus answered, 'I am the way and the truth and the life. No one comes to the Father except through me.'" Jesus then told us the place He was going in verse 12, "I tell you the truth, anyone who has faith in me will do what I have been doing. He will do even greater things than these, ***because I am going to the Father***." (Emphasis added) Now, we know that Jesus is the way. We know that Jesus has gone to the Father, so we know where He is. Now look at what Jesus said in verse 15-17a, "If you love me, you will obey what I command. And I will ask the Father, and He will give you another Counselor to be with you forever-the Spirit of truth." Then He said in verse 23, "If anyone loves me, he (she) will obey my teaching. My Father will love him (her), and we will come to him (her) and make our home with him (her)." (Parentheses added)

Therefore, if you love Jesus, you know exactly where He, His Father, and the Holy Spirit are. They are in our heart, soul and body. We read in 1 Corinthians 6:19, "Do you not know that your body is a temple of the Holy Spirit, who is in you, whom you have received from God? You are not your own; ..." While we are "travelers" on this earth, we know, from the Bible, that Jesus is in us. When Jesus physically left this world, He went to be with His Father in heaven. He told us in John 14:2, "In my Father's house are many rooms; if it were not so, I would have told you. I am going there to prepare a place for you." Yes, Jesus will be physically waiting for us in heaven at our death in Him. Claim it today, and go out and make this a great day.

In the resurrection morning, when the trump of God shall sound,
Then the saints will come rejoicing and no tears will e'er be found,
In the resurrection morning, we shall meet Him in the air,
And be carried up to glory, to our home so bright and fair.

J. E. Thomas - (No Date)

December 5

"No discipline seems pleasant at the time, but painful. Later on, however, IT PRODUCES A HARVEST OF RIGHTEOUSNESS AND PEACE FOR THOSE WHO HAVE BEEN TRAINED BY IT." Hebrews 12:11

As you can imagine, harvest time was a really big time for my family during my childhood years. Fortunately, we had a diversity of crops so we did not have only one time of the year for a harvest. This did not, however, lessen our excitement for the coming harvest, whether it be for wheat, corn, alfalfa, milo, hogs or cows. I learned through watching Dad, and my own study, that it takes careful planning, self-discipline, hard work and the right conditions to produce a bountiful harvest. The careful planning takes time and thought. The hard work involves many days of labor in hot or cold weather, which is very tiring. The right conditions depends to a large extent on God. Yes, a good harvest is available for those who have the discipline to prepare for it.

Such is the case in today's promise. I know that discipline is sometimes unpleasant and painful. (I received my share of spankings while growing up.) I firmly believe the discipline administered with love and fairness by my parents made me better. I always knew there was love in my home. I also believe their discipline resulted in the harvest of accomplishments (however modest), and the peace of mind I now have in those accomplishments. The love Momma and Dad had for me pales in comparison to the love of God for me, for God is love. The fairness of the discipline of my parents for me pales in comparison to the fairness of my heavenly Father. The same can be said for you, however much your parents loved you. While the discipline administered by my parents resulted in a better, more productive person, the discipline of my heavenly Father is far more rewarding-it results in my fully turning to God as my Savior through Jesus Christ my Lord. This leads to an eternity of joyous celebration and worship in heaven.

It would have been foolish for me to ignore the lessons of my parent's discipline, just as it is foolish for any of us to ignore the discipline of God. See Proverbs 15:5, "A fool spurns his father's discipline, but whoever heeds correction shows prudence." Ignoring some of their discipline could have led to situations which could have resulted in my death, just as ignoring God and His discipline leads to eternal death. See verse 10, "Stern discipline awaits him who leaves the path; he who hates correction will die." I could have laughed at my parent's discipline, and mocked them, just as I could do about the discipline God gives me through the Bible, sermons and quiet time, but that would not have been wise as stated in verse 12, "A mocker resents correction; he will not consult the wise." No, I cared too much for myself, my future on earth and eternity to ignore the discipline of my parents and God. See verse 32, "He who ignores discipline despises himself, but whoever heeds correction gains understanding."

Respond positively to the love and discipline of God. It may be unpleasant and painful, but it is administered in love and fairness. Now go out and make this a great day.

Love becomes a way of life when there's love at home;
Sweet insistent end to strife when there's love at home.
Glad submission each one's gift, willing pledge to love and life,
Healing balm for every rift when there's love at home.

Gloria Gaither - 1942-

December 6

"THAT EVERYONE MAY EAT AND DRINK, AND FIND SATISFACTION IN ALL HIS TOIL - THIS IS THE GIFT OF GOD." Ecclesiastes 3:13

Do you enjoy the work you perform? Many people go to work each work day dreading the thought of spending the time they must put in on the job. I really feel sorry for those people! I enjoyed my work on the farm during my childhood years (though I am sure Dad would have told you I complained about it enough.) I enjoyed the jobs I had while I was a student. I really loved teaching Chemistry at the college level. My ten years in politics held many interesting, unusual, fascinating and difficult assignments, but I had a great time working at each one. The twenty plus years I spent as an insurance agent was mostly enjoyable, however, I never enjoyed telling a client that a loss was not covered, and explaining the reason why. My thirty years in the National Guard were absolutely wonderful as they were filled with comradery, learning and preparation. These jobs were very different, but I was able to support myself and my family and find satisfaction in each one.

I think there are two secrets to enjoying our work. First, is to be where God wants you to be. If God wants you to be a teacher, you will never be happy doing nothing but research. If God wants you in sales, you will never be happy in management. If God wants you in mission work, you will never be happy as a business owner teaching Sunday School. The proper question to ask a young person IS NOT: What do you want to do with your life? Rather IT IS: What does God want you to do with your life? You should know the truth of Jeremiah 29:11, "'For I know the plans I have for you,' declares the Lord, 'plans to prosper you and not to harm you, plans to give you hope and a future.'" Yes, God does have plans for your life. Second, is to follow the advice of Paul in Colossians 3:23-24, "Whatever you do, work at it with all your heart, as working for the Lord, not for men, since you know that you will receive an inheritance from the lord as a reward. It is the Lord Christ you are serving." Your supervisor may perform your evaluations, he may be able to hire or fire you, but you do not work for him alone. You are working for the Lord! If working for the Lord is your motivation, you will find slights from you supervisor or fellow workers easier to bear. Your forgiving attitude will place you in good stead with your supervisor and your fellow workers. Will some try to take advantage of you because of your Christian attitude and practices? Perhaps, but read Matthew 5:10, "Blessed are those who are persecuted because of righteousness, for theirs is the kingdom of heaven." Jesus was criticized, scorned, doubted, questioned, plotted against, etc. Why do you think your lot should be better?

When your heart is right with God, you are following the plans He has prepared for you, you will know the full truth of today's promise. You will have enough for your family to eat and drink, and find satisfaction in all phases of your work. This peace of mind concerning your occupation is a wonderful gift from God! Now go out and make this a great day.

I want to be a worker strong and brave, I want to trust in Jesus' power to save;
All who will truly come, shall find a happy home, in the vineyard of the Lord.
I want to be a worker, help me Lord, to lead the lost and erring to Thy word,
That points to joy on high, where pleasures never die, in the vineyard of the Lord.

I. Baltzell - (19th Century)

December 7

"A PERVERSE MAN STIRS UP DISSENSION, AND A GOSSIP SEPARATES CLOSE FRIENDS." Proverbs 16:28

My dictionary defines "**perverse**" as: **1**. *deviating from what is considered right or good; wrong, improper, corrupt, wicked, etc.; perverted* **2**. *persisting in error or fault; stubbornly contrary* **3**. *obstinately disobedient or difficult; intractable* **4**. *characterized by or resulting from obstinacy or contrariness.* From that definition, it is easy to imagine such a man stirring up dissension. It defines "**dissension**" as: *a difference of opinion; disagreement or violent quarreling or wrangling.* Isn't it easy to see how someone who deviates from what is considered right or good, or who is wrong, improper, corrupt or wicked could stir up disagreement or violent quarreling or wrangling? Isn't it easy to see how someone who persists in error or fault to the point of being stubbornly contrary could stir up disagreement or violent quarreling or wrangling? Isn't it easy to see how someone who is obstinately disobedient or difficult could stir up disagreement or violent quarreling or wrangling? Would you like to be around such a person for a very long time? Of course not! It would take all our Christian love and patience to continue to tolerate such a person. I suspect, however, that reaction to such a person would bring close friends together in common defense against that type of an attitude.

Today's promise indicates a gossip is worse because he separates close friends. Solomon was so strongly against gossiping that he wrote six proverbs, including this one, against gossip. Paul put the sin of gossip in very tough company in 2 Corinthians 12:20 when he wrote, "For I am afraid that when I come I may not find you as I want you to be, and you may not find me as you want me to be. I fear that there may be quarreling, jealousy, outbursts of anger, factions, slander, gossip, arrogance and disorder." Any one of the sins on Paul's list can lead to a disagreeable split in a church, which is one of the worst things that can happen to a church family. Gossip, however, is the most subtle, sneaky and anonymous sins in that it tends to be whispered to one person at a time behind closed doors. There tends to always be a grain of truth, however tiny it may be, in every gossip morsel. This tends to give the gossiper credibility he does not deserve. This also tends to give the morsel of gossip "legs" to increase the speed at which it is passed. Close friends are separated fastest when one of them is the gossiper, spreading tales to others about his "friend." Close friends are also separated when other people tell one of them a morsel of gossip, which reflects poorly on the one, supposedly said by the other. How devastating!

What can we do about it? First, we should not gossip. Second, we should not listen to gossip. Third, if you are told some gossip, supposedly said by another person, use the Scriptural solution as found in Matthew 18:15-17. Read it! We all need an update on the method from time to time. Remember the charge from God's gracious word. He also suffered untruths which were said about Him. You, too, can survive the pain. Now go out and make this a great day!

According to Thy gracious word, in meek humility,
This will I do, my dying Lord, I will remember Thee.
Remember Thee and all Thy pains, and all Thy love to me:
Yea, while a breath, a pulse remains, will I remember Thee.

James Montgomery - 1771-1854

December 8

> "The Holy Spirit also testifies to us about this. First He says: 'THIS IS THE COVENANT I WILL MAKE WITH THEM AFTER THAT TIME, SAYS THE LORD. I WILL PUT MY LAWS IN THEIR HEARTS, AND I WILL WRITE THEM ON THEIR MINDS.'"
> Hebrews 10:15 & 16

Our mind is such a wonderful part of us. It controls all our motor skills, including those which are automatic, such as breathing and heart-beat. It also records all we see, hear, smell, taste and touch, as well as all we emotionally feel and everything that happens to us. Now, recalling each of those items is an entirely different matter! Recently I began reading a new book, and soon felt I was in familiar territory. I continued to read until I had read about a third of the book. At that time I was sure I had read the book before, and I began to search my reading list of years gone by. I soon discovered I had read the book some years before. (It was such a good book I finished it a second time.) We don't tend to have total recall of everything in our minds. What we seem to be able to recall are those things in which we are most interested. We also find we are able to memorize verses, sayings, poems, etc. which are most interesting to us. Why? Because they affect our heart! Then, they are easier to memorize in our minds.

Isn't that what today's promise is all about? This is a New Testament verification of what Jeremiah wrote in chapter 31. Jeremiah was influenced to write what he did based upon Moses' speech to the Israelites recorded in Deuteronomy 6:4-9, "Hear, O Israel: The Lord our God, the Lord is one. Love the Lord your God with all your heart and with all your soul and with all your strength. These commandments that I give you today are to be upon your hearts. Impress them on your children. Talk about them when you sit at home and when you walk along the road, when you lie down and when you get up. Tie them as symbols on your hands and bind them on your foreheads. Write them on the doorframes of your houses and on your gates." Do you know the commandments of God? If not, perhaps you should do some, or all, of what Moses asked the Israelites to do. First, love the Lord your God with all your heart, soul and strength. Second, teach the commandments to members of your family, and talk about them quite often. Third, write them down and carry them on your person all day, every day. Fourth, write them down and place those written words where you will see them often: your bathroom mirror, your refrigerator door, on the desk where you pay bills, etc.

Why do we need to know the commandments? Because Jesus said in John 15:14, "You are my friends if you do what I command." We need to study those and do all we can to learn them and obey them. Will we always be perfect, according to all the commandments of Jesus? Will failing in some ways doom us? NO! NO! For it is by grace you are saved! Most of all, love God, and follow the leading to the Holy Spirit! Learn God's commands. Count on God's grace. Now go out and make this a great day.

> Hast Thou not bid us love Thee, God and King? All, all Thine own-soul, heart and mind!
> I see Thy cross-there teach my heart to cling; O let me seek Thee, and O let me find!
> Teach me to love Thee as Thine angels love, One holy passion filling all my frame;
> The baptism of the heaven-descended Dove: My heart an altar, and Thy love the flame.
> George Croly - 1780-1860

December 9

> "In reply Jesus declared, 'I tell you the truth, NO ONE CAN SEE THE KINGDOM OF GOD UNLESS HE IS BORN AGAIN.'" John 3:3

Have you ever watched a birth? My daughter was born before the time a husband was allowed in the delivery room. However, I had watched the births of many animals on the farm as I was growing up. I knew what was happening, and I also knew many of the things which could go wrong. I tried to remain calm, but I was a basket case. I watched, or helped the birth of many of our cows and hogs, as those births were one of the "harvests" we had on the farm. I then watched the animals grow to the time they were sold, or they were put into our herds and had babies of their own. I have also watched my daughter grow to be an adult, with a child of her own. What a miracle is represented by each birth! When I look at a newborn baby, I see the creative hand of our loving God.

I can imagine the perplexity of Nicodemus when Jesus gave him today's promise. I suspect most of us would have asked, as did Nicodemus in John 3:4, "How can a man be born when he is old? Surely he cannot enter a second time into his mother's womb to be born!" Nicodemus was a Pharisee so he knew and understood the law. He had told Jesus in verse 2, "Rabbi, we know you are a teacher who has come from God. For no one could perform the miraculous signs you are doing if God were not with him." He didn't yet know that Jesus was the Messiah, and most who then thought He was the Messiah, thought He would establish His Kingdom on earth and reign in Jerusalem.

Put yourself in Nicodemus' position. Would you have understood when Jesus went on in verses 5-6, "I tell you the truth, no one can enter the kingdom of God unless he is born of water and the Spirit. Flesh gives birth to flesh, but the Spirit gives birth to spirit." This was the start of Jesus' explanation to Nicodemus and us that we must believe in Him, as so clearly pointed out in verse 16, "For God so loved the world that He gave His one and only Son, that whoever believes in Him shall not perish but have eternal life." Paul states very clearly how we first express this belief when he wrote in Romans 10:9, "That if you confess with your mouth, 'Jesus is Lord,' and believe in your heart that God raised Him from the dead, you will be saved." Jesus went on to explain to Nicodemus how he should live after being born again. In John 3:19-20 He said, "This is the verdict: Light has come into the world, but men loved darkness instead of light because their deeds were evil. Everyone who does evil hates the light, and will not come into the light for fear that his deeds will be exposed." John clearly stated this in 1 John 1:7, "But if we walk in the light, as He is in the light, we have fellowship with one another, and the blood of Jesus, His Son, purifies us from all sin." This promise and concept is why we call ourselves "saved", or "born again Christians." Are you "born again?" Follow directions given in this paragraph with a sincere, honest and heartfelt attitude and you WILL BE! Now go out and make this a great day.

O do not let the World depart, and close thine eyes against the light;
Poor sinner, harden not your heart, be saved, O tonight.
Our blessed Lord refuses none who would to Him their souls unite;
Believe on Him, the work is done, be saved, O tonight.
Elizabeth Reed - 1794-1867

December 10

"He who did not spare His own Son, but gave Him up for us all - HOW WILL HE NOT ALSO, ALONG WITH HIM, GRACIOUSLY GIVE US ALL THINGS?" Romans 8:32

After we had been retired for over three years, we decided our home of thirty years near the University of Oklahoma was getting too busy and noisy for the life we wished to live. We found a nice wooded lot with a green belt to the immediate east, and built a smaller house for our retirement years. The move to the new home necessitated our giving Jan's grandmother's bedroom furniture and our antique dining room furniture to her son, Kevin Lane. Along with that went lamps, mirrors, paintings, etc. We gave my daughter, Katy Brown, our refrigerator and washer and dryer, as our new home needed new colors. Everything we gave them was put to immediate use, which made both us and them very grateful. We were grateful because we knew the items we gave would make their lives easier and more comfortable, and we knew items we had come to love would always be used in the family. They were grateful because the gifts saved them a considerable amount of money which would have been necessary to purchase the items they needed, and the purchased items would have been of lesser quality. We had enough furniture left to fill our new home and make it very comfortable and accessible in our retirement years.

In today's promise, Paul assures us that God will graciously give us all things. How could Paul be so sure? Because, he reminds us, God gave His own Son to die on the cross for our sins. If God loves us so much, He gave that most precious gift to us, won't He also, along with the gift of His Son, graciously give us all things? Of course He will! Jesus told us in the Sermon on the Mount, recorded in Matthew 7:7-11, "Ask and it will be given to you; ... For everyone who asks receives; ... Which of you, if his son asks for bread, will give him a stone? Or if he asks for a fish, will give him a snake? If you, then, though you are evil, know how to give good gifts to your children, how much more will your Father in heaven give good gifts to those who ask Him!" Matthew told us Jesus' words in 21:22, "If you believe, you will receive whatever you ask for in prayer." Mark records Jesus' words on this in 11:24, "Therefore, I tell you, whatever you ask for in prayer, believe that you have received it, and it will be yours." This is very powerful Scriptural assurance that we can believe, and claim, today's promise.

Do we, then, get everything we ask for? No! Why? Read James 4:1-3, "What causes fights and quarrels among you? Don't they come from your desires that battle within you? You want something but don't get it. You kill and covet, but you cannot have what you want. You quarrel and fight. You do not have, because you do not ask God. When you ask, you do not receive, because you ask with wrong motives, that you may spend what you get on your pleasures." Are you getting "all things" from God? Are you asking with the right motives? Do you believe as you ask? It is interesting how our concept of "all things" changes when our heart is totally right with God. Is yours? Claim the promise, and go out and make this a great day.

Whenever I'm weary He comes to me, so gladly my burdens He'll share;
No night is so dark that I cannot see; I rest for I'm safe in His care.
He's been so good to me: My needs He has supplied, my longings satisfied;
He's been so good to me. The Lord's been so good to me.

R. Douglas Little - 1954-

December 11

"FOR HE WILL COMMAND HIS ANGELS CONCERNING YOU TO GUARD YOU IN ALL YOUR WAYS; THEY WILL LIFT YOU UP IN THEIR HANDS, SO THAT YOU WILL NOT STRIKE YOUR FOOT AGAINST A STONE." Psalm 91:11 & 12

Have you ever been in command of other people? People in the military, police forces and fire departments understand command perhaps better than most others. In those type units the commander must often send their subordinates into danger. It isn't an easy thing to do, however, proper training, planning, equipping and discipline will lessen the danger. The centurion who came to Jesus in Capernaum (Matthew 8:5-13) understood the authority, and responsibilities, of command. He came to Jesus to ask Him to heal his servant, who was suffering terribly. This points out one of the very important aspects of command-taking care of those under your command. I know it gives a police officer, firefighter or member of the military and their commander a really good feeling when they put themselves in danger to remove someone else from that same danger. The training, planning, equipping and discipline of the professional makes the danger far less to them than it is to the non-professional, but it is still a danger.

The Psalmist understood rescue operations very well when he wrote today's promise. He also knew the Commander! We have a great and wonderful God who is in command of all the angels. What a professional we have commanding in today's promise! How comforting it is to know the God referred to in Matthew 10:30 and Luke 12:7, "...the very hairs of your head are all numbered." is the God who watches us closely enough to command His angels to guard us as we go all our ways. He commands them to catch us in their hands so we will not fall if we trip over a stone. When Satan was tempting Jesus after His forty days in the wilderness, before His ministry on earth, Satan took Jesus to the holy city and had Him stand on the highest point of the temple and mocked Him by saying,"If you are the Son of God, throw yourself down. For it is written:..." He then quoted today's promise. What did Jesus answer? He quoted other Scripture, Deuteronomy 6:16 when He said, "It is also written: 'Do not put the Lord your God to the test.'"

I recently read an article in the newspaper of a two year old child who was playing with her twin in her parents third floor suite in a hotel. She leaned against the screen of an open window, the screen gave way, and she fell the three stories and landed on concrete. Witnesses, who saw the child land, say she landed on her diaper, got to her feet and began crying. Now I firmly believe she was the recipient of today's promise at the time of her fall. I am sure you have heard the expression, "God takes care of little children and fools." Well, I know for sure He takes care of little children, because we are told Jesus said in Matthew 18:10, "See that you do not look down on one of these little ones. For I tell you that their angels in heaven always see the face of my Father in heaven." Yes, because of God's perfect love for us, He will command His angels to protect us, and He will clutch us up to His bosom. Claim it, and go out and make this a great day.

Jesus, Lover of my soul, let me to Thy bosom fly,
While the nearer waters roll, while the tempest still is high!
Hide me, O my Savior, hide, till the storm of life is past.
Safe into the haven guide. O receive my soul at last!

Charles Wesley - 1707-1788

December 12

> "ANYONE WHO BREAKS ONE OF THE LEAST OF THESE COMMANDMENTS AND TEACHES OTHERS TO DO THE SAME WILL BE CALLED LEAST IN THE KINGDOM OF HEAVEN, BUT WHOEVER PRACTICES AND TEACHES THESE COMMANDS WILL BE CALLED GREAT IN THE KINGDOM OF HEAVEN."
> Matthew 5:19

When I took a course in biology in college, I was taught about evolution. Based on my Christian upbringing, I was skeptical of the concept, and asked for further evidence. My teacher could not give me any concrete evidence then, nor can any teacher give concrete evidence now. There is not one shred of fossil evidence of evolution from one species to another (macro-evolution). There is a lot of fossil evidence of evolution change within a species, such as horses, dogs, cats, etc (micro-evolution). To deny the existence of micro-evolution is to deny solid evidence. To claim the existence of macro-evolution is to deny the need for any evidence. From all we have learned through fossil study over the last century, we can safely say that those who teach the Darwin theory of evolution are practicing false teaching. In our religious studies, as in our scientific studies, we should not follow false teachings. We are told in 2 Timothy 4:3-5, "For the time will come when men will not put up with sound doctrine. Instead, to suit their own desires, they will gather around them a great number of teachers to say what their itching ears want to hear. They will turn their ears away from the truth and turn aside to myths. But you, keep your head in all situations, endure hardship, do the work of an evangelist, discharge all the duties of your ministry." Today's promise states precisely what will happen to false teachers.

Today's promise also gives us great hope because of the great promise to those of us who practice and teach the Biblical commands of God. We do not, and we should not, teach them as the Pharisee's did. No, we teach them in the full light of the love and grace of God. We must remember that following commands would be classified as "works," and we do not gain salvation by works. Don't ever forget Ephesians 2:8-9, "For it is by grace you have been saved, through faith-and this not from yourselves, it is the gift of God-not by works, so that no one can boast." We are not saved BY works, but we are saved FOR works! Jesus told us in Matthew 6:1, "Be careful not to do your 'acts of righteousness' before men, to be seen by them. If you do, you will have no reward from your Father in heaven." How do we get a reward from our Father? Read Jesus' words in Luke 12:33-34, "Sell your possessions and give to the poor. Provide purses for yourselves that will not wear out, a treasure in heaven that will not be exhausted, where no thief comes near and no moth destroys. For where your treasure is, there your heart will be also." Our good works here on earth provide treasures for us in heaven for eternity.

Are you following the commands of God? Are you teaching others to do likewise? You teach best by example! God wants to reward you when your life on earth is finished. When He calls the roll, will you be there? Make sure right now, and go out and make this a great day.

> Let us labor for the Master from the dawn 'til setting sun,
> Let us talk of all His wondrous love and care;
> Then when all of life is over and our work on earth is done
> And the roll is called up yonder, I'll be there!
>
> James M. Black - 1856-1938

December 13

> "Brothers, as an example of patience in the face of suffering, take the prophets who spoke in the name of the Lord. As you know, we consider blessed those who have persevered. You have heard of Job's perseverance and have seen what the Lord finally brought about. THE LORD IS FULL OF COMPASSION AND MERCY." James 5:10 & 11

Recently I heard of a man who was very ill. He was a member of a sister church of ours, and had lived a long life of service to God. As he lay in his bed the last few days of his life, he loved to have his family and friends sing hymns and pray with him. He would continue to tell all of them of his love for God, his pleasure of serving Him throughout his life, and his joy and willingness in the knowledge that he would soon see Him. His final days were an inspiration to all who came in contact with him. He had not had a life of ease and plenty. He had not had a life free from sickness and other trouble. He was blessed because he had persevered. He was blessed because he had followed the instruction of God in Proverbs 22:6, "Train a child in the way he should go, and when he is old, he will not turn from it." He had seen his children and grandchildren grow up to be Christians.

Even in his pain, he died with joy in his heart and a smile on his face. He was a wonderful example of today's promise that the Lord is full of compassion and mercy. How, you might ask, does this story show the compassion of the Lord? Because God gave the man the total assurance that he would spend his eternity in heaven. God gave joy to the man during his last illness. He gave the promise of being united with his family throughout eternity. God gave the man the love of his family and friends. Finally, God gave the mercy of escape from illness through a peaceful death during his sleep. I feel very confident that if that man could talk to us today, he would confirm the truth of today's promise.

Does your life seem to be full of trouble and woe? Do you seem to have more accidents, illness, money problems, or more relationship problems than those around you? Do you feel you have been forgotten by God in His great plan for all mankind? Are you fearful and anxious about what might come tomorrow? Does God seem to be so far away from you that you can't feel His presence, can't seem to make your prayers be heard by Him, and can't ever get an answer? You are not alone in those feelings. David wrote in Psalm 10:1, "Why, O Lord, do you stand far off? Why do you hide yourself in times of trouble?" David told God exactly how he felt. Do you do that? Or do you feel you have to hide your true feelings from God? Do you really think you can hide anything from God? Claim today's promise, along with 1 Peter 5:7, "Cast all your anxiety on Him because He cares for you." Is it easy? Of course it isn't always easy, but if you fully believe God, remain faithful and claim today's promise, you will be able to say, like Job did in Job 23:12, "I have not departed from the commands of His lips; I have treasured the words of His mouth more than my daily bread." Now go out and make this a great day.

> Mortals, join the happy chorus which the morning stars began;
> Father love is reigning o'er us, brother love binds man to man.
> Ever singing, march we onward, victors in the midst of strife,
> Joyful music leads us sunward in the triumph song of life.
>
> Henry Van Dyke - 1852-1933

December 14

"IN THAT DAY YOU WILL NO LONGER ASK ME ANYTHING. I TELL YOU THE TRUTH, MY FATHER WILL GIVE YOU WHATEVER YOU ASK IN MY NAME. UNTIL NOW YOU HAVE NOT ASKED FOR ANYTHING IN MY NAME. ASK AND YOU WILL RECEIVE, AND YOUR JOY WILL BE COMPLETE." John 16:23 & 24

The story is told about the widow who took in laundry to make her living. She never seemed to have enough customers to make enough money to live on. She always seemed to be in poor health and to have more than her share of bad luck. She did attend church on a regular basis, and one Sunday a friend asked her, "Why don't you pray about your problems?" She replied, "Oh, I do pray, but I don't expect God to help a poor washer woman like me." That woman asked God, but she didn't ask in the spirit of Mark 11:24, "Therefore I tell you, whatever you ask for in prayer, believe that you have received it, and it will be yours." You must **believe** you will receive, before you will receive! That is not to say all prayers are answered. The biggest reason for unanswered prayers is sin. You cannot claim Mark 11:24 without verse 25, "And when you stand praying, if you hold anything against anyone, forgive him, so that your Father in heaven may forgive you your sins." You must have a forgiving heart to have a forgiven heart, and that must precede your expectation of receipt of your request to God.

God always answers the prayer of a forgiving and forgiven person. He has three answers, "Yes," "Wait," and "I have a different plan." Consider the time just before the arrest of Jesus. He prayed to God, saying, "My Father, if it is possible, may this cup be taken from me." Jesus knew the agony of His approaching death, and, as a man, He didn't want to face it. However, as the Son of God, He knew He must face it. He wanted nothing more than to obey the Father in all things, therefore, He added the sentence, "Yet not as I will, but as you will." You see, God had a different plan than to spare Jesus the agony of the cross! Jesus was willing to accept that different plan. Are you willing to accept the plans of God which are different from your own?

The words of Jesus in today's promise were said to His disciples between the Last Supper and the time of His arrest in the Garden of Gethsemane. He knew of His approaching death, burial, resurrection and ascension. He knew He would soon be with His Father in heaven. He also told them in John 16, 27-28, "The Father Himself loves you because you have loved me and have believed that I came from God. I came from the Father and entered the world; now I am leaving the world and going back to the Father." Jesus would be with the Father for eternity. He was, therefore, giving His latest instructions on prayer in today's promise: We are to ask the Father in the name of the Son, Jesus Christ! We are also to believe we will receive that for which we ask! We are also to be willing to accept the will of the Father! Do you have a regular hour to pray? Do you ask for your needs to be fulfilled? Do you believe you will receive? Do you ask in the name of Jesus? Do so, and go out and make this a great day.

Sweet hour of prayer, sweet hour of prayer, that calls me from a world of care,
And bids me at my Father's throne make all my wants and wishes known:
In seasons of distress and grief my soul has often found relief
And oft escaped the tempter's snare by thy return, sweet hour of prayer.
William W. Walford - 1772-1850

December 15

> "BLESSED ARE THOSE WHO HUNGER AND THIRST FOR RIGHTEOUSNESS, FOR THEY WILL BE FILLED." Matthew 5:6

Those of us in the United States have very little knowledge of true hunger or thirst. We have a system of government which encourages individual incentive and industry. This has allowed us to develop a great nation with the capability of providing adequate food and water for the population. Does this mean everyone has plenty? No! We find pockets of lack. We find areas where good, clean water is a problem. However, we also find those problems addressed by individuals, groups or the government when they are brought to light. Wouldn't it be wonderful if we could so readily address the needs of those who hunger and thirst after righteousness? Have you hungered and thirsted after righteousness? Have you been filled? Have you helped others who have also hungered and thirsted? We are charged by Jesus to do so! First, in Matthew 28:19-20, "Therefore go and make disciples of all nations, baptizing them in the name of the Father and of the son and of the Holy Spirit, and teaching them to obey everything I have commanded you. And surely I am with you always, to the very end of the age." Also in Acts 1:8, "But you will receive power when the Holy Spirit comes on you; and you will be my witnesses in Jerusalem, and in all Judea and Samaria, and to the ends of the earth." In this charge, "Jerusalem" is your home town, "Judea" is your country, "Samaria" is persons of other cultures or groups, and "the ends of the earth" is the rest of the world. Are you faithful to this great commission?

We read in Matthew 5:13, "You are the salt of the earth. But if the salt loses its saltiness, how can it be made salty again? It is no longer good for anything, except to be thrown out and trampled under foot." Have you ever eaten a piece of good country ham? It has been tossed into a hot skillet, and served piping hot with the edges slightly curled and a little brittle in a place or two, and has some dimples of soft ham with a little juice in them. You cut into it, put a piece into your mouth, and begin to chew. You can just close your eyes and see the ham-maker rubbing the salt into the ham, hanging it in the smoke-house to let the smoke cure the ham. You know he occasionally took the ham down and rubbed more salt into it so it would cure in the proper way. You finish the ham and in just a few minutes what do you want more than anything on earth? A big drink of water! You ask the waitress for a glass of water. You just have to have it! In the same way Jesus asked the Samaritan woman at the well for a drink of water. She said to Jesus, "You are a Jew, and I am a Samaritan woman. How can you ask me for a drink?" In John 4:10 we read, "Jesus answered her, 'If you knew the gift of God and who it is that asks you for a drink, you would have asked Him and He would have given you living water.'" Are you God's salt of the earth? When unbelievers come in contact with you, does your Christian saltiness develop a thirst for the living water that only God can give? Are you fulfilling your mission in life?

Carry to others the message of the cross of Christ, and go out and make this a great day.

> Rejoice, ye pure in heart, rejoice, give thanks and sing;
> Your festal banner wave on high, the cross of Christ your King.
> Then on, ye pure in heart, rejoice, give thanks and sing;
> Your glorious banner wave on high, the cross of Christ your King.
>
> Edward H. Plumptre - 1821-1891

December 16

"All the days of the oppressed are wretched, BUT THE CHEERFUL HEART HAS A CONTINUAL FEAST." Proverbs 15:15

The story is told about the young man, in his late teens, who was caught near the end of the college semester stealing backpacks. At the time he was caught he had 95 pounds of backpacks in his car. When he was brought before a wise old judge, he was sentenced to carry a total weight on his body all day, each and every day for a year. The judge told him he could carry the weight in any way he wanted to, as long as the total weight was 95 pounds. When the young man would carry the weight in a backpack, his shoulders would become chafed. When he carried it around his waist, his hips would become chafed. When he carried it in his arms, his shoulders and arms would become tired and cramped. When he spread it all over his body, his entire body would become chafed, tired and sore. At all times, his feet would be sore and bruised because of the extra weight. He was losing weight and his body was deteriorating. He found he could no longer enjoy life, or even enjoy his food. He considered the sentence to be oppressive, unjust and unfair. He was leading a wretched life. Don't you know that fictional young man is a lot like those who are continually carrying the burden of sin and guilt? When they try to carry their load hidden in their hearts, they have terrible heartaches. When they try to cover their burden with alcohol or drugs, they wake up sick and tired, and find their bodies deteriorating. When they try to cover their burden with loose living, they find they are susceptible to diseases, and they find they must have greater and greater "thrills" to satisfy their hunger. They are living a life which is oppressive, unjust and unfair. They are leading a wretched life.

Contrast that with the promise we have for today: A person who has asked God, through Jesus Christ, to remove his burden has a cheerful heart. Without the burden of guilt and sin, a Christian has continual joy, whether he are always happy or not. He find he enjoys all of life, especially the fellowship of a meal around a dining table with fellow Christians. He feels like David must have felt when he wrote Psalm 34:8, "Taste and see that the Lord is good; blessed is the man who takes refuge in Him." He finds when he tastes and sees the Lord is good, he has such a cheerful heart he has a continual feast! He is not exposed to many of the diseases and debilitations common to many who carry their load of sin and guilt. He rests in the peaceful knowledge that the Lord protects him and has promised him eternal life. He knows his time on earth is the preparation for where he will spend eternity, and he has the promise of spending that eternity with his Lord Jesus Christ in heaven. He is content with his life.

What about you today? Are you carrying a load of sin and guilt? Do you have a heartache, headache or the results of deterioration brought on by loose living? Do you run from party to party to try to put joy in your life, only to find more loneliness and heartache? Turn your burdens to Jesus for a cheerful heart and a continual feast. Now go out and make this a great day.

Days are filled with sorrow and care, hearts are lonely and drear;
Burdens are lifted at Calvary, Jesus is very near.
Troubled soul, the Savior can see every heartache and tear;
Burdens are lifted at Calvary, Jesus is very near.

John M. Moore - 1925-

December 17

"When we are judged by the Lord, we are being disciplined SO THAT WE WILL NOT BE CONDEMNED WITH THE WORLD." 1 Corinthians 11:32

Over the years, I have read many stories about judges who, during sentencing of persons convicted in their courts, took the opportunity to explain the reason behind the sentence. In doing so, those judges provided explanations to make sure those convicted knew they were being disciplined, and why they were being disciplined. In several cases the stories go on to explain how the judges words, and the sentences given, turned their lives around so they were lived so as to never again appear before a judge to be sentenced. By accepting the judgement given them, and by taking the discipline to heart, those people turned from a life of crime which could have resulted in very harsh judgement and condemnation at some time in the future.

In the same way, we are often disciplined by the Lord so we might see the sin in our lives, turn from it, and avoid the condemnation which is coming to those who are not children of God's. That is the wonderful truth about today's promise! Those of us who are children of God are not perfect people who never sin in any way. No, we are still of this world, and we are tempted by Satan to sin. We are then judged by the Lord, and He disciplines us. He does this just as our parents disciplined us as children, or those judges disciplined those who were convicted before them. He does this so we might see the error of our ways, repent of our sins, and grow to be more and more like Jesus. When we do repent we have the promise of God that we will not be judged with the world (those who do not profess Jesus as their Lord and Savior.)

We are told in Psalm 118:18, "The Lord has chastened me severely, but He has not given me over to death." How true that is! No matter how severely we are disciplined, we still have the promise of eternal life. Sure we will suffer the physical death, but that is nothing compared to the spiritual death of those who are not Christians. In fact, as Christians, we realize that our lives on this earth are only temporary. The main thing we do during our lives on earth is to determine where we will spend eternity. That decision is of such great importance that it is no surprise that our Lord would discipline us to make sure we stay on the right path. In the same way, a parent takes great pains to ensure their children learn those extremely important lessons in life, and will discipline a child who go astray of those teachings. They do this, not to just exert their authority, rather to insure the child will not suffer death from his disobedience.

Have you gone through a period of discipline from the Lord? How did you handle the experience? Were you contrite and broken hearted about your actions, or did you rebel against the discipline? We are told in Psalm 51:17, "The sacrifices of God are a broken spirit; a broken and contrite heart, O God, you will not despise." When we are disciplined by God He does not want our sacrifices. He wants us to be truly repentant and broken hearted at our transgressions.

Accept God's discipline, God will give you a crown. Go out and make this a great day.

To him that o'er cometh God giveth a crown;
Thro' faith we shall conquer, though often cast down;
He who is our Savior, our strength will renew;
Look ever to Jesus, He will carry you through.

Horatio R. Palmer - 1834-1907

December 18

"If you then, though you are evil, know how to give good gifts to your children, HOW MUCH MORE WILL YOUR FATHER IN HEAVEN GIVE THE HOLY SPIRIT TO THOSE WHO ASK HIM!" Luke 11:13

When I was four years old my eight year old sister and ten year old brother had taken a considerable amount of time teaching my six year old sister how to read as they did their homework for their next school day. All three of my siblings worried about me because I could not read. They were concerned that my illiteracy might be a permanent situation. So great was their concern that they all took turns giving me reading lessons. As a result of three hours reading lessons each day I became a very good reader during the summer I was four. When it came time for school to start I was ready to go. When Dad and Momma took us all to the school and left my three siblings, left to take me home, I cried with a broken heart because everyone told me I was too young to go to school. My parents were very wise. They knew they had to get something to take my mind off school so they stopped at the store as we were driving home and bought me a pretty, rugged tricycle. That gift caused my tears to immediately cease and my smile was as wide as my face as I rode it down the sidewalk leading my parents to the car. What a nice gift that was! My siblings still use that gift as the prime example to tell me how spoiled I was. That's okay. I still use that gift as an example of the wisdom and generosity of our parents.

I think of that gift and how happy and loved it made me feel when I consider today's promise. We humans are evil in the sense that we are sinners, saved by the grace of God through the death of Jesus Christ on the cross. If in that sense, we who are evil, know how to give good gifts to our children can't you just imagine how much greater is the love and generosity of our heavenly Father who, if we just ask Him, will give us the Holy Spirit. Paul told us, regarding Jesus, in Ephesians 2:18, "For through Him we both have access to the Father by one Spirit." If we believe in Jesus Christ in our hearts and confess Him with our mouths, we are saved to eternal life, and we also receive the Holy Spirit as a gift from God. John gave us Jesus' words in John 4:23-24, "Yet a time is coming and has now come when the true worshipers will worship the Father in spirit and truth, for they are the kind of worshipers the Father seeks. God is spirit, and His worshipers must worship in spirit and in truth." John told us Jesus' words regarding how we are to worship in spirit and truth in John 16:13, "But when He, the Spirit of truth, comes, He will guide you into all truth. He will not speak on His own; He will speak only what He hears, and He will tell you what is yet to come."

When we have the gift of the Holy Spirit we will bear the fruit of the Spirit Paul told us about in Galatians 4:22-23, "But the fruit of the Spirit is love, joy, peace, patience, kindness, goodness, faithfulness, gentleness and self-control. Against such things there is no law." Do you have the Holy Spirit? Ask God for that great gift, and go out and make this a great day.

There's a sweet, sweet Spirit in this place, and I know that it's the spirit of the Lord:
There are sweet expressions on each face, and I know they feel the presence of the Lord.
There are blessings you cannot receive 'til you know Him in His fullness and believe;
You're the one to profit when you say, "I am going to walk with Jesus all the way."

Doris M. Akers - 1922-

December 19

> "But when you give a banquet, invite the poor, the crippled, the lame, the blind, and you will be blessed. Although they cannot repay you, YOU WILL BE REPAID AT THE RESURRECTION OF THE RIGHTEOUS." Luke 14:13 & 14

One of the most rewarding events you can ever take part in is the preparation and serving of Thanksgiving dinner for a homeless shelter. The gratitude on the faces of those who are being served a hot, nourishing, plentiful dinner in a warm place makes for a delightful experience. As the people go through the line you get all sorts of comments, from a softly spoken "thank you," to loud praise, to a dropped head from someone who hopes they are not recognized. What makes such an event even better is when warm clothes and coats can also be handed out. Add to that a few toys for the children, and you have topped off a remarkable experience.

Jesus must have been thinking about such an event when he made today's promise. He knew people of such circumstances could never repay you for your thoughtfulness and kindness. He also knew the looks on the faces of these who had just enjoyed a satisfying meal and received a warm coat was payment enough for this world. Jesus went on with today's promise to tell us when we do such things in His name we will be repaid during our time in eternity. When you consider what a short time we spend on this earth in relation to eternity, shouldn't we be storing up such treasures for ourselves in heaven? There can be no question about what Jesus is saying in this promise. Read the parable of Jesus about the Sheep and the Goats in Matthew 25: 31-40. It ends in verse 40 by Jesus stating, "The King will reply, 'I tell you the truth, whatever you did for one of the least of these brothers of mine, you did for me.'" That is confirmation of today's promise. We do not have righteousness of our own. We have righteousness only if it is given to us as part of the righteousness of Jesus. In verse 40 when we read the word "least" as it is used, it is not to describe someone of lower value. It is used instead to describe someone less capable to provide for themselves. Those are the very people Jesus told us to invite to the banquet.

What about your actions? Have you behaved as Jesus said you should to those less fortunate than yourself? Have you provided them with food, clothing, fresh water or a place to stay? Have you visited them in the hospital, the nursing home or in prison? You may say, "I can't invite strangers into my house to feed, clothe and provide a place for the night." I agree. In our world today that would not be a safe thing to do. There are many Christian organizations, however, which provide those very necessities for people in need. You can give money and time to those organizations. You can visit hospitals, nursing homes and prisons to visit lonely, hurting people who need to know God has not forgotten them. It is not just a nice thing for a Christian to do. No! It is a command of Jesus that we do it, and that we do it in His name. They cannot repay you, but Jesus has promised us that He will repay us. Provide those services today, and go out and make this a great day.

> Rescue the perishing, care for the dying, snatch them in pity from sin and the grave;
> Weep o'er the erring one, lift up the fallen, tell them of Jesus, the mighty to save.
> Rescue the perishing-duty demands it! Strength for thy labor the Lord will provide;
> Back to the narrow way patiently win them, Tell the poor wanderer a Savior has died.
>
> Fanny J. Crosby - 1820-1915

December 20

"THE LORD WILL KEEP YOU FROM ALL HARM - HE WILL WATCH OVER YOUR LIFE; THE LORD WILL WATCH OVER YOUR COMING AND GOING BOTH NOW AND FOREVERMORE." Psalm 121:7 & 8

One of the most comforting things that ever happened to me was during my sixth grade when I walked to a one-room schoolhouse just over a mile from our house. On a very cold winter day I walked through the kitchen door upon arriving home from school, to find a bowl of hot chicken noodle soup setting on the table waiting for me. I looked at Momma and asked, "How did you know I would get home at this very time?" She just smiled and said, "Oh, I saw you coming." I knew the road to school very well, and I knew there was only one place at the top of a hill about a quarter of a mile away where you could see someone for only a few seconds when you are watching from our house. What made me feel so comforted was the knowledge that Momma was waiting and watching for me, even at my advanced age to be in the sixth grade.

I think of that time when I read today's promise. This promise is the last two verses of one of my favorite Psalms. Just like Momma would wait and watch for me coming home from school so she could have a bowl of hot soup to warm me up, so the Lord watches over our life. While it was very possible for Momma to miss seeing me in the short time I would have been visible to her, it is impossible for the Lord to miss seeing us at all times. Our promise is all-inclusive! He will watch over all our life! He will watch over our coming and going right now, and He will do it for the rest of our lives! He will keep us from all harm! Does that mean we will never suffer physical injury? Of course not! It means those of us who have put our trust in Him need never fear anything on this earth. Whatever happens to us on this earth will, at the most, end our physical lives. Our eternal life is secure because of Jesus Christ, our Lord and Savior.

Our Lord will watch over us to protect us from our enemies. Who are our enemies? We see that when we read Ephesians 6:12, "For our struggle is not against flesh and blood, but against the rulers, against the authorities, against the powers of this dark world and against the spiritual forces of evil in the heavenly realms." Satan's evil forces are the only things which can effect our eternal life. Those are the enemies we must be alert to. How do we fight them? That Scripture goes on to tell us to wear our full armor which is a belt of truth, a breastplate of righteousness, the gospel of peace fitted on our feet, a shield of faith, a helmet of salvation and the sword of the Spirit. Notice that the first five items mentioned are for defense. Only one is an offensive weapon, and that is the sword of the Holy Spirit! With all our study of the Bible, our doing our best to live as Jesus would have us live, our prayer and faithfulness we can, at best, just hunker down in a defensive posture. It is the Lord watching over us to unleash the Holy Spirit to fight the evil spirits which provides us the victory over evil. Yes, the Lord will watch over our lives! Claim it, and go out and make this a great day.

All the way my Savior leads me-what have I to ask beside?
Gives me grace for every trial, feeds me with the living bread.
Though my weary steps may falter and my soul athirst may be,
Gushing from the Rock before me, Lo! A spring of joy I see.
Fanny J. Crosby - 1820-1915

December 21

"I press on toward the goal to win the prize for which God has called me heavenward in Christ Jesus. All of us who are mature should take such a view of things. And if on some point you think differently, THAT TOO GOD WILL MAKE CLEAR TO YOU. Only let us live up to what we have already attained." Philippians 3:14-16

I associate today's promise Scripture with what Paul said in 1 Corinthians 9:24-27, "Do you not know that in a race all the runners run, but only one gets the prize? Run in such a way as to get the prize. Everyone who competes in the games goes into strict training. They do it to get a crown that will not last; but we do it to get a crown that will last forever. Therefore I do not run like a man running aimlessly; I do not fight like a man beating the air. No, I beat my body and make it my slave so that after I have preached to others, I myself will not be disqualified for the prize." When I was in high school I ran the mile run in track. Since I was the one assigned the duty of going into the pasture to round up the cows and drive them into the barn lot so we could milk them, I was used to running long distances. In my Senior year I thought I was pretty good and would be able to win every race until I reached the State Track Meet. In the last qualification track meet for State I was in the lead starting the fourth lap when suddenly a shorter runner passed me. I speeded up to try to keep close, but he continued to draw away. Running as fast as I could I still lost that race by about fifty yards. I did not get that prize for winning the race. You see, I had not trained hard enough, and I did not run the race with the correct strategy to enable me to win. I still qualified for State, and had a wonderful experience running in that meet.

Today's promise assures us that in the race for the high calling to which God has called us we can make an error in our view of things from time to time, but when we think differently from God, He will make clear to us what is the truth. When we accept Jesus Christ as our personal Savior, God gives us the Holy Spirit, who actually lives within us. We see this in 1 Corinthians 6:19, "Do you not know that your body is a temple of the Holy Spirit, who is in you, whom you have received from God? You are not your own." As you press on toward the goal to win the prize for which God has called you heavenward in Christ Jesus you should always be in a prayerful attitude about every decision. As you mature, you will find the communication with the Holy Spirit will make clear to you the view you should take of every situation. The times you stray from God will be the times you have not been in close communication with God. Don't ever take that chance. Always confess your sins to God, ask for forgiveness, and prayerfully ask for direction in all matters relating to your life.

Paul concludes today's promise Scripture by saying, "Only let us live up to what we have already attained." What have we attained? The most remarkable prize of all: Eternity spent in heaven with our Lord Jesus Christ in the presence of God! So press on toward the goal to win the prize of glory which God has promised. Now go out and make this a great day.

When all my labors and trials are o'er, and I am safe on that beautiful shore,
Just to be near the dear Lord I adore will through the ages be glory for me.
When by the gift of His infinite grace, I am accorded in heaven a place,
Just to be there and to look on His face will through the ages be glory for me.
Charles H. Gabriel - 1856-1932

December 22

> "For this very reason, make every effort to add to your faith goodness; and to goodness, knowledge; and to knowledge, self-control; and to self-control, perseverance; and to perseverance, godliness; and to godliness, brotherly kindness; and to brotherly kindness, love. FOR IF YOU POSSESS THESE QUALITIES IN INCREASING MEASURE, THEY WILL KEEP YOU FROM BEING INEFFECTIVE AND UNPRODUCTIVE IN YOUR KNOWLEDGE OF OUR LORD JESUS CHRIST." 2 Peter 1:5-8

I remember many lessons Dad taught me as we worked together doing the chores, cutting wood, putting up hay or working in the fields. I think those conversations built the character by which I have lived my life. Dad would stress over and over the need for honesty. He would tell me of someone who was not honest with him in the past, and what problems that caused for both Dad and the other person. He stressed the need to always be a help to other people. I can recall many times we would do the chores for a neighbor who had to be away from home over night. We would always harness the team to pull vehicles out of a mud hole or a snow bank when they would get stuck on the rural roads near our farm. Dad taught me self control by always being calm and talking more softly than normal when he felt he was losing control of his temper. He would assure me that you never gained anything by getting mad and ranting and raving. I wish I could write that I always followed Dad's training, but that was not always the case. I did develop qualities which served me well throughout my life thus far.

When considering today's promise, I always think back to the many lessons Dad spent so many hours teaching me. I am sure that Peter learned many of these traits he lists here during the three years he spent walking and talking with Jesus. Peter was not an educated man. He was a man of the sea, where he made his living by the hard work of his hands with nets and ropes catching the fish to supply the surrounding area. He was a rough, work hardened man who must have had a heart as big as all outdoors. He probably learned some of the same good qualities from his dad that I learned from mine. Jesus knew of those good qualities and built on them while He was training His disciples. Peter then used those good qualities to be a great, effective, productive Christian leader in the early church. Peter wrote these words over thirty years after the crucifixion, burial, resurrection and ascension of Jesus. He knew his time on earth was limited and wanted Christians everywhere to know the lessons he had learned. He had seen the great effectiveness of the other disciples who had learned the same character trait qualities from Jesus. In his great love for Jesus, he passed those lessons on to us.

This entire process Peter describes is the very process that leads to becoming a mature Christian. Becoming a mature Christian is knowing more about Jesus and becoming more like Jesus. Then you become a more effective and productive witness. How far along the road to maturity are you? Follow Peter's advice, and go out and make this a great day.

More about Jesus; in His word, holding communion with my Lord;
Hearing His voice in every line, making each faithful saying mine.
More about Jesus on His throne, riches in glory all His own;
More of His kingdom's sure increase; more of His coming, Prince of Peace.
Eleiza E. Hewitt - 1851-1920

December 23

"IF WE CONFESS OUR SINS, HE IS FAITHFUL AND JUST AND WILL FORGIVE US OUR SINS AND PURIFY US FROM ALL UNRIGHTEOUSNESS." 1 John 1:9

One of the things most children learn at an early age is to tell your parents the truth. I know I learned that lesson very well. Dad and Momma would ask each of their four children to explain what happened when something was amiss. We learned that if we had done something wrong, we should confess it, apologize for it, and ask for forgiveness. They showed they could be very sympathetic to our misdeeds when we did confess, but they had absolutely no tolerance for dishonesty. When I was very young I learned to pull the cabinet drawers out in a stair-step fashion and use them as a ladder to get to the counter to get cookies. One time Momma had a bowl on the counter getting ready to fix our dinner. She left the kitchen and I climbed up to get a cookie. In doing so I knocked the bowl off the counter onto the floor, breaking it. I hurriedly climbed down, pushed the drawers shut, and ran outside to play. When Momma talked to me about the broken bowl I denied any knowledge of it. Since I had been outside when Momma left the kitchen and outside when she entered the kitchen, she could not say with certainty that I was the guilty culprit. I carried the burden of that lie around into the next day. Momma later told me that I came to her late the next day crying, confessing and asking her to forgive me. Yes, she forgave me, but it was after she had paddled me for telling a lie.

Just as our parents want us to be honest with them, so our Father in heaven wants us to be honest with Him. Today's promise is very precious to us because it assures us that every time we confess our sins He is faithful and just. He will forgive us for our sins. He will purify us from all unrighteousness. He will then never remember those sins again! We read in Psalm 103:12, "As far as the east is from the west, so far has He removed our transgressions from us." Hebrews 10:17b also says, "Their sins and lawless acts I will remember no more." In other words, they are GONE! Yes! God is faithful and just! He forgives and purifies us!

Paul said in Romans 15:5-6, "May the God who gives endurance and encouragement give you a spirit of unity among yourselves as you follow Christ Jesus, so that with one heart and mouth you may glorify the God and Father of our Lord Jesus Christ." All sin, in its basic form, is failing to give God glory. We fail to glorify God when we sin, but God still is faithful to forgive us our sins when we confess them. As we become mature Christians, we find we know when we sin and we immediately ask God's forgiveness, not just "for my sins," but "for this specific sin." To mature as Christians is to become more like Jesus. Paul told us in 2 Corinthians 3:18, "And we, who with unveiled faces all reflect the Lord's glory, are being transformed into His likeness with ever-increasing glory, which comes from the Lord, who is the Spirit." Are you gaining maturity as a Christian? Do you confess your specific sins to God and ask His forgiveness? He is faithful and just, and will forgive and purify you! Now go out and make this a great day.

Hast thou dominion o'er self and o'er sin? Is thy heart right with God?
Over all evil without and within? Is thy heart right with God?
Is thy heart right with God, washed in the crimson flood,
Cleansed and made holy, humble and lowly, right in the sight of God?

Elisha A. Hoffman - 1839-1929

December 24

> "But the angel said to her, 'Do not be afraid, Mary, you have found favor with God. You will be with child and give birth to a son, and you are to give him the name Jesus. He will be great and will be called the Son of the Most High. The Lord God will give Him the throne of His father David, and He will reign over the house of Jacob forever; His kingdom will never end.' 'How will this be,' Mary asked the angel, 'since I am a virgin?' The angel answered, 'THE HOLY SPIRIT WILL COME UPON YOU, AND THE POWER OF THE MOST HIGH WILL OVERSHADOW YOU. SO THE HOLY ONE TO BE BORN WILL BE CALLED THE SON OF GOD.'" Luke 1:30-35

Reread the above promise for today. If you are a female reading this today put yourself in the place of Mary. You are a single virgin and an angel comes to you to tell you what was told to Mary. How do you react? Are you surprised? I am sure you would be. Are you afraid? I am sure you would be. Are you embarrassed? I am sure you would be. Would you, like Mary, ask, "How will this be since I am a virgin? I expect you would. Do you really think this is from God? You answer that one. Think about what Mary must have been thinking on that day two thousand years ago. To be unmarried and pregnant would be such a devastating thing. I thank God for Mary and for her obedience to God at that time. What a wonderful gift she gave the world by that obedience. Now, would you ultimately respond like Mary did by saying, "I am the Lord's servant. May it be to me as you have said."?

If you are a male reading this today put yourself in the place of Joseph. When you find out the woman you are to marry, the one with whom you have not had sex, is pregnant, what do you think? Do you suspect another man? I expect you would. Do you feel betrayed? I am sure you would. Do you want to run away? Probably! Joseph was such a good man and a righteous man that he decided not to expose Mary to disgrace. He decided to marry her and then quietly divorce her. This tells me that he strongly suspected another man. Now assume you had the same thought late in the evening and then went to bed. During your sleep an angel of the Lord appears to you in a dream and says, "(Your name), do not be afraid to take Mary home as your wife, because what is conceived in her is from the Holy Spirit. She will give birth to a son, and you are to give him the name Jesus, because He will save His people from their sins." Now what do you do? Are you obedient to God like Joseph was? Joseph woke up and did what the angel of the Lord had commanded him and took Mary home as his wife.

So from this most unusual process came the greatest gift the world has ever known, the birth of Jesus, whose life, death and resurrection has changed the world more than the life of any other person in the history of the world! Is God asking you to do something with your life which you really don't want to do and don't think you can do? You can do it and you should do it. Be obedient to God, and go out and make this a great day!

> What child is this, who, laid to rest, on Mary's lap is sleeping?
> Whom angels greet with anthems sweet, while shepherds watch are keeping?
> So bring Him incense, gold and myrrh - come, rich and poor, to own Him;
> The King of kings salvation brings - let loving hearts enthrone Him.
> William C. Dix - 1837-1898

December 25

"And there were shepherds living out in the fields nearby, keeping watch over their flocks at night. An angel of the Lord appeared to them, and the glory of the Lord shone around them, and they were terrified. But the angel said to them, 'Do not be afraid. I BRING YOU GOOD NEWS OF GREAT JOY THAT WILL BE FOR ALL THE PEOPLE. TODAY IN THE TOWN OF DAVID A SAVIOR HAS BEEN BORN TO YOU; HE IS CHRIST THE LORD.'" Luke 2:8-11

Christmas day! One of the most joyous times in Christendom! Who hears about this joyous event first? Shepherds! At that time shepherds were considered to be very lowly people. They didn't have an education. They didn't have financial wealth. They didn't have social stature. They spent their time out of doors with their flocks almost all the time. Isn't is interesting that God chose them to have the angels tell of the birth of Jesus? The shepherds had a very special place in Jesus' heart. During His ministry He referred to their occupation many times and likened Himself to a shepherd and mankind as His flock.

Now, consider yourself as one of the shepherds. You are out in the pasture on a cold, quiet night with your flock bedded down and sleeping except for the occasional bleating of an ewe for her lamb or the quiet footsteps of the shepherd who has duty to make the continuous rounds to ensure the night time safety of the flock. All of a sudden there is an apparition before you and a bright light shining, where before there was darkness, and this apparition, this angel, speaks. Even though the first words were, "Do not be afraid.", aren't you about scared to death? I think I would be! What do you make of the following message, which is today's promise? As you are still pondering the words of the angel there is suddenly a great company of the heavenly host with the angel, and they are praising God and saying, "Glory to God in the highest, and on earth peace to men on whom His favor rests." Having been out in the blackness of night taking care of animals, I can just picture this scene taking place. As I do so I am filled with wonder and awe just reading the words of Luke, chapter 2!

That angel is still speaking to us, to me and to you! That message is one of great joy. That promise of today is that a savior has been born to me, and to you! We had a perfect man sent to earth by God to live in the flesh of mankind, to experience the same feelings of cold, heat, hunger, thirst, love the discipline. He had to learn lessons, just as we do. He had to learn a trade, just as we do. The difference between Him and us is His perfection and His mission in life. He was sent to live, teach and die for us. He came to shed His blood as atonement for the sins of the entirety of mankind. Galatians 4:4-5 says, "But when the time had fully come, God sent His Son, born to a woman, born under law, to redeem those under law, that we might receive the full rights of sons." By the birth, death and resurrection of Jesus Christ we have the way to become fully the sons of God. Accept this great gift today, and go out and make this a great day.

Away in a manger, no crib for a bed, the little Lord Jesus laid down His sweet head;
The stars in the sky looked down where He lay, the little Lord Jesus, asleep on the hay.
Be near me, Lord Jesus, I ask Thee to stay close by me forever, and love me, I pray;
Bless all the dear children in Thy tender care, and fit us for heaven, to live with Thee there.
John Thomas McFarland - 1851-1913

December 26

"WHETHER YOU TURN TO THE RIGHT OR TO THE LEFT, YOUR EARS WILL HEAR A VOICE BEHIND YOU, SAYING, 'THIS IS THE WAY; WALK IN IT.'" Isaiah 30:21

Have you ever played the game of "blind man's guide?" It is played by cutting out squares of about twelve inches each (we used the backs of "Big Chief" tablets), writing the numbers from 1 to 10 on them, turning them face down and shuffling them, then placing them face up on the floor about a foot apart. The distance between them should be plus or minus a foot by several inches. Someone who has not seen the numbers laid out is blindfolded and led into the room. Another person who has not seen the numbers laid out then enters the room to "talk" the "blind man" through the numbers from 1 through 10, in order, without stepping on a wrong number, by simply giving the directions they should turn and how far to step. The "blind man's guide" is not allowed to move while giving the instructions. When the first pair finishes another "blind man" is brought into the room by a guide to walk through the numbers. The pair who gets through the numbers in proper sequence the fastest, or who have the least number of errors, wins. The last couple into the room could barely hear the instructions because of the laughter and catcalls. This is a fun, silly game which we played as children.

Today's promise relates to the very serious effort we make as mature Christians to walk in the way God has planned for us. Paul gave us a great way to keep our ears tuned to God when he wrote in 1 Thessalonians 5:16-18, "Be joyful always; pray continually; give thanks in all circumstances, for this is God's will for you in Christ Jesus." When we follow Paul's advice we will always be able to discern the voice of God, through the Holy Spirit, leading us in the correct way. Don't be confused by the erroneous leading of Satan's demons. That leading will not be in accordance with Biblical teachings. God's leading will never be in opposition to the teachings you have learned in the Bible. That is one of the reasons it is of vital importance to have at least fifteen minutes a day of quiet time with God, spend time each day reading God's Word, and spend time in fervent prayer. In your quiet times you will hear God's voice. God will direct your path as you read a passage of Scripture, or He will direct you by the comments or suggestions of another mature Christian.

Does this sound just a little bit questionable? Not at all! This is a promise of God! You can claim it and count on it. Does that mean the answer will always come immediately? No! We are told by David in Psalm 27:14, "Wait for the Lord; be strong and take heart and wait for the Lord." When you ask for guidance from God you can be as sure to receive it as Micah when he reported in 7:7, "But as for me, I watch in hope for the Lord, I wait for God my Savior; my God will hear me." Yes, your God will hear you and you will hear His voice saying, "This is the way, walk in it." Hold God's hand, and go out and make this a great day.

When I wander through the valley dim toward the setting of the sun,
Lead me safely to a land of rest if I a crown of life have won;
I have put my faith in Thee, dear Lord, that I may reach the golden strand,
There's no other friend on whom I can depend, blessed Jesus, hold my hand.
Albert E. Brumley - 1905-

December 27

"We ought always to thank God for you, brothers, and rightly so, BECAUSE YOUR FAITH IS GROWING MORE AND MORE, AND THE LOVE EVERY ONE OF YOU HAS FOR EACH OTHER IS INCREASING." 2 Thessalonians 1:3

Jan and I are members of CrossPointe Church in Norman, Oklahoma. The mission statement of our church is, "A church with a heart. A heart for God, a heart for one another, and a heart for a lost world." It is impossible to explain what our church means to us. We have found our worship to be so intense and so profound as we find ourselves worshiping and talking directly to God, who is, indeed, present in every service. We have found so many people to love, and to be loved by. We have found so much help for us in so many ways, and we have found so many people we have been able to help. Our love for our friends in our church just keeps on growing. We have found our church to be increasingly committed to mission support by sending both people and money dedicated to evangelism in our home town and across the world. We have found our faith has grown immeasurably during our membership in our church.

In writing to the Christians of Thessalonica, Paul is expressing a great truth. He tells them he is constantly thanking God for them because their faith is growing stronger and their love for each other continues to increase. The great truth is that as our faith grows stronger, our love for other Christians increases also! The reverse is also true. As our love for other Christians increases, our faith in God grows stronger! Why is this so? Because with an increase in faith, you are becoming more like Jesus. Remember the story in Matthew 14 of the disciples seeing Jesus walking toward them on the water? They thought He was a ghost until He spoke to them. Peter said, "Lord, if it's you, tell me to come to you on the water." Jesus did just that. As he walked toward Jesus, Peter became afraid of the wind and waves and began to sink. He cried, "Lord, save me!" Jesus reached out His hand and caught Peter and said, "You of little faith, why did you doubt?"

The reverse is true because with an increase in love, you are becoming more like Jesus. We read in 1 John 4:16-17, "And so we know and rely on the love God has for us. God is love. Whoever lives in love lives in God, and God in him. In this way, love is made complete among us so that we will have confidence on the day of judgment, because in this world we are like Him." We learn from God just how to love. We are told in 1 John 4:19, "We love because He first loved us." The way you show love is the best evidence of your Christlikeness! We show our love for others by praying for them. Paul gives us an example of this in today's promise when he says, "We ought always to thank God for you, brothers, and rightly so." Go read Colossians 1:3-11 to see how to pray for others. Praying for others is a very special way of showing our love for them. They may not always know of your prayers, but God will honor them.

Let your faith grow. Love one another, and go out and make this a great day.

I thought I had to seek and feel, to prove that what I loved was really real,
But passion turned to ashes, things I held to dust,
I found reality in simple trust.
My faith still holds on to the Christ of Calvary.

William J. - 1936- & Gloria Gaither - 1942-

December 28

"Behold, I AM COMING SOON! BLESSED IS HE WHO KEEPS THE WORDS OF THE PROPHECY IN THIS BOOK." Revelations 22:7

When I left home at age 17 to attend college Momma took me in our family car. Dad had to stay home to do the chores and continue the late summer farm work. I had rented a room on an earlier visit so I knew where I would be staying. When Momma left me at my room I knew I would not see her until the Thanksgiving break, and to see my parents then I would need to arrange transportation. I had been away from them all summer as I had worked for a custom combine crew which started in north Texas and cut wheat all the way to northern North Dakota. It still left a lump in my throat when Momma drove away in the car. I looked forward to the letters from my parents to keep me informed of all going on at home. When I was able to make arrangements for a ride home for Thanksgiving I wrote to tell them when I would be home. The letter in response closed with the words, "I will be seeing you soon." It really brought into focus how much I had missed them and how great it would be to see them again. Rereading the letter from time to time made me feel closer to them and let me know how blessed I was to have them as my parents.

In today's promise we have the words of Jesus, "I am coming soon!" Some say this promise is not true as it has been over two thousand years and He has not returned. We should remember that God's time is not the same as our time. Moses wrote in Psalm 90:4, "For a thousand years in your sight are like a day that has just gone by, or like a watch in the night." I think of the number of days which had to pass before I saw my parents after I had received the letter which said, "I will be seeing you soon." When I consider what Moses said, that could have been several thousand years when considering time as God considers time. The point is, we know Jesus will return. We know He will bless those who keep the words of the prophecy in the Bible. Jesus said this about His coming in Matthew 24:36, "No one knows about that day or hour, not even the angels in heaven, nor the Son, but only the Father." What are we to do in the meantime? Jesus answered that in Mark 13:35-37, "Therefore keep watch because you do not know when the owner of the house will come back-whether in the evening, or at midnight, or when the rooster crows, or at dawn. If He comes suddenly, do not let Him find you sleeping. What I say to you, I say to everyone; Watch!"

Paul told us in 2 Thessalonians 1:9-10, "They [the evil] will be punished with everlasting destruction and shut out from the presence of the Lord and from the majesty of His power on the day He comes to be glorified in His holy people and to be marveled at among all those who have believed. This includes you, because you believed our testimony to you." Yes, those of us who believe in Jesus Christ will be blessed because we kept the words of prophecy of the Bible. We will be in the throngs who marvel at Jesus' return! Now go out and make this a great day.

When Jesus comes to claim His own, the living saints and those gone on
Will all as one together rise to meet the Saviour in the skies.
No mortal knows when Christ will come; perhaps before this life is done;
So let us keep the narrow way, and live for Jesus every day.

I. J. Blackwelder - 1896-1980

December 29

> "FOR I AM CONVINCED THAT NEITHER DEATH NOR LIFE, NEITHER ANGELS NOR DEMONS, NEITHER THE PRESENT NOR THE FUTURE, NOR ANY POWERS, NEITHER HEIGHT NOR DEPTH, NOR ANYTHING ELSE IN ALL CREATION, WILL BE ABLE TO SEPARATE US FROM THE LOVE OF GOD THAT IS IN CHRIST JESUS OUR LORD." Romans 8:38 & 39

The story is told of the young man who wrote a love note to his sweetheart. He wrote: "My love for you is too great to ever tell. It is so great that for you I would climb the highest mountain; I would swim the deepest sea; I would walk across the broadest, driest, hottest desert; I would struggle through the coldest blizzard; I would crawl through the strongest tornado; I would fight the fiercest wild animals; I would conquer the most severe pain; and I would surmount the most formidable obstacles to be by your side. By the way, I will be over next Saturday night if it doesn't rain." We laugh at the obvious insincerity expressed by this young man, but aren't we much the same way when it comes to our actions regarding the love of God?

Paul wrote in today's promise in a very sincere manner what that young man wrote in an obviously insincere manner. How do we know Paul was sincere? Read all of Paul's writings in the New Testament and you will not be able to doubt his sincerity in today's promise! Do we always claim God's promise in this Scripture? How do we handle the death of a loved one? Do we lean on God for His peace and comfort as Jesus promised? Read John 14:27, "Peace I leave with you; my peace I give you. I do not give to you as the world gives. Do not let your hearts be troubled and do not be afraid." Do we worry about how little we have at present and wonder what we will do in the future? Shouldn't we claim God's promise in Jeremiah 29:11, "'For I know the plans I have for you,' declares the Lord, 'plans to prosper you and not to harm you, plans to give you hope and a future.'" Shouldn't we have faith in the future, as God has promised to prosper us and not to harm us? We do not see it yet, but God is in control. Read Hebrews 11:1, "Now faith is being sure of what we hope for and certain of what we do not see." Yes, have faith!

When everything is going well for us do we feel we are in charge and forget our dependence on God? When we are in the depths of depression do we feel things are so bad with us that even God could not help us? Paul clearly tells us today that "neither height not depth" can separate us from the love of God. I might add, that neither can they separate us from the NEED for God!

How wonderful it is to know that regardless of whatever comes along we can always count on the love of God that is in Christ Jesus our Lord. NOTHING can ever separate us from that love, and NOTHING can ever separate us from His presence, for it is written in Joshua 1:5b, "I will never leave you nor forsake you." Now claim it, and go out and make this a great day.

> I am so glad that our Father in heaven tells of His love in the Book He has given;
> Wonderful things in the Bible I see-this is the dearest, that Jesus loves me.
> Though I forget Him and wander away, still He doth love me wherever I stray;
> Back to His dear loving arms I would flee, when I remember that Jesus loves me.
>
> Philip P. Bliss - 1838-1876

December 30

"AFTER THAT, WE WHO ARE STILL ALIVE AND ARE LEFT WILL BE CAUGHT UP TOGETHER WITH THEM IN THE CLOUDS TO MEET THE LORD IN THE AIR. AND SO WE WILL BE WITH THE LORD FOREVER." 1 Thessalonians 4:17

Have you ever taken a vacation to a foreign land? You don't speak the language, you don't come from the same culture, you don't know the city, you don't know the geography of the country, and you may not share the religion. When you return home you feel so comfortable being in familiar surroundings, language, etc. You may have enjoyed your vacation a lot. I know I have enjoyed my vacations in foreign lands, and learned a lot. There could be no doubt, though, that I was a foreigner, a traveler, a sojourner, a stranger, a visitor, an alien in the land in which I was vacationing. There is just something wonderful about being home!

We Christians should consider our lives here on earth in much the same way we consider a vacation to a foreign land. This is not all there is! Everyone will spend eternity somewhere. The most important thing anyone can do on earth is to decide where they will spend eternity. We should study God's Word to make sure we spend eternity in heaven. We need to be, and say, like the Psalmist in 119:19, "I am a stranger on earth; do not hide your commands from me." We have a Father in heaven who has promised us eternal life for our belief in, and acceptance of, Jesus Christ. Peter told us in 1 Peter 1:17, "Since you call on a Father who judges each man's work impartially, live your lives as strangers here in reverent fear." We are to live our lives in worship of our Lord Jesus Christ! God clearly tells us we are different from the non-believers. We read in Philippians 3:19-21, "Their destiny is destruction, their god is their stomach, and their glory is in their shame. Their mind is on earthly things. But our citizenship is in heaven. And we eagerly await a Savior from there, the Lord Jesus Christ, who, by the power that enables Him to bring everything under His control, will transform our lowly bodies so that they will be like His glorious body."

The verse preceding today's promise (see October 30) says, "For the Lord Himself will come down from heaven, with a loud command, with the voice of the archangel and with the trumpet call of God, and the dead in Christ will rise first." Now we have the promise of today that carries to all Christians who are still alive. They will be caught up together, with those Christians who have died before Jesus returns to earth, in the clouds to meet our Lord Jesus Christ in the air. We will then be with our Lord forever! Hallelujah! What a wonderful promise from God! We will leave this land where we are foreigners, travelers, sojourners, strangers, visitors, and aliens, and be with our Lord and Savior in heaven for eternity! We will be HOME!

Are you ready to meet Jesus when He returns and you see Him face to face? Do you believe in your heart, and have you confessed with your mouth that Jesus is the Son of God? Have you asked Him for forgiveness? Do it today! Now go out and make this a great day.

Face to face with Christ my Savior, face to face-what will it be-
When with rapture I behold Him, Jesus Christ who died for me?
Only faintly now I see Him, with the darkened veil between,
But a blessed day is coming when His glory shall be seen.
Carrie S. Breck - 1855-1934

December 31

"TO HIM WHO OVERCOMES, I WILL GIVE THE RIGHT TO SIT WITH ME ON MY THRONE, JUST AS I OVERCAME AND SAT DOWN WITH MY FATHER ON HIS THRONE." Revelation 3:21

Each two years I like to watch either the Summer Olympics or the Winter Olympics. It is exciting to me to see people who have trained their bodies to such a magnificent point compete to see who is the best, or who can overcome. Whether it is an individual event or a team event, the winners mount the medal stands for the gold medal to be draped around their necks and have their national anthem played in recognition of their being a champion. Only the best in the event have the right to stand on the top level of the medal stand. As Paul said in 1 Corinthians 9:24-27, "Do you not know that in a race all the runners run, but only one gets the prize? Run in such a way as to get the prize. Everyone who competes in the games goes into strict training. They do it to get a crown that will not last; but we do it to get a crown that will last forever. Therefore I do not run like a man running aimlessly; I do not fight like a man beating the air. No, I beat my body and make it my slave so that after I have preached to others, I myself will not be disqualified for the prize." Paul is very clear that we must go into strict training to insure we are able to overcome and claim today's promise.

How do we train? We train by our daily study of God's Word, meditating on His Word, and memorizing His Word . We are told in Psalm 119:9,11 & 15, "How can a young man keep his way pure? By living according to your Word." "I have hidden your word in my heart that I might not sin against you." "I meditate on your precepts and consider your ways." We train by our daily quiet time to commune (or abide) with God, or as Jesus told us in John 15:5 (KJV), "I am the vine; ye are the branches: He that abideth in me, and I in him, the same bringeth forth much fruit: for without me ye can do nothing." We train through our prayers to God. Paul told us in 1 Thessalonians 5:17, "Pray continually."

We read in 2 Corinthians 7:1, "Since we have these promises, dear friends, let us purify ourselves from everything that contaminates body and spirit, perfecting holiness out of reverence for God." This book contains but 373 of the wonderful promises God has made to us. When we purify ourselves from sin we can rightly claim each and every one of these promises, as well as all the others contained in God's Word, as our very own. How do we purify ourselves from sin? We read in 1 John 1:9, "If we confess our sins, He is faithful and just and will forgive us our sins and purify us from all unrighteousness."

Are you sure you have the right to claim today's promise? Read 1 John 4:4, "You, dear children, are from God and have overcome them, because the one who is in you is greater than the one who is in the world." Have Jesus in your heart and you will shout and sing the victory!

Now go out and make this a great life!

Sing the wondrous love of Jesus, sing His mercy and His grace;
in the mansions bright and blessed He'll prepare for us a place.
When we all get to heaven, what a day of rejoicing that will be!
When we all see Jesus, we'll sing and shout the victory.

Eliza E. Hewitt - 1851-1920

Good Friday

"But God demonstrates His own love for us in this: WHILE WE WERE STILL SINNERS, CHRIST DIED FOR US." Romans 5:8

Today is a very special day in the life of a Christian. This is the day we recognize receipt of the greatest gift in the history of the world. This is the day fulfilling the promise of John 3:16. This is the day Jesus died on the cross for us. Jesus shed His blood to atone for each and every sin of each and every person. In the Old Testament the book of rules is Leviticus. We read in 17:11, "For the life of a creature is in the blood, and I have given it to you to make atonement for yourselves on the altar; it is the blood that makes atonement for one's life." A blood sacrifice was a command of God to the Israelites. That command was superceded in the New Testament when Jesus Christ shed His blood and died on the cross.

A story circulating on e-mail tells of a pastor who introduced an older minister in the evening service as one of his dearest childhood friends and asked the man to share whatever he wanted to say. The older minister told of a man, his son and his son's friend who went sailing off the Pacific coast. A fast approaching storm kept them from reaching shore and, as the waves got much higher, the boat capsized. The father grabbed the boat and enough rope to save one boy. He knew his son was a Christian, and the friend was not, so calling out, "I love you son!" he threw the rope to the friend and saved him. The son's body was never found. The guest minister said, "How great is the love of God that He should do the same for us. Our Heavenly Father sacrificed His only begotten Son that we could be saved." After the service two teenage boys who had listened intently came to the older minister and said, "That was a great story, but not very realistic for a father to sacrifice his son's life for the life of his son's friend." "You are right, it isn't very realistic," said the minister. "But I'm standing here today to tell you that story gives me a glimpse of what it must have been like for God to give up His Son for me. You see - I was that father, and your pastor is my son's friend."

I like that story. It reminds me that if I were the only person on earth who had sinned, God would still have sacrificed His Son on the cross to atone for my sins. My sins were so bad that God felt He had to let His Son die to save me. What a sacrifice He made for ME! Oh, that I will be worthy of that sacrifice. Oh, that I will follow His leading all the days of my life!

Today, know that Jesus died on the cross for YOU! Today, know that Jesus' death was made necessary because of YOUR sins. God's love for you is infinite. Yes, I know Romans 3:23, "For all have sinned and fall short of the glory of God." I know Jesus died for all, but especially, He died for ME and YOU! Ask Him to forgive you of your sins, vow to always serve Him and be worthy of His sacrifice, and go out and make this a great day.

Must Jesus bear the cross alone and all the world go free
No, there's a cross for ev'ry one, and there's a cross for me.
The consecrated cross I'll bear till death shall set me free,
and then go home my crown to wear, for there's a crown for me.

Thomas Shepherd - 1665-1739

Easter Sunday

> "The angel said to the women, 'Do not be afraid, for I know that you are looking for Jesus, who was crucified. HE IS NOT HERE; HE HAS RISEN, JUST AS HE SAID. Come and see the place where He lay. Then go quickly and tell His disciples: 'He has risen from the dead and is going ahead of you into Galilee. There you will see Him.' Now I have told you.'" Matthew 28:5-7

This is a day celebrated more by Christians second only to the day of Jesus' birth. This is the day that separates Christianity from all other religions. This is the day that Jesus rose from the dead as He promised He would do. This is the day He left us an empty tomb. No other religion has an empty tomb. A God who can sacrifice His Son as atonement for our sins and then raise Him from the dead can do ALL He has promised to do!

You can imagine how difficult it was for those who followed Jesus to believe the He had risen from the dead, even though they were told in advance. In Matthew 16:21 we see, "From that time on Jesus began to explain to His disciples that He must go to Jerusalem and suffer many things at the hands of the elders, chief priests and teachers of the law, and that He must be killed and on the third day be raised to life." So Jesus had prepared the disciples and had taught them what would happen, but still . . .! How can this be? How can such a thing happen? One of the times Jesus appeared to the disciples is described in John 20:24-29, "Now Thomas (called Didymus), one of the Twelve, was not with the disciples when Jesus came. So the other disciples told him, 'We have seen the Lord!' But he said to them, 'Unless I see the nail marks in His hands and put my finger where the nails were, and put my hand into His side, I will not believe it.' A week later His disciples were in the house again, and Thomas was with them. Though the doors were locked, Jesus came and stood among them and said, 'Peace be with you!' Then He said to Thomas, 'Put your finger here; see my hands. Reach out your hand and put it into my side. Stop doubting and believe.' Thomas said to Him, 'My Lord and my God!' Then Jesus told him, 'Because you have seen me, you have believed; blessed are those who have not seen and yet have believed.'"

We won't see Jesus in person on this earth, however, we believe! Our Lord is risen from the dead. He sits at the right hand of God, His Father, and He will welcome us to heaven to rejoice with Him for evermore. Today you can count on this very precious promise. You know that Jesus rose from the dead. You know that He forgives us our sins. You know that He leads us throughout our lives. You know that He provides for us, His sheep. You know that He cares for us. You know that He restores health to us and heals us of our wounds. You know that He lives today, because He lives within your hearts.

Believe it, claim it, live it, and go out and make this a great day.

> Let us sing of Easter gladness that rejoices every day,
> Sing of hope and faith uplifted; Love has rolled the stone away.
> Lo, the promise and fulfillment, Lo, the man whom God hath made,
> Seen in glory of an Easter Crowned with light that cannot fade.
>
> Frances Thompson Hill (No Date)

Mother's Day

> "Honor your father and mother - which is the first commandment with a promise - THAT IT MAY GO WELL WITH YOU AND THAT YOU MAY ENJOY LONG LIFE ON THE EARTH." Ephesians 6:2 & 3

I thank God for a Christian mother! I remember so many wonderful times with her which are so meaningful to me now, as they were then. Mother always included a remembrance for each one of her children (she had four - my brother, two sisters and then me) in her morning prayer. She was always interested in our school work and in our chores. She expected us to carry our load of work in the house and on the farm. As the youngest, I was the one who always had to go to the cellar. I always told her that for every jar of food we ate, I made four trips to the cellar. One to get the jars to do the canning, one to take the full jars down, one to go get the jars of food for the table, and one to take the jars back to the cellar. I miss her since her death in 1979!

One time in Sunday School, she was teaching a group of boys my age the story of Jesus leading up to His death on the cross. She was reading us Matthew 26:34 (KJV), "Jesus said unto him, 'Verily I say unto thee. That this night, before the cock crow, thou shalt deny me thrice." I was joking with one of the other boys about "thrice" and making silly rhymes with it. Mother cut me short and made me understand that I was to never again make fun of the word of God, but I was to respect it always. I promise you, that lesson took with me!

What a wonderful promise we have for today! We have the commandment - "Honor your father and mother" - followed by a promise - "That it may go well with you and that you may enjoy long life on the earth." Does that mean that if we honor our father and mother we will live longer? YES! Studies have shown that Christian people live longer and are healthier than non-Christians. I realize that everyone who honors their parents are not Christians; however, I feel that the greatest way to honor one's parents is to be a Christian, regardless of whether or not the parents were Christians.

My mother was always proud of me and tried to attend every event which was meaningful to me. She would often tell me during the time I was not close to God that she wished I would live closer to God. She would tell me that I had too much talent not to offer it to God. I have always remembered that conversation. I am just sorry that I did not spend more time with her, but thankful for the time I was able to spend.

Today is a good time to take stock of your own situation. Do you have any conflicts with your parents? Do you have any conflicts with any of your children? If so, now is the time to clear the air. Ask them if you have hurt them or offended them in any way. If so, ask, "Will you forgive me?" This is a question which will require a response. It is non-threatening and shows that you really want to establish "honor". Do it, and go out and make this a great day.

> Faith of our mothers, living still in cradle song and bedtime prayer;
> In nursery lore and fireside love, Thy presence still pervades the air.
> Faith of our mothers, Christian faith, in truth beyond our stumbling creeds,
> Still serve the home and save the church, and breathe Thy Spirit through our deeds
>
> A. B. Patten (No Date)

Memorial Day

> "FOR AS IN ADAM ALL DIE, SO IN CHRIST ALL WILL BE MADE ALIVE." 1 Corinthians 15:22

I thank God for the privilege of being born and allowed to live in this country! Many of our forefathers came to this country to escape religious persecution. One branch of my own family has been traced back to the mid 1500's through the records of the Quaker church, and they came to this country in 1682 to escape persecution of the Quakers in London. Our great country was founded on Christian principles. Many of our early leaders were devout Christians. I strongly support Christians who get involved in politics and urge you to do likewise.

Today, we honor not only those who died to defend our freedoms, but all those who have gone on before us. Sin, and, therefore, death, came into this world through one man - Adam. We mourn our loved ones who have died. We cherish the memories they have left us. We are comforted by the fact that Jesus died for all of us so that we need not die indeed, but we die to life everlasting through Jesus Christ our Lord.

The souls of our loved ones who were God's children are with God right now. When Jesus comes again to this earth, we will all rise in body to meet Him and live with Him forevermore. That is such a comforting thought for today. I know there are many of our loved ones who were not Christians. They will not be with us. What that should cause us to do is to redouble our efforts to bring all our loved ones on earth now to a point where they will ask forgiveness of their sins and give their hearts and lives to Jesus Christ our Lord. I know that when I die, I will be joined with my parents and grandparents and many of my aunts, uncles, cousins and other relatives and friends. I pray continually for my relatives still on this earth who have not given their souls to Christ, and on this particular day, I pray especially hard for them.

We can each one face death with the full knowledge that Jesus stands just on the other side of death waiting for us to arrive home. He will welcome us to heaven and join in the celebration for one of His dear children coming home. We need not fear death. Yes, we love life here on earth. We love our families, our friends, our church, our homes, etc., but the thought of life eternally with Jesus in heaven is so very comforting.

Do you have that comfort in your heart today? If not, you can have it. Just confess your sins to Jesus and ask Him to wash them away with the blood He shed on the cross and to make you a new person. He will do it right then. You will be a new person in Christ and never again fear death or the afterlife. What a comforting, blissful thought for this particular day. A new person who will never die! Wondrous, glorious eternity with Jesus! Do it!

Bring peace to your soul with Jesus. Remember your loved ones and those who died to defend our country, and go out and make this a great day.

> Love divine, so great and wondrous! All my sins He then forgave!
> I will sing His praise forever, for His blood, His pow'r to save.
> In life's even-tide, at twilight, at His door I'll knock and wait:
> by the precious love of Jesus I shall enter heaven's gate.
>
> Fredrick A. Blom - 1867-1927

Father's Day

"As a father has compassion on his children, SO THE LORD HAS COMPASSION ON THOSE WHO FEAR HIM." Psalm 103:13

As I write this day's promise, my own father is still alive. He is not as spry as he used to be, he doesn't see as well as he used to see, he doesn't hear as well as he used to hear, but he is still the father I have known and loved my entire life. He has taught me so much and said so many prayers for me that it would be impossible to tell the total. I report many of his lessons in this devotional. My fondest memory of my childhood years is that of finishing the morning chores, washing our hands and face, and gathering around the breakfast table for Dad to bring out the Bible to read a passage followed by a lesson from the devotional book. He would then lead us by saying a morning prayer. Each of the children would say a prayer and mother would close with her prayer. Even if we had company, everyone was urged to say a prayer. I think that memory is the strongest example of a father's compassion there could possibly be.

It is a father's duty to God to pass on a knowledge of the scripture and a Christian heritage. In Psalm 78:1-7 we read, "O my people, hear my teaching; listen to the words of my mouth. I will open my mouth in parables, I will utter hidden things, things from of old - what we have heard and known, what our fathers have told us. We will not hide them from their children; we will tell the next generation the praiseworthy deeds of the Lord, His power, and the wonders He has done. He decreed statutes for Jacob and established the law in Israel, which He commanded our forefathers to teach their children, so the next generation would know them, even the children yet to be born, and they in turn would tell their children. Then they would put their trust in God and would not forget His deeds but would keep His commands." If you are a father, are you obeying the command of God regarding this matter? If not, then you should start to do so today.

The Lord has compassion on those who fear Him. Fear in this case is properly defined as "awe, respect, reverence" and is fully shown by obeying the passage in Psalm. What better way to train our children than through the Bible lessons which I learned from my father and which we have an obligation to pass on to our children. Many passages in Proverbs speak to the duties of a father. Read them and act upon them.

Whether your earthly father showed you the Christian compassion or not, you have the promise of God that your Heavenly Father will show you the compassion of a loving, providing, healing, fair Father. Too many earthly fathers are "missing in action" today. This can never be said about our Heavenly Father! He will always respond! In Romans 10:12 we read that the Lord "richly blesses all who call upon Him."

Call on Him, trust Him, serve Him, and go out and make this a great day.

Faith of our fathers, living still in spite of dungeon, fire and sword
O how our hearts beat high with joy whene'er we hear that glorious word!
Faith of our fathers, we will love both friend and foe in all our strife;
and preach Thee too, as love knows how, by kindly words and virtuous life.
Frederick W. Faber - 1814-1863

Labor Day

"To whom He said, 'THIS IS THE RESTING PLACE, LET THE WEARY REST'; and, 'THIS IS THE PLACE OF REPOSE' - but they would not listen." Isaiah 28:12

Today we celebrate a holiday devoted to the workers. Work is mentioned many times in the Bible and God fully intended us to work. In Colossians 3:23-24 we are told, "Whatever you do, work at it with all your heart, as working for the Lord, not for men, since you know that you will receive an inheritance from the Lord as a reward. It is the Lord Christ you are serving." That speaks directly to us about our work and how we are to approach it. In 1 Thessalonians 4:11 we are told, "Make it your ambition to lead a quiet life, to mind your own business and to work with your hands, just as we told you, so that your daily life may win the respect of outsiders and so that you will not be dependent on anybody."

The haven provided by the Lord God IS a resting place! Today, let the weary rest, rest in the Lord our God. This land and this country was founded on God. Our forefathers put together our government fully under the influence of God. God blessed our land at that time and since. This is a resting place, and this is a place of repose so long as we keep it a land of God. However, wherever you are, you can have rest in Christ. Matthew 11:28 says, "Come to me, all you who are weary and burdened, and I will give you rest." The very best rest you will ever have is when you come fully to Christ. Lay your burdens on the altar, confess your sins, ask for forgiveness and you WILL be saved. Then any place you are will be a resting place and a place of repose. Please listen to these words. They are the most important words you will ever hear and obey!

Whether you work daily in a job that requires hard work with your hands, intricate work with your hands, artistic work with your hands, typing and input with your hands, nursing or surgical work with your hands, teaching and showing with your hands, or management and supervisory work, you should be involved in a labor of love. You will be a witness for the Lord in all that you do if you do it with the love of God and the love for your neighbor in your heart.

Avoid being lazy. The story is told about the man who was so lazy he would not go outside to see if it were hot or cold, wet or dry or windy or still. He would just call in the dog to check. A friend said he could understand how you can determine if it is hot or cold or if it is wet or dry, but how can you tell if it is windy or still? "Well, if he don't come in, it means he done bin blowed away in the wind," was the reply.

So today, this is the resting place, let the weary rest, and when you work tomorrow, do so with all your heart, as working for the Lord, because that is what you are doing. Make this a restful day, and make it a great day.

Work, for the night is coming. Work thru the sunny noon;
fill brightest hours with labor - rest comes sure and soon.
Give ev'ry flying minute something to keep in store;
work for the night is coming when man works no more.
Annie L. Coghill - 1836-1907

Thanksgiving

"YOU WILL LIVE IN THE LAND I GAVE YOUR FOREFATHERS; YOU WILL BE MY PEOPLE, AND I WILL BE YOUR GOD." Ezekiel 36:28

I chose this promise for today because Thanksgiving is a uniquely American holiday. I also feel that God gave this land to our forefathers. I pray that we will start turning back more and more to God and become ever more His people. I agree with Joshua in Joshua 24:15, "But if serving the Lord seems undesirable to you, then choose for yourselves this day whom you will serve, whether the gods your forefathers served beyond the River, or the gods of the Amorites, in whose land you are living. But as for me and my household, we will serve the Lord." Yes, He will be my God! Today, I thank Him for this great land. I thank Him for His providing for me. I thank Him for my home. I thank Him for my family. I thank Him for my church. I thank Him, most of all, for giving me His Son to die on the cross for my sins.

Whether we have plenty or minimal provisions we should render thanks to our Lord. In

1 Thessalonians 5:16-18 we are told, "Be joyful always; pray continually; give thanks in all circumstances, for this is God's will for you in Christ Jesus." Remember, it is God's will for you in Christ Jesus that you give thanks in ALL circumstances! Not just in those really great circumstances. Not just in those circumstances which are a little favorable. Not just in those circumstances which we can barely tolerate. NO, give thanks IN ALL circumstances, for this is God's will for you in Christ Jesus!

In "The Hiding Place" by Corrie ten Boom (if you haven't read this book, I would really recommend you do so!), she and her sister, Betsie, were moved to Ravensbruck concentration camp and placed in Barracks 28. They were shown to the center of the barracks and assigned to the second level platform (of three levels) and had to crawl across three other straw-covered platforms to reach the one that they would share with others. When they lay down to get some rest Corrie suddenly sat up and cried, "Fleas! Betsie, the place is swarming with them!" Betsie followed the admonition, prayed to God and gave thanks for the fleas though Corrie could find no reason to do so. Several days later, as Corrie returned from a wood-gathering foray outside the walls she was greeted by Betsie with her eyes twinkling. "Corrie, I have found a reason to give thanks for the fleas," she said. "You know we've had so much freedom in the big room. I have found out why." They found out that the bad flea infestation was the reason the guards did not come into the building. They were able to read the Bible, hold services and say their prayers without interruption. Now, if those two ladies could give thanks to God for fleas in a concentration camp in Germany, I know we can give thanks in ALL circumstances here in America!

Give thanks to our God for His blessings, and go out and make this a great day.

Thanks, O God, for boundless mercy from Thy gracious throne above;
Thanks for ev'ry need provided from the fullness of Thy love!
Thanks for daily toil and labor and for rest when shadows fall;
Thanks for love of friend and neighbor and Thy goodness unto all!
August Ludvig Storm - 1862-1914

Daily Promises of God Scripture Verses

Verse	Date
Exodus 23:7	9-28
Exodus 23:25	11-9
Deuteronomy 7:9	8-16
Deuteronomy 8:5	6-16
Deuteronomy 11:13-15	6-25
Deuteronomy 20:4	8-13
Deuteronomy 25:13-16	8-23
Deuteronomy 28:3	9-16
Deuteronomy 28:6	10-27
Deuteronomy 28:7	11-23
Deuteronomy 28:13	6-9
Deuteronomy 30:8-9	7-2
Deuteronomy 31:8	10-9
Deuteronomy 32:12	5-28
Deuteronomy 33:27	4-24
Joshua 1:5	5-12
Joshua 1:9	5-30
1 Samuel 2:30	3-15
1 Chronicles 28:9	5-16
2 Chronicles 15:7	1-6
2 Chronicles 16:9	5-13
Nehemiah 8:10	10-10
Job 5:17	7-31
Job 5:21	6-23
Job 5:26	6-24
Job 17:9	5-20
Job 36:11	2-21
Psalm 4:6-7	6-14
Psalm 4:8	6-29
Psalm 8:4-5	2-23
Psalm 9:9	8-22
Psalm 9:10	12-3
Psalm 22:24	10-21
Psalm 23:3	6-17
Psalm 23:4	10-15
Psalm 32:7	6-1
Psalm 32:8	5-2
Psalm 34:8	4-5
Psalm 34:9	11-16
Psalm 34:18	2-14
Psalm 37:21-22	8-15
Psalm 37:23	4-29
Psalm 37:24	5-7
Psalm 37:28	7-15
Psalm 37:39	7-22
Psalm 40:1-2	9-8
Psalm 40:3	11-4
Psalm 40:5	6-5
Psalm 48:14	3-2
Psalm 68:10	1-28
Psalm 73:23-25	8-6
Psalm 84:11	11-24
Psalm 91-4	11-26
Psalm 91:11-12	12-11
Psalm 95:6-7	1-14
Psalm 103:12	3:20
Psalm 103:13	Father's Day
Psalm 112:9	3-28
Psalm 121:3	11-18
Psalm 121:7-8	12-20
Psalm 145:18	10-1
Psalm 145:19	9-11
Psalm 145:20	5-14
Psalm 146:7	11-20

366 Days plus 7 Special Holidays equals
373 Scriptures

CPSIA information can be obtained
at www.ICGtesting.com
Printed in the USA
FFHW011651290119
50353504-55443FF